ONTARIO CORPORATE PROCEDURES

FOURTH EDITION

Prof. Midge Day

Edited by

Bernie Aron B.A. LL.B.

CARSWELL

A THOMSON COMPANY

The paper used in this publication meets the minimum requirements of the American National Standard for Information Sciences — Permanence of Paper for Printed Library Materials, ANSI Z39.48-1984.

National Library of Canada Cataloguing in Publication Data

Day, Midge, 1934-1999.
Ontario corporate procedures

4th ed. / edited by Bernie Aron.
Includes index.
ISBN 0-459-26194-0

1. Corporation law—Ontario. 2. Corporation law—Canada. 3. Corporation law—Ontario—Forms. 4. Corporation law—Canada—Forms. I. Aron, Bernie II. Title.

KEO389.D39 2001 346.713'066 C2001-903881-X

CARSWELL
A THOMSON COMPANY

One Corporate Plaza
2075 Kennedy Road
Scarborough, Ontario
M1T 3V4

Customer Care:
Toronto 1-416-609-3800
Elsewhere in Canada/U.S. 1-800-387-5164
Fax 1-416-298-5094
World Wide Web: http://www.carswell.com
E-mail: orders@carswell.com

PREFACE

It is a privilege to continue the tradition of this important work in law clerk studies. Professor Midge Day was the author of the first three editions of this essential reference resource in the corporate area of practice. As a professor in the Legal Assistant/Law Clerk Program at Durham College in Oshawa, Midge Day was a tireless advocate for the appropriate recognition of the important role of law clerks in law firms and legal departments of corporations and government ministries. With her untimely death, her legacy will be her contribution to the professionalism and pride of the law clerk profession. Professor Day was also an inspiration to me in my teaching endeavours for The Institute of Law Clerks of Ontario. For the past fifteen years, I have taught Corporate Law at Humber College, Centennial College and currently at George Brown College in Toronto. The *Ontario Corporate Procedures* publication has been a constant companion for the teacher and students in chronicling developments in corporate law and procedure in Ontario.

The Fourth Edition of *Ontario Corporate Procedures* features recent developments in automating various corporate procedures including:

- business registrations and name searches in Ontario
- incorporation process
- ONBIS searches
- annual return filings for Ontario and federal corporations
- bankruptcy searches

In addition, the extensive selection of corporate forms has been updated including the requisite annual returns for Ontario and federal corporations, the corporate tax returns, and the Ontario Business Registration Application. With the generous support of Dye and Durham Company Inc., the sample NUANS search, corporate by-laws, standard minutes for annual meetings, and share certificates have been updated for the publication. At Dye & Durham, I wish to thank Jackie Warren, Legal Forms & Product Development Co-Ordinator for her permission to use the various forms. I also wish to acknowledge the kind assistance of Rosanna Conteduca, Director, Search and Registration Services and Joanne Hendry, Manager, Search and Registration Services at Dye and Durham's downtown location in arranging for the various corporate forms. On a further note, I wish to thank Rosanna Conteduca and Joanne Hendry for their support of paralegal training at Humber College, in the area of corporate searches, with their participation as members of the Advisory Committee of the Court and Tribunal Agent program.

At Carswell, I wish to thank the Product Development Manager, Todd Pinsky, for the support and encouragement he has provided me during the writing and production phases. During the production phase, I have valued the calm professionalism of the Production Editor, Rajbir Sandhu, who has guided this work through the different stages of the production process.

I wish to especially thank my wife, Linda, for her love, support and understanding that is a source of constant inspiration, guidance and comfort.

TABLE OF CONTENTS

Preface iii

Part I Forms of Business Organization

Chapter 1 **Sole Proprietorships and Partnerships** 3
1. Sole Proprietorship 3
   (a) Business Name Registration 3
   (b) Name Search and its Importance 6
   (c) Cancellation of Registration 7
   (d) Licensing or Permits 8
   (e) Bank Account 8
2. Partnerships Generally 9
   (a) Introduction 9
   (b) *Partnerships Act* 10
3. General Partnerships 14
   (a) Introduction 14
   (b) Registration — *Business Names Act* 14
   (c) Dissolution or Withdrawal 16
4. Limited Partnerships 17
   (a) Declaration 17
   (b) Rights of a Limited Partner 19
   (c) Extra-provincial Limited Partnership 21
   (d) Records 22
   (e) Bank Account 23
5. Limited Liability Partnership (LLP) 23
6. Ontario Business Registration Application (Ontario Business Connects) 25
7. Federal-Provincial Business Registration (Business Registration On-line) 28

Chapter 2. **Corporations** 31
1. Introduction 31
2. Historical Origins of Corporations 31
3. Fundamental Concepts of a Corporation 32

Part II Provincial Corporations

Chapter 3 **Directors and Officers of Corporations** 39

1. Directors 39
   - (a) Board of Directors 39
   - (b) First Directors 40
   - (c) Increasing or Decreasing Number of Directors 41
   - (d) Qualifications of Directors 43
   - (e) Election of Directors 44
   - (f) Cumulative Voting for Directors 44
   - (g) Quorum of Directors 46
   - (h) Vacancies 47
   - (i) Place of Meetings 48
     - (i) By Telephone and Other Communication Facilities 49
     - (ii) Calling Meetings of Directors 49
     - (iii) Notice 49
   - (j) Duties 50
   - (k) Conduct of Business 50
   - (l) Managing Director 50
   - (m) Disclosure by Director of Interest in Contracts 51
   - (n) General Notice of Interest 53
   - (o) Liability of Directors 53
   - (p) Consent of Director at Meeting 57
   - (q) Liability of Directors for Wages 57
   - (r) Limitation of Liability 57
   - (s) Removal of Directors 58
2. Officers 59
3. Standards of Care 60

Chapter 4 **ONBIS — Companies Branch Automation** 63

1. ONBIS — The System 63
   - (a) Special Notices 64
   - (b) Failure to File Special Notice(s) 65
2. ONBIS — The Public Record 66
3. The Automation Process 66
4. Conversion to Automation 67
5. Current Conversion Status 67

6. Electronic Filing 69
7. Forms 70
8. MyBIS 71

Chapter 5 **The Act of Incorporation** 73
1. Clearance of Name 73
(a) Restrictions 74
(b) Requirements 75
(c) Form of Documents 79
(d) Fees 80
2. Corporate Powers 81
(a) General 81
(b) Power to Act Outside Ontario 82
(c) Acting Outside Powers 82
(d) Loans to Shareholders, Directors, etc. 82
3. Contracts 84
(a) Elements of Contracts 84
(i) Offer and Acceptance 84
(ii) Consideration 84
(iii) Competent Parties 85
(iv) Genuine Consent 85
(v) Legal Purpose 85
(b) Types of Contracts 85
(i) Contracts in Writing under Seal 85
A. Executor's promise 86
B. Guarantee 86
C. Marriage settlements/dowry 86
D. Contracts for the sale of land 86
E. Contracts for more than one year 87
(ii) Contracts in Writing not under Seal 87
(iii) Parol Contract 88
(iv) Power of Attorney 88
(v) Pre-incorporation Contracts 88
A. Adoption of pre-incorporation Contracts ... 89
B. Non-adoption of pre-incorporation contracts 89
C. Exception to subsection (1) 89
4. Shares 90

(a) Rights of Shareholders 90
(b) Shares within a Class Equal 91
(c) Equality of Shares of a Class 94
5. Other Provisions in Articles of Incorporation 95
6. Preparation of Articles of Incorporation 97
7. Consent of First Director 110
8. Filing Articles of Incorporation 110

Chapter 6 **Organizing the Corporation** 115
1. Corporate Records 115
2. Corporate Seal 118
(a) Desk Seal 119
(b) Corporate Embosser 119
(c) Pocket Seal 119
3. Share Certificates 119
4. By-Laws 123
(a) General 123
(b) Preparing By-laws 123
(c) Multiple Director By-Laws 124
(i) Section 2.01 Powers 124
(ii) Section 3.10 Casting Vote 125
(iii) Section 5.01 Appointment of Officers 125
(iv) Section 7.02 Lien for Indebtedness 125
(v) Section 9.01 Financial Year 126
(vi) Section 11.01 Signing Officers 126
(vii) Section 11.02 Corporate Seal 126
(viii) Section 13.01 Repeal 127
(ix) By-law No. 2 127
(x) By-law No. 3 127
(d) Single Director By-law 128
5. Organizational Resolutions 129
(a) Election or Appointment of Officers 129
(b) Issue Share(s) to Incorporator(s) 130
(c) Approve the Form of Share Certificates Required for Authorized Capital of the Corporation 130
(d) Adoption of Corporate Seal 130
(e) Banking Resolution 131
(f) Site of Registered (Head) Office 131

(g) Financial/Fiscal Year End 131
(h) Subscription for Share(s) 132
(i) Confirmation that Resolutions Passed 132
(j) Pre-incorporation Contract 133
(k) Shareholders 133
(i) Election of Director(s) 133
(ii) Waiver of Audit 134
A. Appointing an auditor 134
B. Persons disqualified as auditors 134
C. Annual audit/auditor's report 134
D. Report of auditor to the shareholders 135
(iii) Appointment of Accountant 136
(iv) Confirmation Clause 136
(l) Directors 137
6. Post-Organizational Resolutions of Directors 138
7. Summary of Organizational Resolutions 139
8. Registers 140
(a) Directors' Register 141
(b) Securities Register 141
(c) Register of Transfers 142
(d) Shareholders' Register 143
(e) Shareholders' Ledger 143
9. The Corporate Bank Account 145
(a) Banking Resolution 146
(b) Certificate of Incumbency 147
(c) Service Charges and Fees/Financial Services 147
(d) Specimen Signature Card(s) 148
(e) Corporate Seal 149
(f) Safety Deposit Box 150
10. The *Corporations Information Act* 150
(a) Initial Return/Notice of Change — Form 1 151
(i) Annual Return (Page 1) 153
(ii) Schedule A 154
(iii) Director Information 154
(iv) Officer Information 155
(v) Schedule K 155
11. Corporations Tax 155

12. Exemption From Filing Corporate Tax Returns 156
13. General Consent for Destruction of Books and Records 158
  (a) Conditions 159
  (b) Corporation Tax Account Number 161

Chapter 7 **Reports** 163
1. Report to Client 163
  (a) Incorporation 164
  (b) Authorized Capital 164
  (c) Restrictions on Business 165
  (d) Registered Office 165
  (e) Organization 166
  (f) Directors and Officers 166
  (g) Execution of Instruments 167
  (h) Auditors/Accountants 167
  (i) Financial Year 167
  (j) Issued Shares 167
  (k) Annual Returns 167
  (l) Corporation Tax Status 168
  (m) Corporate Records 168
2. Legal Account for Services Rendered 168
3. Report to Auditor or Accountant 169

Chapter 8 **Sharholders'Agreements** 171
1. Purpose 171
2. Contents Check-list 172
  (a) General Preamble 172
  (b) Specific Clauses to Consider Including 173
  (c) Other Provisions 175
    (i) Share Restrictions 175
    (ii) Board of Directors 175
    (iii) Financing 175
    (iv) Employment Contracts 176
    (v) Corporate Bank Account 176
    (vi) Waiving Appointment of Auditor 176
    (vii) Shareholder Defaults 177
  (d) Miscellaneous Provisions 177
3. Unanimous Shareholder Agreements 178

Chapter 9 **Articles of Amendment** 181

1. Introduction 181
2. Fundamental Changes 181

Chapter 10 **Annual Meetings** 185
1. Requirements 185
(a) Notice of Meetings 185
(b) Record Date 186
(c) Place of Meetings 187
(d) Voting Rights 187
(e) Proxy 187
(f) Special Business 188
(g) Minutes or Resolutions 188
2. Minutes and Resolutions 189
(a) Preliminary Directors' Meetings 189
(b) Annual Meeting of Shareholders 190
(c) Adjourned/Reconvened Preliminary Directors' Meeting 191
3. Sole Director/Sole Shareholder Resolutions 192
4. Sole Director/Multiple Shareholder Resolutions 193
5. Auditors 193
(a) Exemptions from Audit Provisions 193
(b) Persons Prohibited 195
(c) Auditor's Report 195
(d) Right to Attend Meetings 195
(e) Amending Auditor's Report 195
6. Financial Statements 196

Chapter 11 **Extra-Provincial Corporations** 197
1. Introduction 197
2. Classes of Extra-Provincial Corporations 197
3. Name Clearance 200
4. Class 3 Applications 202
5. Application for Extra-Provincial Licence 203
6. Application for Amendment to Extra-Provincial Licence 203
7. Application for Termination of Extra-Provincial Licence 204
8. Signatures on Documents 204
9. Forms on the Internet 204

10. Certificates 204
11. Initial Return — *Corporations Information Act* 205

Chapter 12 **Searches** 207

1. Outline of Searches Made 207
2. Search Fees 207
3. ONBIS and Automation 208
4. Types of Searches 209
   (a) Partnership or Proprietorship/Business Search 209
   (b) Name/Style Registration Search 210
   (c) Corporate Search 210
      (i) Ontario Corporations 210
      (ii) Bonds/Debentures 211
         A. Corporations of Microfiche Index 216
      (iii) Federal Corporations 219
         A. Deposit Account 220
      (iv) Automated Fax Information Sources 221
      (v) On-Line Services 222
      (vi) Other Jurisdictions 223
   (d) *Personal Property Act* Search 223
      (i) Financing Statement/Claim for Lien — Form 1C 229
      (ii) Financing Change Statement/Change Statement — Form 2C 229
      (iii) Financing Change Statement/Change Statement — Form 3C 229
      (iv) Motor Vehicle Schedule — Form 4C 230
      (v) PPSA Enquiry Process 231
         A. Procedure in making PPSA search 232
         B. In-person search 234
         C. Written enquiries 234
         D. Up-date search 234
   (e) Section 427 Search Under the *Bank Act* 236
   (f) Bankruptcy Search 239
      (i) General 239
      (ii) Making the Search 241
   (g) Ontario Securities Commission Search (Micromedia) 244

(i) OSC Bulletin PLUS 246
(ii) Prospectus Researcher PLUS 246
(h) Executions 247
(i) Patents Search 247
(j) Motor Vehicle Search 248

Part III Federal Corporations

Chapter 13 **Federal Incorporations** 253
1. Introduction 253
2. Glossary of Terms 253
3. Incorporation 255
(a) Name and NUANS System 255
(b) Key to Reading Computer Printout 258
(c) Name Clearance 259

Chapter 14 **Incorporation — Federal Jurisdiction** 267
1. Introduction 267
2. Objectives of the *Canada Businss Corporations Act* 268
3. Advantages of Federal Incorporations 268
4. Effecting the Incorporation 270
(a) Articles of Incorporation 270
(b) Notice of Registered Office or Notice of Change of Registered Office — Form 3 279
(c) Notice of Directors or Notice of Change of Directors — Form 6 279
(d) Filing Articles of Incorporation 280
(e) Electronic Filing Centre 282
5. Directors and Officers 283
6. Shares and Securities 287

Chapter 15 **Organization** 291
1. Corporate Supplies 291
2. By-laws 291
3. Organizational Resolutions of Directors 292
4. Organizational Resolutions of Shareholders 293
5. Post-Organizational Resolutions of Directors 293
6. Registers 294
7. Report to Client 294

Chapter 16 **Articles of Amendment** 295

1. Fundamental Changes 295
2. Filing Articles of Amendment 296

Chapter 17 **Annual Meetings of Shareholders** 297
1. Requirements 297
2. Notice and Matters Considered 298

Chapter 18 **Annual Returns** 301
1. Requirements 301
2. Standard Industrial Classification Code ("S.I.C.C.") 302

Part IV Forms

1. Sole Proprietorship and Partnerships

1.1 Registration — *Business Names Act* — Form 1 305
1.2 Registration — *Business Names Act* — Form 2: For Corporations (formerly known as Name/Style Registration) 307
1.3 Declaration — *Limited Partnerships Act* — Form 3 309
1.4 Registration — *Business Names Act* — Form 6: For Ontario Limited Liability Partnership, Extra-Provincial Limited Liability Partnership, Extra-Provincial Limited Liability Company 311
1.5 Ontario Business Registration Application 313
1.6 Services Requisition in Respect of Unincoprorated Businesses 324
1.7 Toronto-Dominion Bank — Business Banking Agreement — Sole Proprietorship/Partnership/Association/Corporation/ Joint Venture 326
1.8 Toronto-Dominion Bank — Checklist — Business Accounts 331
1.9 Toronto-Dominion Bank — Specimen Signature Card 333

5. The Act of Incorporation

5.1 Articles of Incorporation — *Business Corporations Act* — Form 1 335
5.2 Consent to Act as a First Director — *Business Corporations Act* — Form 2 343
5.3 NUANS Name Search — Ontario Biased 344
5.4 Sample Form of Certificate Endorsed on Articles of Incorporation by Companies Branch 352

6. Organizing the Corporation

6.1 Common Share Certificate — Ontario 353
6.2 Preference Share Certificate — Ontario 355
6.3 Non-Designated Share Certificate — Ontario 357
6.4 (Ontario) *Business Corporations Act* By-law (For Corporations with more than 1 Director) 359
6.5 (Ontario) *Business Corporations Act* By-law (For 1 Director — 1 Shareholder Corporations) 382
6.6 Declaration of Trust 392
6.7 Directors' Register 393
6.8 Officers' Register 394
6.9 Register of Debt Obligations 395
6.10 Stock Transfer Register 396
6.11 Shareholders' Register 397
6.12 Shareholders' Ledger 398
6.13 Canadian Imperial Bank of Commerce — Resolution of Directors Regarding Banking and Security 399
6.14 Certificate as to Non-Adoption of a Corporate Seal 403
6.15 Initial Return/Notice of Change by an Ontario Corporation — *Corporations Information Act* — Form 1 404
6.16 Schedule A to *Corporations Information Act* — Form 1 406
6.17 Annual Return — *Corporations Tax Act* 408
6.18 Initial Return/Notice of Change by an Extra-Provincial Corporation — *Corporations Information Act* — Form 2 412
6.19 Corporations Tax Return — *Corporations Tax Act* — CT23 414

9. Articles of Amendment

9.1 Articles of Amendment — *Business Corporations Act* — Form 3 422

10. Annual Meetings

10.1 Minutes of a Meeting of the Board of Directors 426
10.2 Minutes of the Annual Meeting of Shareholders 428
10.3 Alternative Clauses for Annual Meeting of Shareholders 431
10.4 Alternative Set-up for Annual Meeting of Shareholders Where Proxy or Proxies are Present 433
10.5 Minutes of the Adjourned Meeting of the Board of Directors 434
10.6 Resolutions of the Sole Director 435
10.7 Minutes of an Annual Meeting of Shareholders 436

10.8 Auditor(s) Consent and Waiver of Notice 438

11. Extra-Provincial Corporations

11.1 Application for Extra-Provincial Licence — *Extra Provincial Corporations Act* — Form 1 439

11.2 Appointment of/Revised Appointment of Agent for Service — *Extra Provincial Corporations Act* — Form 2 442

11.3 Application for Amendment to Extra-Provincial Licence — *Extra Provincial Corporations Act* — Form 3 443

11.4 Application for Termination of Extra Provincial Licence — *Extra Provincial Corporations Act* — Form 4 445

12. Searches

12.1 Registration or Renewal of Business Name or Style — *Business Names Act* — Form 2 446

12.2 Request for Corporate Information 447

12.3 Industry Canada Purchase Order/Invoice 448

12.4 *Personal Property Security Act* — Financing Statement/Claim for Lien — Form 1C 452

12.5 *Personal Property Security Act* — Financing Change Statement/ Change Statement — Form 2C 453

12.6 *Personal Property Security Act* — Motor Vehicle Schedule — Form 4C 454

12.7 Personal Property Security Registration Service Request 455

12.8 *Personal Property Security Act* — Enquiry Request 456

12.9 Notice of Intention — *Bank Act* 457

12.10 Bankrtupcy Certificate 458

12.11 Application for Vehicle Record Search 459

13. Federal Incorporations

13.1 Federal Name Granting Policy Compendium 460

14. Incorporation — Federal Jurisdiction

14.1 Articles of Incorporation — *Canada Business Corporations Act* — Form 1 519

14.2 Notice of Registered Office or Notice of Change of Registered Office — *Canada Business Corporations Act* — Form 3 523

14.3 Notice of Directors or Notice of Change of Directors — *Canada Business Corporations Act* — Form 6 525

14.4 Common Share with Restriction — Canada 527

14.5 Preference Share Certificate — Canada 529

15. Organization — Federal Corporation

15.1 By-law No. 1 531

16. Articles of Amendment

16.1 Articles of Amendment — *Canada Business Corporations Act* — Form 4 551

18. Annual Returns

18.1 Annual Return (Section 256) — *Canada Business Corporations Act* — Form 22 553

18.2 T2 Corporation Income Tax Return 555

18.3 Industry Canada — Annual Return — *Canada Business Corporatons Act* 563

18.4 Notice of Change of Directors, *Canada Business Corporation Act* 567

Appendices

Appendix A — Frequently Used Addresses and Telephone Numbers 571

Appendix B — Schedule of Current Fees 593

Appendix C — Ontario Business Connects Service Locations 603

Index 613

Part I

Forms of Business Organization

1

SOLE PROPRIETORSHIPS AND PARTNERSHIPS

1. Sole Proprietorship

A sole proprietorship is where an individual carries on business for the purpose of profit. This is the simplest method by which an individual can carry on business in Ontario. The sole proprietorship is less expensive than a corporation to set up, and usually involves fewer regulations. As a sole proprietor, the individual is allowed to write off business losses against his or her personal income. In the early stages of the business, this can be an attractive advantage. At the same time, all profits from the business are taxable at the personal rate of the sole proprietor. As the sole proprietor has unlimited liability to creditors for business debts and expenses, the individual's business and personal assets, with certain exceptions, are available to satisfy creditors of the business. In a proprietorship, one individual performs all the functions required for the successful operation of the business. The proprietor obtains the capital, establishes and operates the business, owns all the assets, assumes all the risks, derives all the profits, suffers all the losses, and pays all the taxes. The proprietor is said to be self-employed, and the success of the business depends on his or her management skills and decision-making.

(a) Business Name Registration

Under the *Business Names Act*, R.S.O. 1990, c. B.16, which came into force on May 1, 1991, a sole proprietor, who carries on business under a name other than his or her own name, must register that name using the prescribed Form 1 under the Act. For example, if Mary Mott conducts business as "Mary Mott", she does not need to register the name. However, if she operates as "Mary Mott's Marketing Services" or "Mott's Marketing Services", she will have to register the name. The Form 1 is a dual form to be also used for registration of a general partnership's business name where that name is different from the names of the partners. The registration places the business name in the public record maintained by the Companies Branch of the Ontario Ministry of Consumer and Business Services, and allows consumers and business people to find the owners or principals behind a business name. The registrant must set out the name and address of the business, and a description of the business activity to be carried out. The registration fee is currently $80, and the registration is effective for five years from the date it is accepted for registration by the Registrar. The business name registration can be renewed prior to the end of the five-year term, and the fee is also $80. Form 1, which can be used either for a new registration, or renewal, is registered at the Companies Branch Public Office of the Ministry of Consumer and Business Services at 393 University Avenue, Suit 200 in the City of Toronto, or submitted by mail. The Forms are available at the Public Office or local land registration offices across the province.

Currently, the Companies Branch will accept personal cheques in payment of registration fees. Registration fees formerly were payable either in cash, by money order, solicitor's cheque or certified personal cheques. Personal cheques will only be accepted with suitable identification such as a valid driver's licence with a photograph of the individual. The current registration fees are set out in Appendix B. All cheques or other negotiable instruments submitted in payment of registration fees are payable to the Ontario Minister of Finance and the required fee must accompany the appropriate registration form when it is presented for registration.

The Ontario Business Registration Application, which includes business name registration, has been recently developed by the Ministry and can be submitted over the Internet or using a computer terminal at one of the Ontario Business Connects self-help workstations. The fee for the electronic registration is $60. This Application can also be registered using designated private-sector service providers. This new development in business name registration is discussed in section 6 below.

In selecting a business name, the regulations under the *Business Names Act* should be reviewed in order to ensure the acceptability of the proposed business name. In particular, under the regulation entitled *Restrictions Respecting Names*, certain words or expressions cannot be used:

- ☐ words or expressions, in any language, that are obscene or objectionable in nature;
- ☐ words that imply the business is a different type of organization. For example, the sole proprietor may not imply that a sole proprietorship is a partnership by using the word "partners" in the name;
- ☐ words that imply the business is associated with the Crown or the Government of Canada, any province of Canada or any municipal government may not be used without the written consent of the appropriate authority; and

- ☐ names of specific individuals may not be used unless the individual has a material interest in the business activity at any time before or during the registration period of the name and the individual consented to the use of his or her name. If the individual is not living and the name is used within 30 days of the date of death, the written consent of the estate must be obtained;

Business names must be registered in the Roman alphabet including English, French, Spanish, Italian, and Latin, and may contain Arabic numerals. The following marks may also be included in the name, but may not be used as the first character: ! “ ” « » # $ % & ’ ( ) * + , - . / \ : ; < = > ? [ ] , ’ ‘ ^ ”

The prescribed form must be fully completed with the information requested in block capital letters, either typewritten or in legible printing suitable for microfilming. Failure to provide any of the necessary information or to comply with the other instructions provided with the form will prevent registration. Both copies of Form 1 are to be submitted, and the registrant's "client copy" will be returned with a validation in the bottom right-hand corner. In addition, the registrant is given a Business Identification Number (BIN) and the expiry date for the registration. The Companies Branch does not issue reminders prior to the expiry of the five-year registration period, and it is the responsibility of the registrant to ensure that the business name registration is renewed on time.

Once the prescribed Form 1 is registered, further filings will only be required in the following circumstances:

1. A change of business name or sole proprietor. This is considered to be a new registration and the prescribed fee must be paid when filing the new Form 1.
2. A change in address or a change in activity. This is considered an amendment to the information in the Form 1, and the amended Form 1 must be filed within 15 days of the change. There is no filing fee in this instance.
3. A renewal of the registration is required every five years and the appropriate fee must be paid when the renewal is filed.
4. Should the proprietorship stop using the business name, a cancellation should be filed. There is no charge for filing a cancellation.

The Form 1 is designed as a multi-purpose form that is to be used for all of the above filings.

Beginning in May, 2001, registrants who register, renew or amend a business name at the Companies Branch Public Office in Toronto or by mail will receive a Master Business Licence (MBL). For the time being, the Companies Branch will continue to provide registrants with their copy of the Form 1. The Master Business Licence can be used as proof of business name registration at financial institutions and to facilitate any other business-related registration with the Ontario government. This one licence will eventually replace many of the government forms, permits, licences and certificates held by businesses.

(b) Name Search and its Importance

Before making a final decision on the business name, a search should be conducted to determine if someone else is already using the name, and where that business is located. When conducting a name search, the Companies Branch will look only for the specific name requested. Accordingly, it is suggested that more than one search be made in order to discover whether variations of a particular name are being utilized. For example, "Smith's Shoe Shop" and "Smith's Shoe Shoppe" are considered two separate searches. Searches can be conducted at the Companies Branch Public Office in Toronto, at Ontario Business Connects workstations throughout Ontario, and through private service providers, Business Access, Create-a-Co., and OnCorp Direct Inc. The *Business Names Act* does not prohibit registration of identical names but if an identical name is used or the selected name is confusingly similar to an existing name, it could result in a lawsuit. The fee for a search at the Companies Branch Public Office, or through the mail, is $12 while a search through the Internet, or one of the Ontario Business Connects workstations is $8. A sample of the requisition form used for this search is included in Part IV — Forms (Services Requisition in Respect of Unincorporated Businesses, Form 1.6). At the same time, a search should be made of the master microfiche index of corporations incorporated and/or carrying on business in Ontario. This index of the corporate names is located in the Public Office and there is no charge for a personal search of this index.

The name search is processed using the Ontario Business Information System (ONBIS) that the Companies Branch introduced on June 27, 1992. ONBIS contains a record of virtually all registered businesses and non-profit corporations that have operated, or are currently carrying on business, in Ontario. When conducting a name search, a Business Names Report is requested from the ONBIS database which report displays current information on the public record for business names registered on or after April 1, 1994. In particular, this report displays the business names of sole proprietorships and general partnerships (Form 1), and business corporations (Form 2). The report includes the business name, registration date, expiry date, business address, business activity, registrant name(s) and address(es), documents filed and filing dates and the Business Identification Number (BIN).

There are certain sanctions under the *Business Names Act* for non-compliance with its provisions. If a business name is not registered as required under the Act, it is a provincial offence contrary to s. 10 of the Act, and the individual can be fined up to $2,000. A further sanction is the individual not being able to maintain a court action in the Ontario courts. Under s. 7 of the Act, a person carrying on business in contravention of the Act is not capable of maintaining a proceeding in Ontario in connection with that business except with leave of the court. Leave of the court shall only be granted if the person can prove that: (a) the failure to register was inadvertent; (b) the public has not been deceived or misled; and (c) the person was not in contravention of the Act when the application was made to the court. The person would, it appears, have to register before filing an application for leave with the court.

Furthermore, it is important that the business name selected is distinctive and not confusing or deceptively similar to an existing registered name. Under s. 6 of the Act, a person who suffers damages by reason of the registration of a name that is the same or deceptively similar to another person's registered name is entitled to recover compensation from the registrant for damages suffered because of the registration. The term ''person'' is defined under the Act as including an individual, a sole proprietorship, a corporation, or an unincorporated association or organization. Although, there is a cap of $500 for the award of damages for proceeding under the Act, the court can also order the Registrar to cancel the registration that was the cause of action (s. 6(3)). This can result in significant losses to the business through damage to any goodwill created under that business name, and by being forced to change its promotional material, stationery, business documentation, and office signage.

There is also the common law cause of action of ''passing off'' where the proposed name is similar to, or the same as, that of an existing business. In some circumstances, an existing business may have the right to request that a new business change its name. Failure to comply with this request could result in a court action for attempting to ''pass off'' the new business to the public by trading on the business reputation of the existing successful business. Alternatively, if the existing business was unsuccessful or had gained a bad business reputation, it would be more important to eliminate the possibility of confusion in the minds of potential customers or suppliers. If, for example, the existing business had a reputation of slow payment or non-payment of debts, it could adversely affect the obtaining of credit by the new business. This potential problem can be eliminated by searching the name before registration is made.

(c) Cancellation of Registration

When a sole proprietor decides to cease business, the Form 1 should be filed requesting cancellation by marking the appropriate box on the form. The Business Identification Number (BIN) previously assigned by the Registrar is also to be included on the form. It is important that the cancellation be registered because it is evidence that the personal liability of the sole proprietor for debts of the business has terminated. A cancellation may arise where a business that was commenced as a sole proprietorship has become a runaway success and the principal decides to incorporate a corporation in order to limit personal liability and obtain the other benefits incorporation can bring. The business is then purchased by the corporation from the sole proprietor. By registering the Form 1 requesting cancellation, the public is informed of when the sole proprietor ceased to be responsible for the contracts and debts of the business and when the corporation assumed these responsibilities. Of course, personal liability will continue for a transitional period of time until the sole proprietor is released from existing contractual obligations. There is no filing fee for the cancellation.

(d) Licensing or Permits

The sole proprietor should also be aware of any licence, permit or other related government regulations governing the particular business activity. Persons who provide professional services generally must be licensed to practise the particular specialty in the province. The legislation governing professions such as medicine, dentistry, law, architecture and engineering is usually provincial. Many semi-professional and skilled trade activities are also subject to provincial licensing or registration. Individuals operating a business in the beverage alcohol or gaming sector may need to be licensed under the Liquor Licence Act or Gaming Control Act. If the sole proprietor is engaged in the retail trade, a provincial sales tax permit is required and a federal goods and services tax (GST) registration may be also required. Municipalities often impose their own registration or licensing of certain business activity in order to protect or control that activity. Skilled trades, the operation of taxis, and various service-oriented businesses frequently require municipal licences to operate within the municipal area. For assistance in starting up a new business, the Ontario Ministry of Economic Development, Trade and Tourism operates self-help offices across the province that offer information or advice in conducting market analysis and developing business plans.

(e) Bank Account

A sole proprietor or sole owner will need a bank account for the business. The requirements for the particular financial institution at which the account is to be opened should be checked and the proper forms obtained, together with the requisite signature card. Some banks may require more than one signature card. An example of the forms required by the Toronto-Dominion Bank [now TD Canada Trust] are shown in Part IV — Forms. These are generic forms designed to accommodate all types of businesses such as sole proprietorships, partnerships, associations, corporations and joint ventures. Under the federal *Proceeds of Crime (Money Laundering) Act*, S.C. 1991, c. 26, banks require a minimum of two pieces of identification from each new client of the bank when an account is opened. Each signing officer on a bank account is required to produce a passport, driver's licence or birth certificate.

2. Partnerships Generally

(a) Introduction

A partnership is the business relationship existing between two or more persons or corporations which has been formed by those involved to make a profit from a common enterprise. The governing legislation for general partnerships in Ontario is the *Partnerships Act*, R.S.O. 1990, c. P.5. Section 2 of this Act defines a "partnership" as "the relation that subsists between persons carrying on a business in common with a view to profit. . . ." This definition excludes all associations and organizations which are not carried on for profit such as social clubs, charitable organizations and amateur sports groups.

The first partnerships were formed by merchants who united for mutual protection against thieves in trading ventures. In those times, travellers were at risk in making journeys of any kind and especially if they carried merchandise. Persons travelling alone often failed to reach their destination or were never heard of again. Marco Polo travelled by caravan to Cathay and was subject to attacks by robbers. Survival depended on strength of arms, not the strength of the law and its enforcement that is relied on today. Eventually the merchants extended their association for protection to include the trading itself and shared the risks and profits of the trading ventures.

Partnerships had developed into a common form of business organization by the time of the Roman Empire and were used for the buying and selling of goods in distant places. If a trading venture involved a high risk or a large amount of capital, a group of people would join together in a partnership. These early partnerships were founded on mutual respect, trust and confidence between the partners.

Partnerships continued to flourish in feudal England and adequately served the needs of the business community because capital requirements were not large. However, the discovery of distant markets in the New World in the 15th and 16th centuries increased the need for capital. This need for more capital led to a change in the structure of partnerships and eventually, in England, to joint stock companies. A joint stock company was basically a partnership in which those investing remained liable for all debts but delegated the management to a board of management. Today, depending on the success of the particular partnership, management may be delegated to other individuals but the partners are still personally liable for all debts, unless the partnership agreement states otherwise.

General partnerships and limited partnerships have elements in common, but also specific differences. In order to determine if a partnership exists, the parties must agree to take part in the business to make a profit. It is not sufficient to merely call themselves partners. The partnership is collectively called a "firm" and the name under which the business is carried on is referred to as the "firm name". Partnerships can often be recognized by the use of the word "company", which is often added to the name or names of the partners used in the firm name. Another indication that a business is a partnership is the use of the words "and Son", i.e., J.M. Jones & Son.

(b) Partnerships Act

The *Partnerships Act* contains various provisions to safeguard customers and the public dealing with partnerships. The Act provides that persons dealing with a partnership are entitled to rely on the following:

1. Each partner is an agent for the partnership for the purpose of the business (section 6).
2. The acts of each partner bind the firm and all other partners unless the partner had no authority to act in a particular matter and informed the party involved in the particular matter, or the party knew that the partner lacked the authority, or the party knew or believed that the person was not a partner (section 6).
3. Each partner is responsible or liable along with the other partners for all debts of the partnership/firm while a partner and the obligation continues after death. The estate of a partner is liable, after payment of other debts of the deceased (section 10).
4. Each partner is liable for any wrongful act or omission of any of the partners which causes loss or injury to anyone not a member of the firm (section 11).
5. Notice given to a known partner in connection with the partnership business is all that is required to give notice to all members of the partnership. One exception to this general rule is in cases of fraud on the firm committed by or with the consent of that partner (section 17).
6. A partner is only liable for debts of the partnership from the date on which the person joined the partnership until the date he or she ceases to be a partner. However, this provision can be amended by the terms of the partnership agreement that exists among the partners (section 18).
7. A continuing guarantee given by the partnership to a third party in respect of transactions of the partnership is revoked as to future transactions by

any change in the constitution of the partnership unless there is agreement to the contrary (section 19).

8. After a dissolution, the accounts between the partners are settled in accordance with the partnership agreement. If there is no partnership agreement, then provision is made under section 44 of the Act as to how these matters are to be handled. Generally speaking, losses and deficiencies of capital are to be paid first out of profits, next out of capital and lastly, if necessary, by the individual partners on the same ratio that each partner was entitled to share in profits. The assets of the firm, which include any sums contributed by the partners to make up losses or deficiencies of capital, are to be applied first in paying the debts and liabilities due to persons not partners in the firm.

Refer to section 44 for details on the priority of payments to be made when all debts and liabilities have been settled.

The legislation also deals with many aspects of the business relationship within the partnership:

1. The mutual rights and duties of partners may be varied by the consent of all the partners, whether express or implied from the course of dealing of the partners, regardless of whether the mutual rights or duties are set out under the statute or in an agreement (section 20).

2. Partnership property is defined as all property, rights and interests in property brought into the partnership or acquired on behalf of the firm/partnership for the purposes of the partnership. Partnership property is owned by the firm, not by the individual members of the partnership (section 21).

3. Property purchased with partnership money is deemed to have been purchased for the firms unless the contract purchasing the property states otherwise (section 22).

4. Rules as to the duties and interests of the partners are set out under the Act and unless an agreement states otherwise, all partners are entitled to share equally in capital and profits and must contribute equally towards all losses. In addition, the firm must indemnify every partner in respect of payments made and personal liabilities incurred either in the ordinary course of business or done for the preservation of the business or property of the firm. The Act also provides that:

   (i) any advances or payments made by a partner beyond the amount of capital he has agreed to subscribe is entitled to annual interest of five per cent from the date such advance or payment is made;

   (ii) every partner may take part in the management of the business;

   (iii) no partner is entitled to be paid for taking part in the business;

(iv) all existing partners must consent to a person being introduced into the business as a partner;

(v) until profits are calculated, a partner is not entitled to interest on the capital subscribed;

(vi) a change in the nature of the partnership business requires the consent of all existing partners. A change in any ordinary business matters may be decided by a majority of the partners. This means that a majority of the partners could decide, for instance, to change suppliers of certain goods. However, any decision to fundamentally change the business of the partnership would have to be made by all partners (section 24).

5. A partner cannot be expelled from the partnership by a majority of the partners unless the power to make this expulsion has been included in the partnership agreement (section 25).

6. If the term of the partnership has not been determined, that is, the length of time the partnership shall carry on business has not been stated, the partnership is said to exist "at will". A partnership at will can be dissolved by one of the partners:

(i) at any time giving notice to all the other partners to end the partnership. If the partnership was entered into by written agreement, then notice in writing must be given (section 26);

(ii) dying or becoming insolvent, unless the agreement among the partners provides otherwise (section 33);

(iii) permitting his share of the partnership property to be pledged under the Act for his personal debt (section 33).

If the partnership is established for a fixed term, that is, either for a number of years or perhaps as a joint venture for a single purpose, then the partnership ends at the time specified in the agreement. There is provision under the Act that where a partnership for a fixed term continues without any new agreement, the rights and obligations of the partners remain the same as before, so far as they are consistent with a partnership at will. When the fixed term of a partnership has expired and the business still continues, for instance the assets of the partnership are not sold and the partners paid out the capital invested, it is presumed under the Act that the business is a continuance of the partnership (section 27).

7. Partners are required to supply true accounts and full information about the business to any partner or legal representative, i.e., an executor of the estate of a deceased partner or a lawyer acting on behalf of a disgruntled partner (section 28).

8. If a partner acquires any personal benefit from a transaction involving the

partnership or from the use of the partnership name, property or business connections without the consent of the other partners, that partner must account to the firm for such benefit. This provision also applies to transactions undertaken after the dissolution of a partnership by death of a partner and before its affairs are completely wound up. It makes no difference if the transactions are undertaken by representatives of the deceased partner or by a surviving partner (section 29).

9. A partner cannot carry on a private business which is the same as that carried on by the partnership, without the consent of the other partners. Should a partner breach this provision of the Act, all profits made from this private business must be turned over to the partnership (section 30).

10. Certain circumstances, set out under number 6 above, can dissolve a partnership. A partnership is also dissolved in every case by the occurrence of any event:

    (i) that makes it unlawful for the business to be carried on; or

    (ii) that makes it unlawful for the members of the firm to carry on the business in partnership (section 34).

11. There is provision under the Act that a partner may apply to the court for dissolution of the partnership on various grounds, such as mental incompetence, a partner's permanent incapacity to carry out commitments under the partnership agreement, a partner wilfully and knowingly breaching or breaking the terms of the partnership agreement or acting in such a manner that his conduct adversely affects the carrying on of the partnership business, when the business can only be carried on at a loss or when, in the opinion of the court, circumstances have arisen that make it just and equitable that the partnership be dissolved (section 35).

The legislation further provides that if the rules of equity and of common law applying to partnership conflict with any express provisions of the Act, the provisions of the Act prevail (section 45). In addition, the *Partnerships Act* is to be read and construed as subject to the *Limited Partnerships Act*, R.S.O. 1990, c. L.16, and the *Business Names* Act.

As stated earlier, the parties involved in a partnership agreement must intend to take part in a business which will make a profit. The receipt by a person of a share of the profits from the business is considered *prima facie* evidence that that person is a partner. It is not necessary to participate in losses of the business to be a partner.

3. General Partnership

(a) Introduction

As a business becomes larger, the need for more capital, and for new and varied management skills may require a change in the form of the organization. This can result in a transformation to a general partnership where two or more persons carry on business for the purpose of profit. Alternatively, it may be decided initially to commence the business as a general partnership due to the capital requirements and the need to pool the management skills and business experience of various participants. For the partnership, the "persons" carrying on business can be individuals and/or corporations. The governing legislation for general partnerships is the *Partnership Act*, R.S.O. 1990, c. P.5. Section 2 of this Act defines a "partnership" as "the relation that subsists between persons carrying on business in common with a view to profit ...". This definition excludes all associations and organizations which are not carried on for profit such as social clubs, charitable organizations and amateur sports groups. Many business relationships are also not partnerships within the meaning of the law such as the debtor-creditor relationship and the joint ownership of property.

A general partnership is one in which the partners are jointly responsible for the liabilities of the firm and all may actively take part in the management of the business. In addition, each partner:

1. is an agent of the partnership for business purposes;
2. can bind the partnership unless his or her authority to act is restricted by the other partners and the person with whom the partner is dealing knew he or she had no authority to act;
3. is liable for all debts while a partner; the estate of a deceased partner may be liable unless exempted by the partnership agreement;
4. is liable for the wrongful acts or omissions of other partners;
5. is liable for any guarantees given in the name of the partnership unless there are contrary provisions in the partnership agreement;
6. is liable to the extent of all personal assets for all debts of the partnership;
7. is taxed on all profits received at the personal rate of income tax.

(b) Registration — Business Names Act

The Registrar of Partnerships established a central registry for all declarations, certificates and records under the Act at the office of the Registrar of Partnerships, Companies Division, Toronto, effective as of January 1, 1975.

Prior to this date registration was effected in the local land registry office in the geographical area where the business was carried on. Records prior to 1974 are filed in the Archives of Ontario at 77 Grenville Street, Toronto, Ontario. The records are on film and anyone residing in the City of Toronto must make a personal search. Non-residents can mail a search request to the Archives of Ontario and the search will be made without charge, provided that the pages copied do not exceed six pages. A photocopy charge is made for each page beyond that number.

The *Business Names Act* requires partnerships operating under a name other than the names of the partners to register that business name. This Act does not apply to limited partnerships carrying on business under the *Limited Partnership Act* which is discussed in section 4 below. Form 1 under the *Business Names Act* is a dual form to be used for registration of a sole proprietorship or a partnership composed of individuals, or a corporation, or a combination thereof. Accordingly, the particular type of ownership must be checked off on the form. The same considerations in selecting a business name and the consequences for not registering a business name apply to a partnership as were discussed for sole proprietors in section 1.

Regulation 121/91 under the *Business Names Act*, and in particular, sections 2, 2.1 and 3, governs the registration of the business name. The form may be submitted on behalf of the partnership by one of the partners. If the partnership has 10 or fewer partners, the names and addresses of all partners must be included with the registration (s. 2). Where there are more than 10 partners, this is to be noted on the form, and the partnership may choose one of the partners to register the business name, eliminating the need to file information on all partners (s. 3). In this instance, the designated partner must keep the required information (the partners' names, home addresses or addresses where legal papers can be served) on record at the place of business. These records must also contain a list of persons who joined the partnership after May 1, 1991, and who subsequently left the partnership. The designated partner may delete from the records information concerning a partner who has left the partnership once six years have elapsed after the departure. Upon request, any partner must permit any person to inspect the record during normal business hours and take extracts or make a copy free of charge. The registration period is five years, after which the registration must be renewed and a renewal fee paid.

Effective July 15, 1996, an existing general partnership may register an additional business name other than the firm name of the partnership. This is provided for under section 2.1 of Regulation 121/91, as amended. If the partnership has a place of business in Ontario where it uses the name, the registrant shall set out that address as well as the mailing address of the partnership. If the partnership does not have a place of business in Ontario where it uses that name, but uses that name outside of Ontario, then the registrant shall provide that address where the name is used. Form 5 under the *Business Names Act* is utilized for registering the business name.

If there is a change in information set out in the registration, the registrant shall register an amended registration, showing the change, using Form 1. The Business Identification Number (BIN) assigned by the Registrar shall also be included on the form. Changing the name of the partnership business is considered a new registration and the applicable fee applies. Amendments to the registration may be submitted on behalf of the partnership by one of the partners, or the designated partner, in the case of a partnership having more than 10 partners. Alternatively, the partnership can authorize an attorney acting under a power of attorney to submit the form on behalf of the partnership. There is no filing fee for the amended registration.

Corporate partners must provide the following information when completing a registration (shown as Form 1.2):

1. *corporation name* — inserted in box 8 in the "Additional Information" section;
2. *Ontario corporation number* — assigned on incorporation by the Companies Branch and inserted in box 8 in the "Additional Information" section;
3. *address of the registered (or head) office* — include the number, street, municipality and postal code (a post office box is not acceptable) in box 8; and
4. *name of person authorizing registration* — as the person authorizing the registration is a corporation, and not an individual, the name of the corporation is inserted in the "Additional Information" section in box 9.

The registration fee may be paid in cash, money order or cheque payable to the Ontario Minister of Finance. A handling fee of $35 will be charged for an NSF cheque.

(c) Dissolution or Withdrawal

The duties and rights of a partner on retirement from the partnership or on the dissolution of the partnership are set out in the *Partnerships Act*. Retirement is dealt with under section 26 and when dissolution of the partnership is contemplated, reference should be made to sections 32 to 35.

In addition to the requirements of the *Partnerships Act* and/or the partnership agreement dealing with dissolution or retirement, there are certain requirements under the *Business Names Act* which must be met. Subsection 4(4) of the Act requires that a prescribed form must be registered when any change in the information set out in a registration occurs. These changes could be, for example, a change in address or change in activity, i.e., business. Penalties are provided for any person who contravenes the provisions of the Act or the Regulations or who knowingly makes a false or misleading statement in any document, material, evidence or information submitted or required under the Act. On conviction such a person is liable to a fine of not more than $2,000 or, if the person is a corporation, to a maximum fine of $25,000 (section 10).

Another very valid reason for ensuring that a prescribed form is registered when a partner either retires or leaves a partnership is to determine the date when the liability of that partner ceases. Until a prescribed form is registered updating the public record, it would prove difficult to prove he or she ceased to be a partner so far as creditors are concerned. Since withdrawal from a partnership usually occurs due to death, retirement or a disagreement among the partners, it is essential to the partner withdrawing, or the partner's estate, that this date be established.

4. Limited Partnerships

The governing legislation for limited partnerships is the *Limited Partnerships* Act and the Regulations under that Act.

A limited partnership is defined under subsection 2(1) of the Act:

> A limited partnership may, subject to this Act, be formed to carry on any business that a partnership without limited partners may carry on.

This definition is very broad in scope. A general partnership is described as "the relationship that subsists between persons carrying on a business in common with a view to profit".

In order to qualify as a limited partnership there must be:

1. one or more persons who are general partners; and
2. one or more persons who are limited partners.

(a) Declaration

As soon as the required declaration is filed with the Registrar the limited partnership is formed. The prescribed declaration, Form 3 (Form 1.3 in Part IV — Forms), is a multipurpose form and is used to:

1. register a new limited partnership;
2. record a change in address, activity or information regarding general partners;
3. renew a registration; and
4. cancel an existing registration by filing a declaration of withdrawal.

A Business Identification Number (''BIN'') is assigned by the Registrar to all new registrations filed after April 1, 1994, and must be included in all renewals, changes, dissolutions or withdrawals.

A declaration filed prior to April 1, 1994, acquires a BIN when the first new declaration is filed after that date. The BIN must be set out in all subsequent declarations.

The information regarding general partners in item 7 of Form 3 must be completed by all general partners. If there is more than one general partner, then the requisite information in item 7 must be set out on additional Form 3s as required. In addition, the declaration must be signed by all the general partners in the ''Signature'' space. If the general partner is a corporation, then the name of the corporation and the Ontario Corporation Number are set out in the ''Additional Information'' space. An authorized signing officer of the corporation must sign the declaration, and the name of the officer must be printed under the signature. Where a person is signing for the general partner under a power of attorney, that person must sign the ''Signature'' space, and check the ''Power of Attorney'' box.

The general partners of every limited partnership must keep a record of the limited partners at the principal place of business in Ontario. This information must be made available to the public upon request. It must include the full name and residence address or address for service of each limited partner and the contribution made to the limited partnership.

As with general partnerships, the limited partnership may register an additional business name other than the firm name of the limited partnership. Form 5 under the *Business Names Act* is utilized for this purpose.

Fees for registrations and renewals may be paid in cash, money order or cheque, including personal cheques. A ''handling fee'' of $35 is charged for an NSF cheque. The fees charged for Searches, certified copies of documents or filing of declarations are shown in Appendix B.

Fees are not payable when filing a change, a dissolution or a withdrawal.

The firm name can only contain the surname or a distinctive part of the corporate name of a limited partner if the surname or distinctive part of the corporate name are the same as one of the general partners (section 6). Failure to comply with this provision means that the limited partner is liable to any creditor of the limited partnership to the same extent as a general partner, if that creditor did not have actual knowledge that the limited partner is not a general partner. The declaration expires five years after the filing date unless cancelled or replaced. The filing fee for this declaration is set out in Appendix B.

Failure to file a renewal at the end of the five-year period does not mean that the limited partnership is dissolved. Subsection 3(4) of the Act provides specifically that the limited partnership is not dissolved if the declaratic expire. However, there is an additional fee payable when the new decla is filed and the limited partner may lose his or her limited liability. When reporting to clients on the formation of a limited partnership it would be advisable to emphasize the importance of renewing the declaration prior to, or at, the expiry date in order to avoid this late renewal filing fee and to preserve the limited liability status of the limited partner.

Subsection 3(1) provides that a limited partnership is formed when a declaration is filed with the Registrar in accordance with the Act.

(b) Rights of Limited Partner

There is provision under subsection 5(1) of the Act that a person may be both a general partner and a limited partner at the same time in the same limited partnership. Such a person has the same rights and powers and is subject to the restrictions and liabilities of a general partner, except so far as his or her contribution as a limited partner is concerned. Insofar as his or her contribution as a limited partner, he or she has the same rights against the other partners as any limited partner.

A limited partner may contribute money and property, but not services, to the limited partnership (section 7). A limited partner's liability is confined to the value of the money or other property he or she has contributed, or agreed to contribute, to the limited partnership as set out in the declaration (section 9).

A limited partner, like a general partner, has the right to inspect the partnership books and to take extracts or make copies from these books at any time. The right to full and true information concerning all partnership matters exists under section 10 of the Act. This information must be provided on demand of the limited partner. The right to obtain dissolution of the limited partnership by court order also exists under this section.

Under section 11 a limited partner has, subject to the Act, the right to share in the profits of the limited partnership and to have his contribution returned. There is provision under subsection 11(2) that no payments will be made to either a limited partner or a general partner if the remaining capital would be insufficient to pay the liabilities of the limited partnership to persons who are not limited or general partners.

A limited partner is permitted to transact business with the limited partnership, subject to the restrictions set out in section 12 of the Act. In addition, a limited partner may examine the partnership business, advise on its management, and act as a contractor for, or an agent or employee of, the limited partnership or a general partner, or act as surety for the partnership business.

A limited partner may retain that status only so long as he or she does not take part in the control of the business (section 13).

Under section 15 a limited partner may demand and receive the return of his or her contribution to the business:

1. upon dissolution of the limited partnership;
2. at the time specified in the partnership agreement;
3. if no time is specified in the agreement for the return of the contribution or for the dissolution of the limited partnership, after six months' notice in writing to all of the other partners; and
4. upon the consent of all partners

provided that all liabilities, other than capital contributions, of the limited partnership have been paid or there are sufficient assets to pay them and the partnership agreement is either terminated or amended to reflect the change in the contributions of the partners.

The limited partner can only demand and receive money for his or her contribution to the limited partnership as listed above unless the partnership agreement states otherwise or all the partners consent to some other manner of returning the contribution.

In situations where the limited partner has demanded and not received his or her contribution, or where creditors remain unpaid and there are not sufficient partnership assets to pay such creditors, the limited partner is entitled to have the limited partnership dissolved and its affairs wound up.

The interest of a limited partner may be assigned either before or after his or her death. An assignee who is admitted to all the rights and powers of an outgoing limited partner is known as a "substituted limited partner" provided:

1. the assignor, if authorized in the partnership agreement, so constitutes the assignee; or
2. all partners, except the assignor, consent in writing.

The assignment and substitution as a limited partner does not become effective until a new declaration is filed with the Registrar. A Form 3 signed by at least one general partner shall be filed. This declaration of change expires at the same time as the original declaration.

A dissolution of the limited partnership occurs on the retirement, death or mental incompetence of a general partner or the dissolution of a corporation general partner, unless the remaining general partners continue the business. In order to continue the business the right to do so must be set out in the partnership agreement and the remaining partners must consent (section 21).

The legal representative of a deceased limited partner has all the rights and powers of a limited partner for the purposes of settling the estate and whatever power the limited partner had under the partnership agreement to constitute his assignee or substitute limited partner. The estate is liable for all the liabilities of the deceased limited partner (section 22).

A declaration of dissolution, signed by at least one general partner, shall be filed when the limited partnership is dissolved or all of the limited partners cease to be limited partners. The declaration of dissolution cancels the declaration previously filed by the limited partnership.

In settling the accounts of a limited partnership on dissolution, the business creditors shall be paid first and then, unless the partnership agreement or other agreement provides otherwise, the liabilities of the limited partnership shall be paid as follows:

1. the limited partners shall receive their share of the profits and other compensation by way of income on their contributions to the business;
2. the limited partners shall receive their contributions;
3. the general partners shall then receive:
   (i) any amounts due except for capital and profits;
   (ii) any profits; and
   (iii) any capital.

(c) Extra-provincial Limited Partnership

Provision is made in the Act for "extra-provincial limited partnership" which is defined as a limited partnership organized under the laws of a jurisdiction other than Ontario.

An extra-provincial limited partnership is required to file a declaration with the Registrar in the prescribed form before commencing business in Ontario. Subsection 25(2) states that business is being carried on by such limited partnership if it:

1. solicits business in Ontario;
2. has a listing in a telephone directory for any part of Ontario;
3. shows its name in an advertisement showing an Ontario address;
4. has a resident agent or representative or a warehouse, office or place of business in Ontario;
5. owns real estate in Ontario;
6. effects a distribution of securities in Ontario by way of a prospectus filed with the Ontario Securities Commission that complies with the *Securities Act*, R.S.O. 1990, c. S.5, and Regulations thereunder or;
7. it otherwise carries on business in Ontario.

In addition to the declaration, an extra-provincial limited partnership must file with the Registrar a power of attorney naming a resident of Ontario as its representative. The power of attorney shall be in Form 4 under the Act. A change in the name or address of the attorney would necessitate the filing of a new power of attorney. Similarly, if there is a change in the name of the extra-provincial limited partnership, a new declaration and power of attorney must be filed.

Cancellation of the declaration and the power of attorney can be effected by filing a declaration of withdrawal signed by a minimum of one general partner (section 25).

An extra-provincial limited partnership which has not filed the required declaration and power of attorney is not capable of maintaining any action in the provincial courts in connection with any contracts or torts arising from its business (section 28).

A general or limited partner may give written permission for some other person to sign any document required under the Act on his behalf. However, the person signing must indicate that he or she is signing on behalf of a general or limited partner (section 32).

(d) Records

Every limited partnership is required to keep the following records at its principal place of business in Ontario:

1. a copy of the partnership agreement;
2. a copy of the declaration, together with any declarations of change that may be filed;
3. a copy of any court order made under section 34 which orders compliance with the provisions of the Act;
4. a copy of the written authority to any person signing on behalf of a general or limited partner;
5. for extra-provincial limited partnerships, a copy of the power of attorney filed with the Registrar. If the partnership does not have a principal place of business, these documents shall be kept by the attorney at the address shown in the power of attorney.

During the normal business hours of the partnership, any partner or any person who has a business relationship with the partnership may examine any of the documents referred to above.

If a person who is required under the Act to sign or permit inspection of a document refuses to do so, an application may be made to the court to have that person comply with the provisions of the Act. The court may order compliance or make any other order the court considers appropriate (section 33).

Any person who contravenes the Act or the Regulations or knowingly makes a false or misleading statement regarding any material fact is guilty of an offence. On conviction a person is liable to a fine of not more than $2,000 and a corporation is liable to a fine of not more than $20,000. If a corporation is found guilty of an offence, every director, officer or attorney acting for an extra-provincial corporation is also guilty and on conviction may be fined to a maximum of $2,000 (section 35).

The Lieutenant Governor in Council may make regulations prescribing fees, information to be set out in a declaration filed under the Act, information to be included in a record of limited partners and prescribing forms and their use (section 36).

(e) Bank Account

The partnership will need a business bank account and once the particular chartered bank is chosen, the bank's forms must be obtained, completed and filed with the appropriate branch. The forms and requirements often vary from branch to branch of the same bank. The Toronto-Dominion Bank [now TD Canada Trust] has business accounts ranging from sole proprietorships and partnerships to corporations and joint ventures. The required forms are included in Part IV — Forms.

5. Limited Liability Partnership (LLP)

In 1998, the *Partnership Act* was amended to provide for limited liability partnerships (LLP). Unlike a general partnership, in which individual partners are liable for the partnership's debts and obligations, an LLP provides each of its individual partners protection against personal liability for certain partnership liabilities. In Ontario, a partner in a limited liability partnership is not liable, by means of indemnification, contribution, assessment or otherwise, for debts, obligations and liabilities of the partnership or any partner arising from negligent acts or omissions that another partner or an employee or agent of the partnership commits in the course of the partnership business (s. 10(2)). However, the partner in a limited liability partnership is still liable for his or her own negligence or the negligence of a person under the partner's direct supervision or control (s. 10(3)). A partner in a limited liability partnership is not a proper party to a proceeding by or against the limited liability partnership for the purpose of recovering damages or enforcing obligations arising out of the negligent acts or admissions of another partner (s. 10(4)).

An Ontario limited liability partnership is formed when two or more persons enter into a written agreement that designates the partnership as a limited liability partnership, and states that the *Partnership Act* governs the agreement (s. 44.1(1)). An existing general partnership may be continued as a limited liability partnership if all of the partners enter into an agreement that continues the partnership as a limited liability partnership and states that the *Partnership Act* governs the agreement, or amend an existing agreement to so provide (s. 44.1(2)). A limited liability partnership may carry on business in Ontario only for the purpose of practising a profession governed by an Act and only if,

(a) that Act expressly permits a limited liability partnership to practice the profession;

(b) the governing body of the profession requires the partnership to maintain a minimum amount of liability insurance; and

(c) the partnership complies with the registration requirements under the *Business Names Act*.

Currently, only chartered accountants and law firms can form a limited liability partnership.

No limited liability partnership formed or continued by an agreement governed by the *Partnership Act* shall carry on business unless it has registered its firm name under the *Business Names Act* (s. 44.3(1)). For registration purposes, the Form 6 under the *Business Names Act* is to be utilized. The name of a limited liability partnership shall contain the words "Limited Liability Partnership" or the abbreviations "LLP" or "L.L.P.", or the French equivalent, as the last words or letters of its name. The limited liability partnership cannot carry on business under a name other than its registered firm name. If there is more than one place of business, one is to be selected as the principal place.

The name and residential address or address for service for each partner is set out in items 8 and 9 of the form. If there are more than two partners and up to 10 partners, additional Form 6 with the additional names and addresses is to be completed and attached. If there are more than 10 partners, the registrant may set out the name and address of a designated partner(s) and check the box marked "more than 10 partners". Then the full name and residential address or address for service for the designated partner(s) is set out in items 8 and 9 of the form. Information on all partners carrying on business in Ontario must be kept and made available at the LLP's business address in Ontario. In item 10, the name of the person authorizing the registration is set out which would be a partner of the LLP. To amend, renew or cancel a registration of its firm name, a limited liability partnership shall register an amendment, renewal or cancellation of the registration using Form 6.

An extra-provincial limited liability partnership can also operate and register its business name in Ontario. Effective February 15, 2001, pursuant to section 44.4 of the *Partnership* Act, an extra-provincial limited liability partnership can carry on business in Ontario if it registers its name under the *Business Names Act*. Form 6 under the *Business Names Act* is utilized, and the jurisdiction in which the extra-provincial LLP was formed is set out in item 7. The extra-provincial limited liability partnership, however, cannot carry on business under a name other than its registered business name. For the principal place of business in Ontario, where the business address is outside of Ontario, the words ''not applicable'' are set out in item 4, and the mailing address which includes the street address of the principal place of business outside of Ontario is set out in item 3. The information requirements concerning each partner are similar to that of the Ontario limited liability partnership discussed above. Information on all partners carrying on business in Ontario must be kept and made available to the public at the registrant's business address in Ontario.

A person may serve a notice or document on an extra-provincial limited liability partnership at its Ontario place of business, if any, or its address required to be maintained under the laws of the jurisdiction of formation or its principal office address (s. 44.4(5)).

6. Ontario Business Registration Application (Ontario Business Connects)

The Ontario Business Registration Application is the culmination of a provincial government initiative called ''Clearing the Path for Business Success'' that began in September, 1994. This initiative was aimed at streamlining the registration and reporting requirements for business in Ontario. Prior to this initiative, a new business would be required to contact anywhere from seven to ten provincial ministries and agencies to commence its business. In addition, the new business had to identify the applicable legislation and regulations, obtain and correctly complete the necessary registration forms and then send these forms to proper ministries.

Clearing the Path began with 16 self-help computer workstations that were set up in communities across the province. The mandate of this project was to:

1. initiate a ''single window'' registration process allowing new businesses to register and complete other applications, such as retail sales tax and health tax; and
2. introduce unified reporting which will permit businesses to report and pay selected taxes, fees and premiums due in any month with a single payment.

The introduction of Ontario Business Registration Access (OBRA) in September, 1994 initiated the ''single window'' registration process. This first phase of implementation was facilitated through selected business self-help and regional land registration offices located throughout Ontario. There are currently over 75 self-help workstations available in Ontario, including 50 located at Government Information Centres (GIC) listed in the appendices, and 16 located at Canada Customs and Revenue Agency (CCRA) offices, where a federal business number (BN) can be obtained for GST registration, and payroll deductions. The target is to have a workstation network of over 150 workstations in the near future.

Ontario Business Connects (OBC) of the Ontario Ministry of Consumer and Business Services (formerly the Ministry of Consumer and Commercial Relations) is responsible for implementing the government's Electronic Service Delivery Strategy for the business community. Its mandate is to streamline and simplify access to government programs by business clients. OBC has a website [*www.cbs.gov.on.ca/obc*] for on-line registration, or to print and mail in registration forms. In addition, it operates the self-help workstations across the province at the OBC service locations. The computer workstations are designed for the first-time computer user or someone who is "computer literate". The software includes a tutorial right up front and a user is assisted by colour capped keys that correspond to the material shown in the tutorial which assists a user in accessing the system.

Pursuant to the Business Regulation Reform Act, 1994, the Province of Ontario has developed the Ontario Business Registration Application form to simplify business registration. This form combines the four most commonly required business registration applications into one easy-to-use form. The four applications are for the following:

- ☐ business names registration or renewal of registration;
- ☐ retail sales tax (RST) vendor permit for businesses which make regular taxable sales and/or provide taxable services;
- ☐ employee health tax (EHT) which is a tax paid by all employers who have a permanent establishment in Ontario with two or more employees; and
- ☐ Workplace Safety and Insurance Board (WSIB) registration where the WSIB pays benefits to workers injured on the job or who develop an occupational disease. This coverage can also extend to a sole proprietor, partner or the officers of a corporation.

These applications are required by most entrepreneurs starting a new business or expanding an existing business. All businesses, whether a sole proprietorship, general partnership or corporation, that operate under a name other than the name(s) of the sole proprietor, partners or corporation must register their business name, which is then placed in the public record. This registration lasts five years, and then must be renewed. The Application form can be located using the Ontario Business Connects website [*www.cbs.gov.on.ca/obc*], and clicking onto "Register/Renew/Amend".

The registrant can submit this application in three ways:

(a) Register the business on-line using Netscape Navigator or Microsoft Internet Explorer. The Ontario Business Registration Application is downloaded, and completed using either the mouse or "enter" button to move through the form. The form is then submitted electronically by hitting the SUBMIT button. Within two weeks, the Ontario Master Business Licence will be received as confirmation of registration from Ontario Business Connects, MCBS. The registration is effective as of the date submitted. The offices of RST, EHT and WSIB will contact the registrant directly. The fee for electronic registration is $60, and can be paid by credit card.

(b) Download and complete the application and send it by mail to Ontario Business Connects, P.O. Box 1028, Station B, Toronto, M5T 3H3. The Ontario Master Business Licence will be returned in the mail in two to four weeks. The fee for a mailed-in business name registration or a business name renewal is $80. A name search can also be made through the mail, and the fee is $12.

(c) Locate the closest Ontario Business Connects registration workstation in order to register the business name instantly using the Ontario Business Registration Application. In addition, an instant business name search can be conducted to determine whether another business has the same name. Applicants can also apply for their federal Business Number, discussed below, at the self-help workstations located at Canada Customs and Revenue Agency offices. There is no fee for using the workstation. A listing of the Ontario Business Connects workstation locations is found at the end of the Forms and Precedents for this chapter. The fee for registering the business name at the workstation is $60 while a business name search is $8. The fee can be paid by cash, personal cheque, certified cheque or credit card.

Information on business registration can now be changed and handled electronically through the Ontario Business Connect's website. An amendment application can be submitted if the business has had one or more of the following changes to the registration information:

- ☐ activity
- ☐ address of one or more of the following: sole proprietor, partner, corporation, corporation officer or director, business, mailing
- ☐ partner(s): one of the original partners must be listed on the amendment
- ☐ sole proprietor name (for example, a personal name changed from the "maiden name" to the "married" name)
- ☐ corporation name.

A cancellation application, however, must be submitted, and a new registration made where one or more of the following changes occurs:

☐ ownership

1. sole proprietor: to a different sole proprietor, or to a general partnership or to a corporation.
2. general partnership: to a complete change of partners, or to a sole proprietor or to a corporation.
3. corporation: to a different corporation, or to a sole proprietor or to a general partnership.

☐ business name

The cancellation application is also used if the business wants to cancel its business registration in its entirety.

The OBC application guides clients through the completion of the electronic form in about 10 minutes, and helpful online tips help to ensure that the amendment or cancellation will be accepted for filing by the Companies Branch. After completing the information requested, clients will receive a Portable Document Format (PDF) version of the information they provided for their records. Confirmation by mail that the business information was successfully updated to the public record will be received from the Companies Branch within three weeks. This service can be accessed directly at *www.cbs.gov.on.ca/obc/english/4TG2AW.htm.* The user must scroll half way down the page and select item #2 under the heading "Amend" to report a change in the registration information or select #3 under the heading "Amend" to cancel a business name registration. For more information about OBC services, there is the OBC Helpline at (416) 314-9151 or toll free in Ontario at 1-800-565-1921.

In addition to the Ontario Business Connects website and workstations at service locations, OBC services can be obtained through licensed private-sector service providers. These private companies offer a variety of customized services and complementary services that are bundled and priced individually. The following companies are licensed to provide OBC services:

☐ Business Access, a division of Dye & Durham Co. Inc. [www.dyedurham.ca].

☐ OnCorp Direct Inc. [www.oncorp.com].

☐ Create-a-Co TM , a division of The Legal Link Corporation [www.legallink.ca].

7. Federal-Provincial Business Registration (Business Registration On-line)

In February, 2001, the Canada Customs and Revenue Agency (CCRA) announced the availability of registration for both Ontario and CCRA business programs during a single computer session. The integrated CCRA/Ontario Business Connects online registration provides a single-window for both levels of government, and is known as Business Registration Online (BRO). It eliminates the need for businesses to provide different levels of government with the same information, and simplifies the registration process when starting up or expanding a business. The CCRA has partnered with the Ontario Ministry of Consumer and Business Services' Ontario Business Connects to provide integrated registration services to their common business clients. The integrated service is available over the internet at the Canada Customs and Revenue Agency website using the "Tax", "Business" and "Electronic services" headings, or at self-help workstations located in CCRA offices. In Ontario, the CCRA offices are located in Ottawa, Toronto Centre, Scarborough, North York, Mississauga, Hamilton, St. Catharines, Kitchener, London, Windsor, Barrie, Peterborough, Kingston, Belleville, Sudbury and Thunder Bay.

During the registration session, the users will be asked to provide their credit card number (VISA, Mastercard, or American Express only) to pay for the $60 fee that Ontario Business Connects charges for a Business Name registration request. From the self-help workstations, the business can register for the CCRA programs and obtain its Business Number. The CCRA programs comprise goods and services tax, corporate income tax, payroll deductions, and the import/export accounts. The business will need to register with CCRA if any of these programs apply to the business. The CCRA Registration Summary, printable from the self-help workstations, provides a business its federal Business Number (BN) and its account number for these programs. At the end of the Ontario Business Name Registration, the client can print the Ontario Master Business Licence. This licence is a legal document that can be presented to financial institutions as proof of a business name. The following information appears on the licence: the nine-digit Business Number, the legal name of the business, the business type, address information, the Business Name registered, the Ontario Business Identification Number (BIN) assigned, and the effective and expiry dates of the Ontario Business Name. While registering its Ontario Business Name, the entrepreneur can also apply for Ontario Retail Sales Tax, Ontario Employer Health Tax and Ontario Workplace Safety and Insurance Board accounts.

If the applicant wants to submit a hard copy version of the business registration form, the applicant can visit the CCRA web site at *www.ccra.adrc.gc.ca/menu/EmenuHAB.html* and print the form. In order to order the form, the applicant can call toll-freee at 1-800-959-2221. Once the form is completed, it can be mailed, faxed, or delivered to a Tax Services Office listed at *www.ccra.adrc.gc.ca/contact/tso-e.html.*

Prior to the Ontario Business Name registration, a name search can be conducted which will tell the applicant whether another business in Ontario is using the proposed name, and in regard to what business activity. Registering a business name does not in itself give the applicant exclusive use of the business name, and does not prevent the applicant from registering a name that is already in use. A unique name, however, will help the applicant to identify and distinguish his or her business to customers and clients. Moreover, it is important that the name is not misleading or confusing in its description of the goods or services provided so that the business activity stands out from its competitors, and does not trigger allegations of passing off the business' goods and services as those of another. The registration information also allows consumers and business people to find out the owners or principals behind a business name in order to pursue a business opportunity or deal with a dispute that may have arisen. Where the applicant requests a business name search by mail and the records show that the name being searched is already in use, the business name will not be registered. The business name application and fee will be returned.

2

CORPORATIONS

1. Introduction

The decision to incorporate is made in consultation between lawyer and client. The production and processing of the paperwork involved rests with members of the legal support staff. It is essential that this staff be capable of not only producing the proper documents involved in an assigned task but also be fully cognizant of the reasons and the areas of law involved in each task. It is only in this way that lawyers will reap the full benefit of qualified individuals working as paralegal law clerks, legal assistants or paralegal secretaries in their offices. Proper utilization of these skilled individuals will result in efficient and accurate legal services being made available to the public at a reduced cost.

The following chapters should provide answers to most of the questions which arise in connection with basic incorporation and related matters.

2. Historical Origins of Corporations

Records show that corporations, in one form or another, have existed since the time of the Phoenicians.

In Italy, during the lifetime of Michelangelo (early 15th century) artists and craftsmen gathered together to discuss matters of mutual concern, such as the division of labour and hours of work. As a group they would petition the local king or monarch to correct problems they had in common. Since these people usually gathered to discuss over meals, they were known as "*cum panis*" organizations, which means "with bread". It is not difficult to see how a *cum panis* organization came to be known as a "company", a term applicable to modern organizations.

The important concept that grew out of the *cum panis* organizations was that the organization was thought of as something quite separate and apart from the members. Eventually, as this perception grew, people began to talk about the organization's position on current matters of the day. According to the law of the tine, the organization had no legal status. It could not purchase anything, vote, or own assets.

The concept of the organization as a separate entity spread across Europe and eventually arrived in England. The merchants in England gathered together in organizations known as guilds. These merchants met to discuss problems in their area of trade, and as time passed, the concept that a guild was separate from its members expanded. It was decided that since these organizations or guilds were considered to be separate entities, and there were advantages in having them thought of in this way in law, they should be treated as such. This was done by issuing royal charters or letters patent. Once created the company existed as long as the monarch wanted it to exist. The company had all the rights of a person — it could own property, carry on business, sue and be sued under the law. The only way a company could die was if the ruling monarch issued a proclamation cancelling the charter.

King Charles II was petitioned by a group of merchants for permission to explore the New World. The King granted their petition, but granted an exclusive right to the company, not the merchants, to explore the New World. Charles II reasoned that by granting the right to the company, the exploration would continue regardless of what happened to the merchants, since the company could not die. The original name of this company was The Governors and Company of Adventurers of England Trading into Hudson's Bay, which was later known as the Hudson's Bay Company, and today is called The Bay. The royal charter forming this company was issued on May 2, 1670.

3. Fundamental Concepts of a Corporation

A corporation is a separate entity which is capable of indefinite life, created by law and formed by one or more persons, to carry on a business from which it is anticipated profits will be made. The corporation's existence can be ended if the shareholders decide to wind it up or to surrender its charter.

The corporation is separate from its shareholders. The shareholders own and control the corporation and can end its corporate existence, but are not the actual corporation. This relationship is often referred to as the "corporate veil".

around 1970

The following are the fundamental concepts of the corporate form of business organization:

1. a corporation is a separate entity from its shareholders;
2. a corporation is created by law and the articles of incorporation are, in effect, its "birth certificate";

3. a corporation never dies, which means that although the shareholders may die and new individuals become shareholders, the corporation continues its existence from the date on which the charter is issued until its existence is terminated by its shareholders, a court or a governmental body as provided under the incorporating statute; and

4. a corporation is formed to carry on a business by one or more persons with a view to making a profit.

The concept of a number of people creating a corporation was brought forward from English law and applied in Ontario until 1971, and federally until 1975. Prior to these years, three people were required to incorporate a corporation either federally or in Ontario.

The *Ontario Business Corporations Act*, R.S.O. 1990, c. B.16 and the *Canada Business Corporations Act*, R.S.C. 1985, c. C-44, permit a single person to create or incorporate a corporation.

As mentioned earlier, when The Hudson's Bay Company was formed in 1670 the group of merchants and traders could not simply decide to create a corporation. It was necessary to petition the ruling monarch for a royal charter or letters patent. Under modern law, creation of a corporation is a matter of right, not privilege. Individuals no longer have to petition the ruling monarch or a governing body for permission to incorporate. However, the articles of incorporation must comply with the legislation of the relevant jurisdiction in order to issue. If the articles of incorporation meet the requirements in law of either the federal or provincial jurisdiction, the applicants are automatically entitled to incorporate.

When a client consults a lawyer to consider whether or not formation of a corporation is the answer to his or her particular needs, the various general advantages to incorporation may be discussed:

1. Unlike sole proprietorships and partnerships, whether general or limited, the primary advantage of incorporation is limited liability. Creditors can seize only the assets owned by the corporation for debts, except in circumstances where there is evidence of attempts to defraud creditors and in specific cases where directors and officers may be liable for certain debts of the corporation.

2. If additional capital is required for the business, a corporation is more attractive to those with money to invest. An investor can purchase stock or shares in the corporation in return for money advanced and the corporation then has the additional capital required for the business.

3. A corporation may set up pension plans and profit sharing stock option plans for the benefit of its employees.

4. When a shareholder, director or officer dies, the corporation continues to

operate and carry on business. It does not cease operation as may happen on the death of a sole proprietor or member of a partnership.

If the business to be carried on by the corporation is one which in all probability will not grow beyond provincial boundaries, then the lawyer will usually advise provincial incorporation. If, on the other hand, there is a possibility that at some point in the future the business might be carried on outside provincial boundaries, then the lawyer will probably recommend federal incorporation.

There are several distinct advantages to federal incorporation, primarily:

1. the right to carry on business in any province in Canada so long as the corporation complies with provincial legislation regarding notifying local governmental authorities of its intention to commence business in a province or provinces; and

2. the right to carry on business in any province under its own name even though a provincially incorporated corporation with the same or similar name may exist in the same jurisdiction.

Although Shakespeare said, "What's in a name?", in business a name becomes very important as a corporation becomes known to the public in its particular area of commerce.

Unlike a federal corporation, an Ontario corporation cannot carry on business outside the province without registering as an extra-provincial corporation. There is one exception to this rule. Ontario and Quebec each have reciprocal legislation which permits Ontario corporations to carry on business in the province of Quebec and Quebec corporations to carry on business in Ontario. However, the corporations must comply with all provincial laws respecting corporations and Ontario corporations contemplating extending business to Quebec must, when incorporating, provide a French translation of the English version of the corporate name. Certain other matters must also be considered at this time. These matters are covered in Chapter 5 ("The Act of Incorporation").

The *Business Corporations Act* is the governing statute in Ontario for "offering" and "non-offering" corporations, except where it is otherwise expressly provided. This statute does not, for example, apply to non-profit corporations, co-operatives, insurance corporations or to a corporation incorporated for the construction and working of a railway, or a corporation within the meaning of the *Loan and Trust Corporations Act*, R.S.O. 1990, c. L.25, except as may be provided in that Act. Prior to the enactment of the *Business Corporations Act*, corporations were referred to as "public" and "private" corporations. These words were replaced under the present Act by the concepts of the "offering" and "non-offering" corporations. An "offering corporation" means a corporation, any securities (that is, shares, debentures or other securities) of which are listed for trading on a stock exchange or in respect of which a prospectus or similar document has been filed. A ''non-offering corporation'' is the converse of an offering corporation. A corporation must, in order to be exempted from certain provisions of the *Securities Act*, set out certain provisions in its articles of incorporation. The term ''private company'' is still used in the *Securities Act* and the provisions which must be so included in the articles of incorporation are set out in the definition of ''private company'' contained in subsection 1(1) of the *Securities Act*.

Under subsection 1(1), a corporation is a private company if its articles:

1. restrict the transfer of shares;
2. limit the number of shareholders, exclusive of employees, to 50; and
3. prohibit any invitation to the public to subscribe for its securities.

Part II

Provincial Corporations

3

Directors and Officers of Corporations

In sole proprietorships and partnerships, it is the persons involved who carry on and run the business. A corporation is slightly different. Since a corporation is recognized at law as being a separate entity from its shareholders, there is a problem: a corporation cannot communicate or deal with the outside world or carry on its business without the assistance of people. The titles and functions of the people involved are discussed in this chapter.

Should it prove necessary to confirm the meaning of a term or word used, reference to subsection 1(1) of the *Business Corporations Act*, R.S.O. 1990, c. B.16 (''BCA'''), may assist. This subsection sets out definitions for words or terms used in the statute and will assist in understanding the reference and the context in which it is used. A good legal dictionary, such as *Osborn's Concise Law Dictionary*, 8th ed. (London: Sweet & Maxwell, 1993) may also prove to be a useful source for general legal terms. This dictionary is available from Thomson Professional Publishing Canada.

1. Directors

Directors are the governing body of a corporation. The Board of Directors makes the general policy and major decisions as to how the business of the corporation will be carried on by passing resolutions and by-laws. A record of the by-laws and resolutions is kept in a minute book. Sections 115 to 137 of the BCA set out the duties, powers and general responsibilities of directors and officers. There are other sections throughout the Act which also mention directors but the various sections mentioned here set out the general requirements for, and what is expected of, directors.

(a) Board of Directors

Subsection 115(1) provides that subject to any unanimous shareholder agreement, the directors shall manage or supervise the business and affairs of the corporation. Subsection (2) sets out the composition of the Board of Directors as follows:

1. A corporation not offering its securities to the public (non-offering corporation) must have at least one director. The maximum number of directors is decided by the individuals involved in each corporation.
2. The Board of a corporation offering its securities to the public (an offering corporation) must have a minimum of three individuals, of whom at least one-third are not officers or employees of the corporation or of any affiliate corporation.

According to subsection 118(3) of the BCA, a majority of the directors of every corporation, except a non-resident corporation, shall be resident Canadians. If a corporation has only one or two directors, the Act requires that the one individual or one of the two individuals, as the case may be, shall be resident Canadians.

The definition of a ''non-resident corporation'' means a corporation not deemed to be resident in Canada under subsection 250(4) of the *Income Tax Act*, R.S.C. 1985, c. 1 (5th Supp.). The result of this definition is, in effect, that a non-resident corporation, for the purposes of the BCA, is a corporation which was incorporated before April 27, 1965, never carried on business in Canada and never was a resident of Canada (that is, it never exercised its management in Canada).

(b) First Directors

The Act clearly states that each person named in the articles of incorporation as a first director is a director of the corporation from the date of endorsement of the certificate of incorporation until the first meeting of shareholders. The first directors named in the articles have all the powers and duties and are subject to all the liabilities of directors. A first director shall not be permitted to resign his or her office unless a successor is elected or appointed and such election or appointment is effective at the same time as the resignation. Depending on the situation, this could occur during the organization of the corporation. If the clients decided not to proceed after incorporation, the temporary shareholders of the corporation could hold a meeting and elect the permanent directors of the corporation, relieving the lawyer and his or her staff of their obligations as first directors. The Act has additional sections concerning first directors. Subsections 119(4) to (8) deal with the following:

1. *Subsection (4):* Subject to clause 120(a), the shareholders of a corporation shall at their first meeting elect directors to hold office for a term expiring not later than the close of the third annual meeting of shareholders following the election. This means that the shareholders have the option of electing directors for varying lengths of time. The shareholders can elect

directors for a minimum of one year to a maximum of three years. Depending on the approach adopted by the shareholders at their first meeting, it may not be necessary to have an election of directors at each annual meeting of shareholders. It would, however, be necessary to at least elect directors at the third annual meeting of shareholders following the first meeting of the shareholders of the corporation at which the directors were elected. Alternatively, directors could be elected annually by the shareholders.

2. *Subsection (5):* All directors elected at a meeting of shareholders need not hold office for the same term or length of time. As mentioned previously, a director may be elected for a one-year term and others may be elected for two- or three-year terms. This approach would only be adopted in situations where it would be advantageous to the corporation to have some directors available to assist in the transition as new directors come "on board". (The usual practice is to hold annual elections of directors.) Known as a "rotating Board", this approach is designed to ensure continuity in the proper management and direction of the business of the corporation. This approach may be adopted by corporations with numerous directors or by non-profit corporations served by volunteer directors.
3. *Subsection (6):* If a director is not elected for a specific term, for example two years, that director ceases to hold office at the close of the first annual meeting of shareholders following his or her election to office.
4. *Subsection (7):* If the shareholders of a corporation do not elect directors as provided under this section, this subsection authorizes the incumbent directors to continue in office until their successors are elected.
5. *Subsection (8):* If the shareholders fail to elect the number of directors required by the articles or by section 125 because of the disqualification, incapacity or death of one or more candidates, the elected directors, provided they constitute a quorum, may exercise all the powers of the directors of the corporation until the holding of a meeting of shareholders in accordance with subsection 124(3). Under this subsection, if the directors lack a quorum or if there has been a failure to elect the required number of directors, the directors then in office are required to call a special meeting of shareholders to fill the vacancy. If there are no directors in office, or if they fail to call a meeting, any shareholder of the corporation may call the meeting.

(c) Increasing or Decreasing Number of Directors

Subsection 125(1) provides that a corporation may increase or decrease the number of its directors by applying for articles of amendment as provided under clause 168(1)(m). A decision to decrease the number of directors of the corporation will not shorten the term of office of an incumbent director. This subsection also provides that a corporation may increase or decrease the minimum or maximum number of the directors if a fixed number is not set out in its articles.

Under section 125 of the BCA, the increase or decrease in the number of directors, or the minimum or maximum number of directors if this is provided for in its articles, is accomplished by articles of amendment. The articles of amendment will issue provided the provisions of section 120, which deals with cumulative voting for shareholders, and section 125, are not contravened.

Where the articles of incorporation provide for a minimum to maximum number of directors, the number of directors shall be determined or decided from time to time by a special resolution of the shareholders. This authority can, however, be delegated to the directors of the corporation. Refer to section (h) titled "Vacancies", below, for further information on the restrictions that apply to this delegation of authority.

The decision to incorporate with a minimum to maximum number of directors is made in circumstances where flexibility in this area may be required in the future. For example, a corporation in its articles provides for a minimum of one director up to a maximum of seven. Initially the shareholders decide that four directors are sufficient and a certified copy of this special resolution is filed with the Companies Branch. At a subsequent annual meeting the shareholders, or the directors if the authority has been delegated by the shareholders, decide to increase the number to six. A certified copy of the appropriate resolution must be filed with the Companies Branch within ten days of its passing. The appropriate resolution would vary depending on the individual circumstances that exist — that is, who made the decision. The resolutions that would apply are:

- ☐ decision made by shareholders — special resolution; and
- ☐ decision made by directors — resolution (sometimes referred to as an "ordinary resolution").

This would occur where the corporation has provided for a minimum to maximum number of directors in its articles. The decision would be made by the shareholders unless this authority has been delegated by a special resolution of the shareholders to the directors of the corporation.

Failure to file the required certified copy does not affect the validity of the resolution making the change in the number of directors.

In the event that the shareholders, or the directors as the case may be, fail to pass the appropriate resolution under subsection 125(3) fixing the number of directors, then subsection 125(4) applies. This subsection states that the number of directors shall be the number named in the articles. The articles make provision for inserting the number of directors whether a fixed number or a minimum to maximum number as may be decided by the persons filing the articles of incorporation.

A change of directors triggers the filing of Form 1 (Notice of Change) required under the *Corporations Information Act*, R.S.O. 1990, c. C.39. Under subsection 2(1), every corporation must file the notice of change within 15 days after the change takes place. It is not necessary, however, to file a notice of change in respect of a director's retirement and subsequent re-election for the next term of office.

(d) Qualifications of Directors

The minimum age for a director of a corporation is 18 years. In addition, a director cannot be of unsound mind so found by a court in Canada or elsewhere, or have status of a bankrupt. Under the Act, a person who is not an individual is also disqualified (subsection 118(1)). The reference here to a "person who is not an individual" means a human being. The term "person" under the BCA includes, in addition to an individual (human being), a sole proprietorship, partnership, unincorporated syndicate, organization, trust or a body corporate and a natural person acting as trustee, executor, administrator or other legal representative.

Subsection 118(3) of the Act requires that a majority of the directors of every corporation shall be resident Canadians, except for a non-resident corporation. "Non-resident corporation" in the BCA means a corporation incorporated before April 27, 1965 that is not deemed to be resident in Canada for the purposes of the *Income Tax Act* (Canada), subsection 250(4).

"Resident Canadian" under subsection 1(1) means an individual who is:

(a) a Canadian citizen ordinarily resident in Canada,

(b) a Canadian citizen not ordinarily resident in Canada who is a member of a prescribed class of persons; or

(c) a permanent resident within the meaning of the *Immigration Act* (Canada), and ordinarily resident in Canada.

The Regulations set out the following classes of persons who are deemed to be prescribed as "resident Canadians":

1. full time employees of the federal or any provincial government or of an agency of such governments, or of a federal or provincial Crown corporation;

2. full time employees of a body corporate in which more than 50% of the voting shares are held or controlled by resident Canadians or in which a majority of the directors are resident Canadians, where the principal reason for the residence outside Canada is to act as such employees;

3. full time students at a university outside of Canada or other educational institution outside of Canada recognized by the province;
4. full time employees of an international association or organization of which Canada is a member; and
5. persons who were ordinarily resident in Canada when they became 60 years of age and who have been resident outside Canada since that time (R.R.O. 1990, Reg. 62, section 26).

Formerly, a person who was elected or appointed a director had to consent before the appointment was valid. While this provision does not specifically appear in the BCA, subsection 135(3) states that every director who was absent from a meeting at which a resolution was passed or action was taken is deemed to consent unless he or she makes his or her dissent known within seven days after becoming aware of the resolution. If present at the meeting, all directors are deemed to have consented to all business at the meeting unless they make their dissent known.

(e) Election of Directors

The directors of a corporation are elected under section 119 of the Act at the first meeting of shareholders and at each succeeding annual meeting at which such an election is required. The directors can hold office for up to a maximum term of three years. Their term of office expires at the close of the third annual meeting of shareholders following their election. All directors elected at a meeting of shareholders can hold office for different periods of time. If there is provision for a rotating board, as mentioned under the sub-heading "(b) First Directors", above, then the directors may very well hold office for varying lengths of time. If the term of office of a director is not expressly stated, the director ceases to hold office at the close of the first annual meeting of shareholders following his or her election. Should the shareholders, in spite of the provisions under the Act, fail to elect directors at a meeting of shareholders, the directors then in office continue until their successors are elected.

There is also provision under this section for the procedures to be followed if the shareholders failed, for various reasons, to elect the required number of directors set out in the articles. As mentioned earlier, if the directors elected constitute a quorum, they may exercise all the powers of the directors of the corporation until a meeting of shareholders is held to elect the appropriate number of directors.

(f) Cumulative Voting for Directors

Section 120 of the Act states that where the articles provide for cumulative voting, each shareholder entitled to vote at an election of directors has the right to cast votes which equal the number of votes attached to the shares held by that shareholder, multiplied by the number of directors to be elected. Usually each share has only one vote and the shareholder decides how to cast these votes. The shares can be voted in favour of one candidate or may be distributed among the candidates in any manner decided upon by the shareholders.

A separate vote shall be held for each candidate nominated for director unless a resolution is passed unanimously permitting two or more persons to be elected by a single vote. If a shareholder votes for more than one candidate without specifying how the votes are distributed, they shall be deemed to have divided their votes equally among the candidates. If the candidates nominated exceed the number of directors to be elected, those who receive the least number of votes shall be eliminated until the number of candidates remaining equals the number of directors to be elected.

Example 1

The corporation is to elect two directors but four persons are nominated by the shareholders, requiring a vote. John, Elizabeth, Janet and Robert are the nominees for the board of directors. There are four shareholders, each owning ten Class ''A' common shares of the corporation with one vote attached to each share. The first ballot is taken and the (40 possible) votes cast tally as follows:

John, Elizabeth and Janet — 13 votes each;

Robert — 1 vote

A second ballot is cast and the votes tally this time as follows:

John — 15 votes

Janet— 15 votes

Elizabeth — 10 votes

Example 2

There is a motion to remove a director or to decrease the number of directors from three to two. There are four shareholders holding a total of 51 Class ''A'' or common shares of the corporation with one vote attached to each share. Angela holds 10 shares, Adam holds 10 shares, Sonia holds 18 shares and Robert holds 13 shares. Will the motions mentioned in the following situations pass or fail?

1. Sonia and Robert vote against the motion.
2. Angela, Adam and Sonia vote in favour of the motion.

Each director ceases to hold office at the close of the first annual meeting of shareholders following his or her election.

A motion to remove a director or decrease the number of directors will be defeated provided the votes against such a motion would be sufficient to:

(a) elect the director that was to be removed; or

(b) elect a director;

and, in both cases, the number of directors required by the articles were then being elected. In addition these votes could be voted cumulatively at an election at which the same total number of votes was being cast.

Example 3

Five shareholders own 63 Class "A" or common shares of ABC Welding Inc. — one vote attached to each share. The shareholders are:

Bruce	21 shares
Margaret	15 shares
Cynthia	15 shares
Stephanie	4 shares
Marvin	8 shares

A motion is brought by Bruce to decrease the number of directors from five to four. Identify how the shareholders must vote:

(a) to defeat the motion; and

(b) to pass the motion.

When there is provision for cumulative voting in the articles, the directors of the corporation must be a fixed number, rather than a minimum and maximum number of directors (section 120).

(g) Quorum of Directors

A quorum is the number of directors or shareholders of any corporation that must be present for the legal transaction of business at a meeting of directors or shareholders, as the case may be.

Subject to the articles or by-laws and subsection 126(4), if the number of directors of the corporation is fixed, a majority of these should constitute a quorum. If the articles provide for a minimum to a maximum number of directors, the minimum number required by the articles constitutes a quorum at any meeting of directors. However, a statutory quorum shall not be less than two-fifths of the number of directors or of the minimum number of directors, whichever applies. If a corporation has fewer than three directors, all directors must be present at any meeting to constitute a quorum (subsections 126(3) and (4)).

Section 124(3) of the BCA states that if there are not sufficient directors in office to constitute a quorum, they shall forthwith call a special meeting of shareholders to fill the vacancy or vacancies. If the remaining directors fail to call a shareholders' meeting, or there are no directors then in office, a shareholder may call the required meeting.

Section 121 of the Act outlines when a director ceases to hold office, which occurs upon:

1. death or, subject to subsection 119(2), resignation (subsection 119(2) requires that a first director must have a successor elected or appointed before the resignation becomes effective);
2. removal in accordance with section 122, which outlines how a director may be removed from office by the shareholders of a corporation (a director may be removed by an ordinary resolution passed at an annual or special meeting of shareholders; if elected by the holders of any class or series of shares, a director elected by these shareholders may be removed by an ordinary resolution at a meeting of the holders of the class or series); or
3. disqualification under subsection 118(1) which outlines how a person may be disqualified as a director (this topic is discussed under the heading "(d) Qualifications of Directors", above).

(h) Vacancies

Subject to subsections 124(2), (4) and (5), a quorum of directors may fill a vacancy among the directors except a vacancy caused by the shareholders' failure to elect the number of directors required for the corporation. The directors cannot fill a vacancy that results in an increase in the number of directors unless the increase follows the provisions of subsection 124(2), nor can they change the maximum number of directors, if the articles of the corporation provide for a minimum number and a maximum number of directors.

Where the vacancy occurs in the board and a quorum of directors remains, the remaining directors may appoint a person to fill the vacancy for the remainder of the term; however, the articles may provide that such vacancy may only be filled by a vote of the shareholders. If the vacancy occurs among the directors elected by a class or series of shares, the articles may provide that a vacancy among the directors shall only be filled by a vote of the holders of that class or series of shares having an exclusive right to elect such director or directors.

Where a minimum and maximum number of directors of a corporation is provided for in its articles, the number of directors to be elected at the annual meeting of shareholders shall be the number determined from time to time by special resolution. The term "special resolution" means a resolution that is submitted to a special meeting of the shareholders of a corporation called for the purpose of considering the resolution and passed, with or without amendment, at the meeting by at least two-thirds of the votes cast. A special resolution may be consented to in writing by each shareholder of the corporation entitled to vote at a special meeting, or by his or her attorney authorized in writing.

The shareholders may, in their special resolution, authorize the directors to determine by resolution the number of directors of the corporation (subsection 125(3)). Under subsection 124(2) where the directors are empowered to determine the number of directors of the corporation, the directors may not between meetings of shareholders appoint another director if, after such appointment, the total number of directors would be more than one and one-third times the number of directors required to have been elected at the last annual meeting of shareholders.

For example, if the shareholders decided at the annual meeting to elect three directors for the corporation and also authorized the directors to determine the number of directors of the corporation, the directors could increase the maximum number of directors so long as the total number did not exceed four. The increase from three to four directors of the corporation would not exceed the guidelines set out under subsection 124(2) of the Act.

If the directors lack a quorum, or if the required number has not been elected, the directors in office shall immediately call a special meeting of shareholders to fill the vacancy. If the directors fail to call a meeting, or if there are no directors in office, such a meeting may be called by any shareholder of the corporation.

Some corporations may include as a provision of their articles the right of the holders of a class or series of shares to elect one or more directors of the corporation. If a vacancy occurs among these directors, the remaining directors elected by that class or series may fill the vacancy unless the vacancy resulted from:

1. an increase in the number of directors for that class or series; or
2. from a failure to elect the number of directors provided for in the articles.

If there are no remaining directors elected by those particular shareholders, any holder of shares of that class or series may call a meeting for the purpose of filling the vacancy (section 124).

The usual practice is to fill the vacancy by appointment made by the remaining directors provided they constitute a quorum.

(i) Place of Meetings

Subject to subsection 126(2), a meeting of the Board of Directors shall be held at the registered office of the corporation (subsection 126(1)). Where the by-laws so provide, meetings of directors may be held at any place within or outside Ontario but in any financial year, a majority of the meetings shall be held within Canada. There is an exception for non-resident corporations (subsection 126(2)).

A majority of the directors present must be resident Canadians in order to transact business at a meeting In addition, the Act provides that the directors may transact business at a meeting where a majority of resident Canadian directors are not present provided an absent resident Canadian director approves in writing, by telephone or by other communication facilities the business transacted at the meeting and the required majority would have been present had that director been present at the meeting. An exception to the residency requirement is a non-resident corporation (subsections 126(6) and (7)).

(i) By Telephone and Other Communication Facilities

Subject to the by-laws of the corporation, and provided all directors consent, meetings may be held by conference telephone or by such other electronic or other communication facilities that permit all persons participating in the meeting to communicate with each other simultaneously and instantaneously. All participants in such a meeting are deemed to be present (subsection 126(13)).

If a majority of the directors participating in a meeting held under subsection 126(13) are in Canada, the meeting shall be deemed to be held in Canada (subsection 126(14)).

(ii) Calling Meetings of Directors

In addition to any other provisions in the articles or by-laws of a corporation for the calling of meetings, a quorum of the directors may at any time call a meeting of directors for transaction of any business so long as the notice states the general nature of the business (subsection 126(8)).

(iii) Notice

If the by-laws make no other provision regarding notice of meetings called under subsection 126(8), notice of the time and place of the meeting shall be given to every director of the corporation by sending notice at least ten days prior to the meeting, to his or her latest address as shown on the records of the corporation. More notice of the meeting can be given if warranted by the circumstances existing at the time the decision to call a meeting is made (subsection 126(9)).

The definition of "day" is set out under subsection 1(1) of the Act and defines the manner in which periods of time referred to in the statute are to be calculated. According to the definition, notice of a meeting of directors would require a minimum of 12 days to follow the provisions of the Act. The extra days are required because the period of days allowed for notice is deemed to commence the day after the notice has been given and to end at midnight on the last day in the period of days. In order to give the proper minimum notice under the Act for meetings of directors, the period of days cannot end on the day on which the directors' meeting would be held because, in all likelihood, the meeting would occur prior to midnight. If the last day of the notice period falls on a Sunday or holiday, the notice period shall end at midnight on the next working day. Saturday is not excluded when calculating the required days of notice.

(j) Duties

Subject to any unanimous shareholder agreement, the directors shall manage or supervise the management of the business and affairs of the corporation (subsection 115(1)).

(k) Conduct of Business

Subject to the articles or by-laws, subsection 126(5) provides that where there is a vacancy or vacancies in the Board of Directors, the remaining directors may exercise all of the powers of the Board so long as:

(a) a quorum of the Board remains in office; and

(b) a majority of directors present are resident Canadians.

An exception is made on the residency requirement for non-resident corporations (subsection 126(5)). Where a corporation has only one director, that director may, under subsection 126(12), constitute a meeting.

(l) Managing Director

Subject to the articles or by-laws, directors of a corporation, either offering or non-offering, may appoint a resident Canadian as a managing director, or a committee of directors, and delegate any of their powers. A majority of a committee of directors must be resident Canadians. The power to delegate authority, set out under subsection 127(1), is limited under subsection 127(3). This subsection states various prohibitions which a managing director and committee of directors cannot undertake. For example, a managing director or committee of directors of a non-offering corporation is not permitted:

(a) to submit matters to the shareholders that require their approval;

(b) to fill a vacancy among the directors or in the office of auditor;

(c) to appoint or remove any chief executive officer, chief financial officer, the chairman or the president of the corporation;

(d) subject to section 184, to issue securities except in the manner and on the terms authorized by the directors;

(e) to declare dividends;

(f) to purchase, redeem or otherwise acquire shares issued by the corporation;

(g) to pay a commission referred to in section 37;

(h) to approve an amalgamation under section 177 or an amendment to the articles under subsection 168(2) or (4); nor

(i) to adopt, amend or repeal by-laws.

There does not appear to be a specific quorum established for this committee of directors.

The remaining provisions in this subsection apply specifically to offering corporations.

(m) Disclosure by Director of Interest in Contracts

Section 132 of the Act states that a director or officer of a corporation shall disclose his or her interest in any contract, or proposed contract, with the corporation. These disclosure requirements are triggered when a director or officer is:

(a) a party to an actual or proposed material contract or transaction; or

(b) a director or officer of, or has a material interest in, any person who is a party to an actual or proposed material contract or transaction with the corporation.

The definition of the term "person" would be that supplied under subsection 1(1) of the BCA.

If a director is already involved in the proposed contract or transaction, disclosure must be made at the first meeting of directors when the contract is considered. If the director's involvement occurs after this first meeting, then disclosure must be made at the first meeting after the director becomes interested in the contract.

An officer of a corporation who is not a director shall make this disclosure as soon as he or she becomes aware:

1. that the actual or proposed contract will be considered; or
2. that the actual or proposed contract has been considered.

If such an officer becomes interested after the contract or transaction is entered into, then the interest must be disclosed at that time.

A general notice in writing sent to the corporation would be a sufficient disclosure of interest for an officer or director for the purposes of this section. The notice would state that the director or officer has a material interest in a "person" and is to be regarded as interested in any actual or proposed contract or transaction with that person.

These guidelines appear to apply particularly to contracts with the corporation that require joint approval of the directors and shareholders. If a director or officer has an interest in a contract that falls within the "ordinary course of business of the corporation" and does not require approval of either the directors or shareholders, then that person shall:

1. disclose the nature of their interest in writing to the corporation; or
2. request that the nature and extent of their interest be recorded in the minutes of the meeting.

This shall be done forthwith after that person becomes aware of the actual or proposed contract or transaction.

A director shall refrain from voting on any resolution to approve the contract or transaction unless it falls within the exceptions listed under subsection 132(5) which are:

1. any arrangements to secure money loaned or obligations undertaken by the director for the benefit of the corporation-or an affiliate;
2. his or her remuneration as a director, officer, employee or agent of the corporation or an affiliate;
3. indemnity for actions taken honestly and in good faith as a director or officer of the corporation or the purchase of liability insurance for his or her protection; and
4. a contract or transaction with an affiliate.

Once the disclosure has been made, the director or officer is not accountable to the corporation or its shareholders for any profit or gain. The contract is not void or voidable because:

(a) a party is a director or officer of the corporation, or
(b) the director is present or counted to determine a quorum at the meeting that authorized the contract or transaction,

provided the contract is fair and reasonable to the corporation when it was approved and the interested director or officer was acting honestly and in good faith.

However, in order to retain the profits or benefits, the contract or transaction must be confirmed by a special resolution of the shareholders passed at a meeting called for that purpose. The notice calling the meeting of shareholders must disclose in reasonable detail the nature and extent of the interest of the director or officer.

Subject to subsections (7) and (8), when a director or officer of a corporation fails to disclose his or her interest in a material contract or a transaction as provided under section 132, the corporation or a shareholder thereof may apply to the court for an order setting aside the contract or transaction and directing that the director or officer account to the corporation for any profit realized. Depending on the evidence supplied, the order applied for may be granted.

(n) General Notice of Interest

The language in the Act under subsection 132(6) is clear because the word "person" has been included under the definition section of the Act. A "person" includes an individual, sole proprietorship, partnership, unincorporated association, unincorporated syndicate, unincorporated organization, trust, body corporate, and a natural person acting as a trustee, executor, administrator or other legal representative.

An officer or director may disclose by a general notice to the directors that he or she is a director or officer of, or has the material interest in, a person and is to be regarded as interested in any contract or any transaction entered into with that person. Such a disclosure made by a director of the corporation is considered sufficient regarding any contract or transaction entered into by the corporation with that person (subsection 132(6)).

(o) Liability of Directors

Section 130 deals generally with the liability of directors of a corporation who vote for or consent to various matters that would be encountered during the normal business transacted by a corporation. Section 23 of the BCA empowers the directors to issue shares at such time and for such consideration as the directors may determine. These powers are subject to the articles, by-laws, any unanimous shareholder agreement and section 26. This section further provides that a share shall not be issued until the consideration is fully paid in money, or in property or past services equivalent to its cash or money value. Directors who vote for or consent to a resolution authorizing the issue of a share for property or past services which are of less value than the fair equivalent of its cash value are jointly and severally liable to make good any loss suffered by the corporation. Their actions contravened section 23 and accordingly these directors became jointly liable to the corporation for its losses (subsection 130(1)).

Subsection 130(2) of the BCA sets out potential areas of liability for directors as follows:

(a) any financial assistance contrary to section 20;

This section provides generally for financial assistance by the corporation to any person for any purpose by means of a loan, guarantee or otherwise. Subsection 20(2), however, requires a corporation to disclose to its shareholders all material financial assistance that the corporation gives to:

☐ a shareholder

☐ a beneficial owner of a share

☐ a director

☐ an officer, or

☐ an employee

of the corporation, an affiliate of the corporation, or an associate of any of them, or

☐ any person for the purpose of, or in connection with, a purchase of a share, or a security convertible into or exchangeable for a share issued or to be issued by the corporation or an affiliate of the corporation.

Pursuant to subsection 1(4), a corporation shall be deemed to be "affiliated" with another corporation if one of them is the subsidiary of the other or both are subsidiaries of the same corporation or each of them is controlled by the same person.

In addition, subsection 20(3) provides that the corporation is not required to disclose to its shareholders any financial assistance that it gives

☐ on account of expenditures incurred or to be incurred on its behalf;

☐ in the ordinary course of business, if the lending of money is part of the ordinary course of business of the corporation;

☐ to its holding company if it is a wholly owned subsidiary;

☐ to a subsidiary body corporate; or

☐ to employees of the corporation or any of its affiliates in accordance with a plan for the purchase of shares of the corporation or any of its affiliates.

Where disclosure is required, a corporation that is a non-offering or private corporation shall make disclosure by giving a notice to all shareholders within 90 days after giving the financial assistance (s. 20(5)). For an offering or public corporation, the corporation shall make disclosure in the management information circular sent to its shareholders in respect of the next annual meeting held after it gives the financial assistance, and in respect of each annual meeting thereafter so long as the financial assistance remains outstanding (s. 20(6)).

(b) a purchase, redemption or other acquisition of shares contrary to section 30, 31 or 32;

Section 30 provides for the purchase of issued shares.

Section 31 states that, subject to its articles and to remaining solvent (able to meet all of its obligations to creditors and shareholders), a corporation may purchase or otherwise acquire shares or warrants issued by it to:

☐ settle a debt or claim asserted by or against the corporation;

☐ eliminate fraction shares; or

☐ fulfil the terms of a non-assignable agreement under which it has an option, or is obliged to purchase shares owned by a current or former director, officer or employee.

Warrants are documents issued by a corporation guaranteeing, for example, a right to purchase additional shares at a stated price for a certain period of time.

The BCA states the purchase of issued shares or warrants is "subject to its articles" rather than "where authorized by its articles" as formerly required. This might be interpreted to mean that a corporation can purchase any of its issued shares:

☐ if this provision is included in the articles; or

☐ if the articles are "silent", that is, if no mention is made in this area at all in the articles.

This section also empowers the corporation to purchase or otherwise acquire issued shares to:

☐ satisfy the claim of a dissenting shareholder under section 185;

☐ comply with a court order under section 248 which provides an oppression remedy for a complainant who feels he or she has been unfairly dealt with by the corporation or its agents.

(c) a commission contrary to section 37;

Section 37 of the Act authorizes the directors to pay a commission to any person who buys shares of the corporation or obtains purchasers for shares of the corporation. However, no direction is given as to how this should be done. Presumably a resolution of directors would be sufficient. Confirmation by the shareholders of this resolution would ensure the validity of the action taken by the directors.

(d) a payment of a dividend contrary to section 38;

Under section 38, and subject to its articles and any unanimous shareholder agreement, the directors may declare, and a corporation may pay, a dividend by issuing fully paid shares of the corporation or options or rights to acquire fully paid shares of the corporation. A corporation may pay a dividend in money or property provided that the payment will not render the corporation insolvent.

(e) a payment of an indemnity contrary to section 136; or

Under this section a corporation may indemnify a director or officer of a corporation who is being sued in that capacity so long as the director or officer acted honestly and in good faith and in the best interest of the corporation. If the action against the director or officer is either criminal or administrative, the corporation may indemnify that individual so long as he or she had reasonable grounds for believing that their conduct was lawful.

(f) a payment to a shareholder contrary to section 185 or 248,

These sections refer to the rights of a dissenting shareholder and the oppression remedy which were briefly discussed earlier in reference to section 31.

Any director who contravenes the provisions of section 130 is jointly and severally liable to reimburse the corporation for any amounts that have been distributed or paid and are not otherwise recovered by the corporation (subsection 130(2)).

A director who has paid a judgment obtained under this section is entitled to receive contributions from any other directors who voted for or consented to the unlawful act upon which the judgment was founded (subsection 130(3)).

A director liable under subsection (2) is entitled to apply to the court for an order compelling a shareholder or any other recipient to pay or deliver to the director any money or property that was paid or distributed contrary to sections 20, 30, 31, 32, 37, 38, 136, 185 or 248. The court may, if it deems it equitable to do so:

(a) order a shareholder/recipient to pay or deliver any such money or property to the director;

(b) order a corporation to return or issue shares to a person which had been purchased, redeemed or otherwise acquired; or

(c) make any further order it thinks fit (subsection 130(5)).

A director is not liable under subsection (1) provided he or she can prove that they did not know, and could not reasonably have known, that the share was issued for less than the corporation would have received if the share has been issued for money (subsection 130(6)).

A complainant has two years in which to commence an action to enforce a liability under this section. The time begins to run from the date of the resolution that authorized the action which is the basis of the complaint (subsection 130(7)).

(p) Consent of Director at Meeting

A director who is present at a meeting of directors or committee of directors is deemed to have consented to any resolution passed or action taken unless:

(a) his or her dissent is entered into the minutes of the meeting;

(b) the written dissent is filed with the secretary of the meeting before adjournment; or

(c) the dissent is sent by registered mail or delivered personally to the registered office of the corporation, immediately after the adjournment of the meeting (subsection 135(1)).

A director who voted in favour of, or consents to, a resolution is not entitled to dissent under subsection (1) (subsection 135(2)). Under subsection 135(3), a director who is absent from the meeting at which a resolution was passed or action taken is deemed to have consented unless within seven days after becoming aware of the resolution he or she causes his or her dissent to be placed with the minutes of the meeting; or sends his or her dissent by registered mail or delivers it to the registered office of the corporation.

The requirement of consent includes any resolution passed or action taken at a meeting. Formerly, the matters were restricted to those which required the consent of a director at a meeting.

Subsection (4) exempts a director from liability under section 130 or 134 of the Act if he or she relies in good faith upon financial statements of the corporation, or a written report of the auditor regarding the financial position of the corporation, or a report of a lawyer, accountant, engineer, appraiser or person whose profession lends credibility to a statement made by that person.

(q) Liability of Directors for Wages

Directors are jointly and severally liable to employees of the corporation:

1. for all debts not exceeding six months' wages that became due while they are directors for services performed for the corporation;
2. for the vacation pay accrued while they are directors for not more than 12 months under the *Employment Standards Act*, R.S.O. 1990, c. E.14, and the Regulations thereunder; or
3. under any collective agreement made by the corporation (subsection 131(1)).

(r) Limitation of Liability

A director is liable under subsection 131(1) if the action is commenced within six months after the debts became payable, and, under clause 131(1)(b):

(i) the corporation is sued in the action against the director and execution against the corporation is returned unsatisfied in whole or in part, or
(ii) before or after the action is commenced the corporation goes into liquidation, is ordered to be wound up or makes an authorized assignment under the *Bankruptcy Act* (Canada) [now the *Bankruptcy and Insolvency Act*], or a receiving order under the *Bankruptcy Act* (Canada) is made against it, and in any such case, the claim for the debts is proved.

Where an execution has issued against the corporation, the amount recoverable from a director is the amount remaining unsatisfied after execution.

A director who pays the debt under subsection (1) is entitled to any preference that the employee would have been entitled to and, where a judgment has been obtained, is entitled to an assignment of the judgment.

A director who has paid a claim under this section is entitled to contributions from the directors who are liable for the claim (section 131).

(s) Removal of Directors

Subject to clause 120(f), the shareholders of a corporation may by ordinary resolution at an annual or special meeting remove any director or directors from office (subsection 122(1)).

The term ''special meeting'' is not defined under the Act but is referred to in the definition for ''special resolution'' set out in subsection 1(1) of the Act. A special resolution is one that is:

(a) submitted to a special meeting of the shareholders of the corporation called to consider the resolution and passed, with or without amendment, at the meeting by at least two-thirds of the votes cast; or

(b) consented to in writing by each shareholder or a shareholder's attorney authorized in writing.

Presumably then the shareholders could draft a resolution removing a director or directors and then call a special meeting to consider the resolution, even though the subsection refers to an ''ordinary resolution''.

Where a class of shares carries an exclusive right to elect one or more directors, such a director may only be removed by an ordinary resolution of the shareholders of that class or series. The term ''ordinary resolution'' means a resolution that is submitted to a meeting of the shareholders of the corporation and passed, with or without amendment, at the meeting by at least a majority of the votes cast. Subject to clauses 120(a) to (d), a vacancy created by the removal of a director may be filled at the meeting of the shareholders or filled under the provisions of section 124.

As mentioned, there are other sections dealing with directors which should be noted. The sections set out above are, however, of primary importance for a general understanding of the duties and responsibilities of directors.

In a small, closely held corporation, the directors are the most important persons in relation to a corporation, as they are usually the actual proprietors. The directors are usually responsible, depending on the size of the corporation, for the daily management of the business of the corporation. They make the important day-to-day decisions, such as whether or not to lease property, build a registered office, formerly head office, or expand the business by acquiring another corporation or business. Other people assist in the operation of the corporation but the directors are elected by the shareholders to manage or supervise the management of the business of the corporation. The directors enact by-laws governing the general operation of the corporation and by resolution make the other decisions affecting the corporation. A record of the by-laws, resolutions, ownership of shares of the corporation and registers of the directors, officers and shareholders are kept in the corporate records (or minute books) of the corporation.

Larger corporations, as occasion demands, consult with experts in areas in which the directors or officers lack expertise. Substantial public corporations, such as Ford Motor Company of Canada, Ltd., hire professional management people. In contrast, Henry Ford, the founder of the present corporation, ran the business singlehandedly. In order to function today, this corporation requires experts in a great many areas such as design, manufacturing, marketing and accounting.

2. Officers

The second group of individuals through which a corporation acts are its officers. The officers are elected or appointed by the directors of the corporation. This is one of the first acts taken by the first directors named in the articles of incorporation after they pass the organizational resolutions. The officers perform the administrative functions of a corporation. It is their responsibility to see that the decisions made by the directors are carried out.

The important provisions dealing with both directors and officers are found under Part IX, sections 115 to 137 of the Act. Several of these sections refer to both directors and officers, and have already been discussed in detail under the section concerning directors. Accordingly, only the sections which apply to both directors and officers will be discussed here.

Section 132 requires officers of a corporation to make the same disclosures concerning a possible conflict of interest as is required from directors under this section. An officer of a corporation who is either an officer of, or has a material interest in, any person who is a party to a proposed or actual contract shall disclose this interest in writing to the corporation or ask that this information be noted in the minutes of the meeting of directors. Section 133 provides that subject to the articles, the by-laws or any unanimous shareholder agreement, the directors may designate the offices of the corporation, appoint officers, specify their duties and delegate to them powers to manage the general business and affairs of the corporation. There are some powers which directors are unable to delegate, and sections 184 and 127(3) should be checked to ensure that the directors do not contravene the new Act.

Section 184 provides that the directors may by resolution, unless restricted by the articles, by-laws or a unanimous shareholder agreement, delegate any or all of the borrowing powers set out under this section to a director, a committee of directors or an officer.

Section 127 provides for the appointment of a managing director, who is a resident Canadian, or a committee of directors chosen from the current directors of the corporation. A majority of the members of the committee shall be Canadian residents unless the corporation is a non-resident corporation. There are certain limitations on the authority of the managing director or committee of directors for both offering and non-offering corporations which are set out under subsection 127(3). These limitations are summarized under the subheading ''(1) Managing Director'', above.

Section 133 states that a director may be appointed to any office of the corporation and that the same person may hold two or more offices of the corporation.

Formerly, a corporation was required to have a president and a secretary and such other officers as are provided for either in the by-laws or the resolutions of the directors. The same person could hold two or more offices. Now the choice of the offices, the officers and the assignment of duties is left up to the directors.

Unless there is a requirement in the articles, the by-laws or any unanimous shareholder agreement, there is no requirement under the Act that the Chairman of the Board or the President must be a director of the corporation. However, a director may be appointed to any office of the corporation.

It is a common practice for non-offering corporations, i.e., those that do not offer their shares to the public, to appoint a president and a secretary or secretary-treasurer in the initial organizational resolutions. Additional officers that could be appointed, as the need arises, are one or more vice-presidents, an assistant secretary or treasurer or a manager.

3. Standards of Care

The BCA requires every director and officer of a corporation to exercise the powers and discharge the duties of his or her office honestly, in good faith and in the best interest of the corporation. Directors and officers are required to exercise the degree of care, diligence and skill that a reasonably prudent person would exercise in similar circumstances. Subsection 134(2) requires that every director and officer of a corporation shall comply with the Act, the regulations, articles, by-laws and any unanimous shareholder agreement.

Subsection 134(3) states that subject to subsection 108(5), no provision in a contract, the articles, the by-laws or a resolution relieves a director or officer from the duty to act in accordance with this Act and the regulations, nor from liability for a breach thereof.

Subsection 108(5) provides that where a shareholder is a party to a unanimous shareholder agreement, that shareholder has all the rights, powers, duties and liabilities of a director of the corporation to the extent that the agreement restricts the discretion or powers of the directors to manage or supervise the management of the business and affairs of the corporation. In these circumstances the directors are relieved of the duties and liabilities set out in a unanimous shareholder agreement.

Directors and officers act in a fiduciary capacity for the corporation. The term ''fiduciary'' means the relationship of one person to another, where the former is bound to exercise rights and powers in good faith for the benefit of the latter. A person in a fiduciary position is not entitled to make a personal profit, unless this is specifically set out under the governing statute or agreement, or to put himself or herself in a position where his or her duty and interest conflict.

4

ONBIS — Companies Branch Automation

1. ONBIS — The System

ONBIS is the acronym for the Ontario Business Information System, a system that has been under consideration and development by the Companies Branch of the Ministry of Consumer and Commercial Relations [now Ministry of Consumer and Business Services] since early 1988. In order to initiate the process, in April of that year, the Companies Branch conducted a client survey in the Public Office over a one-week period and requested responses from the clients in the following areas:

- ☐ waiting time for request to be completed
- ☐ how long the request should have taken
- ☐ whether assistance was required
- ☐ whether the service was adequate
- ☐ office convenience
- ☐ staff knowledge
- ☐ staff courtesy
- ☐ rating of service time involved

covering the areas of incorporations, corporate and debenture searches, partnerships registrations and partnerships searches.

The decision to implement ONBIS resulted from the increased use, by the public and by government agencies, of the services offered by the Companies Branch. The Companies Branch responds to more than 500,000 information requests annually and demand continues. The Companies Branch is the sole provider of information on corporations, partnerships, sole proprietorships and name/style registrations. In the fast-paced business world of the nineties, the automated Companies Branch records provide up-to-date information and, through ONBIS, offer online access to a vast databank of business registration information.

Through the Companies Branch registration files, clients determine, for example:

- ☐ the identity of sole proprietorships, partnerships and corporations, including corporations operating under a name or style
- ☐ the names and addresses of corporate directors and officers
- ☐ business addresses.

The information extracted depends on the requirements of the individual client at the time the files are searched.

The staff of the Companies Branch involved in this computerization process reviewed the existing legislation and formulated changes which would have to be made to permit computerization. At the same time consideration was given as to the currency of the information in the registration files and how the legislation might contribute to the failure to comply, for example, with the requirement for filing a notice of change or a new declaration when a change or changes occurred in the original information for a business or a corporation. It is not unusual, for example, during the five-year registration period for a business to change one or more of the following at least once:

- ☐ its business address;
- ☐ its mailing address;
- ☐ the address(es) of the partners or sole proprietor; or
- ☐ the description of its business which may change due to diversification.

Prior to September 1, 1988, each of these changes involved a fee of $11 or a total of $44 for the above examples. To encourage its clients to report changes, the Companies Branch consolidated fees. One fee is paid when a partnership or sole proprietorship is registered and all other fees for changes, dissolution or withdrawal have been eliminated.

In conjunction with the necessary changes in legislation, the Companies Branch has undertaken a phased mailout to the approximately 600,000 corporations and 500,000 active business registrations to update the information and ensure the accuracy of the database.

(a) Special Notices

A component of the above-mentioned phased mailout was the requirement to file a Special Notice. Section 6 of the *Corporations Information Act*, R.S.O. 1990, c. C39, provides that the Minister may at any time by written notice require that a corporation, except those in a class exempted by the Regulations, make a special filing for the purposes of establishing or maintaining an electronic record database under section 9. When the request is received, the corporation shall make the special filing in the prescribed form and pay the prescribed fee.

The initial request to file a Special Notice was mailed to all corporations on record with the Companies Branch in 1992. A second request followed to the corporations who had not responded. Any of these corporations that filed the Special Notice only had to file one Special Notice but were required to pay a fee of $100 rather than the usual $50 fee. Special Notice 3 was mailed in December 1994.

(b) Failure to File Special Notice(s)

In June 1994, the Companies Branch initiated the process to dissolve the corporations that had not responded to the initial request to file nor had paid the prescribed fee. Prior to the actual cancellation of the charter, the corporations would have received three letters regarding their legal obligations to file. In addition, several weeks in advance of the cancellation date, a courtesy letter was sent setting out the specific cancellation date. By November 1994, some 118,000 corporations were dissolved for failure to file the Special Notice and pay the prescribed fee. These corporations failed to respond to the initial request to file. This filing was an interim measure to continuously update the public record and has been replaced by annual returns, the legislation for which was proclaimed on April 7, 1995.

Reaction to the dissolutions by the Companies Branch resulted in applications to revive the corporations and complaints about the costs involved. In addition to the filing fee, a consent was required from the Public Guardian and Trustee and a NUANS name search. A consent was also required from the Corporations Tax Branch. The Companies Branch responded by:

1. setting up a last minute filing room to handle the filing of these Special Notices;
2. expanding the last minute filing room to handle revivals; and
3. amending the Regulations under the *Business Corporations Act* to provide for streamlined procedures for revival of corporations dissolved for failure to file special notices. Effective October 12, 1994, in most cases such corporations no longer required consent from the Corporations Tax Branch or the Public Guardian and Trustee. In addition, the revival fee was eliminated but was later reinstated on December 1, 1995.

A large number of dissolved corporations responded to these initiatives and filed articles of revival.

The Companies Branch will continue to provide notice of its intention to cancel or dissolve corporations that fail to respond to the requests for special notices. At least 90 days prior to the cancellation of the charter, a notice of intention to cancel will be mailed to the corporation by the Companies Branch.

A certificate of status ordered for a corporation that has not complied with the filing requirements but, for whatever reason, has not been dissolved will for Ontario corporations show the following:

> This corporation has received a Notice of Intention to Cancel and is subject to cancellation.

This statement will remain until either the corporation has remedied the default in filing or it is dissolved.

2. ONBIS — The Public Record

The electronic ONBIS record is now the public record. All information on notices has been keyed into the system since June 27, 1992, and the electronic public record began on that date. Information filed with the Companies Branch prior to that date, together with information filed after that date but not keyed into ONBIS, is still in microfiche form. The Companies Branch has no plans at present for conversion of microfiche to some other type of storage medium.

3. The Automation Process

The major functions of the Companies Branch are to conduct the following transactions:

- ☐ incorporation and changes in corporate structure;
- ☐ registration of assumed business names of corporations;
- ☐ (voluntary) dissolutions of corporations;
- ☐ cancellations of licences;
- ☐ revivals of corporation;
- ☐ licensing of non-Canadian corporations to carry on business in Ontario as extraprovincial corporations;
- ☐ registrations of proprietorships and partnerships;
- ☐ maintaining and updating public records on business entities in Ontario; and
- ☐ providing searches of public records maintained on corporations, proprietorships and partnerships.

ONBIS has, the Companies Branch advises, not only improved the services offered to its clients, but, by improving access to this information, contributed to a fair and informed marketplace. One of the greatest advantages of computerized information is that multiple users can access the same information at the same time.

4. Conversion to Automation

ONBIS developed in seven releases or stages. This approach supported a smooth, staged introduction of automation into the branch while minimizing inconvenience to clients and maximizing customer service. The seven planned releases or stages were:

Release 1: begin to build the database with information provided by the conversion of partnership and proprietorship records.

Release 2: include records of corporations. The content of these records began with the information provided by the corporate mailout. Also provide an ONBIS online index of names of corporations.

Release 3: allow the Branch to search an ONBIS online name index for partnerships and sole proprietorships.

Release 4: enable online registration of basic data at the counter for partnerships and sole proprietorships.

Release 5: introduce online registration of basic data at the counter for corporations. Computerized accounting will also be implemented.

Release 6: provide additional online searching capabilities and a variety of reports for partnerships and sole proprietorships.

Release 7: introduce full online registration at the counter for partnerships, sole proprietorships and corporations. Information will be immediately available in the database to respond to search requests from the public.

5. Current Conversion Status

The database for partnerships and sole proprietorships permits an automated "look-up". Prior to registration, a search of these records is recommended to avoid registering a name similar to, or exactly the same as, an existing business.

The Companies Branch has available in the Public Office an Electronic Corporate Index (ECI) known as an Alphabetical Corporate Index and there are instructions which walk a person through gaining access to the ONBIS system. The ECI replaced the COM (Corporations on Microfiche) Index and is a new user-friendly electronic version of the COM index with enhanced search features. The first step is to determine the corporation number, the date of incorporation, or any other applicable date, *i.e.*, amalgamation or continuance, all of which can be obtained from the ECI Index. For more information, see Chapter 12, Searches.

Starting with Special Notice 3 mailed December 1994, the actual notices did not appear on the microfiche. These were filmed on a security roll for emergency retrieval.

Several ONBIS products are now online, replacing certain kinds of information previously only available on microfiche:

1. *Corporate Document List:* A report that lists all documents filed on or after June 27, 1992, and which is produced while the person waits at the counter. This report is useful as evidence that a particular document was actually filed with the Companies Branch on a certain date. The List also shows any default notices that may have been sent by the Companies Branch to the corporation.
2. *Certificate of Status:* The Certificate of Status provides the current Status of the corporation. It is available only for Ontario Corporations or for Extra-Provincial foreign corporations. By having the Certificate of Status produced through the ONBIS system, such certificates could be produced immediately instead of within five days as was previously required.
3. *Corporation Profile Report:* This report provides all the current information on file for a corporation which is required under the *Corporations Information Act*. This report includes a listing of the active directors and officers. The Report is produced while the client waits. Some historical information such as amalgamating corporations, where the subject corporation is an amalgamated corporation, and name history are included in the report. Other historical information comes from the microfiche record and takes somewhat longer to generate, but usually only a few hours.
4. *Corporation Business Names List:* This report sets out all business names registered or renewed by the particular corporation within the last five years. The business name, Business Identification Number (BIN), registration date and expiry date are included in this report. If more information on the business name is required such as the status of the registration, business address, and activity, then an Unincorporated Business Name Search can be requested.

As with other information accessed from ONBIS, the Corporate Document List, the Corporation Profile Report and the Corporation Business Names List can be certified.

With the availability of the Corporation Profile Report, certain filings, set out below, will not be added to the corporate microfiche jacket:

1. 1994-1995 Special Notices (year 3);
2. Initial Notices/Notices of Change; and

3. Annual Returns filed on or after January 1, 1995.

In instances where a Corporation Profile Report is not available, the Companies Branch will supply to the client:

1. Corporate Document List;
2. microfiche; and
3. copies of notices filed on or after January 1, 1995.

The province of Quebec enacted on January 1, 1994, a statute titled *An Act Respecting the Legal Publicity of Sole Proprietorships, Partnerships and Legal Persons*, S.Q. 1993, c. 48, pursuant to which data respecting the incorporation and amendment of Quebec corporations is no longer forwarded to the NUANS database.

This data is being recorded in a new provincial system called "CIDREQ". There is ongoing discussion between Industry Canada and provincial authorities but it is anticipated that a method to supply such data to NUANS may be available some time in the future.

Industry Canada recommends that until this temporary gap in data is remedied, any of its clients proposing to carry on business in Quebec should supplement the NUANS search report with a search of the new CIDREQ register. The search report can be obtained by making a written request to:

L'Inspecteur général des institutes financiérs
Direction des entréprises
P.O. Box 1153
Québec, Québec
GlK 7C3

The Notice advises the cost of a search report is $23.93. The request can be sent direct or a private search house may be of assistance in making such a search. In addition, the Office of the Inspector General may be contacted during business hours at the following numbers:

Montréal — (514) 873-5324
Québec — (418) 643-3625

6. Electronic Filing

In keeping with its commitment of providing multiple access channels for the products and services offered, the Companies Branch implemented electronic filing of Articles of Incorporation under the *Business Corporations Act*. Proclamation of the 1994 electronic filing amendments to the *Act* and amendments to Regulation 62 under the *Business Corporations Act* became effective in May, 2000 enabling clients to file Articles of Incorporation electronically. The amendments to the Regulation were published in the Ontario Gazette on

June 3, 2000. The following amendments were made to the *Act* and Regulations to facilitate the electronic filing of the articles of incorporation:

1. The clients may file articles of incorporation and supporting documents electronically through the two primary service providers under contract with the Ministry. These primary service providers are OnCorp Direct Inc. (*www.oncorp.com*) and Cyberbahn Inc. (*www.cyberbahn.ca*) which provide electronic access to the Ministry's electronic database, ONBIS.
2. Clients filing articles of incorporation are not required to submit the NUANS name search report. However, clients must provide the NUANS report reference number, the date of the report and the proposed name searched (s. 18(1.1), Reg. 62). The clients must keep a paper or electronic copy of the NUANS report and any consent or consent and undertaking required under the *Act* or Regulations at the corporation's registered office. Articles of incorporation submitted to the Companies Branch manually will still require the original NUANS report in paper format.
3. Signatures are not required on articles of incorporation filed electronically. Although section 273(4) of the *Business Corporations Act* refers to an electronic signature, the signature requirement is waived under subsection 24.1(3) of Regulation 62. In addition, an incorporator or someone duly authorized to represent and bind the incorporator(s) of a corporation incorporated electronically is required to indicate acceptance of the Terms and Conditions of filing articles of incorporation electronically on the primary service provider interface before the filing is allowed to proceed.
4. Clients who file electronically receive a Certificate of Incorporation. This certificate is prescribed by regulation and is part of the incorporating documents that appear in the public record.

7. Forms

The Ministry of Consumer and Business Services is now making available on its website certain forms under the *Business Corporations Act* (Ontario) and the *Extra-Provincial Corporations Act* that are filed with the Companies Branch. These forms are found selecting the Business Information and then the Companies Branch Forms buttons on the website at *http://www.cbs.gov.on.ca/mcbs/english/business_info.htm*. The following forms, together with instructions, are available:

☐ Business Corporations Act

- Articles of Incorporation (Form 1)
- Consent to Act as a First Director (Form 2)

☐ Extra-Provincial Corporations Act

- Application for Extra-Provincial Licence (Form 1)
- Consent to Act as Agent for Service (Form 2)
- Application for Amended Extra-Provincial Licence (Form 3)
- Application for Termination of Extra-Provincial Licence (Form 4)

The forms can either be printed and then filled out, or filled out on screen (Adobe 4.0 required) and then printed. The forms must be signed in duplicate, and submitted in person to the Companies Branch public office or mailed to the Branch with the appropriate fee to: Companies Branch, 393 University Avenue, Ste. 200, Toronto, M5G 2M2.

8. MyBIS

The Business Information Service (MyBIS) is an Ontario Business Connects (OBC) initiative to expand the business-to-government relationship. By subscribing to this e-mail service, the client can receive relevant links to information quickly and efficiently. The choice of business topics includes taxation, export, import, and intellectual property. When the client subscribes to MyBIS, the client is asked to select options that best fit the client's area of business. Based on the selections, the system searches the database sources and automatically sends personalized e-mail with current and updated hyperlinks specific to the client's business interests. MyBIS subscribers can change their existing preferences at any time by logging on to MyBIS at the OBC website (*http://www.cbs.gov.on.ca/obc/english/MyBIS.htm*).

5

The Act of Incorporation

1. Clearance of Name

Industry Canada in Ottawa has established a database which includes a record of all federal corporations and those received from the various provincial jurisdictions in Canada. NUANS stands for Newly Updated Automated Name Search which is a sophisticated search engine that searches over 8,000,000 records of corporation names, trademarks and business names. While Industry Canada runs the program, Compaq Canada has the contract to manage the "business" end, and in turn, contracts with the private search houses who provide the actual service. When clearing a name for a proposed Ontario corporation, the suggested name is submitted to one of the private search houses which have access to the database in Ottawa. The proposed name is submitted, the computer pulls from the database the names that are most similar and the computer printout is received by the name search house usually within 24 hours of the request being filed. In addition to submitting the name to the database, these private name search houses also do a manual check of copies of microfiche showing the latest provincial and federal names which may not as yet have been added to the database. Although not required to do so, the search houses often make recommendations as to whether or not the name is acceptable. The final decision is made by the lawyer and client as to whether or not to incorporate under a particular name. The Companies Branch of the Ministry of Consumer and Business Services makes no decisions on names for corporations incorporated under the *Business Corporations Act*. This decision is now the joint responsibility of the lawyer involved and the incorporator(s).

The Companies Branch at one time searched and cleared names for extra-provincial corporations, non-profit corporations and, until June 15, 1982, for licences in mortmain (when the statute providing for these licences was repealed). In the fall of 1989 the Companies Branch announced three new policy changes, two of which applied to the names clearance procedures, which were:

1. The Companies Branch would no longer pre-clear or rule on proposed names of extra-provincial corporations. Extra-provincial corporations would be treated in the same manner as corporations incorporated under the *Business Corporations Act, 1982*. This means that the onus is now on the applicants to make certain there is no existing Ontario corporation or business that has the exact, or similar, name as that of the extra-provincial corporation. Refer to Chapter 11 ("Extra-Provincial Corporations") for more information.
2. Pre-clearance of proposed names of organizations applying for incorporation under the *Corporations Act* would cease. The Companies Branch would still rule on names but it would be done at the point of application, that is, when the articles of incorporation are received by the Companies Branch after approval by the Public Guardian and Trustee of applications of a charitable nature or containing charitable clauses.

The third policy change referred to above concerned a change in procedure regarding certain incorporations under the *Corporations Act*.

All applications for non-profit corporations which are of a charitable nature or contain charitable clauses and which use objects specially drafted for that charity must be submitted first to the Office of the Public Guardian and Trustee for clearance. The Public Guardian and Trustee will affix a stamp indicating approval and forward the application to the Companies Branch for further processing. This change eliminates transit time and reduces the turnaround time. There is a charge of $150 to review the application.

Another innovation in the area of not-for-profit incorporations is the adoption of a stamp endorsed on the application, as is done when articles of incorporation issue for business corporations. The Companies Branch no longer prepares the two cover pages for the applications. Any charitable provisions required for a particular applicant will be embodied in the application.

Where the application uses pre-approved objects developed by the Public Guardian and Trustee, then the application can be submitted directly to the Companies Branch for processing. These pre-approved objects are set out in Appendix "A" of Charities Bulletin #2 issued by the Office of the Public Guardian and Trustee.

(a) Restrictions

Section 9 of the BCA sets out restrictions on the names a corporation may use:

9. (1) Subject to subsection (2), a corporation shall not have a name,

(a) that contains a word or expression prohibited by the regulations;

(b) that is the same as or, except where a number name is proposed, similar to,

(i) the name of a known,

(A) body corporate,

(B) trust,

(C) association,

(D) partnership,

(E) sole proprietorship, or

(F) individual,

whether in existence or not, or

(ii) the known name under which any body corporate, trust, association, partnership, sole proprietorship, or individual, carries on business or identifies himself, herself or itself,

if the use of that name would be likely to deceive; or

(c) that does not meet the requirements prescribed by the regulations.

(2) A corporation may have a name described in clause (1)(b) upon complying with conditions prescribed by the regulations.

(3) There shall be filed with the Director such documents relating to the name of the corporation as may be prescribed by the regulations.

(b) Requirements

Section 10 of the BCA establishes the requirements for the legal element in a corporate name. The legal element is the last word of the name of every corporation, and includes the word "Limited", "Limitée", "Incorporated", "Incorporée" or "Corporation" or their corresponding abbreviations. Although this section requires the use of one of the legal elements in a corporate name, the Act states only that it must be part, in addition to any use in a figurative or descriptive sense, of the name of every corporation.

A corporate name should also include distinctive and descriptive elements. A word which will set the corporate name apart from all other corporations and which is not similar to existing corporations is distinctive. A descriptive word must convey to the public some idea of the type of business carried on by the corporation.

Subsection 10(2) of the BCA states that subject to the provisions of this Act and the regulations, a corporation may set out its name in its articles in an English form, a French form, an English form and a French form, a combined English and French form, or an English form and a French form where the forms are equivalent but used separately. The corporation may be legally designated by any such name.

Subsections 10(3) and (4) of the BCA set out the following requirements for the corporate name:

(3) For the purposes of subsections (1) and (2) only letters from the Roman alphabet or Arabic numerals or a combination thereof together with such punctuation marks and other marks as are permitted by regulation, may form part of the name of a corporation.

(4) Subject to the provisions of this Act and the regulations, a corporation may have in its articles of incorporation a special provision permitting it to set out its name in any language and the corporation may be legally designated by that name.

Subsection 10(5) of the Act requires the corporation to set out its name in legible characters in all contracts, invoices, negotiable instruments and orders for goods or services issued or made by or on behalf of the corporation. This requirement extends to all documents sent to the Director under the Act as well.

The Regulations referred to in the above subsections set out in detail definitions of terms or references made in these subsections. Reference should be made to these Regulations. See General Regulation, R.R.O. 1990, Reg. 62.

Regulations generally set out information that assists in implementation of a particular statute and the procedures which must be followed by individuals dealing with matters contained in that statute. For example, section 2 of Reg. 62 sets out particulars of the meaning of the expression "if the use of that name would be likely to deceive" which includes:

1. a name which would infer the corporation is the same as another, whether or not a similar business is carried on, *i.e.*, a person named Ronald McDonald should not incorporate using a name such as Ronald McDonald Hamburgers Limited. This could cause confusion in the minds of the public between the new corporation and McDonald's.
2. a name which would lead the public to think that a corporation bearing the name is or would be associated or affiliated with a person when in fact they are not associated nor will they be associated. The term "person" under the new Act includes a body corporate or corporation. The name "Ronald McDonald Food Enterprises Limited" could cause confusion in the minds of the public since the name "Ronald McDonald" is associated with the McDonald's Corporation. It would be unwise to incorporate under such a name even if one of the incorporators is named Ronald McDonald.
3. a name which is similar to that of a well known individual which would lead the public to think they are in fact dealing with that well known individual because the corporation bears the same or a similar name to that of the well known individual — see the examples set out in 1 and 2 above. The term "person" which is used in clause 2(c) of the Regulations, as defined under the Act, includes an individual, sole proprietorship, partnership, a body corporate and others as set out under subsection 1(1) of the Act.

Provided the Regulations are complied with, a corporation may be incorporated using a name not prohibited under this section. There are several sections under the Regulations which refer to the specific requirements for names of proposed corporations. Reference should always be made to the Regulations prior to choosing a name for a proposed corporation.

Section 18 of Reg. 62 states that the following document shall accompany any articles containing a proposed name for a corporation or a change of corporate name:

> **18.** (1) The following documents shall accompany any articles containing a proposed name for a corporation or a change of corporate name:
>
> 1. An original Ontario biased or weighted computer printed search report for the proposed name from the NUANS automated name search system maintained by the Department of Consumer and Corporate Affairs, Canada [now Industry Canada] dated not more than ninety days prior to the submission of the articles.
> 2. Any consent or consent and undertaking required under the Act or this Regulation and, if applicable, in the Form prescribed.
>
> (2) Where a proposed name is in,
>
> (a) an English form and a French form; or
>
> (b) a combined English and French form,
>
> and the English and French forms of the name are phonetically dissimilar, a separate computer printed search report shall be provided for the English form and the French form of the name.
>
> (3) Subsections (1) and (2) also apply to an application for revival under section 241 of the Act if the articles change the name of the Corporation or at least 10 years have elapsed since the Corporation was dissolved.
>
> (4) No name that is identified in a computer printed search report as proposed shall be used as a corporate name by a person other than the one who proposed the name unless a consent in writing has been obtained from the person who first proposed the name.

Under the law it is the responsibility of the incorporator(s) and the lawyer to:

1. obtain an Ontario biased NUANS name search report through a private search house;
2. make a decision on the availability of the proposed name;
3. ensure articles of incorporation do not contravene the statute and the Regulations;
4. file the articles of incorporation along with the Ontario biased NUANS name search report dated within 90 days of the submission date of the articles of incorporation.

It is recommended that the following steps be taken concerning name clearance:

1. search business names registrations records, partnerships and sole proprietorships;
2. check master microfiche and/or the Electronic Corporate Index (ECI) at the Public Office for existing corporations; and
3. obtain a computer printout from a private search house.

Step 1 must be taken because from time to time, objections have been raised from partnerships/proprietorships because some names are visually quite different but sound somewhat alike. The Director has on occasion issued a certificate of amendment to the articles changing the name of a new corporation. The Director has also received complaints from existing corporations where there is a similarity in name and the type of business. For example, a corporation under the name of ''Smith Realty Limited'' may be in existence. Later, a new corporation, ''Smith Construction Company Limited'' may be incorporated. There is some similarity in the names of the corporations, and both corporations deal with land. A realty corporation could have the right to build houses in addition to developing land. A construction corporation's general business may be to deal in real property (land), which could be interpreted to mean it could carry on business as a realty corporation. In this instance, the first corporation could be successful in having the name of the second corporation changed. The Director's authority to change a name is found under section 12 of the Act.

It is advisable to have an alternative name ready should a name not be cleared. Otherwise a number followed by either ''Ontario Limited'' or ''Ontario Inc.'' will be assigned to the corporation by the Minister. The articles of incorporation are prepared with nine blank spaces in front of the words ''Ontario limited'' or ''Ontario Inc.'', as may be decided. The number is filled in by the staff at the Companies Branch when the articles of incorporation are filed. The number assigned is the file number allotted to the new corporation by the Companies Branch. All applications for incorporation, once they have been checked and approved as to form and content as set out under the statute and the Regulations, are given a file number. This file number, or Ontario corporation number, is inserted in the upper right hand corner of the articles of incorporation and enables the Companies Branch to keep track of the articles of incorporation and all other material filed in connection with a particular corporation.

There are various methods available to law firms in performing preliminary checks on proposed corporate names. Proposed names can be submitted to the private search houses for clearance but this can prove to be a costly venture for the client if the proposed name does not clear. A more economical, and perhaps ultimately a more time saving, method is to make some preliminary investigations concerning a proposed name. This can be done by checking the local telephone directory in the municipality where the business will be carried on, searching the business names registrations, the master microfiche listing of Ontario corporations and/or checking the names by using the Electronic Corporate Index located in the Public Office at the Companies Branch. If there is time, a letter search can be directed to the Companies Branch concerning a proposed name. Sufficient time should be allowed for the letter request to be received by the Companies Branch, the search completed and the letter report received back by the lawyer or law firm initiating the inquiry. This procedure could be expedited by the use of one of the many private courier services if the clearing of the name is a "rush". Mail service usually involves a minimum of 12 to 14 days. There is no charge for personally inspecting the master microfiche listing of Ontario corporations or using the Companies Branch Electronic Corporate Index.

Included in Part III, Federal Corporations, is information on reading the printout (shown as Form 13.2) which would apply equally to a printout for an Ontario corporation. In addition, there may also be some helpful information regarding name selection obtained from the Publication "Choosing a name . . . for your federally incorporated company" prepared by Industry Canada, and the Name Granting Compendium of Industry Canada shown as Form 13.1.

Once the preliminary checks have been made as outlined above, then the proposed name will be submitted to a private search house to obtain the NUANS name search report. Among the private search houses to enter the name clearance field in Ontario and which possess a thorough understanding of the proper procedures involved in checking out a proposed name are:

1. Dye & Durham Co. Inc. (www.dyedurham.ca),
2. Cyberbahn Inc., and
3. OnCorp Direct Inc.

(c) Form of Documents

The Regulations set out the prescribed documents that are to be filed with the Director under the Act and section 24 of Reg. 62 sets out details as to the form such documents must be in to be acceptable for filing:

> **24.** (1) All documents sent to the Director or filed in the office of the Director including all affidavits, applications, assurances, balance sheets, by-laws, consents, dissents, forms, notices and statements shall be printed, typewritten or reproduced legibly and, in the opinion of the Director, suitable for photographing on microfilm, upon one side of good quality white paper that is,
>
> (a) 210 millimetres by 297 millimetres with a margin. of 30 millimetres on the left-hand side; or

(b) 8 1/2 inches by 11 inches, with a margin of 1 1/4 inches on the left-hand side.

(2) A document consisting of two or more pages shall have no backing or binding, and be stapled in the upper left-hand corner and each page shall be numbered consecutively.

(3) Any document that is sent to the Director shall be on good quality white paper of the size prescribed in subsection (1) that is capable of being endorsed by the Director without smudging.

(4) Articles, applications or statements filed with the Director requiring the signature of one or more persons shall be signed manually by each such person and not by an attorney.

Although there is provision under this section of the Regulation for the filing of documents on paper that measures 8½ inches by 11 inches, provided the left-hand side has a 1¼ inch margin, this "letter size" paper is no longer acceptable. The practice of accepting documents on other than prescribed forms or letter size paper was discontinued as of August 5, 1983. The first page of any document submitted on letter size paper must be identical to the first page of the prescribed form or it will not be accepted for filing by the Companies Branch.

(d) Fees

Regulation 62 formerly set out fees to be charged under the Act in connection with incorporations, amendments, amalgamations or any other filing under this Act. Pursuant to the Minister's Order published in the Ontario Gazette (1999) 132 Ontario Gazette 1582, the fees are set out in the Schedule attached to this Order and shall be paid to the Minister of Finance for Ontario upon the filing, examination or copying of the document or before the Director takes the action for which the fee is intended, as the case may be (see Appendix B).

Paragraph 2 of the Minister's Order requires the name of a corporation or the Ontario corporation number on a cheque that is given in payment of a fee. This information should be entered on the "face" of the cheque. The fee is payable on delivery of articles of incorporation, amalgamation or continuance, arrangement or revival.

The Companies Branch will accept cheques from lawyers, corporations or individuals in payment of fees. There is a handling fee of $35 charged for an NSF cheque.

Paragraph 14 of Schedule 1 refers to a certificate issued in respect of a corporation, which is commonly known as a Certificate of Status. This Ontario certificate at one time certified that in addition to being in existence, the corporation was also up to date in its filing. This reference to "up to date" means that the corportion had filed all annual returns that were required, prior to December 7, 1976, from all corporations carrying on business in Ontario. If a corporation was delinquent, the certificate would not issue. The enactment of the *Corporations Information Act*, R.S.O. 1990, c. C.39 temporarily ended the requirement for the filing of annual returns although any corporation in default in this area on the proclamation date of the new statute was required by the Companies Branch to file any annual returns in arrears, to file an Initial Notice required under the *Corporations Information Act* and to pay the annual filing fees for these delinquent returns.

Pursuant to 1995 amendments to the *Corporations Information Act*, which were proclaimed in force on January 1, 2000, the requirement for annual returns was re-instituted. Every corporation that is incorporated, amalgamated or continued in Ontario under the *Business Corporations Act* shall file a return each year with the Minister by delivering it to the Minister of Finance. In addition, every foreign corporation which has a licence endorsed under the *Extra-Provincial Corporations Act* to carry on business in Ontario must file an annual return. The annual return is combined with the Corporations Tax Return and is to be filed even if the corporation is exempt from filing (EFF) the complete return. If the corporation is exempt from filing, as having no Ontario taxable income, the corporation will complete the common page 1 of the CT23 Corporations Tax and Annual Return form, complete the EEF declaration on page 2, and Schedules A or K (see Form 16.19). The combined return can be submitted using the preprinted paper form which is forwarded to the Corporations Tax Branch of the Ministry of Finance. Alternatively, the corporation can complete the electronic filing version of the Annual Return found through the Ministry of Consumer and Business Services website *www.cbs.gov.ca/mcbs/companies*, or submit the preprinted paper version of the Annual Return shown as Form 16.17. If applicable, the corporation would then submit its CT23 return to the Minister of Finance separately.

The certificate of status, which is available only for Ontario corporations or for extra-provincial foreign corporations, now states when the corporation came into existence, and that it has not been dissolved. If a legal opinion is being given in connection with a matter, a corporate search must be made to determine whether the corporation is current in the filings required under the *Corporations Information Act* such as Notices of Change and Annual Returns.

2. Corporate Powers

(a) General

Section 15 of the Act states that a corporation has the capacity and the rights, powers and privileges of a natural person. Subsection 17(2) states that a corporation shall not exercise any of its powers in a manner contrary to its articles nor carry on any business or exercise any power that is restricted by its articles. It has not been usual in the past to limit the powers and presumably this practice will continue, except in special circumstances. However, the articles should always be checked for any such restrictions before reporting to the principal. Subsection 17(3) of the Act states that notwithstanding subsections (2) and 3(2), no act of a corporation, including a transfer of property to or by the corporation, is invalid because the act is contrary to its articles, by-laws, a unanimous shareholder agreement or this Act.

(b) Power to Act Outside Ontario

Section 16 of the BCA specifically sets out the corporation's authority to exercise its powers outside Ontario so far as the law in that particular jurisdiction allows. Each jurisdiction requires the corporate name be cleared. For example, if there is an existing corporation with the same or a similar name, the Ontario corporation could not carry on business in that province under its name. If this situation should occur in Ontario, there is provision for carrying on business under a name style by registering under the *Business Names Act*.

(c) Acting Outside Powers

If a corporation under section 17 of the BCA acts outside its powers, that is the power is restricted in its articles, beyond the limits of its objects, but if the act or transfer is otherwise valid according to law, then the act or the transfer of real or personal property is not invalidated by reason of the lack of capacity of the corporation. No act of a corporation is invalid, including a transfer of property to or by the corporation, because the act is contrary to its articles, by-laws, unanimous shareholder agreement or this Act.

Subsection 17(1) of the Act states that it is not necessary for a by-law to be passed in order to confer any particular power on the corporation or its directors.

(d) Loans to Shareholders, Directors, etc.

Section 20 of the BCA was amended in 1999 to change the prohibition against financial assistance to affiliated corporations or associates to a requirement of disclosure of all material financial assistance. Subsection 20(1) provides that a corporation may give financial assistance to any person for any purpose by means of a loan, guarantee or otherwise. Subject to subsection (3), a corporation shall disclose to its shareholders all material financial assistance that the corporation gives to

(a) a shareholder, a beneficial owner of a share, a director, an officer or an employee of

   (i) the corporation,

   (ii) an affiliate of the corporation, or

   (iii) an associate of any of the persons mentioned in subclause (i) or (ii); or

(b) any person for the purpose of, or in connection with, a purchase of a share, or a security convertible into or exchangeable for a share, issued or to be issued by the corporation or affiliated corporation.

The term "affiliate" is defined in subsection 1(4) of the Act as an affiliated body corporate that is a subsidiary of another corporation, or both are the subsidiaries of the same corporation or each of them are controlled by the same person. The term "associate" is defined in subsection 1(1) of the Act and means, where used to indicate a relationship with any person:

- ☐ any body corporate of which the person beneficially owns, directly or indirectly, voting securities carrying more than 10% of the voting rights attached to all voting securities;
- ☐ any partner of that person;
- ☐ any trust or estate in which the person is either a beneficiary or acts as trustee or in a similar capacity;
- ☐ any spouse or same-sex partner or relative of the person occupying the same house as the person; or
- ☐ any relative of the person's spouse or same-sex partner occupying the same house as the person.

Subsection 20(3) of the Act sets out the circumstances where the corporation is not required to disclose to its shareholders any financial assistance to the persons set out in subsection 20(2). Pursuant to subsection (3), disclosure is not required where the material financial assistance is given to:

1. a person in the ordinary course of business, if the lending of money is part of the ordinary business of the corporation;
2. a person on account of expenditures incurred on behalf of the corporation;
3. its holding body corporation if the corporation is a wholly owned subsidiary of the holding body corporation; or
4. a subsidiary body corporate of the corporation.

The extent of the disclosure required under subsection 20(2) is set out in subsection 20(4) of the Act. The disclosure of financial assistance shall include:

(a) a brief description of the financial assistance, including the nature and extent of the financial assistance given;

(b) the terms on which the financial assistance was given; and

(c) the amount of the financial assistance initially given and the amount, if any, outstanding.

In the case of a non-offering corporation, the disclosure shall be made by giving a notice to all shareholders within 90 days after giving the financial assistance. In respect of an offering corporation, the corporation shall make the disclosure in each management information circular that the corporation is required to send to its shareholders in respect of each meeting held after giving the financial assistance.

The directors of the corporation who vote for or consent to a resolution authorizing any financial assistance contrary to the disclosure requirements under section 20 are jointly and severally liable to restore to the corporation any amounts so distributed or paid and not otherwise recovered by the corporation (s. 130(1)(a)). Pursuant to subsection 20(7), however, although a contract made by a corporation is in contravention of section 20, the contract may be enforced either by the corporation or by the lender.

3. Contracts

(a) Elements of Contracts

The law of contracts is, in itself, a very large subject outside the scope of this work and it is treated in a number of standard textbooks (one example is G.H.L. Fridman, Q.C., *The Law of Contract in Canada*, 4th ed. (Toronto: Carswell, 1999)). However, the basic requirements for an agreement to constitute a legally binding contract are summarized below.

(i) Offer and Acceptance

The offer must be definite and seriously intended, not made jokingly or in anger. For example, a person buys a new car and a series of problems occur. The owner in anger says, ''For $100 I'd sell this car.'' The owner is not seriously offering to sell the car for $100. Therefore, if someone overhearing these words were to say, ''I'll take the car for $100.'' and the owner refused to sell the car for this amount, an action against the owner would fail because of lack of intent. No sane, sober adult would offer to sell a recent model car for $100.

(ii) Consideration

This consists of values exchanged by the parties to a contract and is that which induces them to be bound. Most commonly, this could be cash or an exchange of property or services or mutual promises or both.

(iii) Competent Parties

In law a sane, sober adult is considered capable of managing his or her own affairs and of making binding contracts. Some persons who enjoy the protection of being considered less than fully capable are: minors, insane persons, mentally incompetent persons, and persons who are intoxicated by drugs or alcohol.

(iv) Genuine Consent

There is no consent of contracting parties if obtained through: (a) misrepresentation by a false statement of material fact, either innocent or fraudulent; or (b) undue influence or duress, encompassing improper use of any power exercised over the mind of a contracting party so that consent is not voluntary.

In some cases there is no consent if at the time of entering into the contract both parties are genuinely mistaken about some fundamental aspect of the contract.

(v) Legal Purpose

A contract is not enforceable if its object is contrary to established law or against public policy, *i.e.*, policy in the best interests of the public. A contract to commit a crime or a tortious act is illegal and void.

The directors of a corporation may pass a resolution authorizing certain officers or directors to sign a particular contract. However, if the resolution authorizing the contract does not specify the signing officers on behalf of the corporation, this information can be obtained by checking By-law No. 1 which sets out the officers and/or directors authorized to sign on behalf of the corporation. Every corporation was required under the former BCA to have a corporate seal and it was usually added to all contracts. Under section 13 of the present BCA a corporation may, but need not, have a corporate seal. It may take some time before the use of a corporate seal by corporations will cease.

Subsection 1(7) of the Act provides that duplicate copies of the same document are deemed to be one document for the purposes of the Act.

(b) Types of Contracts

(i) Contracts in Writing under Seal

A corporation may enter into a contract in writing where, by law, such a contract with an individual person would be required to be in writing (subsection 17(1)).

In 1677 the British Parliament passed the Statute of Frauds (29 Car. 2, 1677 (Eng.), c. 3), which set out the types of contracts which had to be in writing in order to be enforceable in a court of law. The purpose of this statute was to prevent persons bringing cases to court based solely on oral or verbal evidence. The statute was later adopted by each Canadian province which operates under the common law system. In Ontario the *Statute of Frauds*, R.S.O. 1990, c. S.19, requires under section 4 that no action shall be brought in the following circumstances unless the agreement, or some note or memorandum thereof, is in writing and signed by the person being sued or someone acting as an agent for that person:

A. *Executor's promise.* An executor under a will is charged with the responsibility of paying the debts of the deceased out of the assets of the estate before any other payments are made to beneficiaries of the estate. If the situation existed where the estate assets were not sufficient to pay all the debts and the executor promised the creditors to pay the debts out of his own personal funds, this promise would have to be in writing to be enforceable in court. If the executor promised to pay a creditor and then failed to do so, the creditor could only sue if that promise was in writing.

B. *Guarantee.* A bank may agree to lend a person money although the borrower is not considered a very good credit risk, provided the borrower is able to get an acceptable person to guarantee the loan. This means that if the borrower does not make the payments to the bank to repay the loan, the payments must be made by the other person. A guarantee is a promise to make any payments due under the loan if the borrower defaults or fails to make the required payments. This guarantee must be in writing to be enforceable in a court of law.

C. *Marriage settlements/dowry.* In feudal England, when a couple married it was essential that the marriage produce children (especially male) who would inherit the family property. Property was passed down by primogeniture (through eldest male heirs). Sons were very important, while daughters were considered as something of a liability. In order to marry off daughters, fathers were required to agree to provide a dowry to the prospective husband. The dowry usually consisted of land, since wealth in the feudal society was based on the ownership of land, but could include money as well. If a father agreed to a dowry, but after the marriage delayed or refused to pay the dowry, payment could only be enforced in court if the agreement was in writing. Although social customs have changed, this law could still apply.

D. *Contracts for the sale of land.* Any agreement concerning real property or land must be in writing to be enforceable in a court. Accordingly, an offer for the purchase or sale of real estate must be in written form.

Similarly, any document that is required to transfer the legal title or ownership from the present owner to the person buying the land must be in writing

In order to comply with the *Statute of Frauds* any document which is required to transfer the legal title or ownership from the present owner to the purchaser must be in writing and under seal.

Today most people are able to read and write but literacy was not always so common. Historically, only certain persons, such as clergymen, lawyers, doctors and teachers, were literate. These people prepared the legal documents for those who were illiterate. Once a legal document was prepared, red sealing wax was melted and dropped on the document and the person affixed his "seal", usually the imprint of a ring bearing a crest. Since many people could not read, those in the nobility adopted a crest which was incorporated in flags, shields and signet rings. This practice, known as heraldry, provided a means of recognizing the person and binding that person to any contracts or agreements made. Today the usual practice is to use a small, round red paper seal on legal documents requiring a seal. A corporation uses a seal made of metal in a frame. The round disc sets out the name of the corporation around the edge of the circle and either the jurisdiction of incorporation or a star is set out in the middle of the disc or seal. The seal of the corporation is imprinted on legal documents by pressure, the paper being placed between the two metal discs that make up the seal.

E. *Contracts for more than one year.* If the contract entered by the parties cannot be completed within one year from the date of the contract, then such a contract must be in writing to be enforceable in law. For example, large corporations with offices in foreign countries may hire persons to work in these offices for periods of three years. If a person was hired for this period and left the employ of the corporation six months after being hired, the corporation could not sue that person unless the employment contract was in writing.

Normally corporations transact business in the contract area in writing under seal. The following provisions cover contracts in writing not under seal and parol contracts.

(ii) Contracts in Writing not under Seal

Any contract an individual would be required to sign in writing, but not under seal, to be valid against the individual, can be entered into by the corporation in writing signed by the person(s) acting under its authority, express or implied.

Express authority means that a by-law or resolution has been passed by the directors and, if necessary, confirmed by the shareholders, authorizing a particular person to sign such a contract. Implied authority means that the person signing the contract has the authority to sign on behalf of the corporation because of the office held in the corporation by that person. So long as the director or officer acts honestly and responsibly in the carrying out of the duties imposed under the Act, and there is no breach of these duties and responsibilities, the contract would be valid and binding on the corporation.

(iii) Parol Contract

Subsection 17(3) of the former BCA authorized a corporation to enter into parol, or oral, contracts which if made by a person would be valid in law if made orally *only* and not reduced to writing, through any person acting on its behalf under either express or implied authority.

These specific references to contracts do not appear in the present BCA presumably because of the provisions of section 15 which states a corporation has the capacity and the rights, powers and privileges of a natural person. A natural person has the right to make parol, simple or specialty contracts.

(iv) Power of Attorney

A corporation has the capacity to appoint any person to act as its attorney, inside or outside Ontario, either as a general attorney or for specific acts.

Documents which by law are required to be under seal and which are signed by the attorney on behalf of the corporation under his or her seal are as binding on the corporation as if executed under the corporate seal of the corporation.

An attorney may be appointed for various reasons but is usually appointed to act on behalf of extra-provincial corporations, which are corporations incorporated outside Ontario wishing to carry on business in Ontario. In addition to being licensed as an extra-provincial corporation, the corporation must appoint an Ontario resident to act as its attorney in the province. The attorney would accept service of documents in any court action and file any annual or other returns required by the government from that corporation.

A corporation through its directors could appoint an attorney if this appointment was deemed necessary to carry out the business of the corporation. The duties of the directors as set out under section 115 of the Act are to manage, or supervise the management of, the business and affairs of a corporation.

(v) Pre-incorporation Contracts

Section 21 of the BCA applies to pre-incorporation contracts. The situation may exist where the incorporators are required by the particular circumstances to acquire land or leasehold premises for the business operation of the new corporation before the articles of incorporation are filed. When this happens, one of the incorporators may enter into the contract, acting in the capacity of a trustee for the corporation to be incorporated. Once the corporation exists, the directors will pass a resolution adopting this pre-incorporation contract. The incorporator is released from all obligations or liabilities which then are assumed by the corporation which is now entitled to all benefits under the contract.

Under the Act, a person who enters into an oral or a written contract in the name of or on behalf of a corporation before it comes into existence is personally bound by the contract and is entitled to the benefits, except as provided in section 21.

A. *Adoption of pre-incorpration contracts.* A corporation may under subsection 21(2), within a reasonable length of time after it is incorporated, by any action or conduct, signify its intention to be bound by the terms of a pre-incorporation contract, whether oral or written.

Once the appropriate corporate action has been taken, the corporation is bound by the contract and is subject to the liabilities and entitled to all benefits. A person who entered into the pre-incorporation contract on behalf of the corporation ceases, subject to the terms of subsection 21(3), to be bound by or entitled to the benefits of the contract. The usual practice is to adopt such pre-incorporation contracts by a resolution of the directors. Presumably, unless special circumstances dictate otherwise, this practice will continue.

B. *Non-adoption of pre-incorporation contracts.* Subject to the provisions of subsection 21(4), whether or not an oral or written contract is adopted by the corporation, a party to the contract may apply to a court for an order fixing obligations under the contract. This application may ask the court to fix the obligations as joint, joint and several, or to apportion liability between the corporation and any other party to the contract. The court may make any order it thinks fit in the circumstances.

C. *Exception to subsection (1).* A person entering into either an oral or written pre-incorporation contract, if this is expressly provided in the said contract, is not bound by the contract or entitled to the benefits thereof. There is always the possibility that persons who intend to set up a business organization via a corporation may change their minds. If one of these persons has entered into a pre-incorporation contract and the plan to incorporate is aborted, unless a specific paragraph were included in the pre-incorporation contract to cover such a situation, the person involved might be held personally liable. Subsections 21(1) and (4) of the BCA clarify the position of a person who enters into either an oral or written pre-incorporation contract. In addition, subsection 21(4) provides a method to protect the person entering into a pre-incorporation contract, whether oral or written, where the decision to incorporate is abandoned. In a written contract the inclusion of a paragraph stating that the person is not in any event bound by the contract or entitled to the benefits would apparently relieve that person of any possible personal liability.

4. Shares

Part III (Corporate Finance) under the Act contains the provisions regarding share capital for corporations.

Shares of a corporation shall, under subsection 22(1) of the BCA, be in registered form and shall be without nominal or par value.

Shares with nominal or par value of a corporation incorporated before the day this section comes into force shall be deemed to be shares without nominal or par value (subsection 22(2)).

The concept of shares in the authorized capital of a corporation with a fixed or par value has ended in Ontario. In the past when Ontario corporations were incorporated with par value shares, the value assigned to such shares was an amount decided upon by the incorporators and their lawyers. The amount was an arbitrary one chosen primarily for convenience and ease of division or multiplication. In most instances the amount chosen did not reflect the actual value of the par value share. A share represents a proportionate interest of the holder in the net worth of the business of the corporation. A share with a par value of $1 may have a market value ranging from 1¢ to $1,000 or more. Its actual or market value would depend on the net worth of the business. The par value concept, which tended to confuse the idea of a proportionate interest, has now been eliminated. When reviewing minute books of corporations incorporated prior to 1982 it will be noted that often the par value assigned to a class of shares was $10 per share or a multiple thereof.

(a) Rights of Shareholders

Under the BCA, when a corporation has only one class of shares, the rights of the holders thereof are equal in all respects and include:

1. voting at all meetings of shareholders; and
2. receiving the remaining property of the corporation upon dissolution (subsection 22(3)).

The articles may provide, as set out in subsection 22(4), for more than one class of shares and in that event:

1. the rights, privileges, restrictions and conditions attaching to the shares of each class shall be set out in the articles; and
2. each of the rights set out in subsection (3) shall be attached to at least one

class of shares; both such rights are not required to be attached to any one class.

In spite of the provisions of subsection 22(4), it is not necessary to set out in the articles the right of the holders of a class of shares to one vote for each share at all meetings of shareholders, except meetings of the holders of another class of shares, or to receive the remaining property of the corporation on dissolution (subsection 22(5)).

(b) Shares within a Class Equal

Except as provided in section 25 of the BCA, which contains provisions regarding special shares in series, each share of a class shall be the same in all respects as every other share of that class (subsection 22(6)).

If shares are allotted to an individual by the corporation, they are usually given in exchange for, or acknowledgement of, services, past or present, or property given to the corporation by the individual.

Shares are issued by a corporation in response to a written subscription for shares, submitted by the individual, addressed to the corporation, at a mutually acceptable price.

Shares are transferred when a current shareholder disposes of his or her shareholding in the corporation either to another shareholder or a stranger. The existing share certificate is assigned by the seller to the purchaser, it is cancelled and a new share certificate in the name of the purchaser is issued.

Subsection 22(4) states that where the articles provide more than one class of shares, the rights, privileges, restrictions, and conditions that attached to each class of shares shall be set out in the articles. The terms "Class A" and "Class B" could be used to designate the class of shares with the right to vote and to receive the remainder of the property of the corporation on dissolution and those shares with the right to receive a dividend. The Class A shares could be determined to be the voting or "common" shares of the corporation. The Class B shares would have the right to a dividend, similar to the former "preference" shares. This right could be extended to provide that before the directors could declare a dividend on the Class A shares of the corporation, a dividend must be declared and paid to the Class B shareholders. A dividend is a sum of money paid out of the profits of the corporation to its shareholders. These dividends can be cumulative, non-cumulative, or partially cumulative. The definitions of these terms are set out below.

1. *Cumulative*—The directors of the corporation are obliged to declare a dividend at the rate fixed for the preference shares in each financial year from the date these shares were created and issued. The right to this annual dividend does not expire at the end of the year. If a dividend is not declared

in one year, the following year before the directors declare a dividend to the holders of the common shares, they must declare a dividend on the preference shares for the prior year and the current year. The right to a cumulative dividend continues from year to year and must be declared for each year before any other dividends can be declared.

If the articles do not state whether the dividend is cumulative or non-cumulative, it is presumed in law that the dividend is to be cumulative.

2. *Non-Cumulative*—This dividend is payable on the preference shares in any year before dividends on the common shares can be paid. If the dividend is not declared by the end of the financial year, the right to a dividend for that year disappears. However, the directors in the following year are obliged to declare a dividend on the preference shares before declaring a dividend on the common shares.

3. *Partially Cumulative*—The articles could provide that the holders of the preference shares will receive a cumulative dividend and after that dividend is paid, these shareholders will share equally with the common shareholders in dividends declared on the common shares.

   The right to share in dividends would not be cumulative. Only the right to the preferential dividend would be cumulative.

Various rights, privileges and conditions can be attached to a class of shares of a non-offering corporation such as:

(a) *Right to cumulative, non-cumulative or partially cumulative dividends.* The right to a dividend based on a dollar value per share or a fixed percentage rate. Before the directors can declare a dividend on the Class A (common) shares of the corporation, a dividend must be declared and paid to the holders of a certain class of shares.

(b) *Preference over any other class(es) of shares as to payment of dividends.* The directors of the corporation would be obliged to declare a dividend to the holders of the Class B (preference) shares before a dividend could be paid to the other shareholders of the corporation.

(c) *Preference over any other class(es) of shares on dissolution or winding up.* If the shareholders of the corporation decide to end its corporate existence and distribute the assets among the shareholders, the Class B (preference) shareholders would be entitled, after payment of the debts of the corporation, to receive the money paid for the shares before any other shareholders.

(d) *Exclusive right to elect a director or directors.* If the Class B (preference) shareholders are entitled to dividends, this right may also contain the privilege of electing one or more directors of the corporation if the dividends are declared but not paid over a certain period of time. This right to elect a director or directors would cease when the declared dividends have all been paid to the shareholders.

(e) *Right to convert shares of one class into shares of another class.* Class B (preference) shareholders could have the right to convert their shares into Class A (common) shares at a fixed price over a certain period of time, usually a few years. If the Class B (preference) shareholders decided to exercise this right they would subscribe for the Class A (common) shares by completing a form on the back of the share certificate. The shareholder would then exchange the Class B (preference) share certificate for a Class A (common) share certificate for the appropriate number of shares. Usually the consideration for the issue of the Class A (common) shares is the return and cancellation of the Class B (preference) shares.

(f) *Right of corporation at its option or the shareholder at his or her option to redeem part or all of the shares of a certain class.* A corporation attracts any additional money it requires by the issuing of special or preference shares. Persons buying these shares do so as an investment since they would earn money through dividends or other privileges attached to the special or preference shares. The only way a corporation can rid itself of these obligations is to redeem the shares when funds are available. The preference or special shares of a corporation are usually described as "redeemable" special or preference shares. This redemption can take place:

1. at the option of the shareholder; or
2. at the option of the corporation.

The articles usually provide that redemption will be at the option of the corporation so that redemption will take place only when the corporation has funds available. If redemption can take place when the shareholder needs the money, the corporation could be placed in the position of having to borrow money at high interest rates to repay the capital a special or preference shareholder has invested in the corporation. The redemption of special or preference shares would be made in accordance with section 32 of the Act.

(g) *Purchase for cancellation by corporation of all or part of shares of a certain class by agreement with holders.* The corporation may decide to cancel a certain class of shares and can only do so if the shareholders agree. The corporation would make an offer to the holders of those shares but if the offer is not accepted, the corporation cannot force the shareholders to give up their shares. The corporation can only offer to buy the shares and this offer can be either accepted or rejected by the shareholders involved. If the offer is accepted, the corporation must comply with section 32 of the Act.

Section 32 provides the right to purchase or recover any redeemable shares issued by a corporation in accordance with the terms for redemption or purchase set out in the articles. A corporation is prohibited from making any such purchase or redemption if the payment would render the corporation insolvent. Subsection 32(1) states that the purchase or redemption of any redeemable shares issued by a corporation shall be at prices either stated, or calculated according to a formula, set out in the articles. It may therefore be possible, should the circumstances warrant, that a corporation could include in its articles the right to purchase and/or cancel shares issued by it.

(h) *Conditions, restrictions, limitations or prohibitions on right to vote at meeting of shareholders.* Preference shares are usually non-voting shares. However, under certain conditions, the preference shareholders may be entitled to a vote. The rights attaching to the preference shares in the articles of incorporation may provide that on dissolution or winding-up of the corporation, the preference shareholders shall have a vote. Provision may also be included that on a sale of the undertaking of the corporation, or a substantial part thereof, the preference shareholders shall have a vote.

If the directors decide to amend or vary any of the conditions, rights or privileges attached to the preference shares, the preference shareholders have the right to vote. Under section 170 of the Act, if the amendment to the charter, regardless of its nature, affects a class of special or preference shares, the holders of these shares must consent to the amendment. Failure to obtain their consent means the amendment cannot proceed.

Paragraph 23 of Reg. 62 states that where shares of a class or series prohibit, limit or restrict the right to vote, a condition attaching to that class or series of shares shall provide that the holders are entitled to notice of meetings of shareholders called either to authorize dissolution of the corporation or the sale of its undertaking, or a substantial part thereof, under subsection 184(3) of the Act. This subsection states that a sale, lease or exchange of all or substantially all of the property of a corporation, other than in the ordinary course of business, requires the approval of the shareholders in accordance with subsections (4) to (8). Subsection (6) provides a right to vote separately as a class or series if a particular class of shareholders is affected differently by the sale than other shareholders of the corporation entitled to vote on such sale, lease or exchange.

(c) Equality of Shares of a Class

Under subsection 22(6) of the Act, except for shares which can be issued in a series, all shares of a class shall be the same. Provision to issue shares in a series is made in the original articles where it may be required by a corporation, thereby avoiding the future possibility of having to amend the articles of incorporation to add this provision. Under section 25 of the Act, the articles may authorize the issue of shares in a series. The shares cannot issue until articles of amendment are filed with the Director in the prescribed form designating such series of shares. The Director shall on receipt endorse a certificate on the articles which shall constitute the certificate of amendment.

The provision for issuance of shares in a series would be used in non-offering corporations where maximum flexibility of share capital may be required to meet future needs of the corporation. This type of share structure eliminates the additional fees, both legal and governmental, involved and any delays that might be occasioned by amending the charter.

5. Other Provisions in Articles of Incorporation

There is provision in the prescribed form of articles of incorporation for other clauses or provisions which must be in the articles to enable the corporation to exercise these powers. Listed below are some of the more standard clauses which were and are included in many applications for non-offering corporations.

1. There is provision to exempt the corporation from the requirements of the *Securities Act*, wherein subsection 35(2) paragraph 10 identifies "securities of a private company where they are not offered for sale to the public" as being exempt from registration.

   The Act defines a "private company" under subsection 1(1) as a company whose constating document (articles of incorporation) contains the following provisions:

   (a) restricts the transfer of its shares;

   (b) limits the number of shareholders to 50; and

   prohibits the public from subscribing for securities (shares) of the corporation.

2. An Ontario corporation intending to carry on business in Quebec, in addition to having a French translation of its name, must have the power to borrow set out in its articles of incorporation.

   This is a requirement set out under a Quebec statute, the *Special Corporate Powers Act*, R.S.Q 1977, c. P-16.

   If the power to borrow is not set out in the articles, and the corporation wished to borrow money in the province of Quebec, an amendment to the articles would be required.

3. The right to purchase any of its issued common or preference shares (section 30).

4. The right to redeem or purchase any of its issued redeemable shares (section 32).

5. If meetings of shareholders can be held outside Ontario as the directors decide, the place or places outside Canada could be specified in the articles (section 93)

6. Lien by the corporation on shares which have been subscribed for but are

not paid for in full. This clause authorizes the corporation to claim a lien for unpaid moneys. This provision may be included in the by-laws but it is preferable to include it in the articles of incorporation (subsection 40(1))

7. If a French version of the name may be required at some time in the future, the clause setting out the French name must be included in the articles under other provisions (subsection 10(4)).

Under section 30 of the BCA a corporation may purchase or redeem any of its issued shares subject to subsection (2) and to its articles. Subsection (2) prohibits a payment to purchase or otherwise acquire shares if it would render the corporation insolvent or reduce the value of the corporation's assets to less than the total of its liabilities and the amount required to pay the holders of shares who have a right to be paid before the holders of shares to be purchased or redeemed. It appears that if a corporation would like to have the right to purchase any of its issued shares, this right, together with any required restrictions on the right, should be included in the articles of incorporation. It could be argued that if the right to purchase any of its issued shares is included in the statute, subject only to what the articles might say and nothing is set out in the articles, the corporation has an implied right to exercise this power so long as it does not contravene any of the other provisions of the statute; therefore it is not necessary to include this right in the articles.

Under section 93 of the Act the directors of the corporation may, subject to the articles and any unanimous shareholder agreement, determine where a meeting of shareholders will be held either in or outside of Ontario. If this decision is not made, there is provision for the shareholders to meet at the registered office (head office) of the corporation. In some instances the incorporators may wish to establish the meeting places outside Ontario and include this provision in the articles; in other cases, if more flexibility is required, a decision may be made to omit this right from the articles of incorporation.

Subsection 40(1) of the Act lays out the provisions relative to a lien by the corporation on shares which have been subscribed for but which are not paid in full. The incorporators have the option of including this provision either in the by-laws or the articles of the corporation.

Subsection 10(4) of the Act provides that subject to its provisions and the regulations, a corporation may have in its articles a special provision permitting it to set out its name in any language and the corporation may be legally designated by that name. Should a corporation see the need for a French version of its corporate name, the French version would have to be set out in its articles of incorporation.

Decisions of this nature, that is, what rights, privileges or conditions will be included under the special provisions section of the articles of incorporation, will be made by the lawyer acting for the particular client. In large law offices a standard policy, indicating the rights to be included, may be adopted. Should this standard policy conflict with the needs of a particular client, then the lawyer, in consultation with the client, would make any necessary changes.

6. Preparation of Articles of Incorporation

The articles of incorporation are drafted in consultation with the lawyer and are then considered jointly by the lawyer in charge and the client. The form prescribed by the Regulations under the BCA is Form 1, shown as Form 5.1.

The following information will assist in drafting articles of incorporation. The numbers below correspond to Form 1:

1. The forms are bilingual. All instructions appear in both French and English.
2. The term "head office" has been replaced by the term "registered office".
3. The number of directors of an Ontario non-offering or offering corporation may be fixed or a minimum to a maximum number determined so long as the required minimum in each case is observed. In the case of an Ontario non-offering corporation, the number could be fixed, *i.e.*, three, or a minimum of one to a maximum, decided on by the lawyer and the client. If the latter course is chosen, the number is decided by a special resolution of the shareholders passed by at least two-thirds of the shareholders present at a special meeting of shareholders or by their unanimous written consent. A certified copy of this resolution is no longer required to be filed with the Director under the BCA.

   If the special resolution of the shareholders authorizes the directors to fix the number of directors, then the number is decided by a resolution of the directors. The director's resolution is also no longer required to be filed.

   A change in the number of directors set out in the articles of incorporation requires Articles of Amendment. In order to avoid the additional legal and filing costs, careful consideration will have to be given to this matter prior to incorporation (subsection 168(1)). An amendment under this subsection requires a special resolution of the shareholders.

. . .

5. The incorporators may, if it is considered desirable, set out restrictions on the type of business the corporation may carry on, or the powers the corporation may exercise.

   For example, section 184 of the BCA provides very broad borrowing powers to the directors of a corporation. This section states that unless the articles or bylaws, or a unanimous shareholder agreement otherwise provide, the articles of a corporation shall be deemed to state that the directors of a corporation may, without authorization of the shareholders, borrow money, issue, reissue, sell or pledge debt obligations of the corporation, give a guarantee, subject to section 20, and mortgage, hypothecate, pledge or otherwise create a security interest in any or all of the property of the corporation.

It is a fairly common practice to include a general borrowing power under the other provisions. This power to borrow in the articles of incorporation is required under the *Quebec Special Corporate Powers Act* if an Ontario corporation carrying on business in Quebec wishes to borrow money. However, the wording used in this power to borrow may restrict the broad powers set out under the above section of the Act.

There is provision in the BCA under section 185 for the rights of dissenting shareholders if an Ontario corporation amends its articles under section 168. A holder of shares of any class or series entitled to vote on the resolution may dissent. One of the amendments to articles that would trigger this shareholders' dissent and its accompanying appraisal remedy, which is set out under subsection (1), would be the addition, removal or change of any restriction on the business or the powers exercised by the corporation.

Review of the current legislation in conjunction with the drafting of the Articles of Incorporation will ensure greater accuracy and reduce the time involved in the actual preparation of Form 1.

6. Under the Act a corporation is not required to set out the number of shares it is authorized to issue. If there are to be two or more classes of shares, the articles must set out out the rights, privileges, restrictions and conditions attaching to each class of shares.

The concept of par value shares has disappeared under the BCA. Subsection 22(1) states that the shares of a corporation shall be in registered form and shall be without nominal or par value. Nominal or par value shares of an Ontario corporation incorporated prior to July 29, 1983, under this section shall be deemed to be without nominal or par value.

Section 23 of the BCA provides that the directors may, subject to the articles, by-laws, unanimous shareholders agreement and any pre-emptive rights that may be set out in any of these areas, issue shares as they may determine. Subsection (3) provides that any such shares shall not be issued until the consideration is fully paid in money, in property or past services that would equal the amount received in money if the shares had been issued for money only.

Each article on Form 1 under the Act is discussed below.

1. *The name of the corporation is:* Insert here in capital letters the name which has been cleared through one of the private name search firms or search houses.

A single capital letter should be inserted in each of the blocks on the form. One blank space must be left between each word making up the corporate name, for example:

S	M	I	T	H		A	D	V	E	R	T	I	S	I	N	G		A	G	E	N	C	I	E	S		I	N	C.	

2. *The address of the registered office is:* Insert here the municipal number and street name, or the R.R. number if applicable, the name of the municipality and the postal code. If the Corporation has its registered office in the City of Toronto, formerly the Municipality of Metropolitan Toronto, the corporation may move its registered office within the city limits, requiring only a resolution of directors to effect the change. In addition, a Notice of Change (Form 1) under the Corporations Information Act must be filed within 15 days of the change (see Form 16.18).

Articles of Amendment were required when the registered office relocated to a different township or municipality, resulting in additional legal and filing costs to clients. Lawyers protested this somewhat Draconian approach to what is essentially a minor change within the corporate structure. As objections to this requirement continued, legislation was introduced in the Legislature to change this process. On January 1, 1987 the *Business Corporations Amendment Act, 1986*, S.O. 1986, c. 57, was proclaimed. Since that date, only a special resolution is needed, and it is no longer required to be filed with the Companies Branch.

Under the BCA a ''special resolution'' is a resolution submitted for consideration to a special meeting of the shareholders called for that express purpose. A two-thirds vote of the shareholders present at the meeting is required to pass, with or without amendment, the resolution presented. Alternatively, the special resolution can be consented to in writing by all of the shareholders of the corporation. If a shareholder would not be available to evidence his or her consent to this special resolution, an attorney could be appointed in writing to give consent.

3. *Number (or minimum and maximum number) of directors is:* Here set out the number of directors the proposed corporation will have. An Ontario non-offering corporation may have a minimum of one director, and up to any number decided by the persons involved in the new corporation. However, as a matter of practice the numbers selected are usually small. The larger the board of directors, the more difficult it is to get all members together, either for meetings or the signing of resolutions.

The number of directors is shown written out in full in words and/or figures such as one, one (1) or 1. The method used is determined by the law office and a common practice is the combination of words and figures.

4. *The first director(s) is/are:* The full names of the persons who will be the first directors of the corporation are inserted here. Initials cannot be used. The

addresses set out for the directors are no longer required to be their residences but are addresses for service purposes such as business addresses. If one of the first directors was John A. Smith, 2975 Bloor Street West, Toronto, Ontario M8X ICI, it would be necessary to find out what the initial "A" represented. If it were ascertained that the "A" stands for "Andrew", the information would be set out in the columns in Form 1 as follows:

First name, initials and surname	Address for service, giving street No. or R.R. No. or municipality and postal code	Resident Canadian state yes or no
John Andrew Smith	2975 Bloor Street West, Toronto, Ontario. M8X IC1	Yes

Any first director named in the articles who is not an incorporator must sign Form 2, Consent to Act as a First Director. An example of this consent is shown as Form 5.2.

Under the BCA subsection 1(1) a "resident Canadian" is defined as:

(a) a Canadian citizen ordinarily resident in Canada,

(b) a Canadian citizen not ordinarily resident in Canada who is a member of a prescribed class of persons, or

(c) a permanent resident within the meaning of the *Immigration Act* and ordinarily resident in Canada.

Under subsection 119(2) of the BCA, any first director named in the articles cannot resign until the first meeting of shareholders unless a successor is elected to replace such director.

The BCA Regulations, R.R.O. 1990, Reg. 62, set out the persons who qualify as "a member of a prescribed class of persons" set out above. Included are full-time employees of the federal or provincial governments, or any agency thereof, full-time students at a university or other educational institution recognized by the province and full-time employees of an international association or organization of which Canada is a member.

Subsection 118(3) requires a majority of the directors of every corporation to be resident Canadians. Corporations with only one director must ensure that person is a resident Canadian. In cases of a two director corporation, at least one director must be a resident Canadian.

5. *Restrictions, if any, on business the corporation may carry on or on powers the corporation may exercise:* Under the BCA it is not required that a corporation set out in the articles a description of the business to be carried on or the powers to be exercised. If a decision is made not to restrict the business to be carried on by the corporation, this approach provides maximum flexibility for the corporation and avoids the possibility of having to amend the articles at

some time in the future. For example, the incorporators may incorporate to carry on the business of constructing both residential and commercial buildings. Should the business develop more in commercial construction, an ancillary business of leasing or managing the properties for their customers could evolve. If there are no restrictions on the type of business set out in the articles, the corporation would be able to branch out into different areas of business as the opportunities arise.

Subsection 3(2) of the Act provides that a corporation may be incorporated with its powers restricted by its articles to:

1. lending and investing money on mortgage of real estate or otherwise;
2. accepting and executing the office of liquidator, receiver, assignee, trustee in bankruptcy or trustee for the benefit of creditors; and
3. accepting the duty of and acting generally in the winding up of corporations, partnerships and estates, except estates of deceased persons.

Any such corporations shall not be deemed to be corporations within the meaning of the *Loan and Trust Corporations Act*, R.S.O. 1990, c. L.25. These corporations are restricted to a maximum of five shareholders, not including persons who are employees, and can only issue debt obligations to, or borrow money from, its shareholders. In addition, such corporations cannot receive money on deposit or offer securities to the public.

If there are no restrictions on the powers or business of the corporations, the word ''None'' is inserted in the appropriate space.

If there are restrictions, and the text is short, the information would be set out under article 5 in Form 1. However, if the restrictions are lengthy, a schedule may be attached to Form 1 containing the details of these restrictions. This information would be inserted under this article in the prescribed form. The wording could be: ''The annexed Schedule [A or 1] is to be included in this form.'' If any amendments are required to the proposed restrictions, it is not necessary to redraft Form 1—changing the schedule is all that would be necessary.

Although objects are now history in Ontario, occasions will arise in which it may be necessary to review the objects of existing corporations incorporated before the new Act was proclaimed to determine if actions taken were within its powers.

6. *The classes and any maximum number of shares that the corporation is authorized to issue:* Section 5 of the BCA states that the articles of incorporation shall follow the prescribed form and set out the prescribed information. The articles shall set out the classes and any maximum number of shares that the corporation is authorized to issue. If there is only one class of shares,

nothing further need be added to the articles because of the provisions of subsection 22(3). This subsection states that

> Where a corporation has only one class of shares, the rights of the holders thereof are equal in all respects and include the rights,
>
> (a) to vote at all meetings of shareholders; and
>
> (b) to receive the remaining property of the corporation upon dissolution.

Subsection 22(4), dealing with the rights of shareholders, states that the articles may provide for more than one class of shares and in that event the articles must set out the rights, privileges, etc., as mentioned above. In addition, each of the rights set out under subsection (3) shall be attached to at least one class of shares. There is no requirement that both rights are to be attached to one class of shares. An incorporation providing for more than one class of shares would set out all of the necessary information on a schedule which would be attached to and form part of the articles. (Suggested wording for such a schedule may be found in Form 14.2, which is an example of a schedule attaching to federal articles of incorporation.) The use of a schedule to detail the various rights, privileges, restrictions and conditions attaching to each class of shares ensures that any required changes can be easily and quickly made without necessitating the redrafting of Form 1.

7. *Rights, privileges, restrictions and conditions (if any) attaching to each class of shares and directors authority with respect to any class of shares which may be issued in series:* If a corporation has more than one class of shares, the rights, privileges, restrictions and conditions attaching to each class are set out under this numbered paragraph in the articles of incorporation. If the space provided is not sufficient, supplementary pages can be added so long as they comply with the Instructions for Completing which accompany Form 1. Subsection 22(4) of the BCA states that the right to vote and to receive the remaining property of the corporation on dissolution must be attached to at least one class of shares. However, both of these rights are not required to be attached to one class of shares. For example, these rights could be attached to the Class A (common) shares or they could be divided between two classes of shares. This decision will be made by the lawyer in consultation with the client involved. The choice of the classes of shares and their attributes are decisions made by the individuals incorporating the corporation.

Some of the usual or standard rights and privileges that could be attached to classes of shares, in addition to those mentioned above, are:

(a) *Right to a fixed, preferential cash dividend.* This right could be attached to the Class B (preference or special) shares to be payable either annually or when declared by the directors. The dividend could be cumulative or non-cumulative. Where the provision for a preferential cumulative dividend is included the directors are obliged to declare a dividend on these issued and outstanding shares before declaring dividends on other classes of issued and outstanding shares in each year. If a dividend is not declared in one year, the right to have a dividend declared does not expire at the end of the financial year. In the following financial year, before dividends can be paid to any other shareholders, the directors must declare dividends on the Class B (preference or special) shares for the current and preceding years.

A non-cumulative preferential dividend is payable on the Class B (preference or special) shares in any given year before dividends may be declared on the Class A (common) or any other shares that rank junior to the Class B shares. If the dividend is not declared by the end of the financial year, the right to this dividend for the current year is extinguished.

The wording of this right can be varied and adapted to carry out the wishes of the incorporators.

(b) *Liquidation, dissolution or winding-up.* Right to receive a fixed sum for each Class B share held in priority to holders of Class A shares, together with all declared and unpaid dividends; no further right to share further in assets or property of the corporation.

(c) *Purchase of shares for cancellation.* Right to purchase outstanding Class B shares at lowest price obtainable, such price not to exceed a fixed amount, together with all unpaid dividends.

(d) *Redemption of outstanding Class B shares.* Right of corporation to redeem outstanding Class B shares on payment to holders of a fixed sum, together with any declared and unpaid dividends. The method of redemption, including notice to be given, must be detailed in the articles.

(e) *Voting or non-voting.* The articles should indicate whether or not the holders have the right to vote. Under the Act there are occasions where the holders of shares have the right to vote even though the shares are normally non-voting — for example, an application for articles of amendment to change the conditions attaching to a class of shares, unless the articles provide otherwise. If the articles state that the holders of the various classes of shares in the corporation shall not be entitled to vote separately as a class upon a proposal to amend the articles as described in subsection 170(1)(a), (b) or (e) of the BCA, then the shareholders lose the right to either approve or disapprove of the proposed amendment. The articles supersede the provisions of the statute.

Set out below are sample clauses of some of the preferences, rights and conditions that could attach to special shares of a corporation:

(a) *Right to non-cumulative dividend.* The holders of the preference shares shall in each year by the discretion of the directors, but always in preference and priority to any payment of dividends on the common shares for such year, be entitled, out of any or all profits or surplus available for dividends, to non-cumulative dividends at the rate of ten per cent (10%) per annum on the amount paid up on the preference shares; if in any year, after providing for the full dividend on the preference shares, there shall remain any profits or surplus available for dividends, such profits or surplus or any part thereof may, in the discretion of the directors, be applied to dividends on common shares; the holders of the preference shares shall not be entitled to any dividend other than or in excess of the non-cumulative dividends at the rate hereinbefore provided for.

(b) *Priority over common shares — dividends and capital.* The preference shares shall rank, both as regards dividends and repayment of capital, in priority to all other shares of the corporation but shall not confer any further right to participate in profits or assets.

(c) *Redemption of shares at option of corporation.* The corporation may, upon giving notice as hereinafter provided, redeem the whole or any part of the preference shares on payment for each share to be redeemed of the amount paid up thereon, together with all dividends declared thereon and unpaid. Not less than thirty (30) days notice in writing of such redemption shall be given by mailing such notice to the registered holders of the shares to be redeemed, specifying the date and place or places of redemption. If notice of any such redemption be given by the corporation in the manner aforesaid and an amount sufficient to redeem the shares be deposited with any trust company or chartered bank in Canada, as specified in the notice, on or before the date fixed for redemption, the holders thereof shall thereafter have no rights against the corporation in respect thereof except, upon the surrender of certificates for such shares, to receive payment therefor out of the moneys so deposited.

(d) *Purchase of shares for cancellation at option of corporation.* The corporation may, at any time and from time to time, purchase for cancellation of the whole or any part of the preference shares at the lowest price at which, in the opinion of the directors, such shares are obtainable, but not exceeding the amount paid up thereon, together with all dividends declared thereon and unpaid.

(e) *Right on dissolution to receive capital first.* In the event of the liquidation, dissolution or winding up of the corporation, whether voluntary or involuntary, the holders of the preference shares shall be entitled to receive, before any distribution of any part of the assets of the corporation among the holders of any other shares, the amount paid up thereon and any dividends declared thereon and unpaid and no more.

(f) *Right to vote.* The holders of the preference shares shall not be entitled to notice of or to vote at shareholders' meetings unless and until the preferential dividend herein shall be declared and unpaid for two consecutive years, at which time the holders of the said preference shares shall be entitled to one vote for each share held by them at all meetings of shareholders until such time as all arrears of dividends have been paid. Provided however, that notice of any meeting of shareholders called for the purpose of dissolution, a sale of a substantial part of the undertaking or any amendment to the articles of the corporation to delete or vary any preference, right, condition, restriction, limitation or prohibition attaching to the preference shares or to create preference shares ranking in priority to or on a parity with the preference shares, shall be given to the holders of the preference shares and in addition to the authorization by a special resolution, may be authorized by at least two-thirds (2/3) of the votes cast at a meeting of the holders of the preference shares duly called for that purpose. The holders of the common shares shall be entitled to one vote for each share held by them at all meetings of shareholders.

Notes: Usually preference shares are non-voting, except in the circumstances described above. If the circumstances warrant it, these shares could be voting shares. Only one class of shares, usually the common Class A shares, are required to be voting shares.

8. *The issues, transfer or ownership of shares is/ is not restricted and the restrictions (if any) are as follows:* The Ontario *Securities Act*, subsection 1(1) defines a ''private company'' as follows:

> ''private company'' means a company in whose constating document,
>
> (a) the right to transfer its shares is restricted,
>
> (b) the number of its shareholders, exclusive of persons who are in its employment and exclusive of persons who, having been formerly in the employment of the company, were, while in that employment, and have continued after termination of that employment to be, shareholders of the company, is limited to not more than fifty, two or more persons who are the joint registered owners of one or more shares being counted as one shareholder, and
>
> (c) any invitation to the public to subscribe for its securities is prohibited.

In order to qualify as a ''private'' or non-offering corporation this section of the Ontario *Securities Act* must be met. A non-offering corporation is often described as one whose shares are ''closely held'', that is the issued and outstanding shares are owned by a few people as opposed to, for example, the shares of Alcan Aluminum or Bell Canada Enterprise. These latter two corporations are ''public'' or offering corporations whose shares are traded on the Toronto and other stock exchanges. Any person may purchase shares of these corporations.

The Ontario *Securities Act* prohibits the distribution of shares of non-offering corporations to the public. The term ''distribution to the public'' under subsection 1(1) is defined as follows:

> "distribution to the public", where used in relation to trading in securities, means a distribution that is made for the purpose of distributing to the public securities issued by an issuer, whether such trades are made directly or indirectly to the public through an underwriter or otherwise.

Subsection 35(2) of the *Securities Act* deals generally with trades in securities that are exempted under the Act. Item 10 under this section states:

> (2) Subject to the regulations, registration is not required to trade in the following securities:
>
> . . .
>
> 10. Securities of a private company where they are not offered for sale to the public.

Under the BCA the following wording can be used in articles of incorporation to restrict the transfer of shares:

> The right to transfer shares of the corporation shall be restricted in that no share shall be transferred without either:
>
> (i) the sanction of the directors of the corporation expressed by a resolution passed at a meeting of the board of directors or by an instrument or instruments in writing signed by a majority of the directors; or
>
> (ii) the sanction of the holders of at least fifty-one per cent (51%) [a possible alternative would be that the sanction of a majority of the shareholders is required, rather than a fixed percentage] of the common shares of the corporation for the time being expressed by a resolution passed at a meeting of the holders thereof or by an instrument or instruments in writing signed by the holders of at least fifty-one per cent (51%) of the common shares,

or it could be varied to suit the practice in a particular law office.

9. *Other provisions, if any, are:* Under this article are included any powers the corporation might require which by law must be included in its charter in order to acquire those rights. Under the BCA certain standard provisions are included, such as:

(a) *Exemption from the Securities Act:* The number of shareholders of the corporation, exclusive of persons who are in the employment of the corporation, is hereby limited to fifty (50), two (2) or more persons holding one (1) or more shares jointly being counted as a single shareholder.

"Any invitation to the public to subscribe for any shares of the corporation is hereby prohibited." This clause in articles of incorporation filed under the Act establishes the corporation as non-offering and qualify it for exemption under the Ontario *Securities Act*.

(b) *If corporation to carry on business in Quebec:* There are requirements under Quebec's *Special Corporate Powers Act*. This Quebec statute requires that the powers to mortgage, charge and hypothecate property in

Quebec be contained in the charter of the corporation. The clause required to comply with this statute can be drafted as follows:

When authorized by special by-law the directors may:

(i) borrow money on the credit of the corporation; or

(ii) issue, sell or pledge debt obligations of the corporation; or

(iii) charge, mortgage, hypothecate or pledge all or any currently owned or subsequently acquired real or personal, movable or immovable property of the corporation, including book debts, rights, powers, franchises and undertaking, to secure any debt obligations or any money borrowed, or other debt or liability of the corporation; or

(iv) delegate to such one or more of the directors or officers of the corporation as may be designated by the directors, all or any of the powers conferred by the foregoing clauses to such extent and in such manner as the directors shall determine at the time of any such delegation;

If the corporation intends now or at some time in the future to carry on business in the province of Quebec, it must comply with the requirements under the *Special Corporate Powers Act* and include the right to borrow and pledge assets in its articles. The borrowing and charging powers under section 184 of the BCA, are quite broad and a decision may be made not to include a power to borrow in the charter. However, until the requirements under this Quebec statute change, it may be advisable to continue to include this clause, or a revised version thereof, in the articles of incorporation. For example, the following could be added at the beginning of the clause to ensure the borrowing powers of the corporation under the Act are not restricted in any way:

Without in any way limiting any other powers the corporation may by law possess, the directors of the corporation may without authorization of the shareholders:

(i) borrow money on the credit of the corporation;

(ii) issue, sell or pledge debt obligations . . .

(c) *Right to purchase common shares:* Subject to the BCA, the corporation may purchase any of its common shares.

Under the Act, subsection 30(1) states that ''[s]ubject to subsection (2) and to its articles, a corporation may purchase or otherwise acquire any of its issued shares or warrants''. Subsection (2) states that a corporation cannot make any payment to purchase or acquire its issued shares if such payment would render the corporation insolvent.

(d) *Meetings of shareholders and directors:*

Meetings of the board of directors and the executive committee (if any) of the corporation may be held at any place within or outside of Ontario but in any financial year of the corporation a majority of the meetings of the board of directors and of the executive committee (if any) must be held at a place within Canada, and meetings of the shareholders of the corporation may be held at the City of New York, in the State of New York, one of the United States of America, or at the City of London, England. [The location chosen would reflect the needs of the particular corporation.]

The portion of the above clause referring to meetings of directors and the executive committee, provided one was established, was authorized under subsection 126(2) of the BCA. This could have been included in the by-laws of the corporation. Some lawyers prefer to see this clause in the articles. It would be necessary to check the procedure followed in a particular law office.

Section 93 of the BCA provides that subject to the articles and any unanimous shareholder agreement, a meeting of shareholders shall be held at such place, either in or outside Ontario, as the directors determine. If the directors fail to choose a location, then under this section a meeting shall be held at the registered office of the corporation. If the articles are silent, the meetings can be held wherever the directors decide. If the client and the lawyer in charge of an incorporation deem it necessary to exercise some control on the location of shareholders' meetings, certain locations may be designated in the articles.

In addition to the usual paragraphs mentioned above, anything that could be the subject matter of a by-law may be inserted under other provisions in the articles of incorporation, such as:

1. Clause 97(a) of the BCA states that unless the Act, articles or by-laws of a corporation or a unanimous shareholder agreement provides otherwise, the chairman presiding at a meeting of shareholders shall not have a second or casting vote in case of an equality of votes.
2. Subsection 96(1) requires a minimum of ten days' notice of a shareholders' meeting be given to shareholders of a non-offering corporation.
3. Subsection 126(3) requires that a quorum of directors, that is the number of directors who must be in office to conduct the business of the corporation, shall be a majority unless a contrary intention is expressed in the articles or by-laws. The minimum quorum is two-fifths of the board of directors or two directors, whichever is greater. Since articles may express a minimum to a maximum number of directors, this section provides that in such cases the minimum number of directors required by the articles constitutes a quorum at any meeting of directors. In situations where there are only two directors, both must be present to constitute a quorum. A single director can constitute a meeting under subsection 126(12).
4. Section 40 states that where the articles or by-laws so provide, the corporation has a lien on shares registered to a shareholder who was indebted to the corporation. This lien extends to shares registered in the name of a legal representative of a shareholder indebted to the corporation. A corporation may enforce such a lien in accordance with its articles or by-laws.
5. Subsection 127(1) of the BCA provides for the appointment of a resident Canadian as a managing director or a committee of directors and delegates to these persons any of the powers of the directors.

These matters, because they are capable of being the subject-matter of by-laws, could be included in the articles of incorporation if more control was needed or the statutory requirements were to be varied. If these two reasons did not apply, then the usual practice would be to include these provisions in the by-laws of the corporation. This approach affords greater flexibility and avoids extra costs if and when changes are required. Any amendment to the charter requires Articles of Amendment and each amendment involves the payment of a government fee and probably legal fees as well.

10. *The names and addresses of the incorporators are:* The full names and addresses of the incorporators are set out as follows:

First name, initials and surname or corporate name	Full address for service or address of registered office or of principal place of business giving Street & No. or R.R. No., municipality and postal code
John Andrew Smith	2975 Bloor Street West, Toronto, Ontario M8X 1C1

If one of the incorporators is a body corporate, that is a corporation, the full corporate name would have to be shown with the full address of its registered office. Under the BCA an incorporator is defined as a person who signs articles of incorporation. The term "person" under the Act includes an individual, sole proprietorship, partnership, unincorporated association, syndicate or organization, trust, body corporate and a natural person acting as a trustee, executor, administrator or other legal representative.

The words "*These articles are signed in duplicate*" appear below this article. Appropriate signature lines should be inserted in the space provided below these words. Individuals who are incorporating a corporation would have their names typed or printed below the signature lines. The usual signature of an individual is sufficient when signing as an incorporator. A body corporate named as an incorporator would have its corporate name typed or printed with the required number of signature lines for its corporate officers to sign on its behalf. The titles of the signing officers would be typed or printed below the appropriate signature lines and, if applicable, the corporate seal would be added. It may be that the laws of the incorporating jurisdiction of the body corporate provide for a corporate seal but the corporations decide whether or not to actually obtain and use a corporate seal. In still other jurisdictions, there may be no requirement for a corporation to have and use a corporate seal in the course of its business.

7. Consent of First Director

There may be occasions when the incorporators of the corporation and the first directors named in the articles of incorporation are not the same persons. If an individual named as a first director is not also an incorporator, that person is required under subsection 5(2) of the BCA to sign a consent to act as a first director. Form 2, prescribed under Reg. 62, subsection 46(2) (see Form 5.2, Consent to Act as a First Director) must be completed and signed by every first director who is not an incorporator of the corporation. The consent form is no longer to accompany the articles of incorporation when submitted to the Companies Branch but is to be kept at the registered office address.

8. Filing Articles of Incorporation

Once the articles of incorporation have been drafted, the lawyer will check the articles and arrange for their execution by the office incorporators or the clients, as the case may be. If the articles are being signed by the clients, then at the same time they attend at the office, sufficient funds should be obtained to cover the out-of-pocket expenses involved. These expenses involve:

1. name clearance search;
2. government incorporation fee;
3. minute book — cover only;
4. share certificate book(s); and
5. corporate seal (usual desk style) — (optional).

See Appendix B for approximate costs of these items. In addition to the minute book cover, consideration will be given to ordering an index, by-law, necessary sheets for the various required registers and having the corporate name imprinted on the spine of the minute book cover. These costs are also included in Appendix B. Economics dictates that at least the disbursements involved in an incorporation be obtained from the client before proceeding. There are always exceptions to this general rule and this should always be checked with the lawyer involved before such a request is made. Some lawyers prefer to get a portion of their fee for incorporating the corporation at the same time.

Once the articles of incorporation are fully executed, together with any necessary consent forms for first directors, the next step is to file the articles with the Ministry of Consumer and Business Services. Since lawyers and incorporators assume the responsibility for the articles of incorporation conforming to law and for the proposed name of the corporation, most law offices in Toronto have an employee attend at the Public Office to file the application, unless there is electronic filing through the private service providers.

Before leaving for the Companies Branch, a final check should be made to ensure that all the necessary documentation is in order and present. In order to successfully file and obtain the articles of incorporation the following will be required:

1. articles of incorporation in duplicate executed by all incorporators, with all pages present and in correct numerical order;
2. a NUANS name search with proposed name of the corporation at the top of the search dated within 90 days of the date of the filing of the articles of incorporation;
3. any consent or consent of first directors required;
4. a cheque for the incorporation fee payable to the Minister of Finance with the name of the corporation typed or printed on the face of the cheque (cheques issued by individuals, solicitors or corporations are acceptable); and
5. a covering letter from the agent acting for the incorporators.

Depending on the day, it is possible to obtain the articles of incorporation with the appropriate certificate endorsed on it by the Companies Branch staff in 15 to 20 minutes, providing there are no defects in the preparation of the documents. The Companies Branch has a Deficiency Notice against which the staff member checks the articles of incorporation. If all of the requirements are met, the articles of incorporation are assigned a Ministry file number, and the file is returned to the person presenting it. That person is asked to take the file to the cashier and pay the incorporation fee by personal cheque, money order or a cheque issued by a lawyer or a corporation.

Pursuant to the Minister's Order under the BCA (1999) 132 Ontario Gazette 1582, a cheque tendered in payment of a fee must have the name of the corporation or the Ontario corporation number on the face. Since the cheque is handed over the counter with the articles of incorporation, prior to the assigning of the Ontario corporation number, the name of the corporation should be typed or printed on the face of the cheque. The cashier accepts the file with the articles of incorporation and the cheque, puts the cheque through the cash register and returns the file. The person filing the articles returns to the inspection counter, hands over the file and waits. A staff member then endorses the articles of incorporation with the certificate and returns a copy of the articles to the person. In addition, an Initial Return Form 1 would also be returned if submitted with the application. This Initial Return containing information about the directors and officers of the Corporation is to be filed within 60 days of the date of incorporation.

In an effort to assist its customers, the Companies Branch offers advance endorsement of articles of incorporation. Provided the request for advance endorsement is made in writing, the articles of incorporation may be endorsed up to 30 days after the date on which the written request and the articles are submitted to the Companies Branch. For example, if the request and articles are submitted on December 1, the articles could be endorsed with any subsequent date up to and including December 30.

If the law office is located outside Toronto, the articles of incorporation, name search, consent or consents and cheque can be forwarded by mail to the Ministry of Consumer and Business Services, Companies Branch. Depending on the mail, it may take three to four weeks to process the articles of incorporation. If the incorporation is urgent, the best approach would be to send the articles to a local agent or by courier to the Companies Branch. The agent or courier could attend at the Companies Branch and personally process the application.

Some of the Regional Land Registry Offices in Ontario provide service to the public by accepting documents under the BCA considered to be more or less straightforward, which, it is indicated, means mainly all articles under the Act. This apparently includes a range from articles of incorporation to amalgamation or dissolution.

The following 14 Regional Land Registry Offices offer these additional services:

Algoma	420 Queen St. East P.O. Box 550 Sault Ste Marie P6A 5M8	(705) 253-8887 Fax (705) 253-9245
Durham	590 Rossland Rd. East Whitby LIN 9G5	(905) 665-4007 Fax (905) 665-5247
Essex	250 Windsor Ave., 3rd Floor Windsor N9A 6V9	(519) 971-9980 Fax (519) 971-9937
Frontenac	Court House 1 Court St. Kingston K7L 4N4	(613) 548-6767 Fax (613) 548-6766
Lambton	700 North Christina St. N., Suite 102 Sarnia N7V 3C2	(519) 337-2393 Fax (519) 337-8371
Middlesex	80 Dundas St., Ground Floor J London N6A 6A7	(519) 675-7611 Fax (519) 675-7633
Niagara South	200 Division St. Welland L3B 4A2	(905) 735-4011/13 Fax (905) 735-2430
Ottawa-Carleton	161 Elgin St. 4th Floor, Court House Ottawa K2P 2KI	(613) 239-1230 Fax (613) 239-1422

Peterborough	300 Water St., 2nd Floor Peterborough K9J 8M5	(705) 755-1342 Fax (705) 755-1343
Simcoe	114 Worsley St. Court House Barrie L4M 1M1	(705) 725-7232 Fax (705) 725-7246
Sudbury	199 Larch St., Suite 301 Sudbury PE3 5P9	(705) 564-4300 Fax (705) 564-4148
Thunder Bay	189 Red River Rd. Suite 201 Thunder Bay P7B 1A2	(807) 343-7436 Fax (807) 343-7439
Waterloo	200 Frederick St., 3rd Floor Kitchener N2H 6N9	(519) 571-6043 Fax (519) 571-6067
Wentworth	119 King St., 4th Floor Ontario Government Bldg., Box 2112 Hamilton L8N 4Y7	(905) 521-7561 Fax (905) 521-7505

Before attending at one of the Regional Land Registry Offices listed above, it might be advisable to confirm that the particular document will be accepted.

Once the certificate, shown as Form 5.4, is endorsed on the articles of incorporation, the corporation is incorporated. The next step in the process is to organize the corporation so it can "get off the ground" and carry on business.

6

Organizing the Corporation

1. Corporate Records

The first step in organizing the corporation is to order the necessary corporate supplies:

1. a minute book and/or record book as described under sections 139, 140, 141 and 143 of the *Business Corporations Act*;
2. a corporate seal if one is chosen to be used (section 13); and
3. a share certificate(s) book(s) (sections 54 to 56).

The BCA, under section 139, requires that a corporation keep a record of all of its business in a bound or looseleaf book or by means of a mechanical, electronic data processing or other information storage device. If a looseleaf book is used, the corporation must take all necessary precautions to see that the records are not falsified.

The corporation is required under the Act to keep in its records the following:

1. A copy of the articles of the corporation. If the articles are amended, a copy of the articles of amendment should be added to the records.
2. All by-laws and amendments thereto, together with minutes and resolutions, including special resolutions, of the directors and shareholders of the corporation.
3. A register or list of debt obligations (security holders) who are or have been within six years registered as shareholders of the corporation or the holders of any debt obligations or warrants of the corporation, alphabetically arranged. The register must include the name, residence address and the number and class of shares, and the class or series and principal amount of the debt obligation. The name, residence address and the class or series and number of warrants held by all persons who are or have been within

six years registered as holders of warrants must also be included. An exception is warrants exercisable within one year from the date of issue.

4. A register of directors setting out the name, residence addresses and dates on which each became or ceased to be a director of the corporation since its incorporation.
5. A register showing the transfer of all issued shares of the corporation since incorporation.
6. A ledger sheet for each shareholder of the corporation showing the class and number of shares of the corporation acquired, transferred and held. Subsection 24(1) states that a corporation shall maintain a separate stated capital account for each class or series of shares it issues and add to the said account the full amount of consideration received for shares issued.
7. A copy of any unanimous shareholder agreement known to the directors.

Subsection 127(1) provides that subject to the articles or by-laws, directors of a corporation may appoint from among themselves:

1. a resident Canadian as a managing director; or
2. a committee of directors, a majority of which must be resident Canadians (an exception to the residency requirement is a non-resident corporation).

There is no requirement for a minimum number of directors before a managing director or committee of directors may be appointed. Subsection 127(3) of the Act sets out specifically the areas in which either a managing director or a committee of directors lacks authority. If a committee of directors is established it would be necessary to retain copies of all minutes and resolutions as part of the corporate records.

The various registers required under the statute are often referred to as follows:

1.	register of security holders	share register
2.	register of directors	directors' register
3.	register showing all transfers of issued shares	share transfer register
4.	ledger sheet for each shareholder	shareholder's ledger or stated capital account

Some law offices have created a special officer's register. By looking at this register it is possible to quickly determine who the current officers of the corporation are at any time.

The corporation is required under subsection 140(2) of the Act to prepare and maintain adequate accounting records. Subject to any special retention requirements of any taxing authority, whether federal, provincial or municipal, to which the corporation is subject, the accounting records need only be retained by the corporation for six years from the end of the last fiscal period to which they relate.

The corporate records detailed under section 140 of the BCA, together with the securities and transfer registers required under section 141, are to be kept at the registered office of the corporation. There is provision under section 143 that the securities register and the register of transfers be kept at the registered office of the corporation or at such other places in Ontario designated by the directors. Where the corporation has a branch office that issues or transfers securities, the branch registers or registers of transfers may be kept at such offices of the corporation or at such other places, either within or outside Ontario, as designated by the directors. There is also provision under section 144 that certain accounting records of a branch of the corporation be kept at the branch office, rather than the registered office of the corporation. A corporation may keep all of its records at a place other than the registered office if the records are available for inspection during regular office hours at the registered office by means of a computer terminal or other electronic technology (s. 144(3)). This provision eliminates the need for an order of the Director appointed under the BCA for the removal of records from the registered office. Usually the corporate records of Ontario non-offering corporations are retained for safekeeping at the office of the lawyer acting on behalf of the corporation.

Section 144 of the Act provides for the examination of the corporate records by directors during normal business hours.

Shareholders and creditors of non-offering and offering corporations also have the right under section 145 to examine the corporate records during the corporation's normal business hours with the following exceptions:

1. accounting records; and
2. minutes of meetings or resolutions of directors or any committee thereof.

These persons are also permitted to make extracts from the corporate records free of charge. A shareholder may request, and is entitled to receive without charge, one copy of the articles, by-laws and any unanimous shareholder agreement. Although not specifically stated, presumably the corporation would also be required to provide the shareholder with any amendments to these documents. In the case of an offering corporation, any other person may examine the corporate records and, upon payment of a reasonable fee, make extracts from the records.

Provided the required statutory declaration has been filed under section 146, a shareholder or creditor, or their agents and legal representatives, may require the corporation to furnish a basic list of shareholders. This basic list must set out the names, addresses and shareholdings of each shareholder as shown on the corporation's records and must be delivered within ten days of the receipt of the statutory declaration. Supplemental lists, showing any changes in the basic list, may be obtained if requested in the statutory declaration. Trafficking in lists is prohibited and any such list is to be used in connection with:

1. an effort to influence the voting by shareholders of the corporation;
2. an offer to acquire shares of the corporation; and
3. any other matter relating to the affairs of the corporation.

A reasonable fee must be paid to the corporation for either the basic or supplemental lists of shareholders and their shareholdings.

There is provision under section 250 of the BCA where the name of a person is, without sufficient cause, either wrongly entered in or omitted from the corporate records for an application may be brought for a court order to correct the records. This course of action could be taken if there was undue delay in showing that a person had ceased to be a security holder of the corporation. The applicant could be the security holder involved, any security holder, aggrieved person or the corporation itself.

There is reference under section 236 of the BCA to the disposal of the records of a corporation that has been wound up, either voluntarily by the shareholders or by court order, and is about to be dissolved. In the case of a voluntary winding up, the records are disposed of as the corporation, by resolution, directs. If the winding-up occurs under an order of the court, then the records would be disposed of according to the terms of the court order. At the expiry of five years from the date of dissolution of the corporation, the responsibility of the liquidator or anyone who was given custody of the corporation's records ends.

2. Corporate Seal

Section 13 of the BCA states that a corporation may, but need not, have a corporate seal. Despite the permissive approach taken, a corporation incorporated or continued under the BCA may still adopt a corporate seal.

If a document appears to be executed by a corporation, but a corporate seal has not been used, then reference should be made to section 19 of the BCA or section 18 of the *Canada Business Corporations Act* if a federal corporation is involved. These sections are a codification of the indoor management rule.

If the document has been signed on behalf of a corporation where the person signing is "held out by a corporation as a director, officer or an agent of the corporation", presumably indicated by the title beneath the signature, then anyone checking the document may assume it was properly authorized, executed and delivered. Should it turn out later that the persons signing did not have the authority, or were not officers or directors of the corporation, although the document is a nullity, the person or persons relying on this section of the Act cannot be held to be negligent. An exception under section 19 of the Act to reliance on the indoor management rule occurs when the person or persons ought to have known, because of either a position held or a relationship with the corporation, that the persons signing could not properly execute the document on behalf of the corporation.

However, a corporation may still decide to have a corporate seal and may choose from the following which are available from Dye & Durham Company Inc. and other legal stationers. The current costs are set out in Appendix B.

(a) Desk Seal

This is an upright desk model which provides the best impression.

(b) Corporate Embosser

This is a lightweight corporate seal with the name inscribed on the brass plate on the top of the seal. It can be stacked for easy storage.

(c) Pocket Seal

As indicated by the name, this corporate seal is portable and includes a small carrying case. A good impression can be produced on single or double pages. This seal would be ordered for a corporation where the documents to be sealed are limited either in size or number. For example, if the corporate seal was to be imprinted on ten pages, the maximum number of pages to be imprinted each time would be two.

3. Share Certificates

At the time the order for the appropriate minute book and corporate seal is placed, an order must also be placed for a share certificate book. The choice of a share certificate book is based on the authorized capital set out in the articles of incorporation.

This is a bound book containing the blank share certificates which are issued to the subscribers for shares in the corporation. It is necessary to subscribe for shares in the organizational resolutions. These are the resolutions passed by the first directors which get the new corporation organized and ready to officially carry on business such as the appointment of officers, the setting up of the corporate bank account and other related matters.

The legal stationers have a variety of share certificate books available which cover the possible variations in the authorized capital of Ontario corporations. The books contain a minimum of 12 share certificates to a maximum of 100 share certificates, all of the same class. There are also books of 12 or 25 certificates "back to back" which means that if the authorized capital has both preference and common shares, one book of 12 certificates each of common and preference share certificates can be ordered. In addition to the convenience of having all of the share certificates in one book, there is a slight saving in the cost. The legal stationer saves money on the binding of the certificates, since only one binding is required instead of two, and can pass this saving on to the customer. Back to back share certificates can also be ordered with 25 certificates for each class of shares. Also available are "non-designated" share certificates which can be tailored to fit the authorized capital of a corporation, a sample of which is shown as Form 6.3.

Share certificates are printed in various colours by the legal stationers. In practice, certificates of a certain colour are chosen by law offices for the different classes of shares, for example common share certificates are brown, while preference or special shares are green and orange. A second colour is provided for special and preference share certificates because a corporation may often have more than one class of such shares. The decision as to the colour that will be used for a class of shares will be made by the lawyer.

When ordering share certificates for corporations, the information required would be:

1. type of share certificates, designated (common/preference), or non-designated or totally blank (see Forms 6.1 to 6.3);
2. whether the shares are with or without restrictions. All certificates, with one excepetion, show a lien on the shares and some show in red lettering the restrictions on the right to transfer shares of the corporation. Non-offering Ontario corporations require share certificates with restrictions;
3. number of certificates required (12 or 25);
4. confirmation that the corporation is incorporated in Ontario. Separate certificates are available for federal corporations.

Subsection 56(1) of the BCA sets out the information which must be shown upon the face of a share certificate:

> **56.** (1) A corporation shall state upon the face of each share certificate issued by it,
>
> (a) the name of the corporation and the words "Incorporated under the law of the Province of Ontario" or words of like effect;

(b) the name of the person to whom it was issued; and

(c) the number and class of shares and the designation of any series that the certificate represents.

These requirements apply to all share certificates issued by a corporation regardless of the class of shares. If, for example, the authorized capital of the corporation is made up of common and special shares, this information would have to appear on the face of all certificates issued in either class of shares by the corporation.

Subsection 56(2)(b) states there must be a legible statement on the certificate of each class and series stating that there are preferences, rights, conditions, restrictions or limitations attaching to these shares and that a copy of the full text thereof can be obtained on demand and without fee from the corporation. If this statement is on the share certificate, the corporation is required to provide a shareholder with a copy of the preferences, rights, and conditions that attach to the share.

If the articles of incorporation include, under other provisions, the right for the corporation to claim a lien on the shares to the extent of the debt owed by the registered shareholder to the corporation, this right must be conspicuously noted on every share certificate issued by the corporation (subsection 56(3)).

If a transferee has no knowledge of a restriction or lien attaching to the share or shares, then such restriction or lien is ineffective against the transferee.

Information concerning restrictions on the transfer of a share certificate issued by a corporation must appear on, or be attached to, the share certificate. Another alternative available under this subsection is to state on the face of the share certificate that there are transfer restrictions and that a full copy of these restrictions can be obtained on demand and without fee from the corporation. The corporation is obligated to furnish a copy of the transfer restrictions on demand by a shareholder without charge (subsection 56(8)).

Subsection 42(1) of the Act states that a corporation may only impose the restrictions on the transfer of shares that are set out in the articles of incorporation. Article 8 in the articles of incorporation deals with the restrictions, if any, on the issue, transfer or ownership of shares of the corporation. It is under article 8 that any restrictions such as these would be shown. Usually the only restrictions that are set out in articles of incorporation refer to the transfer of shares. These restrictions under the BCA constitute the corporation as a non-offering corporation. There is an exception to this general rule under subsection 42(2) which states that a corporation which has restricted the transfer of its shares shall not offer its shares to the public unless the restrictions are necessary

1. under any Act of Canada or Ontario to obtain, hold or renew its authority to engage in any activity necessary to its undertaking;

2. to achieve or preserve its status as a Canadian corporation for the purpose of any Act of Canada or Ontario;

3. to limit the ownership of shares by any prescribed class of person for the purpose of assisting it and any of its affiliates to qualify under the *Securities Act* or similar legislation of other provinces or the Territories to obtain, hold or renew registration, or to qualify for membership in a recognized Ontario stock exchange; or

4. to attain or maintain a level of Canadian ownership or control for the purpose of assisting it and any of its affiliates to qualify for licences, permits, grants, payments or other benefits under any prescribed Act of Canada or a province or territory.

A non-offering corporation is exempted from certain requirements of the Ontario *Securities Act*.

A share certificate is evidence of the shares of the corporation a person may hold. Section 54 states that every shareholder is entitled to a share certificate in respect of the shares held, signed by the proper officers authorized under the by-laws. A corporation is only required to issue one share certificate for shares held jointly by two or more persons. Delivery of such a share certificate to one of the joint registered owners is considered to be delivery of the share certificate to all registered owners. The corporation is limited to charging a fee of not more than $3 for every share certificate issued in respect of a transfer.

The share certificate must under section 55 of the BCA be manually signed by at least one director or officer of the corporation or by or on behalf of a registrar, transfer agent, branch transfer agent or issuing or other authenticating agent, or by a trustee who certifies it in accordance with a trust indenture. The corporation may by by-law provide that any additional signatures required on the share certificate may be printed or otherwise mechanically reproduced. If the share certificate is so signed, it is as valid as if it had been signed manually.

Under section 23, shares may be issued subject to the articles, the by-laws, to any unanimous shareholder agreement and the pre-emptive rights contained in section 26. A "pre-emptive" right is a right that permits existing shareholders of a corporation to take a new issue of shares pro rata, thus protecting their proportionate holdings of the issued share capital of the corporation. The directors continue to have the right to issue shares at any time to any person and to determine the consideration to be paid for the shares. Subsection (2) contains a provision which states that shares issued by a corporation are non-assessable and that the holders are not liable in respect of these shares either to the corporation or its creditors. Under subsection (3), shares are not to issue until fully paid. Under subsection (5), the directors may include reasonable charges and expenses of organization and reorganization or payments for property and past service expected to benefit the corporation when determining the value of property or past service.

4. By-Laws

(a) General

The words used in law today are derived from several different sources and several different languages. The word "by-law" is of Scandinavian origin. The word "byr" in Old Norse meant village. The combination of "byr" with the Old Norse word "law", by-law, meant a local or village law or a municipal ordinance. In Old English the word "by" meant beside or near. The word "by-laws" came to mean subordinate laws by or near a main body of law.

By-laws set out the rules and regulations which govern how the corporation shall act and usually take effect as soon as the directors approve the resolution enacting them.

Section 116 of the BCA empowers the directors to pass by-laws. It also states that unless there are contrary provisions in the articles, the by-laws or a unanimous shareholder agreement, the directors may by resolution make, amend or repeal any by-laws that regulate the business or affairs of a corporation. All by-laws made, amended or repealed are effective on the date of the resolution of directors and continue until confirmed, confirmed as amended or rejected by the shareholders.

It is common practice under the BCA to pass a general by-law which sets out the rules governing how the business of the corporation would be carried on for a non-offering Ontario corporation.

If the corporate banker of the corporation requires a borrowing by-law, then a second by-law may prove necessary in spite of section 184.

(b) Preparing By-laws

There are two possible approaches in the preparation of by-laws. Some law offices draft their own specific form of by-laws while others purchase the form of bylaws supplied by the legal stationers. The by-laws shown as Forms 6.5 and 6.6 are prepared by a legal stationer for use in the organization of an Ontario non-offering corporation. It is essential to keep the following information in mind when ordering by-laws from a legal stationer:

1.	the incorporating jurisdiction:	provincial or federal since the provisions of the by-laws differ. It would reflect badly on the law office if federal by-laws were approved for an Ontario corporation.
2.	single or multiple directors:	Dye & Durham Co. Inc. supplies by-laws prepared for use by corporations having either one director or multiple directors. Although the multiple director/shareholder by-law can be used for a ''one person'' corporation, that is, a single director/single shareholder corporation, an abbreviated form of this by-law is offered for the ''one person'' situation.

(c) Multiple Director By-laws

The printed form of By-law No. I requires the insertion of specific information to complete the by-law. By-law No. 1 (see Form 6.4, By-law (for corporations with more than one director)) requires the insertion of the corporate name in the places marked by asterisks. In addition, the following sections require consideration and completion:

(i) Section 2.01 Powers

The number of directors of the corporation is established under this section. The BCA provides for either a fixed or variable number of directors and both options are printed in this section of the by-law. The articles of incorporation decide which option is applicable for a particular corporation. If the articles show that the corporation can have a minimum of one to a maximum of six directors, these numbers would be inserted in the appropriate spaces and the reference of a fixed board of directors deleted.

Subsection 126(3) of the Act provides that a majority of the number of directors or the minimum number of directors required by the articles constitutes a quorum at any meeting of directors. Except for two director or single director corporations, the minimum quorum permitted is two-fifths of the number of directors for corporations with a fixed or set number of directors. The minimum number of directors, for non-offering corporations with a minimum to maximum number of directors set out in the articles, establishes the minimum quorum for these corporations. Where a corporation has fewer than three directors, either one or both must be present to constitute a quorum. Subsection 126(12) states that where a corporation has only one director, that director may constitute a meeting.

(ii) Section 3.10 Casting Vote

A decision must be made whether or not the chairman of a meeting of the board of directors is to have a second or casting vote. One of the reasons for establishing an odd number of directors is to avoid the possible situation of a tie vote. If, for example, there were four directors and a contentious matter was being discussed, two might vote in favour and two could vote against the proposal, resulting in a tie or equal vote. In time, one of the directors could change his or her mind, but until that occurred the corporation would be powerless to act. The number of directors influences whether or not the chairman would have a second or deciding vote. When the decision has been made, the appropriate blank is either filled by adding the word ''not'' if the decision is negative, or left as is if the chairman is to have a second vote.

(iii) Section 5.01 Appointment of Officers

The decision as to the officers to be appointed for a corporation is made by the client and the lawyer. The by-law sets out the officers and their duties that are most often selected. In addition, under subsection 1(1) of the Act, ''officer'' includes the chair of the board of directors, a vice-chair of the board of directors, the president, a vice-president, the secretary, an assistant secretary, the treasurer, an assistant treasurer and the general manager of a corporation and any other individual designated an officer by by-law or resolution of directors or any other person who performs the duties of an office on behalf of a corporation. Section 133 of the Act empowers the directors to designate the offices of the corporation, appoint officers, specify their duties and delegate to them powers to manage the business and affairs of the corporation, subject to certain exceptions. Two or more offices of the corporation may be held by the same person.

(iv) Section 7.02 Lien for Indebtedness

This form of by-law sets out the claim for a lien on shares registered to a shareholder if the shareholder owes money to the corporation. Subsection 40(1) of the BCA provides that the right to a lien on shares for debts owing by a shareholder to the corporation may be set out in either the articles or by-laws. If the provision is included in the articles, this section should be deleted from the by-laws.

(v) Section 9.01 Financial Year

The form of by-law refers to the "financial or fiscal year" of the corporation. In the past, the term used to describe the 12-month period used as a basis of business reckoning was "fiscal year". The Ontario *Business Corporations Act* now uses the term "financial year", rather than fiscal year.

The *Corporations Tax Act*, R.S.O. 1990, c. C.40, states that the first financial year of a corporation cannot exceed 53 weeks from the date of incorporation. This information is not always available when the organization of the corporation is undertaken. The situation could arise where a lawyer may prefer that clients not sign by-laws in which some information is lacking In order to solve this problem this section could be deleted from the by-law. Later, when the year end has been decided upon, the directors can pass a resolution fixing the financial year end. In many law offices the financial year end is established by resolution, rather than by by-law Should the corporation at any time wish to change its financial year end, it is much simpler to pass a new resolution rather than amend an existing by-law to incorporate any desired change in this area.

(vi) Section 11.01 Signing Officers

This section of the by-law designates that contracts and obligations of the corporation may be signed by the president or a vice-president or a director together with the secretary or treasurer of an assistant to either of these officers. In some instances a corporation may want to restrict the individuals who have authority to execute documents on behalf of the corporation. This decision is made jointly by the client and the lawyer in charge of the incorporation. The section should be brought to the attention of the lawyer in charge so that this section is appropriately completed.

(vii) Section11.02 Corporate Seal

Section 13 of the BCA states that a corporation may, but need not, have a corporate seal. Should a decision be made to have a corporate seal, the method of adoption of the seal appears to be left to the discretion of the principals involved in the corporation. Some law firms may adopt the policy of approving the seal under By-law No. 1; others may elect to approve it by resolution of the directors. This is why 11.02 is still found in the standard stationer's form for By-law No. 1.

Depending on the choice made, it may be necessary to delete this section of the by-law.

(viii) Section 13.01 Repeal

This section provides for the repeal of existing by-laws of the corporation when this by-law comes into force. Depending on the circumstances, this section may or may not be deleted.

If the corporation has been incorporated after July 29, 1983, then this section should be deleted.

Page 19 of the by-law should be completed by adding the date and arranging for the by-law to be signed by two officers of the corporation with their titles added below the signature lines. The form of by-law shows the signing officers to be the president and secretary and these officers usually sign most by-laws. Some corporations may, for example, have a secretary-treasurer, rather than a secretary.

Complete page 20 by adding the date and the necessary signature lines. The names of the persons signing the by-law should be typed below each signature line. This assists clients in signing in the correct place and also makes it easier for anyone looking at the signatures to know the names of the persons who signed the by-law. The same procedure should be followed for confirmation of the by-law by the shareholder(s) on this page.

(ix) By-law No. 2

Section 184 of the BCA confers on the directors the power to borrow and pledge without the authorization of the shareholders of the corporation, subject to any contrary provisions in the articles, by-law or a unanimous shareholder agreement. A policy will have to be adopted by the law office as to what is to be done in this area. The possible choices would appear to be:

1. enact By-law No. 2;
2. include in By-law No. 1 in case proof must be furnished for another jurisdiction; or
3. exclude from the by-laws and rely on the provisions of the statute.

(x) By-law No. 3

In addition to the general power to borrow and pledge, the individual chartered bank may require its form of by-law which authorized the directors to borrow and pledge assets to the bank. This by-law might also appoint the bank as the corporate banker for the corporation.

Although the banks are aware of the provisions of the Act regarding the directors' right to borrow and pledge, either of two approaches may still be adopted:

☐ By Law No. 3 may be required; or

☐ Certificate as to Non-Restriction of Borrowing Powers.

The practice may vary from bank to bank. One bank may not require either the bank form of borrowing by-law or a certificate. Another bank might require the bank form of by-law while a third bank may demand the certificate.

Prior to the preparation of the banking documents needed to open a new corporate bank account, it would be advisable to contact the branch of the particular bank involved and confirm its requirements.

If the bank requires the bank form of borrowing by-law, a copy must be prepared and filed in the corporate records of the corporation. The usual practice is to photocopy the form on minute book paper and add the necessary confirmation clauses, dates and signature lines.

(d) Single Director By-law

This form of By-law No. 1 (see Form 6.5) is intended for a single director and a single shareholder corporation. Section 4 of the by-law (Shareholders) contains provisions to cover more than one shareholder. Should the number of shareholders increase it would not be necessary to pass a new by-law.

Page 9 of this by-law contains the confirmation clauses by the sole director and sole shareholder of the corporation. The use of the word "sole" ensures that there is no confusion as to the number of directors and shareholders involved in the corporation when this by-law was passed and confirmed. This is a good practice to adopt when dealing with single director/single shareholder corporations. If at some future time more than one shareholder signed a confirmation, it would alert the person reviewing the minute book to check on the date the other person or persons in fact became shareholders of the corporation. If there was no resolution issuing a share or shares, this may just be an oversight. On the other hand, it would raise the question as to whether or not the other person or persons are really shareholders. If a client is acquiring the assets of a corporation it is very important to know exactly who the shareholders are since they control the corporation. It is essential that all shareholders of the corporation consented to the sale or acquisition. If a shareholder had not consented, this would raise a question as to the validity of the purchase of the assets.

The form of banking by-law if required by the chartered bank which would act as the corporation's banker would be By-law No. 2. Under the BCA, one-person corporations will only have one by-law enacted immediately after incorporation unless its corporate banker insists on a borrowing by-law on the bank's form.

Section 8.01 (Financial Year) requires insertion of the date on which the year ends.

The by-laws set out here are the minimum by-laws required initially for new corporations.

Any matter can be dealt with at this time but there are certain more or less "standard" matters which are included in all organizations of new corporations.

There are two methods of proceeding, either by way of minutes or by way of resolutions. Minutes are a more formal method and require additional notices and waivers. The more common practice today is to proceed by way of signed resolutions of directors and shareholders. This method eliminates a great deal of paperwork. It is also much easier to add to resolutions if some matter comes up which was not included in the instructions the lawyer received earlier from the clients.

Once the by-laws have been prepared and passed, the organizational resolutions dealing with the routine matters involved in all new incorporations are the next order of business.

5. Organizational Resolutions

It is the responsibility of the first directors to deal with the usual matters that are required in order to get the corporation organized and ready to actually commence business. In cases where the first directors are not the permanent directors of the corporation, once the usual housekeeping type of resolutions are passed, the office incorporators (usually members of the law firm or support staff) resign and appoint the permanent directors so that they make any actual business decisions for the corporation.

The following are the standard matters dealt with by the directors on every incorporation.

(a) Election or Appointment of Officers

The officers carry out the decisions of the directors and are required to sign share certificates for shares issued by the corporation.

Usually at least a president and secretary or secretary treasurer are appointed. Any other officer or officers could be appointed. One person may occupy two offices, such as secretary-treasurer. The president is the chief executive officer of the corporation. The secretary certifies documents and generally takes care of records for the corporation.

Unless the articles, by-laws or any unanimous shareholder agreement states otherwise, under section 133 of the BCA the directors may designate the offices of the corporation and appoint officers.

(b) Issue Share(s) to Incorporator(s)

At least one shareholder is required to confirm the by-laws and enact any resolution that falls within the jurisdiction of shareholders. It is now necessary to include a subscription for at least one Class A (common) share in the organizational resolutions so that the functions reserved under the statute for shareholders can be carried out.

(c) Approve the Form of Share Certificates Required for the Authorized Capital of the Corporation

Under the BCA, the authorized capital can be composed of Class A/common shares and Class B/preference shares or only common shares. Non-offering corporations which restrict the transfer of shares are required under section 56 to set this and other information out on the face of the share certificate.

The terminology used to describe the shares comprising the authorized capital of corporations incorporated under the Act may contain the words "preference" and "common" or may simply denote the shares as Class A and Class B shares.

One of each kind of share certificate is marked "sample" and attached as a schedule to the resolution of the directors adopting the share certificate or certificates for use by the corporation.

(d) Adoption of Corporate Seal

Under the BCA a corporation may but need not have a corporate seal. It also appears that a seal is no longer required in connection with a certified copy of a document filed under the Act. The term "certified copy", in relation to a corporation document, is defined as a copy of the document certified to be a true copy by an officer. This can be accomplished by an officer signing the certificate which states the copy of the document is a true copy. However, situations may still arise in which a corporate seal will be required and since the statute is permissive in this area, it is a decision that will be determined to some extent by the type of business or by the individuals involved.

The standard share certificate form available from the legal stationers provides a place for a seal but there is no statutory requirement that it be added to a share certificate. In practice the seal is usually impressed on each share certificate issued by the corporation.

(e) Banking Resolution

The next matter to be dealt with is the appointing of the signing authorities or officers on the corporate bank account. The banking resolution names by title the officers of the corporation who have authority by resolution of the directors to make deposits to the bank account, sign cheques drawn on this account and authorize the debiting of this account with charges for services made by the bank. A copy of this banking resolution is attached to the resolution of directors as a schedule. Titles, rather than the names of persons, are typed in the appropriate blank spaces in the resolution. While the persons occupying certain offices in the corporation may change, the titles remain the same. If names of persons are used, then each time there is a change it would be necessary to pass a new banking resolution, certify a copy of the new resolution and file it with the bank. However, if titles are used, then it is only necessary to file a Certificate of Incumbency, which is the list of directors and officers supplied to the bank, along with new specimen signature cards.

Situations may occur in which it will be necessary to use an individual's name in a banking resolution. For example, a corporation might want to provide that all cheques on the corporate bank account be signed by any two of the president or secretary-treasurer or John Smith, office manager. Each cheque drawn on the bank account would require two signatures. A new banking resolution would not be required unless the office manager changed.

(f) Site of Registered (Head) Office

The site of the registered office, formerly head office, is set out in the articles of incorporation. The information shown includes the municipal or mailing address of the corporation. Under section 14 of the BCA, a registered office is to be located at the place specified in the articles of incorporation. The statute provides that a corporation can change the location of its registered office by resolution of directors within the same municipality, followed by the filing of the appropriate Notice of the Change or Annual Return.

(g) Financial/Fiscal Year End

The decision as to when the corporation will end its financial or fiscal year is usually made after discussion with an accountant. The client may take care of this matter before consulting the lawyer about incorporation. However, if the client has not done so, the lawyer may advise on the tax implications and assist the client in making this decision. If this is the situation, then the first directors pass a resolution officially establishing the date on which the financial year of the corporation ends.

If a decision has not been made in this area and for whatever reason this matter cannot be decided for some time, this resolution should be omitted from the organizational resolutions. When the financial year end is established, a resolution of the directors can be passed at that time. Another option available is to include the financial year end in By-law No. 1, rather than the organizational resolutions.

However, under the *Corporations Tax Act*, subsection 1(1)(a) and subsection 249.1(1)(a) of the *Income Tax Act*, R.S.C. 1985, c. 1 (5th Supp.), the financial year of the corporation cannot exceed 53 weeks from the date of incorporation. If it would be advantageous to establish a financial year end that would exceed this 53-week period, the first taxation year of the corporation need not be for a full year. The corporation could file returns for a broken portion of a taxation year. This broken portion would extend from the date of incorporation to the end of the month in which the taxation year would end. For example, a corporation may be incorporated on April 30. The first taxation year must end on April 30 the following year, plus one week. If the corporation wanted to establish its financial year end as June 30, the corporation could file returns for the broken portion of the first taxation year. This broken portion would be calculated from April 30 to June 30 in the same year.

(h) Subscription for Share(s)

A subscription for at least one share must be included in the organizational resolutions. A shareholder is required to confirm the by-law or by-laws and to pass the other organizational resolutions that are necessary. If any other shares are to be issued, this matter may be dealt with at the same time. However, many lawyers feel it is at this point that any "office incorporators", who are also first directors, should resign so that this matter is handled by the permanent directors and officers.

(i) Confirmation that Resolutions Passed

After all of these standard resolutions are taken care of, the directors must confirm that all resolutions have been passed. This is accomplished by adding a confirmation clause. There are a number of variations of the closing confirmation clause. Below is one example:

> Each and every of the foregoing (*add appropriate number of resolutions*) resolutions is hereby consented to by the directors of the Corporation pursuant to

the provisions of the Business Corporations Act as evidenced by the respective signatures hereto of all of the directors.

DATED this _____ day of ____________, 20_____.

Below this clause the necessary number of signature lines are added for the number of directors involved in the particular corporation.

As previously stated, where a corporation has only one director, that director may constitute a meeting and only one signature line is required.

(j) Pre-Incorporation Contract

An additional matter which may come up in the organization of a corporation is a pre-incorporation contract. A pre-incorporation contract is one that is entered into prior to the incorporation by one of the principals involved in the proposed corporation. The principal is usually described in the contract as a trustee or as a trustee for a corporation to be incorporated.

In order for the corporation to obtain the benefit of such a contract, it must be adopted by the corporation, preferably when it is being organized after incorporation. At that time the corporation also assumes any liabilities under the pre-incorporation contract and the contractor is released from all liability. It might, for example, be necessary to lease premises or buy land for the purposes of the undertaking or business of the corporation. Rather than lose the opportunity of acquiring a desirable site or piece of land, an offer would be made by one of the principals on behalf of the proposed corporation. If the contract is not adopted by the corporation, the contractor is bound by the terms of the contract, unless it is specifically stated otherwise in the contract. In order to avoid this potential personal liability, any pre-incorporation contract must state that the person purporting to act on behalf of the corporation before it came into existence is not in any event either bound by the contract or entitled to any benefits therefrom.

(k) Shareholders

Under the BCA the shareholders have the right to elect directors. Exceptions, of course, are the first directors who are named in the articles of incorporation. Any first directors not permanently involved in the corporation normally now tender their resignations. The organizational resolutions usually passed by the shareholders are set out below.

(i) Election of Director(s)

The shareholder(s) accept(s) the resignation of the office incorporator(s) who are also first director(s) and elect(s) the permanent director or directors.

(ii) Waiver of Audit

The shareholders of a non-offering corporation have the authority to waive the appointment of an auditor and instead appoint an accountant if all of the shareholders consent in writing to the exemption in respect of the particular financial year.

If the corporation so decides, and all of the shareholders consent in writing, the corporation is exempt from the requirements of the statute concerning auditors for the particular financial year. Consent of all the shareholders must be obtained for each year the exemption is sought.

A. *Appointing an auditor.* Should the corporation require an auditor and the shareholders fail to make such an appointment at their first annual or special meeting, then under subsection 149(1) of the BCA, the directors have the power to appoint an auditor. The directors also have the authority to fill a casual vacancy in the office of auditor. Only the shareholders have the power to remove the auditor from office, except where the appointment is under a court order.

B. *Persons disqualified as auditors.* The Act, under section 152, institutes the *concept of independence* as a necessary qualification for an auditor. The auditor must be independent of the corporation or any affiliates and the directors and officers of the corporation or any of its affiliates. This section states clearly that the independence must be a question of fact and then sets out those persons who would not be considered independent:

1. a business partner of the corporation or its affiliates or of any director, officer or employee of the corporation or its affiliates;
2. a person who owns directly or indirectly or exercises control or direction over, a material interest in the securities of the corporation or any of its affiliates; or
3. anyone who has been a receiver, receiver and manager, liquidator or trustee in bankruptcy of the corporation or any affiliates within two years of the proposed appointment as auditor.

C. *Annual audit/auditor's report.* Section 151 of the BCA deals with the right of the auditor to attend the meeting of shareholders, the right to receive all notices and other communications relating to such meetings and the right to be heard at such meeting on any relevant part of the business.

The specific requirement for an annual audit no longer appears in the BCA. However, since the directors are required to place financial statements before the annual meeting of shareholders, the audit would have to be done on an annual basis. Subsections 153(5) and (6) of the Act set out this right, with right of access through the officers, directors, employees or agents of the corporation. The Act provides that any oral or written statement between the auditor or a predecessor and the directors, officers, employees or agents of the corporation or any subsidiary of the corporation has qualified privilege. This provision offers protection to the auditor against libel and slander in connection with statements made while carrying out the duties of the office. This allows an auditor to discuss matters candidly with any of these persons and assist the effective carrying out of his or her duties. This does not, of course, bar any actions for negligence in performing the duties of the office.

D. *Report of auditor to the shareholders.* Section 154 of the BCA sets out the information to be laid before an annual meeting of shareholders which, among other material, includes financial statements and the auditor's report. The financial statements, under section 155, are to be prepared as prescribed by regulations and in accordance with generally accepted accounting principles ("GAAP"). The Regulations define GAAP as the standards as they exist from time to time set out in the *Handbook of the Canadian Institute of Chartered Accountants* (the "*CICA Handbook*") (Reg. 62, section 40). The establishment of a common basis for the preparation of financial statements will not only enhance their credibility to potential lenders or investors but will allow anyone reading financial statements of various corporations in the same industry to make informed comparisons. Without this common basis for preparation, the financial statements would present problems to anyone reading them, except for the author. The *CICA Handbook* contains general guidelines, usually updated annually, as to alternatives that are acceptable for accounting and disclosure of material in financial statements. Financial statements for non-offering corporations must contain the following:

- ☐ a balance sheet
- ☐ a statement of retained earnings
- ☐ an income statement
- ☐ a statement of changes in financial position.

There is a requirement under GAAP that financial statements be prepared in comparative form, except when such information would not be meaningful. This could occur when:

1. the prior year is not a complete financial year, that is less than 52 weeks; or
2. there is a major change in the operations of the corporation, for example, the buying or selling of substantial assets, a merger or an amalgamation during the year.

In addition, a holding corporation must consolidate its financial statement with its subsidiaries. There is no reference in the BCA or the Regulations to comparative or consolidated financial statements. However, depending on the type of corporation, either comparative or consolidated financial statements may be required to comply with GAAP as set out in the *CICA Handbook*.

Section 104 of the BCA makes provision, with some exceptions, for resolutions in lieu of a meeting of shareholders. A resolution in writing signed by all of the shareholders entitled to vote is valid and satisfies all the requirements of the Act relating to that meeting of the shareholders. Subsection 101(4) states that if a corporation has only one shareholder, or only one holder of any class or series of shares, the shareholder present in person or by proxy constitutes a meeting.

(iii) Appointment of Accountant

There were, at one time, two schools of thought in this area. In some law offices, the procedure was not to appoint an accountant. Lawyers stated, quite correctly, that there was no requirement under the statute. In other offices the accepted practice was to appoint an accountant. Accountants may be concerned that without this resolution the client could claim the accountant had no authority to prepare the financial statements and refuse to pay the account. This situation would only occur if a disagreement arose between the client and the accountant or if the client was unhappy about the amount of the account. The resolution is evidence of his or her official appointment as accountant for the corporation.

The usual reason for waiving the appointment of an auditor is cost. An audit of a corporation's books is a more costly service. For example, the auditor must send out statements to all those who owe money to the corporation and verify the amounts owing A similar check may be made in connection with the debt obligations of the corporation which takes time, and time is money. However, if a chartered accountant is performing an accounting service he or she usually relies on the information in the corporation's books, does a minimum of background checking and bases the financial statements on the figures shown in the books.

(iv) Confirmation Clause

The last item to be added after these standard resolutions of the shareholders required on the organization of a new corporation is the confirmation clause. There are a number of variations of the closing confirmation clause, such as the following:

> Each and every of the foregoing three (*or appropriate number*) resolutions is hereby confirmed/ consented to by the shareholders of the corporation pursuant to the provisions of the Business Corporations Act as evidenced by the respective signatures hereto of all of the shareholders.
>
> DATED THIS _____ day of ____________, 20_____.

Below this clause the necessary number of signature lines are typed for the number of shareholders of the corporation. The names of the shareholders should be inserted below each signature line to assist the clients in signing in the appropriate place.

(l) Directors

If any of the first directors resigned and new directors were elected, in addition to the resolutions, accepting the resignations and election of new directors, the following ancillary documents must be prepared:

1. resignations for those persons resigning as directors or as directors and officers; and
2. consents to act for signature by the new directors.

Pursuant to subsection 119(9), the election or appointment of a director is not effective unless the person elected consents in writing on or within 10 days after the date of such election or appointment. If the person elected or appointed consents in writing after the 10 day period, the electing or appointment is still valid (s. 119(10)).

Certain individuals are not permitted to act as directors of a corporation. Details of the reasons for disqualification are set out below:

- ☐ a person less than 18
- ☐ a person with the status of a bankrupt
- ☐ a person found by a court in Canada or elsewhere to be of unsound mind
- ☐ a person who is not an "individual" (as defined in subsection 1(1)).

If a first director is not an incorporator, then under the Regulations, Form 2 must be signed by the director but Form 2 is no longer required to be filed with the articles of incorporation. Subsection 135(1) states that a director present at a meeting is deemed to have consented to any resolution passed or action taken unless the director,

(a) requests that his or her dissent be or his or her dissent is entered in the minutes of the meeting;

(b) sends a written dissent to the secretary of the meeting before the meeting is terminated; or

(c) sends a dissent by registered mail or delivers it to the registered office of the corporation immediately after the meeting is terminated.

A director not present at a meeting is deemed to have consented to a resolution passed or action taken unless within seven days of becoming aware of the resolution he or she:

1. causes notification of dissent to be placed with the minutes of the meeting; or

2. delivers or sends by registered mail notification of dissent to the registered office of the corporation.

Section 124 provides that a quorum of directors may fill a casual vacancy among the directors, and if the person so appointed was not present at the meeting, some doubt could arise as to the validity of the appointment. By the requirement under subs. 119(9) that all new directors sign a consent to act, this potential problem can be avoided.

6. Post-Organizational Resolutions of Directors

The matters handled in the post-organizational resolutions of the directors are those required to complete the organization of a new corporation. These resolutions are usually passed by the permanent directors of the new corporation. However, in instances where the permanent directors are not available, these matters can be dealt with by the first directors named in the articles of incorporation. Once these resolutions are passed, the office incorporators who are first directors would resign and the permanent directors would be elected or appointed by the shareholders of the new corporation.

The following are the standard matters dealt with on all incorporations:

1. Transfer of Shares—Any share or shares subscribed for by the office incorporators will be transferred to the permanent and beneficial owner or owners.
2. Election of Officers—If the office incorporators who resigned as directors were also officers of the corporation, these persons would have included in their resignation as a director their resignation as an officer of the corporation. It would be appropriate to elect officers to replace these persons who are intended to be the permanent officers of the corporation. It is possible to prepare separate forms of resignations, one as a director and another as an officer. It depends on the practice followed in the particular law office.
3. Confirmation Clause—The last item to be added is the confirmation clause by the directors concerning these resolutions, the date and sufficient signature lines for the number of directors.

These post-organizational resolutions complete all of the resolutions usually required to organize a new non-offering Ontario corporation.

One matter mentioned in the earlier organizational resolutions of directors was the subscription for shares. Some lawyers prefer this matter to be handled in the post-organizational resolutions. The method to be used would have to be confirmed with the particular lawyer acting for the new corporation.

There may be occasions where, for various reasons, the beneficial owner of the shares of a corporation prefers to remain anonymous. In these situations an office incorporator may remain as a permanent director and shareholder of a corporation. To protect the identity of the beneficial or actual owner of the share or shares, a Declaration of Trust should be prepared and signed at the time the organizational resolutions are prepared. A precedent of a Declaration of Trust is shown as Form 6.6. At the same time, the share certificate registered in the name of the trustee should be signed in blank. When the written direction is received from the beneficial owner of the share or shares, it is a simple matter to complete the transfer of the share or shares. The transfer form is completed on the back of the share certificate, the new share issued in the name of the beneficial owner and the appropriate share registers amended. Entries would have to be made in the share transfer register, the shareholders' register and a shareholders' ledger sheet prepared. These registers are discussed in detail in this chapter, under the heading "8. Registers".

7. Summary of Organizational Resolutions

The first directors, those persons named in the articles of incorporation, pass the standard resolutions which are required for all organizations of newly incorporated Ontario corporations:

1. adopting a corporate seal if a decision is made to have a corporate seal;
2. appointing interim officers to sign by-laws;
3. passing banking resolution;
4. adopting form of share certificate(s);
5. establishing financial year end (if known); and
6. subscription for at least one share to confirm by-law(s) and elect permanent director(s).

The other issue of shares may be dealt with by the permanent directors after the organizational resolutions of shareholders are completed.

As soon as these matters are completed, if the fast directors are "office incorporators" (that is, the lawyer or members of the legal support staff) they will usually resign. It is essential to know at all times who the directors and officers of the corporation were when certain actions were taken. It is for this reason that many law offices prefer to record the times all resolutions of directors and shareholders are made when the corporation is being organized. This can be done very simply by adding the time as follows:

Dated this _____ day of ____________, 20_____ at 1:15 p.m. Toronto time.

The resignation of any office incorporator is accepted by the shareholder or shareholders of the corporation. Usually the shareholders are those persons who are beneficially interested in the corporation but, as a matter of convenience, the shareholders may be the lawyer and members of the legal support staff. The shareholders accept the resignation or resignations and elect a permanent director or directors as required in each individual situation.

If the shareholders are beneficially interested in the corporation, a decision will be made either to waive the appointment of an auditor and appoint an accountant, or to appoint an auditor.

If the shareholders are only temporary, the matter of waiving the appointment of an auditor and appointing an accountant and/or electing an auditor may be postponed until the permanent shareholders enter the picture. The practice followed depends on the particular law office.

Once the permanent directors are elected, they usually take care of certain matters:

1. If the shareholder or shareholders are temporary, the directors pass the resolution transferring a share or shares to the permanent shareholder or shareholders.
2. Any office incorporators who also act as temporary officers of the corporation resign and the directors by resolution elect the permanent officer or officers of the corporation.
3. When a decision has been made to incorporate a corporation to carry on either a new business or an existing business, it may be necessary in view of the business to be carried on that an action be taken on behalf of the corporation before it actually exists, such as:
   (a) purchasing real estate so that a building can be constructed for the registered office for the use of the business;
   (b) leasing premises which will be used for the business. For example, if it was a retail store it would be most important to find a good location for "walk by" traffic. If such a location is found, the lessor may want an immediate offer and rather than lose this site, an offer to lease would be made on behalf of the corporation by one of the principals involved as a trustee.

8. Registers

Under section 140 of the BCA a corporation is required to keep certain records.

One of the ancillary duties often overlooked when the corporate records are being completed for a new corporation is the completion of the share registers which reflect the issued and outstanding shares of the corporation and the holders thereof. The registers should be completed at the same time as the organizational resolutions and other organizational matters are dealt with for a new corporation. Failure to complete these registers contravenes the BCA, and in addition, the information set out in the registers is not available when required. It is a relatively simple matter to complete the registers at the same time that all other organizational matters are dealt with and to maintain these registers as the changes take place. There may come a time in the future when the principals involved in the corporation may wish to sell the shares and/or the undertaking of the corporation. If the registers have not been properly set up and maintained, it is then necessary to review all of the corporate records and bring the registers up to date. Checking through the minute book is a time-consuming exercise and occurs when time is minimal. The completion of the various registers is not difficult because the headings and columns are clear-cut. The registers which must be completed are discussed below.

(a) Directors' Register

Section 140 of the BCA sets out in detail the records which must be maintained by a corporation. In addition to the articles and by-laws, together with all amendments thereto, a copy of any unanimous shareholder agreement and minutes of meetings and resolutions of shareholders, a register of directors and a securities register are required. The register of directors must set out the names and residence addresses, including street and number, of all persons who are or have been directors of the corporation. This register must also set out the dates on which each person became or ceased to be a director. (See Form 6.7)

In this register, the director's surname is shown with the initials of the first name(s), together with the date elected and, when applicable, the date on which the director retired. The final column, entitled "office held" allows insertion of the office, if any, held by the director in the corporation.

The columns entitled "M.B. Folio" refer to a fairly common earlier corporate practice of numbering each page in the minute book. Very few law offices follow this practice today, but if the procedure is followed, the number of the page in the minute book on which the director was either elected and/or retired is inserted.

(b) Securities Register

The requirements for the securities register are set out in subsection 141(1) of the BCA. This register must record the securities issued by the corporation in registered form showing with respect to each clause or series of securities:

(a) the names, alphabetically arranged of persons who,

  (i) are or have been within six years registered as shareholders of the corporation, the address including the street and number, if any, of every such person while a holder, and the number and class of shares registered in the name of such holder,

(ii) are or have been within six years registered as holders of debt obligations of the corporation, the address including the street and number, if any, of every such person while a holder, and the class or series and principal amount of the debt obligations registered in the name of such holder, or

(iii) are or have been within six years registered as holders of warrants of the corporation, other than warrants exercisable within one year from the date of issue, the address including the street and number, if any, of every such person while a registered holder, and the class or series and number of warrants registered in the name of such holder; and

(b) the date and particulars of the issue of each security and warrant.

Although this section sets six years as the mandatory time limit for this information to be recorded, presumably this register would set out a record of all holders of any securities from incorporation forward. Provision has been made in the register, entitled Register of Debt Obligations (see Form 6.9) for a column headed "Date Discharged". If the debt obligations included bonds or debentures when these securities were paid off and discharged, for example, this information would be inserted in this column.

(c) Register of Transfers

Subsection 141(2) of the BCA requires every corporation to keep a record of transfers of all securities issued by the corporation in registered form including the date and other particulars of each transfer. The statute refers to a register of transfers but in practice this register may also be referred to as a share transfer register, a stock transfer register or a transfer register. This register (see Form 6.10) includes the date, class of shares, names of the transferor (original owner of security), the transferee (new owner of security), the numbers of the certificates surrendered and a record of the new certificates issued. The term "ledger folio" refers to the numbers that could be assigned to the individual records maintained for each security holder. This is not a common practice today, so these columns usually remain blank. The other column which causes some confusion is headed "transfer number". When a transfer of a security is recorded in the records for a particular security holder, the number assigned should be recorded here. While any number could be chosen to start the transfer register for a new corporation, the usual practice is to start with the figure "1" and continue in sequence for all future transfers. Under the column headed "attorney", there is space for the person charged with this responsibility to add his or her signature. This individual could be an officer of the corporation, usually the secretary, in the case of non-offering corporations. If deemed necessary, a transfer agent could be appointed as provided under section 142.

If it was necessary for a lawyer or a member of the legal support staff to act as a temporary shareholder, this share would usually be transferred immediately on completion of the standard organizational matters. The transfer would be recorded in the register, along with all transfers of issued shares that occurred in the future. It may be necessary, if the corporation has issued other securities which involve the right of transfer, to set up additional transfer registers to record transfers of these securities.

(d) Shareholders' Register

The shareholders' register contains a record of all shares issued by the corporation since incorporation. The register of debt obligations (Form 6.9) complies with the requirements of the BCA so far as other debt obligations of the corporation are concerned (for example, debentures or bonds). The register (see Form 6.11) includes an alphabetical list of the shareholders' names, together with the date of issue and the class of shares held. The description of the class of shares held is inserted in the last column.

Some law offices have adopted the practice of ruling off the name of an individual who has ceased to be a shareholder. This ruling off occurs when the transfer is recorded in the transfer register of the corporation. A notation either of the date of transfer or the transfer number may be added. This method ensures that at any given time the numbers of issued shares of each class and the identities of the shareholders can be easily ascertained.

(e) Shareholders' Ledger

In addition to the general shareholders' register, the corporation also keeps an individual record of each holder of issued shares. The individual holder may have purchased the shares or received the shares via a transfer. This ledger (see Form 6.12) contains the name, address and occupation of the holder, the telephone number and class of shares. There is provision for additional information:

Date: date of issue

Cert. No.: certificate number

Trans No.: transfer number (this is completed only if the share(s) received resulted from a transfer by a shareholder of the corporation)

To or from whom: In this column, the source of the shares is indicated. Shares can be issued from treasury or received by transfer from a shareholder of the corporation. The term "treasury" refers to the authorized or unissued share capital of the corporation. Shares that were subscribed for during the organization of a new corporation are issued from treasury. However, if any shares are transferred from temporary shareholders at this time, the name of the temporary shareholder would be shown here. The following are examples of entries that could appear in this column:

TO OR FROM WHOM
From treasury
From John W Smith*
To George Brown**
*Transferee
**Transferor

Folio: This refers to the number of the transfer register. If this practice of numbering is not used, this column remains blank.

Shares: When shares are issued from treasury the number of shares is entered in the column headed "Acquired". This figure is also entered in the column entitled "Bal. Held".

When shares are received by transfer from a shareholder of the corporation, the number of shares is inserted in the column headed "Transferred". This figure is then entered in the last column on the ledger showing the number of shares held.

At the same time that the new shareholder's ledger sheet is made up, in cases where the shares are received by transfer from a shareholder of the corporation, an amending entry must be made in the ledger sheet for the shareholder who sold or transferred their shares. In the example shown above (the transfer by John W. Smith to George Brown), a new ledger sheet would have to be set up for the transferee, George Brown. At that time, the number of shares transferred would be entered on the ledger sheet in existence for John W. Smith. The number of shares transferred would be deducted from the original number of shares held. The number of shares shown in the column "Bal. Held" would reflect the current share holdings of John W. Smith after the transfer to George Brown had been recorded in the records of the corporation.

It is considered good corporate practice that these registers accurately reflect the information contained in the organizational resolutions and that they be properly maintained from that time forward. Should the lawyer receive requests to inspect the corporate records, it would be a simple matter to screen these requests, if the information in the registers is up to date, to determine who has the right to make such a request.

A corporation may, under section 142 of the BCA, appoint a transfer agent or other agent to keep the register of security holders and the register of transfers, together with one or more branch registers if they should be required.

The register of security holders and the register of transfers, under subsection 143(1) of the Act, are to be kept at the registered office of the corporation or at such other office or place in Ontario designated by the directors. The branch register of security holders or register of transfers may be kept at the branch office of the corporation or at any other place or places, either within or outside Ontario, designated by the directors.

Subsection 143(2) states that registration of the transfer of a security of the corporation in the register of transfers or a branch register of transfers is a complete and valid registration for all purposes. Subsections (3) and (4) provide for the entries in the branch transfer register and in the register of transfers.

Subsection (5) states that a corporation registrar or transfer agent is not liable to produce a security certificate, a warrant or any document that is evidence of the issue or transfer of the security certificate or warrant: (a) in the case of a share certificate, six years from the date of its cancellation; (b) in the case of a warrant, six years from the date of its transfer or exercise; or (c) in the case of a certificate representing a debt obligation, six years from the date of cancellation of that certificate.

There is provision under section 146 of the BCA for a list of shareholders. A shareholder, creditor, agent, or personal representative of such persons can obtain a basic list of all current shareholders, their shareholdings and addresses from the corporation provided that the appropriate statutory declaration has been filed with the corporation or its agent. Where the shareholder or creditor is a body corporate or corporation, the statutory declaration shall be made by a director or officer of the body corporate and an address for service must be shown. The form of statutory declaration is Form 19, prescribed under the Regulations.

A list of shareholders may, under subsection 146(8), only be used in connection with (a) an effort to influence the voting by shareholders of the corporation; (b) an offer to acquire shares of the corporation; or (c) any other matter relating to the affairs of the corporation.

9. The Corporate Bank Account

One of the matters dealt with in the organizational resolutions is the establishment of the corporate bank account at one of the chartered banks and the authorization of officers and any other person working for the corporation who will be involved in either depositing funds, writing cheques on the account or picking up the monthly bank statements and cancelled cheques. Each of the chartered banks has its own special forms for the setting up of the bank account and the requirements vary from bank to bank and from branch to branch of each bank. It may be possible to obtain a supply of the printed forms required by each of the chartered banks in connection with corporate bank accounts by making arrangements with a particular branch of each bank. In the past these forms could be obtained by either telephoning or writing to the stationery departments at the banks but now policy prohibits direct contact with members of the public. However, if one of the branches requisitions the forms, the request will be filled.

The forms required by the Canadian Imperial Bank of Commerce have been chosen to illustrate the minimum number of documents requested by a chartered bank, and are discussed below.

(a) Banking Resolution

This form of banking resolution (Form 6.13) sets out the officers of the corporation who are authorized to sign cheques on the corporate bank account. It is quite common to require two signatures on all cheques issued by the corporation. Sometimes, to provide more flexibility, one signature on a cheque is permitted to a specified amount. Should disputes arise among the principals involved in a corporation, the requirement of two signatures prevents one person from absconding with the funds of the corporation.

Provision can also be made in the resolution for certain other employees of the corporation to make deposits to the account and pick up the monthly bank statements and cancelled cheques.

The first paragraph of the banking resolution sets out the name of the corporation. Under a clause the titles of the authorized signing officers are set out. It is preferable to set out titles rather than names, because the individuals holding the named offices may change, but the names of the offices remain the same. This eliminates having to replace the banking resolution every time there is a change in officers.

If only one signature is required on cheques to a specified amount, this information is inserted under this paragraph.

A provision is also made to add the names of any additional employees of the corporation who would have the power to negotiate or deposit with or transfer to the bank for the credit of the corporation all or any cheques, promissory notes, drafts, acceptances, bills of exchange and orders for the payment of money and for this purpose to sign or endorse these instruments or to deliver them to the bank endorsed with the name of the corporation impressed on the instruments by a rubber stamp. These persons would also have authority to receive all paid cheques and other debit vouchers charged to any account of the corporation and to sign the form of receipt required by the bank.

In order to avoid having an individual endorse the cheques or other negotiable instruments received by the corporation in payment of its accounts receivable, it is common practice to have a rubber stamp prepared with the words "for deposit only to the credit of (*insert name of corporation*)". These cheques are then accepted by the bank for deposit without signature and, should the cheques be lost, they cannot be negotiated by anyone else.

There is a certificate to be completed by the secretary and/or president of the corporation at the bottom or the back of the borrowing by-law and the banking resolution. Other banking forms sometimes make provision in these certificates for the by-law and resolution to be passed either by signature of all the directors of the corporation or passed at a meeting of the directors. In addition, where applicable, similar provisions are made in connection with the shareholders of the corporation.

These certificates must be completed indicating the method by which the by-law and resolution were passed. The certificates indicate where signatures are to be shown, either typed or printed in quotation marks. This indicates that they are copies only and are not an attempt to forge the signatures of the individuals involved. This process is referred to as "truing up" the copies of the document so they are identical to the resolution in the minute book.

(b) Certificate of Incumbency

This certificate, otherwise known as a list of officers and directors, must be filed with the appropriate bank listing the persons acting as directors and officers of the corporation. The certificate requires insertion of the name of the corporation and is then dated and signed by the secretary. If the corporation decides to adopt a corporate seal, it would be required as well.

If the corporation does not adopt a corporate seal, all banking forms must be appropriately amended by deleting all references to a corporate seal.

(c) Service Charges and Fees/Financial Services

Form 1.7 deals with the bank's service charges in connection with operating the corporate bank account. It gives the bank authority to debit the account with cheques and other instruments issued by the corporation and various other matters. This agreement contains full particulars of the commitment made by the customer to the bank. The form requires insertion of the name of the corporation and the date and location of signing above the signature lines. The titles of the officers signing must be shown below the signatures.

(d) Specimen Signature Card(s)

This is a requirement for every corporate bank account. The names and titles of the signing officers are typed in and the individuals sign opposite their names. The bank files this card in its records and should a question arise either as to the person signing a cheque on the account, or whether or not the signatures are genuine, the cheque will be compared with this card. (See Form 1.9.)

The banking forms listed above were all the documents that corporations incorporated under the BCA had to file with a bank to open a corporate account. However, because of potential restrictions on the borrowing powers of a corporation which may be contained in its articles, bylaws or a unanimous shareholder agreement, some chartered banks may request a certificate as to non-restriction of borrowing powers. If the bank has adopted this approach the certificate must be dated and signed by the secretary of the corporation under seal, if the corporation has adopted a corporate seal.

The banking documents referred to above, with one exception, are completed in duplicate. The original is sent or delivered to the appropriate branch of the chartered bank and the copy is retained for the office file. Only one specimen signature card is prepared and it is filed with the bank.

Effective March 1, 1995, pursuant to the *Proceeds of Crime (Money Laundering) Act*, S.C. 1991, c. 26, all banks and other associations or organizations such as cooperative credit associations are required to ensure the identity of their customers and generally, through the use of records outlined in the Act, keep track of transfers to third parties. The primary intent of the legislation it appears is to make it more difficult for persons involved in illegal activities that result in large cash transactions to launder these moneys through legitimate financial institutions. The Proceeds of Crime (Money Laundering) Regulations, SOR/93-75, require, for example, that

> **5.** Every bank, cooperative credit association, cooperative credit society, credit union, caisse populaire, loan company and trust company shall keep and retain the following records:
>
> (a) a signature card in respect of each account holder;
>
> (b) every account operating agreement that is received or created in the normal course of business;
>
> (c) a deposit slip in respect of every deposit that is made to an account;
>
> (d) every debit and credit memo that is received or created in the normal course of business, except debit memos that relate to an account at the same branch of a financial institution that created the debit memo;
>
> (e) a copy of every account statement that is sent to a client, if the information therein is not readily obtainable from other records that are kept and retained pursuant to these Regulations;

(f) every cleared cheque that is drawn on, and a copy of every cleared cheque that is deposited to, an account, unless,

(i) the account on which the cheque is drawn and the account to which it is deposited are at the same branch of the financial institution, or

(ii) the following conditions are met, namely,

(A) an image of the cheque has been recorded on microfilm or on an electronic medium,

(B) an image of the cheque can be readily reproduced from the microfilm or electronic medium,

(C) it is possible to readily ascertain where the image of any particular cheque is recorded, and

(D) the microfilm or electronic medium is retained for a period of at least five years; and

(g) every customer credit file that is created in the normal course of business.

SOR/98-439, s. 4

In addition to financial institutions, every person engaged in the business of dealing in securities, every life insurance company for clients purchasing an immediate or deferred annuity or insurance policy the premium for which is $10,000 or more, and every person, with some exceptions, engaged in the business of foreign exchange, are included in this legislation.

In order to comply with the requirements of this Act, the banks may require a "signatories identification" form be completed by the individual(s) having signing authority on business bank accounts, whether a sole proprietorship, partnership or corporation. A minimum of two pieces of identification is required from each signatory such as:

- ☐ a passport,
- ☐ driver's licence, or
- ☐ birth certificate.

(e) Corporate Seal

One item that was quite often overlooked in the preparation of banking documents for corporations when a corporate seal was mandatory was adding the seal to the forms.

Although a seal is not mandatory under the BCA now, the banking forms still make provision for a seal for the certificates which verify that certain documents are true copies. If the corporation does have a corporate seal, it can simply be added where indicated.

If, however, the corporation does not have a seal, the bank may require that the forms be amended to reflect this fact. In addition, the bank may very well require a certificate from an officer of the corporation verifying that

1. the corporation has not adopted a corporate seal; and
2. there are no provisions in the articles, by-laws or any of the other constating documents requiring a seal.

All references to a seal must be deleted from each banking form. A certificate as to the non-adoption of a corporate seal that is acceptable is shown as Form 6.14. A witness to the signature of the officer signing is required.

(f) Safety Deposit Box

A corporation may occasionally require a safety deposit box. Most of the banks have special documents for execution by a corporation if it requires a safety deposit box.

10. The *Corporations Information Act*

The *Corporations Information Act*, R.S.O. 1990, c. C.39, requires the filing of an Initial Return within 60 days of incorporation, amalgamation or continuation or the date of establishing a registered office or commencing any business activity in Ontario. A form entitled ''Initial Return/Notice of Change'' is provided at the time the articles of incorporation are issued by the Companies Branch. (See Form 6.15.) This form can serve as an initial notice or notice of change, depending on the circumstances. Every time a change in the information filed in the Initial Return occurs, the corporation is required to file a Notice of Change within fifteen days after the change or changes take place. There is no fee for filing these notices with the Companies Branch.

At the time of incorporation a corporation number is assigned by the Companies Branch in accordance with the Regulations. This Ontario corporation number must also be stated in all notices or returns filed under this statute and must also be stated in all correspondence with the Companies Branch.

There is a concerted effort being made by the provincial government to update all areas of corporate and business law in Ontario. The May 1,1991 proclamation of the *Business Names* Act, R.S.O. 1990, c. B.17, repealed section 2 and clause 15(a) of the *Corporations Information Act* (''CIA''). The registration by corporations carrying on business under a name other than the corporate name is now effected under this statute. Any member of the public desiring registration information on any business or corporation will only have to make one search under one statute.

In addition, a corporation carrying on business under a name style is required to set out its corporate name on all contracts, invoices, negotiable instruments, and orders for goods or services.

Section 13 of the CIA provides for a fine of up to $2,000 or imprisonment for a term not more than one year or both for an individual and a fine of up to $25,000 for a corporation upon summary conviction for contravention of the Act.

Section 18 of the CIA provides that where a corporation has failed to file a notice, such as an Initial Return or a Notice of Change, as required by the Act, the corporation is not capable of maintaining any action or other proceeding in any court in Ontario in respect of any contracts made by the corporation.

A duplicate copy of all notices filed under the CIA should be kept at the registered/head office of the corporation or in the corporate file at the law office. Subsection 5(2) of the Act states that a corporation shall retain a duplicate of the last notice filed under the Act. Alternatively, a corporation shall maintain an electronic record of the prescribed information set out in the returns and notices filed under the Act. Further, a corporation must make the record available for examination by any shareholder, member, director, officer or creditor of the corporation at its registered office or principal place of business. Examination of the record is to take place during the normal business hours of the corporation at the appropriate location.

There is also provision under section 17 of the Act for a prescribed late filing fee if a corporation fails to file a notice within the stated time.

All items on every form to be filed must be fully completed. Notices with incomplete items will not be accepted for filing. All information must be typewritten or printed in block capital letters. All documents delivered or filed with the Ministry are microfilmed and therefore must be legible and conform to all of the requirements set out below. Failure to comply with these standards will mean the document is not accepted for filing.

Form 1 can also be filed electronically via the internet using the primary service providers, OnCorp Direct Inc. and Cyberbahn Inc.

Discussed below are the forms currently required for filing under the CIA.

(a) Initial Return/Notice of Change — Form 1

Form 1 under the *Corporations Information Act* must, as set out in section 2, be filed with the Minister within 60 days after the date of incorporation, amalgamation or continuation of the corporation. Form 1 is a two-part form and must set out the prescribed information as of the date of filing.

The first filing of Form 1 is called an Initial Return. The second filing and all subsequent filings of this form are referred to as Notices of Change. A sample Form 1 and Schedule A are shown in Part IV — Forms, as Forms 6.15 and 6.16.

Subsection 4(1) states the Notice of Change updating the information in the Initial Notice shall be filed with the Minister within 15 days after the change takes place.

Up to June, 1995, the Companies Branch administered the processing of the Annual Returns required under the *Corporations Information Act*. After June, 1995, the requirement to file an Annual Return was temporarily suspended. In 1997, the Cabinet Office approved a joint venture between the Ministry of Finance (MOF) and the Ministry of Consumer and Commercial Relations (MCCR) [now the Ministry of Consumer and Business Services] to provide for combined filing and processing of annual and corporate tax returns. Beginning with the 2000 taxation year, corporations that would otherwise have to file a CT23 Corporations Tax Return with MOF and an Annual Return with the MCCR separately will instead file a combined return with the Ministry of Finance. This process streamlines the corporate filing function to allow corporations that have a taxation year ending on or after January 1, 2000 to file a combined CT23 Corporations Tax and Annual Return (see Form 6.19) with MOF. The Ministry of Finance will receive the combined return, separate the Annual Return information and pass it on to the Ministry of Consumer and Business Services, and process the CT23 Corporations Tax Return. Alternatively, a corporation can file the required Annual Return separately using the preprinted form (see Form 6.17) or electronically through the Ministry of Consumer and Business Services website *www.cbs.gov.on.ca/mcbs/companies*. The website will take the user to the two primary service providers for electronic filing, Oncorp Direct Inc. and Cyberbahn Inc.

Every share-capital corporation that is incorporated, amalgamated or continued in Ontario under the BCA must file an Annual Return. Every share-capital foreign extra-provincial corporation which has a licence endorsed under the *Extra-Provincial Corporations Act* to carry on business in Ontario must file an Annual Return. Such foreign extra-provincial corporations are those corporations that are incorporated outside Canada, and are known as ''Foreign Business Corporations''. These corporations also file the combined CT23 Corporations Tax Return or the separate Annual Return form using Schedule K. A corporation that is incorporated, continued or amalgamated in a Canadian jurisdiction other than Ontario is not required to file an Annual Return.

A corporation that is required to file a CT23 and Annual Return is required to deliver an Annual Return within six months after the end of its taxation year. This applies whether the Annual Return is delivered to MOF or delivered electronically to the Ministry of Consumer and Business Services (MCBS). A corporation is only required to file one Annual Return for each calendar year. The Annual Return is considered to be delivered on the day it is received by the MOF unless it is filed electronically through the use of the Value Added Network, then it will be considered as delivered on the day MOF acknowledges receipt and acceptance of the return. If the Annual Return is delivered electronically to MCBS during its business hours, the date of receipt will be considered to be that date. Incomplete Annual Returns are considered to be deficient, and MCBS will contact corporations regarding Annual Return deficiencies. The Annual Return will not be considered filed until the deficiency is corrected. Corporations that do not properly file an annual return may be subject to all penalties, including cancellation, in accordance with the acts to which they are subject, that are administered by MCBS.

A corporation is exempt from filing a CT23 Corporations Tax Return if it meets all of the criteria in subsection 75(5) of the *Corporations Tax Act* such as having no taxable income for the taxation year, and it is not subject to the Corporate Minimum Tax. Such a corporation files an Exempt from Filing Corporations Tax Return Declaration form (EFF Declaration) for each applicable taxation year. An eligible EFF corporation that is required to file an Annual Return will be in compliance with the filing requirements of the *Corporations Tax Act* and the *Corporations Information Act* if it completes the EFF Declaration and the Annual Return portion of the combined return and delivers them to MOF. Alternatively, the EFF Declaration can be filed with MOF, and the Annual Return can be submitted separately or electronically filed with MCBS through the primary service providers.

An Ontario corporation must complete all of the information on page 1 of the combined CT23 and Annual Return form. The MCCR Schedule A will only be required if there has been a change in information previously submitted to MCBS with regard to the directors, officers or administrators of the corporation. A Foreign Business Corporation must complete page one of the combined form together with the MCCR Schedule K if there has been a change in the information previously submitted to MCBS with regard to the Chief Officer/Manager or Agent for Service.

(i) Annual Return (Page 1)

A sample copy of the combined CT23 Short-Form Corporations Tax and Annual Return is shown as Form 6.19. The Annual Return portion will be forwarded to MCBS, be microfilmed and added to the public record of the corporation at the Companies Branch. The document must be both legible and suitable for microfilming which means *the information must be typed or printed in block capital letters using black ink.*

Each corporation must retain a duplicate copy of all Annual Returns and other notices that are required filings or maintain an electronic record of the prescribed information. These copies must be available for examination at the registered office during normal business hours. In order to assist in the completion of the Annual Return, the corporate information currently on file in the database will be printed on the form.

If there is no change in the pre-printed information on the form, then it can just be checked off as "no change" and the authorized person's name inserted. Then the schedules to the form are not required to be submitted.

If the pre-printed information is either wrong or out of date, then the corrections and/or updates of the information are to be inserted in the appropriate places on the the form. All addresses on the form must be completed in full, which means:

1. include street number or name or, if applicable, the lot and concession number;
2. the city or town and, if applicable, the unit or suite number; and
3. the province or state, country and postal code — abbreviations for provinces, states and countries are not acceptable.

Dates must be provided in the following format:

November 15, 2001 would be: 2001 11 15

(ii) Schedule A

Schedule A is used to report current officers and directors of Ontario corporations. If any of the information for a director or officer is either incorrect or out of date, then all required information in the Director/Officer Information section must be completed.

If an officer of the corporation holds more than one office, all current positions held by that person, including the date of appointment, must be completed. Section 133 of the BCA permits one person to hold two or more offices of the corporation.

If the number of directors or officers of the corporation will require more than one Schedule A to provide all current information, the blank Schedule A should be photocopied to provide the extra copy(ies) needed prior to inserting the information.

(iii) Director Information

The following information must be inserted in the appropriate section if the pre-printed information needs to be either corrected or updated for a current director:

1. *Resident Canadian* — place an "X" in the appropriate box; required for directors of business corporations only.

2. *Date first elected* — insert the date on which the person became a director.

When reporting a director not previously listed, complete both the name and address information.

In instances where a person is no longer a director of the corporation, complete the date on which he or she ceased to be a director.

(iv) Officer Information

The following information must be inserted in the appropriate section if the person is a current officer and the pre-printed information needs to be either corrected or updated:

1. date the officer was appointed; and
2. the position(s) held as an officer and the date(s) on which he or she was appointed to the position(s).

If an officer shown in the pre-printed information is no longer an officer of the corporation, then the appropriate section should be completed and the date on which he or she ceased to be an officer should be completed.

Every return must be verified by the certificate of either a director, officer or other individual that has knowledge of the affairs of the corporation, for example, the lawyer acting for the corporation. The name of such authorized person must be printed where indicated at the bottom of the form. An "X" must be placed in the appropriate box identifying the capacity in which the person has verified the information. Signatures are not required on the electronically filed Annual Returns.

(v) Schedule K

Schedule K is completed for foreign business corporations that are incorporated, continued or amalgamated in jurisdictions outside of Canada but have an extra-provincial licence for carrying on business in Ontario. The Schedule K reports information on the Chief Officer/Manager and the Agent for Service for foreign business corporations which have a licence endorsed under the *Extra-Provincial Corporations Act*. The Agent for Service may be an individual or an Ontario corporation. Only one Schedule K may be submitted with the Annual Return.

11. Corporations Tax

Under the *Corporations Tax Act*, R.S.O. 1990, c. C.40 ("CTA") all corporations, with and without share capital, having permanent establishments in Ontario, are liable under this statute. The statute also applies to corporations incorporated outside Canada receiving certain income or capital gains from a source in the province.

Under section 4 of the CTA, ''permanent establishment'' is defined as:

1. a corporation having its registered office in the province of Ontario. The head office or registered office may be designated either in the charter or the by-laws.
2. a corporation having its principal place in which the corporation's business is conducted located in Ontario.
3. a corporation that has substantial machinery and equipment, a branch, mine, oil well, warehouse, agency or other fixed place of business located in Ontario.
4. a corporation that has an employee or agent who has general authority to contract for the corporation or who fills orders from a stock of merchandise owned by the corporation which is located in Ontario.
5. the corporation is an insurance corporation and is registered or has a licence to conduct business in Ontario.
6. a corporation which owns land in Ontario but has a permanent establishment in another province or territory of Canada.
7. a corporation which carries on the growing, mining, creating, manufacturing, fabricating, improving, packing, preserving or constructing of anything in Ontario.
8. a corporation which presents any form of entertainment within Ontario.

The taxes administered and included under the Act are:

1. *Income Tax* — Tax based on taxable income for each taxation year. Corporations incorporated outside Canada, or non-Canadian corporations, licensed to carry on business in Ontario are taxed on taxable income earned in Canada.
2. *Capital Tax* — A tax based on the taxable paid-up capital of the corporation and total assets or gross revenues. Non-Canadian corporations are taxed on the taxable capital employed in Canada.
3. *Premium Tax* — A tax applicable to insurance corporations carrying on business in Ontario and based on the total taxable premiums written in the province.

12. Exemption from Filing Corporate Tax Returns

A corporation will be exempt from filing a corporation tax return for taxation years ending after April 20, 1988, if all of the following requirements are met for that particular taxation year:

- ☐ it is a Canadian controlled private corporation (CCPC) through the taxation year;
- ☐ it files a federal income tax return (T2) with Canada Customs and Revenue Agency;
- ☐ it has no Ontario taxable income;
- ☐ it has no Ontario Corporations Tax payable; and
- ☐ it has provided its Canada Customs and Revenue Agency Business Number to the Ontario Ministry of Finance's Corporations Tax Branch.

Corporations exempted from filing returns should keep adequate records for these non-filing years to support a claim made in other years. Records may have to be kept for more than the required 60 months to prove, for example, losses claimed in subsequent years.

If a corporation files a CT23 for a taxation year that is exempt, the Corporations Tax Branch will destroy the return and will not issue a Notice of Assessment for that taxation year.

Corporations exempt from filing are not subject to the statute-barred time limitations. Time begins to run from the date of mailing of a Notice of Assessment or a notification that no tax is payable for a particular taxation year, as set out under subsection 80(11)(c) of the CTA.

All insurance companies carrying on business in Ontario through a permanent establishment are required to file a corporations tax return, CT8, within six months of the taxation year end.

The first or initial corporation tax return must be filed within six months of the financial year end. Six months is the prescribed time limit and applies to the initial and all subsequent corporation tax returns. A copy of the CT23, Corporations Tax Short Form Return is shown as Form 6.19.

Subsection 1(1)(a) of the CTA and subsection 249.1(1)(a) of the *Income Tax Act* require that the financial year end of a corporation cannot exceed 53 weeks from the date of incorporation. If, for example, a corporation is incorporated on June 1 and the financial year end was established as November 30 in each year, the corporation would be required to file a corporation tax return for the broken period of the first financial year. The corporation tax return would cover the period from June 1, the date of incorporation, to November 30, the end of the first corporate financial year.

If the Corporations Tax Branch is not advised of the date on which the taxation year will end, the financial year end is automatically set at one year from the date of the incorporation, commonly referred to as the "anniversary date of incorporation".

The Companies Branch forwards on a regular basis to the Corporations Tax Branch information on all new incorporations. This information is integrated in the computer master file maintained by the Corporations Tax Branch. Every new corporation is "flagged" as an exempt corporation when entered, and assigned an account number, but the account remains dormant until a CT23 corporations tax return is filed. The onus is on the corporation to file when it becomes liable under the CTA.

In order to acquire and maintain its exempt status for corporation tax, a corporation must file a federal T2 income tax return with Canada Customs and Revenue Agency. The Corporations Tax Branch has a link-up with the computer system of Canada Customs and Revenue Agency from which it can pick up all corporations that no longer qualify as exempt corporations but have not filed the required CT23 Corporations Tax Return.

Providing the correct mailing address for the corporation is very important. The address is stored on the branch computer database and is used to mail all computerized forms, returns and letters to the corporation.

Under the BCA, section 241 states that where the Director is notified by the Minister of Finance that a corporation is in default in complying with the provisions of the *Corporations Tax Act*, or has not complied with sections 77 and 78 of the *Securities Act*, the Director may give notice by registered mail to the corporation or by publishing once in *The Ontario Gazette*, that an order dissolving the corporation will be issued. The corporation has 90 days after the giving of this notice to remedy the default.

Any interested person may apply to revive the corporation. There is no longer the requirement that the application be made before the dissolution. The Director may in his or her discretion by order, upon such terms and conditions as he or she sees fit to impose, revive the corporation. Upon revival, subject to the terms and conditions imposed by the Director and to the rights, if any, acquired by any person during the period of dissolution, the Corporation shall be deemed for all purposes to have never been dissolved. The Corporations Tax Branch notifies the corporation by letter of the impending cancellation of its charter for failure to comply with the provisions of the CTA. If the letter is returned undelivered, the charter could be cancelled without the directors or officers of the corporation being aware that this happened. Cancellation of the charter may result in forfeiture of the corporation's property to the Crown.

13. General Consent for Destruction of Books and Records

A tax information bulletin issued in June, 2000 by the Ministry of Finance advised that a general consent was established for the destruction of books and records held for Ontario tax purposes. As long as the eight conditions outlined in the bulletin are met, written permission is considered to have been given.

(a) Conditions

On the conditions set out below, a business may destroy books and records required to be kept if

1. the books and records are held under the following statutes:
(a) the *Corporations Tax Act*, R.S.O. 1990, c. C.40;
(b) the *Gasoline Tax Act*, R.S.O. 1990, c. G.5;
(c) the *Provincial Land Tax Act*, R.S.O. 1990, c. P.32;
(d) the *Race Tracks Tax Act*, R.S.O. 1990, c. R.1;
(e) the *Retail Sales Tax Act*, R.S.O. 1990, c. R.31
(f) the *Small Business Development Corporations Act*, R.S.O. 1990, c. S.12;
(g) the *Tobacco Tax Act*, R.S.O. 1990, c. T.10;
(h) the *Mining Tax Act*, R.S.O. 1990, c. M.15;
(i) the *Fuel Tax Act*, R.S.O. 1990, c. F.35;
(j) the *Land Transfer Tax Act*, R.S.O. 1990, c. L.6;
(k) the *Income Tax Act* (Ontario), R.S.O. 1990, c. I.2;
(l) the *Ontario Home Ownership Savings Plan Act*, R.S.O. 1990, c. O.20;
(m) the *Employer Health Tax Act*, R.S.O. 1990, c. E.11;
(n) the *Succession Duty Act*; and
(o) the *Community Small Business Investment Funds Act*, S.O. 1992, c. 18.
2. The books and records to be destroyed relate to a fiscal/financial year that ended more than seven years before the beginning of the fiscal/financial year in which the books and records are destroyed.
3. The books and records to be destroyed must relate to a period for which any tax returns required by the statutes mentioned (or by regulations made under such statutes) have been filed and all taxes assessed for that period have been paid.
4. There must be no outstanding discrepancy with the Ontario Ministry of Finance or any other taxing jurisdiction with respect to the period covered by the books and records to be destroyed.
5. The time limit for filing a Notice of Objection or a Notice of Appeal for the period must have expired without the filing of such notice of objection or appeal. If a Notice of Objection or Notice of Appeal has been filed, records must be maintained for the period under objection or appeal until the dispute is resolved.
6. All demands by the Ministry to produce the books and records that are to be destroyed must have been satisfied.

7. The books and records to be destroyed must not be ones that the Ministry has requested, in writing, the corporation to keep.
8. The books and records to be destroyed must not relate to the following:
   (a) A fiscal year for which a corporation has filed a waiver under subclause 80(11)(a)(iv) of the *Corporations Tax Act* or in the form required by subsection 152(4) of the *Income Tax Act* (Canada).
   (b) A fiscal year for which an operator has filed a waiver under subclause 9(1)(a)(iv) of the *Mining Tax Act*.
   (c) A fiscal year for which a taxpayer has filed a waiver under subclause 8(1)(a)(ii) of the *Employer Health Tax Act* waiving the benefit of limitation on assessments contained under clauses 8(1)(b) and 8.1(3)(b) of that Act. Books and records may be destroyed if all the conditions in sections one to seven above have been met, and the audit or refund/rebate entitlement review to which the waiver relates has been conducted by the Ministry of Finance and any related notices of assessment were issued.

Waivers may be cancelled by filing a notice of revocation of waiver under subsection 80(12) of the *Corporations Tax Act* or under subsection 9(2) of the *Mining Tax Act*. A notice of revocation comes into effect one year after the notice is received by the Ministry. When a notice of revocation has been filed, the books and records must be kept until the cancellation comes into effect. Once the waiver has been cancelled, the books and records can be destroyed if all the conditions stated in sections one to eight of this bulletin have been met.

Books and records may be destroyed earlier than outlined in paragraph 2 above if written permission for their disposal is given by the Minister. A written request, signed by an authorized representative, should be sent to the relevant branch or branches of the Ministry of Finance. The request should provide the following information:

(i) a clear indication of which books and records or other documents are to be destroyed;

(ii) the taxation years for which the request applies; and

(iii) details of any special circumstances which would justify their destruction at an earlier time.

As a result of the changes made and the implementation of the new exempt status, it may prove necessary to retain accounting and other records for longer than seven years, referred to under 2 above. Corporations that are exempt from filing corporations tax returns should maintain and keep adequate records for non-filing years to support possible claims made in other years, for example, to substantiate losses claimed in subsequent years.

Some exceptions to this rule are:

1. *Ontario Home Ownership Savings Plan Act* — more than seven years; and
2. *Mining Tax Act* — more than ten years.

Information required concerning the status of the filing of the corporate tax returns for a corporation can be obtained by writing to or telephoning the Corporations Tax Branch. The mailing address and general enquiry telephone number for the Corporations Tax Branch are listed in Appendix A.

If a Corporation Tax Return, CT23, shown as Form 6.19, is not filed by a corporation, the computerized system generates a series of letters, initially requesting and later demanding the return be filed. The final step is to threaten cancellation of the charter or articles of incorporation of the corporation.

The pre-printed Corporations Tax Return, CT23, is supplied in triplicate. The original copy is filed with the Corporations Tax Branch, a duplicate is provided for the corporation and the third copy is a ''working copy'' for the accountant or auditor who prepared the Return. Alternatively, the plain paper return produced with certified computer software or a diskette format may be submitted. In addition, electronic filing of annual returns through private service providers is available via the Internet and dial-up access.

(b) Corporation Tax Account Number

As mentioned earlier, every new corporation is recorded in the computerized system of the Corporations Tax Branch from information supplied by the Companies Branch. An account number is assigned but the account remains dormant until the first CT23 Corporations Tax Return is filed.

All enquiries, correspondence and documents filed with the Corporations Tax Branch require this account number to access the records of a particular corporation. The account number can be obtained by telephoning the Corporations Tax Branch.

7

REPORTS

Once all of the matters involved in the organization of a new corporation have been completed, it is essential that the following be prepared:

1. report to the client on the incorporation;
2. legal account for services rendered; and
3. report to the auditor or accountant.

These matters will be dealt with individually in detail.

1. Report to Client

In this area, as in many other areas of corporate law, there are several approaches to the handling of the report to the client. The approach ranges from the very short one-page report to an extremely detailed report of many pages, including several extensive enclosures such as copies of all the corporation's by-laws, the organizational resolutions of directors and shareholders, the shareholders' and directors' registers and copies of the shareholders' ledger sheets. Others adopt a middle-of-the-road approach, which is the approach that will be discussed here. A report adopting this approach supplies sufficient information to the principal or principals involved in the new corporation so they will have certain information readily available without having to contact a lawyer. This information will be set out in paragraph headings which could be used in a report to clients on the average non-offering corporation.

The reporting letter is usually addressed to the corporation to the attention of its chief executive officer, the president, but again this practice would depend on the policy of the particular law office. The purpose of the report is defined in the opening paragraph, that is, the client is advised that the report is on the incorporation and organization of the new corporation.

The following headings suggest the standard paragraphs which could be included in such a report.

(a) Incorporation

This paragraph sets out the incorporating statute, the method of incorporation and the date on which the charter issued. In Ontario, the incorporating statute is the *Business Corporations Act* and the charter issues under a certificate of incorporation endorsed on the articles of incorporation by the Companies Branch of the Ministry of Consumer and Business Services. The certificate sets out the date on which the articles of incorporation were accepted by the Companies Branch and issued.

In addition, this paragraph usually includes the information that the corporation is subject to the provisions of the articles of incorporation, the *Business Corporations Act* and other relevant statutes and all laws of general application that exist in the province of Ontario.

(b) Authorized Capital

Details of the authorized capital in the articles of incorporation are set out in this paragraph. The information included here will depend on the capital established under the articles of incorporation and could reflect the following.

Under the BCA the wording of this part of the report could read as follows:

> The corporation is authorized to issue an unlimited number of common shares;
>
> or
>
> The corporation is authorized to issue an unlimited number of shares;
>
> or
>
> The corporation is authorized to issue an unlimited number of Class A or Class B shares. The Class B shares have the following rights and privileges attached: (*set out details of and privileges*).

The information contained in this paragraph should accurately reflect the clauses dealing with authorized capital shown in the articles of incorporation.

The information regarding the restrictions on the transfer of shares issued by the corporation may also be included in this paragraph. The usual restrictions imposed on the transfers of shares in a non-offering corporation under the BCA require either a resolution of directors or a resolution of shareholders. A resolution of the directors or the shareholders can be either of the following:

1. An instrument in writing signed by a majority of the directors or by the holders of at least 51% of the issued common shares.
2. A resolution of the directors or the shareholders passed at a meeting at which a quorum is present.

These are the standard restrictions used for most non-offering corporations but can be varied to suit the particular situation. In some instances the resolution of directors consented to in writing might require all of the directors, rather than a majority, to sign the resolution. A resolution of the shareholders consented to in writing could require the consent of all of the holders of the issued common or Class A shares of the corporation.

A brief summary of the restrictions required to exempt a non-offering corporation from the provisions of the Ontario *Securities Act*, R.S.O. 1990, c. S.5 can also be set out here. The client would be reminded that the corporation is limited to 50 shareholders, exclusive of employees, one or more persons holding a share or shares jointly being counted as a single shareholder. In addition, the corporation is prohibited from offering its shares to the public in order to obtain the exemption from certain provisions of the Ontario *Securities Act*.

If any of the other provisions included in the articles of incorporation have any reference to the share capital of the corporation, that information can be included in this paragraph. Examples of the common provisions included in the articles under these other provisions sections could be the right of the corporation to purchase any of its issued common shares and the right to claim a lien on shares registered in the name of a shareholder owing money to the corporation.

A general information section concerning the location of any other provisions under the by-laws which apply to shares and the transfer of shares can be added. A reference can be made to these specific sections of By-law No. 1 of the corporation which contain provisions relating generally to shares and the transfer shares and, in particular, to provisions regarding the signing of share certificates, the allotment and issue of shares. If the client requires this information, the report will be a handy reference to the particular sections of the general by-law which will assist the client in finding this information.

(c) Restrictions on Business

Under the BCA, objects are not required. A corporation has the option of restricting its business. This paragraph will simply state that the corporation is not restricted as to the type of business to be carried on. Alternatively, the paragraph may state that "the corporation may carry on any business except that of" at which point the particulars of the type of business to be restricted are set out.

(d) Registered Office

In this paragraph the municipal address of the office is set out. This information is contained in the articles of incorporation but it may be that the address used was an "office address" because the corporation had not established its permanent address at the time the articles of incorporation were being filed. When drafting the report, the information for this paragraph should be checked both in the articles of incorporation and in the organizational resolutions of the directors.

The client can be notified of the requirements under the BCA to change the location of the registered office and the filing requirements in connection with the change. Appropriate wording could be:

> The location of the registered office within the same municipality may be changed by special resolution of the directors. Notice of this change must be filed with the Companies Branch of the Ministry of Consumer and Commercial Relations within 10 days of the change.

(e) Organization

This paragraph in the report sets out the various by-laws which have been enacted in connection with the organization of the corporation, with a brief explanation of the purpose of each by-law. In most new corporations incorporated under the BCA two by-laws may be passed: By-law No. 1, being a general by-law governing the administration of the affairs of the corporation, and perhaps By-law No. 2, being a general borrowing by-law.

A resolution of directors authorizes the establishment of the corporate bank account at one of the chartered banks at a specific branch. This same resolution appoints the officers of the corporation who are empowered to sign cheques and other negotiable instruments on behalf of the corporation. Any other relevant information regarding the corporate bank account is also included in this paragraph.

(f) Directors and Officers

The client is advised in this paragraph that the Act and/or By-law No. 1 provides that the directors shall manage or supervise the management of the affairs and the business of the corporation. The number of directors shown in the organizational resolutions is set out. In addition, information as to the persons named as the first directors of the corporation in the articles of incorporation is supplied. This paragraph also advises the date on which the first director or directors resigned and the date on which the permanent director, or directors was elected.

The names of the officers, along with their positions, are set out in detail. In case the client should wish to define or confirm the duties of the various officers, the relevant sections of By-law No. 1 are provided.

(g) Execution of Instruments

The authority for designating officers and/or directors of the corporation to execute instruments and obligations on behalf of the corporation is set out under Bylaw No. 1. The usual provision is to require the signature of at least two persons, one holding the office of president, vice-president, general manager or director and the other holding the office of secretary, treasurer, assistant-secretary, assistant-treasurer or director.

These provisions can be modified to fit the particular situation. When preparing this section of the report, the information should be taken from the relevant provisions of By-law No. 1.

(h) Auditors/Accountants

In consultation with a lawyer the client will have made a decision as to whether an auditor or an accountant is to be appointed for the corporation. The information set out here informs the client of the date of the resolution appointing the auditor or the accountant along with the name of the individual or firm involved.

(i) Financial Year

If the financial year end of the corporation has been established, the date is set out here.

However, if the decision as to when the financial year of the corporation will end has not as yet been made, this is drawn to the attention of the client so that the matter will not be overlooked.

(j) Issued Shares

Incorporations under the BCA require a subscription or subscriptions for shares to be included in the organizational resolutions.

A statement is made of the issued and outstanding common/Class A or other shares of the corporation as of a specific date and details of the certificate number, registered holder and the number of common or other shares issued to each registered holder is detailed here.

(k) Annual Returns

Recent amendments to the *Corporations Information Act* continued the filing of the Initial Return/Notice of Change and reintroduced the filing of Annual Returns for corporations. The rationale for the change was two-fold:

1. since 1976, Ontario was the only jurisdiction in Canada not requiring such annual filings; and
2. failure by corporations to file changes adversely affected the Ontario public corporate record and it had become increasingly out of date and unreliable.

Prior to 1976, all corporations operating in Ontario were required to file Annual Corporate Returns and pay a fee. As of January, 2000, corporations once again have to file an Annual Return within six months after the end of taxation year. There is no filing fee for the Annual Return.

(l) Corporation Tax Status

The client would be informed as to whether or not it was an exempt or a liable corporation. If liable, depending on the approach adopted in the individual law office, the client would be:

(a) advised to contact its auditor/accountant concerning the filing requirements for the CT23 return; or

(b) advised that if an auditor/accountant has not as yet been appointed, the CT23 return must be filed, as required under the *Corporations Tax Act*, within six months of the financial year end, and that it is suggested that an accountant/auditor be contacted as soon as possible.

If, on the other hand, the corporation was exempt from filing, this information would be supplied, along with the conditions that must be met as established by the Corporations Tax Branch. Further information regarding these conditions is set out in Chapter 6 under heading "12. Exemption from Filing Corporate Tax Returns".

(m) Corporate Records

Unless the client has expressed a desire to retain the minute book, share certificate book or books and corporate seal, the usual practice is to keep these items in the law office for safekeeping.

The final paragraph in the report to the client encloses the legal account in connection with the incorporation and organization of the corporation.

2. Legal Account for Services Rendered

This account should contain sufficient detail to outline the services performed by the lawyer in connection with the incorporation and organization of the new corporation. In some offices the account is directed to the president of the corporation and in others to the corporation itself. The amount to be charged will be decided by the solicitor and the account can be drafted with this figure left blank. A decision as to the amount charged can be made when the report and account are being reviewed by the lawyer.

In addition, it is essential that all disbursements made on behalf of the client be included. There are certain disbursements which are made for every corporation and should automatically be included, such as:

- ☐ incorporation fee;
- ☐ name search fee; and
- ☐ minute book, seal and share certificate book.

There may be long distance telephone charges, photocopying charges, delivery charges and additional search fees. When preparing the account, it should be confirmed that all outstanding disbursements and time dockets have been forwarded to the accounting department for inclusion in the client's ledger sheet.

Most law offices have precedents of the preferred wording for accounts. However, to assist in this area, a suggested wording is set out below:

> TO PROFESSIONAL SERVICES RENDERED in connection with the above matter including: receiving instructions to incorporate, obtaining name search report, preparing articles of incorporation, arranging for signature and filing with the Ministry of Consumer and Business Services, obtaining the articles of incorporation, preparing organizational resolutions of directors and shareholders, preparing by-laws, share registers, Initial Return and advising Corporations Tax Branch, to preparing and filing necessary banking papers, discussions with you concerning appointing accountant/auditor for the corporation, reporting to accountant/auditor as requested, miscellaneous attendances by telephone and correspondence with you in connection with the foregoing;

To Our Fee		$__________
<u>Disbursements:</u> Paid Name Search	$__________	
Paid Filing Fee	$__________	
Paid for minute book, seal and share certificate book	$__________	

3. Report to Auditor or Accountant

In order to set up the necessary accounting records for the corporation, the accountant or auditor will require information about the incorporation and organization of the corporation. There are two approaches taken by lawyers in connection with reporting to the auditor or accountant. The decision as to how to handle this matter will be made on instructions from the client.

One approach is to report fully and completely to the auditor or accountant and enclose photocopies of the by-laws, the charter, the organizational resolutions of the directors and shareholders, together with copies of the share registers and the shareholders' ledger sheets. The other approach is to arrange for the client to deal with the auditor or accountant directly supplying the necessary information. Instructions from the principal are required as to the method to be used for each new corporation. If the law office is to supply the auditor or accountant with the necessary information, this can be done quite easily by forwarding to that individual or firm a copy of the report to the client, along with a copy of the legal account. A brief covering letter should be sent to the auditor or accountant advising that if there is any further information required, this could be obtained by contacting the lawyer.

8

SHAREHOLDERS' AGREEMENTS

1. Purpose

The preparation of shareholders' agreements may be recommended by the principal when discussing the incorporation with the clients. Many of the non-offering corporations are merely "corporate partnerships". The persons involved in the corporation have chosen to carry on business as a corporation rather than in partnership. In order to qualify as a non-offering corporation, the shareholders are limited to 50 in number, exclusive of employees. In most cases the shareholders are few in number and there is not a ready market for the shares. These shareholders may also want to limit the persons who in future could become shareholders of the corporation and, for this, among other reasons, it is advisable under the BCA that a shareholders' agreement be prepared. This agreement is prepared either before or after incorporation. When a new corporation is just commencing business, the parties involved are usually all on good terms and eager to co-operate to accomplish their mutual goals. The shareholders' agreement provides for the management and financing of the corporation and also deals with the rights and obligations of the shareholders among themselves. Every shareholders' agreement is tailored to the particular incorporation situation but there are certain standard matters which are dealt with under all shareholders' agreements. Matters such as share capital, financing, share transfers, directors, employees, dividends and a buy/sell agreement are usually included.

Consideration is also given as to whether or not the corporation should be a party to the agreement. The purposes and intentions of the shareholders are carried out through the corporation. If the agreement contains provisions which are intended to be binding on or enforceable by the corporation, it is made a party to the agreement. If it is intended that the shareholders' agreement will only govern the relationships among the shareholders, then it was not necessary to add the corporation as a party The decision as to whether or not the corporation will be added as a party to the contract will rest with the lawyer involved.

If the corporation is already incorporated, a copy of the articles of incorporation and the by-laws are attached as schedules to the shareholders' agreement and initialled by the parties for identification.

If the corporation has not as yet been incorporated, the articles and by-laws are usually drafted after the other items in the shareholders' agreement are settled. Decisions are made as to which items would be included in the articles and which should be set out in the by-laws. This decision is made by the lawyer acting for the clients. Articles of incorporation are not as easily amended as by-laws and some of the shareholders involved may want this added protection. If there are certain provisions which the persons involved would not want on the public record, these would also be included in the by-laws rather than the articles of incorporation.

2. Contents Check-list

The preparation of a shareholders' agreement for a corporation incorporated under the BCA can include any requirements the principals or their lawyer considers necessary. Some of the matters common to such agreements are outlined below:

(a) General Preamble

1. *Date:* day, month and year.
2. *Parties:*
   - (a) for each registered and/or beneficial shareholder: name in full, residence address, occupation and how to be described for use in text of the agreement;
   - (b) for corporation: name in full, jurisdiction of incorporation, location of registered office and how the corporation will be described in the text of the agreement.
3. *Authorized capital of corporation:* Full and accurate description of each class of shares and how each class of shares will be described in the text of the agreement.
4. *Issued shares:* number and class of shares issued to each shareholder; description of all trust or other nominative holding of shares.
5. *Statement of consideration:* full description of consideration and receipt thereof for each of the parties entering into agreement.

(b) Specific Clauses to Consider Including

1. *Definitions:* The agreement should contain definitions for various terms used, such as:

> where context permits singular may mean plural, masculine may mean feminine or neuter;

and other convenient short forms for terms or transactions that repeat in the text of the agreement, for example "offered shares", "purchase offer", "sale offer", "vendors" and "purchasers". This ensures clarity and at the same time shortens the length of the agreement.

2. *First right of refusal:* Separate covenants by each shareholder not to bargain, sell, assign, transfer, convey or otherwise dispose of shares in any way (including by way of gift, devise or bequest) except as permitted by the agreement. The percentages and to whom each shareholder wishing to sell must first offer the shares for sale. The mechanical procedures governing a sale of shares, for example, offer to sell to be in writing, time limited for acceptance of offer, price related to other *bona fide* offers, conditions precedent to the making of an offer to sell (other *bona fide* offers received and copies thereof to be delivered to other shareholders, purchasers agreeing to be bound by agreement), time and place of closing a sale if offer accepted, mechanics if offer not accepted for sale by offeror to maker of *bona fide* offer to purchase on identical terms within a limited period of time, if sale not completed shares again subject to agreement, if sale of part of shares of remainder still subject to agreement.

☐ Separate covenants by each shareholder not to mortgage, hypothecate, pledge, charge or otherwise encumber shares without consent of all shareholders.

☐ Permitted sales and transfers if transferee signs agreement, *i.e.*, to corporation and/or a trust owned or set up by shareholders and/or their families, nominees to qualify to be directors, to spouse or children.

3. *Pre-emptive rights:* Statement of number and class of shares not allotted and that same may only be allotted or allotted and issued in accordance with the agreement. If shares or other securities of the corporation are to be issued, such shares or securities to be allotted to existing shareholder in ratio to existing holdings unless the shareholders unanimously consent otherwise. The mechanics involved in offer and acceptance such as the offer to be made in writing, the time for acceptance, time and place of closing and disposition of shares not taken up within the time limit. The mechanics for embodying pre-emptive rights in either the by-laws and/or the articles of incorporation.

4. *Compulsory buy-sell arrangements of death, permanent disability or retirement:*

(a) Compulsory sale by (i) estate of deceased; (ii) permanently disabled; or

(iii) retirement from active employment, bankruptcy or similar situations and purchased by surviving shareholders or trustees for surviving shareholders.

(b) Determination of sale price, *i.e.*, a base price at time of agreement and formula for adjusting the same upwards or downwards by reference to financial statements of corporation, *i.e.*, earnings over 3 years, etc.

- Date of determination of price, *i.e.*, *preceding financial year end.*
- By whom price determined, *i.e.*, auditors or other independent person capable of applying formula.
- Time and method of paying price, *i.e.*, any releases required, down payment, balance in semi-annual instalments over 5 years interest at __ %.
- Disposition and voting of shares until full price paid.
- Payment into court or other release if estate fails to comply with agreement.

(c) Insurance on life of each shareholder.

- Dollar amount, time of policy, policy numbers, acceptable insurer, location of policy.
- Trustee for receiving proceeds of insurance or other arrangements for receiving such proceeds.
- Obtaining of further insurance-mechanics if a party becomes non-insurable.
- Payments of premiums, primary responsibility, mechanics and rights if paid by other than party primarily responsible.
- Non-encumbering of policies and dedication of same as trust property.

(d) Out clause if all survivors die within specified time, *i.e.*, 1 year. Spread clause if more than one shareholder dies within specified time, *i.e.*, 2 years.

5. *Special voting arrangements:*

(a) cause corporation to comply with agreement and not to record transfers except on compliance with agreement;

(b) nominees on board;

(c) other.

6. *Miscellaneous:*

(a) share certificate to be endorsed that same are subject to agreement;

(b) mechanics of amendments to agreement;

(c) further assurances;

(d) notices, names and postal addresses, methods, *i.e.*, service or mail, time;

(e) errors, etc.;

(f) remedies for non-compliance with agreement, *i.e.*, injunction;

(g) acknowledgement by and consent of corporation to agreement;

(h) governing law; and

(i) time of essence.

The list of provisions that could be included in a shareholders' agreement is not all-inclusive. The instructions as to its preparation and content are given by the lawyer involved, including any special clauses that might have been required for an individual corporation.

Giving pre-emptive rights on the issuance of new shares to all the shareholders is a common method of protection against dilution of a shareholder's interest in the corporation unless such dilution was recognized and agreed to by all the shareholders. This protection would only work, of course, if all the shareholders were financially able to take advantage of this right.

(c) Other Provisions

(i) Share Restrictions

Among the most important features in the agreement are the provisions restricting the transfer, mortgage, pledge or other disposition of shares. It is usual to provide that no such disposition take place except in accordance with the provisions of the agreement or on consent of all shareholders. A note of any such restriction should be made on the share certificates for the corporation.

(ii) Board of Directors

A fairly standard provision in the agreement is to provide for the number and composition of the board of directors. There could also be the right for some of the parties to elect members to the board. The BCA requires that a majority of the board of directors, or if only one or two directors, one or both, must be Canadian citizens resident in Canada (section 118).

(iii) Financing

The lawyer discusses the corporation with the clients in the preliminary stages. In these discussions, decisions are made as to how to meet the financial requirements, the obligations of the shareholders in this area and how the shareholders may restrict borrowing by the corporation. The shareholders may decide to advance money to the corporation through loans, and if so, the terms and conditions of such loans would be clearly set out. There should be an obligation on the part of the corporation to repay the loans by a certain date. If in the future the terms of the loans should prove to be unsatisfactory, the shareholders may make whatever changes in the terms they wish by unanimous consent.

(iv) Employment Contracts

If some of the shareholders will also act as employees of the corporation, even if only on a part-time basis, it may prove prudent to detail in the agreement the functions of these various individuals. If the duties and obligations of the shareholders /employees are set out in the agreement, potential future conflicts among the individuals involved in the corporation may be avoided. Employment contracts are useful in situations where some, but not all, of the shareholders are employees, particularly if an employee is also a minority shareholder. Such a person may find, if things go wrong, that they have not only lost a job but, by operation of the agreement, lost their shares in the corporation without receiving adequate compensation for these shares. Usually employment contracts are separate documents which set out in detail the following:

1. duties to be performed by the employee;
2. amount of time to be devoted to the corporation's business;
3. remuneration and the fringe benefits, if any, to be paid and provided;
4. notice to be given if the employee's services are no longer required; and
5. disposal of shares in the corporation if the employment is terminated; together with any other provisions or terms that might be required in the circumstances.

(v) Corporate Bank Account

It is also important to provide for the establishment of a corporate bank account, to authorize the officers to deal with the bank account and possibly to include a limitation on the borrowing powers of officers and employees in dealing with the bank. Depending on the circumstances, the agreement may provide that cheques or withdrawals in large amounts require two signatures from specific officers while smaller cheques and/or withdrawals can be made by one individual.

(vi) Waiving Appointment of Auditor

There is provision under section 148 of the BCA that certain corporations may waive the appointment of an auditor. This is a fairly common practice in most small non-offering corporations. An auditor would be appointed only if there was some specific reason for this appointment.

(vii) Shareholder Defaults

The agreement should also include specific provisions dealing with what would happen if a shareholder defaulted either in financial obligations assumed or duties which are to be performed for the corporation. These provisions usually include notice of default, an opportunity to correct this default and, in the event the default is not corrected, the offending shareholder is required to transfer the shares in accordance with the terms set out in the shareholders' agreement. Normally the price to be paid for the shares would be the lower of cost or book value and would be paid for by the other shareholders of the corporation. However, if the default occasioned any loss or damage to the corporation or the remaining shareholders, these claims could be deducted from the amount due for the shares.

(d) Miscellaneous Provisions

Various miscellaneous provisions can be included in the agreement which are required for the particular corporation. Some of the more or less standard miscellaneous provisions found in most shareholders' agreements are as follows:

1. *Arbitration Clause*—If a disagreement should arise, an arbitration clause encourages the parties to negotiate reasonably rather than risk the arbitration procedures.

2. *Notice Provision*—This is required in order to implement the buy-sell, default and any other similar terms in the agreement.

3. *Nominees*—If some of the directors are nominees of the shareholders, it is important to ensure they act responsibly and in accordance with the provisions of the agreement.

4. *Amendments*—Any amendments to the terms of the agreement shall only be made in writing.

Again, depending upon the circumstances, there may be any number of additional miscellaneous provisions that should be included in the agreement.

As mentioned earlier, the lawyer will discuss all of the matters to be included in the shareholders' agreement with the client or clients and select the provisions to be included in the agreement.

3. Unanimous Shareholder Agreements

The BCA contains the concept of a unanimous shareholder agreement, borrowed from the *Canada Business Corporations Act*, R.S.C. 1985, c. C.44 (''CBCA''). Section 146 of the Act provides that the written agreement may be made:

1. between two or more shareholders and may provide that the voting rights of shares held by them shall be voted according to the agreement;
2. among all the shareholders or among all the shareholders of a corporation and one or more other persons who are not shareholders and may restrict, in whole or in part, the powers of the directors to manage the business and the affairs of the corporation; and
3. by a person who is the beneficial owner of all issued shares of a corporation. The written agreement is in the form of declaration and may restrict in whole or in part the management and supervisory powers of the directors.

Provided notice of a unanimous shareholder agreement is noted conspicuously on the share certificate, a transferee of such shares shall be deemed to be a party to the agreement. Although a transferee of shares is covered, there is no mention of shares issued after the agreement has been signed by the existing shareholders. The holders of any shares of the corporation, whether they are voting or non-voting, must also be added as parties to the agreement. Failure to add these individuals could invalidate a unanimous shareholder agreement since the BCA requires all shareholders to be parties of the written agreement.

In addition to voting rights and restriction of the powers of directors, the written agreement may provide for the amending of the agreement and the appointment of an arbitrator if the parties to the agreement are unable to agree on or resolve any matter. The statute does not indicate whether or not this section applies only to unanimous shareholder agreements executed after the proclamation of the BCA. It may be advisable to review any existing shareholder agreements dated before July 29, 1983, to see if they could be interpreted as unanimous shareholder agreements. If this interpretation could be made, then the shareholders may be liable for the liabilities of the directors if the shareholder agreement restricts or limits the powers of the directors or their freedom to make decisions regarding the management of the business.

Subsection 108(5) provides that a shareholder who is a party to a unanimous shareholder agreement has all the rights, powers, duties and liabilities of a director of the corporation arising under this Act or otherwise. These rights and obligations are limited to the extent the agreement restricts the discretion or powers of the directors to manage or supervise the management of the business and affairs of the corporation. There are several sections or subsections of the Act which are specifically made subject to the provisions of any unanimous shareholder agreement:

1. the duties of the directors (subsection 115(1));
2. designation of the offices and officers of the corporation by the directors (section 133); and
3. the right of the directors to fix their remuneration and the remuneration of officers and employees of the corporation (section 137).

A unanimous shareholder agreement is an effective method of reserving to the shareholders certain areas of the decision-making process normally exercised by the directors. Such an agreement would be particularly useful in the case of a foreign corporation owning a Canadian subsidiary. The shareholder in this situation might, for example, want to control the decisions concerning salaries, the appointment of officers and any financing that might be needed by the corporation in the future.

If a unanimous shareholder agreement is executed, the directors of the corporation should be informed of its existence and the limits on their discretion and powers. Alternatively, as provided in the Act, the directors could be made parties to the unanimous shareholder agreement. The latter method would of necessity include any replacement directors and this may prove to be impractical in some circumstances.

Depending on the practice in law offices, this may, or may not, prove to be an important provision of the Act. In some offices a unanimous shareholder agreement may be common practice. In other offices the preparation of such an agreement would be a rarity.

9

ARTICLES OF AMENDMENT

1. Introduction

Prior to the drafting of the articles of incorporation the solicitor involved will have given very careful consideration to all of the various areas included in articles of incorporation. When interviewing the individuals involved in a new corporation, the solicitor attempts to find out not only what their current intentions are but any possible plans for the future. For example, information is elicited from the clients as to the business to be carried on initially by the corporation and also any other business that might possibly be carried on at some time in the future. By adopting this problem prevention approach, the solicitor attempts to prevent the necessity of applying for Articles of Amendment which would be required if any of the provisions of the articles of incorporation had to be changed. (See Form 9.1.)

2. Fundamental Changes

When a change of name is involved, it is necessary to search the new name and to file with the Articles of Amendment a computer printed name search report obtained from a private search house and produced by the NUANS system. The report must be dated not more than 90 days prior to the delivery of the articles. Names and addresses of private search houses are listed in telephone directories. The following searchouses were included in Chapter 5 ("The Act of Incorporation"):

1. Dye & Durham Co. Inc. (*www.dyedurham.ca*),
2. Cyberbahn Inc., and
3. OnCorp. Direct Inc.

Section 171 of the BCA provides that the Articles of Amendment shall not change the name or decrease the authorized or issued capital of the corporation if it is insolvent or if the amendment would render the corporation insolvent.

Section 168 of the BCA provides that subject to sections 170 and 171, a corporation may amend its articles to add, change or remove any provision that is permitted by this Act. This includes, without limiting the generality of the foregoing:

(a) change its name;

(b) [repealed S.O. 1994, c. 27, s. 71(20)];

(c) add, change or remove any restriction upon the business or businesses that the corporation may carry on or upon the powers that the corporation may exercise;

(d) add, change or remove any maximum number of shares that the corporation is authorized to issue or any maximum consideration for which any shares of the corporation are authorized to be issued;

(e) create new classes of shares;

(f) [repealed S.O. 1994, c. 27, s. 71(20)];

(g) change the designation of all or any of its shares, and add, change or remove any rights, privileges, restrictions and conditions, including rights to accrued dividends, in respect of all or any of its shares, whether issued or unissued;

(h) change the shares of any class or series, whether issued or unissued, into a different number of shares of the same class or series or into the same or a different number of shares of other classes or series;

(i) divide a class of shares, whether issued or unissued, into series and fix the number of shares in each series and the rights, privileges, restrictions and conditions thereof;

(j) authorize the directors to divide any class of unissued shares into series and fix the number of share in each series and the rights, privileges, restrictions and conditions thereof;

(k) authorize the directors to change the rights, privileges, restrictions and conditions attached to unissued shares of any series;

(l) revoke, diminish or enlarge any authority conferred under clauses (j) and (k);

(m) subject to sections 120 and 125, increase or decrease the number, or minimum or maximum number, of directors; and

(n) add, change or remove restrictions on the issue, transfer or ownership of shares of any class or series.

Effective on proclamation of the *Business Corporations Act, 1982* on July 29, 1983, until January 1, 1987, a change in the registered or head office of a corporation required Articles of Amendment. The latter date was the proclamation date of the *Business Corporations Amendment Act, 1986* which changed the requirement from Articles of Amendment to a special resolution to effect a change of registered or head office from one municipality to another municipality in Ontario. A special resolution is a resolution passed by the directors and either submitted to the shareholders at a meeting called to consider and pass the resolution or passed by consent in writing of all shareholders entitled to vote at a meeting.

Subsection 1(1) defines a ''special resolution'' as a resolution either:

(a) submitted to a special meeting of the shareholders of a corporation duly called for the purpose of considering the resolution and passed, with or without amendment, at the meeting, by at least two-thirds of the votes cast; or

(b) consented to in writing by each shareholder of the corporation entitled to vote at such a meeting or the shareholder's attorney authorized in writing

Subsection 104(1) states, with two exceptions, that a resolution in writing signed by all the shareholders entitled to vote on that resolution is as valid as if it had been passed at a meeting of shareholders. The change of the registered or head office may be effected by a resolution in writing. If the change of location is within a municipality, the change may be effected by a directors' resolution (s. 14(3)).

A sample of Form 3, Articles of Amendment, prescribed under the Regulations to the BCA, is shown as Form 9.1. Included in this sample is a form of resolution authorizing a change of name which is acceptable under the BCA.

In addition to the Articles of Amendment in duplicate and a name search report, if required, a filing fee must be paid at the time the Articles of Amendment are filed with the Companies Branch. The current fee is listed in Appendix B. The cheque must be made payable to the Minister of Finance and the name of the corporation must be set out on the face of the cheque.

When the Articles of Amendment are received by the Companies Branch, the documents are checked in accordance with a BCA Deficiency Notice. Provided that all the required documents, executed in accordance with the Act, and the prescribed fees have been received, a certificate of amendment shall be endorsed on the Articles of Amendment. This certificate sets out the day, month and year of endorsement, the corporation number and amends the articles of incorporation effective on the date shown in the certificate.

Section 172 states the Director upon receipt of Articles of Amendment shall endorse a certificate of amendment in accordance with section 273. This latter section sets out the specific requirements for execution, and the filing of the copies submitted.

Section 240 of the BCA authorizes cancellation of certificates by the Director for "sufficient cause". This term is defined as:

(a) failure to comply with subsection 115(2) governing the minimum number of directors required or subsection 118(3), the Canadian residency requirement for directors;

(b) a conviction of the corporation for an offence under the *Criminal Code* (Canada) or any other federal statute or an offence as defined in the *Provincial Offences Act*, in circumstances where cancellation of the certificate is in the public interest; or

(c) conduct described in subsection 248(2) as oppressive or unfairly prejudicial.

In view of the provisions of this section, it would be advisable to ensure that all filings under the *Corporations Information Act* are up to date prior to submitting the Articles of Amendment to the Companies Branch. The default could include an Initial Return or Notice of Change. Beginning in January 2000, when the filing requirements changed, an Annual Return must also be filed.

The section goes on to state that cancellation of a certificate of incorporation or any other certificate takes effect on the date fixed in the Order. In the case of other certificates, *i.e.*, Articles of Amendment, the amendment applied for and which became effective on the issuance of the certificate ends on the specified date in the Order.

10

Annual Meetings

1. Requirements

The *Business Corporations Act* requires under section 94 that a corporation shall hold an annual meeting of its shareholders not later than 18 months after its incorporation and subsequently not more than 15 months after the holding of the last preceding annual meeting. At such meeting, any shareholders shall have an opportunity to raise any matter relevant to the affairs and business of the corporation.

Section 104 of the BCA, while riot specifically mentioning a single shareholder corporation, states that a resolution in writing:

> (a) . . . signed by all the shareholders entitled to vote on that resolution at a meeting of shareholders is as valid as if it had been passed at a meeting of shareholders; and
>
> (b) . . . dealing with all matters required by this Act to be dealt with at a meeting of shareholders, and signed by all shareholders entitled to vote at that meeting, satisfies all the requirements of this Act relating to that meeting of shareholders.

Presumably the provisions of this section would govern in the corporations with only one shareholder where a decision was made to use resolutions rather than prepare minutes of a meeting There is provision under subsection 101(4) that a single shareholder, or one holder of any class or series of shares, present in person or by proxy constitutes a meeting. Minutes could be prepared if that is the preferred practice in a law office.

(a) Notice of Meetings

Section 96 of the BCA requires notice of not less than 21 days for offering corporations and not less than ten days for any other corporations. The maximum notice in all cases is 50 days. The Act also specifies that notice must be given to each shareholder entitled to vote at the meeting, to each director and to the auditor of the corporation.

(b) Record Date

Section 95 of the BCA states that the record date for determining shareholders entitled to receive notice of a meeting fixed by the directors shall be not less than 21 days or more than 50 days preceding the date of the meeting. If the directors fail to fix such a record date, the record date to determine the shareholders entitled to receive notice shall be the close of the business on the day before the date on which the notice is given. If no notice is given, the record date is the day on which the meeting is held.

The record date for determining shareholders for any other purpose required under the Act, except for notice of a meeting or to vote, shall be the close of business on the date on which the directors pass the resolution.

The minimum and maximum time limits for notice to both offering and non-offering corporations are set out above under "(a) Notice of Meetings".

Subsection 154(3) of the BCA requires that the financial statements are to be sent to each shareholder, except shareholders who have informed the corporation in writing that they do not wish to receive a copy of the financial statements. Financial statements must be sent to the shareholders not less than 21 days for offering corporations and ten days for non-offering corporations prior to the annual meeting or the signing of resolutions in lieu of the meeting.

Subject to the Act, the articles or by-laws of a corporation or a unanimous shareholder agreement, section 97 of the BCA states the following:

(a) All questions proposed for the consideration of the shareholders shall be determined by a majority vote at a meeting of shareholders. The chair presiding at the meeting shall not have a second or casting vote in the case of an equality of votes.

(b) The chair of the meeting may with the consent of the meeting, and subject to any conditions the meeting may impose, adjourn the meeting from time to time and from place to place subject to subsections 96(3) and (4).

(c) The president or, in his or her absence, a vice-president who is a director, shall preside as chair of the meeting of shareholders.

However, if there is no president or such a vice-president or if neither is present within 15 minutes after the time appointed for the holding of the meeting, the shareholders present shall choose a person from their number to be the chair.

(d) Unless the ballot is demanded, an entry in the minutes of a meeting of shareholders to the effect that the chair declared a motion to be carried is sufficient proof of the fact without proof of the number or proportion of votes recorded in favour of or against the motion (subsection 103(3)).

(c) Place of Meetings

Section 93 of the BCA states that subject to the articles and any unanimous shareholder agreement, a meeting of shareholders of the corporation shall be held at such place in or outside Ontario as the directors determine. In the absence of such determination, a meeting of shareholders shall be held at the place where the registered office (head office) of the corporation is located.

(d) Voting Rights

Section 102 of the BCA states that each share of a corporation entitles the holder to one vote at a meeting of shareholders, unless the articles provide otherwise. A body corporate or association who is a shareholder of the corporation shall by resolution of its directors or governing body appoint an individual as its representative at meetings of shareholders. This authorized individual can exercise all of the powers such body corporate or association could exercise if it were an individual shareholder.

Where two or more persons hold the same share or shares jointly, any one of such persons present at a meeting of shareholders has the right in the absence of the other or others to vote in respect of such share or shares. However, if more than one of such persons is present or represented by proxy, they shall vote together as one the share or shares jointly held by them (subsection 102(4).

(e) Proxy

Section 109 of the BCA defines "form of proxy" to mean "a written or printed form that, upon completion and execution by or on behalf of a shareholder, becomes a proxy". A "proxy" means a completed and executed form in writing in which a shareholder has appointed a person as his, her or its nominee to attend and act on that person's behalf at a meeting of shareholders. A proxy is used when a shareholder is unable to be personally present at a meeting but wants to exercise his, her or its right to vote at that meeting.

Section 110 of the BCA provides that every shareholder, including a shareholder that is a body corporate, entitled to vote at a meeting of shareholders may by means of a proxy appoint a person, not necessarily a shareholder, as his, her or its nominee to attend and act at the meeting in the manner, to the extent and with the power conferred by the proxy A proxy shall be signed by the shareholder or by the shareholder's attorney authorized in writing. If the shareholder is a body corporate, the proxy must be signed by an officer or attorney thereof duly authorized by the corporation. The proxy ceases to be valid one year from its date. A proxy may be revoked in writing by the shareholder or by the shareholder's attorney authorized in writing. The revocation of the proxy must be deposited either at the registered office of the corporation prior to the meeting, or any adjournment thereof, at which the proxy is to be used, or with the chairman of such meeting. The directors may by resolution fix a time not exceeding 48 hours, excluding Saturdays and holidays, preceding any meeting or adjourned meeting of shareholders, before which time the proxies to be used at that meeting must be deposited with the corporation or an agent thereof. This information must be set out in the notice calling the meeting.

(f) Special Business

Subsection 96(5) of the BCA defines ''special business'' at an annual meeting of shareholders to be any business transacted other than:

1. consideration of the minutes of an earlier meeting;
2. consideration of the financial statements and auditor's report;
3. election of directors; or
4. reappointment of the incumbent auditor.

If special business is to be conducted at the annual meeting the notice shall state the nature of the special business in sufficient detail to permit the shareholder to form a reasoned judgment. If a special resolution or by-law is to be submitted to the meeting, the text of the special resolution or by-law must accompany the notice. This provision for, and definition of, special business did not exist prior to the coming into force of the present BCA.

The foregoing sets out the general requirements for meetings of shareholders including notice, record dates and proxies.

(g) Minutes or Resolutions

The usual practice is to prepare annual minutes for all corporations with more than one shareholder. Resolutions are used to deal with the usual matters covered at annual meetings for single shareholder corporations incorporated under the BCA. This practice will probably continue for single shareholder corporations incorporated under the Act despite the provisions of subsection 101(4) that one shareholder constitutes a meeting

Subsection 96(5) provides that all business transacted either at a special or annual meeting of shareholders shall be deemed to be special business except for the routine matters which are considered at all annual meetings. The notice of the annual meeting mailed to the shareholders sets out the various matters to be dealt with and provides in the last item for ''any other business that may properly come before the meeting''. In the normal non-offering corporation the waivers of notice and the minutes are prepared in the law office and then forwarded to the client for signature and the insertion of dates or other information required. A similar procedure is followed for resolutions in a single shareholder corporation.

Again, there are various approaches to the handling of annual resolutions (or annual maintenance as it is sometimes called). It is necessary to find out what the practice is in a particular office and, at times, even the practice of particular lawyers within an office. Larger law offices are attempting to standardize the handling of these annual resolutions or minutes.

2. Minutes and Resolutions

(a) Preliminary Directors' Meetings

The average Ontario non-offering corporation holds a preliminary directors' meeting, primarily to approve the financial statements for presentation to the shareholders. This meeting is followed by the annual meeting of the shareholders of the corporation. Immediately following the annual meeting of shareholders, at which the directors of the corporation are elected in addition to the other matters usually considered, the directors meet and elect the officers for the ensuing year. If there are any other matters which require action of the directors, they are included in this meeting Alternatively, if resolutions, rather than minutes, are to be used, there will be three individual sets of resolutions with the time of passing noted so a proper sequence is easily determined by anyone reviewing the minute book.

A corporation shall not, under section 159 of the BCA, issue, publish or circulate copies of the financial statements unless they meet the requirements under subsection (1) and, if required, are accompanied by the report of the auditor of the corporation. The directors are required to approve the financial statements and this must be evidenced by the signatures of two directors at the bottom of the balance sheet. In a single director corporation, that director must sign the balance sheet. A typical format for such approval could be:

APPROVED BY THE DIRECTORS:

____

Director

____

Director

This requirement under the BCA may create difficulties for auditors and their clients. Auditors often prepare and send to their clients draft copies of financial statements for discussion purposes prior to preparation and release of finalized statements. Although intended for internal use only, these draft statements could on occasion be circulated to others, perhaps even a bank if a request for a loan or an extension of credit had been made. It may be that such actions would contravene the provisions of the Act.

Minutes or resolutions of the preliminary meeting of directors would be prepared for corporations with multiple directors and shareholders and include:

1. setting out the name, location of the meeting (head office or address where the meeting will be held), the city, date and time;
2. setting out the names of the persons present at the meeting;
3. appointing a chairman and secretary of the meeting;
4. stating that the meeting is properly constituted for the transaction of business and that a quorum is present;
5. approving the minutes of the last meeting of directors held prior to this meeting;
6. approving the financial statement and authorizing the particular directors who will sign the balance sheet to evidence this approval;
7. adjourning the meeting until immediately after the annual meeting of shareholders; and
8. adding signature lines and inserting the titles of chairman and secretary below the signature lines.

A consent and waiver of notice must be prepared for signature by the directors present at the meeting waiving the required notice of the calling of the meeting, and any adjournment thereof, as required under the by-laws of the corporation. The form would include the consent of the directors to the transaction of such business as may come before the meeting.

(b) Annual Meeting of Shareholders

The minutes or resolutions of the annual meeting of shareholders include routine and other matters set out in the formal notice sent to all the shareholders. These routine matters would be covered if the format below is followed:

1. Set out the name of the corporation, the location of the meeting, the city, date and time.
2. Set out the names of the shareholders who are present, either in person or represented by proxy.
3. Appoint a chairman and secretary of the meeting.
4. State that the meeting is properly constituted for the transaction of business and that a quorum of the shareholders is present.

5. Approve the minutes of the last meeting of shareholders held prior to this annual meeting
6. Approve the financial statements and auditor's report, if applicable. Section 154 of the BCA requires that the financial statement for a non-offering corporation shall be for the period that commenced immediately after the end of the last financial year and which ended not more than six months before the annual meeting. If the annual meeting is not held within the required time period, new financial statements may be required. If the financial statements are beyond this time period, it should be drawn to the lawyer's attention and instructions obtained as to procedure to be followed.
7. Elect the directors of the corporation.
8. Appoint the auditor or accountant, depending on the circumstances.
9. Generally confirm all acts taken on behalf of the corporation by the directors and officers. This practice is followed in many offices but there are some law offices which omit this paragraph from the minutes of the annual meeting of shareholders. The procedure to be followed would be decided in consultation with the principal or the accepted office practice would prevail.
10. Adjourn the meeting
11. Add signature lines and insert the titles chairman and secretary below signature lines.

A form of consent and waiver of notice, similar to the form prepared for signature by the directors at the first meeting, should be prepared for the signatures of the shareholders waiving the required notice under the by-laws of the calling of the annual meeting and consenting to the transaction of the business that came before the meeting.

In addition, if the shareholders wish to exempt the corporation from audit requirements, the appropriate form of consent must be prepared and signed.

Many law firms prepare a consent and waiver of notice for signature by the auditor if one has been appointed by the corporation.

(c) Adjourned/Reconvened Preliminary Directors' Meeting

The chairman of the preliminary meeting of directors reconvenes the meeting which had been adjourned to permit the holding of the annual meeting of shareholders. The minutes or resolutions prepared for this adjourned meeting of the directors should:

1. recite that the meeting is an adjourned meeting of directors and set out again the name of the corporation, the address where the meeting is being held, the city, date and time;

2. show the directors present and confirm that a quorum is present;
3. include a recital that the chairman and secretary of this adjourned meeting are the same as those in the first meeting of directors;
4. recite that the meeting is properly constituted and had been adjourned to permit the holding of the annual meeting of shareholders;
5. elect the officers of the corporation;
6. adjourn the meeting; and
7. add the necessary signature lines and insert the titles chairman and secretary below such signature lines.

It is not necessary to prepare any additional forms of consent and waiver of notice since the forms prepared earlier included any possible adjournments of either the annual meeting of shareholders or an adjournment of the meeting of board of directors.

3. Sole Director/Sole Shareholder Resolutions

The accepted practice for sole director and sole shareholder corporations is to deal with the matters outlined above by resolution, rather than minutes. Despite the provision of subsection 126(12), which states that one director may constitute a meeting, it is probable that this practice will continue. In these circumstances, the following resolutions would be appropriate:

1. prepare a director's resolution approving the financial statements for presentation to the shareholder and authorizing the director to sign the balance sheet.
2. prepare resolutions of the sole shareholders as follows:
   (a) approval of financial statements;
   (b) election of director;
   (c) waiver of audit and appointment of accountants; or appointment of an auditor;
   (d) confirmation of all acts of the director and officers of the corporation. This resolution is optional depending on the practice in the particular law office.
3. sole director's resolution electing the officers or officer of the corporation for the ensuing year.

The resolutions of the sole director shown above under numbers 1 and 3 would be prepared on separate sheets of minute paper with the usual confirmation clause, date and signature line. These resolutions and the sole shareholder's resolutions would be timed in sequence to establish the order in which they were passed.

4. Sole Director/Multiple Shareholder Resolutions

Where a corporation has a sole director and multiple shareholders, minutes should be prepared for an annual meeting of shareholders. However, the sole director can pass resolutions to approve the financial statements and elect the officers of the corporation for the ensuing year. Again, there is a variety of approaches depending on the law office involved and some lawyers prefer to prepare resolutions for signature by the shareholders as well as the sole director. It will be necessary to check which procedure is followed in a particular law office.

Forms 10.1 to 10.2 show minutes of meetings of the directors and the shareholders based on the format set out above.

Form 10.3 is an alternative set up for an annual meeting of shareholders where the corporation is exempt from audit provisions and Form 10.4 shows an alternative for shareholders represented by proxy.

Form 10.5 shows minutes of an adjourned meeting of the directors.

Forms 10.6 to 10.9 show a format for a sole director/multiple shareholder corporation.

5. Auditors

Sections 148 to 160 of the BCA outline the duties and responsibilities of auditors and the requirements for financial statements. Reference will be made here only to the sections which deal with matters which normally come before an annual meeting of shareholders.

(a) Exemptions from Audit Provisions

As mentioned in the discussion dealing with the organization of a new corporation, where the shareholders of a corporation consent in writing, the corporation in a financial year is exempt from appointing an auditor. Listed below are the requirements under the BCA which must be met if a corporation is to be exempt:

- ☐ non-offering corporation
- ☐ all shareholders consent, no restriction on number (but must not exceed 50 as required under *Securities Act*)

Section 149 of the Act provides that the shareholders of a corporation at their first annual or special meeting shall appoint one or more auditors to hold office until the close of the first or next annual meeting The directors are authorized to make this appointment if the shareholders fail to do so. This matter was outlined in the organizational resolutions for a new corporation.

Subsection 149(2) provides that the shareholder shall at each annual meeting appoint one or more auditors to hold office until the close of the next annual meeting. If an appointment is not made, the auditor in office continues until a successor is appointed.

Should a casual vacancy arise in the office of auditor, the directors may fill such vacancy. So long as the vacancy continues, the surviving or continuing auditor, if any, may act, as stated under subsection 149(3).

The shareholders may, under subsection 149(4), by a resolution passed by a majority of the votes cast at a special meeting duly called for the purpose, remove an auditor before the expiration of the auditor's term of office. The shareholders shall by a majority of the votes cast at that meeting appoint another auditor as replacement for the remainder of the term. If the shareholders intend to remove the auditor before the expiry of the term, it is required under subsection 149(5) that the corporation must give written notice to the auditor at least 15 days or more before the mailing of the notice of the meeting. In addition, a copy of all material proposed to be sent to the shareholders in connection with the meeting must be supplied to the auditor. These provisions also apply if the incumbent auditor is not being reappointed.

The auditor has a right under subsection (6) of this section to make representations in writing to the corporation three or more days before the mailing of the notice of the meeting concerning:

(a) the auditor's proposed removal as auditor;

(b) the appointment or election of another person to fill the office of auditor; or

(c) the auditor's resignation as auditor.

At the corporation's expense, the notice of the meeting and a copy of any such representation shall be forwarded to each shareholder entitled to receive notice of the meeting

Subsection 149(7) provides that the remuneration of an auditor appointed by the shareholders shall be fixed by the shareholders, or by the directors if they are authorized to do so by the shareholders. The remuneration of an auditor appointed by the directors shall be fixed by the directors.

The corporation is required, under subsection 149(9), to give notice in writing to an auditor of his or her appointment forthwith after the appointment is made. While there is no requirement to notify an accountant of his or her appointment under the Act, the corporation would likely do so.

(b) Persons Prohibited

Section 152 of the BCA stresses that a person is disqualified from being an auditor of the corporation if he or she is not *independent* of the corporation, all of its affiliates, or of the directors or officers of the corporation and its affiliates. Under subsection 152(2)(b) a person is deemed not to be independent if he or she or his or her business partner is involved in business dealings with the corporation or any of its affiliates or acts as a director, officer or employee thereof. The Act also states a person is disqualified from being an auditor if he or she owns directly or indirectly or controls a material interest in the securities of the corporation or has been involved in an official capacity in either insolvency or bankruptcy proceedings of the corporation or its affiliates within two years of the proposed appointment as auditor. The term "material interest" is not defined.

(c) Auditor's Report

The auditor is required to make a report to the shareholders on the financial statements which will be presented at the annual meeting of the corporation during his or her term of office. The auditor shall state in the report whether in his or her opinion the financial statements fairly present the financial position of the corporation and the results of its operation for the period under review in accordance with generally accepted accounting principles, commonly referred to as "GAAP". Under subsection 153(1) of the Act the auditor is required to make such examination as will enable the making of this report to the shareholders.

(d) Right to Attend Meetings

Under subsection 151(1) of the Act the auditor has the right to attend any meeting of shareholders of the corporation and to receive all notices and other communications relating to any such meeting, that the shareholders are entitled to receive. The auditor is also entitled to attend at the corporation's expense and to be heard at any such meeting on any matters at the business meeting relating to the auditor's duties.

(e) Amending Auditor's Report

There are also provisions under section 153 of the BCA which deal with amending the auditor's report if facts are discovered after the statement has been prepared, and various other related matters. The subsections referred to above are relevant to the preparation of minutes of the annual meeting of shareholders or, in the case of a single director, the resolutions covering the matters normally dealt with at such an annual meeting.

Subsection 151(7) provides that any oral or written statement or report made by either the auditor or the former auditor of the corporation has qualified privilege. The term ''qualified privilege'' means that a person (the auditor) is not liable, unless negligent or guilty of malice, for statements made in the course of performing his or her duties, or for reports made or actions taken. This qualified privilege, to some extent, protects the auditor against libel and slander and, at the same time it permits him or her to effectively discharge all duties by being quite open and candid in all written and oral communications with the shareholders, directors, officers and employees of the corporation and with a successor auditor. The auditor would be liable if proved negligent in the performance of his or her duties.

6. Financial Statements

Section 155 of the BCA states that the financial statements required under this Act shall be prepared as in accordance with the regulations and GAAP

A provision under the Act in this area is the requirement under section 156 regarding offering (public) corporations. The Ontario *Securities Act*, R.S.O. 1990, c. S.5, Part XVIII, requires offering corporations to file financial statements with the Ontario Securities Commission. This demand to file financial statements is repeated in the BCA.

Section 157 demands that true copies of the latest financial statements of each subsidiary of a holding corporation shall be retained at the registered office (head office) of the holding corporation. Shareholders of the holding corporation, their agents and legal representatives, may on request during normal business hours make extracts from these financial records at no charge. A corporation has 15 days after receipt of a request to apply to a court for an order barring the right of any person to examine the financial records. If the court decides to grant the application, the order may bar the right, together with any other remedy that the court considers suitable in the circumstances.

11

Extra-Provincial Corporations

1. Introduction

The *Extra-Provincial Corporations Act, 1984*, S.O. 1984, c. 14 [now the *Extra-Provincial Corporations Act*, R.S.O. 1990, c. E.27] (''EPCA'') repealed Part VIII of the *Corporations Act* which formerly governed the registration of corporations incorporated outside Ontario that wanted to carry on business here. Some of the highlights of the legislation are:

- ☐ corporations incorporated in Canada are exempt from licensing requirements;
- ☐ restrictions on the use in Ontario of names of corporations incorporated outside the province;
- ☐ corporations incorporated outside Canada that decide to carry on business in Ontario must obtain an extra-provincial licence;
- ☐ corporations governed by this Act are divided into three classes.

Regulations made under this Act, issued as R.R.O. 1990, Reg. 365, as amended, set out the prescribed forms that must be filed by applicants.

2. Classes of Extra-Provincial Corporations

Subsection 2(1) of the EPCA divides all corporations into three classes:

Class 1. Corporations incorporated or continued by or under the authority of an Act of a legislature of a province of Canada.

Class 2. Corporations incorporated or continued by or under the authority of an Act of the Parliament of Canada or of the legislature of a territory of Canada.

Class 3. Corporations incorporated or continued under the laws of a jurisdiction outside of Canada.

Corporations incorporated under an ordinance of the Northwest Territories or of Nunavut but governed by the corporate laws of a province of Canada are included in Class 1 (subsection 2(2)).

Subject to the terms of this statute, the *Corporations Information Act* and any other Act, an extra-provincial corporation in Classes 1 and 2 may carry on business in Ontario without a licence. Such extra-provincial corporations must file an Initial Return, Form 2, under the Corporations Information within 60 days of commencing business in Ontario. Effective April 1, 2000, Companies Branch policy required that the Initial Return be accompanied with a photocopy of the page of the most recent Articles, containing the correct name and incorporation/amalgamation date, filed with the jurisdiction to which the corporation is subject.

Only corporations incorporated under the laws of a foreign jurisdiction (*i.e.*, any other country in the world) must obtain an extra-provincial licence to do business in Ontario (see Form 11.1). Subsection 4(2) of the Act states that an agent or representative of such an extra-provincial corporation cannot carry on any of its business unless the corporation has a licence.

Every non-Canadian corporation licensed under the Act must under section 19 ensure the continuing appointment of an agent for service in Ontario. This agent must be an Ontario resident aged 18 or older or a corporation having its head or registered office in Ontario. The appointment is made by filing the prescribed Form 2, Appointment of Agent for Service/Revised Appointment for Service (see Form 11.2). This is a dual form used on the original appointment and for notifying the public of any changes in any of the particulars set out in that document. Subsection 19(3) requires the filing forthwith of a revised appointment in the prescribed form where, for example, the agent's address changes or a new agent is substituted. A Class 3 extra-provincial corporation that has not obtained a licence or appointed an agent for service cannot, under section 21, maintain an action in Ontario courts. When the default is corrected, the action may proceed in the courts as if such default had been corrected before the institution of the court action or other proceeding. Section 20 of the Act provides penalties for persons or corporations who contravene this Act, its regulations or a condition of a licence. Failure to comply with an order or direction made under the Act or its regulations may give rise to fines as well. On conviction a person is liable for a fine to a maximum of $2,000 and a corporation to a fine not to exceed $25,000.

If a non-Canadian, or Class 3, extra-provincial corporation

- ☐ changes its name,
- ☐ is ordered to change its name under section 11 of this Act, or
- ☐ is continued under the laws of another jurisdiction,

then it must under subsection 12(1) apply for an amended licence, using prescribed Form 3, Application for Amended Extra-Provincial licence (see Form 11.3).

Subsection 12(2) states that when a Class 3 extra-provincial corporation has not carried on any of its business in Ontario for two consecutive years, it shall terminate its licence by filing prescribed Form 4, Application for Termination of Extra-Provincial Licence (see Form 11.4). The Director has the power under this subsection to order the cancellation of the licence after giving the extra-provincial corporation an opportunity to be heard.

In addition the Director has the power under section 7 to cancel the licence of a Class 3 non-Canadian corporation for sufficient cause after the corporation has had an opportunity to be heard. The term "sufficient cause" in this section includes:

(a) failure to pay any prescribed fee;

(b) failure to comply with section 19;

(c) failure to comply with a filing requirement under the *Corporations Information Act*,

(d) a conviction . . . under the *Criminal Code* (Canada) or . . . the *Provincial Offences Act* whereby cancellation of the licence is in the public interest.

Section 22 of this Act provides that every corporation that is

- ☐ within Class 1 or 2,
- ☐ a licensed Class 3 corporation under this Act, or
- ☐ exempt from licensing under this Act,

has the power to acquire, hold and convey any land or interest in land in Ontario necessary for its actual use and occupation or for carrying on its business.

Prior to March 1, 1985, the proclamation date of the EPCA, licences had been issued to foreign or non-Canadian corporations under Part VIII of the *Corporations Act* (or a predecessor thereof). Licences were also issued to extra-provincial corporations incorporated in other provincial jurisdictions in Canada under the same legislation. Section 23 of the EPCA provides that licences issued to non-Canadian corporations under Part VIII of the *Corporations Act*, or a predecessor statute:

- ☐ remain in effect and are deemed to have been endorsed under this Act;
- ☐ restrict the powers of these extra-provincial corporations to the extent set out in the licences; and
- ☐ retain the previously appointed attorney for service who must operate under the relevant provisions of this Act.

All other extra-provincial licences issued under Part VIII of the *Corporations Act* (or a predecessor thereof) were cancelled on the day this section came into force.

Subsection 24(1) provides that references in other statutes to an extra-provincial corporation, unless the context otherwise requires, are deemed to refer to extra-provincial corporations under this Act. A reference to an extra-provincial corporation that is licensed or required to be licensed under Part VIII of the *Corporations Act* means a Class 1 or Class 3 corporation under this Act.

Subsection 24(2) states that where a Class 1 or Class 2 corporation would, if licensed under this Act, receive a benefit or exemption under another statute, that corporation shall be deemed to have a licence for the purpose of the other statute or Act.

The initial decision to be made is whether or not the extra-provincial corporation is, in fact, carrying on business in Ontario. The definition of extra-provincial corporation in this Act includes a corporation, with or without share capital, incorporated or continued otherwise than by or under the authority of an Act of the Legislative Assembly of Ontario (subsection 1(1)). An extra-provincial corporation is deemed, for the purposes of this Act, to carry on its business in Ontario if:

- ☐ it has a resident agent, representative, warehouse, office or place of business in Ontario;
- ☐ it holds an interest in or owns real property in Ontario, otherwise than by way of security;
- ☐ it otherwise carries on its business in Ontario (subsection 1(2)).

An extra-provincial corporation does not carry on business in Ontario by reason that:

- ☐ it takes orders for or buys or sells goods, wares and merchandise, or
- ☐ it offers or sells services of any type

through the use of travellers or through advertising or correspondence (subsection 1(3)).

3. Name Clearance

Once it has been decided that the extra-provincial corporation falls within the definition of carrying on business in this Act, the next step is to check its corporate name to see if it can be used in Ontario. There is no informal pre-clearance of names of extra-provincial corporations available. Under the BCA the onus is on incorporators to check the availability of the proposed corporate name. The responsibility for checking the corporate name for use in Ontario is assumed by the corporation that wants to do business in Ontario, provided it falls within the Class 1 definition in this Act.

A Class 2 corporation, that is a federal corporation, has the right by federal statute to carry on business in any province in Canada under its corporate name.

A Class 3 corporation, that is a foreign or non-Canadian corporation, is required under Reg. 365 to file an original NUANS Ontario-biased search report, dated not more than 90 days prior to the submission date of the application for an extra-provincial licence (see Chapter 13, heading 3.(a) for more on the NUANS system).

It would be advisable for *all* extra-provincial corporations to order a NUANS Search Report in order to avoid the possibility of contravening the provisions of section 10 of this Act. This section sets out certain prohibitions on the use of a name in Ontario, for example:

- ☐ it cannot contain a word or expression prohibited by the regulations;
- ☐ it cannot be the same or similar to the name of a known body corporate, trust, association, partnership, sole proprietorship or individual, whether in existence or not, if the use of the name would be likely to deceive;
- ☐ it cannot be the same or similar to a name or business style by which any of the above forms of business ownership identifies itself to the public, if the use of the name would be likely to deceive; or
- ☐ it must meet the requirements prescribed by the regulations.

Section 11 provides that the Director may, after giving the extra-provincial corporation an opportunity to be heard, order it to cease using a name that is contrary to the provisions of section 10, whether the use of the name is inadvertent or otherwise.

If there is an Ontario or other corporation carrying on business with a name similar to that of the extra-provincial corporation, a Class 3 corporation may encounter problems in becoming licensed in Ontario. The similar name or names would be revealed in the NUANS Search Report and the Director could refuse to endorse the application as filed. The use of the same or a similar name could very likely confuse or deceive the public and this may be sufficient grounds for refusing to endorse the application. The Director is required under section 6 to give written notice of the refusal, and the reasons therefor, to the person who delivered the application.

Section 9 of this Act states that an extra-provincial corporation may, subject to the *Corporations Information Act* and any other Act, use and identify itself in Ontario by a name other than its corporate name. Previously, a Class 3 extra-provincial corporation could be licensed to use such a name. In other words the extra-provincial corporation could either carry on business, or apply to be licensed, using a name or business style. It could, for example, operate its business or be licensed as ''National Advertising Agencies Inc. carrying on business in the Province of Ontario as Adnat Services''. Effective March 27, 2000, such foreign corporations can no longer be licenced with a business name. They can only be licensed under their corporate name. However, they an carry on business under their business name provided that name is registered under the *Business Names Act.*

Although a Class 1 extra-provincial corporation avoids licensing problems, the use of the same name as, or a name similar to, an existing corporation operating in Ontario could result in difficulties in the future. There is provision for a letter of objection that can be sent by the known business or corporation to the Legal Section of the Companies Branch. This letter should contain the facts on which the objector is relying, including any examples of actual deception in the public mind that the objector knows about. Supporting legal arguments can also be noted in this letter of objection. By permission, a copy of the formal objection is sent directly to the extra-provincial corporation involved to obtain its comments on the issues raised. Letters to the Ministry of Consumer and Business Services are copied by the writers to the other parties so that there is both full disclosure and exchange of information. Once the issues have been defined through correspondence, a decision is made as to whether or not a hearing should be held. If a hearing is not held, a letter is sent from the Legal Section of the Companies Branch providing reasons for the decision and informing the objector of its right of appeal to the Divisional Court pursuant to section 8 of this Act.

If a hearing is to be held, the hearing shall be in writing in accordance with rules made by the Director under the *Statutory Powers Procedure Act*, R.S.O. 1990, c. S.22. The decision of the Director will be forwarded in writing to both parties. Both parties are informed of their right to appeal to the Divisional Court. Under section 11 of this Act, the Director could order the extra-provincial corporation to cease using its name. This could result in a loss of business and additional costs involved in finding a new suitable name under which it can carry on business.

4. Class 3 Applications

A foreign or non-Canadian corporation may apply under section 5 of this Act to be licensed as an extra-provincial corporation. Applications can also be filed for an amended licence or a termination of a licence. The Director endorses the two originals of the application, signed by a director or officer of the corporation, setting out the day, month and year of endorsement and a corporation number. The Director then:

- ☐ files one original of the application with the endorsement; and
- ☐ returns one original of the endorsed application to the corporation or its representative.

The application can be endorsed with the date on which the application, any other required documents and the prescribed fee were received by the

Director. Alternatively, the person who submitted the application can request a later date and, provided the Director agrees, this later date can be endorsed on the application.

5. Application for Extra-Provincial Licence

In order to be licensed, an extra-provincial corporation must submit the following to the Companies Branch:

1. Form 1 — Application for Extra-Provincial Licence, in duplicate, properly completed and executed by a director or officer of the corporation.
2. Form 2 — Appointment of Agent for Service, in duplicate, and executed by the corporation and the person or other corporation who will act as an agent.
3. A Certificate of Status signed by the proper officer, that is the Director, Corporations Branch, of the original jurisdiction in which the applicant was incorporated or continued.
4. A cheque for the prescribed fee payable to the Minister of Finance. The name of the corporation should appear on the face of the cheque.
5. The original NUANS Search Report dated not more than 90 days prior to the submission date of the application.

6. Application for Amended Extra-Provincial Licence

This application would be filed where a Class 3 extra-provincial corporation, through inadvertence or otherwise, has contravened the provisions of section 11 by using a name that is contrary to section 10. The Director can order the corporation to apply for an amended licence. Alternatively where a Class 3 extra-provincial corporation has changed its name in its home jurisdiction, or been continued under the laws of another jurisdiction, an application for an amended licence shall, under section 12 of this Act, be filed. The following must be submitted to the Companies Branch to obtain the required amendment to the licence:

1. Form 3 — Application for Amended Extra-Provincial Licence, in duplicate, properly completed and executed by a director or officer of the corporation.
2. A Certificate of Status signed by the proper officer (the Director, Corporations Branch) of the original jurisdiction in which the applicant was incorporated or continued.
3. The original NUANS Search Report dated not more than 90 days prior to the submission date of the application.

4. A cheque payable to the Minister of Finance for the prescribed fee. The name of the corporation should appear on the face of the cheque.

Where the Director has ordered an amended licence, the application for the amended licence must be submitted within the time period specified in the order. Presumably if the extra-provincial licence restricted the powers of the corporation and a change was deemed necessary, Form 3 would be filed along with the prescribed fee.

7. Application for Termination of Extra-Provincial Licence

Pursuant to subsection 12(2), where a Class 3 extra-provincial corporation has not carried on any of its business in Ontario for any two consecutive years, it is required to make application for termination of its licence or, if it does not do so, the Director, upon giving the corporation a chance to be heard, may by order cancel the licence.

Form 4, Application for Termination of Extra-Provincial Licence, must be prepared and executed in duplicate by a director or officer of the corporation under seal. If the original jurisdiction to which the corporation is subject does not require corporate seals, this must be indicated when submitting the application.

8. Signatures on Documents

All signatures on applications submitted to the Companies Branch must be original signatures. The counter staff test documents when they are presented if there is any question that the signatures are not originals. Applications with photocopied signatures will not be accepted.

9. Forms on the Internet

The *Extra-Provincial Corporations Act* forms are available on the Ministry of Consumer and Business Services website (*www.cbs.gov.on.ca*). The forms can be accessed by selecting the "Business Information" button on the Ministry's home page. The forms can be completed online, and then print the completed forms. Alternatively, a blank form can be printed and subsequently completed.

10. Certificates

Regulation 365 requires that a fee be charged for certificates for each corporation. The Companies Branch issues the following certificates of status for extra-provincial corporations:

- ☐ a certificate that certifies that the extra-provincial corporation named is licensed under the EPCA; and
- ☐ a certificate that states that the corporation named is not required to be licensed in Ontario. This certificate states:

  This certifies that according to the records of the Companies Branch (insert name of corporation), Ontario Corporation Number (insert number), is a corporation of (state original jurisdiction, i.e., Canada/Alberta) and is not required to be licensed under the Extra-Provincial Corporations Act of Ontario.

Each certificate is dated and signed by the Controller of Records for the Companies Branch.

11. Initial Return — *Corporations Information Act*

Section 2 of the *Corporations Information Act* requires that every extra-provincial corporation must, within 60 days after the date it begins to carry on business in Ontario, file an initial notice with the Minister. This notice must set out the prescribed information as of the date of filing

Form 2, Initial Return/Notice of Change is a prescribed, dual form and, when first filed by an extra-provincial corporation, it is described as an initial return. (The second and subsequent filings are made as Notices of Change. Subsection 4(1) of the *Corporations Information Act* requires the filing of a Notice of Change for every change in the information filed in the Initial Return. This Notice of Change is required to be filed within 15 days after the change takes place.)

The Companies Branch advises that all extra-provincial corporations exempted from licensing under the Act must file Form 2 as an Initial Return in order to obtain an Ontario Corporation Number. Class 1 and 2 extra-provincial corporations should complete this filing before commencing business in Ontario. This was the only method through which the Companies Branch learned about Class 1 and 2 extra-provincial corporations that were doing business in Ontario. If, however, corporations fail to file an Initial Return, users of the computer search system who cannot locate any record of a particular extra provincial corporation can inform the Companies Branch. Steps can then be taken to request compliance with this filing requirement.

Effective January, 2000, corporations now are required to file Annual Returns. The Annual Return is combined with the CT23 Corporations Tax Return and are to be filed together. Schedule K is used for extra-provincial corporations licensed under the *Extra-Provincial Corporations Act*. The Class 1 and Class 2 corporations use Schedule A to the Annual Return.

Section 6 of the Act provides for special filings and the provisions of this section were used by the Companies Branch to update corporate information on file for the database being created for ONBIS (see Chapter 4). All extra-provincial corporations carrying on business in Ontario were required to make these filings and pay the prescribed fee. Ontario does not require payment to register, does not require a local agent for service, and provides a number for use by the Ministry of Finance, Corporations Tax Branch. All other Canadian jurisdictions, the Companies Branch advises, require extra-provincial corporations to pay a registration fee.

12

SEARCHES

1. Outline of Searches Made

A corporation may from time to time require additional financing to carry on its business. When this situation arises, the corporation will apply to a bank or another lending institution to borrow the required amount of money. As security for the repayment of the money borrowed, the corporation will pledge some or all of its assets to the lender.

Once the agreement has been made between the lender and the borrower, the lender will forward the necessary documents to be completed, along with instructions as to the searches required, to a law firm. Depending on the nature or type of transaction involved, some or all of the following searches will be required.

1. partnership or proprietorship/business search;
2. style search;
3. corporate search;
4. PPSA search (*Personal Property Security Act*, R.S.O. 1990, c. P10 search), which includes a debenture search;
5. section 427 search under the *Bank Act*, S.C. 1991, c. 46;
6. bankruptcy search;
7. Ontario Securities Commission search; and
8. execution search.

2. Search Fees

The provincial government charges fees for searching the public records to gather information on the various forms of business ownership, i.e., corporations, partnerships, business/style and proprietorships, and for access to any of the records required to perform the searches listed above. See Appendix B for a list of the current fees. Included in these charges is a photocopy of the registration filed by the partnership or proprietorship and the business/style registration filed when a corporation is carrying on business under a name other than its corporate name.

Various other documents, i.e., certificates or certified copies of documents on file are available from the Companies Branch. Certificates, for example certificates of status, are available immediately while the client waits now that this certificate is generated through ONBIS.

The Public Office is open from 8:30 a.m. to 4:30 p.m., Monday to Friday.

3. ONBIS and Automation

As regular users of the services offered by the Companies Branch can attest, the Public Office is always busy. As demand for the services grows, it takes longer and longer to complete the searches, to order certified copies or certificates and to file applications. The delays result from a combination of increased demand from the public and staffing constraints. Despite these pressures, particularly the handling of over 500,000 information requests annually, the Companies Branch has struggled not only to maintain its former level of service but to improve it.

Several new customer-oriented improvements have been introduced by the Companies Branch in an attempt to improve their services such as:

- ☐ after hours mail drop slot in the main door of the Public Office;
- ☐ customer pick-up boxes for regular clients;
- ☐ ONBIS now calculates the search fees required for search requests and counter clerks initialize the forms prior to payment;
- ☐ personal cheques, with appropriate identification, are accepted to pay fees;
- ☐ a new brochure on business registration in seven languages — English, French, Italian, Chinese, Portuguese, Spanish and Greek;
- ☐ corporate search counter — clients sign in and go to the counter only when called on the P.A. system;
- ☐ express line for picking up prepaid search requests only except for certified copies; and
- ☐ fee exempt clients, other government departments or agencies, located in Metro Toronto, have access to a reader/printer facility on a first come first served basis; suitable identification is required plus "take a number" at the corporate pick-up counter.

Through the use of computer terminals at the counter the staff can quickly verify whether or not a registration under the name submitted by the customer exists in the public records. This computer search shows only the registered name and the date of registration. This could prove a problem if there was more than one registration in the records with the same, or very similar, name. The main difference would, of course, be the registration date. It may be that law firms will either record this information or photocopy the actual registration before forwarding it to their clients.

The database supplying the information for the automated look-up for business names is located in Ottawa. This powerful and flexible new computer system now offers online access to an immense databank of business registration information through private service providers, Cyberbahn Inc. and OnCorp Direct Inc. Refer to Chapter 4 (''ONBIS — Companies Branch Automation'') for further information on this system.

4. Types of Searches

(a) Partnership or Proprietorship/Business Search

A search may be ordered for a partnership or proprietorship in order to issue a Statement of Claim on behalf of a client in a civil litigation matter. It is essential that the names of the individuals involved in the partnership or business be obtained, along with the correct name under which the partnership or proprietorship carries on business.

The central registry for these records is located in the Public Office in Toronto. A search can be made in person or by forwarding a request by mail, along with the appropriate search fee, to the Registrar, Companies Branch, at the address listed in Appendix A. Allow about four to six weeks for a mail search. Searches in person may be made at the Public Offce between the hours of 8:30 a.m. and 4:30 p.m., Monday to Friday. If possible obtain the date, or approximate date, of registration of the partnership or proprietorship.

When attending in person at the Public Office to search the records, a Services Requisition in Respect of Unincorporated Businesses must be completed and the appropriate fees paid. A sample of this requisition is shown as Form 1.6.

The fee for the search is charged regardless of whether or not a registration is filed. If there is no trace of the partnership or proprietorship in the records, the clerk will verbally advise that there is nothing on the particular name in the records. Should it be necessary to prove that the search has been made and that the partnership or proprietorship is not registered, a Certificate of Non-Registration can be obtained upon payment of the additional prescribed fee.

Although the search fee includes a copy of the registration on file, if a certified copy of this registration is required, this can be ordered and obtained upon payment of the required fee.

The business name search can also be conducted at some 50 locations throughout Ontario using Ontario Business Connects (OBC) self-serve workstations discussed in Chapter 1, and listed in Appendices C.

These Government Information Centres, which are open from 8:30 am to 5:00 pm, are listed in offices throughout the province. In addition, there are OBC workstations at various Land Registration offices.

The records presently on file at the Companies Branch in the Public Office are made up of the currently active records for a five-year period and the records for the five-year period immediately preceding this. For example, in 2001 the currently active records covered the years 2001 to 1996; the inactive records showed the registration made for the five years prior to 1996. Records of partnerships and sole proprietorships existing prior to these years are filed in the Archives of Ontario in Toronto. The address for the Archives of Ontario is shown in the list of Frequently Used Addresses in Appendix A. The records are on film and may be searched either in person or by mailing a search request to the Archives of Ontario. Particulars regarding the procedures involved and information on file and not on file may be found in Part 1, ''Forms of Business Organization''. An ''expired search'' can be performed by the Companies Branch but it takes a minimum of five working days to obtain the results.

(b) Name/Style Registration Search

If required, a Certificate of Registration or a Certificate of Non-Registration, whichever is applicable to a particular search, can be obtained when the appropriate fee is paid. A certified copy of the actual registration can be obtained on request with payment of the additional fee.

All filings of this nature will be made under the *Business Names Act*, R.S.O. 1990, c. B.17.

(c) Corporate Search

(i) Ontario Corporations

Initially the only information a lawyer may have about a corporation is its corporate name and even that information may not be accurate. The only method of confirming the exact corporate name and the jurisdiction of incorporation is by means of a corporate search. A corporation could be incorporated federally, in Ontario or in one of the other provinces of Canada and registered in Ontario as an extra-provincial corporation.

A corporate search may be required for several reasons:

(a) If a statement of claim is to be issued in a civil litigation matter, it is essential that the name of the corporation is correct in every respect. In addition, it is necessary to know who the officers and directors of the corporation are and the location of its head or registered office for service of the document once it has been issued.

(b) If a corporation is transferring title to real property, a corporate search will ensure that the corporation is in existence and able to transfer title. There have been instances reported where it was discovered that at the time the real estate transaction closed, the corporation did not exist as its charter had been cancelled for failure to file a corporation tax return. Where a corporation's charter has been cancelled, its assets escheat to the Crown. Any transfer by a corporation, once its charter has been cancelled, is null and void.

(c) When a corporation is obtaining financing from a bank or other lending institution, it is essential to confirm that the corporation is in existence and to find out whether or not during its corporate existence the corporation has changed its name. This information is required in order to properly complete the debenture, and to conduct section 427, bankruptcy, *Personal Property Security Act* and other searches. If a name change has occurred, it will be necessary to search under the original name and the current name when performing the other searches.

It is important when reviewing corporate records to keep the following in mind concerning changes that may have occurred in a head/registered office. The BCA and Regulations have been in force since July 29, 1983. Any changes made in the geographic location during the period July 29, 1983 to January 1, 1987, the proclamation date of the *Business Corporations Amendment Act, 1986*, would require Articles of Amendment. Changes made subsequent to the latter date would be effected by a special resolution of the shareholders.

In addition, a Notice of Change would have to be filed under the *Corporations Information Act* to reflect this change on the public record, as required under subsection 4 of this Act.

(ii) Bonds /Debentures

Various methods may be used by corporations to acquire capital. A corporation may mortgage its fixed assets (for example, real estate) or pledge its chattels (equipment) under a chattel mortgage. A corporation also has the option of raising capital through the issue of bonds or debentures. Bonds and debentures represent a pledge of the assets or earning power of the corporation as security for debt. There is no clearly defined legal definition for these terms and they are often used interchangeably when referring to debt obligations of the corporation. Both are instruments acknowledging long-term debt of a corporation, payable either on demand or over a period of time, and they may be unsecured or secured by the assets of the corporation.

Bonds are traditionally associated with government institutions and are therefore unsecured (examples are Ontario Hydro or savings bonds issued by the federal government). These bonds are usually in denominations of $100, $500 or $1,000, rather than a floating sum (not a specific amount). Corporations may issue collateral trust bonds which acknowledge the debt but the debt is secured by assets of the corporation pledged under another instrument. A mortgage could be given on the fixed assets and chattels together with a floating charge on all other assets.

Debentures are usually associated with either offering (public) or non-offering (private) corporations. A debenture may secure some or all of the assets of the corporation (including the undertaking), may be payable on demand or over a fixed period of time, and may be secured by a fixed or floating charge on assets. The payments made may be for interest only or may include periodic payments of principal as well as interest. A debenture holder takes priority over unsecured creditors of a corporation. A floating charge is an equitable charge which affects neither the assets nor operation of the corporation so long as no default occurs under the debenture. If a breach of the terms of the debenture occurs, then the charge is said to "crystallize", that is, it becomes a fixed charge and attaches to the property described in the instrument. For example, a manufacturer of finished goods, which are subject to a floating charge, is free to sell these goods in the normal course of business so long as the terms and conditions of the debt instrument are observed. If a breach occurs, then the debenture holder could, if the situation warranted this action, seize the remaining finished goods and sell them to pay off the debt.

Subsection 244(3) of the BCA was added and proclaimed in force on March 1, 1995. The Companies Branch issued a Notice for the benefit of the legal profession which advises this amendment should be reviewed to determine the need for a corporate search where a previous corporate owner was dissolved at least 20 years before a purchaser's deed or transfer is registered.

The central registry for all corporations carrying on business in Ontario, regardless of the original jurisdiction of incorporation, is located in the Public Office.

A form entitled Request for Corporation Information (see Form 12.2) must be completed indicating the service required. It is used to both search corporations and to order copies, or certified copies, of any documents on file. A Certificate of Status can also be ordered with this form. The service required is noted by placing an "X" in the appropriate column. Particulars of the copies of documents required are set out in detail on the lower half of the form.

The search or document request is then processed. The search fee includes a copy of the microfiche which contains all of the information the Companies Branch has on the particular corporation. Usually this duplicate of the master microfiche can be obtained within approximately 30 minutes. On a busy day this time can increase significantly. Persons working in the City of Toronto can avoid the delay by faxing the names of the corporations to be searched, so long as the microfiche will be picked up. The payment of the required fees is made at that time. The fax number for this service in Toronto is (416) 314-0102.

Effective January 1, 1995, the microfiche does not provide a complete and current corporate record for a corporation as a result of the following notices no longer being added to the corporation microfiche records:

- ☐ Initial Notices or Returns for Ontario corporations filed after December 31, 1994;
- ☐ Notices of Change filed after December 31, 1994;
- ☐ Special Notices (year 3) mailed out during 1994 and 1995 for completion and filing with the Companies Branch; and
- ☐ Annual Returns which were reinstituted effective January, 2000.

The information filed on these forms is now incorporated into ONBIS, the electronic Ontario Business Informations System, which is now the legal public record.

Searchers must, in addition to reviewing the microfiche, consult the corporation Profile Report for current corporation information. The Profile Report is an up to date "snapshot" of current information on the corporation obtained from the most recent notice filed. This Report includes, for example, the current officer and director information as filed by the corporation.

The Corporate Document List, another ONBIS document, lists all of the documents that a corporation has filed on or after June 27, 1992. This List may also provide information that would be helpful to a searcher, for example, amendments to the articles.

The Companies Branch will provide both the Profile Report and Document List where available in addition to the microfiche on the corporation for the basic corporate search fee. The Companies Branch will also provide the corporate microfiche as a stand alone search product. The microfiche provides the incorporating and amending documents but not the Initial Notices or Initial Returns.

The Companies Branch is soliciting feedback on both the Profile Report and the Document List. Comments and suggestions can be sent to:

Companies Branch
Client Liaison Section

Suite 200
393 University Avenue
Toronto, ON
M5G 2M2

If hard copies of material on the microfiche are required, these can be obtained by using the coin-operated printers available in the Public Office.

Another tool available to the public to access the information on file at the Companies Branch is the Electronic Corporate Index (ECI). Through the seven terminals in the Public Office, the Companies Branch is offering electronic access to the ONBIS system instead of using the COM (Corporations on Microfiche) Index, the microfiche listing. The ECI, known as the Alphabetical Corporate Index, permits access to basic information which a searcher would normally obtain from the COM, such as checking for the correct corporate name and the Ontario Corporation Number assigned on incorporation. This Ontario Corporation Number assists the staff in the Public Office in processing a search request because the files are listed under this number.

It is recommended that a search be completed before placing a search request. The purpose is to determine whether or not the corporation falls within the Domestic Extra-Provincial Corporation or Federal Corporation class. The Companies Branch does not issue certificates for these two classes of corporations.

A searcher can obtain the date of incorporation or amalgamation, status and corporation name by looking up the name in the ECI Index. ONBIS can only provide information if the *correct corporate name* is entered into the system. Provided this is done, ONBIS will provide the corporation number.

There are five methods of accessing the ONBIS system:

1. by Ontario Corporation Number (''OCN'');
2. by entering the name as set out in the articles of incorporation *(an error in keying the name could result in a message from the system that the name cannot be found)*;
3. select a starting point and search an alphabetical list of corporations by keying in the corporate name — the system will respond by starting with the corporate name closest to the name entered;
4. a corporate name contains a descriptive element, usually indicating the type of business or a word that makes it unique — *knowing this key word may provide faster results* — ONBIS will display a list of corporations containing the particular key word; and
5. if a corporate name contains punctuation, spaces or special characters, and this information is not entered in the system, the corporation may not be located — a ''similar name search'', may resolve this problem since the

system removes the abovementioned punctuation, spaces or special characters and provides a list of names that to the system are similar.

Outlined below is a brief explanation of the process used to enter corporate names on the COM Index.

Corporations are listed on the master microfiche and the COM Index in alphabetical order and if the corporation's name begins with a popular letter of the alphabet, such as "S", "T" or "C", it may be easier to locate the corporation by choosing the second word in the corporate name. If the name of the corporation includes initials, there may be some difficulty in locating the name on the master microfiche. A name or style search, for example, would disclose the name of the corporation that had registered the name or style. It would then be necessary to search the corporation behind the name or style. If, for example, the name of the corporation was J. C. J. Restaurant Limited, you would expect to find the listing under the first initial, that is "J". However, the practice of the Ministry when listing corporations with initials is to first list the corporation under the letter of the alphabet, *i.e.*, under the letter "J" for the above corporation, and then to place it in the following order:

1. initials plus an ampersand — no period (J&C);
2. initials with spaces between but no periods (J C J);
3. initials with a period after each and a space between the period and the next initial (J. C. J.);
4. initials with an ampersand — with a period and a space before the next initial (J. & C.);
5. initials — with no period after each initial and no spaces between (JCJ).

In other words, there were five possible listings to be checked in order to locate this corporation. Using the key word approach may speed up the process of locating the correct corporate name and the Ontario Corporation Number for the service requisition.

The possibility always exists that the name of the corporation shown on the name and style registration as operating the style or business might not be correct. This should especially be kept in mind when the corporate name shown involves initials as part of the name. The corporation shown above was finally located under category 5. The corporate name shown in this case was wrong.

At the present time it is anticipated by the staff in the Public Office that the COM Index will always be available. Should the ONBIS system "go down" at some time, search requests could still be processed.

There are several "readers" available in the Public Office for use in reading the microfiche obtained for the corporation or corporations. In addition, there is a growing trend for the large law offices to have a reader available in the office. The microfiche can then be picked up from the Public Office by a messenger and delivered to the lawyer or law clerk who can then complete the search in the office, rather than attending personally at the Companies Branch. The microfiche is usually attached to the report forwarded to the lawyer who ordered the corporate search.

A. *Corporations on Microfiche Index*. The Corporations on Microfiche Index, usually referred to as the COM Index, is a computer-generated alphabetical listing of corporations on microfiche. This index includes both active and inactive corporations which have registered and/or carried on business in Ontario. The weekly updated listing contains information on all new incorporations or registrations to the end of the working day on the previous Monday. These weekly updates are incorporated into the new master listing which is printed approximately every six months. The COM Index can be accessed at no charge in the Public Office during normal business hours. Microfiche readers are available for public use.

There are two types of searches which may be requested in connection with corporations. If the information required is to be used in a litigation matter, the information required for that search would be:

1. exact name of the corporation in full;
2. names and addresses of the current directors and officers which would be obtained from the last Initial Return or Notice of Change or the Last Annual Return filed as required under the *Corporations Information Act*;
3. registered office (head office) address;
4. mailing address of the corporation if it is different from the registered office (head office) address; and
5. names of the solicitors acting for the corporation if this information is on file.

Service of any legal documents on a corporation is effected by serving either a director or officer of the corporation, who are usually located at the registered office of the corporation. If all attempts fail, a last resort may be to serve the solicitors who are on the record as acting for the corporation.

If the information on the corporation is required in connection with a financing (the advance of money by a lender to a corporation), the solicitor will require what is known as a "full corporate search". When reporting on a full corporate search, the searcher will have to be familiar with the differences which apply to corporations incorporated under the BCA and those corporations incorporated under earlier predecessor statutes.

In addition to the information set out above, which is required for litigation purposes, the lawyer would require a summary of the following information:

(a) The business or businesses the corporation is authorized to carry on as described in the objects set out in the articles of incorporation. Corporations incorporated under the former BCA may have many objects. Under the present Act a corporation is only required to set out in its articles any restrictions on the business the corporation may carry on or on the powers that the corporation may exercise. There may be no restrictions set out in the articles and this would be included in the report.

(b) The authorized capital of the corporation. The capital structure of a corporation incorporated under the former BCA could comprise common shares only, a combination of common and preference shares or a more complex capital structure. Corporations incorporated under the present Act must set out the classes and any maximum number of shares the corporation is authorized to issue. If there are two classes of shares, then the rights, privileges, restrictions and conditions attaching to each class of shares must be included. If the authorized capital has been amended, Articles of Amendment would be shown on the microfiche and this information should be noted next to the details of the original authorized capital.

(c) If the corporation is a private or non-offering corporation, there are restrictions set out in the articles of incorporation relating to the transfer of shares. Usually the restrictions require a resolution of the directors or shareholders of the corporation to transfer the issued shares.

(d) Information on any special clauses in the letters patent or articles of incorporation. A corporation incorporated prior to December 31, 1971 was incorporated by a charter document called "Letters Patent". After the proclamation of the original *Business Corporations Act*, the charter document incorporating a corporation was called "Articles of Incorporation". If there are clauses included under "other provisions" in the articles of incorporation, this information will be set out in detail at this point in the report.

(e) The lawyer would be interested in knowing whether or not the corporation was up-to-date in the filings required under the *Corporations Information Act*. Every corporation carrying on business in Ontario is required to file an Initial Return and/or Notice of Change. Each time there is a change in the information filed in the Initial Return filed, the corporation is required to file a Notice of Change within 15 days of the date of such change. The corporation is in default under the *Corporations Information Act* if the required Notice of Change is not filed. Effective January, 2000, Annual Returns must now be filed by corporations under the Act.

If a corporation has not filed the Annual Returns, Initial Return or Notice of Change, this information should be reported to the lawyer. Usually a requisition is made by the lawyer to have the filings updated prior to the advancing of any funds.

(f) When performing a corporate search or any other type of search, an assistant is acting as "the eyes of the lawyer" and the search report should include the information filed either on the last Annual Return or the last Initial Return or Notice of Change. The date of the filing of the Annual Return, Initial Return or Notice of Change should also be noted in the report. The report would ultimately include all of the information set out in the notice or Annual Return from which it is being obtained.

(g) If a corporation has registered a business name or style, this information would be included in the report along with particulars of the name or style, the business carried on, the date of registration, and the expiry date of registration. Every registration expires five years from the date of registration. If the registration has expired and a renewal or a withdrawal of business name or style has not been filed, this information should also be noted (see Form 12.1).

(h) If there have been any amendments to the charter of the corporation, particulars of these amendments should be summarized in one section of the report for the convenience of the lawyer. These amendments could include supplementary letters patent or articles of amendment, together with sufficient information on the type of amendment. It was mentioned earlier that if the original authorized capital had been amended, this information should be noted in the section of the report dealing with the authorized capital. Repeated here are the date and the name of the instrument amending the charter, that is, the supplementary letters patent, the date of issue, and the fact that it dealt with an amendment to the authorized capital. A notation would be made here that details have been supplied in the section of the report dealing with authorized capital.

If the amending instrument dealt with a revision to some other provision or provisions of the original charter, in addition to naming the instrument and supplying the date of issue, full particulars of the amendment or amendments set out in the amending instrument are added in the appropriate section of the report.

(i) If there is any record of the solicitor or solicitors who acted on behalf of the corporation, the latest information on the file should be included in the report. If problems arise in contacting the principals involved in the corporation, a possible alternative open to the lawyer would be to contact the solicitor or solicitors of record.

Depending on the volume of business, requests for either certified copies of microfiche or Certificates of Status may take some time to obtain. Certificates of Status can be obtained while the person waits or on the same day if the request is faxed in and the certificate is picked up from the Public Office.

Certified copies require three to five working days to supply. The Companies Branch, effective February 13, 1995, requires payment for certified copies of documents ordered at the time the request is submitted. There is a minimum fee payable which can be paid by cheque, money order or cash. Cheques and money orders are made payable to the Minister of Finance. The maximum number of pages provided for this fee is ten. Should the page count exceed that number, the person making the request must pay the extra charges before the certified copies will be released.

(iii) Federal Corporations

If the corporate search made at the Public Office reveals that the corporation is incorporated federally, or if this information was known in advance of the search, information can be obtained from the Corporations Directorate, Industry Canada, located in Ottawa. Federal corporations incorporated under the *Canada Business Corporations Act*, R.S.C. 1985, c. C-44 (''CBCA'') are required to file certain notices along with the articles of incorporation. The Notice of Registered Office, Form 3, sets out the address of the registered or head office of the corporation. The Notice of Directors, Form 6, lists the directors of the corporation along with their addresses.

Subsections 19(4) and 113(1) of the CBCA require that within 15 days of any change of address of its registered office or any change among its directors, a corporation shall send to the Director, the government official in charge of enforcing the statute, a notice in the prescribed forms setting out the change. A director of the corporation shall file any such notice. Forms 3 and 6 previously mentioned are dual forms which are used initially as a Notice of Directors and a Notice of the Registered Office, respectively, and later to record a change in any of the information filed in the original notices.

Subsection 266(1) of the CBCA provides that any person who has paid the prescribed fee is entitled during usual business hours to examine a document required under this Act or the Regulations which must be filed with the director. The only exception to this general rule is an order appointing an inspector under subsection 230(2) of the Act.

Subsection 266(2) provides that the director appointed under the Act shall furnish any person with a copy or a certified copy of a document required by the Act or the Regulations, with the exception of the report referred to under subsection 230(2) above.

There are two options available when searching federal corporations:

1. Letters may be sent to the Corporations Directorate, Industry Canada, Ottawa, along with the corporation name and other pertinent information.
2. Telephone the information to a clerk, who will provide the results of the search in approximately 48 hours. Telephone searches can be made Monday to Friday (8:30 a.m. to 4:30 p.m.) provided a deposit account has been established with Industry Canada.

If copies of any of the documents on the file are required, they can be ordered at the time the name of the corporation is submitted to be searched, and payment can be made by cheque, Visa, MasterCard or through a deposit account. There is no charge for either a letter or telephone search of a federal corporation. Should you require copies of any of the material on file, or a certified copy of any such material, charges do apply. The required purchase order form must be completed as indicated in the following discussion of deposit accounts (see Form 12.3), or the request can be faxed and payment made by Visa or MasterCard.

If a corporation falls under the provisions of subsection 160(1) of the CBCA, copies of the financial statement must be filed with the Director. Any corporation offering its securities to the public must file financial statements not less than 21 days before each annual meeting and not later than 15 months after the date of the last annual meeting.

If financial statements are requested for more than three corporations, the search must be submitted by letter. Otherwise, the request may be telephoned.

A. *Deposit Account*—The CBCA Regulations, SOR/79-316, were amended as follows:

> **82.** (1) The fee in respect of the filing, examination or copying of any document or in respect of any action that the Director is required or authorized to take under the Act, set out in column I of an item to Schedule II shall be
>
> (a) the applicable fee set out in column II of that item; and
>
> (b) paid to the Director on the filing, examination or copying of the document or before the Director takes the action in respect of which the fee is payable.

A cheque payable to the Receiver General for Canada must be sent with the request to open a deposit account with Industry Canada. Cheques issued whether by individuals or firms need not be certified.

In order to establish a deposit account a letter can be sent to the Supervisor, Revenue Control, Finance Branch, Industry Canada, at the address listed in Appendix A. The following information is required:

1. name of client and full mailing address including postal code;
2. name and telephone number of the contact person or persons who will be responsible for the use of the deposit account;
3. list the branches or departments that will be supplying the required services (for example, if corporate searches and the filing of articles of incorporation are the primary use, the Corporations Directorate would be listed; if other services will be needed, the proper name of the branch or department supplying the service should be obtained and listed);
4. the signature of the contact person and the date should also be included in the letter.

Alternatively, Industry Canada, Finance Branch, has a form available which can be obtained, completed and filed. This form is called a Request for Opening a Deposit Account and requires the information outlined above.

Each client is assigned a unique deposit account number which must be quoted on all cheques, purchase order forms and correspondence relating to the deposit account.

A purchase order form is required to order services and a few copies can be obtained when the deposit account number is assigned. Additional copies are available by writing to Industry Canada, Finance Branch.

A minimum deposit of $100 is required but it is suggested that if frequent use is made of these services, a larger amount be deposited. Telephone requests for copies or certified copies will only be taken from those persons or law firms having deposit accounts. Before preparing the documents ordered, a check will be made to ensure sufficient funds are in the account to pay for the service ordered.

If a deposit account has not been opened and the need for services is urgent, payment can be made by Visa, MasterCard or cheque. If either credit card is used, the account number and expiry date must be provided.

Deposit accounts will be opened if a particular organization or law office makes frequent use of the services offered by Industry Canada or other federal departments or agencies.

If pressed for time, it may be necessary to retain an Ottawa law firm to act as an agent and deliver the necessary order form to Industry Canada or the particular government department providing the required service.

Another alternative available to the public in the City of Toronto is to deliver letters addressed to federal departments or offices to the Ontario regional office of Industry Canada at the address shown in Appendix A.

A covering letter or ''note'' should be enclosed with the delivery requesting the letter be delivered to the appropriate government department in Ottawa. If, for example, the letter was intended for the Corporations Directorate, Industry Canada, this information should be included in the covering letter. The regional office sends a bag of Priority Post mail on a daily basis to Ottawa. These letters are included and delivery is usually made on the next working day. There is no charge for this service.

(iv) Automated Fax Information Sources

On June 25, 1993, a merger took place between the Department of Consumer & Corporate Affairs and the Department of Industry. Now known as Industry Canada, the activities formerly carried on by Consumer & Corporate Affairs are handled by the Corporations Directorate. In addition, on August

15, 1994, the Corporations Directorate moved to new offices in Ottawa to the address shown in Appendix A.

The Corporations Directorate has provided an automated fax information system for clients wishing to obtain forms, policies and guidelines by facsimile equipment using a touch tone telephone. This automated fax information system, or FLASHFAX, can be accessed by telephoning:

(613) 941-0200 or (613) 942-0199.

This bilingual system is user friendly and the minimum requirement is knowing the numbers assigned to the information that is required. The following list provides the initial requests that will assist you in making use of the system:

☐ Service Level Guide	1101
☐ Directory of Documents Available	1105
☐ Fee Schedule	1106

(v) On-Line Services

Industry Canada has introduced a number of fully interactive web-based tools for businesses and their legal advisers. The Canada Business Corporations Act (CBCA) administrative forms are a collection of various administrative forms from the CBCA including Articles of Incorporation and Articles of Dissolution. These forms can be accessed and downloaded through Industry Canada's Strategis web-site at *http://strategis.ic.gc.ca/SSG/cs00058e.html*.

There is also information available at the *strategis.ic.gc.ca* website for persons starting up a business including:

☐ *Business Management* — programs and services related to operating a business, *i.e.*, incorporation requirements, including incorporation kits, certain guidelines and regulations.

☐ *Business Start-Up* — programs and services related to starting up a business, *i.e.*, financial assistance information, researching markets, and using electronic commerce.

☐ *Information Services* — information centres such as the Canada-Ontario Business Service Centres (COBSC) and its website *http://www.cbcs.org/ontario*, directories and research tools. There is available through COBSC an Online Small Business Workshop which is a step-by-step web-based program designed to help start a new venture or improve an existing small business.

(vi) Other Jurisdictions

If a corporate search is required for a corporation incorporated in any of the other provinces or territories in Canada, it can be done by either writing or telephoning the appropriate jurisdiction. The procedure to be used will vary depending on the incorporating jurisdiction. The time lapse between the request and the answer to the request can range anywhere from one hour to two weeks. If there is some urgency in obtaining the information, it is often better to contact a local law firm in the appropriate jurisdiction and arrange to have the search completed by that law firm. If a corporate search is required in any of the other provinces, a request should be directed to the appropriate province at the address listed in Appendix A.

(d) Personal Property Security Act Search

The *Personal Property Security Act*, R.S.O. 1990, c. P.10 (''PPSA''), changed and updated the former systems for registration of security interests. The primary purpose of this statute is to make business deals involving security interests simpler and to provide a single uncomplicated system for registering security interests in personal property. A security interest, for example, would be the rights of the mortgagee under a chattel mortgage or of a conditional seller under a conditional sale agreement. The collateral is the property to which a security interest attaches, which may be almost any kind of personal property. Personal property may include book debts, inventory, equipment or motor vehicles. Proper registration in the system, using the appropriate prescribed form, of the security agreement perfects or establishes the creditor's right to the security interest in the particular personal property of the debtor. Priority of right is determined by the date and time of registration of the security agreement. Should the debtor default in repayment of the debt, the creditor could take the steps required to realize (take possession of) the collateral.

The PPSA permits registration at branch offices which are usually located in the local land registry offices. The information from the branch offices is forwarded on the computerized system to the central registry, located in Toronto, which is a computer-based storage system. A search can be made at the central registry or any branch office to ascertain whether or not a security interest is claimed in personal property located anywhere in Ontario. A creditor who fails to register his or her security interest as provided under the PPSA loses the protection afforded by the statute. A subsequent creditor making a proper registration would obtain a security interest in the personal property in priority to any unregistered security interest.

The Personal Property Registration Branch manages the Personal Property Security Registration (''PPSR'') System and administers the PPSA. The PPSR system provides a method whereby a seller of personal property or a lender of money can secure the purchase price or the loan by the registration of a financing statement. It also acts as an inquiry service for a purchaser of personal property, or a lender accepting it as collateral for a loan, to check for a lien on the personal property The PPSR system permits a potential buyer or lender to find out whether or not the personal property has been pledged by the owner to anyone else.

Searches under the PPSA are made by directing inquiries to the PPSR system, which is both centralized and computerized, and replaces the old manual version. A person requiring the information need only contact the particular branch or the central office either by writing or calling the Personal Property Registration Branch. The information is recorded in the central office on a computer file under the name of the debtor. The business hours for telephone inquiry purposes are 8:00 a.m. to 5:00 p.m.

Provided the person or law firm has online access, enquiries can be made and fees paid either through a deposit account, arranged with the Ministry of Consumer and Business Services, or by Visa or MasterCard. The telephone call is made and the information is keyed in by the searcher.

A deposit account permits the user to deposit moneys in advance against which enquiry fees can be debited. The account holder is then able to place an enquiry from any telephone. The method of establishing this account and the minimum requirements will be discussed later in this section.

Registrations made under the PPSA and the *Repair and Storage Liens Act*, R.S.O. 1990, c. R.25, and their predecessors or other statutes fall under the PPSR system of registration.

The PPSA includes the registration of debentures and the transfer of an account or chattel paper, even though the transfer may not secure payment or performance of an obligation. Under section 4, specific transactions are exempted from the authority of the Act. For example, the PPSA does not apply:

☐ to a transfer of an interest or claim in or under any policy of insurance or contract of annuity;

☐ to an assignment for the general benefit of creditors to which the *Assignments and Preferences Act*, R.S.O. 1990, c. A.33, applies;

☐ to an assignment of accounts made solely to facilitate the collection of accounts for the assignor;

☐ to the creation or assignment of an interest in real property, including a mortgage, charge or lease of real property, other than:

— an interest in a fixture; or

— an assignment of a right to receive payment under a mortgage, charge or lease where the assignor retains the interest in the real property.

(Refer to section 4 for a complete listing of all of the exempted transactions.)

Section 1 of the PPSA defines the term "security interest" to mean an interest in personal property that secures payment or performance of an obligation. This definition includes the interest of a transferee of an account or chattel paper, whether or not the interest secures payment or performance of an obligation. The term "chattel paper" means one or more writings that evidence both a monetary obligation and a security interest in, or lease of, specific goods. "Goods" under this section are defined as, tangible personal property, other than chattel paper, documents of title, instruments, money and securities, and include fixtures, growing crops, the unborn young of animals, timber to be cut, and minerals and hydrocarbons to be extracted. "Consumer goods" are those used or acquired primarily for personal, family or household purposes. "Collateral" is defined as personal property that is subject to a security interest. The term "inventory" can include goods which are held by a person for sale or lease or which are or have been furnished under a contract of service. The term can also include raw materials, work in process, or materials used or consumed in a business or profession. Any items that do not fall in the above-mentioned categories for consumer goods or inventory are described as "equipment" under this statute.

There is also provision under the PPSA for registration of collateral which includes fixtures, or goods that may become fixtures, crops, oil, gas or other minerals to be extracted, or timber to be cut. Subsection 54(1) of the PPSA states that a Notice of Security Interest, prescribed Form 5, may be registered in the proper land registry office. R.R.O. 1990, Reg. 912 states that Form 6, a Notice of Security Interest, be registered if the security interest under subsection 54(1) is a right to payment under a mortgage, charge or lease of real property. If the collateral is consumer goods, the Notice of Security Interest, or any extension thereof, authorized under subsection 54(2), must set out an expiration date. This expiration date shall not be later than the fifth anniversary of the registration date and the notice or extension notice is effective until the end of the expiration date.

The PPSA requires that certain prescribed forms be used to record the information in the system. Form 1C, Financing Statement/Claim for Lien, is the document which must be registered to perfect a security interest by registration. This is a dual form which can be registered in the PPSR system to perfect a security interest arising under the PPSA or the *Repair and Storage Liens Act* ("RSLA"). The completion of the appropriate box under the file number printed in the upper right hand corner of Form 1C identifies the statute to which the registration applies.

Form 2C, Financing Change Statement/Change Statement and Form 4C, Motor Vehicle Schedule follow the same principle and are also registerable under both Acts. The terminology that applies to the PPSA for Form 1C is Financing Statement and Form 2C is a Financing Change Statement. Samples of these prescribed forms are shown as Forms 12.4, 12.5 and 12.6. These forms no longer are available to the public over the counter in the Central Registration Branch or any of the branch offices but must be purchased from Dye & Durham Co. Inc.

Form 3C, also described as a Financing Change Statement/Change Statement, is generated by the PPSR system and acts as a verification statement. When a Financing Statement/Claim for Lien is registered, Form 3C and a verification statement are automatically produced and mailed to each secured party or lien claimant named in the registration. The term ''secured party'' refers to persons registering under the PPSA. Lien claimant refers to persons registering under the RSLA. This form permits the persons registering Form 1C to check the accuracy of the information obtained from Form IC and recorded in the PPSR system.

Form 3C is also the prescribed form used to register a complete discharge or a renewal. This form cannot be used by a registrant for a partial discharge. The PPSR system links all registrations through the use of a file number to the original Form 1 C filed by the secured party or lien claimant. This file number must appear on all subsequent filings that apply to Form 1C. This procedure is referred to as ''linking of registrations''. Form 1C is referred to as the ''head of the family'' and all Forms 2C referenced to it are described as ''members of the family''. It is imperative that the file number be correctly recorded on all filings that relate to the head of the family. If an incorrect file number is recorded on a Form 2C, there are two possible results:

1. Form 2C may, through the incorrect number, link up with another family, provided that number is recorded in the PPSR system; or
2. if the incorrect number is not already in the PPSR system, Form 2C forms a family of its own.

Form 2C may be used to record amendments or changes to Form 1C and may also be used to file a renewal or complete discharge. However the Registration and Enquiry Guide recommends that Form 3C be used when possible because most of the information on this form is preprinted by the PPSR system. This will reduce the possibility of error on the part of the registrant.

Financing statements may be registered in person at any branch office or the central office in Toronto. A second alternative is to forward the financing statement by mail to the Central Registration Branch. Branch offices forward copies of all financing statements and any amending statements to the central office.

The *Electronic Registration Act (Ministry of Consumer and Commercial Relations Statutes)*, S.O. 1991, c. 44 (''ERA''), was proclaimed in force March 1, 1992, enabling the Ministry of Consumer and Commercial Relations (now Ministry of Consumer and Business Services) to accept information in an electronic format.

The PPSA was the first Act to be designated under the ERA to use electronic filing. Clients using this process send an electronic filing to the PPSR in the form of a computer tape or through a telephone line. These registrations are processed overnight and added to the PPSR database. They are referred to as "Batch Electronic Filings". In 1994, the PPSR allowed clients to be connected to its computer system and register online electronically. Documents are filed immediately directly into the PPSR database. Any errors made by these online clients must be corrected by the clients involved. Corrections to electronic registrations cannot be made by the PPSR staff. Electronic searches and filings can also be made through private service providers, OnCorp Direct Inc. and Cyberbahn Inc.

Clients who file paper registrations are required to pay an administrative fee per registration. A client filing electronically does not have to pay this fee.

The registration becomes effective at the time shown in the registration number. A sample registration number for a financing statement under the PPSR system could be 20010211 1019 0043 2884. By reading the registration number from left to right, the following information can be obtained:

Date of registration—20010211 — February 11, 2001

Time—1019-10:19

This means the registration was effected at 10:19 in the morning. If the figures shown here were 1400, it would mean the registration was effective at 2:00 in the afternoon.

Branch number—0043

Shows registration in Toronto. If registered in one of the branch offices, the appropriate number would appear here.

Instrument number—2884

A copy of the financing statement with the registration particulars is returned to the individual or law firm registering the statement after the registration has been entered in the system. Only the financing statement is submitted for registration. The security agreement, to which the financing statement refers, is retained by the parties to the agreement. There is provision under subsection 18(l)(d) of the PPSA that a secured party must supply a copy of the security agreement on request. Alternatively the lender can be asked to disclose the location of the security agreement, or a true copy thereof, to permit inspection by the debtor or anyone who has an interest in the collateral. An authorized representative may act on behalf of any such interested person. In addition to discovering what the outstanding liabilities of an individual or corporation are, another purpose of this search is to verify that the same goods or equipment have not been already pledged to another creditor. This provision prevents the debtor from pledging the same assets to more than one lender.

The secured party may under subsection 18(7) require payment in advance of the prescribed charge for each statement or copy of the security agreement requested under subsection (1). R.R.O. 1990, Reg. 912 states that the charge for a true copy of the security agreement shall not exceed 50¢ per page.

Section 10 of the PPSA states that where a security agreement is in writing, the secured party shall deliver a copy of this agreement to the debtor within ten days of its execution. If the copy is not delivered to the debtor within the stated time period or after it has been requested by the debtor, then the debtor may apply to the Ontario Superior Court of Justice.

Registration periods under the PPSA can range from 1 to 25 years and there is provision for a "perpetual registration" which is valid until discharged by the secured party. A financing statement is effective only during its registration period and only whole, not partial, years are permitted. Subsection 51(1) of the PPSA states that the registration period may be for a perpetual period or for the period of years set out in the financing statement. Subsection 51(5) states that where the collateral is or includes consumer goods, the deemed registration period is five years unless:

(a) a shorter registration period is shown on the financing statement; or

(b) the registration is extended by the registration of the financing change statement.

Current registration charges are shown on the Fee Schedule, Appendix B. Registration can be effected in person or by mail at the Central Registration Branch or in person at any of the Regional Land Registry Offices participating in the PPSR System. A list of these Regional Land Registry Offices is included in Appendix A.

The information on all of the prescribed forms filed in the PPSR System should be recorded through the use of a typewriter or a computer printer in capital letters only. Using only capital letters reduces the possibility of error where the similarity of a character and a numeral might, during the conversion process into a computer file, result in a misinterpretation of a character. On many keyboards, for example, the lower case character "1" and the figure "1" are the same.

When a registrant mails in a financing statement, a Form 3C/Verification Statement is produced by the system and mailed to the registrant. A two-part form, the top half (Form 3C) can be removed and used later to record a discharge or renewal. The bottom half of the form can be used to check the accuracy of the computer input and the information filed. If the form filed contained any inaccuracies, a courtesy notice may be included listing the problems in the form that has been registered.

The prescribed forms currently used in the PPSR System are designed to implement registrations under the PPSA or the RSLA. The registrant designates on the prescribed form which statute applies to each registration by use of the letter "P" or "R" (The letter "P" refers to the PPSA, while the "R" indicates the RSLA.) Detailed instructions for the completion of these dual forms can be found on the back of each form. The following lists the prescribed forms and their uses in the PPSR System:

(i) Financing Statement/Claim for Lien — Form 1C

This is the basic document registered under the PPSA and the RSLA.

(ii) Financing Change Statement/Change Statement — Form 2C

This is the form used to record any change in the information in Form 1C or on another Form 2C and updates or corrects the information filed in the PPSR System. A "Letter for Change Code" is inserted on line 22 of this form. Some of these Letter for Change Codes apply to both Acts while others are limited only to the PPSA. The uses of this form and the applicable Letter for Change Codes are:

PPSA/RSLA	*PPSA ONLY*
A—Amendment	E—Transfer by Debtor
B—Renewal	G—Assignment of security interest in part of collateral by secured party
C—Discharge	H—Transfer of part of collateral by debtor
D—Assignment by secured party/lien claimant	J—Other change
F—Partial discharge	

Full instructions for the appropriate change are listed on the back of Form 2C.

(iii) Financing Change Statement/Change Statement — Form 3C

The Personal Property Security Registration and Enquiry Guide refers to this form as "Form 3C and Verification Statement". This document is perforated and Form 3C may be separated from the Verification Statement. Unlike the other prescribed forms, which are available in paper form, this form is generated by the PPSR System and mailed to, depending on the particular prescribed form that triggered Form 3C, the secured party, lien claimant or registering agent that may have acted on their behalf. A Form 3C and Verification Statement is produced for every Form 1C, 2C or 3C registered.

If Form 3C results from the registration of a Form 1C, the registrant is advised to keep Form 3C for future use. The information on the Financing Change Statement/ Change Statement is preprinted which reduces the chance of error when either a renewal or complete discharge is registered. This form can only be used for a registration having the same reference file number as the pre-printed number on the form. The procedure of ''linking registrations'' was discussed earlier in this chapter. In the event that this form is lost, a renewal or complete discharge may be registered using Form 2C.

The Verification Statement reproduces the information recorded in the PPSR System and allows the registrant to check its accuracy The PPSR System is designed to inform the registrant about possible errors in the registered statement. The particular problem is listed, along with a brief explanation. Some of the common errors that occur are:

1. *Using the incorrect registration number.* A PPSA search can be made to obtain the current 9-digit file number.

   If the incorrect number is included in the Financing Change Statement (Form 2C) and does not link up, or the registration has expired, a new Form 2C can be prepared and filed. If the courtesy notice indicates that a ''new file number has been assigned'', that number cannot be used as it has been assigned by the system to the invalid registration.

   If a discharge has been filed, and a courtesy notice is received stating ''discharge indicated, registration will not be removed from the file'', it means that unnecessary information was included in the discharge. A discharge applies to all registrations in a file and a single particular registration cannot be discharged. If the file is to be removed from the computer system, a new discharge should be prepared and registered.

2. The letter entered in the ''Enter Letter for Change'' and the appropriate sections that apply to the letter entered have not been completed or there is a conflict between the letter entered and the information supplied.

3. Required information is missing or incorrect, such as the individual debtor's date of birth, incomplete or missing address for a debtor, an invalid date of maturity which is either a non-existent date, for example April 31, or the date is in the past.

4. The information indicates that it is a registration against consumer goods and includes a motor vehicle but details describing the motor vehicle are omitted.

(iv) Motor Vehicle Schedule — Form 4C

A motor vehicle schedule is always registered with either a Form IC or 2C, never alone. It becomes part of the registered statement and is used when there are more than two motor vehicles to be described. Forms 1C and 2C provide for the registration of either one or two motor vehicles.

In the centre at the top of Forms 1C and 2C are two sections titled:

1. Account No. (if applicable); and
2. Registration Account Code.

These sections are only completed if the user of the PPSR System has established an invoice billing account with the Central Office and pays the registration fees through this account. Account holders have ''Account Identifiers'' made up of 17 alphanumeric characters. The Account Number includes:

- ☐ a six-character Master Account Number; and
- ☐ a four-character Sub-Account Number.

This ten-character Account Number is entered in the section headed ''Account No.''.

Each sub-account can have a maximum of two codes, one for search enquiries and one for registration of documents. These codes produce the last seven characters of the Account Identifier. The Registration Account Code ends in the letter ''R'', which distinguishes it from the Enquiry Account Code. The appropriate seven-character code must be entered in the section headed ''Registration Account Code''.

A person or firm that wishes to establish an invoice billing account with the Central Office of the PPSR System can obtain an information brochure by writing to the Central Office. The mailing address for the Central Office is listed in Appendix A.

(v) PPSA Enquiry Process

The registrations included in the PPSR System are:

- ☐ financing statements and financing change statements registered under the PPSA;
- ☐ claims for lien and change statements registered under the RSLA;
- ☐ entries made by the Registrar with the registration particulars made under the *Corporation Securities Registration Act*, R.S.O. 1980, c. 94 (''CSRA'') [repealed S.O. 1989, c. 16, s. 84(1)5], which were not discharged before October 10, 1989 with any financing change statements which relate to these entries together.

An enquiry response includes all unexpired registrations which correspond to the search information submitted. The PPSR System is described as a notice filing system, which means that the actual document is not registered, only a notice. Details of individual transactions are not available but may be obtained from the secured party, lien claimant or the debtor.

A copy of the instrument filed pursuant to the CSRA may be obtained from the Central Office upon payment of the prescribed fees.

Registrations are reported by "family" in reverse chronological order and commence with the "head of the family". The details of the head of the family will be followed by any financing change statements/change statements which relate to it. The head of the family could be:

☐ a financing statement/claim for lien; or

☐ an entry by the Registrar of a CSRA registration.

The first family reported will be the latest registration in the PPSR System and then the report will go backwards in time until all of the families that meet the search requirements are listed.

A bilingual enquiry service is available in either French or English and registrants can complete the information required in the prescribed forms in either language. This is not, however, a translation service. A request can be made for a bilingual enquiry operator and that operator will communicate in French, refer to the headings on the registered forms in French, but will not translate English text into French.

A. *Procedure in making PPSA search.* This search may be made by telephoning the local PPSA office or the Toronto office provided the searcher has a deposit account. The Toronto office can be reached at (416) 325-8847 or (long distance) 1-800-267-8847. The following is the procedure used in Toronto:

1. The operator will mention a number which should be noted, *i.e.*, operator number 24, and will then ask for:

   (a) Account Number—a ten-digit number, combined with an enquiry code which is a mix of seven alphanumeric characters.

   The first six numbers of the account number are known as the "Master Account Number", which is the only number that appears on correspondence between the Account Holder and the Personal Property Registration Branch. The next four numbers represent the "Sub-Account Number" and any quantity of sub-accounts can be assigned to an account up to a maximum of 9,999. These can be assigned by the Account Holder to authorized users in an organization.

   (b) Enquiry Code—a mix of seven alphanumeric characters, *i.e.*, ABC-S54E; each sub-account will have a unique enquiry code which, on request, can be changed to prevent unauthorized use of a sub-account.

   These files will normally be current to two days immediately preceding the day on which the call is made.

2. The operator will then ask the category of search, i.e., individual specific, individual non-specific, business debtor or the motor vehicle identification number. An *individual specific search* requires first given name, initial of second given name, if any, surname and date of birth; *individual non-*

specific search requires the first given name and surname; and a *business debtor search* requires the name of the business debtor as set out in its charter, including the French version, if any, of the corporate name and any trade or business names the corporation may use. Although the Regulations do not require a trade name to be entered on any of the prescribed forms to effect registration in the PPSR System, through inadvertence a registrant may use a trade name, rather than the corporate name, of a business debtor. If such an error is made, the registration would be included in the enquiry response by searching trade or business names.

When a motor vehicle is manufactured in Canada a standardized 17-character alphanumeric VIN, vehicle identification number, must be attached to each vehicle. It can be found on a plate, usually located on the dashboard, and is unique to that vehicle. Prudent persons will not rely on the VIN as printed on the vehicle permit or ownership as errors do occur. If there is a difference between the VIN on the plate and the VIN in the ownership, it may be advisable to search both numbers as an added precaution.

3. The next request will be the type of search, i.e., verbal or certificate. If a certificate is ordered, it can be picked up at the PPSA office. The operator is advised to this effect and the certificate will be available after 10:30 a.m. the following day. If the search is performed on a Friday, the certificate will be available on the Monday immediately following. If a verbal search is requested, the operator will then check through the system for the name of the debtor as supplied. As soon as the name is located in the system, the operator calls up a screen which shows the financing statements registered, together with any amendments or discharges thereof, in the system. The operator will then ask whether or not full information is required. Normally all of the information in the file is requested and the operator then proceeds to read out all the information contained in the family, as mentioned before, including the registration number. A careful note should be made of all of the details and if not certain of any detail, it should be checked immediately with the operator before proceeding to the next financing statement. Accuracy is particulary required in connection with telephone searches under the Act.

There are sometimes problems distinguishing the letters of a name being spelled over the telephone. Operators use the following letter identification phrases to eliminate this problem:

A for Adam	N for Nancy
B for Bob	O for Ocean
C for Charlie	P for Peter
D for David	Q for Queen
E for Easter	R for Roger

F for Frank	S for Susan
G for George	T for Tennis
H for Henry	U for Union
I for Island	V for Victoria
J for John	W for William
K for King	X for X-ray
L for Lola	Y for Yellow
M for Mary	Z for Zebra

For example, if the name of the corporation being searched is Widget Incorporated, the operator might spell it as follows:

William, **I**sland, **D**avid, **G**eorge, **E**aster, **T**ennis
Incorporated—in full

Another aid in eliminating errors in telephone searches under the PPSA is to use a search memorandum in the same format as the financing statement filed. A search memorandum can be used to record information received on telephone searches. A telephone search is often made to provide "instant" information, which is confirmed by ordering a certificate. The order is placed immediately after obtaining the results of the verbal search from the branch. If this procedure is followed, the searcher would check verbal and then order a certificate as well.

B. *In-person search.* If time demands that a personal attendance be made at the PPSA office, then the Enquiry Request, shown as Form 12.8, must be completed and handed to the clerk at the counter.

C. *Written enquiries.* A user of the system may complete an Enquiry Request Form, shown as Form 12.8, with the information required to obtain the desired search, that is identifying the type of search and providing the necessary information. This written enquiry is then mailed to the Central Office's Enquiry Department, along with a cheque for the appropriate fee payable to the Minister of Finance. A copy of the Enquiry Request Form is included as Appendix G in the *PPSA Guide* and may be duplicated or copies of this form are available at any of the branch offices. Refer to Appendix A for the full mailing address of the Enquiry Department.

There is provision for the production, copying and certifying of copies of all documents registered in the PPSR System available from the Central Office. In addition the Branch Offices can produce or retrieve and copy a chattel mortgage, conditional sales contract or an assignment of book debts included in its records. See Appendix B for the fees required for any of these services.

D. *Up-date search.* A user of the PPSR System who has already conducted a full search would want to check to see whether or not any other registrations had been made against the debtor since the original search. Provided a full search has been done, any such person could request an up-date search, also known as a sub-search.

An up-date search, or sub-search, would include only details of any registrations made subsequent to the date of full search. The "currency date" on the full search should be submitted with this up-date request to ensure that all registrations recorded since the date of the full search are disclosed.

If you would like to obtain a copy of the Personal Property Security Registration and Enquiry Guide or of the Accounts brochure, these can be obtained free of charge by writing to:

Personal Property Registration
Central Registration Branch,
PO. Box 21100, Postal Station A
TORONTO, Ontario
M5W 1W6

and are available in either French or English. Along with the request, a stamped, self-addressed envelope, minimum size of 254mm X 333mm, or 10" X 13", must be sent for each publication ordered. Sufficient postage should be attached for the weights listed below:

☐ English version—300 grams;

☐ French version—370 grams.

Copies can also be obtained from any Regional Land Registry Office that accepts PPSA registrations.

There is also provision for the production, copying and certifying of a copy of any Financing Statement or Financing Change Statement upon payment of the required fees.

In Toronto, certified copies of these statements can be obtained from the Personal Property Security Office. The registration number must be supplied and the name searched and it must be stated that a certified copy of either a financing statement or a financing change statement is required.

The Certificate attached to the copy of the requested statement states as follows:

CERTIFIED COPY OF A FINANCING STATEMENT

I hereby certify that the attached photocopy of a financing statement registered as number

20010315 1212 0043 3354

is a true copy of the said financing statement, registered on the 15th day of March, 2001, at 12:12 in the afternoon, in the Central Registration Branch bearing sequence number 3354.

Certified under my hand and seal this 18th day of March, 2001, at Toronto.

____

Registrar of Personal Property Security

(e) Section 427 Search Under the *Bank Act*

Banks, in addition to safeguarding money for their depositors, are in the business of lending money by way of secured loans to businesses or individuals as provided under the *Bank Act*. The borrower must sign the required bank form which vests in the bank a preferential lien on the goods or equipment involved. The security interest of the bank may be extended to include goods or materials received after the signing of the required form. In order to protect its security, the bank must register a Notice of Intention with the Bank of Canada (see Form 12.9).

Subsection 427(1) of the *Bank Act*, S.C. 1991, c. 46 sets out the types of security upon which a bank is authorized to lend money and make advances:

> **427.** (1) **Loans to certain borrowers and security.**—A bank may lend money and make advances
>
> (a) to any wholesale or retail purchaser or shipper of, or dealer in, products of agriculture, products of aquaculture, products of the forest, products of the quarry and mine, products of the sea, lakes and rivers or goods, wares and merchandise, manufactured or otherwise, on the security of such products or goods, wares and merchandise and of goods, wares and merchandise used in or procured for the packing of such products or goods, wares and merchandise,
>
> (b) to any person engaged in business as a manufacturer, on the security of goods, wares and merchandise manufactured or produced by that person or procured for such manufacture or production and of goods, wares and merchandise used in or procured for the packing of goods, wares and merchandise so manufactured or produced,
>
> (c) to any aquaculturist, on the security of aquacultural stock growing or produced in the aquaculture operation or on the security of aquacultural equipment or aquacultural implements,
>
> (d) to any farmer, on the security of crops growing or produced on the farm or on the security of agricultural equipment or agricultural implements,
>
> (e) to any aquaculturist
>
> (i) for the purchase of aquatic broodstock or aquatic seedstock, on the security of the aquatic broodstock or aquatic seedstock and any aquatic stock to be grown therefrom,
>
> (ii) for the purchase of pesticide, on the security of the pesticide and any aquatic stock to be grown from the site on which the pesticide is to be used, and
>
> (iii) for the purchase of feed, veterinary drugs, biologicals or vaccines, on the security of the feed, veterinary drugs, biologicals or vaccines and any aquatic stock to be grown in the aquaculture operation on which the feed, veterinary drugs, biologicals or vaccines are to be used,

(f) to any farmer

(i) for the purchase of seed grain or seed potatoes, on the security of the seed grain or seed potatoes and any crop to be grown therefrom, and

(ii) for the purchase of fertilizer or pesticide, on the security of the fertilizer or pesticide and any crop to be grown from land on which, in the same season, the fertilizer or pesticide is to be used,

(g) to any aquaculturist on the security of aquatic plants and animals, but security taken under this paragraph is not effective in respect of any aquatic plants and animals that, at the time the security is taken, by any statutory law that is then in force, are exempt from seizure under writs of execution and the aquaculturist is prevented from giving security for money lent to the aquaculturist,

(h) to any farmer or to any person engaged in livestock raising, on the security of feed or livestock, but security taken under this paragraph is not effective in respect of any livestock that, at the time the security is taken, by any statutory law that is then in force, is exempt from seizure under writs of execution and the farmer or other person engaged in livestock raising is prevented from giving as security for money lent to the farmer or other person,

(i) to any aquaculturist for the purchase of aquacultural implements, on the security of those aquacultural implements,

(j) to any farmer for the purchase of agricultural implements, on the security of those agricultural implements,

(k) to any aquaculturalist for the purchase or installation of aquacultural equipment or an aquacultural electric system, on the security of that aquacultural equipment or aquacultural electric system,

(l) to any farmer for the purchase or installation of agricultural equipment or a farm electric system, on the security of that agricultural equipment or farm electric system,

(m) to any aquaculturist for

(i) the repair or overhaul of an aquacultural implement, aquacultural equipment or an aquaculture electric system,

(ii) the alteration or improvement of an aquacultural electric system,

(iii) the erection or construction of fencing or works for drainage in an aquaculture operation for the holding, rearing or protection of aquatic plants and animals or for the supply of water to such plants and animals or the disposal of effluent from them,

(iv) the construction, repair or alteration of or making of additions to any building or structure in an aquaculture operation, and

(v) any works for the improvement or development of an aquaculture operation for which a loan, as defined in the *Canada Small Business Financing Act*, a business improvement loan, as defined in the *Small*

Business Loans Act, or a farm improvement loan, as defined in the *Farm Improvement Loans Act*, may be made, (S.C. 1993, c. 6, s. 6; 1998, c. 36, s. 21.)

on the security of aquacultural equipment or aquacultural implements, but security taken under this paragraph is not effective in respect of aquacultural equipment or aquacultural implements that, at the time the security is taken, by any statutory law that is then in force, are exempt from seizure under writs of execution and the aquaculturist is prevented from giving as security for money lent to the aquaculturist,

(n) to any farmer for

(i) the repair or overhaul of an agricultural implement, agricultural equipment or a farm electric system,

(ii) the alteration or improvement of a farm electric system,

(iii) the erection or construction of fencing or works for drainage on a farm,

(iv) the construction, repair or alteration of or making of additions to any building or structure on a farm,

(v) any works for the improvement or development of a farm for which a farm improvement loan as defined in the *Farm Improvement Loans Act* may be made, and

(vi) any purpose for which a loan as defined in the *Farm Improvement and Marketing Cooperatives Loans Act* may be made,

on the security of agricultural equipment or agricultural implements, but security taken under this paragraph is not effective in respect of agricultural equipment or agricultural implements that, at the time the security is taken, by any statutory law that is then in force, are exempt from seizure under writs of execution and the farmer is prevented from giving as security for money lent to the farmer,

(o) to any fisherman, on the security of fishing vessels, fishing equipment and supplies or products of the sea, lakes and rivers, but security taken under this paragraph is not effective in respect of any such property that, at the time the security is taken, by any statutory law that is then in force, is exempt from seizure under writs of execution and the fisherman is prevented from giving as security for money lent to the fisherman, and

(p) to any forestry producer, on the security of fertilizer, pesticide, forestry equipment, forestry implements or products of the forest, but security taken under this paragraph is not effective in respect of any such property that, at the time the security is taken, by any statutory law that is then in force, is exempt from seizure under writs of execution and the forestry producer is prevented from giving as security for money lent to the forestry producer,

and the security may be given by signature and delivery to the bank, by or on behalf of the person giving the security, of a document in the prescribed form or in a form to the like effect.

A bank may secure advances to a manufacturer by taking security under subection 427(3) on the inventory. If the funds are not repaid, the bank can seize the inventory and sell it to settle the debt.

The only registration required is a Notice of Intention (see Form 12.9) which is filed with the branch of the Bank of Canada, or its authorized representative, located in the area of the borrower's principal place of business or residence.

In the case of a corporation, whether federal or provincial, this would be the place where the head/registered office is located. If, for example, the borrower's residence or head/registered office, as the case may be, is located in the City of Toronto, a search is made at the Bank of Canada's authorized representative, Canadian Securities Registration System (CSRS) located at 439 University Avenue, Suite 2000, Toronto. A letter search can be made but this process costs slightly more and is time-consuming. An ''in person'' search at the business premises of CSRS for section 427 searches is faster and cost-efficient. On payment of the required fee, and the completion of a request form, the staff of CSRS conduct a computer search and provide a search certificate detailing the name of the debtor, the address of the debtor, the date of registration, the registration number, and the name of the bank.

A letter search can be made and an individual computer-generated search certificate is sent by Canadian Securities Registration Systems.

The bank can only acquire security under section 427 if the advance is made:

1. at the time such security is acquired; or
2. if the advance is made upon the customer's written promise that a section 427 assignment will be given.

The bank will require the borrower to execute an application for a line of credit for a definite period, perhaps one year. In the application the borrower agrees that any advance under the credit will be secured by an assignment under section 427 given by the borrower.

Notices of Intention are cancelled after five years unless the bank involved gives notice that they are still in effect.

The bank will also require the borrower to execute an assignment of the property. In the event of non-payment, the bank has the right to sell all or any of the assigned property.

(f) Bankruptcy Search

(i) General

There is a risk when money is loaned that the debtor will not be able to repay the loan. If a debtor is unable to pay any debts as they fall due, he or she is said to be insolvent, not bankrupt. Insolvency frequently precedes bankruptcy. Under the *Bankruptcy and Insolvency Act*, R.S.C. 1985, c. B-3, bankruptcy arises when an individual has debts of more than $1,000 and has committed an act of bankruptcy. There are ten specific acts of bankruptcy under the statute which include an assignment of property to a trustee for the benefit of creditors or leaving the country to avoid or delay his creditors. A debtor in financial difficulties may attempt to resolve related problems by:

1. making a proposal to the creditors;
2. making a voluntary assignment in bankruptcy; or
3. permitting the creditors to petition for a receiving order.

The decision to use either of the first two methods is made solely by the debtor. The third procedure may be undertaken by the creditors alone or jointly with the debtor. Regardless of the method adopted, a licensed trustee will be appointed to administer the assets or estate of the bankrupt. The trustee collects all of the assets of the bankrupt and if possible converts them into cash, which is then distributed among the creditors. Assets that are subject to security interests are made available to the creditor who is known as a "secured creditor". Any moneys left over after the disposition of the property by the secured creditor are given to the trustee to be included in the distribution to other creditors. If the debt owed to a secured creditor is not paid in full by the sale of the secured property, the secured creditor can claim the unpaid balance as an unsecured creditor. Unsecured creditors share *pro rata* any balance remaining after all prior claims have been satisfied. Until a bankrupt is discharged by the Bankruptcy Court that individual is not released from his or her debts. Any moneys earned before the discharge may, if the court orders, be paid to creditors.

A bankrupt must not carry on business without disclosing that he or she is an undischarged bankrupt. That person cannot purchase goods on credit, except for necessities. The amount must not exceed $500, unless the bankrupt discloses his or her status to the seller. The trustee generally applies for a discharge of the bankrupt within 12 months after proceedings are instituted. If the bankrupt is an individual who, for example, is simply unable to handle credit and "got in over his or her head" the application for discharge may be made anywhere from three to six months in cases where it is obvious no attempt has been made to defraud the creditors. A discharge releases the bankrupt from all debts and obligations with certain exceptions involving fines and penalties imposed by law for wrongdoing or amounts due under a maintenance or separation agreement or court order. A corporation must pay all of the creditors' claims to obtain a discharge.

(ii) Making the Search

A search is made, either at an area office or in the Bankruptcy Court Office, Toronto, to ascertain whether or not proceedings have been instituted to declare a corporation or individual a bankrupt. The general purpose of this search is to make sure that proceedings have not been started. If bankruptcy proceedings are in progress, the debtor cannot be sued as all proceedings are stayed or stopped.

A bankruptcy search might be requested in situations where a particular customer requested a line of credit, or where inventory might be on consignment with a particular customer or in connection with a purchase of assets of a corporation by a third party.

Set out below is a list of Bankruptcy Offices and the geographical areas included under the jurisdiction of each office:

OTTAWA HEAD OFFICE

(613) 941-1000

TORONTO—DIVISION #31

(416) 973-6486

AJAX	HAVELOCK	PARRY SOUND
ALGOMA	HUNTSVILLE	PICKERING
ALLISTON	KENORA	RICHMOND HILL
BEAVERTON	KESWICK	SCARBOROUGH
BOWMANVILLE	KIRKLAND LAKE	SIMCOE
BRACEBRIDGE	LINDSAY	STOUFFVILLE
BURKETON	MACTIER	SUTTON
CAMPBELLFORD	MANITOULIN	TEMISKAMING
COBOURG	MIDLAND	TIMMINS
COCHRANE	MUSKOKA	TOTTENHAM
COLLINGWOOD	NIPISSING	UXBRIDGE
CONCORD	NORTH BAY	WEST HILL
ELMVALE	NORTHUMBERLAND	WHITBY
GRAVENHURST	ORILLIA	YORK
HALIBURTON	OSHAWA	

HAMILTON—DIVISION #32

(905) 572-2847

ACTON	FORT ERIE	NIAGARA FALLS
BOLTON	GEORGETOWN	NORFOLK
BRAMALEA	GRIMSBY	NORVAL

BRAMPTON	HAGERSVILLE	OAKVILLE
BRANT	HALTON	PEEL
BURLINGTON	LINCOLN	ST CATHARINES
CALEDON,	MILTON	WELLAND
CALEDON EAST	MISSISSAUGA	WENTWORTH

LONDON—DIVISION #35

(519)645-4034

BRUCE	GREY	OXFORD
CAMBRIDGE	GUELPH	PERTH
CHATHAM	HURON	SARNIA
CLARKSBURG	KENT	TILLSONBURG
DRESDEN	KITCHENER	WALKERTON
DUFFERIN	LAMBTON	WALLACEBURG
ELGIN	MIDDLESEX	WATERLOO
ESSEX	ORANGEVILLE	WELLINGTON
FERGUS	OWEN SOUND	WINDSOR

OTTAWA—DIVISION #33

(613) 995-2994

ADDINGTON	HASTINGS	PRESCOTT
ARNPRIOR	HAWKESBURY	PRINCE EDWARD
BELLEVILLE	KINGSTON	RENFREW
BROCKVILLE	LANARK	RUSSELL
CARLETON	LEEDS	SMITHS FALLS
DUNDAS	LENNOX	STORMONT
FRONTENAC	PERTH	VANIER CITY
GLENGARRY	PEMBROKE	
GRENVILLE	PICTON	

Included in Appendix A is a list of offices of the Superintendent of Bankruptcy in Canada.

In addition to making the search at the appropriate Bankruptcy Office, it is also essential to telephone the Official Receiver in the particular area where the debtor resides. There is approximately a two-week time lapse between the time the assignment or proposal is filed with the Official Receiver and when notice of the proceedings reach the Bankruptcy Court Office. The assignment is a voluntary act of bankruptcy and the proposal is made when the debtor cannot satisfy in full the claims of its, his or her debtors. The debtor attempts to persuade the creditors that they would fare better under the proposal than under a petition in bankruptcy.

An on-site bankruptcy search can be made at the office of the Official Receiver in Toronto. (Information on pending bankruptcies is available in the public section of the office.)

Either on-line personal searches or certificate searches can be made at the Bankruptcy Court Offices located in London, Ottawa or Toronto. There is counter access in Toronto to the user-friendly computerized system. The information updates are scheduled for every two weeks but sometimes exceed this time-frame. The file currency date is shown on the computer display and there are complete instructions on how to access the system. In addition there is a back-up microfiche listing which can be checked but, since updates are no longer received, this microfiche listing cannot be relied on for currency of information. It may be that a bankrupt will appear on the microfiche but not appear in the computer system. Only Ontario bankruptcies are listed in the computer system. Bankruptcies that occur in other provinces, but where the bankrupts have offices in Ontario, and Ontario bankruptcies are listed on the microfiche. A check should also be made of the Petitions Book, also referred to as the Day Book, for bankruptcies not as yet listed in the computer system.

When the search of the records is completed, or if a Certificate is ordered, the searcher can order the printing of the Certificate by the computer system. The Certificate is held until the correct fees, shown on the cash control slip completed by the staff and handed to the searcher, are paid in the appropriate office area. Presentation of the receipt obtains the printed Certificate. See Form 12.10 for a sample of the Certificate. Fees apply only if a Certificate is ordered.

An online insolvency name search can be conducted via the internet through the website of the Office of the Superintendent of Bankruptcy Canada at *http://strategis.ic.gc.ca/sc_marksv/bankrupt/engdoc/general.html*. The database accessed contains a record of all bankruptcies and proposals filed in Canada from 1978 to date. It also contains a record of all private and court appointed receiverships filed in Canada from 1993 to date. All petitions that have been registered in the district offices of the Office of the Superintendent are also available in the database. There is a minimum $8.00 charge for each search, including those which result in ''no record''. In the case of multiple hits, the charge is $8.00 for each group of 10 matches or less, utilizing the same search criteria. Users are able to redefine their search criteria in order to limit their costs. A template is utilized in submitting the name of the debtor searched and indicating whether the debtor is an individual or corporation.

Payment must be made either online, using the Strategis secure financial server with a valid Mastercard or Visa credit card, or by setting up a client account with the Office of the Superintendent of Bankruptcy for billing purposes.

Industry Canada has prepared a publication titled ''Dealing with Debt: A Consumer's Guide'' which is available to the public. This guide outlines everything from recognizing the danger signals of a financial crisis to a guide to the legal process involved in declaring bankruptcy. Should a member of the public contact the office of the Superintendent of Bankruptcy in Toronto enquiring about the bankruptcy process, this publication, an application for bankruptcy services and a list of trustees in bankruptcy are forwarded. The Office of the Superintendent is also involved in a Debtor Assistance Service. If a trustee cannot be found, and if the person feels that declaring bankruptcy is the course to be followed, the enquirer is advised to contact the Toronto office which will help the person find a trustee through the Debtor Assistance Service. This service is available where the debts are mostly personal rather than business-related.

The address and telephone number for the Toronto office are listed in Appendix A.

(g) Ontario Securities Commission Search (Micromedia)

A public corporation lists its shares on the American Stock Exchange, or on the Stock Exchanges in Toronto, New York, or the Canadian Venture Exhange (CDNX) based in Montreal. Searches of OSC files on public corporations can only be made at the offices of the Ontario Securities Commission. Current files are retained in the OSC office and older files are stored in off-site storage facilities. It normally takes about two days to obtain files that are in storage.

Another option open to the public in Toronto for information on offering (public) corporations is Micromedia Limited. Micromedia Limited (''Micromedia'') is the official documents agent for the Ontario Securities Commission. Its services were expanded to cover Canadian corporate reports from all Canadian jurisdictions. Its CanCorp Demand Documents Services now covers over 13,000 corporations, including corporations which became inactive in that period. Micromedia has produced a comprehensive guide, ''CanCorp Guide to Canadian Corporate Reports'', which contains information on:

- ☐ where to find specific items in corporate filings;
- ☐ the differences between U.S. and Canadian public disclosures; and
- ☐ Canadian corporate registration.

A copy of this Guide can be obtained by contacting the Information Centre of Micromedia.

Micromedia can be contacted by telephone: 1-800-387-2689, in Toronto (416) 369-2599, or via email at demanddocs@micromedia.on.ca.

Micromedia also indicates in this Guide that it has available, at no charge, ''Disclosure's Guide to SEC Corporate Filings''. Canadian corporations that plan on raising funds in the United States through public issues must comply with all Security Exchange Commission (''SEC'') filings.

Chapters of the Guide list the corporate information services available from Micromedia. Documents can be supplied through Subscription, Demand or Monitoring Services. Subscription documents are delivered on microfiche and customers may select only the documents required or all documents or a certain type or only documents from the selected corporation. Clients may order documents through the Demand Documents Service by telephone, email, fax or mail. They will be received the same day in Toronto or on the next day elsewhere. A limited reading room facility is available in Micromedia's Toronto office. If necessary a searcher could go to the office, access the microfiche to select the documents required and copies would be made while the searcher waits. There is little or no delay in complying with such requests, depending on how busy the office is on any given day. If a Monitoring Service is chosen then the Information Centre will watch for the specific filings requested. When the document appears it will be prepared and forwarded to the customer on the same day. Full information on all services with time-frames for delivery can be obtained by ordering a copy of the Guide.

CanCorp Financials is a web-based product that provides financial and management information extracted from the corporate documents of over 13,000 Canadian companies. Based on its Canadian Corporations database, CanCorp provides corporate details, seven years of financials, ratios, operating statistics and five to seven year history of stock performance data for virtually all active public companies. Archival information is maintained on an additional 8,000 public, private and Crown Corporations.

Information on additional services offered, or more details on those mentioned here, may be obtained directly from Micromedia.

One area of particular interest to law offices would be the information on corporations in the United States which are required to file with the Securities Exchange Commission in Washington. The records on file at Micromedia include annual reports, 10K and 10Q filings. The term ''10K'' describes a filing which contains more detailed information than an annual report, for example, particulars of the principal products produced by the corporation or the raw materials available. The term ''10Q'' is a quarterly filing of interim financial reports. Information at hand on OSC filings includes insider reports, annual reports, annual information returns, prospecti, interim financial statements, Toronto Stock Exchange material, shareholders' meetings material, private placements (Form 20 under the Act lists officers and shareholders of the corporation) and other reports.

Micromedia introduced two additional products, the OSC Bulletin PLUS, available since June 1995, and the Prospectus Researcher PLUS, available since September 1995, both on CD-ROM, Web, email or print. The highlights are as follows:

(i) *OSC Bulletin PLUS*

The OSC Bulletin PLUS on CD-ROM offers instant access to the OSC Bulletin, excluding insider trading, directly from a PC. This enables retrieval, display and print of historical content of the OSC Bulletin in a matter of seconds. Included are:

- ☐ insider trading (Chapter 7) from January, 2000 to present;
- ☐ full text of all OSC Bulletin chapters, with the exception noted above, from January 1995 to present and all text chapters from January 1995 to present;
- ☐ complete historical index of the contents of all OSC Bulletins from January 1988 to December 1999;
- ☐ complete index of OSC company filings from 1985 to December 1999 (on a separate CD-ROM);
- ☐ updated monthly and fully searchable using Folio Views; and
- ☐ public filings (Chapter 10) from January 2000.

The OSC Bulletin hard copy version is available as an annual subscription, with weekly updates. Back issues are available on microfiche or as hard copy.

(ii) *Prospectus Researcher PLUS*

Prospectus Researcher PLUS on CD-ROM is, Micromedia advises, the most comprehensive archival prospectus research tool available today. It can find prospectuses which meet the specific criteria, locate information to support development of new prospectuses or determine the leading advisory firms in various industries. Included are:

- ☐ data from all prospectuses in 1994 (delivery September 1995) and 1995 (delivery December 1995) — a full list of fields and sample records is available on request;
- ☐ complete index of OSC company filings from 1986 to 1994;
- ☐ beginning in 1996, monthly updates of the service;
- ☐ fully searchable using *Folio Views*; and
- ☐ it is available in both Windows and Macintosh versions and fully networkable.

Prospectus Researcher PLUS will end the tedious task of reviewing or scanning hundreds of prospectuses to find the information and precedents required.

Micromedia states that either, or both, of the above services are indispensable tools for all securities industry professionals. These services will be of interest to professionals involved in the Canadian securities industry such as brokers, investment dealers, securities professionals, corporate secretaries, lawyers, accountants, fund managers and librarians.

(h) Executions

Executions lodged in the local Sheriff's office result from successful action taken by a creditor in the courts to collect moneys owed by a debtor in default. Court action is usually a last resort after all other attempts to collect the debt have failed. The execution search is essential in real estate transactions but may be required in corporate financings as well. If, for example, a debtor owns real property and this real property is registered in the Land Titles System, notice of the judgment has to be registered with both the local Sheriff's Office and the appropriate Land Registry Office. In order to improve service to the public, the execution search services in many areas have been relocated to the local Land Registry Offices and the equivalent services offered by the Sheriff's Office and the Land Titles Division have been amalgamated. Through the computerization of the system, initiated in 1987, all new filings of writs of execution or renewals are automatically included in the Land Titles System Index of Writs. Copies of writs and the filing of new writs or renewals will continue to be handled by the Sheriff's Office. The search fees are listed in Appendix B.

The corporate name to be searched should be taken from its charter documents to ensure accurate search results. For example, if the corporate name includes the word "The", but this is not included, or the legal element is wrong, the results could be unreliable, as outlined below:

Name Searched—The KM Company Limited

Included	*Not Included*
The KM Company Limited	The KM Company Inc.
KM Company Limited	KM Company Incorporated

Omission of the word "The" would result in a "no match" indicating that there were no executions lodged against the corporation, when in fact this might not be correct.

(i) Patents Search

Any individual or corporation wishing to protect an invention from being copied must file a patent application with the Patents Office of the federal government in Ottawa. Before filing such an application, a search of the existing records will be made to see if the particular invention is already on record. General information on the process involved can be obtained by telephoning (819) 997-1936 or by attending personally at the regional office of Industry Canada located at 25 St. Clair Avenue East in Toronto. Copies of the rules and regulations regarding such applications can be purchased from Renouf Publishing Company (Ontario) Ltd., 12 Adelaide St. West, Toronto, or at its Ottawa office. A preliminary patent search can be made at the Metropolitan Toronto Library and information as to the procedures involved can be obtained by telephone. It is indicated by the regional office of Industry Canada that the records on file there are not guaranteed to be complete or up to date. They are sufficient, however, to meet the requirements for a preliminary search and are filed numerically and by subject-matter. If searching for records of an existing patent, it would be helpful to have the patent number under which the invention is registered in Ottawa.

Depending on the results of this preliminary search, a decision must then be made as to whether or not the person wishes to travel to the Patents Office in Ottawa to make a further search or hire a patent attorney to undertake the recording of the invention by patent. Patent attorneys specialize in this area and are listed in the local telephone directory. It would be advisable when meeting with a patent attorney for the first time to request an estimate of the fee for all services involved in completing the patent registration in full, including the Ottawa search. The patent attorney, rather than personally attending in Ottawa, may hire a local person to act as an agent to perform the search. These costs would be added to the patent attorney's fee.

Fundamental changes to the *Patent Act*, R.S.C. 1985, c. P-4, were passed by Parliament in November 1987 (S.C. 1987, c. 41) and proclaimed on October 1, 1989. The amendments represented a major effort to update the Act, and have resulted in earlier notice to the public of applications involving new technologies.

The changes impact primarily on the areas of early publication, first to file, absolute novelty, term of protection and the Patent Cooperation Treaty. Information and copies of Canadian and foreign patent documents are available from Micromedia's Technical Information Centre. Canadian patent applications are, according to the *Micromedia Monitor*, indexed in the *Canadian Patent Office Record*, issued weekly by Industry Canada.

(j) Motor Vehicle Search

The Ministry of Transportation maintains the records on motor vehicles registered in Ontario. Should it become necessary to either know or confirm the owner of a motor vehicle, a search can be made of these records. The searcher must complete the Application for Vehicle Record Search, shown as Form 12.11, and mail or deliver this form, along with the prescribed fee listed on the form, to the address shown for the record search. This address is also listed in Appendix A.

The Ministry of Transportation also provides online services in the driver, vehicle and commercial areas. In the vehicle area, a confirmation letter can be requested confirming the status of an Ontario motor vehicle registration. The letter will contain the Vehicle Identification Number (VIN), the vehicle owner's name, plate number, validation sticker number, date of issue, and expiry, plus a full description of the vehicle. The fee is $6.00 for the hardcopy letter, and an additional fee of $6.00 for certification.

Part III

Federal Corporations

13

Federal Incorporations

1. Introduction

If, during discussions with clients, it appears that the business of the proposed corporation will be carried on in several provinces in Canada, and particularly if using the name of the proposed corporation is essential to business, lawyers often recommend incorporation in the federal jurisdiction. This jurisdiction will be recommended if it will best serve the interests of the particular clients.

2. Glossary of Terms

The CBCA has a special vocabulary and some of the terms from the statute which are used in this text are set out below

articles of continuance:	the articles sent to the Director when applying for a Certificate of Continuance under the CBCA.
body corporate:	a company, or other body corporate, whenever or however incorporated.
corporation:	a body corporate, incorporated or continued under the CBCA or not discontinued under the Act.
Director:	the individual appointed by the Minister to carry out the duties and exercise the powers of the Director under the statute.
director:	a person acting as a director of a corporation.
distributing corporation:	a federal corporation that distributes its securities to the public, the federal equivalent of the Ontario offering corporation.

exporting corporation:	a federally incorporated corporation, either incorporated or continued under the CBCA, which has applied to leave the federal jurisdiction for a provincial jurisdiction.
importing corporation:	a corporation not federally incorporated, that is, incorporated provincially or in a foreign jurisdiction.
non-distributing corporation:	a corporation that does not distribute its securities to the public, the federal equivalent of the Ontario non-offering corporation.
ordinary resolution:	a resolution passed by a majority of the votes cast by the shareholders who voted in respect of that resolution.
person:	includes an individual, partnership, association, body corporate, trustee, executor, administrator or legal representative.
prescribed:	means required under the CBCA Regulations.
redeemable share:	a share issued by a corporation which it may redeem or purchase on demand or which it is required by its articles to redeem or purchase at a specified time or on the demand of a shareholder or at a specified time.
resident Canadian:	a Canadian citizen ordinarily resident in Canada; a Canadian citizen not ordinarily resident in Canada who is a member of a prescribed class of persons; or a permanent resident within the meaning of the *Immigration Act* and ordinarily resident in Canada, except one ordinarily resident in Canada for more than one year after becoming eligible to apply for Canadian citizenship.
security:	a share of any class or series of shares or a debt obligation of a corporation and includes a certificate evidencing such a share or debt obligation.
special resolution:	a resolution passed by a majority of not less than two-thirds of the votes cast by the shareholders who voted in respect of that resolution or signed by all the shareholders entitled to vote on that resolution.

unanimous shareholder agreement:	an otherwise lawful written agreement among all the shareholders or among all the shareholders and a person who is not a shareholder, that restricts, in whole or in part, the powers of the directors to manage the business and affairs of the corporation; or a declaration signed by a sole shareholder.

3. Incorporation

(a) Name and NUANS System

The initial step when incorporating a federal corporation is to clear the proposed name.

The name clearance process is the same for both provincial and federal incorporations. All proposed names must be submitted through a private search house which accesses the NUANS (Newly Updated Automated Name Search) database located in Ottawa. This database was established, and is maintained, by Industry Canada through the use of a service bureau. The NUANS name search requests received from a search house must be weighted for the jurisdiction in which the application for articles of incorporation will be filed. For example, a name could not be submitted and cleared for a provincial incorporation and then filed with a federal application. Federal applications for incorporation must be submitted or filed with a federally-biased name search report. Name searches biased for different jurisdictional levels are not interchangeable. When ordering a name search report from a search house the jurisdiction in which the application will be filed must be supplied.

The computer printout received from the search house is merely a recommendation that the proposed name is available for incorporation. In Ontario the responsibility for the decision to incorporate rests with the incorporators and the lawyer acting on their behalf. This decision is made on the basis of the NUANS name search report, biased for Ontario, and in accordance with the provisions of the BCA and the Regulations.

The recommendation made by a search house on the availability of a federally proposed name is made on the basis of the Name Granting Compendium published by the Corporations Branch of the Corporations Directorate, Industry Canada. A copy of the most recent publication is included as Form 13.1. This recommendation however does not automatically guarantee that the application will be granted by the Corporations Branch when it is received. If the incorporators want to be certain that the application will be approved, a copy of the NUANS Search Report can be submitted to the Corporations Directorate, by fax, prior to filing articles requesting a decision on the proposed name. There is no fee for this service and the fax number is (613) 941-5782. Once a favourable decision is received, then the proposed name is reserved for 90 days retroactive to the date of the NUANS Search Report. Anyone else submitting a similar or identical name to the approved name during the 90-day reservation period would be advised the name is not available. The only exception to this general rule would be instances where one client has proposed both names. The name remains on the database for a period of 180 days unless the incorporation has been filed and granted. It is then purged from the system.

If the search house has recommended in the NUANS Search Report that the name is not available, the incorporators can forward a copy of the search report to the Corporations Directorate, Industry Canada, requesting a review. The decision as to the availability of the name is made by the Corporations Directorate.

Some concern has been expressed about the currency of the information in the database on which the search houses base their recommendations. Information is added to this database from several sources on a continuing basis such as:

1. As names are submitted for clearance, they are automatically retained on the database for varying periods of time. For example, federal and Alberta name clearances remain on the database for 180 days while Ontario name submissions are purged after 150 days.
2. Weekly tapes are received from Ontario, Manitoba, New Brunswick, Prince Edward Island, Quebec and Saskatchewan listing recent incorporations. British Columbia and Alberta send a monthly tape and Nova Scotia forwards a similar tape every three months.
3. Information from Newfoundland, the Northwest Territories and the Yukon on new incorporations and proposed names are added from their tapes and keypunched from issues of the respective Gazettes.
4. In September 1990, Alberta added about 300,000 business names and, since the legislation does not require a renewal of the original registration, it is not known which of these business names represent active, or inactive, businesses.
5. Registered trade-marks and pending applications are also added to the NUANS database. The current federal policy is to place corporations on the inactive list if the file is dormant over a period of time. The corporations remain on this inactive list for about three years and, although Industry Canada retains the records, the names are then removed from the NUANS database. The provincial statutes governing corporations are rather vague as to when a corporation becomes inactive. Names of corporations received from Ontario, Manitoba, Saskatchewan and Alberta will remain on the database until this situation is clarified. British Columbia has a policy for

placing corporations on the inactive list and when this occurs, deletes the names from its tapes and then the NUANS database is updated. Information on Quebec's inactive corporations will be kept on the system for two years and then removed.

A NUANS report is only valid for a period of 90 days. After this, the search is considered "stale-dated" and a new search must be obtained and filed with the articles of incorporation.

A list of private search houses can be obtained from Industry Canada, which has a list of all search houses in Canada. However, care should be taken in the selection of a search house in order to ensure a quality report for the clients of the law office. A good choice, in the Toronto area, would be either of the following:

1. Dye & Durham Co. Inc. (D & D); or
2. Canadian Securities Registration Systems.

These search houses, in an effort to supply a quality search, augment the computer printout with a manual search of microfiche which are purchased from Industry Canada. These microfiche are a duplicate of the microfiche in the offices of Industry Canada.

There are certain instances in which a name search report is not required:

1. *Amalgamation:* a search is not necessary for either an Ontario or federal company, provided the name used is identical to one of the amalgamating corporations;
2. *Continuance:* a search is not required for the continuance of a federal Special Act corporation (one that was incorporated by an Act of Parliament) to the *Canada Business Corporations Act*, provided the name remains identical in every respect. Any other type of continuance requires a NUANS Search Report;
3. *Changes:* in the legal element, *i.e.*, Limited to Ltd., Corp. to Corporation, does not require a search. If the change involves adding or deleting punctuation, this may significantly alter the name and any such change should be discussed with the searchouse or the Corporations Directorate before proceeding. Hyphens, periods or parentheses are treated as word separators in the NUANS system, that is, as blank spaces between two words.
4. *Acquisition:* of all, or substantially all, of the property of an affiliated body corporate. The corporate name may be used provided its affiliate undertakes in writing to dissolve or change its name before the corporation adopts the name; and
5. *Successor Corporation:* to the business of a body corporate which has ceased, or will cease to carry on business and undertakes in writing to dissolve forthwith or change its name before the corporation proposing to

use a similar corporate name adopts it. The body corporate so undertaking must be a federal corporation. A NUANS microfiche search is sufficient.

There are also circumstances in which two searches may be required if' a bilingual name for the corporation is proposed. Generally speaking, a bilingual name will require an additional search only in instances where the English version is phonetically different from the French version when the descriptive element is translated, such as:

Rainbow Paint Distributors Inc./ Distributeurs de Peinture Arc—en-Ciel Inc.-two searches are required;

Dustbane Enterprises Ltd./Les Entreprises Dustbane Ltée.—one search only is required.

A sample NUANS computer printout for Sandusky Construction Inc. is shown as Form 13.3.

If the name is extremely long, it may be a problem since the NUANS system can only accept a maximum of 39 characters. Anything over this maximum number must be shortened by omitting ''familiar'' words in the NUANS dictionary, such as the word ''Association''. Another alternative is to omit any articles, conjunctions or prepositions contained in the proposed name, such as ''the'', ''and'' or ''of'', and retaining the major elements of the proposed name. The reporting letter received from the searchouse would show the full proposed name but the NUANS printout would show only the major elements of the proposed name. It is possible to search and incorporate long names provided the appropriate steps are taken.

(b) Key to Reading Computer Printout

When the NUANS computer printout is received, there are several abbreviations which provide useful information, provided the reader is aware of their meanings.

The following information will prove helpful in reading these printouts:

Column 1 lists the similar names;

Column 2 lists the type or form of business ownership and its jurisdiction; and

Column 3 lists the incorporation and/or registration date.

The abbreviations used for the calendar months and the various provinces are:

Months		*Provinces*	
January	JA	Alberta	AB
February	FE	British Columbia	BC
March	MR	Manitoba	MB
April	AL	New Brunswick	NB

May	MA	Newfoundland	NF
June	JN	Nova Scotia	NS
July	JL	Ontario	ON
August	AU	Prince Edward Island	PE
September	SE	Quebec	QC
October	OC	Saskatchewan	SK
November	NO	Northwest Territories	NT
December	DE	Yukon	YK
		Canada	CD

Corporations and business names appear on the first three pages of the NUANS Search Report. Trade-marks information appears on the last two pages of the Search Report.

(c) Name Clearance

The Corporations Directorate of Industry Canada publishes a name granting policy statement entitled Name Granting Guidelines which includes information that will assist persons who will be submitting applications for which a NUANS Search Report is required.

Section 10 of the CBCA sets out the statute requirements for names as follows:

1. *Names:* generally the "legal" element to be included or that which can be included or that which can be included in the name of a corporation (subsections 10(1) and (1.1));
2. *Alternate Name:* a corporation can set out its name in its articles in: an English form; a French form; an English form and a French form; or in a combined English and French form (subsection 10(3));
3. *Alternative Name Outside Canada:* a corporation may set its name out in any language in its articles for use outside Canada (subsection 10(4));
4. *Publication of Name:* shall set out its name legibly in all contracts, invoices, negotiable instruments and orders for goods or services issued or made by or on behalf of the corporation (subsection 10(5));
5. *Other Name:* right to carry on business under or identify itself by a name other than its corporate name, subject to subsection (5) (the publication of the name) and subsection 12(1), if that other name does not contain, other than in a figurative or descriptive sense, the legal element of its corporate name (subsection 10(6)).

In addition, the Regulations, SOR/79-316, as amended, set out certain requirements so far as the proposed name is concerned under Part II (Corporate Names). These are as follows:

PART II

CORPORATE NAMES

Interpretation

12. In this Part,

''confusing'', in relation to a corporate name, means a corporate name the use of which causes confusion with a trade mark or trade name in the manner described in section 13; *(prête à confusion)*

''distinctive'', in relation to a trade name, means a trade name that actually distinguishes the business in association with which it is used by its owner from the business of others or that is adapted so as to distinguish them; *(distinctif)*

''secondary meaning'', in relation to a trade name, means a trade name that has been used in Canada or elsewhere by any applicant or his predecessors so as to have become distinctive in Canada as at the date of filing an application for a corporate name; (*sens dérivé*)

''trade mark'', means a trade mark as defined by the *Trade Marks Act, (marques de commerce)*

''trade name'' means the name under which any business is carried on, whether it is the name of a body corporate, a trust, a partnership, a proprietorship or an individual; *(nom commercial)*

''use'' means actual use by a person that carries on business in Canada or elsewhere. (*emploi*)

Confusion of Names

13. A corporate name is confusing with

(a) a trade mark if the use of both the corporate name and the trade mark is likely to lead to the inference that the business carried on or intended to be carried on under the corporate name and the business connected with the trade mark are one business, whether or not the nature of the business of each is generally the same; or

(b) a trade name if the use of both names is likely to lead to the inference that the business carried on or intended to be carried on under the corporate name and the business carried on under the trade name are one business, whether or not the nature of the business of each is generally the same.

Consideration of Whole Name

14. Subject to section 19, when determining whether a trade name is distinctive, the name as a whole and not only its separate elements shall be considered.

Reservation of Corporate Name

15. (1) A request, pursuant to section 11 of the Act, to reserve a corporate name that is not a designating number shall be made by submitting to the Director the original of a Canada-biased NUANS search report dated not more than 90 days before the date of its submission.

(2) Where the corporate name requested has an English form and a French form or a combined English and French form in a single name, and the English and French forms are phonetically dissimilar, the originals of separate NUANS search reports shall be submitted for both the English and the French forms.

15.1 For the purposes of section 15, "NUANS search report" means the computer-generated search report that identifies trade names which are phonetically similar to the corporate name in respect of which the search is performed and that is produced by the Newly Upgraded Automated Name Search (NUANS) system, which uses the national data bank of existing and reserved trade names, and registered and applied-for trademarks, in Canada.

15.2 For the purposes of paragraph 12(1)(a) of the Act, a corporate name is prohibited in respect of a request to reserve if it is the same as, or is confusing with, a corporate name that has, before the date of the request, been reserved by the Director for another person, unless

(a) written consent has been obtained from the person for whom the corporate name was reserved; or

(b) the 90-day reservation period referred to in subsection 11(1) of the Act has expired without the person for whom the corporate name was reserved having made a renewed request to reserve the corporate name.

15.3 Sections 15 to 15.2 apply in respect of an application for revival submitted to the Director in accordance with section 209 of the Act.

Prohibited Names

16. For the purposes of paragraph 12(1)(a) of the Act, a corporate name is prohibited where the name contains any of the following:

(a) "Air Canada";

(b) "Trans Canada Airlines" or "Lignes aériennes Trans Canada";

(c) "Canada Standard" or "CS";

(d) "Cooperative", "Coopérative", "co-op" or "pool" when it connotes a cooperative venture;

(e) "Parliament Hill" or "Colline du Parlement";

(f) "Royal Canadian Mounted Police", "Gendarmerie Royal du Canada", "RCMP" or "GRC"; or

(g) "United Nations", "Nations Unies", "UN" or "ONU".

17. For the purposes of paragraph 12(1)(a) of the Act, a corporate name is prohibited where the name connotes that the corporation

(a) carries on business under royal, vice-regal or governmental patronage, approval or authority, unless the appropriate government department or agency requests the name in writing;

(b) is sponsored or controlled by or is affiliated with the Government of Canada, the government of a province, the government of a country other than Canada or a political subdivision or agency of any such government, unless the appropriate government, political subdivision or agency consents in writing to the use of the name;

(c) is sponsored or controlled by or is affiliated with a university or an association of accountants, architects, engineers, lawyers, physicians, surgeons or any other professional association recognized by the laws of Canada or a province unless the appropriate university or professional association consents in writing to the use of the name; or

(d) carries on the business of a bank, loan company, insurance company, trust company, other financial intermediary or a stock exchange that is regulated by a law of Canada or a province unless the appropriate government department or agency consents in writing to the use of the name.

18. For the purposes of paragraph 12(1)(a) of the Act, a corporate name is prohibited where the name contains a word or phrase that is obscene or connotes a business that is scandalous, obscene or immoral.

19. For the purposes of paragraph 12(1)(a) of the Act, a corporate name is prohibited where the name is not distinctive because

(a) it is too general,

(b) it is only descriptive, in any language, of the quality, function or other characteristic of the goods or services in which the corporation deals or intends to deal,

(c) it is primarily or only the name or surname used alone of an individual who is living or has died within 30 years preceding the date of the request to the Director for that name, or

(d) it is primarily or only a geographic name used alone,

unless the person requesting the name establishes that it has, through use, acquired and continues to have secondary meaning at the time of the request.

20. For the purposes of paragraph 12(1)(a) of the Act, a corporate name is prohibited where the name is confusing having regard to all the circumstances, including

(a) the inherent distinctiveness of the whole or any elements of any trade mark or trade name and the extent to which it has become known;

(b) the length of time the trade mark or trade name has been in use;

(c) the nature of the goods or services associated with a trade mark or the nature of the business carried on under or associated with a trade name, including the likelihood of any competition among businesses using such a trade mark or trade name;

(d) the nature of the trade with which a trade mark or trade name is associated, including the nature of the products or services and the means by which they are offered or distributed;

(e) the degree of resemblance between the proposed corporate name and any trade mark or trade name in appearance or sound or in the ideas suggested by them; and

(f) the territorial area in Canada in which the proposed corporate name or an existing trade name is likely to be used.

21. For the purposes of paragraph 12(1)(a) of the Act, a corporate name is prohibited where an element of the name is the family name of an individual, whether or not preceded by his given name or initials, unless the individual or his heir or legal representative consents in writing to the use of his name and the individual has or had a material interest in the corporation.

22. For the purposes of paragraph 12(1)(a) of the Act,

(a) a corporate name is prohibited where its use is likely to lead to the inference that the business carried on or intended to be carried on under it and the business of a body corporate that is dissolved are one business, whether or not the nature of their business is generally the same; and

(b) the name of a revived corporation is prohibited where it is confusing with a name acquired by another corporation between the date of dissolution and revival of the revived corporation.

Deceptively Misdescriptive Names

23. For the purposes of paragraph 12(1)(a) of the Act, a corporate name is deceptively misdescriptive if it misdescribes, in any language,

(a) the business, goods or services in association with which it is proposed to be used;

(b) the conditions under which the goods or services will be produced or supplied or the persons to be employed in the production or supply of those goods or services; or

(c) the place of origin of those goods or services.

Certain Names Not Prohibited

24. A corporate name is not prohibited only because it contains alphabetic or numeric characters, initials, punctuation marks or any combination thereof.

25. A corporate name that is confusing with the name of a body corporate that has not carried on business in the 2 years immediately preceding the date of a request for that corporate name shall not for that reason alone be prohibited if the body corporate that has that name

(a) consents in writing to the use of the name; and

(b) undertakes in writing to dissolve forthwith or to change its name before the corporation proposing to use the name commences to use it.

26. A corporate name containing a word that is the same as or similar to the distinctive element of an existing trade mark or trade name shall not for that reason alone be prohibited if

(a) the person who has the trade mark or trade name consents in writing to the use of the corporate name; and

(b) the corporate name is not confusing

27. (1) A corporate name that is confusing with the name of a body corporate shall not for that reason alone be prohibited if

(a) the corporate name is the name of an existing or proposed corporation that is the successor to the business of the body corporate and the body corporate has ceased or will, in the immediate future, cease to carry on business under that corporate name and undertakes in writing to dissolve forthwith or to change its corporate name before the successor corporation commences carrying on business under that corporate name; and

(b) subject to subsection (2), the corporate name of the existing or proposed corporation sets out in numerals the year of incorporation or the year of the most recent amendment to the corporate name, in parentheses, immediately before the word or expression "Limited", "Limitée", "Incorporated", "Incorporée", "Corporation", "Société par actions de régime federal" or "Société commerciale canadienne" or the abbreviation "Ltd", "Ltée", "Inc.", "Corp.", "S.A.R.F." or "S.C.C.".

(2) The reference in a corporate name to the year of incorporation or the year of the most recent amendment to the corporate name may be deleted two years after its use is introduced, if the corporate name so changed is not confusing.

28. (1) When two or more corporations amalgamate, the name of the amalgamated corporation shall not be prohibited if

(a) it is the same as one of the amalgamating corporations;

(b) it is a distinctive combination of the names of the amalgamating corporations and is not otherwise confusing or prohibited; or

(c) it is a distinctive new name that is not confusing.

(2) Where an existing corporation has acquired or will, in the immediate future, acquire all or substantially all of the property of an affiliated body corporate, the use by the corporation of the corporate name of the body corporate is not prohibited if the body corporate undertakes in writing to dissolve, or to change its corporate name, before the corporation commences using the corporate name.

(3) Where a proposed corporation will, in the immediate future, acquire all or substantially all of the property of a body corporate that is to be an affiliate of the proposed corporation, the use by the proposed corporation of the corporate name of the body corporate is not prohibited if the body corporate undertakes in writing to dissolve, or to change its corporate name, before the proposed corporation commences using the corporate name.

Section 11 of the CBCA sets out the provisions for reserving a name and the designation of a proposed corporation by number on the request of the incorporators. These provisions are:

1. *Reserving Name:* the Director can reserve a name for 90 days. When a name is cleared federally through a search house there is an automatic reservation of all names for this 90-day period at no extra charge. This is part of the service provided in the federal search area (subsection (1));
2. *Designating Number:* incorporators can request a number name if there is a rush to incorporate just as can be done under the BCA (subsection (2)).

Section 12 of the *CBCA* sets out the circumstances in which a name may be prohibited and what avenues are open to the Director when this occurs. A name may be prohibited under section 12 for the following reasons:

> **12.** (1) **Prohibited names.**—A corporation shall not be incorporated or continued as a corporation under this Act with, have, carry on business under or identify itself by a name
>
> (a) that is, as prescribed, prohibited or deceptively misdescriptive; or
>
> (b) that is reserved for another corporation or intended corporation under section 11.
>
> (2) **Directing change of name**—If, through inadvertence or otherwise, a corporation
>
> (a) comes into existence or is continued with a name, or
>
> (b) on an application to change its name, is granted a name
>
> that contravenes this section, the Director may direct the corporation to change its name in accordance with section 173.
>
> (3) **Name of continued corporation.**—[Repealed S.C. 1994, c. 24, s. 7(2).]
>
> (4) **Idem.**—If a corporation has a designating number as its name, the Director may direct the corporation to change its name to a name other than a designating number in accordance with section 173.
>
> (4.1) **Undertaking to change name.**—When a corporation acquires a name as a result of a person undertaking to dissolve or to change names, and the undertaking is not honoured, the Director may direct the corporation to change its name in accordance with section 173, unless the undertaking is honoured within the period specified in subsection (5).
>
> (5) **Revoking name.**—When a corporation has been directed under subsection (2), (4) or (4.1) to change its name and has not within sixty days from the service of the directive to that effect changed its name to a name that complies with this Act, the Director may revoke the name of the corporation and assign a name to it and, until changed in accordance with section 173, the name of the corporation is thereafter the name so assigned.

Under section 13 of the Act the Director is required to issue a certificate of amendment to a corporation which has been directed under subsection 12(5) to change its name but has not within 60 days from the service of the directive changed its name to one that complies with the statute. The Director may revoke the name and assign to it a name which shall be the name of the corporation until changed in accordance with section 173 which sets out the amendments which may be made to a charter. The articles of the corporation are amended as of the date shown in the certificate of amendment. Notice of the name change is published in the Canada Gazette or a periodical available to the public.

14

INCORPORATION — FEDERAL JURISDICTION

1. Introduction

If, during discussions with clients, it appears that the business of the proposed corporation will be carried on in several provinces in Canada, and particularly if using the name of the proposed corporation is essential to business, lawyers often recommend incorporation in the federal jurisdiction. This jurisdiction will be recommended if it will best serve the interests of the particular clients.

The *Canada Business Corporations Act*, S.C. 1974-75-76, c. 33, offered distinct advantages to members of the public over the *Business Corporations Act* in force at that time in Ontario, such as:

- ☐ unlimited capital;
- ☐ objects not required;
- ☐ directors — fixed minimum or maximum number; and
- ☐ unanimous shareholder agreement which could restrict the powers of the director or directors.

These advantages were not incorporated in the Ontario statute until 1982.

In order to update the records of federal corporations, the approach adopted by the federal authorities was to require all existing federal corporations to file Articles of Continuance under the new legislation in order to continue their corporate existence. If a federal corporation failed to make this decision within the prescribed time, the charter would be cancelled and the assets of the corporation would, in theory at least, escheat to the Crown. The aim was to eliminate from the records of Consumer and Corporate Affairs Canada [now the Corporations Directorate, Industry Canada] all inactive or defunct corporations.

The *Canada Business Corporations Act*, R.S.C. 1985, c. C-44 (the "BCA"'), is now the governing legislation for federal corporation.

2. Objectives of the *Canada Business Corporations Act*

The CBCA has two expressed objectives:

1. to provide a federal law that permits efficient administration and equitable treatment of the competing interests of management, shareholders and creditors of federal corporations; and
2. to serve as a model to business corporation law to advance the cause of uniformity of corporation law in Canada.

Implicit in the objectives set out above is a third objective — to encourage large corporations which carry on business in more than one province in Canada to incorporate at the federal level. It appears from the increased number of applications for incorporation under the CBCA that the first objective has been met. The second objective has also met with some degree of success. Alberta, Manitoba and Saskatchewan have already enacted business corporation laws based on this statute and several other provinces are considering revisions to their existing corporate law which will result in greater uniformity across Canada.

3. Advantages of Federal Incorporations

As mentioned earlier, the primary advantages of federal incorporation are:

1. a corporation has the right to carry on business in any province in Canada under its own name, regardless of whether or not there is a provincial or extra-provincial corporation carrying on business under the same or similar name; and
2. since the articles of incorporation do not require detailed objects or authorized capital, there is greater flexibility in these areas than formerly existed under Ontario law.

In addition, Industry Canada's Corporations Directorate offers online federal incorporation at the Strategis web site. Through the Corporations Directorate's Electronic Filing Centre, the Articles of Incorporation can be completed and filed online. Online submissions received before 1 p.m. (EST) each business day are processed before 5 p.m. (EST) the same day. The web site is located at *http://www.strategis.ic.g.c.ca/corporations*.

A non-distributing corporation incorporated under the CBCA is the federal equivalent of the Ontario non-offering corporation. Generally speaking, a non-distributing corporation has very few shareholders, most of whom participate in the management of the business affairs of the corporation. Some may be salaried employees of the corporation. In some cases, a non-distributing corporation may be the subsidiary of a larger non-distributing corporation.

A concern of many persons considering incorporation, as opposed to a partnership, is the lack of control over the acquisition of an interest in a corporation by "outsiders". In the partnership, if one of the partners decides to assign his or her share of a continuing undertaking to someone else, unanimous consent is normally required from the remaining partners. In this way the partners exercise control of the person or persons who can acquire an interest in the partnership. This difficulty was solved under the CBCA by subsection 146(2) which provides that the shareholders of the corporation have the option of entering into a unanimous shareholder agreement. This written agreement can either be among all of the shareholders of a corporation or among all of the shareholders and a person who is a not a shareholder. The unanimous shareholder agreement can restrict, in whole or in part, the powers of the directors to manage the business affairs of the corporation. Presumably this agreement could contain whatever provisions the lawyer and the clients mutually agreed upon are necessary. It could, for example, set out the terms and conditions upon which an outsider might acquire an interest in the corporation if this was deemed advisable by the lawyer for a particular incorporation.

Provision is also made under this section for a written declaration to be made by a single shareholder who is the beneficial owner of all of the issued shares of the corporation. This declaration can restrict, in whole or in part, the powers of the directors to manage the business affairs of the corporation. This declaration is deemed to be a unanimous shareholder agreement.

Subsection 146(5) provides that a shareholder who is a party to a unanimous shareholder agreement has all the rights, powers and duties of a director of a corporation to which the agreement relates. The shareholder has these rights to the extent that the agreement restricts the powers of the directors to manage the business and affairs of the corporation. The directors are thereby in theory relieved of their duties and liabilities, including any liabilities under section 119, to the same extent. Section 119 refers to the liability of directors for wages. Directors of a corporation are jointly and severally liable to employees of the corporation for all debts, not exceeding six months wages, due to each such employee for services performed for the corporation. This liability is limited to the period of time that the person or persons are directors of corporation.

There are certain other conditions prescribed under s. 19 which must be met to establish this liability:

(a) the corporation has been sued for the debt within six months after it has become due and execution has been returned unsatisfied in whole or in part;

(b) the corporation has commenced liquidation and dissolution proceedings or has been dissolved and a claim for the debt has been proved within six months after the earlier of the date of commencement of the liquidation and dissolution proceedings and the date of dissolution; or

(c) the corporation has made an assignment or a receiving order has been made against it under the *Bankruptcy and Insolvency Act* and a claim for the debt has been proved within six months after the date of the assignment or receiving order.

A successful judgment creditor will issue a writ of execution against a judgment debtor in order to collect the money due. Under this section, a director is only liable for the amount that is outstanding after execution has been levied on the assets of the judgment debtor. When a director pays such a debt, the director is entitled to any preference to which the employee would have been entitled. Where a judgment has been obtained, the director is entitled to an assignment of the judgment.

In addition, a director who has satisfied a claim under this section is entitled to contribution from the other directors who are liable for the claim.

An employee must sue a director during that director's term of office or within two years after he or she has ceased to be a director. If this time limit is not met, a director is not liable under this section of the Act.

Generally speaking, a non-distributing corporation is not subject to as great a degree of regulation as a corporation which offers its securities to the public.

4. Effecting the Incorporation

Once the incorporating jurisdiction has been decided by the lawyer and the clients, the necessary steps to prepare the documentation required to effect the incorporation must be implemented.

The initial step is to clear the proposed name for the new corporation. The search of the proposed name is submitted, as is done for an Ontario non-offering corporation, through a private search house to the database in Ottawa (the NUANS System).

Local customers of a search house normally receive a telephone report 24 hours after the submission of the name. Arrangements can be made at that time, depending on the practice in the particular law office, to either pick up the name search report or have it delivered.

(a) Articles of Incorporation

The format of the documents must conform to sections 5 to 10 of the Regulations of the CBCA, unless the documents are submitted online, which provisions are as follows:

5. All documents referred to in subsection 4(1) shall be

(a) on good quality white paper approximately 8 1/2 by 11 inches in size;

(b) printed or typewritten; and

(c) legible and suitable for microfilming and photocopying.

6. Where possible, each individual item in a document shall be set out in one or more contiguous, sequentially numbered paragraphs and each such item shall be preceded by an appropriate heading.

7. (1) Numbers in a document shall be in numerals and not in words.

(2) Information in a document shall, where practical, be set out in tabular form.

8. Abbreviations in a document shall,

(a) if formed by the truncation of a word, be followed by a period; and

(b) if formed by the deletion of alphabetic characters from the middle of a word, not be followed by a period, but a corporate name may contain alphabetic characters that are not followed by a period.

9. (1) If an item of information required to be disclosed in a form does not apply, it shall be so indicated by the phrase "not applicable", by the abbreviation "N/A" or by a brief explanatory statement.

(2) If information is set out in response to one item in a document, it may be referred to in response to any other item in that document by a cross reference.

10. (1) Where

(a) any provision required to be set out in a form furnished by the Director is too long to be set out in the space provided in the form, or

(b) an agreement or other document is to be incorporated by reference in and to be part of the form,

the person completing the form may, subject to subsection (2), incorporate the provision, agreement or other document in the form by setting out in the space provided in the form the following sentence: "The annexed Schedule I (or as the case may be) is incorporated in this form." and by annexing the provision, agreement or other document to the form as that schedule.

(2) A separate schedule is required in respect of each item that is incorporated in a form by reference pursuant to subsection (1).

The documents referred to in subsection 4(1) of the Regulations are all of the prescribed forms of documents required to be sent to the Director or to be issued by the Director under the Act.

In order to proceed with the drafting of the articles of incorporation, certain information is required from the client. The prescribed Form 1, Articles of Incorporation, under the CBCA is shown as Form 14.1. Many lawyers will include their paralegal secretary or law clerk in the initial interview with new clients and at that time the information necessary to complete the articles of incorporation can be obtained. However, if the principal interviews the clients alone, most law firms use a memorandum setting out in point form the information required to complete the prescribed form for articles of incorporation.

The approaches taken to drafting articles of incorporation are as varied as the individuals who practise law. Many corporate commercial lawyers take the same basic approach to drafting articles for a federal corporation as they do when drafting articles for an Ontario corporation.

Careful consideration is given to the potential future of the corporation so that possible changes can be anticipated before the articles are prepared. In this way, the client may not be required to amend the charter in the immediate future.

The forms for articles of incorporation are prepared in triplicate on sensitized papers so carbon paper is not required to produce the duplicate copies of the form. Care must be taken in the typing of the forms to avoid typing errors as mistakes cannot be erased or "whited out". The ribbon copy of Form 1 is returned by the Corporations Directorate along with the Certificate of Incorporation (see Form 14.3). The duplicate copy is retained by the Corporations Directorate for its file in Ottawa.

The articles of incorporation forms are completed as follows:

1. *Name of Corporation*

The NUANS System is used.

2. *The place in Canada where the registered office is to be situated*

The information to be inserted under this numbered section is the geographical, as opposed to the municipal address, of the registered or head office of the corporation.

It is essential that this information be accurate because a change of registered office requires articles of amendment. If the registered office is to be located in a large urban centre, the largest possible geographical area would be chosen. If, for example, the registered office of the corporation is to be located in the city of Mississauga, the location of the registered office would be shown as the Regional Municipality of Peel, Ontario. This would allow the registered office of the corporation to be located in any of the cities or towns that make up the Regional Municipality of Peel without requiring amendment of the articles of incorporation.

Subsection 19(1) of the CBCA requires that a corporation shall at all times have a registered office in Canada as specified in its articles. Subsection (2) states that a notice of registered office in prescribed form shall be sent to the Director, along with any articles that designate or change the place of the registered office of the corporation. The directors of a corporation may, under subsection 19(3), change the address of the registered office within the place specified in the articles. Under subsection (4) a corporation is required to send to the Director, within 15 days of any change of address of its registered office, notice in the prescribed form. If a decision is made to move the registered office from its initial location, the change would be recorded in the minute book of the corporation by resolution of the directors. Form 3 (see Form 14.4) is a dual form which can be used either as a notice of registered office or as a notice of change of registered office, and should be filed with the Director within 15 days of the date on which the address of the registered office changed. It is not necessary to set out a specific street address in the articles of incorporation because that information is included in Form 3.

3. *The classes and any maximum number of shares that the corporation is authorized to issue*

Subsection 6(1)(c) sets out the information that is required here as follows:

(i) if there will be two or more classes of shares, the rights, privileges, restrictions and conditions attaching to each class of share, and

(ii) if a class of shares may be issued in series, the authority given to the directors to fix the number of shares in, and to determine the designation of, and the rights, privileges, restrictions and conditions attaching to, the shares of each series.

Since the space in the form is somewhat limited, it is recommended that a schedule be attached to the articles of incorporation containing all of the necessary information. If this approach is adopted, wording such as "The annexed Schedule A is incorporated in this form." could be inserted under this numbered section. A sample Schedule A to Form 1 is shown as Form 14.2.

Another section of the Act to be aware of when considering the class or classes or shares is subsection 24(3) which states:

(3) Where a corporation has only one class of shares, the rights of the holders thereof are equal in all respects and include the rights

(a) to vote at any meeting of shareholders of the corporation;

(b) to receive any dividend declared by the corporation; and

(c) to receive the remaining property of the corporation on dissolution.

If the corporation has only one class of shares, the following wording is often used and is acceptable to the Corporations Directorate, "The corporation is authorized to issue an unlimited number of shares of one class."

Subsection 24(4) states:

(4) The articles may provide for more than one class of shares and, if they so provide,

(a) the rights, privileges, restrictions and conditions attaching to the shares of each class shall be set out therein; and

(b) the rights set out in subsection (3) shall be attached to at least one class of shares but all such rights are not required to be attached to one class.

In these circumstances, the wording below would be acceptable to the Corporations Directorate:

> The Corporation is authorized to issue an unlimited number of Class A and Class B shares. The Class A shares shall be entitled to vote at all meetings of shareholders, except meetings at which only holders of a specified class of shares are entitled to vote, and to receive such dividends as the directors in their discretion shall declare. Subject to the provisions of the Canada Business Corporations Act, the Class B shares shall be non-voting. Upon liquidation or dissolution, the holders of the Class A and Class B shares shall share equally remaining property of the Corporation.

If the incorporators wish to continue the concept of ''common'' shares and ''preferred'' shares often used under the CBCA, this can be achieved by adopting the following style:

> The corporation is authorized to issue:
>
> 1. Class A shares (common shares), the holders of which are entitled:
>   (a) to vote at all meetings of shareholders; and
>   (b) to receive the remaining property of the Corporation on dissolution;
> 2. Class B shares (preferred), which shall carry the right:
>   (a) to a dividend as fixed by the Board of Directors; and
>   (b) upon liquidation or winding up of the Corporation, repayment to the amount paid for such shares (plus any declared and unpaid dividends) in priority to the Class A shares, but they shall not confer the right to any further participating in profits or assets;
> 3. The holders of the Class B shares shall (not)* be entitled to vote at all meetings of shareholders.
>
> ***Note**—If the Class B shareholders are not to be entitled to vote, add ''except as otherwise specifically provided in the Canada Business Corporations Act''.

Section 27 of the Act states that the articles may authorize the issue of any class of shares in one or more series. In addition, the articles may authorize the directors to fix the number of shares and determine the designations, rights, privileges, restrictions and conditions attaching to the shares of each series, subject to the limitations set out in the articles. If the articles are to include provision for the issuance of shares in a series, the following wording as set out in the policy statement would be acceptable:

> The directors may authorize the issue of one or more series of shares within each of ________ classes of shares, and may fix the number of shares in each series, and determine the designations, rights, privileges, restrictions and conditions attaching to the shares of each series.

Section 28 of the CBCA states that if the articles so provide, no shares of a class shall be issued unless the shares have first been offered to the shareholders holding shares of that class. These shareholders have a pre-emptive right to acquire the offered shares in proportion to their holding of the shares of that class, at such price and on such terms as those shares are to be offered to others. Under subsection (2), shareholders have no pre-emptive right in respect to shares issued:

(a) for a consideration other than money;

(b) as a share dividend; or

(c) pursuant to the exercise of conversion privileges, options or rights previously granted by the corporation.

4. *Restrictions if any on share transfers*

If the corporation is to be a non-distributing corporation (one that is not offering its securities to the public), the articles of incorporation must include a restriction on the transfer of shares.

These restrictions are required in the articles of incorporation in order to exempt the federal corporation from the requirements of securities legislation in the various provinces dealing with public or distributing corporations. The following wording would be acceptable to the Corporations Directorate:

> No shares of the capital of the Corporation shall be transferred without either (a) the sanction of the majority of the directors of the corporation or alternatively (b) the sanction of the majority of the shareholders of the Corporation.

or

> No shares of the Corporation shall be transferred without the approval of the directors evidenced by a resolution of the board, provided that approval of any transfer may be given as aforesaid after the said transfer has been effected upon the records of the corporation, in which event, unless the said resolution stipulates otherwise, the said transfer shall be valid and shall take effect as from the date of its entry upon the books of its corporation.

Subsection 2(7) of the Act sets out the definition of ''distribution to the public''. A distribution to the public occurs where in respect of a security there has been a filing of a prospectus, statement of material facts, registration statement, securities exchange take-over bid circular or a similar document under the laws of Canada, a province or a jurisdiction outside Canada. If the incorporators wish to include restrictions on the transferred shares to ensure that the corporation is a non-distributing corporation within the meaning of the Act, the following sentence could be included, ''The Corporation shall not make a distribution to the public of any of its securities.''

The incorporators could also add the following clause in order to clarify the corporation's status as a non-distributing corporation for the purposes of provincial security regulations:

> The number of shareholders of the Corporation is limited to 50, not including persons who are in the employment of the Corporation and persons, who, having been formerly in the employment of the Corporation, were, while in that employment, and have continued after the termination of that employment, to be shareholders of the Corporation, two or more persons holding one or more shares jointly being counted as a single shareholder.

In the event that the proposed restrictions on the transfer shares require more space than that allowed on the prescribed form, it is recommended that a schedule be prepared setting out these various restrictions desired and the following wording inserted under item 4, "The attached Schedule B is incorporated in this form."

5. *Number (or minimum and maximum number) of directors*

A variable number of directors can be specified or the number of directors can be fixed. If cumulative voting is permitted, the number of directors must be fixed. Subsection 102(2) provides that a non-distributing corporation shall have one or more directors. A distributing corporation, one that issues its securities to the public, must have not fewer than three directors, at least two of whom are not officers or employees of the corporation or its affiliates.

If the decision is made to have a variable number of directors, the following wording would be acceptable: "a minimum of one and a maximum of seven".

6. *Restrictions if any on business the corporation may carry on*

The concept of "objects", formerly required for both Ontario and federal corporations, was abandoned under this statute.

If the incorporators do not wish to restrict the kind of business the corporation may carry on, this section is left blank or "N/A" may be inserted. If the incorporators decide to restrict the types of business the corporation may carry on, the following wording is suggested: "The business of the Corporation shall be limited to the following".

Particulars of any business the corporation is prohibited from carrying on would be set out below this wording. The approach taken in this area is that rather than setting out the business a corporation is actually involved in, which could restrict flexibility in the future, information here should state the areas of business in which the corporation cannot participate.

7. *Other provisions if any*

There are a number of provisions under the CBCA which may be contained in the articles of incorporation. In addition, incorporators may include clauses to satisfy requirements of other legislation.

The following list sets out various provisions that could be included under this item in the articles of incorporation in a form that is acceptable to the Corporations Directorate:

(a) If the corporation will be carrying on business in the province of Quebec, in order to comply with the provisions of the Quebec *Special Corporate Powers Act*, R.S.Q. 1977, c. P-16, the right of directors to borrow must be included in the articles. The wording would be:

> If authorized by by-law which is duly made by the directors and confirmed by ordinary resolution, the directors of the Corporation may from time to time:
>
> (i) Borrow upon the credit of the Corporation;
>
> (ii) Issue, reissue, sell or pledge debt obligations of the Corporation; and
>
> (iii) Mortgage, hypothecate, pledge or otherwise create a security interest in all or any property of the Corporation, owned or subsequently acquired to secure any debt obligation of the Corporation.
>
> Any such by-law may provide for the delegation of such power by the directors to such officers or directors of the Corporation to such extent and in such manner as may be set out in the by-law.
>
> Nothing herein restricts the borrowing of money by the corporation on bills of exchange or promissory notes made, drawn, accepted or endorsed by or on behalf of the Corporation.

(b) If cumulative voting for directors is to be permitted, the following wording would be acceptable: "There shall be cumulative voting for directors." If this is provided, the number of the directors must be fixed.

(c) Under the Act, a simple majority vote of shareholders is required to pass a resolution. If the incorporators wish to increase this majority vote, the wording below is suitable:

> In order to effect any ordinary and/or special resolution passed at a meeting of shareholders, a majority of not less than _____ per cent of the votes cast by the shareholders who voted in respect of that resolution shall be required.

The CBCA specifies a simple majority for an ordinary resolution and a two-thirds vote for a special resolution. Therefore, any figures set out in the articles would be greater than the statutory majority.

(d) If a foreign version of the corporate name is to be used outside Canada, wording such as that below can be used:

> It is hereby provided that the Corporation may use and be legally designated by the following name outside Canada:

The foreign version of the corporate name would appear below the above words.

(e) If a pre-emptive right is to be included, the following paragraph is acceptable:

> It is hereby provided that no shares of class shall be issued unless the shares have been offered to the shareholders holding shares of the class, those shareholders have a pre-emptive right to acquire the offered shares in proportion to their

holdings of the shares of that class, at such price and on such terms as those shares are to be offered to others.

(f) Under the Act, the directors are not required to own shares of the corporation. If the incorporators wish to provide for the directors to own shares, the wording used could be:

> No person otherwise qualified shall be elected or appointed as a director unless such person beneficially owns at least one share issued by the Corporation.

(g) If the incorporators decide to provide for the filling of any vacancies that may occur on the board of directors by the shareholders, the following sentence could be used: "Any vacancy among the directors shall be filled by a vote of shareholders."

(h) Subsection 114(2) provides that subject to the articles or by-laws, a majority of the number of directors, or the minimum number of directors required by the articles, constitutes a quorum at any meeting of directors. If the incorporators wish to establish a quorum other than that set out under the statute, the wording could be: "The quorum for any meeting of the board of directors shall be ____________."

There are certain other standard provisions that are often included in addition to those set out above:

(i) *Lien on shares*—If a shareholder of the corporation is indebted to the corporation, provision can be made under this item for a lien on any share registered in the name of such shareholder or that shareholder's legal representative until the debt is paid. Acceptable wording is:

> Subject to the Canada Business Corporations Act, the Corporation has lien on any share of a shareholder who is indebted to the Corporation, whether the share is registered in the name of the shareholder or his or her legal representative.

(j) *No public offering*—In order to exempt the corporation from provincial securities legislation, a provision prohibiting the offering of securities to the public would be included here, such as, "Any invitation to the public to subscribe for any security of Corporation is prohibited."

(k) *50 shareholders*—Limiting the number of shareholders of the corporation to 50 also exempts the corporation from the provisions of provincial securities legislation. An acceptable form of wording is set out below:

> The number of shareholders of the corporation is limited to fifty, not including employees of the Corporation or former employees who were shareholders while so employed and have continued to be shareholders since ceasing to be employed, and counting joint registered owners as one shareholder.

8. *Incorporators*

The full name and residence address of each of the incorporators is set out under this item. The incorporator(s) sign under the signature column on the right hand side of the Form. Each incorporator must sign the articles of incorporation. Although this is an obvious requirement, it is frequently overlooked. This is a deficiency so far as the articles of incorporation are concerned and the application will be returned if any of the incorporators fails to sign the form.

Detailed instructions for the completion of Form 1, Articles of Incorporation, are printed on the back of the form.

(b) Notice of Registered Office or Notice of Change of Registered Office — Form 3

Form 3, Notice of Registered Office (see Form 14.2) is a prescribed form as required under the Regulations of the CBCA. This is a dual form and must be filed with the Articles of Incorporation. The form sets out the municipal address of the registered or head office of the corporation. The following items (numbered to correspond to the form) should be completed when the form is being used as a Notice of Registered Office.

1. *Name of Corporation*—If the name is shown in French as well as English both names must appear under this item.
3. *Place in Canada where registered office is situated*—The place in Canada where the registered office is situated as indicated in the articles.
4. *Address of the registered office*—The municipal address, including a suite number if applicable, must be inserted here.

Item 2 (Corporation No.) is completed by Industry Canada when the application is received.

Items 5 (Effective date of change) and 6 (Previous address of registered office) are only completed when the form is being used as a Notice of Change of Registered Office of the corporation.

The form is dated at the bottom and signed by one of the incorporators. A corporation does not have either officers or directors until the certificate of incorporation has been issued by Industry Canada.

When a notice of a change in the registered office is being filed, this form would be signed by an officer or director of the corporation.

(c) Notice of Directors or Notice of Change of Directors — Form 6

This form is also prescribed under the Regulations of the Act and is designed as a dual form (see Form 14.3). Form 6 must also be filed with an application for articles of incorporation. When serving this purpose the following items must be completed:

1. *Name of Corporation:*

Insert the name of the corporation as shown in the articles of incorporation.

5. *The directors of this corporation now are:*

List the individuals who will be the first directors of the corporation. These persons need not necessarily be the same as the incorporators shown in the articles of incorporation. However, the incorporators and first directors are often the same people.

The full names of the directors, together with residence addresses, occupations and citizenships must be set out. Citizenship is important because the Act requires that a majority of directors of the corporation are to be ''resident Canadians''. Subsection 2(1) defines a ''resident Canadian'' as an individual who is,

(a) a Canadian citizen ordinarily resident in Canada,

(b) a Canadian citizen not ordinarily resident in Canada who is a member of a prescribed class of persons, or

(c) a permanent resident within the meaning of the Immigration Act and ordinarily resident in Canada, except a permanent resident who has been ordinarily resident in Canada for more than one year after the time at which he first became eligible to apply for Canadian citizenship.

The form is dated and signed by one of the incorporators when it is being filed as a Notice of Directors.

When a change occurs in the directors named in the notice filed with the articles of incorporation, this notice must be filed within 15 days of the change as required under subsection 113(1) of the Act. When this form is being filed as a notice of a change in the directors, items 1 to 5 must be completed with the appropriate information. Detailed instructions are set out on the back of the form regarding the completion.

Pursuant to an amendment to the Regulations under the Act, SOR/79-316, which came into force on January 1, 1999, the Notice of Change of Directors may be sent to the Department of National Revenue attached to a T2 Corporation Income Tax Return where the form is required to be sent to the Director. Subsection 4(1.1) was added to the Regulation and provides that Schedule 81 (Notice of Change of Directors) can be utilized when reporting a coinciding change among directors and can be filed along with the T2 Tax Return (see Form 18.2).

Where changes among its directors do not coincide with the filing due date of the corporation income tax return, the corporation will have to notify Industry Canada within 15 days using Form 6.

(d) Filing Articles of Incorporation

Once the appropriate forms, along with any ancillary schedules, have been prepared and the documents are properly signed, the next step is to file the application with the Corporations Directorate of Industry Canada. All documents filed with the Corporations Directorate must be in duplicate. The forms are pre-pared in three different colors. The ribbon copy is white, the second copy is yellow and the file copy is pink. It is this pink copy which is retained by the law office.

A covering letter directed to the Corporations Directorate of Industry Canada should be forwarded with the following:

1. Form 1 — Articles of Incorporation;
2. Form 3 — Notice of Registered Office;
3. Form 6 — Notice of Directors;
4. NUANS report;
5. A cheque payable to the Receiver General for Canada for the prescribed incorporation fee, which is set out in Appendix B.

Provided care has been taken in the preparation of the information contained in the articles of incorporation and supporting documents, the application should issue. A Deficiency Notice will issue if the application is not correct.

Once the final check of all the documents has been made, the application and the covering letter should be mailed to Industry Canada, Corporations Directorate, Ottawa.

A list of personnel and telephone numbers for Industry Canada is set out in Appendix A and may prove to be of assistance in obtaining information or status reports on applications filed.

The Corporations Directorate accepts filings submitted by way of facsimile equipment for the following:

Form 3 — Notice of Registered Office/Notice of Change of Registered Office

Form 6 — Notice of Directors/Notice of Change of Directors.

Corporations and/or their representatives are expected to keep the originals of any documents sent to the Director by fax as part of the normal business record keeping procedures.

An informal receipt for filing would be the transmission slip if one is generated by the fax machine. If a formal receipt from the Director is required, an acknowledgement should be prepared and sent with a return envelope and submitted in hard copy form.

Documents must be legible and suitable for microfilming, imaging or photocopying. Original forms should be used and the information typed or written in heavy black pen. All faxes should be sent using fine resolution.

Failure to comply with these requirements could result in the fax filing being rejected and returned to the originator.

The fax number to be used for these filings is (613) 941-0999.

(e) Electronic Filing Centre

The Corporations Directorate of Industry Canada provides through its Electronic Filing Centre the online completing and filing of Articles of Incorporation. The fee for online filing is $200 as compared to $250 for filing by mail. This incorporation fee may be charged to the user's Visa or Mastercard credit card account using the Corporations Directorate's secure on-line payment facility.

Filing online offers the following distinct advantages:

- ☐ *convenience*: the electronic filing centre is open seven days a week, 24 hours a day;
- ☐ *reduced delivery costs*: traditional delivery expenses and delays are eliminated with online submissions;
- ☐ *immediate acknowledgment of filing*: the user knows precisely when its submission has been received; and
- ☐ *prompt articles processing*: direct electronic submissions to the Corporations Directorate's database enable expedient processing either the same day or next day, depending on the time of filing and complexity of the application.

In order to file the Articles of Incorporation online, the user must first go to the Electronic Filing Centre featured on the Corporations Directorate Strategis website *http://www.strategis.ic.gc.ca/corporations*. Next, the user registers with the Strategis Secure Server Facilities to access the Electronic Filing Home Page. The Strategis Registration form is used to obtain a username and password for access purposes. At the Electronic Filing Home Page, the user will choose "articles of incorporation" from the list of menu choices available and select one of the four incorporation options available:

1. incorporation of a numbered corporation, e.g., 1234567 Canada Inc.
2. incorporation of a corporation with a name pre-approved by the Directorate (a NUANS search in electronic format is required to accompany the submission); or
3. incorporation of a corporation where name approval is to be sought (a NUANS search in electronic format is required to accompany the submission);
4. incorporation of a numbered name corporation that has been pre-reserved.

Amendments to the CBCA Regulations enacted in 1999 provided for the filing of documents in electronic format, without an original certificate. It should be noted, however, that originally signed copies of all documents must be maintained in the records of the corporation.

The user follows the menus provided to complete the necessary documents online and then, using their Visa or Mastercard account, charges the prescribed $200 filing fee through the secure online payment facility. Assuming that the corporate name is accepted, if the articles are submitted before 1 p.m. (EST) any business day, the incorporation certificate should be processed same day by 5 p.m. (EST).

5. Directors and Officers

Part X of the CBCA sets out the powers, qualifications and responsibilities of the directors of the corporation under sections 102 to 125. Subsection 102(1) states that the directors shall manage the business and affairs of the corporation, subject to any unanimous shareholder agreement. Subsection (2) provides that a non-distributing corporation shall have one or more directors. A corporation offering its securities to the public shall have a minimum of three directors, at least two of whom are not officers or employees of the corporation or its affiliates, if any.

While all sections dealing with directors are important, there are specific sections to which particular attention is directed:

> **103.** (1) **By-laws.**—Unless the articles, by-laws or a unanimous shareholder agreement otherwise provide, the directors may, by resolution, make, amend, or repeal any by-laws that regulate the business or affairs of the corporation.
>
> (2) **Shareholder approval.**—The directors shall submit a by-law or an amendment or a repeal of a by-law made under subsection (1) to the shareholders at the next meeting of shareholders, and the shareholders may, by ordinary resolution, confirm, reject or amend the by-law, amendment or repeal.
>
> (3) **Effective date.**—A by-law, or an amendment or a repeal of a by-law, is effective from the date of the resolution of the directors under subsection (1) until it is confirmed, confirmed as amended or rejected by the shareholders under subsection (2) or until it ceases to be effective under subsection (4) and, where the by-law is confirmed or confirmed as amended, it continues in effect in the form in which it was so confirmed.
>
> (4) **Idem.**—If a by-law, an amendment or a repeal is rejected by the shareholders, or if the directors do not submit a by-law, an amendment or a repeal to the shareholders as required under subsection (2), the by-law, amendment or repeal ceases to be effective and no subsequent resolution of the directors to make, amend or repeal a by-law having substantially the same purpose or effect is effective until it is confirmed or confirmed as amended by the shareholders.

(5) **Shareholder proposal.**—A shareholder entitled to vote at an annual meeting of shareholders may, in accordance with section 137, make a proposal to make, amend or repeal a by-law.

104. (1) **Organization meeting.**—After issue of the certificate of incorporation, a meeting of the directors of the corporation shall be held at which the directors may

(a) make by-laws;

(b) adopt forms of security certificates and corporate records;

(c) authorize the issue of securities;

(d) appoint officers;

(e) appoint an auditor to hold office until the first annual meeting of shareholders;

(f) make banking arrangements; and

(g) transact any other business.

(2) **Exception.**—Subsection (1) does not apply to a body corporate to which a certificate of amalgamation has been issued under subsection 185(4) or to which a certificate of continuance has been issued under subsection 187(4).

(3) **Calling meeting.**—An incorporator or a director may call the meeting of directors referred to in subsection (1) by giving not less than five days notice thereof by mail to each director, stating the time and place of the meeting.

Section 105 under the CBCA sets out the qualifications of a director. The following persons are disqualified from being a director of a corporation:

1. anyone under 18 years of age;
2. anyone of unsound mind and has been found so by a court in Canada or elsewhere;
3. a person who is not an individual; or
4. a bankrupt.

Subsection (2) states that a director of a corporation is not required to hold shares issued by the corporation unless the articles state otherwise. A majority of the directors must be resident Canadians, as required under subsection (3), unless the corporation involved is a holding corporation. Under subsection (4), not more than one-third of the directors of a holding corporation need be resident Canadians so long as the corporation earns in Canada directly or through its subsidiaries, less than five per cent of the gross revenues of the holding corporation and all its subsidiary bodies corporate together.

The remaining sections to be considered are:

106. (1) **Notice of directors.**—At the time of sending articles of incorporation, the incorporators shall send to the Director a notice of directors in prescribed form and the Director shall file the notice.

(2) **Term of office.**—Each director named in the notice referred to in subsection (1) holds office from the issue of the certificate of incorporation until the first meeting of shareholders.

(3) **Election of directors.**—Subject to paragraph 107(b), shareholders of a corporation shall, by ordinary resolution at the first meeting of shareholders and at each succeeding annual meeting at which an election of directors is required, elect directors to hold office for a term expiring not later than the close of the third annual meeting of shareholders following the election.

(4) **Staggered terms.**—It is not necessary that all directors elected at a meeting of shareholders hold office for the same term.

(5) **No stated terms.**—A director not elected for an expressly stated term ceases to hold office at the close of the first annual meeting of shareholders following his election.

(6) **Incumbent directors.**—Notwithstanding subsections (2), (3) and (5), if the directors are not elected at a meeting of shareholders the incumbent directors continue in office until their successors are elected.

(7) **Vacancy among candidates.**—If a meeting of shareholders fails to elect the number or the minimum number of directors required by the articles by reason of the disqualification, incapacity or death of any candidates, the directors elected at that meeting may exercise all the powers of the directors if the number of directors so elected constitutes a quorum.

(8) **Appointment of directors.**—The directors may, if the articles of the corporation so provide, appoint one or more directors, who shall hold office for a term expiring not later than the close of the next annual meeting of shareholders, but the total number of directors so appointed may not exceed one third of the number of directors elected at the previous annual meeting of shareholders.

. . .

108. (1) **Ceasing to hold office.**—A director of a corporation ceases to hold office when

(a) he dies or resigns;

(b) he is removed in accordance with section 109; or

(c) he becomes disqualified under subsection 105(1).

(2) **Effective date of resignation.**—A resignation of a director becomes effective at the time a written resignation is sent to the corporation, or at the time specified in the resignation, whichever is later.

109. (1) **Removal of directors.**—Subject to paragraph 107(g), the shareholders of a corporation may by ordinary resolution at a special meeting remove any director or directors from office.

(2) **Exception.**—Where the holders of any class or series of shares of a corporation have an exclusive right to elect one or more directors, a director so elected may only be removed by an ordinary resolution at a meeting of the shareholders of that class or series.

(3) **Vacancy.**—Subject to paragraphs 107(b) to (e), a vacancy created by the removal of a director may be filled at the meeting of the shareholder at which the director is removed or, if not so filled, may be filled under section 111.

. . .

111. (1) **Filling vacancy.**—Notwithstanding subsection 114(3), but subject to subsections (3) and (4), a quorum of directors may fill a vacancy among the directors, except a vacancy resulting from an increase in the number or minimum number of directors or from a failure to elect the number or minimum number of directors required by the articles.

(2) **Calling meeting.**—If there is not a quorum of directors, or if there has been a failure to elect the number or minimum number of directors required by the articles, the directors then in office shall forthwith call a special meeting of shareholders to fill the vacancy and, if they fail to call a meeting or if there are no directors then in office, the meeting may be called by any shareholder.

. . .

113. (1) **Notice of change of directors.**—Within fifteen days after a change is made among its directors, a corporation shall send to the Director a notice in prescribed form setting out the change and the Director shall file the notice.

(2) **Application to court.**—Any interested person, or the Director, may apply to a court for an order to require a corporation to comply with subsection (1), and the court may so order and make any further order it thinks fit.

114. (1) **Meeting of directors.**—Unless the articles or by-laws otherwise provide, the directors may meet at any place, and upon such notice as the by-laws require.

(2) **Quorum.**—Subject to the articles or by-laws, a majority of the number of directors or minimum number of directors required by the articles constitutes a quorum at any meeting of directors and, notwithstanding any vacancy among the directors, a quorum of directors may exercise all the powers of the directors.

(3) **Canadian majority.**—Directors, other than directors of a corporation referred to in subsection 105(4), shall not transact business at a meeting of directors unless a majority of directors present are resident Canadians.

(4) **Exception.**—Notwithstanding subsection (3), directors may transact business at a meeting of directors where a majority of resident Canadian directors is not present if

(a) a resident Canadian director who is unable to be present approves in writing or by telephone or other communications facilities the business transacted at the meeting; and

(b) a majority of resident Canadian directors would have been present had that director been present at the meeting.

(5) **Notice of meeting.**—A notice of a meeting of directors shall specify any matter referred to in subsection 115(3) that is to be dealt with at the meeting but, unless the by-laws otherwise provide, need not specify the purpose of or the business to be transacted at the meeting.

(6) **Waiver of notice.**—A director may in any manner waive a notice of a meeting of directors; and attendance of a director at a meeting of directors is a waiver of notice of the meeting, except where a director attends a meeting for the express purpose of objecting to the transaction of any business on the grounds that the meeting is not lawfully called.

(7) **Adjournment.**—Notice of an adjourned meeting of directors is not required to be given if the time and place of the adjourned meeting is announced at the original meeting.

(8) **One director meeting.**—Where a corporation has only one director, that director may constitute a meeting

(9) **Participation by telephone.**—Subject to the by-laws, a director may, if all the directors of the corporation consent, participate in a meeting of directors or of a committee of directors by means of such telephone or other communications facilities as permit all persons participating in the meeting to hear each other, and a director participating in such a meeting by such means is deemed for the purposes of this Act to be present at that meeting

Under section 120, a director or officer of a corporation who is a party to a material contract or proposed material contract with the corporation, or is a director or officer who has a material interest or proposed material interest in any person who is a party to a material contract or proposed material contract, shall disclose in writing to the corporation or request to have entered into the minutes of directors the nature and extent of that interest. An officer who is not a director must disclose his or her interest as soon as the officer is aware the contract or proposed contract is to be considered or has been already considered.

6. Shares and Securities

Part V (Corporate Finance) of the CBCA sets out the provisions for securities/ shares of a corporation.

Under subsection 24(1) shares of a corporation shall be in registered form and shall be without nominal or par value.

If a body corporate is continued under this Act with shares with nominal or par value issued by the corporation before it was continued, such shares shall be deemed, for the purposes of subsection (1), to be shares without nominal or par value.

Class or classes of shares are also discussed under subsection 24(3):

(3) Where a corporation has only one class of shares, the rights of the holders thereof are equal in all respects and include the rights

(a) to vote at any meeting of shareholders of the corporation;

(b) to receive any dividend declared by the corporation; and

(c) to receive the remaining property of the corporation on dissolution.

Subsection 24(4) sets out what must be done if there is more than one class of shares:

(a) the rights, privileges, restrictions and conditions attaching to the shares of each class shall be set out therein; and

(b) the rights set out in subsection (3) shall be attached to at least one class of shares but all such rights are not required to be attached to one class.

Section 25 provides that, "[s]ubject to the articles, the by-laws and any unanimous shareholder agreement and to section 28, shares may be issued at such times and to such persons and for such consideration as the directors may determine." Shares must be paid for, either in cash or in consideration other than money, before they are issued.

Subsection 49(7) of Part VI (Security Certificates, Registers and Transfers) sets out what must be stated upon the face of each certificate issued by a corporation:

(a) the name of the corporation;

(b) the words "Incorporated under the *Canada Business Corporations Act*";

(c) the name of the person to whom it was issued; and

(d) the number and class of shares and the designation of any series that the certificate represents.

Subsection 49(4) requires that a security certificate shall be signed manually by at least one director or officer of the corporation or by or on behalf of a registrar, transfer agent or branch transfer agent of the corporation, or by a trustee who certifies it in accordance with a trust indenture. Any additional signature required may be printed or otherwise mechanically reproduced thereon.

Under subsection 49(1) every security holder is entitled at his or her option to a security certificate which complies with the Act. Another alternative provided under this subsection, in lieu of a security certificate, is a non-transferable written acknowledgment of his or her right to obtain a security certificate from a corporation in respect of the securities held by that person.

Legal stationers supply share certificates, shown as Forms 14.4 to 14.5, for corporations incorporated under the CBCA. Although there are no "common" and "preferred" shares under the Act, the authorized capital may be so designated in the schedules attached to the articles of incorporation. There are lawyers who prefer to draft their own wording to be put on the face of the certificates so the certificate will more closely comply with the terms of the CBCA. The blank form shows the "frame" of the share certificate with the interior left blank. These certificates are available in brown, green, orange or purple borders and can be completed to suit the individual lawyer.

It should be noted that there is provision on all of these share certificates for a corporate seal to be added. Section 23 of the Act states that an instrument or agreement, executed on behalf of a corporation by a director, officer or an agent of the corporation, is not invalid merely because a corporate seal is not affixed thereto. This section is interpreted by many lawyers to mean that a corporate seal is not mandatory under the Act. They argue, quite reasonably, that if there is provision on a share certificate for a seal, a security holder will likely demand that a seal be added. Some law firms, for this and the other reasons stated above, have had certificates printed with wording that complies with the provisions of the CBCA for the use of their corporate clients. This is a possible alternative to be considered if the lawyer is dissatisfied with the certificates provided by the legal stationers.

15

ORGANIZATION

1. Corporate Supplies

Once the certificate of incorporation has been issued, the next step is to order the corporate supplies. Although a corporate seal is not mandatory under the Canada *Business Corporations Act*, lawyers often order a seal for the corporation. Most banks and other lending institutions are now accustomed to the concept that a corporation is bound by an agreement or contract even though it is not signed under seal. In addition, a minute book and share certificate book will be required.

2. By-laws

A general borrowing by-law is not required for corporations incorporated under the CBCA because of the provisions of section 189 which deal with borrowing powers. This section states that unless the articles, by-laws or a unanimous shareholder agreement otherwise provide, the articles of a corporation are deemed to state that the directors of the corporation may, without authorization of the shareholders:

(a) borrow money on the credit of the corporation;

(b) issue, reissue, sell or pledge debt obligations of the corporation;

(c) subject to section 44, give a guarantee on behalf of the corporation to secure performance of an obligation of any person; and

(d) mortgage, hypothec, pledge or otherwise create a security interest in all or any property of the corporation, owned or subsequently acquired, to secure any obligation of the corporation.

In addition, providing there is no prohibition to the contrary, the directors may by resolution delegate the powers to a director, a committee of directors or an officer. (See Form 15.1.)

3. Organizational Resolutions of Directors

Section 104 of the CBCA sets out the various matters that may be dealt with by the directors once the certificate of incorporation has issued. Under subsection (3), an incorporator or director may call the meeting of directors by giving not less than five days notice thereof by mail to each director, stating the time and place of the meeting. Subsection 114(6) provides that a director may in any manner waive notice of a meeting of directors. Attendance of a director at a meeting of directors is a waiver of notice of the meeting unless the director attends for the express purpose of objecting to the transaction of any business on the grounds that the meeting was not lawfully called. Generally, notice of the first meeting is waived by the first directors.

The following are the standard matters dealt with at the first meeting of directors of a corporation incorporated under the CBCA:

1. pass a resolution enacting By-Law No. 1;
2. adopt the form(s) of security certificates/share certificates;
3. authorize the issue of at least one share to qualify a shareholder for the purposes of organization;
4. appoint officers of the corporation;
5. appoint the banker of the corporation, including enacting any by-law the bank might require. Most banks no longer request a borrowing by-law because they are aware of the provisions of section 189. The banks will require a banking resolution, certificate of incumbency, operation of account agreement, specimen signature card and a certificate as to any restrictions on borrowing that might exist in the by-laws or articles or a unanimous shareholder agreement;
6. approve a corporate seal, provided the corporation will have a corporate seal;
7. establish by resolution the site of the registered office, even though this information is set out in the Notice of Registered Office filed with the articles of incorporation. Some lawyers, instead of passing such a resolution, merely file the copy of the Notice of Registered Office in the minute book. What will be done depends on the practice in the particular law office;
8. add the confirmation clause, below which all the directors of the corporation sign, evidencing their presence and approval of the organizational resolutions.

In addition, section 20 sets out other matters to be included:

> **20.** A corporation shall prepare and maintain, at its registered office or at any other place in Canada designated by the directors, records containing

(a) the articles and the by-laws, and all amendments thereto, and a copy of any unanimous shareholder agreement;

(b) minutes of meetings and resolutions of shareholders;

(c) copies of all notices required by section 106 [Notice of Directors] or 113 [Notice of Change of Directors]; and

(d) a securities register complying with section 50. [Details of this register are supplied, below, under ''Registers''.]

The directors can by resolution establish the place in Canada where the corporate records are to be maintained.

Under subsection 114(8) where a corporation has only one director, that director may constitute a meeting.

4. Organizational Resolutions of Shareholders

The shareholder of the corporation will either confirm the by-law in writing or pass a resolution confirming the by-law.

Other standard matters the shareholder will deal with regarding the average non-distributing corporation are:

1. The election of directors, if one or more of the first directors named in the Notice of Directors was only acting in a temporary capacity.
2. The appointment of an auditor or, if the corporation is a non-distributing corporation, the dispensing with an auditor (see Chapter 17, ''Annual Meetings of Shareholders'', subheading ''2. Notice and Matters Considered'').

Section 163 states: ''The shareholders of a corporation that is not required to comply with section 160 may resolve not to appoint an auditor.'' Section 160 requires the forwarding of financial statements to the Director if the corporation distributes its securities to the public.

3. The addition of the confirmation clause, below which the shareholder or shareholders sign, evidencing their presence and approval of the organizational resolutions.

5. Post-Organizational Resolutions of Directors

The matters that could be dealt with at this point in the organization of the corporation are:

1. The transfer of a share to the beneficial owner from a temporary shareholder.
2. The election of permanent officers to replace any temporary officers.

6. Registers

Various registers are required to be set up under the CBCA for holders of debt obligations, transfer registers and individual securities registers for each shareholder, arranged in the minute book in alphabetical order.

The legal stationers have the usual registers available but these do not conform to the precise wording of the Act. The available forms can be adapted by changing the headings. Some law firms have created special registers that comply with the Act.

7. Report to Client

The reporting letter to the client on the incorporation and organization of the federal corporation would report on the following matters:

1. articles of incorporation — A copy of the certificate of incorporation, with the articles attached, could be enclosed with the reporting letter. Special mention would be made of
   - (a) authorized capital — classes and whether limited or unlimited;
   - (b) restrictions on share transfers;
   - (c) number of directors — if a minimum and maximum number was set out in the articles, the number established by resolution of the directors;
   - (d) summary of the "other provisions" included in the articles;
2. a copy of the Notice of Registered Office would be forwarded; and
3. a copy of the Notice of Directors would be enclosed.

In addition, information and filing requirements, if there is the possibility of any change in the registered office or the directors, would be supplied to the client.

Other paragraphs included in the report would provide particulars on the corporate banker and signing officers of the bank account, information as to the issued shares of the corporation and any special provisions under the by-laws that a lawyer might want to bring to the attention of the client.

At the same time, an account for services would be prepared and enclosed with the report to the client.

16

ARTICLES OF AMENDMENT

1. Fundamental Changes

Subsection 173(1) under Part XV (Fundamental Changes) of the *Canada Business Corporations Act*, states that subject to sections 176 and 177, the articles of a corporation may by special resolution be amended to:

(a) change its name;

(b) change the place in which its registered office is situated;

(c) add, change or remove any restriction on the business or businesses that the corporation may carry on;

(d) change any maximum number of shares that the corporation is authorized to issue;

(e) create new classes of shares;

(f) reduce or increase its stated capital, if its stated capital is set out in the articles;

(g) change the designation of all or any of its shares, and add, change or remove any rights, privileges, restrictions and conditions, including rights to accrued dividends, in respect of all or any of its shares, whether issued or unissued;

(h) change the shares of any class or series, whether issued or unissued, into a different number of shares of the same class or series or into the same or a different number of shares of other classes or series;

(i) divide a class of shares, whether issued or unissued, into series and fix the number of shares in each series and the rights, privileges, restrictions and conditions thereof;

(j) authorize the directors to divide any class of unissued shares into series and fiat the number of shares in each series and the rights, privileges, restrictions and conditions thereof;

(k) authorize the directors to change the rights, privileges, restrictions and conditions attached to unissued shares of any series;

(l) revoke, diminish or enlarge any authority conferred under paragraphs (j) and (k);

(m) increase or decrease the number of directors or the minimum or maximum number of directors, subject to sections 107 and 112;

(n) add, change or remove restrictions on the issue, transfer or ownership of shares; or

(o) add, change or remove any other provision that is permitted by this Act to be set out in the articles.

2. Filing Articles of Amendment

A ''special resolution'' is defined under subsection 2(1) of the Act to mean ''a resolution passed by a majority of not less than two-thirds of the votes cast by the shareholders who voted in respect of that resolution or signed by all the shareholders entitled to vote on that resolution''.

Once the special resolution has been passed by the directors and confirmed by the shareholders as required under the statute, Form 4, articles of amendment (see Form 16.1) as prescribed under the CBCA must be forwarded in duplicate to the Director of the Corporations Directorate, Industry Canada, Ottawa, along with the required fee. The cheque is payable to the Receiver General for Canada. If the amendment involves a change of name, a NUANS report must also be submitted. If the proper documentation is filed, Form 5, Certificate of Amendment will issue.

If the proposed amendment involves a change in the registered office or in the number of directors, then the appropriate Notice of Change must also be submitted with the articles of amendment. Before mailing the documents, reference should be made to the instructions on the back of the form.

17

ANNUAL MEETINGS OF SHAREHOLDERS

1. Requirements

The duties of the directors of a corporation are set out under section 127 of the *Canada Business Corporations Act*:

133. Callling meetings.—The directors of a corporation

(a) shall call an annual meeting of shareholders not later than eighteen months after the corporation comes into existence and subsequently not later than fifteen months after holding the last preceding annual meeting; and

(b) may at any time call a special meeting of shareholders.

134. (1) **Fixing record date.**—For the purpose of determining shareholders

(a) entitled to receive payment of a dividend,

(b) entitled to participate in a liquidation distribution, or

(c) for any other purpose except the right to receive notice of or to vote at a meeting,

the directors may fix in advance a date as the record date for such determination of shareholders, but such record date shall not precede by more than fifty days the particular action to be taken.

(2) **Notice of meeting.**—For the purpose of determining shareholders entitled to receive notice of a meeting of shareholders, the directors may fix in advance a date as the record date for such determination of shareholders, but such record date shall not precede by more than fifty days or by less than twenty-one days the date on which the meeting is to be held.

(3) **No record date fixed.**—If no record date is fixed,

(a) the record date for the determination of shareholders entitled to receive notice of a meeting of shareholders shall be

(i) at the close of business on the day immediately preceding the day on which the notice is given, or,

(ii) if no notice is given, the day on which the meeting is held; and

(b) the record date for the determination of shareholders for any purpose other than to establish a shareholder's right to receive notice of a meeting or to vote shall be at the close of business on the day on which the directors pass the resolution relating thereto.

(4) **When record date fixed.**—If a record date is fixed, unless notice of the record date is waived in writing by every holder of a share of the class or series affected whose name is set out in the securities register at the close of business on the day the directors fix the record date, notice thereof shall, not less than seven days before the date so fixed, be given

(a) by advertisement in a newspaper published or distributed in the place where the corporation has its registered office and in each place in Canada where it has a transfer agent or where a transfer of its shares may be recorded; and

(b) by written notice to each stock exchange in Canada on which the shares of the corporation are listed for trading

2. Notice and Matters Considered

Section 135 requires that notice shall be sent to each shareholder not less than 21 days prior to the date of the meeting and not more than 50 days in advance of the proposed meeting. This section also provides that at the annual meeting the shareholders shall consider:

1. the financial statements and the auditor's report;
2. the election of the directors; and
3. the reappointment of an incumbent auditor.

This section also states that any business transacted at an annual meeting of shareholders, except consideration of the financial statements, auditor's report, election of directors and reappointment of the incumbent auditor, is deemed to be special business.

Pursuant to subsection 135(6), notice of a meeting of shareholders at which special business is to be transacted shall state:

(a) the nature of that business in sufficient detail to permit the shareholder to form a reasoned judgment thereon; and

(b) the text of any special resolution to be submitted to the meeting.

Under section 136 of the Act, a shareholder or any other person entitled to attend a meeting of shareholders, for example the auditor, can waive notice of the meeting in any manner.

Section 142 of the CBCA makes provision for the shareholders to sign resolutions covering all matters normally dealt with at an annual meeting of shareholders and these resolutions are as valid as if passed at a meeting.

Section 155 of the Act sets out requirements for the information that must be included in the annual financial statements and requires the report of the auditor, if an auditor has been appointed.

In addition, section 160 requires that copies of the financial statements be filed with the Director, the government official in charge of administering the statute, if any securities are offered to the public by the corporation. Non-distributing corporations are exempt from filing copies of financial statements with the Director if all shareholders consent to the exemption.

Section 163 makes provisions for dispensing with an auditor by corporations which are not required to comply with the provisions of section 160.

18

ANNUAL RETURNS

1. Requirements

Subsection 263(1) of the *Canada Business Corporations Act* requires the filing of an Annual Return. The section states that every corporation shall, on the prescribed date, send to the Director an Annual Return in prescribed form and the director shall file it. Subsection (2) makes provision for the issuance of a certificate of compliance by the Director. This certificate would state that a corporation has sent to the Director a document required to be sent under this Act.

Section 4 of the Regulations made under the Act was amended by SOR/95-364 which came into force on January 1, 1999. Pursuant to the amendments, federally incorporated corporations are able to file the annual return, Form 22 (see Form 18.1), by sending it to the Director under the *Canada Business Corporations Act*, or file when required under the Act with their corporate income tax return. Corporations were previously required to file their annual return within next 60 days following the anniversary date of incorporation. Corporations that choose this latter option can use Schedule 80, Industry Canada Annual Return — Canada Business Corporations Act (see Form 18.2) which is attached to the T2 Corporation Income Tax Return. The corporation can use the same form to report a coinciding change in the address of its registered office. To report a change of directors coinciding with the filing of its annual return, a corporation can use Schedule 81, Notice of Change of Directors — Canada Business Corporations Act (see Form 18.3). The annual return filing fee has been reduced to $40, effective April 1, 2001. Corporations using Schedules 80 and 81 should include their payment with the return they file with the CCRA. The CCRA will forward the payment to Industry Canada.

The Canada Customs and Revenue Agency (CCRA) and Industry Canada are developing a joint-filing initiative for federally incorporated corporations. This new initiative serves to streamline reporting and eliminate duplication.

Instead of sending Industry Canada an annual return required under the Act, federal corporations are able to file this information with Revenue Canada by including Schedule 80 with its corporate income tax return. Industry Canada is harmonizing the filing date of the annual return to coincide with the CCRA's corporate income tax return (i.e., six months after the end of the tax year). This new date applies to corporations filing Schedule 80, or filing Form 22 separately.

2. Standard Industrial Classification Code (''S.I.C.C.'')

The only information which might prove to be something of a problem is the response required under number 5 on Form 22. The instruction on the back of the Form reads as follows:

> **Item 5**
>
> State the main actual business or businesses of the corporation, indicating, where possible, the corporation's standard industrial classification code (S.I.C.C.).

The S.I.C.C. is found under the CBCA Regulations. There are eleven divisions, each subdivided into major groups. It will be necessary to find out the major business of the corporation and then check through the S.I.C.C. until the appropriate classification is found. This S.I.C.C. number is then inserted under item 5 in the Annual Return.

After its completion, the Annual Return is mailed to the Director, Corporations Directorate, Industry Canada. A cheque for the prescribed fee, payable to the Receiver General for Canada, should be forwarded with the Annual Return. The mailing address is listed in Appendix A.

The Corporations Directorate accepts facsimile filings of Annual Returns provided the client has a deposit account and is in good standing with Industry Canada. The provision for the deposit account is to pay the prescribed fee for the Annual Return.

The originals of the Annual Return are to be retained by the corporation as part of its record keeping process.

The notice concerning fax filings also sets out specific requirements for the quality of the fax filing. These particulars can be reviewed in Chapter 14, Incorporation — Federal Jurisdiction.

Part IV

Forms

(There are no forms for chapters 2, 3, 4, 7, 8 and 17.)

1. Sole Proprietorships and Partnerships

1.1 Registration—*Business Names Act*—Form 1

Ontario

Ministry of Consumer and Commercial Relations
Ministère de la Consommation et du Commerce

Registration under the Business Names Act - Sole Proprietorship / Partnership
Enregistrement en vertu de la *Loi sur les noms commerciaux* (Entreprise personnelle / société en nom collectif)

Form 1
Formule 1

INSTRUCTIONS **It is important to read these notes before completing the attached form.**

Print all information clearly in CAPITAL LETTERS using black ink.

Complete all sections of the form. Incomplete forms will be returned.

Fees:
- there is a fee payable for new registrations and renewals;
- fees may be paid in cash, money order or cheque;
- payable to the **Ontario Minister of Finance;**
- do not send cash in the mail;
- a handling fee of $35 will be charged for a non-negotiable cheque.

Please forward both copies of the enclosed form to the Ministry of Consumer and Commercial Relations. The Client copy will no longer be certified consistent with Ontario Regulation 175 / 94 Section 4. The Client copy will be **returned**, with a validation in the bottom right-hand corner.

Return completed forms to: Ministry of Consumer and Commercial Relations
Companies Branch
393 University Ave., Suite 200
Toronto ON M5G 2M2

Please do not separate the form.

Refer to these notes while completing form.

1. Registration Type - Check the appropriate box:
   New (Fee payable)
   - a new registration is the first filing of the business name
   - a change of business name, sole proprietor, or a complete change of partners, is considered a new registration

   Renewal (Fee payable)
   - a registration expires in five years and must be renewed

   Amendment (No fee payable)
   - an amendment should be filed whenever there is a change in address or change of activity

   Cancellation (No fee payable)
   - a cancellation should be submitted if you stop using the business name

   BIN
   For renewal, amendment or cancellation, enter "Business Identification No." (BIN) if previously issued.

2. Business Name - Please print the business name. This is the name you are registering. The business name must be set out in Block Capital Letters in the squares provided and must commence on the first line of the "grid" in the first square. Each square of the grid represents a letter of the alphabet, a punctuation mark, or a space. If there is not sufficient space on the grid for the name, please use additional form(s). Please complete all items on additional form(s) and note the number of each additional page in the top right-hand corner of each form.

3. Mailing Address - Include street number, name, municipality and postal code. Your copy of the registration will be mailed to this address.

4. Address of Principal Place of Business in Ontario - Include street, number, name, municipality and postal code. A post office box is not acceptable in a business address. If there is more than one place of business, select one as the principal place.
   Where the business address is outside Ontario, set out the words "Not Applicable" in Item 4. If this is the case, please ensure that Item 3, the mailing address, includes the street address of the principal place of business outside of Ontario, as a post office box is not acceptable.

5. Activity - Include a brief description of the activity being performed.

6. Type of Registrant - Check the appropriate box. If you are registering a partnership with more than 10 partners, you may set out the name and address of a designated partner(s), and check the box marked "More than 10 Partners". Information on all partners carrying on business in Ontario must be kept and made available to the public at the partnership business address.

7/8. Registrant Information - Include the full name and residential address or address for service of the sole proprietor, each partner, or designated partner(s). A post office box is not acceptable. For partnerships with more than two partners, please fill out and attach another form(s) with the additional names and addresses.

   Additional Information - If the registrant is **not** an individual, enter the name of the business or corporation in "Additional Information". Also enter the address of the business or corporation in Item 8. If the registrant is a corporation, enter the corporation number in the space titled "Ontario Corporation No."

9. Print the name of the person authorizing this registration, (either a sole proprietor, or a partner, or a person acting under a power of attorney).

   Additional Information: If the person authorizing the registration is not an individual, (e.g. corporation, trust, syndicate) set out the name in "Additional Information" and do not complete the boxes for the last, first and middle names.

1.1 (continued)

Ontario

Ministry of Consumer and Commercial Relations / Ministère de la Consommation et du Commerce

Registration under the *Business Names Act* - Sole Proprietorship / Partnership

Enregistrement en vertu de la *Loi sur les noms commerciaux* (Entreprise personnelle / société en nom collectif)

Form 1 / Formule 1

Page_____ of / de_____

Print clearly in CAPITAL LETTERS / Écrivez clairement en LETTRES MAJUSCULES

1. Registration Type / Type d'enregistrement

BIN / NIE — If B, C, or D enter "Business Identification Number" / En cas de B, C ou D, inscrivez le nº d'identification de l'entreprise

A New / Nouveau — B Renewal / Renouvellement — C Amendment / Modification — D Cancellation / Révocation

2. Business Name / Nom commercial

3. Mailing Address / Adresse postale

Street Number / Nº de rue — Street Name / Nom de la rue — Suite No. / Bureau nº

City / Town / Ville — Province / Province — Country / Pays — Postal Code / Code postal

4. Address of principal place of business in Ontario / Adresse de l'établissement principal en Ontario — Same as above / comme ci-dessus

Street Number / Nº de rue — Street Name / Nom de la rue — Suite No. / Bureau nº

City / Town / Ville — Province / Province **Ontario** — Postal Code / Code postal

Should NOT too broad

5. Give a brief description of the ACTIVITY being carried out under the business name / Résumez brièvement le genre d'ACTIVITÉ exercée sous le nom commercial

6. Type of Registrant / Type de personne enregistrée

A Sole proprietorship / Entreprise personnelle **OR / OU** B Partnership / Société en nom collectif

More than 10 Partners: records at business address / Plus de 10 associés : dossiers à l'adresse d'affaires

Registrant Information / Renseignements sur la personne enregistrée

7. Last Name / Nom de famille — First Name / Prénom — Middle Initial / Initiale (2º prénom)

8. Street Number / Nº de rue — Street Name / Nom de la rue — Suite No. / Bureau nº

City / Town / Ville — Province / Province — Country / Pays — Postal Code / Code postal

Additional Information / Renseignements supplémentaires — Ont. Corporation No. / Nº matricule de la personne morale en Ontario

7. Last Name / Nom de famille — First Name / Prénom — Middle Initial / Initiale (2º prénom)

8. Street Number / Nº de rue — Street Name / Nom de la rue — Suite No. / Bureau nº

City / Town / Ville — Province / Province — Country / Pays — Postal Code / Code postal

Additional Information / Renseignements supplémentaires — Ont. Corporation No. / Nº matricule de la personne morale en Ontario

9. Print name of person authorizing this registration (either the sole proprietor, a partner or a person acting under power of attorney). If the person is a corporation, complete additional information below only. / Indiquez en lettres majuscules le nom de la personne autorisant l'enregistrement (propriétaire unique, associé ou personne habilitée en vertu d'une procuration). (Si c'est une personne morale qui autorise l'enregistrement, complétez les renseignements supplémentaires ci-dessous.)

Last Name / Nom de famille — First Name / Prénom — Middle Name / 2º prénom

OR If person authorizing the registration is not an individual (eg. corporation, trust, syndicate), print name below and do *not* complete last, first and middle names above.

OU Si la personne qui autorise l'enregistrement n'est pas un individu (c'est-à-dire une personne morale, un trust ou syndicat) et *ne pas* remplir le nom de famille, prénom et 2º prénom.

Additional Information / Renseignements supplémentaires

MINISTRY USE ONLY - RÉSERVÉ À L'USAGE DU MINISTÈRE

07219(04/99)

1.2 Registration—*Business Names Act*—Form 2: For Corporations (formerly known as Name/Style Registration)

Ontario

Ministry of Consumer and Commercial Relations — Ministère de la Consommation et du Commerce

Registration
under the Business Names Act – Corporations
Enregistrement
en vertu de la Loi sur les noms commerciaux (Personnes morales)

Form 2
Formule 2

INSTRUCTIONS

It is important to read these notes before completing the attached form

Print all information clearly in CAPITAL LETTERS using black ink.

Complete all sections of the form. Incomplete forms will be returned.

Fees
- there is a fee payable for new registrations and renewals
- fees may be paid in cash, money order or cheque
- payable to the **Ontario Minister of Finance**
- do not send cash in the mail
- a handling fee of $35 will be charged for a non-negotiable cheque.

Please forward both copies of the enclosed form to the Ministry of Consumer and Commercial Relations. The Client's copy will no longer be certified consistent with Ontario Regulation 175 / 94 Section 4. The Client's copy will be **returned**, with a validation in the bottom right hand corner.

Return completed forms to: Ministry of Consumer and Commercial Relations
Companies Branch
393 University Ave., Suite 200
Toronto, ON M5G 2M2

Please do not separate the form.

Refer to these notes while completing form

1. Registration Type – Check the appropriate box
   New (Fee payable)
   - a new registration is the first filing of the business name
   - a change of business/identification name is considered a new registration

   Renewal (Fee payable)
   - a registration expires in five years and must be renewed

   Amendment (No fee payable)
   - an amendment should be filed whenever there is a change in address, activity or corporation name

   Cancellation (No fee payable)
   - a cancellation should be submitted if you stop using the business name

   BIN
   For renewal, amendment or cancellation enter "Business Identification No." (BIN) if previously issued.
2. Business Name – Please print the business name. This is the name you are registering. The business name must be set out in Block Capital Letters in the squares provided and must commence on the first line of the "grid" in the first square. Each square of the grid represents a letter of the alphabet, a punctuation mark, or a space. If there is not sufficient space on the grid for the name, please use additional form(s). Please complete all items on additional form(s) and note the number of each additional page in the top right-hand corner of each form.
3. Mailing Address – Include street number, name, municipality and postal code. Your copy of the registration will be mailed to this address.
4. Business Address in Ontario – include street number, name, municipality and postal code. A post office box is not acceptable in a business address. If there is more than one place of business, select one as the principal place. Where the business address is outside Ontario, set out the words "Not Applicable" in Item 4. If this is the case, please ensure that Item 3, the mailing address, includes the street address of the principal place of business outside of Ontario, as a post office box is not acceptable.
5. Activity – include a brief description of the activity being performed.
6. Corporation Name – the name of the corporation that is registering the business name.
7. Ontario Corporation Number – the number assigned to the corporation named in item 6.
8. Jurisdiction – the name of the jurisdiction in which the corporation was incorporated. Please do not use abbreviations.
9. Address of the Head or Registered Office of the corporation – include the number, street, municipality and postal code of the head or registered office address. **A post office box is not acceptable.**
10. Print the name of the person authorizing the registration, (either an officer, or a director, or a person acting under a power of attorney.)

    Additional Information: If the person authorizing the registration is not an individual, set out the name in "Additional Information", and do not complete the boxes for the last, first and middle names.

1.2 (continued)

Ontario

Ministry of Consumer and Commercial Relations / Ministère de la Consommation et du Commerce

Registration
under the Business Names Act – Corporations

Enregistrement
en vertu de la Loi sur les noms commerciaux (Personnes morales)

Form 2

Formule 2

Print clearly in CAPITAL LETTERS / Écrivez clairement en LETTRES MAJUSCULES

Page ___ of / de ___

1. Registration Type / Type d'enregistrement
   A. New / Nouvel   B. Renewal / Renouvellement   C. Amendment / Modification   D. Cancellation / Révocation

2. Business or identification Name / Nom commercial ou d'identification

3. Mailing Address / Adresse postale
   City/Town / Ville   Province   Country / Pays   Postal Code / Code postal

4. Business address in Ontario / Adresse d'affaires en Ontario
   Same as above / Même que ci-dessus
   Street Number / N° de rue   Street Name / Nom de la rue   Suite No. / Bureau n°
   City/Town / Ville   Province: Ontario   Postal Code / Code postal

5. Give a brief description of the **ACTIVITY** being carried out under the business/identification name
   Résumez brièvement le genre d'**ACTIVITÉ** exercée sous le nom commercial ou d'identification

6. Corporation Name / Personne morale

7. Ontario corporation number / Numéro matricule de la personne morale en Ontario

8. Jurisdiction in which the corporation was incorporated / Le territoire de compétence où la personne morale a été constituée

9. Address of Head or Registered Office of the corporation / Adresse du siège social ou du bureau enregistré de la personne morale
   Street Number / N° de rue   Street Name / Nom de la rue   Suite No. / Bureau n°
   City/Town / Ville   Province   Country / Pays   Postal Code / Code postal

10. Print name of person authorizing this registration
    Indiquez en lettres majuscules le nom de la personne autorisant l'enregistrement
    Last Name / Nom de famille
    First Name / Prénom
    Middle Name / 2e prénom
    OR / OU
    Additional information / Renseignements supplémentaires

MINISTRY USE ONLY / RÉSERVÉ AU MINISTÈRE

07197 (01/95) CD441   MINISTRY COPY / COPIE DU MINISTÈRE

1.3 Declaration—*Limited Partnerships Act*—Form 3

Ontario

Ministry of Consumer and Commercial Relations | Ministère de la Consommation et du Commerce

INSTRUCTIONS **It is important to read these notes before completing the attached form**

Print all information clearly in CAPITAL LETTERS using black ink.

Complete all sections of the form. Incomplete forms will be returned.

Fees:
- there is a fee payable for new declarations and renewals
- fees may be paid in cash, money order or cheque
- payable to the **Ontario Minister of Finance**
- do not send cash in the mail
- a handling fee of $35 will be charged for a non-negotiable cheque.

Please forward both copies of the enclosed form to the Ministry of Consumer and Commercial Relations. The Client copy will no longer be certified consistent with Ontario Regulation 175 / 94 Section 4. The Client copy will be **returned**, with a validation in the bottom right-hand corner.

Return completed forms to: Ministry of Consumer and Commercial Relations
Companies Branch
393 University Ave., Suite 200
Toronto ON M5G 2M2

Please do not separate the form

Refer to these notes while completing form

1. Registration Type - Check the appropriate box:
New (Fee payable)
- a new declaration is the first filing of the firm name
- a change of firm name is considered a new declaration (For name change check box marked ***New*** as well as box marked ***Name Change***)

Renewal (Fee payable)
- a declaration expires in five years and must be renewed
- (For name change check box marked ***Renewal*** as well as box marked ***Name Change***)

Change (No fee payable)
- a change should be filed when there is a change in address, activity or information regarding general partners

Dissolution (No fee payable)
- Limited Partnerships formed in Ontario may cancel the Declaration by filing a declaration of dissolution

Withdrawal (No fee payable)
- Extra-provincial Limited Partnerships in Ontario may cancel the Declaration by filing a declaration of withdrawal

BIN
For a new declaration or renewal with name change or a renewal, change, dissolution or withdrawal, enter **Business Identification No. (BIN)**, if previously issued.

2. Firm Name - Please print the business name of the Limited Partnership. The firm name must be set out in Block Capital Letters in the squares provided and must commence on the first line of the grid in the first square. Each square of the grid represents a letter of the alphabet, a punctuation mark, or a space. If there is not sufficient space on the grid for the name, please use additional form(s). Please complete all items on additional form(s) and note the number of each additional page in the top right-hand corner of each form.

3. Mailing Address - Include street number, name, municipality and postal code. Your copy of the registration will be mailed to this address.

4. Address of Principal Place of Business in Ontario - Include street, number, name, municipality and postal code. A post office box is not acceptable in a business address. If there is more than one place of business, select one as the principal place.

5. General Nature of Business - include a brief description of the activity being carried on by the firm.

6. Jurisdiction of Formation - the name of the jurisdiction in which the Limited Partnership was formed. Please do not use abbreviations.

7. Information regarding General Partners:

Item 7 must be completed by all general partners. If there is more than one general partner, set out the information in Item 7 on additional Form 3's as required.

The general partners of every limited partnership must keep a record of limited partners at the principal place of business in Ontario. This information must be made available to the public upon request. It must include the full name and residence address or address for service of each limited partner and the contribution made to the Limited Partnership.

If the general partner is not an individual or a corporation, then set out the general partner's name in the "Additional Information" space.

Where a person is signing for the general partner under power of attorney, that person must sign in the "Signature" space and check the "Power of Attorney" box.

If a **New Declaration or Renewal** is being filed, each general partner must sign the form. If the general partner is a corporation, set out the corporation name in the Additional Information box and include the Ontario Corporation Number. An authorized signing officer must sign. Print the name of the officer under the signature.

If a **Change, Withdrawal or Dissolution** is being filed, at least one general partner must sign the form. If the general partner is a corporation, an authorized signing officer must sign. Print the name of the officer under the signature.

8. Information Regarding Attorney/Representative for an Extra-Provincial Limited Partnership:

In the case of an Extra-Provincial Limited Partnership, the Limited Partnership shall execute a power of attorney in the prescribed form (Form 4 as set out in the Limited Partnerships Act, Regulation 578), to appoint a person resident in Ontario or a corporation having its head or registered office in Ontario to be the attorney and representative in Ontario of that Extra-Provincial Limited Partnership. The representative's name, Ontario address and signature must be set out in Item 8. If a corporation is appointed, an authorized signing officer must sign. Print the name of the officer under the signature and set out the Ontario Corporation Name & Number.

If the representative is not an individual or a corporation, then set out the representative's name in the "Additional Information" space.

Upon request, the representative must make available to the public, at its Ontario address, both the executed power of attorney and a record of the limited partners.

1.3 (continued)

Ontario

Ministry of Consumer and Commercial Relations / Ministère de la Consommation et du Commerce

Declaration

Déclaration

Form 3
Formule 3

Page ____ of / de ____

Print clearly in CAPITAL LETTERS / Écrivez clairement en LETTRES MAJUSCULES

1. Declaration Type / Type déclaration — A ☐ New / Nouvelle — B ☐ Renewal / Renouvellement — C ☐ Change / Changement — D ☐ Dissolution / Dissolution — E ☐ Withdrawal / Retrait

For Name Change, check also box A or B and enter BIN / Si modification de la raison sociale, cochez aussi A ou B et indiquer le NIE — ☐ Name Change / Modification de la raison sociale — Enter Business Identification Number if A or B with Name Change or B, C, D or E. / Indiquer le numéro d'identification d'entreprise si A ou B avec modification de la raison sociale ou B, C, D ou E — BIN / NIE

2. Firm Name / Raison sociale de la société en commandite

3. Mailing Address / Adresse postale — Street Number / Nº de rue — Street Name / Nom de la rue — Suite No. / Bureau nº — City / Town / Ville — Province / Province — Country / Pays — Postal Code / Code Postal

4. Principal Place of Business in Ontario / Établissement principal en Ontario — ☐ Same as above / comme ci-dessus
Street Number / Nº de rue — Street Name / Nom de la rue — P.O. Box not acceptable / Case postale non acceptable — Suite No. / Bureau nº
City / Town / Ville — Province / Province **Ontario** — Postal Code / Code Postal

5. General Nature of Business / Nature générale de l'activité exercée

6. Jurisdiction of Formation / Territoire de la création

7. Information Regarding General Partner(s) / Renseignements sur le ou les commandités
Last Name / Nom de famille — First Name / Prénom — Middle Initial / Initiale (2e prénom)
Street Number / Nº de rue — Street Name / Nom de la rue — P.O. Box not acceptable / Case postale non acceptable — Suite No. / Bureau nº
City / Town / Ville — Province / Province — Country / Pays — Postal Code / Code Postal
Additional Information / Renseignements supplémentaires
Ontario Corporation No. / Nº de la personne morale en Ontario
☐ Power of Attorney / Procuration
Signature / Signature X
Print Name of Signatory / Nom du signataire en lettres moulées

8. Information Regarding Attorney/Representative / Renseignements sur le procureur/représentant d'une société en commandite extraprovinciale
Last Name / Nom de famille — First Name / Prénom — Middle Initial / Initiale (2e prénom)
Street Number / Nº de rue — Street Name / Nom de la rue — P.O. Box not acceptable / Case postale non acceptable — Suite No. / Bureau nº
City / Town / Ville — Province / Province — Country / Pays — Postal Code / Code Postal
Additional Information / Renseignements supplémentaires
Signature / Signature X
Print Name of Signatory / Nom du signataire en lettres moulées
Corporation Name / Personne morale
Ontario Corporation No. / Nº de la personne morale en Ontario

MINISTRY USE ONLY - RÉSERVÉ À L'USAGE DU MINISTÈRE

07191(01/99)

MINISTRY COPY / COPIE DU MINISTÈRE

1.4 Registration—*Business Names Act*—Form 6: For Ontario Limited Liability Partnership, Extra-Provincial Limited Liability Partnership, Extra-Provincial Limited Liability Company

Ontario

Ministry of Consumer and Commercial Relations | Ministère de la Consommation et du Commerce

Registration

Ontario Limited Liability Partnership
Extra-Provincial Limited Liability Partnership
Extra-Provincial Limited Liability Company

Société à responsabilité limitée de l'Ontario
Société à responsabilité limitée extraprovinciale
Société de capitaux extraprovinciale

Form 6
Formule 6

INSTRUCTIONS

It is important to read these notes before completing the attached form.

Print all information clearly in CAPITAL LETTERS using black ink.

Complete all sections of the form. Incomplete forms will be returned.

Fees:
- there is a fee payable for new registrations and renewals;
- fees may be paid in cash, money order or cheque,
- payable to the **Ontario Minister of Finance;**
- do not send cash in the mail;
- a handling fee of $35 will be charged for a non-negotiable cheque.

Please forward both copies of the enclosed form to the Ministry of Consumer and Commercial Relations. The Client copy will no longer be certified consistent with Ontario Regulation 175 / 94 Section 4. The Client copy will be **returned**, with a validation in the bottom right-hand corner.

Return completed forms to: Ministry of Consumer and Commercial Relations
Companies Branch
393 University Ave., Suite 200
Toronto ON M5G 2M2

Please do not separate the form.

Refer to these notes while completing form.

1. Registration Type - Check the appropriate box:
New (Fee payable)
- a new registration is the first filing of the business name
- a change of business name, or a complete change of partners, is considered a new registration

Renewal (Fee payable)
- a registration expires in five years and must be renewed

Amendment (No fee payable)
- an amendment should be filed whenever there is a change in address or change of activity

Cancellation (No fee payable)
- a cancellation should be submitted if you stop using the business name

BIN
For renewal, amendment or cancellation, enter "Business Identification No." (BIN) if previously issued.

2. Business Name - The name must contain the legal element which identifies the entity, for example; Limited Liability Partnership, LLP, Limited Liability Company, LLC or the equivalent French or other similar terms required under the law where the entity was formed. Please print the business name in Block Capital Letters in the squares provided, commencing on the first line of the "grid" in the first square. Each square of the grid represents a letter of the alphabet, a punctuation mark or a space. If there is not sufficient space on the grid for the name, please use additional form(s) and write the number of each additional page in the top right-hand corner of each form.

3. Mailing Address - Include street number, name, municipality and postal code. Your copy of the registration will be mailed to this address.

4. Address of Principal Place of Business in Ontario - Include street, number, name, municipality and postal code. A post office box is not acceptable in a business address. If there is more than one place of business, select one as the principal place. For an Extra-Provincial Limited Liability Partnership or an Extra-Provincial Limited Liability Company where the business address may be outside of Ontario, set out the words "Not Applicable" in item 4. If this is the case, please ensure that item 3, the mailing address, includes the street address of the principal place of business outside of Ontario, as a post office is not acceptable.

5. Activity - Include a brief description of the activity being performed.

6. Type of Registrant - Check the appropriate box. If you are registering an Ontario Limited Liability Partnership or an Extra-Provincial Limited Liability Partnership with more than 10 partners, you may set out the name and address of a designated partner(s) and check the box marked "More than 10 Partners". Information on all partners carrying on business in Ontario must be kept and made available to the public at the Limited Liability Partnership's business address in Ontario.

7. Jurisdiction of Formation - Enter the name of the jurisdiction in which the Ontario Limited Liability Partnership, the Extra-Provincial Limited Liability Partnership or the Extra-Provincial Limited Liability Company was formed. Please do not use abbreviations.

8/9. Registrant Information - This item applies only to an Ontario Limited Liability Partnership or to an Extra-Provincial Limited Liability Partnership (it is not required for an Extra-Provincial Limited Liability Company). Include the full name and residential address or address for service of each partner or designated partner(s). A post office box is not acceptable. If there are more than two partners, please fill out and attach another form(s) with the additional names and addresses.

Additional Information - If the registrant is **not** an individual, enter the name of the business or corporation in "Additional Information". Also enter the address of the business or corporation in item 9. If the registrant is a corporation, enter the Ontario Corporation No.

10. Print the name of the person authorizing this registration, (either a partner for a Limited Liability Partnership, a general manager/representative for a Limited Liability Company or a person acting under power of attorney).

Additional Information: If the person authorizing the registration is not an individual, (e.g. corporation, trust, syndicate) set out the name in "Additional Information" and do not complete the boxes for the last, first and middle names.

1.4 (continued)

Ontario
Ministry of Consumer and Commercial Relations / Ministère de la Consommation et du Commerce

Registration under the Business Names Act
Enregistrement en vertu de la Loi sur les noms commerciaux

Ontario Limited Liability Partnership
Extra-Provincial Limited Liability Partnership
Extra-Provincial Limited Liability Company
Société à responsabilité limitée de l'Ontario
Société à responsabilité limitée extraprovinciale
Société de capitaux extraprovinciale

Form 6
Formule 6

Page ...... of / de ......

Print clearly in CAPITAL LETTERS / Écrivez clairement en LETTRES MAJUSCULES

1. Registration Type / Type d'enregistrement
   BIN / NIE
   A. New / Nouveau — B. Renewal / Renouvellement — C. Amendment / Modification — D. Cancellation / Révocation

2. Business Name / Nom commercial

3. Mailing Address / Adresse postale
   Street Number / Nº de rue — Street Name / Nom de la rue — Suite No. / Bureau nº
   City / Town / Ville — Province / Province — Country / Pays — Postal Code / Code postal

4. Address of principal place of business in Ontario / Adresse de l'établissement principal en Ontario — Same as above / comme ci-dessus
   Street Number / Nº de rue — Street Name / Nom de la rue — Suite No. / Bureau nº
   City / Town / Ville — Province / Province **Ontario** — Postal Code / Code postal

5. Give a brief description of the ACTIVITY being carried out under the business name / Résumez brièvement le genre d'ACTIVITÉ exercée sous le nom commercial

6. **Type of Registrant / Type de personne enregistrée**
   A. Ontario Limited Liability Partnership / Société à responsabilité limitée de l'Ontario
   OR / OU
   B. Extra-Provincial Limited Liability Partnership / Société à responsabilité limitée extraprovinciale
   More than 10 Partners; records at business address / Plus de 10 associés; dossiers à l'adresse d'affaires
   OR / OU
   C. Extra-Provincial Limited Liability Company / Société de capitaux extraprovinciale

7. Jurisdiction of formation / Territoire de la création

Registrant Information / Renseignements sur la personne enregistrée

8. Last Name / Nom de famille — First Name / Prénom — Middle Initial / Initiale (2ᵉ prénom)

9. Street Number / Nº de rue — Street Name / Nom de la rue — Suite No. / Bureau nº
   City / Town / Ville — Province / Province — Country / Pays — Postal Code / Code postal
   Additional information / Renseignements supplémentaires — Ont. Corporation No. / Nº matricule de la personne morale en Ontario

8. Last Name / Nom de famille — First Name / Prénom — Middle Initial / Initiale (2ᵉ prénom)

9. Street Number / Nº de rue — Street Name / Nom de la rue — Suite No. / Bureau nº
   City / Town / Ville — Province / Province — Country / Pays — Postal Code / Code postal
   Additional information / Renseignements supplémentaires — Ont. Corporation No. / Nº matricule de la personne morale en Ontario

10. Print name of person authorizing this registration
    Indiquez en lettres majuscules le nom de la personne autorisant l'enregistrement
    Last Name / Nom de famille — First Name / Prénom — Middle Name / 2ᵉ prénom

OR / OU

Additional information / Renseignements supplémentaires

MINISTRY USE ONLY - RÉSERVÉ À L'USAGE DU MINISTÈRE

07195(01/99)

MINISTRY COPY / COPIE DU MINISTÈRE

1.5 Ontario Business Registration Application

Ontario Ministry of Consumer and Commercial Relations | Ministère de la Consommation et du Commerce | Ontario Business Connects PO Box 1028 STN B Toronto ON M5T 3H3 | Entreprises branchées de l'Ontario CP 1028 SUCC B Toronto ON M5T 3H3

The Ontario Business Registration Application

The **Ontario Business Registration Application** is part of the Ontario government's service to cut red tape and simplify business registration. In order to use this application your business must be one of the following:

- ✔ **A sole proprietorship** (an individual who operates a business)
- ✔ **A general partnership** (a business consisting of two or more partners who carry on business together)
- ✔ **An existing corporation** (already incorporated)

What's Inside

- ✔ **Business Start-up Checklist**
- ✔ **Business Name Record Search Request**
- ✔ **Ontario Business Registration Application**

•The **Ontario Business Registration Application** combines four business registration applications into one easy-to-use form. These applications are required by most entrepreneurs starting a new business or expanding an existing business.

•Please complete the **Ontario Business Registration Application** and return it to us at Ontario Business Connects, P.O. Box 1028, Station B, Toronto, Ontario M5T 3H3.
The four applications are listed on the next page.

Helpline

If you have any questions about the enclosed material, if you need to follow up on your registration application, or if you have any comments or suggestions to improve this registration kit, please call the Ontario Business Connects Helpline.

In Toronto, call (416) 314-9151
All other regions, call toll free 1-800-565-1921
TTY (for the hearing/speech impaired) users dial (416) 326-8566

Cette trousse d'enregistrement est aussi disponible en français

1.5 (continued)

The Ontario Business Registration Application

Business Name Registration or Business Name Renewal: All businesses that operate under a name other than the owner's must register their business name, which is then placed in the public record. This registration lasts five years, after which time it must be renewed. *The fee for a mailed-in Business Name registration or a Business Name renewal is $80. Please include your pre-printed cheque, payable to the Minister of Finance, with this completed application. It takes about four weeks to receive your Master Business Licence as your confirmation of registration from Ontario Business Connects, Ministry of Consumer and Commercial Relations.*

Business Name Search: A name search is **optional.** It will tell you whether another business in Ontario is using the name you've chosen. For more information, please see the enclosed Business Name Record Search Request. *The fee for a Business Name search is $12.*

Retail Sales Tax Vendor Permit: You need a vendor permit if your business makes regular taxable sales and/or provides a taxable service. You must collect tax and send it on a regular basis to the Ministry of Finance. For more help deciding if you need a vendor permit, please call 1-800-668-5810 or call your local Retail Sales Tax office listed in the Blue Pages of the telephone directory. *It takes about two weeks for registration and you should expect a follow-up phone call or letter from the Ministry of Finance.*

Employer Health Tax: This tax is paid by all employers who have a permanent establishment in Ontario with one or more employees. It is calculated on the total Ontario wages and salaries paid to employees. *It will take about two weeks for registration. You should receive follow-up information in the mail within six weeks from the Ministry of Finance.*

Labour Law: You also have legal obligations under the Occupational Health and Safety Act and the Employment Standards Act. Contact your local Ministry of Labour for more information.

Workplace Safety and Insurance Board: When you hire employees or contractors, in most cases you must register with the Workplace Safety and Insurance Board (WSIB). The WSIB pays benefits to workers who are injured on the job or who develop an occupational disease. If you do not hire workers, you may still want coverage for a sole proprietor, partner or the officers of a corporation. *You will receive information or a phone call within four to six weeks from the WSIB.*

Business Number: This is part of a numbering system used by the federal government for the following important Revenue Canada programs: Goods and Services tax (GST); payroll deductions; corporate income tax; and/or import/export. If you have not applied for a federal Business Number, we will get one for you. In future, it will increasingly be used by the Ontario government when dealing with your business. You still need to register with Revenue Canada if any of their programs apply to your business.

1.5 (continued)

START-UP CHECKLIST FOR ONTARIO BUSINESSES

Business Plan

Have you developed your **business plan**? Preparing a business plan is the first step in starting any new venture. Also, you will probably need a business plan to get financing.

Your business plan should include:

- what you are trying to do and how you are going to do it;
- your assessment of the market opportunity and an analysis of your equipment and space needs;
- an assessment of the risks and opportunities, and projected expenditure and income flows, leading to an assessment of financial performance and a forecast of future earnings;
- a tested sales and marketing strategy and human resources plan.

Preparing a business plan is not easy, and to do a good one you will need to talk to other people, both to get advice on how to prepare the plan and to find out from others how businesses really grow and succeed.

You can contact the Business Self-Help office nearest you by calling (416) 954-4636 or 1-800-567-2345. Their services are free of charge, and the business consultants can help you with your business plan and advise you on all topics for starting a business. You can also obtain a free guide called "Business Start Up Info". For $3.50 you can purchase a publication called "Starting a Small Business in Ontario" by calling Publications Ontario at (416) 326-5300 or 1-800-668-3398.

Market Research and Planning

For help in this area, contact your local Chamber of Commerce for information about your business community. You can also call the Ontario Chamber of Commerce at (416) 482-5222 or access its Web site at http://www.occ.on.ca. This site enables you to visit all Ontario Chambers of Commerce that have a Web site. In addition, you can call the Canada-Ontario Business Call Centre at (416) 954-4636 or 1-800-567-2345 to get a free copy of "A Small Business Guide--Market Research". The Web site is http://www.cbsc.org/english/ontario/bis/7067.html

Financial Assistance

There are several organizations offering assistance to new and existing businesses. The Canada-Ontario Business Call Centre offers two free guides: "Business Start-Up Financing" and "Existing Business Finance." You can obtain a copy of these guides by calling (416) 954-4636 or 1-800-567-2345.

The Business Development Bank of Canada has strategic alliances with Canadian financial institutions, federal/regional development agencies and other private and public sector partners. The bank offers innovative financial services that address the unique needs of today's small and medium-sized businesses. To find out the kinds of programs they have please call (416) 973-0341 or 1-888-463-6232, or visit their Web site at http://www.bdc.ca

The Small Business Loans Administration Program provides business improvement loans to finance the purchase or improvement of fixed assets for new and expanding businesses. You can obtain a brochure on this program by calling (416) 954-4636 or 1-800-567-2345. You can also visit the Web site at http://strategis.ic.gc.ca/sc_mangb/smallbus/engdoc/sbla.html

1.5 (continued)

START-UP CHECKLIST FOR ONTARIO BUSINESSES

The Canadian Bankers Association can provide you with a detailed list of Canadian banks that give credit to small and medium-sized businesses. Call them at (416) 362-6092 or 1-800-263-0231 or visit their Web site at http://www.cba.ca

For on-line help to find the right kind of financing for you, Industry Canada has developed a Web site to guide you to the different types of financing that are available for a specific industry. The Web site is http://strategis.ic.gc.ca/SSG/so00611e.html

Registration/Licensing

To register for the federal Goods and Services Tax (GST) call 1-800-959-5525, in the local Toronto area call (416) 954-3400 or contact the Revenue Canada Tax Services office nearest you. Revenue Canada's Web site is http://www.rc.gc.ca

To find out about possible municipal licensing and zoning requirements, contact your municipality clerk to see whether your home-based business needs to be registered. You can also buy an Ontario Municipal Directory which lists all municipalities in Ontario, telephone numbers, municipal associations and other useful municipal-related information. To order a copy please call 1-800-358-9778.

To find out about other provincial and federal business regulations and licences, call the Canada-Ontario Business Call Centre at (416) 954-4636 or 1-800-567-2345. Its Web site is http://www.cbsc.org/ontario

For information regarding employment standards and occupational health and safety regulations, call your local Ministry of Labour office listed in the Blue Pages of your telephone directory. For $5 you can purchase the "Employer's Guide to the Employment Standards Act." Call (416) 326-5300 or 1-800-268-7095.

Information on bonding and business insurance is regularly provided by insurance agents and brokers.

Other Resources

A great deal of useful information can often be obtained through related trade associations and organizations.

Contact your local community college/university to find out more about courses, seminars and workshops. It's a great way to network and get up-to-date information. For more information, call the Council of Ontario Universities at (416) 979-2165 or for a Canadian directory contact the Association of Universities and Colleges at (613) 563-1236. For on-line access to colleges and universities contact Industry Canada's Web site at http://strategis.ic.gc.ca/SSG/mi04419e.html

Your public library's collection of business and industry directories can help you locate suppliers of products and potential distributors. Industry Canada has a Web site library with more than 450 educational articles and self-help guides by leading business experts. The Web site is http://strategis.ic.gc.ca/SSG/mi03933e.html#library

1.5 (continued)

Before you mail this application back, have you:

- ✔ Included **ALL** pages of the application?
- ✔ Answered **ALL** questions on the form, unless instructed otherwise?
- ✔ Correctly identified your home/business address? Note: Rural Routes and P.O. Boxes are **NOT** acceptable as home and/or business addresses.
- ✔ Left a phone number for us to contact you during daytime hours?

If you have any questions about completing this application, please contact the Ontario Business Connects Helpline at:

In Toronto, call (416) 314-9151
All other regions, call toll free 1-800-565-1921
TTY (for the hearing/speech impaired) users dial (416) 326-8566
Cette trousse d'enregistrement est aussi disponible en français.

98/C1

1.5 (continued)

Business Name Record Search Request

All businesses that operate under a name other than the owner's must register their business name. Registering your business name does not give you exclusive use of the business name. Likewise, you are not prevented from registering a name that is already in use. However, a unique name will help to identify your business to customers and clients.

If you want to find out if another Ontario business has already registered the **specific** business name you want to use, you may request a search through the record of registered business names. **The search is an identical name match only**; it does not check for business names that are similar.

A business name search is optional. The fee is $12 for each business record searched. If you want a name search, please complete and return this form along with your fee and your Ontario Business Registration application.

When you request a business name search by mail and records show that the name you are searching is already in use, your business name will **not** be registered. Your business name application and fee will be returned.

I want to conduct a search for the following business name:

____

(please print clearly)

Date: ____________________________

Name: ____________________________

Mailing Address ____

Fees

Business Name Registration	$ 80.00
Business Name Search (copy of record)	$ 12.00
Total fees enclosed	$ 92.00

(Make pre-printed cheque payable to Minister of Finance. Do not send cash.)

99/C1

1.5 (continued)

Ontario

Ontario Business Registration Application

Print clearly in capital letters   Please check your language preference for future correspondence: ☐ English ☐ French

Business Ownership

Please check your business ownership type:

☐	Sole Proprietorship	(An individual who operates a business)
☐	General Partnership	(A business with 2 or more partners, who carry on business together)
☐	Corporation	(An incorporated business)

If your business is NOT a sole proprietorship, general partnership or corporation, do not complete this form.

The federal business number is a new numbering system. Businesses get a unique identifier that does not change regardless of how many or what types of Revenue Canada accounts a business may have.

Business Number:
(if you have one) ☐

Individual Information

Enter information about the sole proprietor or an officer/director of the corporation.

Name	First	Middle	Last
Home Address	Street No. & Name / Lot No. / Concession & Township / Suite No.		City / Town
	Province / State	Country	Postal Code / Zip Code
Telephone Number	Area Code ( )		

If the business is a corporation, complete this section.

Corporation Name	Ontario Corporation Number

Jurisdiction (Province/State) in which the corporation was incorporated: ☐

Partnership Information

If you are a partner in a general partnership, please provide information about yourself and your partner(s). If the partner is an individual, enter the partner's full name, home address and telephone number. If the partner is not an individual, enter the name of the corporation, business address and telephone number.

How many partners are there in the business? ☐

A partnership with more than 10 partners may name one or more designated partners. The designated partner(s) must keep information on all their partners at their business location and make it available to the public.

Are you listing only (a) designated partner(s)? ☐ Yes ☐ No

Complete the following information about 2 partners. **(If you have more than 2 partners, attach a list of additional partners, including their full name and address.)**

1.5 (continued)

Partner Name	First	Middle	Last
	Corporation Name		Ontario Corporation Number
Address	Street No. & Name / Lot No. / Concession & Township / Suite No.		City / Town
	Province / State	Country	Postal Code / Zip Code
Telephone Number	Area Code ( )		

Partner Name	First	Middle	Last
	Corporation Name		Ontario Corporation Number
Address	Street No. & Name / Lot No. / Concession & Township / Suite No.		City / Town
	Province / State	Country	Postal Code / Zip Code
Telephone Number	Area Code ( )		

Business Name Information

A business operating under the owner's name does not need to register its business name. However, if it chooses to do so, the business name field must be completed and the registration fee is applicable.

Business or trade name
(If different from owner's name)

Complete the following to register your new business name or renew your registration with the Ministry of Consumer and Commercial Relations. The fee for a new registration or a renewal is $80.

Have you registered this business name before? ☐ Yes ☐ No

If **No**, you must register your business name.

If **Yes**, do you want to renew your business name registration?
Your registration is valid for 5 years. ☐ Yes ☐ No

If you answered **No** to the above, go to the next section - **Business Location**.

The individual authorizing the business name registration must be the sole proprietor, a partner in a general partnership, an officer or director of a corporation, or an individual with power of attorney for one of these.

Name of individual authorizing registration	First	Middle	Last

Do you want a Business Name Search? ☐ Yes ☐ No

If **Yes**, complete the Business Name Record Search Request. It costs $12 for a Business Name Search.

Make your pre-printed cheque or money order payable to the Minister of Finance and attach it to this form. Do not send cash.

1.5 (continued)

Business Location

Business Address

Street No. & Name / Lot No. / Concession & Township / Suite No.		City / Town
Province / State	Country	Postal Code / Zip Code

Telephone Number — Area Code ( )

Fax Number — Area Code ( )

Is the mailing address the same as the business address? ☐ Yes ☐ No

If **No**, complete the following:

Mailing Address

Street No. & Name / P.O. Box / R.R. No. / Suite No.		City / Town
Province / State	Country	Postal Code / Zip Code

Your registration confirmation will be sent to the mailing address.

If your business is a corporation, complete the following:

Is the address of the registered or Head office the same as the business address?: ☐ Yes ☐ No
If **No**, complete the following:

Head/registered office address

Street No. & Name / Lot No. / Concession & Township / Suite No.		City / Town
Province / State	Country	Postal Code / Zip Code

Business Activity

The business operates ☐ full-time ☐ part-time

Briefly describe your main business activity.

Describe in detail the products or services you sell. Include the type of machinery or equipment you use and materials used in your product.

Retail Sales Information

Your business needs a vendor permit if it regularly sells taxable items (eg. alcoholic beverages, cigarettes, snack foods) or provides taxable services (eg. labour to repair items such as cars, clothing). For more specific information, please call the Retail Sales Tax Branch of the Ministry of Finance at 1-800-668-5810.

1.5 (continued)

Does your business sell taxable goods or provide taxable services? ☐ Yes ☐ No

If you answered **No,** go to the next section.

A **Retail Sales Tax Vendor Permit** is assigned to the legal ownership of a business. The same permit can be used for different locations or different businesses if the ownership remains the same.

Do you have a Vendor Permit for another business? ☐ Yes ☐ No

If you answered **Yes**, go to the next section.

Business Start Date [YY MM DD]

Do you have more than one business location? ☐ Yes ☐ No

If your business does not operate for a full 12 months, enter an "**x**" for each month you are open.

JAN	FEB	MAR	APR	MAY	JUN	JUL	AUG	SEP	OCT	NOV	DEC

If you purchased an existing business, complete the following:

Previous business or trade name:

Taxable business assets can be any equipment that is NOT permanently attached and are usually listed on your bill of sale.

Have you paid Retail Sales Tax on the business equipment? ☐ Yes ☐ No

What was the value of the taxable business equipment? $

How much did you pay to buy the business? $

Employee Information

Have you hired employees or will you hire employees? ☐ Yes ☐ No

Date Help First Employed [YY MM DD]

Have you hired contractors or will you hire contractors? ☐ Yes ☐ No

Contractor Hiring Date [YY MM DD]

If you answered **No** to both of the above questions, go to the section - **Workplace Safety and Insurance Board Information**.

If you answered **Yes** to either question, indicate the estimated annual gross payroll for employees and/or contractors of this business. (The estimated gross payroll for the business in a year is the amount before any deductions and includes benefits.) $

1.5 (continued)

Payroll Information

Do you have, or have you already applied for an Employer Health Tax number? ☐ Yes ☐ No

If you answered **Yes**, go to the section - **Workplace Safety and Insurance Board Information**.

Revenue Canada Taxation, employer account number (if you have one). [ ]

If your business has more than one location in Ontario, will each location remit Employer Health Tax under separate accounts? ☐ Yes ☐ No

If your business does not have a payroll every month, enter an "x" for each month you will have a payroll.

JAN	FEB	MAR	APR	MAY	JUN	JUL	AUG	SEP	OCT	NOV	DEC

Workplace Safety and Insurance Board Information

Do you have, or have you already applied for an account with the Workplace Safety and Insurance Board (WSIB)? (formerly known as Workers' Compensation Board) ☐ Yes ☐ No

Does the business owner, a partner or an executive officer of this business want to apply for personal coverage under the Workplace Safety and Insurance Act, 1997? ☐ Yes ☐ No

If you answered **Yes** to the above, the Workplace Safety and Insurance Board will contact you.

Freedom of Information and the Protection of Privacy Act

You are responsible for the accuracy and completeness of this information.

Please note that by providing this information to Ontario Business Connects, you are consenting to its use by the Ministries of Consumer and Commercial Relations, Finance and the Workplace Safety and Insurance Board for the purpose of administering the Business Names Act, the Employer Health Tax Act, the Retail Sales Tax Act and the Workplace Safety and Insurance Act, 1997. This information is collected for the purpose of administering these programs only and will not be retained by Ontario Business Connects in paper format.

Questions about the collection, storage, use and disclosure of the information should be directed to:
Ministry of Consumer and Commercial Relations, Business Names Act, Information Officer, Companies Branch, Suite 200, 393 University Avenue, Toronto, ON M5G 2M2, (416) 314-8880, or toll free 1-800-361-3223
Ministry of Finance, Employer Health Tax Act, Freedom of Information Liaison Officer, Employer Health Tax Branch, 33 King Street West, Oshawa, ON L1H 8H7, (905) 436-4489
Ministry of Finance, Retail Sales Tax Act, Freedom of Information Coordinator, Retail Sales Tax Branch, 33 King Street West, Oshawa, ON L1H 8H7, (905) 433-6170
Workplace Safety and Insurance Board, Workplace Safety and Insurance Act, 1997, Revenue service representative, 200 Front Street West, Toronto, ON M5V 3J1, (416) 344-1013, or toll free 1-800-387-8638

07209-CTP001
99/01

1.6 Services Requisition in Respect of Unincorporated Businesses

Ontario Ministry of Consumer and Commercial Relations / Ministère de la Consommation et du Commerce — Companies Branch / Direction des compagnies

Services Requisition In Respect of Unincorporated Businesses

Demande de recherche sur des entreprises non constituées en personne morale

Please use separate forms for electronic and non-electronic products.
Searches for business names ending in "Corporation", "Limited" or Incorporated", or any abbreviated thereof, cannot be processed on this form.
See instructions and description of products on reverse.
Please check appropriate box for product requested and whether uncertified or certified.

Veuillez utiliser des formules distinctes si vous désirez obtenir des documents électroniques et non électroniques.
Les recherches ne peuvent pas être effectuées sur des entreprises constituées en personne morale, notamment celles dont le nom comporte, en entier ou en abrégé, le mot «limitée» ou «incorporée».
Les instructions et les descriptions des documents se trouvent au verso.
Veuillez cocher les cases appropriées pour indiquer les documents désirés et s'ils doivent être certifiés ou non.

Electronic Search Products
Documents électroniques

For speedier service, please provide the Business Identification Number below.
Afin d'accélérer le service, veuillez indiquer ci-dessous le numéro d'identification de l'entreprise.

	Unincorporated Business Name Raison Sociale de l'entreprise non constituée en personne morale	Business Identification Number N° d'identification de l'entreprise	A Business Names Report Rapport sur les noms commerciaux	B Document Replica Copie de document	C BNLP Document List Liste des documents - NC/SC	D Partnership Business Names List Liste des noms commerciaux(SNC/SC)	E Certificate of Non-Registration Certificat de nonenregistrement
1.							
2.							
3.							
4.							

Please use separate forms for electronic and non-electronic products.
See instructions and description of products on reverse.
Please check appropriate box for product requested and whether uncertified or certified.

Veuillez utiliser des formules distinctes si vous désirez obtenir des documents électroniques et non électroniques.
Les instructions et les descriptions des documents se trouvent au verso.
Veuillez cocher les cases appropriées pour indiquer les documents désirés et s'ils doivent être certifiés ou non.

Non-Electronic Search Products
Documents non électroniques

For speedier service, please provide the Business Identification Number below.
Afin d'accélérer le service, veuillez indiquer ci-dessous le numéro d'identification de l'entreprise.

	Unincorporated Business Name Raison Sociale de l'entreprise non constituée en personne morale	Business Identification Number, if known N° d'identification de l'entreprise, si connu	Expired Search Période de recherche expirée F
1.			
2.			
3.			
4.			

Client Name/Nom du/de la client(e) : ____________ Attention / Personne à contacter : ____________

Address / Adresse ____________

Signature / Signature ____________ Date/Date ____________ Telephone No. / N° de téléphone ____________

Mail out/ Envoyer par courrier Pick-up/Prendre livraison	Pick-up box #/ N° de la boîte	Account #/N° de compte	Sub-Account/Compte auxiliaire	Access I.D./Mot de passe

Ministry use only/Réservé au ministère

Request#/N° de la demande	Pull/Retrait	Copies/Copies	Time In/Arrivé	Time Out/Départ	Pages/Pages	Fee/Droits	Clerk/Commis

07095(12/98)

1.6 (continued)

SEARCH PRODUCTS: DESCRIPTION / GUIDE

Electronic Search Products

A. Business Names Report
This report displays current information on the public record for business names registered on or after April 1, 1994, including information filed on amendments and cancellations.

B. Document Replica
An electronic replica of any one specific BNLP document (eg; new, renewal, amendment/change, cancellation/dissolution/withdrawal) filed in the last 5 years.

C. BNLP Document List
The BNLP Document List is available for sole proprietorships, general partnerships, corporation business names limited partnerships, limited liability partnerships and partnership business names registered on or after April 1, 1994. This report sets out all documents that have been filed in relation to the business name registered, including the filing date for each document.

D. Partnership Business Names List
The Partnership Business Names List sets out all additional business names registered or renewed by the firm since July 15, 1996.

E. Certificate of Non-Registration
This certificate states that there is no record of the registration under the Business Names Act or a declaration under the Limited Partnerships Act in the subject name or BIN (Business Identification Number).

Non-Electronic Search Products

F. Expired Search
This search covers a 5 year period of expired records. Records which have been expired for more than 5 years are stored in the Archives of Ontario.

BNLP refers to an unincorporated business registered under either the **Business Names Act** or the **Limited Partnerships Act.**

DESCRIPTION DES DOCUMENTS FAISANT L'OBJET D'UNE RECHERCHE

Documents électroniques

A. Rapport sur les noms commerciaux
Ce rapport fournit les renseignements à jour qui se trouvent dans les dossiers publics sur les raisons sociales enregistrées à partir du 1er avril 1994, y compris l'information déposée sur les modifications et les annulations.

B. Copie de document
Copie électronique de tout document spécifique déposé au cours des 5 dernières années, aux termes de la *Loi sur les noms commerciaux* ou de la *Loi sur les sociétés en commandite* (p. ex.: Enregistrement/Déclaration, renouvellement, modification/changement, révocation/dissolution, retrait).

C. Liste des documents - NC/SC
On peut obtenir une liste des documents (NC/SC) pour les entreprises enregistrées sous un nom commercial depuis le 1er avril 1994 - -entreprises personnelles, sociétés en nom collectif, sociétes en commandite, noms commerciaux enregistrés par des personnes morales, sociétés à responsabilité limitée ou par des sociétés en nom collectif ou en commandite. Cette liste indique tous les documents qui ont été déposés relativement au nom commercial enregistré, y compris la date de dépôt de chaque document.

D. Liste des noms commerciaux (SNC/SC)
Cette liste indique les noms commerciaux supplémentaires qu'une société en nom collectif (SNC) ou une société en commandite (SC) a enregistrés ou dont elle a renouvelé l'enregistrement depuis le 15 juillet 1996.

E. Certificat de non-enregistrement
Ce certificat atteste qu'il n'existe aucun dossier concernant un enregistrement aux termes de la *Loi sur les noms commerciaux* ou le dépôt d'une déclaration aux termes de la *Loi sur les sociétés en commandite* relativement au nom ou au numéro d'identification d'entreprise indiqué.

Documents non électroniques

F. Période de recherche expirée
Cette recherche est effectuée dans des dossiers qui sont expirés depuis cinq ans ou moins. Les dossiers expirés depuis plus de cinq ans sont conservés aux Archives publiques de l'Ontario.

NC/SC - Cette abréviation indique une entreprise sans personnalité morale qui est enregistrée aux termes de la *Loi sur les noms commerciaux* (NC) ou de la *Loi sur les sociétés en commandite* - (SC).

1.7 Toronto-Dominion Bank—Business Banking Agreement—Sole Proprietorship/Partnership/Association/Corporation/Joint Venture

TD

BUSINESS BANKING AGREEMENT

Banking Relationship

1. This agreement between The Toronto-Dominion Bank, TD Mortgage Corporation and TD Pacific Mortgage Corporation *(collectively we, our and us)* and the undersigned customer *(you and your)* sets out the terms and conditions that will govern your banking relationship with us, in addition to agreements between us and you for specific products and services.

Name of Business

2. You declare that you are carrying on business as:

(tick one)

- ❑ Sole Proprietorship
- ❑ Partnership
- ❑ Association
- ❑ Corporation
- ❑ Joint Venture

under the name:

**Enter the name of the business. If the business operates under a trade name, enter the trade name only.*

* ____.

You also declare that this name is the correct name of the business *(your "Business Name")*. You appoint us as your banker.

Signing Officers (except Sole Proprietorship)

3. (a) ** ____

____

(the "Signing Officers") are authorized on your behalf from time to time:

***Partnership- Insert "any one partner", "all partners", "any two partners", or otherwise as required. For Limited Partnership, same as above but use general partner(s). If a partner is a corporation, indicate name of partner corporation together with title.*
Corporation, Association, Joint Venture - Use titles only where possible. If two or more must act together, use words showing joint action, e.g. "the President and the Treasurer jointly" or "the President, the Treasurer and the Secretary or any two of them". If one of two or more may act alone, add "or any one of them". For Joint Venture, also indicate name of member corporation together with title.

(i) to conduct all aspects of your banking relationship with us (whether under corporate seal or not);

(ii) to authorize any person or persons to do any one or more of the following:

(1) to receive from us any (i) cash or securities, (ii) bills of exchange (including cheques), promissory notes, orders for payment of money, securities, coupons, clearing items or other value items, and other instruments *(each of which we individually call an "Instrument")* or (iii) other property, or to give instructions to us for the delivery or other transfer of any such cash, securities, Instruments or other property to any party named in those instructions;

(2) to deposit with, negotiate or transfer to us, for your credit, cash or any security, Instrument or other property, endorsed (by rubber stamp or otherwise) with your Business Name; and

(3) to settle your accounts with us and to receive from us, and provide receipt of, statements, passbooks, debit vouchers and other items (including paid and unpaid cheques).

(b) You agree to provide us with: (i) a list of the names and positions of the Signing Officers certified by the Signing Officers; (ii) specimens of their signatures; and (iii) an original of any authorization made by the Signing Officers under sub paragraph 3(a)(ii) of this agreement.

You will be bound by any such document until each of our branches where you have an account receives a new document repealing or replacing it.

Non-Restriction (except Sole Proprietorship)

(c) There are no provisions in the Memorandum of Association, Articles of Incorporation or in any of your by-laws or resolutions, or in any unanimous shareholder agreement, or in any other agreement, that restrict or limit in any way your powers or the powers of your directors on your behalf (except the provisions of *** ______________________ a true copy of which is attached to this agreement).

****If applicable, list articles, by-laws, agreement, etc.*

1.7 (continued)

Your Liability

4. You agree that you are liable to us (if a partnership or joint venture jointly and severally) for:

(a) all transactions and agreements entered into by you or in your Business Name;

(b) for all Instruments made, drawn, accepted, endorsed (by rubber stamp or otherwise) or signed (manually or by facsimile signature):

(i) by you in your Business Name, or

(ii) by your appointed attorney, if you are a sole proprietorship, or

(iii) by you, as provided in Section 3, if you are a partnership, corporation, association or joint venture; and

(c) for all Instruments credited to you.

We may, from time to time, provide you with the terms of our services or products. Your use of those services or products will act as your acceptance of and agreement to be bound by their terms.

Waiver of Protest

5. You waive presentment, protest and notice of dishonour on all Instruments which you have drawn, made, accepted or endorsed and which are delivered to us for any purpose.

Use of Agents

6. We may use any third party to provide any service, including the Canadian Payments Association for clearing arrangements, without responsibility for any loss occasioned thereby. That party is considered to be your agent.

Charges to Account

7. We may charge any of your accounts, even if that creates or increases an overdraft, with the amount of the following:

Instruments Drawn on Us

(a) any Instrument drawn by you on any of our branches;

Unpaid Instruments

(b) any Instrument cashed or negotiated by us for you or credited to any of your accounts for which payment is not received by us or which is returned to us later by reason of a forged, unauthorized or missing endorsement, plus any expenses incurred by us in that connection. You agree that the charging of any unpaid Instrument will not be considered to be payment of it and that our rights against all parties liable on the Instrument are preserved;

Lost, Stolen Instruments

(c) any Instrument received by us for credit to any of your accounts if it is lost, stolen or otherwise disappears from any cause, other than our negligence;

Recovery

(d) any amounts you owe us and any costs to recover them, including legal fees on a solicitor and their own client basis, as well as any legal fees and disbursements charged by our legal department; and

Service Charges and Fees

(e) any service charge for the operation of any of your accounts and our fees for other services and products used by you, in effect from time to time.

Overdrafts

8. Unless we agree, you may not overdraw your account. You will repay the amount of any overdraft plus interest immediately without notice from us. Unless otherwise agreed, we will charge you interest at our standard rate charged from time to time for overdrafts.

1.7 (continued)

Verification of Account

9. (a) We will periodically forward to you, your employee or agent a statement of your account by any means including ordinary mail to your last provided address. You will:

- advise us promptly if you have not received the statement within 10 days of the date upon which you normally receive it;
- if you have a passbook, present it to us periodically for updating;
- carefully and promptly verify the completeness and correctness of each statement or update and immediately notify us in writing of any errors or omissions.

(b) **If we don't receive notice from you within 30 days of the statement date or update, subject to (i) and (ii) below, you accept the statement or update as correct, and we will be released from any claim with respect to any and every item on the statement or update and from any other claim for negligence, breach of trust, breach of fiduciary duty or otherwise.** At any time, we may correct:

(i) amounts credited to your account by mistake; or

(ii) amounts charged to your account as a result of a forged or unauthorized endorsement of the payee of an Instrument drawn on your account. You must notify us in writing of any forged or unauthorized endorsement on any Instrument as soon as you discover it.

Electronic Communications

10. Any electronic communication between you and us will take place according to the provisions of this section. The term "electronic communication" means any communication of instructions by telex, telephone, wire or other method of telecommunication or electronic transmission, including a facsimile transmission.

We will consider any electronic communication received from you or in your name to be duly authorized by you and binding on you. You authorize us to rely and act on any such communication. If the communication is by facsimile transmission, we will be entitled to act upon any signature purporting to be your signature or that of your Signing Officer. If we try to verify the signature on a facsimile transmission or the validity of any instructions electronically communicated (though we are not obligated to do so) and are unable to do so to our satisfaction, we may delay in acting on or refuse to act on such instructions.

You agree that our records regarding any electronic communications will be admissible in any legal, administrative or other proceedings as if such records were original written documents. Our records will be conclusive proof of the information contained in such electronic communications.

Internal Supervision

11. You will at all times have in place commercially reasonable procedures to prevent and detect losses due to forged or unauthorized signatures, and fraud or theft involving Instruments or instructions.

Limitation on Our Liability

12. **Although we are liable for direct losses or damages caused by our negligence, we will not be liable for indirect or consequential loss or damage regardless of the cause of action.**

In no event will we be liable for any loss or damage resulting from:

(a) the actions, or any failure to act, of any other person;

(b) a forged or unauthorized signature or a material alteration on any Instrument, unless you prove (i) it was made by a person who was at no time your employee or agent; and (ii) its occurrence was beyond your control;

(c) our failure to perform or fulfill any obligation due to any cause beyond our control; or

(d) incomplete or incorrect information supplied to us by you.

1.7 (continued)

Partnership/ Joint Venture Terms

13. You are liable under this agreement regardless of the admission or withdrawal of any partner of a partnership or member of a joint venture. You will not be liable for obligations under this agreement which are incurred after we receive written notice that you are no longer a partner or a member signed by you or your legal representative, provided that in the event of dissolution of the partnership or joint venture, you will remain liable until the obligations to us under this agreement, whether incurred before or after the dissolution, are paid in full. This notice will be effective at each of our branches when the branch where you have an account receives it.

Heirs, Executors, etc.

14. This agreement is binding on us, our successors and assigns. It is also binding on you, your heirs, executors and administrators and other legal representatives, successors and assigns.

Amendments and Waiver

15. We may amend this agreement by sending you a notice or by posting a notice in all our branch offices. No waiver of any breach of any term of this agreement will be effective unless in writing. It will not be considered to be a waiver of any other breach of such term or other term of the agreement.

Copy of Agreement

16. You have received a copy of this agreement and our Schedule of Business Account Service Charges (or About TD Deposit Accounts and Related Services if applicable).

Officers/Directors (except Sole Proprietorship)

If more space required, add separate schedule.

17. The following are the names of your officers and directors (where applicable):

Officers	Directors
President	....
Vice President	....
Secretary	....
Treasurer	....
....	....
....	....

Consent

18. You authorize us to obtain credit or other information to the extent permitted by law, and to give other credit grantors and credit bureaus information about this application and subsequent credit experiences, if applicable.

Dated this__________day of ____________________________, 20________.

(Please print name below respective signature.)

Obtain signatures of:
Sole Proprietorship - sole proprietor
Partnership - all partners and for Limited Partnership, all general partner(s). If partner is corporation, partner to sign under corporation name. If more than 8, add separate schedule
Corporation - the Signing Officers as set out in paragraph 3(a) under the corporation name - no corporate seal required
Association - the Signing Officers as set out in paragraph 3(a)
Joint Venture - all members under the corporation name if member is corporation - no corporate seal required

X____________________________ X____________________________
Signature
Name:
Signature
Name:

X____________________________ X____________________________
Signature
Name:
Signature
Name:

X____________________________ X____________________________
Signature
Name:
Signature
Name:

X____________________________ X____________________________
Signature
Name:
Signature
Name:

TD COPY

1.7 (continued)

FOR TD USE

Documents Required:	
1. Corporation - Copy of Certificate of Incorporation - First page indicating the company name only	Date corporation incorporated *(if applicable)* __________ Date of Articles of Continuance *(if applicable)* __________ Corporation Act* __________ *(specify applicable corporations legislation)*
2. Copy of Certificate of Registration	Trade Name Registration/Partnership declaration *(if applicable)* recorded in the __________ __________ *(specify applicable registration office)* on the ____ day of __________ **20** ____.
3. Borrowing Authority	*A borrowing authority must be completed for any corporation whose applicable corporations legislation as indicated on the Certificate of Incorporation **is not** listed below:

Newfoundland	The Corporations Act (except incorporated associations)
New Brunswick	Business Corporations Act
Ontario	Business Corporations Act
Manitoba	The Corporations Act
Saskatchewan	The Business Corporations Act
Alberta	Business Corporations Act
British Columbia	Company Act Society Act
Yukon Territory	The Business Corporations Act
Canada	Business Corporations Act
U.S.	The business corporations statute of any State

In **Quebec,** a borrowing authority must be completed for any corporation opening an account even if it was incorporated outside of Quebec.

Where a borrowing authority must be completed, see your Guide to Documentation Required - Business Accounts, form 14080, for instructions.

1.8 Toronto-Dominion Bank—Checklist—Business Accounts

TD Know Your Customer Checklist - Business Accounts

☐ New customer ☐ Existing customer

About the customer

Business name ______________________ *(you)* Business Number ________

Business address ______________________

Parent company ______________ Nature of business/occupation ______________

Phone no. ________ Fax no. ________ No. yrs.: In business ______ At present location ______

No. employees ________ Annual sales $ ________ Fiscal year end *(month, day)* ________

Introduced/referred by ______________ Previous banker ______________

Accountant ______________ Lawyer ______________

Services required

	Yes	No
Need to deposit at other branch(es)?	☐	☐
Branches ______________		
Need to deposit outside regular branch hours?		
Night deposit service	☐	☐
Need to bank from office or home?		
TD Business Bankline	☐	☐
TD Business Service Plan	☐	☐
Need balance and activity reporting?	☐	☐
Need merchant services?		
Merchant VISA	☐	☐
Direct Payment for Retailers	☐	☐

	Yes	No
Does business use an IBM compatible PC?	☐	☐
Type and version of accounting software used ______________		
Payroll services performed in-house?	☐	☐
Outside agency ______________		
Need credit services?		
TD Business Overdraft Protection	☐	☐
TD Business VISA	☐	☐
Need business financing?	☐	☐
Credit Application given to customer?	☐	☐
May we arrange transfers of any business or personal accounts from other financial institutions?	☐	☐

Name of customer contact to discuss any of the above ______________________

About the account

Account no.(s) ______________ ☐ General ☐ Payroll ☐ Trust ☐ Other ________

Statement frequency
- ☐ Month-end *(standard)* **OR:**
- ☐ Daily
- ☐ Weekly *(day)* ________ *(and month-end)*
- ☐ Specific date(s) *(0-31)* ________ *(and month-end)*

Statement delivery
- ☐ Post office mail
- ☐ Pick up, this branch
- ☐ Pick up, TD branch # ________

Cheque order
- ☐ TD printer, date ordered ________
- ☐ Outside printer *(provide spec sheet, form 10460)*

Chargeback delivery
- ☐ Post office mail
- ☐ Pick up, this branch
- ☐ Pick up, TD branch # ________

☐ Endorsement stamp needed, date ordered ________ Classification/SIC code ________

Hold on funds
- ☐ No Approved by ______________
- ☐ Yes During the 30 business days after the first transaction on the account and at any time after that at the Bank's option, funds for each non-cash deposit will be placed on a minimum 7 business day hold.

Consent You authorize the Bank to obtain credit or other information to the extent permitted by law, and to give other credit grantors and credit bureaus information about this application and subsequent credit experiences, if applicable. The Bank will keep a copy of this agreement for its records.

X ______________ X ______________ X ______________

Branch Copy Date ______________ **Branch transit** ______________

14038 (6-97)

1.8 (continued)

Documentation Required

Refer to the **GUIDE TO DOCUMENTATION REQUIRED - BUSINESS ACCOUNTS** (form 14080) for guidance.

Any application to open an account by a currency dealer must be referred to your Division Office.

About the Signing Officers *(Federal Regulations require identification of at least 3 Signing Officers. If fewer than 3 Signing Officers, ALL to be identified.)*

1. Name and title ______________________________

   Address ______________________________ Birth date __________
   (Obtain and record 2 pieces of signed I.D. below, preferably 1 with photo.)

   Type __________ No. __________ Type __________ No. __________

2. Name and title ______________________________

   Address ______________________________ Birth date __________
   (Obtain and record 2 pieces of signed I.D. below, preferably 1 with photo.)

   Type __________ No. __________ Type __________ No. __________

3. Name and title ______________________________

   Address ______________________________ Birth date __________
   (Obtain and record 2 pieces of signed I.D. below, preferably 1 with photo.)

   Type __________ No. __________ Type __________ No. __________

Due diligence *(at Branch Management's discretion)*

Initial deposit *($50 recommended to cover initial cheque order)* $ __________ Source of funds __________

Information obtained/verified	Yes	No*		Initial	Date
CustomerLink checked for existing profile and comments (business and Signing Officers)	☐	☐			
Address and phone verified	☐	☐			
Former financial institution called	☐	☐	**Interviewed by**	______	______
Credit Bureau report obtained	☐	☐			
Site visited	☐	☐			
Financial statements/annual report obtained	☐	☐	**All account opening forms**		
PPSA search obtained	☐	☐	**completed and in order**	______	______
Thank You/Welcome letter sent	☐	☐			

*(*If necessary, please explain any "No's" under Additional comments)*

Date business registered *(if applicable)* __________ **Verified by Branch Manager** ______ ______

Assigned to Account Manager ______________________________ Team no. __________

Additional comments ______________________________

____

____

____

1.9 Toronto-Dominion Bank—Specimen Signature Card

13848

Forward to ChequeMate

Branch Transit

Account Number

Branch stamp ______________________

______________________ Operating name of account

(*Include designation of account* ie. Payroll Account)

Specimen Signature	Position and/or Name

SEE REVERSE

Message Code(s)

(✓)

☐ 1. Power of Attorney
☐ 2. Both to sign
☐ 4. Any two to sign
☐ 5. Any three to sign
☐ 6. All to sign
☐ 8. Multiple Style of Signature
☐ 9. Both P/A's to sign
☐ 11 Sole owner
☐ 12. President alone
☐ 13. President & Treasurer together
☐ 14 President & Secretary together
☐ OTHER - *SEE REVERSE*

1.9 (continued)

☐ – Other (free format text message/additional signing authority instructions)

Specimen Signature	Position and/or Name

5. The Act of Incorporation

5.1 Articles of Incorporation—*Business Corporations Act*—Form 1

Ontario Ministry of Consumer and Business Services | Companies Branch | 393 University Ave Suite 200 Toronto ON M5G 2M2

Articles of Incorporation
Form 1
Business Corporations Act

INSTRUCTIONS FOR COMPLETING

Articles in duplicate may be mailed to the Toronto address listed above. For over-the-counter service they may also be filed in person at the Toronto office or at one of the following Land Registry Offices: Hamilton, Kingston, Kitchener, London, Whitby, Sudbury, Barrie, Sarnia, Ottawa, Peterborough, Sault Ste.Marie, Thunder Bay, Windsor or Welland.

FEE

$360.00 BY MAIL - Cheque or money order payable to the Minister of Finance.
IN PERSON (at the Toronto office) - cash, cheque or money order payable to the Minister of Finance, Visa, MasterCard, American Express or debit card. (If you are filing the documents at a Land Registry Office, call first to confirm whether credit or debit cards are acceptable).

SUPPORTING DOCUMENTS

NAME SEARCH

If you are incorporating under a name instead of a number name, you must obtain an Ontario-biased NUANS name search report. NUANS stands for New Updated Automated Name Search. It is a five-page computer-printed search report consisting of corporate names, business names and trademarks that have already been incorporated/registered and are similar to the proposed corporate name. This search must be submitted together with the duplicate Articles of Incorporation within 90 days from production by the NUANS system.

The NUANS name search must be obtained from a private name search company. These companies are listed in the Yellow Pages under the heading "Searchers of Records". The Ministry does not provide this search. It is the applicant's responsibility to check the search for similar/identical names and to obtain any consent that may be required.

The Ministry will not grant a name that is identical to the current name or former name of another corporation operating in Ontario whether active or not, unless it has been more than ten years since the other corporation dissolved or changed its name. The only exception to this rule is when the corporation meets the requirements of Subsection 6(2) of the Regulations, under the *Business Corporations Act*. In this case, Companies Branch policy requires that a legal opinion accompany the articles being filed. The legal opinion must be on legal letterhead and must be signed by an individual lawyer (not a law clerk). It must also clearly indicate that the corporations involved comply with Regulation 6(2) by referring to each clause specifically.

BILINGUAL NAMES

When incorporating a corporation with an English and French version of the name (where the versions can be used separately), a name search is required for each version of the name (English and French). There should be a forward slash (/) separating the two versions of the name.

NUMBER NAMES

You do not require a name search for a number name. In Article one on the form, leave nine empty boxes, then type or print in block capital letters the word "ONTARIO" followed by one of the legal elements...LIMITED, LIMITÉE, INCORPORATED, INCORPOREE, CORPORATION or the corresponding abbreviation LTD., LTEE., INC., or CORP. The Director of Companies Branch will assign a number to the corporation.

APPEARANCE OF DOCUMENTS

The Articles of Incorporation must be completed in duplicate on a Form 1 as prescribed by Minister's Order. All documents must be legible and compatible with the microfilming process, with the information typed or hand printed in block capital letters, on one side of good quality , white bond paper 8 1/2" X 11".

The Article headings are numbered 1 to 10 and should remain in that order. Do not leave out any of the headings. If a section does not apply type "nil" or "not applicable". When additional pages are required, due to lack of space, they should be the same size as all the other pages and should be inserted after the applicable heading with the same number as the heading page with the addition of alphabet characters to indicate sequence. For example, pages inserted after page 3 would be numbered 3A, 3B, etc.

07116 (05/2001)

5.1 (continued)

ARTICLE 1 Set out the name of the corporation in block capital letters starting from the first box of the first line on the left with one letter per box and one empty box for a space. Punctuation marks are entered in separate boxes. Complete one line before starting in the first box of the next line. The name entered must be exactly the same as that on the name search report.

E	A	S	T		S	I	D	E		I	N	V	E	S	T	M	E	N	T		A	N	D		M	A	N	A	G
E	M	E	N	T		L	T	D	.																				

ARTICLE 2 The address (where multi-office building include room or suite number) of the registered office of the corporation must be set out in full including the street name, street number, suite, municipality, province, country and the postal code. A post office box is not an acceptable address. If there is no street and number, set out the Lot and Concession numbers. The registered office must be in Ontario.

ARTICLE 3 Set out the number of directors. This can be a set number of directors or a minimum and maximum number, (i.e., minimum 1, maximum 10).

ARTICLE 4 The name(s) (including first name, middle name and surname) and the address for service for each of the directors must be set out. The address should include the street name, number suite, municipality, province, country and postal code. State if the director(s) is/are Resident Canadian(s). A majority of the directors must be Resident Canadians. Where a corporation has only one or two directors, one shall be a resident Canadian. If a director is listed who is not signing the form as an incorporator (see Article 10), then a Form 2, Consent to Act as a First Director must be completed and kept at the registered office of the corporation. The directors must be individuals, not corporations.

ARTICLE 5 Set out restrictions, if any, on the business the corporation may carry on or on the powers that the corporation may exercise. If none, state so.

ARTICLE 6 Set out the classes and any maximum number of shares that the corporation is authorized to issue. This item should be completed (e.g., unlimited common shares).

ARTICLE 7 Set out the rights, privileges, restrictions and conditions etc. (if any) attached to each class of shares, and directors' authority with respect to any class of shares which is to be issued in series.

ARTICLE 8 Set out restrictions on issue, transfer or ownership of shares (if any).

ARTICLE 9 Set out other provisions (if any).

ARTICLE 10 Set out name(s) and address(es) for service of incorporator(s). If the incorporator(s) is/are a corporation, set out the registerd office address(es).

EXECUTION Both copies of the Articles must have original signature(s) of the incorporator(s). If the incorporator(s) is/are a corporation(s), set out the name of the corporation(s) above the signature(s) and the office held in the corporation by the signatory(ies). (e.g., President)

Articles (in duplicate), original Ontario-biased NUANS name search report (if applicable), covering letter and filing fee should be mailed or delivered to:

COMPANIES BRANCH
MINISTRY OF CONSUMER AND BUSINESS SERVICES
393 UNIVERSITY AVENUE, SUITE 200
TORONTO ONTARIO M5G 2M2

07116 (05/2001)

5.1 (continued)

1

For Ministry Use Only
À l'usage exclusif du ministère

Ontario Corporation Number
Numéro de la société en Ontario

Form 1
Business Corporations Act

Formule 1
Loi sur les sociétés par actions

ARTICLES OF INCORPORATION
STATUTS CONSTITUTIFS

1. The name of the corporation is: (Set out in BLOCK CAPITAL LETTERS)
Dénomination sociale de la société : (Écrire en LETTRES MAJUSCULES SEULEMENT)

2. The address of the registered office is:
Adresse du siege social :

(Street & Number or R.R. Number & if Multi-Office Building give Room No.)
(Rue et numéro ou numéro de la R.R. et, s'il s'agit d'un édifice à bureaux, numéro du bureau)

ONTARIO

(Name of Municipality or Post Office)
(Nom de la municipalité ou du bureau de poste)

(Postal Code)
(Code postal)

3. Number (or minimum and maximum number) of directors is/are:
Nombre (ou nombres minimal et maximal) d'administrateurs :

minimum/*minimal* maximum/*maximal*

4. The first director(s) is/are:
Premier(s) administrateur(s) :

First name, middle names and surname *Prénom, autres Prénoms et nom de famille*	Address for service, giving Street & No. or R.R. No., Municipality, Province, Country and Postal Code *Domicile élu, y compris la rue et le numéro, le numéro de la R.R. ou le nom de la municipalite, la province, le pays et le code postal*	Resident Canadian? Yes or No *Résident canadien? Oui/Non*

07116 (05/2001)

5.1 (continued)

5. Restrictions, if any, on business the corporation may carry on or on powers the corporation may exercise.
Limites, s'il y a lieu, imposées aux activités commerciales ou aux pouvoirs de la société.

6. The classes and any maximum number of shares that the corporation is authorized to issue:
Catégories et nombre maximal, s'il y a lieu, d'actions que la société est autorisée à émettre :

5.1 (continued)

3

7. Rights, privileges, restrictions and conditions (if any) attaching to each class of shares and directors authority with respect to any class of shares which may be issued in series:
Droits, privilèges, restrictions et conditions, s'il y a lieu, rattachés à chaque catégorie d'actions et pouvoirs des administrateurs relatifs à chaque catégorie d'actions qui peut être émise en série :

07116 (05/2001)

5.1 (continued)

4

8. The issue, transfer or ownership of shares is/is not restricted and the restrictions (if any) are as follows:
L'émission, le transfert ou la propriété d'actions est/n'est pas restreint. Les restrictions, s'il y a lieu, sont les suivantes :

07116 (05/2001)

5.1 (continued)

5

9 Other provisions if any:
Autres dispositions, s'il y a lieu :

07116 (05/2001)

5.1 (continued)

6

10. The names and addresses of the incorporators are:
Noms et adresses des fondateurs :

First name, middle names and surname or corporate name *Prénom, autres prénoms et nom de famille ou dénomination sociale*	Full address for service or address of registered office or of principal place of business giving street & No. or R.R. No., municipality and postal code *Domicile élu au complet, adresse du siège social ou adresse de l'établissement principal, y compris la rue et le numéro ou le numéro de la R.R., le nom de la municipalité et le code postal*

These articles are signed in duplicate.
Les présents statuts sont signés en double exemplaire.

Signatures of incorporator(s) /
Signatures des fondateurs

07116(05/2001)

5.2 Consent to Act as a First Director—*Business Corporations Act*—Form 2

Form 2
Business Corporations Act

Formule 2
Loi sur les sociétés par actions

CONSENT TO ACT AS A FIRST DIRECTOR
CONSENTEMENT DU PREMIER ADMINISTRATEUR

I,/*Je soussigné(e),* ____________________

(First name, middle names and surname)
(Prénom, autres Prénoms et nom de famille)

address for service
domicile élu

____

(Street & No. or R.R. No., Municipality, Province, Country & Postal Code)
(Rue et numéro, ou numéro de la R.R., nom de la municipalité, province, pays et code postal)

hereby consent to act as a first director of
accepte par la présente de devenir premier administrateur de

____

(Name of Corporation)
(Dénomination sociale de la société)

____

(Signature of the Consenting Person)
(Signature de l'acceptant)

07117 (06/01)

5.3 NUANS Name Search—Ontario Biased

AC 16.3

DYE & DURHAM

393 University Avenue
Suite 1519
Toronto, Ontario
Canada, M5G 1E6
Telephone: (416) 595-7177
Canada Toll Free Telephone: 1-800-668-8208

CORPORATE NAME SEARCH REPORT

UNIVERSITY NON-ACCOUNT SALES

Request #: N477780
Reference #: 999971
Date: Oct 23/01

Service: NUANS NAME SEARCH-NON ACCOUNT

Choice #01: =SANDUSKY= CONSTRUCTION INC.

Significance of keyword: COINED

Required for: NEW INCORP. WITH SHARE CAPITAL

IMPORTANT NOTICE:

An indication that a proposed name appears to be available at this time is based only on the information derived from the NUANS automated name search system and additional searches may be required to determine conformity with the laws of the incorporating jurisdiction. Dye & Durham Co. Inc. is not responsible and will not be liable for any inaccuracies or omissions in the NUANS search report. All decisions respecting name selection and use are the responsibility of the incorporator and his legal adviser.

This NUANS Report is valid for use within 90 days from the date of the report. Articles must be accompanied by an original, valid NUANS Report. Photocopies are not accepted.

5.3 (continued)

CORPORATE NAME SEARCH REPORT

FEDERAL CORPORATIONS

The recommendation concerning availability of a Federally proposed name as indicated below has been made in accordance with Name Policies as published by the Federal Corporations Branch, but should not be construed as an undertaking that the said name will automatically be granted when articles are submitted. The NUANS Search Report together with any consents required must accompany all articles submitted. A name which meets the requirements of the Federal Corporations Branch is automatically reserved for 90 days from the date of the NUANS Search Report. If you are dissatisfied with the recommendation in this report, please consult the Corporations Branch directly *in writing*, for their binding decision: Industry Canada, Corporations Directorate, 9th Floor, 365 Laurier Avenue West, Ottawa, Ontario K1A 0C8.

ONTARIO CORPORATIONS WITH SHARE CAPITAL

Under the Business Corporations Act, incorporators must make a decision on the availability of the proposed name in accordance with the Regulations under that Act on the basis of an Ontario biased NUANS search report. The NUANS search must accompany the Articles when they are filed with Ontario Companies Services Branch.

COMMENTS MADE BY DYE & DURHAM CO. INC. OR ITS EMPLOYEES ARE PROVIDED TO ASSIST ITS CLIENTS IN REACHING A DECISION ON THE AVAILABILITY OF THE PROPOSED NAME AND MUST NOT BE CONSIDERED A LEGAL OPINION.

☐ The proposed name appears to be available for incorporation purposes subject to and conditional upon the incorporator assuming full responsibility for any risk of confusion with existing business names and trade marks, provided that the conditions set forth in the paragraph(s) "✓" are met. Acceptance of such responsibility will comprise an obligation to change the name to a dissimilar one in the event that representations are made and established that confusion occurs.

☐ 1. The proposed name appears to contain a surname and may be available with the consent (to accompany the articles) of the person(s) whose name(s) appears in the name of the corporation and with his proof of material interest. If such person is an incorporator or first director, such consent and undertaking is not necessary.

☐ 2. The proposed name appears to be available with the consent of the present business and the undertaking of the present business to dissolve forthwith or to change its name before the corporation proposing to use the name commences to use it, such consent and undertaking to accompany the articles. There must be an affidavit stating that all partners have signed such consent or in the alternative an affidavit of sole proprietorship.

☐ 3. If the corporation will be applying for registration under the Real Estate and Business Brokers Act, we would suggest that the proposed name and objects be cleared with the Registrar under that Act.

☐ 4. The Insurance Act requires the approval by the Superintendent of Insurance of articles incorporating Insurance Agencies. We would suggest that you have the proposed name and objects cleared with the Agency Licencing Officer, Insurance Division before submitting the articles.

☐ 5. As "Engineering"/"Engineer" is included in the proposed name, the name appears to be available with the written consent of the Association of Professional Engineers of Ontario.

☐ 6. The proposed name appears to be available with the consent of "X" indicated on printout.

☐ 7. The proposed name appears to be available if the articles will be accompanied by the undertaking of the corporation indicated in paragraph 6 above, to dissolve forthwith or to change its name before the corporation proposing to use the name commences to use it.

☐ 8. Please note trade names/trademarks indicated as "X" on enclosed printout.

☐ 9. We suggest that a better descriptive element be added.

☐ 10. Other

☐ Your proposed name is not recommended for incorporation purposes as

☐ 1. It is too general in nature.

☐ 2. It is only descriptive of the nature of the company business, services or products.

☐ 3. The key word is primarily or only a surname.

☐ 4. The key word is primarily or only a geographic name.

☐ 5. It may be confusing with the trade names/trademarks indicated on the attached report.

☐ 6. It is deceptively descriptive of the proposed company business, services or products, or of the origin of those services or products.

☐ 7. Such a name is prohibited under regulation No.

☐ 8. We suggest that a better descriptive element be added.

☐ 9. We suggest that a distinctive element be added.

☐ 10. We suggest that a first name/initial be added.

☐ 11. Other:

5.3 (continued)

NUANS® REPORT RAPPORT NUANS ®

1"THE PROVISION OF THE INFORMATION CONTAINED IN THIS REPORT IS SUBJECT TO THE
TERMS AND CONDITIONS CONTAINED ON THE BACK HERE OF."

Industry Canada, NUANS 5PAGE D & D AVN477780

? SANDUSKY CONSTRUCTION INC. 72025980 PAGE 1/5
ONTARIO 2001Oc23

==

SANDUSKY CONSTRUCTION INC	ON 72025980 PROP.D & D		2001Oc23
PHIL SANDUSKY CONTRACTING LTD DORCHESTER O	ON 1192432		1996Se18
SANDUSKY ENTERPRISES LTD	BC 0490681		1995Fe16
P.J.SANDUSKY HOLDINGS LTD SCARBOROUGH	ON 571100		1983No28
J.B.SANDUSKY HOLDINGS LTD SCARBOROUGH	ON 571099		1983No28
P. J. SANDUSKY INVESTMENTS LTD SCARBOROUGH	ON 571172		1983No29
P. J. SANDUSKY INVESTMENTS LTD SCARBOROUGH	ON 1327768	New_Amalg	1998De01
SANDUSKY FARMS LTD DORCHESTER O	ON 382798		1978Ma05
J. B. SANDUSKY INVESTMENTS LTD SCARBOROUGH	ON 571170		1983No29
SANDUSKY REAL ESTATE INVESTMENT CORPORATION SHAKER HEIGH	ON 351900 Inactive	US Cancelled	1974De12 1994Jl23
J. B. SANDUSKY INVESTMENTS LTD SCARBOROUGH	ON 1327767	New_Amalg	1998De01
P.J.SANDUSKY HOLDINGS LTD SCARBOROUGH	ON 571100 Inactive	Old_Amalg	1983No28 1998De01
SANDUSK CONSTRUCTION LIMITED MIDLAND ONTA	ON 226680 Inactive	Cancelled	1969Au11 1980Jl07
H. SANDHU REALTY LTD NORTH YORK O	ON 827145	Restored	1989Mr22
SANTOWSKI HOLDINGS LIMITED OTTAWA ONTAR	ON 1101345		1994De23
SANDU ENTERPRISES TORONTO	OB 100867621	Sole_Prop	2000Au03
SANDHU & SONS ENTERPRISES LTD MISSISSAUGA	ON 841396	Restored	1989Ma29

ACCEPTANCE OF THIS REPORT CONSTITUTES ACCEPTANCE OF THE TERMS AND CONDITIONS ON THE REVERSE SIDE OF THIS FORM.

EN ACCEPTANT LE PRÉSENT RAPPORT, VOUS ACCEPTEZ ÉGALEMENT LES CONDITIONS ÉNONCÉES À L'ENDOS DU FORMULAIRE.

COMPAQ

5.3 (continued)

NUANS® REPORT RAPPORT NUANS ®

1"LES RENSEIGNEMENTS CONTENUS DANS CE RAPPORT SONT SUJETS AUX CLAUSES ET CONDITIONS ENONCEES A L'ENDOS DE CE DOCUMENT."

Industry Canada, NUANS 5PAGE D & D AVN477780

? SANDUSKY CONSTRUCTION INC.	72025980 ONTARIO	PAGE 2/5 2001Oc23
SANDARSKY INC NEWMARKET ON	ON 1437570	2000Se01
J.B.SANDUSKY HOLDINGS LTD SCARBOROUGH	ON 571099 Inactive Old_Amalg	1983No28 1998De01
SANDUSK GOLF CLUB INC JARVIS ONTAR	ON 957907	1991No12
SAN-DUR BUILDING MAINTENACE SERVICES MISSISSAUGA	OB 970018651	1997Ja07 Sole_Prop
SANDHURST DEVELOPMENTS SCARBOROUGH	OB 970923652	1997Jl29 Genl.Part
SANDUSK DEVELOPMENT INC WATERDOWN ON	ON 859769 Inactive Cancelled	1989No10 1994Jl09
SANDHU & SONS HOLDINGS LTD	BC 0604060	2000Mr27
SUNDUSK HOMES LTD	ON 307437	1975Jl25
SANDHU & SONS INVESTMENTS LTD	Ab 0204983456	1991Jn20 2001Jn07
SANDHURST PROPERTIES INC	BC 0318744	1986De10
TUSCANY CONSTRUCTION SERVICES MISSISSAUGA	OB 101303196 ON-0947342	2000De04 Bus.Style
POLYGON SANDHURST DEVELOPMENT LTD	BC 0497066	1995Ma24
CANDUSCO LIMITED SARNIA ONTAR	ON 139598	1965Al05
J & R SANDHU PROPERTIES LTD	BC 0487776	1995Ja10
SANDHURST CONDOMINIUM SALES INC	Ab 0208146282 1-15Drs	1999Ja15 2001Ja17
SANDY SUE LTD OTTAWA ONTAR	CN 2001425	2001Fe13
SANDU CRAFTS AND GIFTS RR 2 KESWICK	CB 971039268	1997Au28 Genl.Part
TUSCANY DEVELOPMENTS LIMITED MISSISSAUGA	ON 218621 Restored	1968De31
P. J. SANDUSKY INVESTMENTS LTD SCARBOROUGH	ON 571172 Inactive Old_Amalg	1983No29 1998De01

ACCEPTANCE OF THIS REPORT CONSTITUTES ACCEPTANCE OF THE TERMS AND CONDITIONS ON THE REVERSE SIDE OF THIS FORM.

EN ACCEPTANT LE PRÉSENT RAPPORT, VOUS ACCEPTEZ ÉGALEMENT LES CONDITIONS ÉNONCÉES À L'ENDOS DU FORMULAIRE.

COMPAQ

5.3 (continued)

NUANS® REPORT RAPPORT NUANS ®

1"THE PROVISION OF THE INFORMATION CONTAINED IN THIS REPORT IS SUBJECT TO THE TERMS AND CONDITIONS CONTAINED ON THE BACK HERE OF."

Industry Canada, NUANS 5PAGE D & D AVN477780

? SANDUSKY CONSTRUCTION INC.	72025980 ONTARIO	PAGE 3/5 2001Oc23

===

SANDTON DEVELOPMENT LIMITED	BC 0232777	1981A123
SANDSU HOLDINGS INC LISTOWEL ONT	ON 1326639	1998No23
H.SANDHU MALTON	OB 990371015	1999A106 Sole_Prop
DUSCHINSKY ENTERPRISES INCORPORATED NORTH YORK O	ON 639747	1985Oc01
SANDHU S MISS	OB 991332891	1999De20 Sole_Prop
SANDHURST HOLDINGS LTD	BC 0229163	1981Mr11
DOS SANTOS ENTERPRISES MISSISSAUGA	OB 980691380	1998Jn19 Sole_Prop
SANDHURST INVESTMENTS INC VANCOUVER BR	ON 1488169 BC	1994Jn13
SYNDICAU DEVELOPMENT INC REGINA SASKA	ON 1253467 SK	1996De30
TUSCANY ESTATE DEVELOPMENTS LIMITED LONDON ONTAR	ON 1336585	1999Mr19
TUSCANY CONSTRUCTION CO LTD	BC 0508159	1995No10
SANDHURST HOLDINGS LIMITED HALIFAX	NS 1156800 NLC	1980Ja02
SANDHURST ENTERPRISES LTD	BC 0569929	1998Au11
SANDHURST TAX SERVICES RR#1 BATH	OB 100151687	2000Fe09 Sole_Prop
SANDHUS JANITORIAL SERVICE LTD	BC 0389387	1990Jn20
SANDUKE INVESTMENTS INC MISSISSAUGA	ON 983257 Restored	1992A108
SANTOS HOLDINGS INC TORONTO ONTA	ON 1025751	1993A106
SANDHU DEVELOPMENT LIMITED	BC 0635122	2001Oc04
THE SANDHURST SHORES RATEPAYERS BATH ONTARIO	ON 338689	1977A105

ACCEPTANCE OF THIS REPORT CONSTITUTES ACCEPTANCE OF THE TERMS AND CONDITIONS ON THE REVERSE SIDE OF THIS FORM.

EN ACCEPTANT LE PRÉSENT RAPPORT, VOUS ACCEPTEZ ÉGALEMENT LES CONDITIONS ÉNONCÉES À L'ENDOS DU FORMULAIRE.

COMPAQ

5.3 (continued)

NUANS® REPORT RAPPORT NUANS ®

```
CONTENTS OF THIS REPORT ARE DEPENDENT ON THE INPUT PARAMETERS
SELECTED BY THE USER. PENDING APPLICATIONS ARE UPDATED WHERE NECESSARY
AT ADVERTISEMENT AND REGISTRATION.  TYPICALLY THERE IS A 6 WEEK LAPSE
BETWEEN FILING & AVAILABILITY FOR SEARCH.  ERRORS/OMISSIONS SHOULD BE
REPORTED TO THE TRADE MARKS OFFICE BY TELEPHONING (819) 953-8098.

Industry Canada NUANS - TRADEMARK REPORT          D & D   AVT477780 V
                 72025980               CLASS=37          PAGE 4/5
                                                          2001Oc23.
         ? SANDUSKY
                                                   *
SANDBURY HOMES ;         439565 TMA 243404        42,37,19,Home building services,
         Use-1977Se 1979Ma10 1980Al18  namely, building and supplying homes to
                                                     th>  SANDBURY BUILDING CORP
                                                   *
SANDUSKY                 981168 PBRA 94-169                                  31
         Denominatn 1994Se02  Granted                  YODER BROTHERS, INC.
                                                   *
SANDISK ULTRA            1106402                     9.Solid state memory devices.
         Prop.use    2C01Jn13  Formalized              SANDISK CORPORATION,
                                                   *
SANDISK ULTRA ;          1110635                     9.Solid state memory devices.
         Prop.use    2001J125  Formalized              SANDISK CORPORATION,
                                                   *
PENGUIN DESIGN (PENGUIN HOLDING ICE CREA                30.Ice cream novelties.
         Formalized 1077933
         Use-2000Ma 2000Oc06                           GREAT PACIFIC INDUSTRI
                                                   *
SANDPLAY                 1104244       11.Decorative water fountains, with pumps for
         Prop.use    2001Ma25  Formalized            water circulation, sold>
                                                       SALTON, INC., A DELAWA
                                                   *
ON A TRANSPARENT GROUND, A CONTINUOUS...                  30.Sandwich buns.
                         221798 UCA 46297
         Use-1953Se02 1953Oc27 1953Oc27                WESTON FOODS INC.
                                                   *
SANDUSKY POLYCAST        284078 TMA 140698  10,7,6,12.Centrifugally cast cylinders.
         Use-1964Jn30 1964Au12 1965Jn11                SANDUSKY INTERNATIONAL
                                                   *
SANDMAN MOTEL            299028 TMA 152395          42,35,Providing hotel/motel
                         1966Au16 1967Au04  accommodation and restaurant and eating
                                                 faci>  SANDMAN HOTELS AND INN
                                                   *
KANATA NORTH BUSINESS PARK ;           41,35,42,Administration and operation of a
                         412744 TMA 246554          business park for a township.
                         1977J106 1980Jn13                 THE CITY OF KANATA
                                                   *
LOUIE'S SUBMARINE THE BEST ON LAND OR SE      42,30;Sandwiches namely; submarine
                         658687 TMA 399545                          sandwiches.
                         1990Ma25 1992Jn26 Operation of res>  LOUIE'S SUBMARINE INC
                                                   *
SANDCHERRY HOMES         768311 TMA 465774  36,40,37,35,Real estate development and
         Use-1994Fe01 1994No15 1996No05   operating a business developing real
                                                     e>  RICK D'ANDREA,
                                                   *
SANDCHERRY HOMES ;       768543 TMA 449215  36,40,37,35,Real estate development and
         Use-1994Fe01 1994No15 1995Oc20   operating a business developing real
                                                     e>  RICK D'ANDREA,
                                                   *
SANDOZ                   271458 TMA 135750          1,5,3,24.Chemical products for
         Use-1923    1962Se18 1964Ma15      industry, namely, disinfectants and
                                                soaps fo>  NOVARTIS AG( NOVARTIS
```

ACCEPTANCE OF THIS REPORT CONSTITUTES ACCEPTANCE OF THE TERMS AND CONDITIONS ON THE REVERSE SIDE OF THIS FORM.

EN ACCEPTANT LE PRÉSENT RAPPORT, VOUS ACCEPTEZ ÉGALEMENT LES CONDITIONS ÉNONCÉES À L'ENDOS DU FORMULAIRE.

COMPAQ

5.3 (continued)

NUANS® REPORT — RAPPORT NUANS ®

LE CONTENU DE CE RAPPORT DE MARQUE DE COMMERCE EST DEPENDANT DES PARAMETRES DES DONNEES CHOISIS PAR L'UTILISATEUR. LES DEMANDES EN SUSPENS SONT MISES-A-JOUR LORSQUE NECESSAIRE, LORS DE L'ANNONCE ET DE L'ENREGISTREMENT. TYPIQUEMENT, IL Y A UN DELAI DE 6 SEMAINES ENTRE LE DEPOT ET LA DISPONIBILITE POUR FIN DE RECHERCHE. TOUTES ERREURS /OMISSIONS DOIVENT-ETRE RAPPORTEES AU BUREAU DES MARQUES DE COMMERCE EN TELEPHONANT A (819) 953-8098.

Industrie Canada NUANS - TRADEMARK REPORT D & D AVT477780 V
72025980 CLASS=37 PAGE 5/5
20010c23.

? SANDUSKY

*

SANDUVOR 385632 TMA 214865 1,11,16,9.Stabilizers, namely,
Use-1973Au21 1975Ma07 1976Jl16 ultra-violet absorbers used to delay
photo-ox> NOVARTIS AG(NOVARTIS

*

SANDSATIONAL 518027 TMA 302125 42,20,6,35.Giftware items, namely, sand
1984Mr05 1985Al19 sculptures, sand castings and sand fi>
MQE INVESTMENTS LTD.,

*

SANDY'S INN - WE SELL SLEEP 42,Motel services.
595388 TMA 349884
Use-1979Ma01 1987No16 1989Ja13 CONCORD ENTERPRISES LI

*

SANDWASH SILK BY BIANCA 25.Ladies' silk clothing, namely; jackets, skirts,
644611 TMA 379735 blouses, tops, pan>
1989No14 1991Fe08 NYGARD INTERNATIONAL L

*

SANDSATIONS 766255 TMA 450806 28,16,14.Toys namely, a child's craft
1994Oc14 1995No24 kit with which to create play jewelle>
IRWIN TOY LIMITED,

*

SANDISK 787181 TMA 492653 9,7,42,41.Semiconductor memories and
1995Jl12 1998Al08 memory controllers, namely, an
intellig> SANDISK CORPORATION,

*

SANDISK ; 787182 TMA 475349 9,7,42,41.Semiconductor memories and
1995Jl12 1997Al28 memory controllers, namely, an
intellig> SANDISK CORPORATION,

*

SANDUSKY FLAREX 330782-TMA 174569 7,1,6,29.Metallic cylinders for use in
Expunged 1970Mr06 1971Fe19 pulp and papermaking machines.
SANDUSKY FOUNDRY & MAC

*

SANDOKAN 400024-TMA 232005 42,16;Revue.
Expunged 1976Jl09 1979Mr02 Service d'editio> EDITIONS ATLAS, A SOC

*

COMFORT.CA BY LADY SANDRA OF CANADA LTD. 24,20,16,22.Coverlets, comforters,
Formalized 1089629 quilts, duvet covers, comforter covers, sle>
Prop.use 2001Ja18 LADY SANDRA OF CANADA

*

SANDOZ 214482 UCA 42071 14,9.Montres en tous genres, leurs
Use-1946 1952Mr25 1952Mr25 parties et articles d'horlogerie, no>
COMPAGNIE DES MONTRES

*

COLONEL SANDERS; 327804 TMA 178469 42,30,The services of preparing,
Use-1956Ja24 1969No17 1971Se24 serving and/or selling foods and
bevera> TRICON FRANCHISE (CANA

TM Update 20010c23 ApplNo 1117800 Filed 20010c09

ACCEPTANCE OF THIS REPORT CONSTITUTES ACCEPTANCE OF THE TERMS AND CONDITIONS ON THE REVERSE SIDE OF THIS FORM.

EN ACCEPTANT LE PRÉSENT RAPPORT, VOUS ACCEPTEZ ÉGALEMENT LES CONDITIONS ÉNONCÉES À L'ENDOS DU FORMULAIRE.

COMPAQ

5.3 (continued)

TERMS AND CONDITIONS

Definitions:

"Customer" refers to a person who receives a NUANS® Report directly from CDSCL pursuant to a written agreement with CDSCL.

"CDSCL" shall at all times refer to CONTROL DATA SYSTEMS CANADA, LTD.

(a) There are no warranties expressed or implied, oral or written, in fact or by operation or law or otherwise, except as herein expressly stated. In no event shall CDSCL be liable for any indirect, special or consequential damage for any reason whatsoever including any damage arising out of the existence, furnishing, functioning or the Customer's use of services provided for in the Agreement between the Customer and CDSCL, including responsibility or liability resulting from the inaccuracy and/or omissions of NUANS® Reports.

(b) CDSCL liability for direct damages with respect to its Agreement with the Customer shall be limited to the total charge for services performed therein to date. The Customer agrees to submit in writing proper documentation to CDSCL supporting any alleged customer problem within fifteen (15) days of receipt of invoice.

(c) The Customer agrees that CDSCL's sole liability in the event of
(i) the failure by CDSCL to deliver to its established FOB points the Customer's requested NUANS® reports by 10:00 a.m. (local time) on the working day next following submission of such request; or
(ii) the requirements of Customer to re-request an identical NUANS® report because of the failure of CDSCL to produce the first requested report;
shall be the waiver by CDSCL of all charges with respect thereto, provided that in all such cases CDSCL shall not be liable for any failure in the case of an Act of God, riots, insurrection or any other event beyond CDSCL's direct contro, and provided in all cases that the Customer provides CDSCL with satisfactory documentation evidencing one of the above-mentioned failures within fifteen (15) days of the alleged date of such failure.

(d) In the event a Customer's acknowledged request for a NUANS® report fails to produce that report, the Customer shall re-enter it at the next appropriate time. The Customer shall then advise CDSCL in writing within fifteen (15) days of the event and provide CDSCL with adequate documentation in support of the problem report, proving at least the double submission of an identical request, upon which, if it accepts liability, CDSCL agrees to waive charges for both the original request and for the re-run request.

(e) The Customer agrees to indemnify CDSCL and to hold it harmless from any loss or liability to the Customer, or to any third parties, for any injuries or damages not caused by CDSCL's negligence which result from the Customer's use and operation of any machines in the control of CDSCL, from the Customer's use of CDSCL's premises or premises which CDSCL is authorized to use, or from any error or inaccuracy in the preparation and formulation of a request for a NUANS® report.

(f) The Customer acknowledges that CDSCL is subject to certain time and other restrictions in compiling its data base for purposes of delivering a NUANS® report, and the Customer shall so advise any third party to whom it disseminates a NUANS® report. CDSCL agrees to provide the Customer with a monthly status report detailing the currency of the data base of CDSCL, based on the various registers and name lists used by CDSCL to compile its data base

CONDITIONS

Délimitations:

Le "Client" désigne toute personne qui, aux termes d'une entente écrite, reçoit un rapport NUANS® directement de CDSCL

"CDSCL" désigne LES SYSTEMES CONTROL DATA CANADA, LTEE.

(a) Il n'existe aucune garantie, explicite ou implicite, orale ou écrite, de fait ou en vertu d'une loi ou autrement, que celle expressément énoncée ici. CDSCL ne saurait, en aucun cas ou pour quelque raison que ce soit, être tenu responsable de dommages indirects, particuliers ou consécutifs, y compris les dommages résultants de l'existence, de la fourniture, du fonctionnement ou de l'utilisation qu'en fait le Client des services prévus au contrat signé par le Client et CDSCL incluant toutes responsabilitées résultant de l'inexactitude et/ou omission du rapport NUANS®.

(b) Aux termes de ce contrat, la responsabilité de CDSCL quant aux dommages directs se borne au coût total des services rendus ici à date. Le Client s'engage à soumettre par écrit, dans les quinze (15) jours suivant la réception de la facture, toute documentation pertinente à l'appui d'un problème allégué.

(c) Le Client convient que
(i) à défaut de livraison, au point FAS prescrit, à 10h (heure locale) du jour ouvrable suivant la demande de rapport NUANS® du Client; ou
(ii) si le Client se voit dans l'obligation de réitérer sa demande initiale de rapport NUANS® suite au défaut de CDSCL d'avoir originairement produit lesdits rapports;
la responsabilité de CDSCL se limite à renoncer à tous frais afférent à l'incident, à la condition que dans les 15 jours suivant ledit incident, le Client en informe CDSCL par écrit en ayant soin d'inclure dans sa documentation tous les détails corroborant son grief; CDSCL ne saurait être tenu responsable en cas de force majeure, d'émeute, d'insurrection ou d'autres cas fortuits hors de son contrôle direct.

(d) Si, suite à une demande confirmée de rapport NUANS®, le Client ne reçoit pas ledit rapport, il doit resoumettre sa demande dès la prochaine occasion. Le Client devra, dans les quinze (15) jours qui suivent l'incident, en faire part à CDSCL par écrit en ayant soin de lui fournir, à l'appui du rapport de grief, toute documentation corroborant la soumission de deux demandes identiques, après quoi, si elle en prend la responsabilité CDSCL s'engage à assumer les frais encourus pour le traitement original ainsi que pour la reprise du traitement.

(e) Le Client conviendra de tenir CDSCL quitte et indemne de toute perte ou obligation envers le Client ou envers des tiers, pour tous dommages ou blessures qui ne seraient pas dus à la négligence de CDSCL mais qui résulteraient de l'utilisation ou de l'exploitation qu'en ferait le Client des machines sous la juridiction de CDSCL, ou de l'utilisation par le Client des locaux appartenant à CDSCL ou dont CDSCL a la jouissance, ou de toute erreur d'exactitude dans la préparation et la formulation d'une demande de rapport NUANS®.

(f) Le Client connaît les contraintes de temps ou d'autre nature auxquelles CDSCL est assujetti dans la compilation des données servant à la production de rapport NUANS® et convient d'en aviser toute tierce partie récipiendaire de tels rapports. CDSCL s'engage à fournir au Client un rapport mensuel de statut de la banque de données, à partir de divers registres et listes de dénominations servant à compiler sa banque de données.

5.4 Sample Form of Certificate Endorsed on Articles of Incorporation by Companies Branch

Ontario

Ministry of Consumer and Commercial Relations

Ministère de la Consommation et du Commerce

CERTIFICATE

This is to certify that these articles are effective on

CERTIFICAT

Ceci certifie que les présents statuts entrent en vigueur le

....

Director
Companies Branch

Le Directeur
Direction des compagnies

6. Organizing the Corporation

6.1 Common Share Certificate—Ontario

DYE & DURHAM

COMMON SHARE CERTIFICATE

Certificate No. ____________
For ____________ Shares
Issued to
____
____
Dated ____________ *(year)*

From whom transferred
____
Dated ____________ *(year)*
No. Original Certificate ____________
No. Original Shares ____________
No. of Shares Transferred ____________

Received Certificate No. ____________
for ____________ Shares
this ______ day of ______ *(year)*
____
____
____

No. ______ INCORPORATED UNDER THE LAW OF THE PROVINCE OF ONTARIO ______ **Shares**

This is to Certify that ....

is the registered holder of .... Common Shares of

The class or series of shares represented by this certificate has rights, privileges, restrictions or conditions attached thereto and the Corporation will furnish to the holder, on demand and without charge, a full copy of the text of,

(i) the rights, privileges, restrictions and conditions attached to the said shares and to each class authorized to be issued and to each series insofar as the same have been fixed by the directors, and

(ii) the authority of the directors to fix the rights, privileges, restrictions and conditions of subsequent series, if applicable.

COMMON

RESTRICTIONS ON TRANSFER. There are restrictions on the right to transfer the shares represented by this Certificate.

IN WITNESS WHEREOF the Corporation has caused this Certificate to be signed by its duly authorized officers this .... day of .... *(year)*

____________ ____________

NO PAR VALUE

D&D "COMMON" 8½ x 11

6.1 (continued)

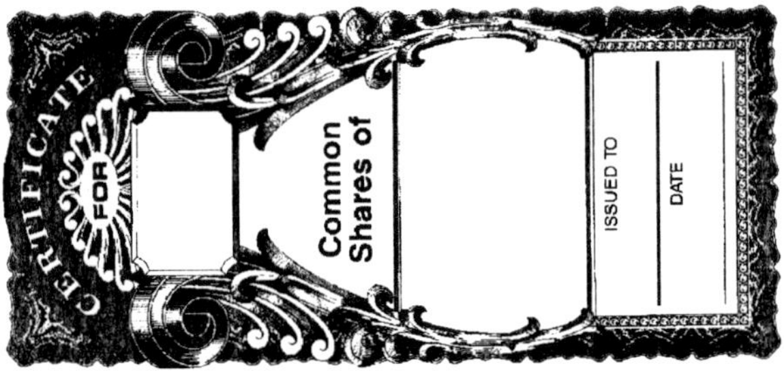

For Value Received, _____ *hereby assign and transfer unto*

______________________________________ ______________

______________________________________ *Common Shares*

____

represented by the within Certificate.

Dated ____________________ (year) ________

In the presence of ____________________

____

NOTICE THE SIGNATURE OF THIS ASSIGNMENT MUST CORRESPOND WITH THE NAME AS WRITTEN UPON THE FACE OF THE CERTIFICATE IN EVERY PARTICULAR, WITHOUT ALTERATION OR ENLARGEMENT OR ANY CHANGE WHATEVER

6.2 Preference Share Certificate—Ontario

DYE & DURHAM

PREFERENCE SHARE CERTIFICATE

Certificate No. ______________

For ______________ Shares

Issued to

____

____

Dated ______________ *(year)*

From whom transferred

____

Dated ______________ *(year)*

No. Original Certificate ______________

No. Original Shares ______________

No. of Shares Transferred ______________

Received Certificate No. ______________

for ______________ Shares

this ______________ day of ______________ *(year)*

____

____

No. **INCORPORATED UNDER THE LAW OF THE PROVINCE OF ONTARIO** ______________ **Shares**

This is to Certify that ....

is the registered holder of .... Preference Shares of

The class or series of shares represented by this certificate has rights, privileges, restrictions or conditions attached thereto and the Corporation will furnish to the holder, on demand and without charge, a full copy of the text of,

(i) the rights, privileges, restrictions and conditions attached to the said shares and to each class authorized to be issued and to each series insofar as the same have been fixed by the directors, and

(ii) the authority of the directors to fix the rights, privileges, restrictions and conditions of subsequent series, if applicable.

RESTRICTIONS ON TRANSFER. There are restrictions on the right to transfer the shares represented by this Certificate.

IN WITNESS WHEREOF the Corporation has caused this Certificate to be signed by its duly authorized officers this .... day of .... *(year)*

______________ ______________

NO PAR VALUE

D&D "PREFERENCE" 8½ x 11

6.2 (continued)

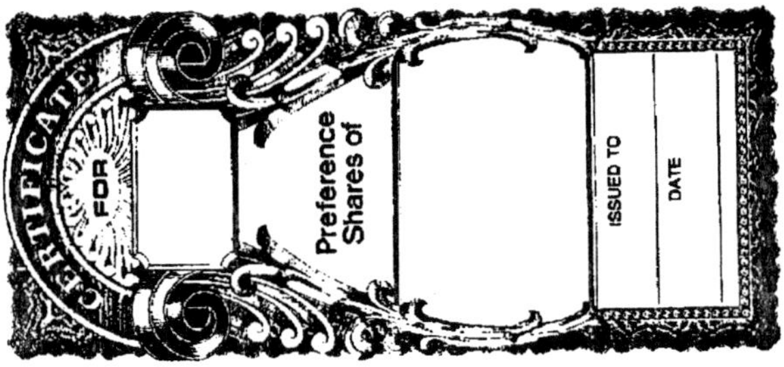

For Value Received, ____ *hereby assign and transfer unto*

____

____________________________________ *Preference Shares*

represented by the within Certificate.

Dated ______________ __

In the presence of ______________________

____

6.3 Non-Designated Share Certificate—Ontario

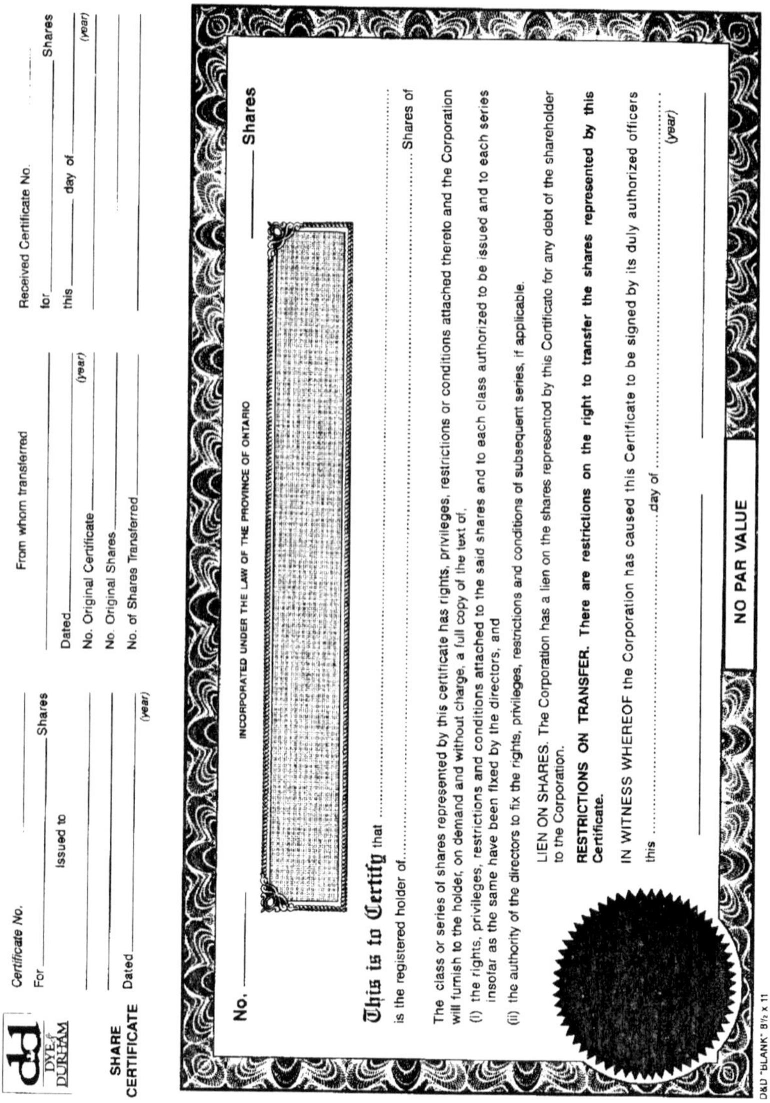

DYE & DURHAM

SHARE CERTIFICATE

Certificate No. ______

For ______ Shares

Issued to ______

Dated ______ *(year)*

From whom transferred ______

Dated ______ *(year)*

No. Original Certificate ______

No. Original Shares ______

No. of Shares Transferred ______

Received Certificate No. ______

for ______ Shares

this ______ day of ______ *(year)*

No. ______ ______ Shares

INCORPORATED UNDER THE LAW OF THE PROVINCE OF ONTARIO

This is to Certify that ....

is the registered holder of .... Shares of

The class or series of shares represented by this certificate has rights, privileges, restrictions or conditions attached thereto and the Corporation will furnish to the holder, on demand and without charge, a full copy of the text of,

(i) the rights, privileges, restrictions and conditions attached to the said shares and to each class authorized to be issued and to each series insofar as the same have been fixed by the directors, and

(ii) the authority of the directors to fix the rights, privileges, restrictions and conditions of subsequent series, if applicable.

LIEN ON SHARES. The Corporation has a lien on the shares represented by this Certificate for any debt of the shareholder to the Corporation.

RESTRICTIONS ON TRANSFER. There are restrictions on the right to transfer the shares represented by this Certificate.

IN WITNESS WHEREOF the Corporation has caused this Certificate to be signed by its duly authorized officers

this .... day of .... *(year)*

NO PAR VALUE

D&D "BLANK" 8½ x 11

6.3 (continued)

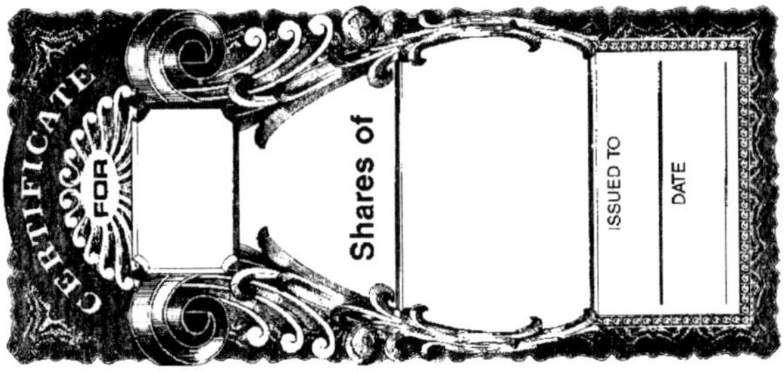

For Value Received, ______ *hereby assign and transfer unto*

____

____ *Shares*

____

represented by the within Certificate.

Dated ______________________ *(year)* __________

In the presence of ______________________

____

NOTICE: THE SIGNATURE OF THIS ASSIGNMENT MUST CORRESPOND WITH THE NAME AS WRITTEN UPON THE FACE OF THE CERTIFICATE IN EVERY PARTICULAR WITHOUT ALTERATION OR ENLARGEMENT OR ANY CHANGE WHATEVER

6.4 (Ontario) *Business Corporations Act* By-law (For Corporations with more than 1 Director)

DYE & DURHAM

D.31
ONTARIO CORPORATION

BY-LAW No.1

(with No. 2 'BORROWING' BY-LAW included)

for use under the Ontario Business Corporations Act

For corporations with *more than 1 director*

Revised 1999

This form of by-law is suitable for use by non-offering corporations incorporated pursuant to the Ontario Business Corporations Act as amended.

It has been designed for use by the typical small corporation and contains those provisions which have been found to be most applicable for the majority of such companies.

Depending on the requirements, additions to or deletions from this by-law may be necessary prior to its use and the incorporators are advised to consult with legal counsel before completion.

Although it *can* be used by corporations with only *one* director and *one* shareholder, **an alternate and abbreviated form of by-law is available for 'one person' corporations (No.D238).**

Sections 2.01 ***(Powers)****, 3.10* ***(Casting Vote)****, 6.12* ***(Votes to Govern)****, 9.01* ***(Financial Year)*** *and 13.01* ***(Repeal)*** *of this by-law should be reviewed by the incorporators and completed as the circumstances require.*

DYE & DURHAM CO. INC.

OTTAWA	TORONTO	LONDON
739-8200	321-1000	685-0101
(Toll Free: 1-800-267-2718)	(Toll Free: 1-800-668-9011)	(Toll Free: 1-800-265-4687)

6.4 (continued)

BY-LAW NO. 1

A by-law relating generally to the conduct of the business and affairs of

(herein called the "Corporation")

CONTENTS

1. Interpretation
2. Directors
3. Meetings of Directors
4. Remuneration and Indemnification
5. Officers
6. Meetings of Shareholders
7. Shares
8. Dividends
9. Financial Year
10. Notices
11. Execution of Documents
12. Effective Date
13. Repeal

BE IT ENACTED as a by-law of the Corporation as follows:

1. INTERPRETATION

1.01 In this by-law and all other by-laws and resolutions of the Corporation, unless the context otherwise requires:

(a) "Act" means the Ontario *Business Corporations Act* together with the Regulations made pursuant thereto and any statute or regulations that may be substituted therefor, as amended from time to time;

(b) "articles" means the articles of incorporation of the Corporation as amended or restated from time to time;

(c) "board" means the board of directors of the Corporation;

(d) "by-laws" means this by-law and all other by-laws of the Corporation as amended from time to time, and from time to time in force and effect;

(e) "Corporation" means this Corporation;

6.4 (continued)

(f) "meeting of shareholders" means any meeting of shareholders, whether annual or special; and "special meeting of shareholders" means a special meeting of all shareholders entitled to vote at an annual meeting of shareholders and a meeting of any class or classes of shareholders entitled to vote on the question at issue;

(g) "person" includes an individual, sole proprietorship, partnership, unincorporated association, unincorporated syndicate, unincorporated organization, trust, body corporate, and a natural person in his capacity as trustee, executor, administrator, or other legal representative;

(h) "recorded address" means, in the case of a shareholder, his address as recorded in the shareholders' register; and, in the case of joint shareholders, the address appearing in the shareholders' register in respect of such joint holding or the first address so appearing if there are more than one; and, in the case of a director, officer, auditor or member of a committee of the board, his latest address recorded in the records of the Corporation; and

(i) "unanimous shareholder agreement" shall have the meaning ascribed to such term under the Act.

D&D (No. D.31)
BY-LAW—ONTARIO CORP (more than 1 Director)
Revised 1996

1.02 In this by-law where the context requires, words importing the singular include the plural and vice versa and words importing gender include the masculine, feminine and neuter genders.

1.03 Save as aforesaid, all the words and terms appearing in this by-law shall have the same definitions and application as in the Act.

2. DIRECTORS

2.01 Powers - Subject to any unanimous shareholder agreement, the business and affairs of the Corporation shall be managed or supervised by a board of directors.

Until changed in accordance with the Act, the board shall consist of

(Delete as applicable.)

a fixed number of directors.

not fewer than the minimum number and not more than the maximum number of directors provided for in the articles.

2.02 Resident Canadians - Except where the Corporation is a non-resident Corporation,

6.4 (continued)

a majority of the directors shall be resident Canadians but where the Corporation has only one or two directors, that director or one of the two directors, as the case may be, shall be a resident Canadian.

2.03 Qualifications - No person shall be qualified for election as a director if he is less than 18 years of age; if he is of unsound mind and has been so found by a court in Canada or elsewhere; if he is not an individual; or if he has the status of a bankrupt.

2.04 Election and Term - The election of directors shall take place at the first meeting of shareholders and at each succeeding annual meeting at which an election of directors is required. The directors shall hold office for an expressly stated term, which shall expire not later than the close of the third annual meeting of shareholders following the election. A director not elected for an expressly stated term ceases to hold office at the close of the first annual meeting of shareholders following his election. Incumbent directors, if qualified, shall be eligible for re-election. If an election of directors is not held at the proper time, the incumbent directors shall continue in office until their successors are elected.

2.05 Resignation - A director who is not named in the articles may resign from office upon giving a written resignation to the Corporation and such resignation becomes effective when received by the Corporation or at the time specified in the resignation, whichever is later. A director named in the articles shall not be permitted to resign his office unless at the time the resignation is to become effective a successor is elected or appointed.

2.06 Removal - Subject to the provisions of the Act, the shareholders may, by ordinary resolution passed at a meeting of shareholders, remove any director or directors from office before the expiration of his or their respective terms and may, by a majority of the votes cast at the meeting, elect any person in his place for the remainder of his term.

2.07 Vacation of Office - A director ceases to hold office when he dies, resigns, is removed from office by the shareholders, or becomes disqualified to serve as a director.

2.08 Vacancies - Subject to the provisions of the Act, where a vacancy occurs on the

6.4 (continued)

board, a quorum of the directors then in office may appoint a person to fill the vacancy for the remainder of the term. If there is not a quorum of directors or if there has been a failure to elect the number of directors required by the articles or in the case of a variable board as required by special resolution, the directors then in office shall forthwith call a special meeting of shareholders to fill the vacancy and, if they fail to call a meeting or if there are no directors then in office, the meeting may be called by any shareholder.

3. MEETINGS OF DIRECTORS

3.01 Place of Meetings - Meetings of the board may be held at any place within or outside Ontario and it shall not be necessary that, in any financial year of the Corporation, a majority of the meetings of the board be held at a place within Canada.

3.02 Meetings by Telephone - Where all the directors present at or participating in the meeting have consented thereto, any director may participate in a meeting of the board or of a committee of the board by means of conference telephone, electronic or other communication facilities as permit all persons participating in the meeting to communicate with each other simultaneously and instantaneously and a director participating in such a meeting by such means is deemed for the purposes of the Act and these by-laws to be present at the meeting. If a majority of the directors participating in such a meeting are then in Canada, the meeting shall be deemed to have been held in Canada.

3.03 Calling of Meetings - Meetings of the board shall be held from time to time at such place, at such time and on such day as the president or a vice-president who is a director or any two directors may determine, and the secretary shall call meetings when directed or authorized by the president or by a vice-president who is a director or by any two directors. Notice of every meeting so called shall be given to each director not less than 48 hours (excluding any part of a Sunday and of a holiday as defined by the Ontario *Interpretation Act)* before the time when the meeting is to be held, except that no notice of meeting shall be necessary if all the directors are present or if those absent have waived notice of or otherwise signified their consent to the holding of such meeting. A notice of a meeting of directors need not specify the purpose of or the business to be transacted at the meeting except where the Act requires such purpose or business to be specified.

6.4 (continued)

3.04 Regular Meetings - The board may appoint a day or days in any month or months for regular meetings at a place and hour to be named. A copy of any resolution of the board fixing the place and time of regular meetings of the board shall be sent to each director forthwith after being passed, but no other notice shall be required for any such regular meetings except where the Act requires the purpose thereof or the business to be transacted thereat to be specified.

3.05 First Meeting of New Board - Each newly elected board may without notice hold its first meeting immediately following a meeting of shareholders at which such board is elected, provided that a quorum of directors is present.

3.06 Quorum - Where the Corporation has fewer than three directors, all directors must be present at any meeting of directors to constitute a quorum. Subject to the articles or by-laws of the Corporation, a majority of the number of directors or minimum number of directors required by the articles constitutes a quorum at any meeting of directors but in no case shall a quorum be less than two-fifths of the number of directors or less than the minimum number of directors, as the case may be.

3.07 Resident Canadians - Directors shall not transact business at a meeting of the board unless a majority of the directors present are resident Canadians or, where the Corporation has fewer than three directors, one of the directors present is a resident Canadian. However, directors may transact business at a meeting of the board where a majority of resident Canadian directors is not present if

(a) a resident Canadian director who is unable to be present approves in writing or by telephone or other communications facilities the business transacted at the meeting; and

(b) a majority of resident Canadian directors would have been present had the director been present at the meeting.

3.08 Chairman - The chairman of any meeting of the board shall be the first mentioned of such of the following officers as have been appointed and who is a director and is present at the meeting:

6.4 (continued)

(a) Chairman of the Board;
(b) President; or
(c) a Vice-President.

If no such officer is present, the directors present shall choose one of their number to be chairman.

3.09 Votes to Govern - At all meetings of the board, every question shall be decided by a majority of the votes cast on the question.

(Complete accordingly.)

3.10 Casting Vote - In the case of an equality of votes on any question at a meeting of the board, the chairman of the meeting shall be entitled to a second or casting vote.

3.11 Disclosure of Interests in Contracts - Every director or officer of the Corporation who is a party to a material contract or transaction or proposed material contract or transaction with the Corporation, or is a director or officer of or has a material interest in any person who is a party to a material contract or transaction or proposed material contract or transaction with the Corporation, shall disclose in writing to the Corporation or request to have entered in the minutes of the meeting of directors the nature and extent of his interest at the time and in the manner required by the Act. Any such contract or proposed contract shall be referred to the board or shareholders for approval even if such contract is one that in the ordinary course of the Corporation's business would not require approval by the board or the shareholders, and a director interested in a contract so referred to the board shall not vote on any resolution to approve the same except as provided by the Act.

3.12 Resolution in Lieu of Meeting - A resolution in writing, signed by all the directors entitled to vote on that resolution at a meeting of directors or committee of directors, is as valid as if it had been passed at a meeting of directors or committee of directors. A copy of every such resolution shall be kept with the minutes of the proceedings of the directors or committee of directors.

3.13 Delegation - Directors may appoint from their number a managing director who is a resident Canadian or a committee of directors and delegate to such managing director or

6.4 (continued)

committee any of the powers of the directors. If the directors appoint a committee of directors, a majority of the members of the committee must be resident Canadians. Unless otherwise determined by the board and subject to the Act, each committee shall have the power to fix its quorum at not less than a majority of its members, to elect its chairman and to regulate its procedure.

4. REMUNERATION AND INDEMNIFICATION

4.01 Remuneration - Subject to the provisions of the Act, the articles, and the by-laws of the Corporation or any unanimous shareholder agreement, the board may fix the remuneration of the directors. Nothing contained herein shall preclude any director from serving the Corporation in any other capacity and receiving remuneration therefor. In addition, directors shall be paid such sums in respect of their out-of-pocket expenses incurred in attending board, committee or shareholders' meetings or otherwise in respect of the performance by them of their duties as the board may from time to time determine.

4.02 Limitation of Liability - Every director and officer of the Corporation, in exercising his powers and discharging his duties, shall act honestly and in good faith with a view to the best interests of the Corporation, and exercise the care, diligence and skill that a reasonably prudent person would exercise in comparable circumstances. Subject to the foregoing, no director or officer shall be liable for the acts, receipts, neglects or defaults of any other director or officer or employee, or for joining in any receipt or other act for conformity, or for any loss, damage or expense happening to the Corporation through the insufficiency or deficiency of title to any property acquired for or on behalf of the Corporation, or for the insufficiency or deficiency of any security in or upon which any of the monies of the Corporation shall be invested, or for any loss or damage arising from the bankruptcy, insolvency or tortious acts of any person with whom any of the monies, securities or effects of the Corporation shall be deposited, or for any loss occasioned by any error of judgment or oversight on his part, or for any other loss, damage or misfortune whatever, which shall happen in the execution of the duties of his office or in relation thereto, unless the same are occasioned by his own willful neglect or default; provided that nothing herein shall relieve any director or officer from the duty to act in accordance with the Act or from liability for any breach thereof.

6.4 (continued)

4.03 Indemnity of Directors and Officers - Subject to the provisions of the Act, the Corporation shall indemnify a director or officer of the Corporation, a former director or officer of the Corporation, or a person who acts or acted at the Corporation's request as a director or officer of a body corporate of which the Corporation is or was a shareholder or creditor, and his heirs and legal representatives, against all costs, charges and expenses, including an amount paid to settle an action or satisfy a judgment, reasonably incurred by him in respect of any civil, criminal or administrative action or proceeding to which he is made a party by reason of being or having been a director or officer of such Corporation or body corporate if

(a) he acted honestly and in good faith with a view to the best interests of the Corporation; and

(b) in the case of a criminal or administrative action or proceeding that is enforced by a monetary penalty, he had reasonable grounds for believing that his conduct was lawful.

4.04 Insurance - Subject to the limitations contained in the Act, the Corporation may purchase and maintain such insurance for the benefit of its directors and officers as such, as the board may from time to time determine.

5. OFFICERS

5.01 Appointment - Subject to the provisions of the Act, the articles or any unanimous shareholder agreement, the board may from time to time appoint a president, one or more vice-presidents (to which title may be added words indicating seniority or function), a secretary, a treasurer and such other officers as the board may determine, including one or more assistants to any of the officers so appointed. The board may specify the duties of and, in accordance with this by-law and subject to the provisions of the Act, delegate to such officers powers to manage the business and affairs of the Corporation. Save for the chairman of the board and the managing director, an officer may but need not be a director and one person may hold more than one office.

5.02 Term, Remuneration and Removal - The terms of employment and remuneration of all officers elected or appointed by the board (including the president) shall be determined

6.4 (continued)

from time to time by resolution of the board. The fact that any officer or employee is a director or shareholder of the Corporation shall not disqualify him from receiving such remuneration as may be determined. All officers, in the absence of agreement to the contrary, shall be subject to removal by resolution of the board at any time with or without cause.

5.03 Chairman of the Board - The board may from time to time also appoint a chairman of the board who shall be a director. If appointed, the board may assign to him any of the powers and duties that are by any provisions of this by-law capable of being assigned to the president; and he shall, subject to the provisions of the Act, have such other powers and duties as the board may specify. During the absence or disability of the chairman of the board, his duties shall be performed and his powers exercised by the president.

5.04 Managing Director - The board may from time to time appoint a managing director who shall be a resident Canadian and a director. If appointed, he shall be the chief executive officer and, subject to the authority of the board, shall have general supervision of the business and affairs of the Corporation; and he shall, subject to the provisions of the Act, have such other powers and duties as the board may specify. During the absence or disability of the president, or if no president has been appointed, the managing director shall also have the powers and duties of that office.

5.05 President - The board may from time to time appoint a president. The president shall be the chief operating officer of the Corporation and, if no managing director has been appointed, and subject to the authority of the board, shall have the general supervision of the business and affairs of the Corporation and he shall have such other powers and duties as the board may specify. During the absence or disability of the managing director, or if no managing director has been appointed, the president shall also have the powers and the duties of that office.

5.06 Vice-President - The board may from time to time appoint one or more vice-presidents. A vice-president so appointed shall have such powers and such duties as the board or the chief executive officer may prescribe.

6.4 (continued)

5.07 Secretary - The board may from time to time appoint a secretary. The secretary shall attend all meetings of the directors, shareholders and committees of the board and shall enter or cause to be entered in books kept for that purpose, minutes of all proceedings at such meetings; he shall give, or cause to be given, when instructed, notices required to be given to shareholders, directors, auditors and members of committees; he shall be the custodian of the stamp or mechanical device generally used for affixing the corporate seal of the Corporation and of all books, papers, records, documents and other instruments belonging to the Corporation; and he shall perform such other duties as may from time to time be prescribed by the board.

5.08 Treasurer - The board may from time to time appoint a treasurer. The treasurer shall keep, or cause to be kept, proper accounting records as required by the Act; he shall deposit, or cause to be deposited, all monies received by the Corporation in the Corporation's bank account; he shall, under the direction of the board, supervise the safekeeping of securities and the disbursement of the funds of the Corporation; he shall render to the board, whenever required, an account of all his transactions as treasurer and of the financial position of the Corporation; and he shall perform such other duties as may from time to time be prescribed by the board.

5.09 Other Officers - The duties of all other officers of the Corporation shall be such as the terms of their engagement call for or the board requires of them. Any of the powers and duties of an officer to whom an assistant has been appointed may be exercised and performed by such assistant, unless the board otherwise directs.

5.10 Variation of Duties - From time to time and subject to the provisions of the Act, the board may vary, add to or limit the powers and duties of any officer.

5.11 Agents and Attorneys - The board shall have power from time to time to appoint agents or attorneys for the Corporation in or outside of Ontario with such powers of management or otherwise (including the power to sub-delegate) as may be thought fit.

5.12 Fidelity Bonds - The board may require such officers, employees and agents of the

6.4 (continued)

Corporation, as it deems advisable, to furnish bonds for the faithful performance of their duties, in such form and with such surety as the board may from time to time prescribe.

5.13 Conflict of Interest - An officer shall disclose his interest in any material contract or transaction or proposed material contract or transaction with the Corporation in accordance with Section 3.11 herein.

6. MEETINGS OF SHAREHOLDERS

6.01 Annual Meetings - Subject to Section 6.16 herein, the directors shall call the first annual meeting of shareholders not later than eighteen months after the Corporation comes into existence and, subsequently, not later than fifteen months after holding the last preceding annual meeting. The annual meeting of shareholders of the Corporation shall be held at such time and on such day in each year as the board may from time to time determine, for the purposes of receiving the reports and statements required by the Act to be laid before the annual meeting, electing directors, appointing auditors and fixing or authorizing the board to fix their remuneration, and for the transaction of such other business as may properly be brought before the meeting.

6.02 Special Meetings - The board may at any time call a special meeting of shareholders for the transaction of any business which may properly be brought before such meeting of shareholders. All business transacted at an annual meeting of shareholders, except consideration of the financial statements, auditor's report, election of directors and reappointment of the incumbent auditor, is deemed to be special business.

6.03 Place of Meetings - Meetings of shareholders shall be held at the registered office of the Corporation, or at such other place within or outside of Ontario as the board from time to time determines.

6.04 Notice of Meetings - Notice of the time and place of each meeting of shareholders shall be sent not less than 10 days and not more than 50 days before the date of the meeting to the auditor of the Corporation, to each director, and to each person whose

6.4 (continued)

name appears on the records of the Corporation at the close of business on the day next preceding the giving of the notice as a shareholder entitled to vote at the meeting. Notice of a special meeting of shareholders shall state:

(a) the nature of the business to be transacted at the meeting in sufficient detail to permit the shareholders to form a reasoned judgment thereon; and

(b) the text of any special resolution or by-law to be submitted to the meeting.

A shareholder and any other person entitled to attend a meeting of shareholders may in any manner and at any time waive notice of or otherwise consent to a meeting of shareholders.

6.05 Persons Entitled To Be Present - The only persons entitled to attend a meeting of shareholders shall be those entitled to vote thereat, the directors and the auditor of the Corporation and others who although not entitled to vote are entitled or required under any provision of the Act or by-laws of the Corporation to be present at the meeting. Any other persons may be admitted only on the invitation of the chairman of the meeting or with the consent of the meeting.

6.06 Quorum - Subject to the provisions of the Act, the holders of a majority of the shares entitled to vote at a meeting of shareholders present in person or by proxy constitute a quorum for the transaction of business at any meeting of shareholders.

6.07 One-Shareholder Meeting - If the Corporation has only one shareholder, or only one holder of any class or series of shares, the shareholder present in person or by proxy constitutes a meeting.

6.08 Right to Vote - At any meeting of shareholders, unless the articles otherwise provide, each share of the Corporation entitles the holder thereof to one vote at a meeting of shareholders, subject to the provisions of the Act.

6.09 Joint Shareholders - Where two or more persons hold the same share or shares jointly, any one of such persons present at a meeting of shareholders may in the absence of the other vote the shares but, if two or more of such persons who are present in person or by proxy, vote, they shall vote as one on the shares jointly held by them.

6.4 (continued)

6.10 Proxies - Every shareholder entitled to vote at a meeting of shareholders may, by means of a proxy, appoint a proxy holder or one or more alternate proxy holders who are not required to be shareholders to attend and act at the meeting in the manner and to the extent authorized by the proxy and with the authority conferred by the proxy. A proxy shall be in writing and executed by the shareholder or by his attorney authorized in writing and shall conform with the requirements of the Act. The board may by resolution fix a time not exceeding 48 hours, excluding Saturdays and holidays, preceding any meeting or adjourned meeting of shareholders, before which time proxies to be used at that meeting must be deposited with the Corporation or an agent thereof, and any period of time so fixed shall be specified in the notice calling the meeting. A proxy shall be acted upon only if, prior to the time so specified, it shall have been deposited with the Corporation or an agent thereof specified in such notice or, where no time is specified in such notice, the proxy has been received by the secretary of the Corporation or by the chairman of the meeting or any adjournment thereof prior to the time of voting.

6.11 Scrutineers - At each meeting of shareholders one or more scrutineers may be appointed by a resolution of the meeting or by the chairman with the consent of the meeting to serve at the meeting. Such scrutineers need not be shareholders of the Corporation.

6.12 Votes to Govern - Subject to the provisions of the Act, the articles and the by-laws of the Corporation or any unanimous shareholder agreement, all questions proposed for the consideration of the shareholders at a meeting shall be decided by a majority of the votes cast thereon. In case of an equality of votes either on a show of hands or on a poll, the chairman of the meeting *shall / shall not* be entitled to a second or casting vote. (Delete accordingly.)

6.13 Show of Hands - Subject to the provisions of the Act, at all meetings of shareholders every question shall be decided by a show of hands unless a ballot thereon be required by the chairman or be demanded by a shareholder or proxyholder present and entitled to vote. Upon a show of hands, every person present and entitled to vote has one vote regardless of the number of shares he represents. After a show of hands has been taken upon any question, the chairman may require, or any shareholder or proxyholder present and entitled to vote may demand, a ballot thereon. Whenever a vote by show of

6.4 (continued)

hands shall have been taken upon a question, unless a ballot thereon be so required or demanded, a declaration by the chairman that the vote upon the question has been carried or carried by a particular majority or not carried and an entry to that effect in the minutes of the meeting shall be prima facie evidence of the fact without proof of the number or proportion of the votes recorded in favour of or against the question. The result of the vote so taken and declared shall be the decision of the Corporation on the question. A demand for a ballot may be withdrawn at any time prior to the taking of the ballot.

6.14 Ballots - If a ballot is required by the chairman of the meeting or is demanded and the demand is not withdrawn, a ballot upon the question shall be taken in such manner as the chairman of the meeting directs.

6.15 Adjournment - The chairman of a meeting of shareholders may, with the consent of the meeting and subject to such conditions as the meeting may decide, adjourn the meeting from time to time and from place to place.

6.16 Resolution in Lieu of Meeting - Except where a written statement with respect to the subject matter of the resolution is submitted by a director or the auditors in accordance with the Act,

(a) a resolution in writing signed by all the shareholders entitled to vote on that resolution at a meeting of shareholders is as valid as if it had been passed at a meeting of the shareholders; and

(b) a resolution in writing dealing with any matter required by the Act to be dealt with at a meeting of shareholders, and signed by all the shareholders entitled to vote at that meeting, satisfies all the requirements of the Act relating to that meeting of shareholders.

7. SHARES

7.01 Allotment - Subject to the provisions of the Act, the articles and any unanimous shareholder agreement, the board may from time to time allot or grant options to purchase the whole or any part of the authorized and unissued shares of the Corporation at such time and to such persons and for such consideration as the board shall determine, provided that no share shall be issued until it is fully paid as provided by the Act.

6.4 (continued)

- 15 -

7.02 Lien for Indebtedness - Subject to the provisions of the Act, the Corporation shall have a lien on shares registered in the name of a shareholder indebted to the Corporation. Such lien may be enforced, subject to any other provision of the articles and to any unanimous shareholder agreement, by the sale of the shares thereby affected or by any other action, suit, remedy or proceeding authorized or permitted by law or by equity and, pending such enforcement, the Corporation may refuse to register a transfer of the whole or any part of such shares.

7.03 Share Certificates - Every holder of one or more shares of the Corporation is entitled, at his option, to a share certificate, or to a non-transferable written acknowledgment of his right to obtain a share certificate, stating the number and class or a series of shares held by him as shown on the records of the Corporation. Share certificates and acknowledgments of a shareholder's right to a share certificate shall be in such form as the board shall from time to time approve. Any share certificate shall be signed in accordance with Section 11.01 herein and need not be under the corporate seal.

D&D (No. D.31)
BY-LAW: ONTARIO CORP. (more than 1 Director)
Revised 1988

7.04 Replacement of Share Certificates - Subject to the provisions of the Act, the directors may by resolution prescribe, either generally or in a particular case, the conditions upon which a new share certificate may be issued to replace a share certificate which has been defaced, lost, stolen or destroyed.

7.05 Transfer Agent and Registrar - The board may from time to time appoint a registrar to maintain the securities register and a transfer agent to maintain the register of transfers and may also appoint one or more branch registrars to maintain branch security registers and one or more branch transfer agents to maintain branch registers of transfers, but one person may be appointed both registrar and transfer agent. The board may at any time terminate any such appointment.

7.06 Joint Shareholders - If two or more persons are registered as joint holders of any share, the Corporation shall not be bound to issue more than one certificate in respect thereof, and delivery of such certificate to one of such persons shall be sufficient delivery to all of them. Any one of such persons may give effectual receipts for the certificate issued in respect thereof or for any dividends, bonus, return of capital or other money payable or warrant issuable in respect of such share.

6.4 (continued)

8. DIVIDENDS

8.01 Declaration - Subject to the provisions of the Act, the articles and to any unanimous shareholder agreement, the board may declare and the Corporation may pay dividends to the shareholders according to their respective rights and interests in the Corporation. Dividends may be paid by issuing fully paid shares of the Corporation or options or rights to acquire fully paid shares of the Corporation or, subject to the provisions of the Act, may be paid in money or property.

8.02 Payment - A dividend payable in cash shall be paid by cheque drawn on the Corporation's bankers or one of them to the order of each registered holder of shares of the class in respect of which it has been declared, and mailed by ordinary mail postage prepaid to such registered holder at his recorded address, unless such holder otherwise directs. In the case of joint holders, the cheque shall, unless such joint holders otherwise direct, be made payable to the order of all of such joint holders and mailed to them at their recorded addresses. The mailing of such cheque as aforesaid shall satisfy and discharge all liability for the dividend to the extent of the sum represented thereby plus the amount of any tax which the Corporation is required to and does withhold, unless such cheque be not paid on due presentation.

8.03 Non-Receipt of Cheque - In the event of the non-receipt of any cheque for a dividend by the person to whom it is so sent as aforesaid, the Corporation shall issue to such person a replacement cheque for a like amount on such terms as to indemnity, reimbursement of expenses and evidence of non-receipt and of title as the board may from time to time prescribe, whether generally or in a particular case.

9. FINANCIAL YEAR

9.01 Financial Year - The financial year of the Corporation shall end on the   day of   in each year, until changed by a resolution of the board.

6.4 (continued)

10. NOTICES

10.01 Method of Giving Notice - Any notice, communication or other document required by the Act, the regulations, the articles or the by-laws to be given by the Corporation to a shareholder, director, officer, or auditor or member of a committee of the board of the Corporation under any provision of the Act, the articles or by-laws or otherwise shall be sufficiently given if delivered personally to the person to whom it is to be given or if delivered to his recorded address or if mailed to him at his recorded address by prepaid ordinary mail or if sent to him at his recorded address by any means of any prepaid transmitted or recorded communication. A notice so delivered shall be deemed to have been given when it is delivered personally or delivered to the recorded address as aforesaid; a notice so mailed shall be deemed to have been received on the fifth day after mailing; and a notice so sent by any means of transmitted or recorded communication shall be deemed to have been given when dispatched or delivered to the appropriate communication company or agency or its representative for dispatch. The secretary may change or cause to be changed the recorded address of any shareholder, director, officer or auditor of the Corporation in accordance with any information believed by him to be reliable. The recorded address of a director shall be his latest address as shown in the records of the Corporation or in the most recent notice filed under the Ontario *Corporations Information Act*, whichever is the more current.

10.02 Computation of Time - In computing the date when notice must be given under any provision requiring a specified number of days' notice of any meeting or other event, "day" means a clear day and a period of days shall be deemed to commence on the day following the event that began the period and shall be deemed to terminate at midnight of the last day of the period except that if the last day of the period falls on a Sunday or holiday the period shall terminate at midnight of the day next following that is not a Sunday or holiday.

10.03 Omissions and Errors - The accidental omission to give any notice to any shareholder, director, officer or auditor, or the non-receipt of any notice by any shareholder, director, officer or auditor or any error in any notice not affecting the substance thereof shall not invalidate any action taken at any meeting held pursuant to such notice or otherwise founded thereon.

6.4 (continued)

10.04 Notice to Joint Shareholders - All notices with respect to any shares registered in more than one name may, if more than one address appears on the records of the Corporation in respect of such joint holding, be given to such joint shareholders at the first address so appearing, and notice so given shall be sufficient notice to all the holders of such shares.

10.05 Persons Entitled by Death or Operation of Law - Every person who by operation of law, by transfer or the death of a shareholder or otherwise becomes entitled to shares is bound by every notice in respect of such shares which has been duly given to the registered holder from whom he derives title prior to his name and address being entered on the records of the Corporation (whether such notice was given before or after the happening of the event upon which he became so entitled) and prior to his furnishing to the Corporation the proof of authority or evidence of his entitlement prescribed by the Act.

10.06 Waiver of Notice - Any shareholder (or his duly appointed proxy), director, officer or auditor may waive any notice or abridge the time required for any notice required to be given under any provision of the Act, the articles or by-laws of the Corporation or otherwise, and such waiver or abridgement, whether given before or after the meeting or other event of which notice is required to be given, shall cure any default in the giving or in the time of such notice, as the case may be. Any such waiver or abridgement shall be in writing except a waiver of notice of a meeting of shareholders or of the board or a committee of the board which may be given in any manner.

10.07 Signatures to Notices - The signatures to any notice to be given by the Corporation may be written, stamped, typewritten or printed or partly written, stamped, typewritten or printed.

11. EXECUTION OF DOCUMENTS

11.01 Signing Officers - Deeds, transfers, assignments, contracts and obligations of the Corporation may be signed by the president or a vice-president or a director together with the secretary or treasurer or an assistant secretary or assistant treasurer or another director. Notwithstanding this, the board may at any time and from time to time direct the manner in

6.4 (continued)

- 19 -

which and the person or persons by whom any particular deed, transfer, contract or obligation or any class of deeds, transfers, contracts or obligations may be signed.

11.02 Seal - Any person authorized to sign any document may affix the corporate seal thereto.

12. EFFECTIVE DATE

12.01 Effective Date - This by-law shall come into force when enacted by the directors, subject to the provisions of the Act.

D&D (No. D.31)
BY-LAW—ONTARIO CORP. (more than 1 Director)
Revised 1999

13. REPEAL

(Delete this section if inapplicable.)

13.01 Repeal - Upon this by-law coming into force, By-law Number of the Corporation is repealed provided that such repeal shall not affect the previous operation of such by-law so repealed or affect the validity of any act done or right, privilege, obligation or liability acquired or incurred under the validity of any contract or agreement made pursuant to any such by-law prior to its repeal.

ENACTED by the board the day of *(year)*

President	Secretary

(Corporate Seal)

CONFIRMED by the shareholders the day of *(year)*

Secretary

(Corporate Seal)

6.4 (continued)

Resolved that the foregoing by-law is hereby enacted by the directors of the Corporation, pursuant to the Ontario Business Corporations Act as evidenced by the respective signatures hereto of all the directors.

Dated the day of *(year)*

In lieu of confirmation at a general meeting of the shareholders, we the undersigned, being all of the shareholders of the Corporation entitled to vote at a meeting of shareholders, hereby confirm in writing the above by-law in accordance with the Ontario Business Corporations Act.

Dated the day of *(year)*

6.4 (continued)

- 21 -

BY-LAW NO. 2

A by-law respecting the borrowing of money and the issuing of securities by:

(herein called the "Corporation")

BE IT ENACTED as a by-law of the Corporation as follows:

1. Without limiting the borrowing powers of the Corporation as set forth in the Ontario *Business Corporations Act* (the "Act"), the Directors of the Corporation may, from time to time without the authorization of the Shareholders:

(a) borrow money upon the credit of the Corporation;

(b) issue, re-issue, sell or pledge debt obligations of the Corporation;

(c) subject to Section 20 of the Act, give a guarantee on behalf of the Corporation to secure performance of an obligation of any person; and

(d) charge, mortgage, hypothecate, pledge or otherwise create a security interest in all or any property of the Corporation, owned or subsequently acquired, to secure any obligation of the Corporation.

2. The Directors may, from time to time, by resolution delegate any or all of the powers referred to in paragraph 1 of this by-law to a director, a committee of directors or one or more officers of the Corporation.

ENACTED by the Directors and sealed with the Corporation's seal

the day of *(year)*

President (Corporate Seal)

Secretary (Corporate Seal)

6.4 (continued)

- 22 -

Resolved that the foregoing by-law is hereby enacted by the directors of the Corporation, pursuant to the Ontario *Business Corporations Act* as evidenced by the respective signatures hereto of all the directors.

Dated the day of *(year)*

In lieu of confirmation at a general meeting of the shareholders, we the undersigned, being all of the shareholders of the Corporation entitled to vote at a meeting of shareholders, hereby confirm in writing the foregoing by-law in accordance with the Ontario *Business Corporations Act*.

Dated the day of *(year)*

6.5 (Ontario) *Business Corporations Act* By-law (For 1 Director—1 Shareholder Corporations)

DYE & DURHAM

D.238
ONTARIO CORPORATION

BY-LAW

for use under the Ontario *Business Corporations Act*

For 1 Director — 1 Shareholder Corporations

Revised 1999

This form of by-law is suitable for use by non-offering corporations incorporated pursuant to the Ontario Business Corporations Act and having only one (1) shareholder and only one (1) director.

It has been designed for use by the typical "one person" corporation and contains those provisions which have been found to be most applicable for the majority of such companies.

Depending on the requirements, additions to or deletions from this by-law may be necessary prior to its use and the incorporator is advised to consult with legal counsel before completion.

If for any reason, the number of shareholders or directors of the corporation using this by-law is increased, a revised general by-law should be adopted. **An alternate and more detailed form of by-law (D.31) suitable for corporations with more than one shareholder or more than one director is available.**

*Section 10.01 **(Repeal)** of this by-law should be reviewed by the incorporator and completed as the circumstances require.*

DYE & DURHAM CO. INC.

OTTAWA	TORONTO	LONDON
739-8200	321-1000	685-0101
(Toll Free: 1-800-267-2718)	(Toll Free: 1-800-668-9011)	(Toll Free: 1-800-265-4687)

6.5 (continued)

BY-LAW NO. 1

A by-law relating generally to the conduct of the business and affairs of

(herein called the "Corporation")

CONTENTS

1. Interpretation
2. Director
3. Disclosure and Indemnification
4. Officers
5. Meetings of Shareholders
6. Notices
7. Execution of Documents
8. Financial Year
9. Effective Date
10. Repeal

BE IT ENACTED as a by-law of the Corporation as follows:

1. INTERPRETATION

1.01 In this by-law and all other by-laws and resolutions of the Corporation, unless the context otherwise requires:

(a) "Act" means the Ontario *Business Corporations Act* together with the Regulations made pursuant thereto and any statute or regulations that may be substituted therefor, as amended from time to time;

(b) "articles" means the articles of incorporation of the Corporation as amended from time to time;

(c) "board" means the director acting as a board;

(d) "by-laws" means this by-law and all other by-laws of the Corporation as amended from time to time, and from time to time in force and effect;

(e) "Corporation" means this Corporation.

1.02 In this by-law where the context requires, words importing the singular include the plural and vice versa and words importing gender include the masculine, feminine and neuter genders.

6.5 (continued)

1.03 Save as aforesaid, all the words and terms appearing in this by-law shall have the same definitions and application as in the Act.

2. DIRECTOR

2.01 Powers - The business and affairs of the Corporation shall be managed or supervised by a board composed of one director who may exercise all such powers and do all such acts and things as may be exercised or done by the Corporation and are not by the by-laws or by the Act expressly directed or required to be done by the Corporation at meetings of the shareholder.

2.02 Place of Meetings - Meetings of the board may be held at any place within or outside Ontario and it shall not be necessary that, in any financial year of the Corporation, a majority of the meetings of the board be held at a place within Canada.

2.03 Resolution in lieu of Meeting - A resolution in writing, signed by the sole director, is as valid as if it had been passed at a meeting of the director. A copy of every such resolution shall be kept with the minutes of the proceedings of the director.

2.04 Resident Canadian - Except where the Corporation is a non-resident Corporation, the director shall be a resident Canadian.

2.05 Qualifications - No person shall be qualified for election as the director of the Corporation if he is less than 18 years of age; if he is of unsound mind and has been so found by a court in Canada or elsewhere; if he is not an individual; or if he has the status of a bankrupt.

2.06 Election and Term - The election of the director shall take place at the first meeting of shareholders and at each succeeding annual meeting at which an election of the director is required. The director shall hold office for an expressly stated term, which shall expire not later than the close of the third annual meeting of shareholders following his election. A director not elected for an expressly stated term ceases to hold office at the close of the first annual meeting of shareholders following his election. The incumbent director, if qualified, shall be eligible for re-election. If an election of the director is not held at the proper time, the incumbent director shall continue in office until his successor is elected.

6.5 (continued)

2.07 Vacancy - If a vacancy occurs on the board, the shareholder shall forthwith fill the vacancy.

3. DISCLOSURE AND INDEMNIFICATION

3.01 Disclosure of Interests in Contracts - Every director or officer of the Corporation who is a party to a material contract or transaction or proposed material contract or transaction with the Corporation, or is a director or officer of or has a material interest in any person who is a party to a material contract or transaction or proposed material contract or transaction with the Corporation, shall disclose in writing to the Corporation or request to have entered in the minutes of the meeting of directors the nature and extent of his interest at the time and in the manner required by the Act. Any such contract or proposed contract shall be referred to the board or shareholders for approval even if such contract is one that in the ordinary course of the Corporation's business would not require approval by the board or the shareholders, and a director interested in a contract so referred to the board shall not vote on any resolution to approve the same except as provided by the Act.

3.02 Indemnity of Directors and Officers - Subject to the provisions of the Act, the Corporation shall indemnify a director or officer of the Corporation, a former director or officer of the Corporation, or a person who acts or acted at the Corporation's request as a director or officer of a body corporate of which the Corporation is or was a shareholder or creditor, and his heirs and legal representatives, against all costs, charges and expenses, including an amount paid to settle an action or satisfy a judgment, reasonably incurred by him in respect of any civil, criminal or administrative action or proceeding to which he is made a party by reason of being or having been a director or officer of such Corporation or body corporate if

(a) he acted honestly and in good faith with a view to the best interests of the Corporation; and

(b) in the case of a criminal or administrative action or proceeding that is enforced by a monetary penalty, he had reasonable grounds for believing that his conduct was lawful.

6.5 (continued)

4. OFFICERS

4.01 Appointment - Subject to the provisions of the Act, the board may from time to time appoint a president, one or more vice-presidents (to which title may be added words indicating seniority or function), a secretary, a treasurer and such other officers as the board may determine, including one or more assistants to any of the officers so appointed. One person may hold more than one office.

4.02 Term, Remuneration and Removal - The terms of employment and remuneration of all officers elected or appointed by the board (including the president) shall be determined from time to time by resolution of the board. The fact that any officer or employee is a director or shareholder of the Corporation shall not disqualify him from receiving such remuneration as may be determined. All officers, in the absence of agreement to the contrary, shall be subject to removal by resolution of the board at any time with or without cause.

4.03 President - The president shall be the chief executive officer of the Corporation and as such shall, subject to the provisions of the Act, have the general supervision of the business and affairs of the Corporation, and he shall have such other powers and duties as the board may specify.

4.04 Secretary - The secretary shall attend all meetings of the board and shareholders and shall enter or cause to be entered in books kept for that purpose, minutes of all proceedings at such meetings and all resolutions passed and consented to by the director and all resolutions of the shareholder; he shall give, or cause to be given, when instructed, notices required to be given to the shareholder, the director and the auditor; he shall be the custodian of the stamp or mechanical device generally used for affixing the corporate seal of the Corporation and all books, papers, records, documents and other instruments belonging to the Corporation; and he shall perform such other duties as may from time to time be prescribed by the board.

4.05 Other Officers - The duties of all other officers of the Corporation shall be such as the terms of their engagement call for or the board requires of them. Any of the powers and duties of an officer to whom an assistant has been appointed may be exercised and performed by such assistant, unless the board otherwise directs.

6.5 (continued)

D&D (No. D.238)
BY-LAW—ONTARIO CORP. (1 DIRECTOR)
Revised 1994

5. MEETINGS OF THE SHAREHOLDER

5.01 Annual Meetings - Subject to Section 5.05 herein, the director shall call the first annual meetings of the shareholder not later than eighteen months after the Corporation comes into existence and, subsequently, not later than fifteen months after holding the last preceding annual meeting, for the purpose of receiving the reports and statements required by the Act to be laid before the annual meeting, electing the director, appointing auditors and fixing or authorizing the board to fix their remuneration, and for the transaction of such other business as may properly be brought before the meeting.

5.02 Special Meetings - The board may at any time call a special meeting of the shareholder for the transaction of any business which may properly be brought before such meeting of the shareholder.

5.03 Place of Meetings - Meetings of the shareholder shall be held at the registered office of the Corporation, or at such other place within or outside of Ontario as the board may determine.

5.04 Joint Shareholders - If shares are held jointly by two or more persons, any one of them present at a meeting of shareholders may, in the absence of the other, vote in respect of such share or shares; but, if more than one shall vote such shares, they shall vote together as one on the share or shares jointly held by them.

5.05 Resolution in Lieu of Meeting - Except where a written statement with resect to the subject matter of the resolution is submitted by the director or the auditors in accordance with the Act,

(a) a resolution in writing signed by the shareholder entitled to vote on that resolution at a meeting of the shareholder is as valid as if it had been passed at a meeting of the shareholder; and

(b) a resolution in writing dealing with any matter required by the Act to be dealt with at a meeting of the shareholder, and signed by the shareholder entitled to vote at that meeting, satisfies all the requirements of the Act relating to that meeting of shareholder.

6.5 (continued)

6. NOTICES

6.01 Method of Giving Notice - Any notice, communication or other document required by the Act, the regulations, the articles or the by-laws to be given by the Corporation to a shareholder, director, officer, or auditor of the Corporation under any provision of the Act, the articles or by-laws or otherwise shall be sufficiently given if delivered personally to the person to whom it is to be given or if delivered to his recorded address or if mailed to him at his recorded address by prepaid ordinary mail or if sent to him at his recorded address by any means of any prepaid transmitted or recorded communication. A notice so delivered shall be deemed to have been given when it is delivered personally or delivered to the recorded address as aforesaid; a notice so mailed shall be deemed to have been received on the fifth day after mailing; and a notice so sent by any means of transmitted or recorded communication shall be deemed to have been given when dispatched or delivered to the appropriate communication company or agency or its representative for dispatch. The secretary may change or cause to be changed the recorded address of any shareholder, director, officer or auditor of the Corporation in accordance with any information believed by him to be reliable. The recorded address of a director shall be his latest address as shown in the records of the Corporation or in the most recent notice filed under the Ontario *Corporations Information Act*, whichever is the more current.

6.02 Computation of Time - In computing the date when notice must be given under any provision requiring a specified number of days' notice of any meeting or other event, "day" means a clear day and a period of days shall be deemed to commence on the day following the event that began the period and shall be deemed to terminate at midnight of the last day of the period except that if the last day of the period falls on a Sunday or holiday the period shall terminate at midnight of the day next following that is not a Sunday or holiday.

6.03 Omissions and Errors - The accidental omission to give any notice to any shareholder, director, officer or auditor, or the non-receipt of any notice by any shareholder, director, officer or auditor or any error in any notice not affecting the substance thereof shall not invalidate any action taken at any meeting held pursuant to such notice or otherwise founded thereon.

6.5 (continued)

6.04 Notice to Joint Shareholders - All notices with respect to any shares registered in more than one name may, if more than one address appears on the records of the Corporation in respect of such joint holding, be given to such joint shareholders at the first address so appearing, and notice so given shall be sufficient notice to all the holders of such shares.

6.05 Persons Entitled by Death or Operation of Law - Every person who by operation of law, by transfer or the death of a shareholder or otherwise becomes entitled to shares is bound by every notice in respect of such shares which has been duly given to the registered holder from whom he derives title prior to his name and address being entered on the records of the Corporation (whether such notice was given before or after the happening of the event upon which he became so entitled) and prior to his furnishing to the Corporation the proof of authority or evidence of his entitlement prescribed by the Act.

6.06 Waiver of Notice - Any shareholder (or his duly appointed proxy), director, officer or auditor may waive any notice or abridge the time required for any notice required to be given under any provision of the Act, the articles or by-laws of the Corporation or otherwise, and such waiver or abridgement, whether given before or after the meeting or other event of which notice is required to be given, shall cure any default in the giving or in the time of such notice, as the case may be. Any such waiver or abridgement shall be in writing except a waiver of notice of a meeting of shareholders or of the board which may be given in any manner.

6.07 Signatures to Notices - The signatures to any notice to be given by the Corporation may be written, stamped, typewritten or printed or partly written, stamped, typewritten or printed.

7. EXECUTION OF DOCUMENTS

7.01 Signing Officers - Deeds, transfers, assignments, contracts and obligations of the Corporation may be signed by the president. Notwithstanding this, the board may at any time and from time to time direct the manner in which and the person or persons by whom any particular deed, transfer, contract or obligation or any class of deeds, transfers, contracts or obligations may be signed.

6.5 (continued)

7.02 Seal - Any person authorized to sign any document may affix the corporate seal thereto.

8. FINANCIAL YEAR

8.01 Financial Year - The financial year of the Corporation shall end on the day of in each year until changed by a resolution of the board.

9. EFFECTIVE DATE

9.01 Effective Date - This by-law shall come into force when enacted by the director, subject to the provisions of the Act.

10. REPEAL

(Delete this section if inapplicable.)

10.01 Repeal - Upon this by-law coming into force, By-law Number of the Corporation is repealed provided that such repeal shall not affect the previous operation of such by-law so repealed or affect the validity of any act done or right, privilege, obligation or liability acquired or incurred under the validity of any contract or agreement made pursuant to any such by-law prior to its repeal.

6.5 (continued)

ENACTED by the board the ______ day of ______ *(year)* .

______________________ President

______________________ Secretary

(Corporate Seal)

CONFIRMED by the sole shareholder ______ day of ______ *(year)* .

______________________ Secretary

(Corporate Seal)

Resolved that the foregoing by-law is hereby enacted by the sole director of the Corporation, pursuant to the Ontario Business Corporations Act as evidenced by his signature hereto.

Dated the ______ day of ______ *(year)* .

____

The foregoing by-law is hereby confirmed by the sole shareholder of the Corporation, pursuant to the Ontario Business Corporations Act as evidenced by his signature hereto.

Dated the ______ day of ______ *(year)* .

____

6.6 Declaration of Trust

DECLARATION OF TRUST

KNOW ALL MEN BY THESE PRESENTS

THAT I, the undersigned Trustee, hereby declare and acknowledge that I hold ____________* (common) shares in the capital stock of:

____

(hereinafer called the "Corporation")

as nominee of and in trust for

____

(hereinafter called the "Beneficial Owner")

and that I did not contribute directly or indirectly to the purchase price of the said shares; and that I have no beneficial interest in the said shares; and that all dividends, profits and advantages accruing on the said shares or arising therefrom including any proceeds of or from the sale or other disposition thereof are and shall be held by me and my heirs, executors and administrators for the sole and only use and benefit of the Beneficial Owner; and I agree, on demand, to transfer the said shares to the Beneficial Owner or to his nominee and do hereby irrevocably appoint the Beneficial Owner my true and lawful attorney for me and in my name to so transfer and set over the said shares on the books of registration; and I hereby authorize and direct the Corporation to pay any and all dividends or other distributions from time to time paid or payable in or in respect of the said shares to the Beneficial Owner.

IN WITNESS WHEREOF I have hereunto set my hand and seal this ______________.

SIGNED, SEALED AND DELIVERED)
in the presence of:)
)
______________________) ______________________ LS

THE undersigned hereby acknowledges that he is the Beneficial Owner of the shares referred to in the above declaration of trust and hereby agrees to and confirms the authorization and direction therein contained and agrees to indemnify and save harmless the Trustee against all liabilities of the Trustee that arise by reason of the Trustee being the registered holder of the said shares and/or acting as a Director and/or acting as an Officer of the Corporation.

IN WITNESS WHEREOF the undersigned has executed these presents this ____________.

SIGNED, SEALED AND DELIVERED)
in the presence of:)
)
______________________) ______________________ LS

---

*Amend description to suit situation

6.7 Directors' Register

DIRECTORS' REGISTER

NAME	INITIALS	ELECTED		RETIRED		OFFICE HELD
		DATE	M.B. FOLIO	DATE	M.B. FOLIO	

D & D

6.8 Officers' Register

OFFICERS' REGISTER

NAME AND ADDRESS	OFFICE HELD	DATE BECAME AN OFFICER			DATE CEASED TO BE AN OFFICER		
		DA	MO	YR	DA	MO	YR

D & D

6.9 Register of Debt Obligations

REGISTER OF DEBT OBLIGATIONS

Date of Debt	Nature of Debt Obligation Incl. Class or Series	Name and Address of Holder of Debt Obligation	Principal Amount of Debt Obligation	Date Discharged

DYE & DURHAM CO. LIMITED
DEBT OBLIGATIONS

6.10 Stock Transfer Register

STOCK TRANSFER REGISTER

D&D

TRANSFER NUMBER	DATE			CLASS OF SHARES	CERTIFICATES SURRENDERED		TRANSFEROR		TRANSFEREE		NEW CERTIFICATES ISSUED	
	MONTH	DAY	YEAR		NO.	SHARES	TRANSFERRED FROM	LEDGER FOLIO	TRANSFERRED TO	LEDGER FOLIO	NO.	SHARES

6.11 Shareholders' Register

SHAREHOLDERS' REGISTER

DATE		NAME	INITIALS	SHARES HELD	
				CLASS	CLASS

D & D

6.12 Shareholders' Ledger

SHAREHOLDERS' LEDGER

NAME

ADDRESS

OCCUPATION

PHONE NOS. - OFFICE: RESIDENCE: CLASS OF SHARES

DATE	CERT. No.	TRANS No.	TO OR FROM WHOM	FOLIO	SHARES		
					TRANS-FERRED	ACQUIRED	BAL. HELD

D 3 D

6.13 Canadian Imperial Bank of Commerce—Resolution of Directors Regarding Banking and Security

6818-96/03

CIBC

Account Number ______________________

Account Name ______________________

Trade Name ______________________

Use for Incorporated Businesses

Contents:

- Resolution Re: Banking and Security
- Certificate of Officers and Directors
- Borrowing By-Law

Complete the appropriate sections only. Delete and initial if not appropriate.

6.13 (continued)

6818-96/03

General Banking Resolution

Resolution of the board of Directors of ______________________________

Also insert trade name, if applicable.

______________________________ (the "Corporation")

[1] It is preferable that official positions be designated rather than the names of the authorized signing officers.

[2] Insert "one", "two", etc. as appropriate.

Resolved that:

1. **CIBC as banker.** The Corporation appoints **Canadian Imperial Bank of Commerce** ("CIBC") as its banker.

2. **Authorized Signing Officers.** [1] ______________________________

   or any [2] __________ of them (each being an "Authorized Signing Officer") is/are authorized for and on behalf of the Corporation from time to time to:

   a) sign or endorse any cheques, promissory notes and evidences of indebtedness, whether or not an overdraft is created in any Account as a result;
   b) provide any authority to any CIBC officer to accept and/or pay any and all drafts, bills of exchange or promissory notes on the Corporation's behalf;
   c) enter into any securities-related transactions with CIBC or any of its securities subsidiaries;
   d) receive from CIBC or any of its subsidiaries any stocks, bonds or other property of our firm;
   e) sign receipts for and orders relating to any of the Corporation's property held by or on behalf of CIBC or any of its subsidiaries;
   f) borrow money or otherwise obtain credit from CIBC by way of loans, advances, overdrafts or otherwise; and to give security over any or all of the Corporation's currently owned or after-acquired, real or personal, movable or immovable property to secure any such credit obtained by CIBC, and to sign all documents necessary to do so;
   g) guarantee to CIBC the indebtedness and liability of any person, firm or corporation, in either a limited or unlimited amount and either with or without security; and
   h) sign any agreement with or authority to CIBC or any of its subsidiaries relating to the Corporation's banking and financial services needs, whether generally or with regard to any particular transaction (including, among other things, (i) the Account Operation Agreement; (ii) interest rate, foreign exchange and commodity-related banking arrangements, and (iii) CIBC's service agreements for centralized cash control, third party payments, electronic data interchange, money market trader and any other of CIBC's cash management services).

3. **Delegation of Authority.** Any [2] __________ of the Authorized Signing Officers may, from time to time, delegate authority in writing to one or more delegatees to do any or all of the actions described in clause 2. Such delegation may be for either a limited or unlimited period of time. The delegation letter will identify by name and title, and contain specimen signatures of, each delegatee.

4. **Deposits, etc.** Any of the Authorized Signing Officers as well as any of the following [1] ____________________

   ____

   is authorized for and on behalf of the Corporation from time to time to negotiate for deposit with CIBC (but for the credit of the Account only) any and all cheques, promissory notes, bills of exchange and payment orders.

   The Corporation's endorsement on any item deposited to an Account may be made by means of a rubber stamp or any other device.

5. **Trade name.** If the Corporation operates any Account under one or more business or trade names, the terms of this resolution apply to each such Account.

6. **Accounts.** In this resolution, the phrase "Account" means each and every account of the Corporation maintained with CIBC, whether in a trade name or otherwise;

7. **CIBC's reliance.** CIBC may rely on everything that is done and on all documents signed on the Corporation's behalf in accordance with this resolution. All such documents will be valid and binding upon the Corporation whether or not the Corporation's corporate seal (if there is one) has been placed on any such document.

8. **Copy of this Resolution.** The Corporation will provide CIBC with a certified true copy of this resolution and a list of the names of all individuals authorized to act in accordance with this resolution, as well as specimens of their signatures. Each office and branch of CIBC may act in accordance with those documents and this resolution until due written notice has been given to and received by a responsible CIBC officer.

We certify that the above is a true copy of a resolution passed by the Board of Directors of the Corporation on __________

______________________________ and recorded in the Minute Book of the proceedings of the Board of Directors, and that the said resolution is now in full force and effect.

Dated ____________________ ____________________ ____________________

Signature of President Signature of Secretary

6.13 (continued)

6818-96/03

Certificate of Officers and Directors

for corporations

We certify on behalf of ____ (the "Company") that:

(1) Last name and position or title of each officer of the Company.

1. **Officers.** The following are the officers of the Company [(1)]

NAME	TITLE	NAME	TITLE

(2) Last name only of each director of the Company.

2. **Directors.** The following are the directors of the Company [(2)]

________________________ ________________________

________________________ ________________________

________________________ ________________________

3. **Borrowing Powers.** Either the directors of the Company may, without authorization of the shareholders, or all necessary corporate action has been taken to authorize the directors of the company to:
   a) borrow money or otherwise obtain credit upon the credit of the Company;
   b) issue, reissue, sell or pledge debt obligations of the Company;
   c) give a guarantee on behalf of the Company to secure performance of an obligation of any person;
   d) mortgage, hypothecate, pledge, assign, transfer or otherwise create a security interest in all or any property of the Company, currently owned or subsequently acquired, to secure any obligation of the Company; and
   e) delegate any of the powers of the directors in regard to the foregoing to one or more directors, a committee of directors or one or more officers of the Company.

4. **Notice of Changes.** The Company undertakes to notify **Canadian Imperial Bank of Commerce** ("CIBC") of any changes respecting the powers of the Company or its directors or officers to do any of the things listed in paragraph 3. The Company further undertakes to notify CIBC of any changes respecting (i) the authority of any director, officer or employee to sign on the Company's behalf or (ii) any resolutions of the directors or shareholders of, or any unanimous shareholder agreement relating to, the Company of which CIBC holds copies.

5. **Reliance of CIBC.** Each branch of CIBC with which any dealings are had by the Company may rely upon this certificate and upon any and all documents referred to herein until notice to the contrary or of any change has been given in writing to the Manager or Acting Manager of such branch.

Dated ________________ ________________________ ________________________

Signature of President Signature of Secretary

NOTE: If the Charter Documents (Articles of Incorporation, Letters Patent, Memorandum of Association, etc.) or any amendments thereto, the by-laws or any unanimous shareholder agreement require the authorization of the shareholders or other persons in order to exercise any of the powers listed in paragraph 3, then certified copies of (i) the provisions requiring the authorization and (ii) the authorization given by the shareholders or such other persons should be referred to the supervising office.

6.13 (continued)

6818 96/03

Borrowing By-Law

for corporations referred to in BMO IV-1-3

By-Law Number ______________________

A By-Law respecting the borrowing of money, the issuing of securities and the securing of liabilities by ____________

____ (the "Company").

Be it enacted as a By-Law of the Company as follows.

The directors of the Company may from time to time:

a) borrow money or otherwise obtain credit upon the credit of the Company in such amounts and upon such terms as may be considered advisable;
b) issue, reissue, sell or pledge debt obligations of the Company, including without limitation, bonds, debentures, debenture stock, notes or other securities or obligations of the Company, whether secured or unsecured for such sums, upon such terms, covenants and conditions and at such prices as may be deemed expedient;
c) charge, mortgage, hypothecate, pledge, assign, transfer or otherwise create a security interest in all or any currently owned or subsequently acquired real or personal, movable or immovable property of the Company, including among other things, book debts and unpaid calls, rights, powers, franchises and undertaking, to secure any money borrowed or any other debt or liability of the Company;
d) guarantee to CIBC the indebtedness and liability of any person, firm or corporation, in either a limited or unlimited amount and either with or without security; and
e) delegate to such one or more of the officers and directors of the Company as may be designated by the directors all or any of the powers conferred by the foregoing clauses of this By-Law to such extent and in such manner as the directors shall determine at the time of each delegation

Passed by the directors on ____

______________________ Signature of President ______________________ Signature of Secretary

We certify that the foregoing is a true copy of a By-Law duly passed by the directors on ______________________

______________________ and duly confirmed by the shareholders/members and recorded in the Minute Book of the proceedings of the directors and shareholders/members of the Company, and that the By-Law is now in full force and effect.

Dated ______________________ ______________________ Signature of President ______________________ Signature of Secretary

6.14 Certificate as to Non-Adoption of a Corporate Seal

**CERTIFICATE AS TO NON-ADOPTION
OF A CORPORATE SEAL**

TO: (name and branch of bank)

Re: (name of corporation)

I, the undersigned (insert title, i.e. President, Secretary) of the Corporation, do hereby certify to you that:

1. the Corporation has not adopted a corporate seal; and
2. there are no provisions in the articles of incorporation, by-laws or any of the other constating documents requiring the Corporation to have a seal.

DATED this day of

Witness	(title of officer signing)

6.15 Initial Return/Notice of Change by an Ontario Corporation—*Corporations Information Act*—Form 1

Ontario Ministry of Consumer and Business Services / Ministère des Services aux consommateurs et aux entreprises
Companies Branch, 393 University Ave Suite 200, Toronto ON M5G 2M2 / Direction des compagnies, 393 ave University, bureau 200, Toronto ON M5G 2M2

For Ministry Use Only / À l'usage du ministère seulement
Page/Page 1 of/de ______

Form 1 - Ontario Corporation/
Formule 1 - Personnes morales en Ontario

Initial Return/Notice of Change/
Rapport initial/Avis de modification
Corporations Information Act/Loi sur les renseignements exigés des personnes morales

Please type or print all information in block capital letters using black ink.
Prière de dactylographier les renseignements ou de les écrire en caractères d'imprimerie à l'encre noire.

1.

	Initial Return / Rapport initial	Notice of Change / Avis de modification
Business Corporation/ Société par actions	☐	☐
Not-For-Profit Corporation/ Personne morale sans but lucratif	☐	☐

For Ministry Use Only / À l'usage du ministère seulement ☐

2. Ontario Corporation Number / Numéro matricule de la personne morale en Ontario ☐

3. Date of Incorporation or Amalgamation/ Date de constitution ou fusion — Year/Année ☐ Month/Mois ☐ Day/Jour ☐

For Ministry Use Only / À l'usage du ministère seulement

4. Corporation Name Including Punctuation/Raison sociale de la personne morale, y compris la ponctuation

5. Address of Registered or Head Office/Adresse d'affaires ou du siège social

For Ministry Use Only/ À l'usage du ministère seulement

c/o / a/s

Street Number/Numéro civique — Street Name/Nom de la rue — Suite/Bureau

Street Name (cont'd)/Nom de la rue (suite)

City/Town/Ville — **ONTARIO, CANADA**

Postal Code/Code postal

6. Mailing Address/Adresse postale

☐ Same as Registered or Head Office/ Même que celle du siège social

☐ Not Applicable/ Ne s'applique pas

Street Number/Numéro civique

Street Name/Nom de la rue — Suite/Bureau

Street Name (cont'd)/Nom de la rue (suite)

City/Town/Ville

Province, State/Province, État — Country/Pays — Postal Code/Code postal

7. Language of Preference/Langue préférée — English - Anglais ☐ French - Français ☐

8. **Information on Directors/Officers must be completed on Schedule A as requested.** If additional space is required, photocopy Schedule A./**Les renseignements sur les administrateurs ou les dirigeants doivent être fournis dans l'annexe A, tel que demandé.** Si vous avez besoin de plus d'espace, vous pouvez photocopier l'annexe A.

Number of Schedule A(s) submitted/Nombre d'annexes A présentées ☐ (At least one Schedule A must be submitted/Au moins une annexe A doit être présentée)

9. (Print or type name in full of the person authorizing filing / Dactylographier ou inscrire le prénom et le nom en caractères d'imprimerie de la personne qui autorise l'enregistrement)

I/Je ______

certify that the information set out herein, is true and correct.
atteste que les renseignements précités sont véridiques et exacts.

Check appropriate box
Cocher la case pertinente

D) ☐ Director/Administrateur

O) ☐ Officer /Dirigeant

P) ☐ Other individual having knowledge of the affairs of the Corporation/Autre personne ayant connaissance des activités de la personne morale

NOTE/REMARQUE: Sections 13 and 14 of the **Corporations Information Act** provide penalties for making false or misleading statements or omissions. Les articles 13 et 14 de la **Loi sur les renseignements exigés des personnes morales** prévoient des peines en cas de déclaration fausse ou trompeuse, ou d'omission.

FOR MINISTRY USE ONLY / À L'USAGE DU MINISTÈRE SEULEMENT ☐ See Deficiency Letter enclosed / Voir l'avis d'insuffisance ci-joint

07200(03/01)

6.15 (continued)

This information is being collected under the authority of The Corporations Information Act for the purpose of maintaining a public data base of corporate information.

La Loi sur les renseignements exigés des personnes morales autorise la collecte de ces renseignements pour constituer une banque de données accessible au public.

The completed form must be mailed or delivered to:
Ministry of Consumer and Business Services
Companies Branch
393 University Ave Suite 200
Toronto ON M5G 2M2

La formule dûment remplie doit être envoyée par la poste ou livrée à l'adresse suivante :
Ministère des Services aux consommateurs et aux entreprises
Direction des compagnies
393 ave University, bureau 200
Toronto ON M5G 2M2

6.16 Schedule A to *Corporations Information Act*—Form 1

Form 1 - Ontario Corporation/Formule 1 - Personnes morales en Ontario

Schedule A/Annexe A

For Ministry Use Only
À l'usage du ministère seulement
Page/Page _____ of/de _____

Please type or print all information in block capital letters using black ink.
Prière de dactylographier les renseignements ou de les écrire en caractères d'imprimerie à l'encre noire.

For Ministry Use Only / À l'usage du ministère seulement	Ontario Corporation Number / Numéro matricule de la personne morale en Ontario	Date of Incorporation or Amalgamation / Date de constitution ou fusion (Year/Année Month/Mois Day/Jour)	For Ministry Use Only / À l'usage du ministère seulement

DIRECTOR / OFFICER INFORMATION - RENSEIGNEMENTS RELATIFS AUX ADMINISTRATEURS/DIRIGEANTS

Full Name and Address for Service/Nom et domicile élu

Last Name/Nom de famille | First Name/Prénom | Middle Names/Autres prenoms

Street Number/Numéro civique | Suite/Bureau

Street Name/Nom de la rue

Street Name (cont'd)/Nom de la rue (suite)

City/Town/Ville

Province, State/Province, État | Country/Pays | Postal Code/Code postal

*OTHER TITLES (Please Specify) / *Autres titres (Veuillez préciser)

Chair	☐ Président du conseil
Chair Person	☐ Président du conseil
Chairman	☐ Président du conseil
Chairwoman	☐ Président du conseil
Vice-Chair	☐ Vice-président du conseil
Vice-President	☐ Vice-président
Assistant Secretary	☐ Secrétaire adjoint
Assistant Treasurer	☐ Trésorier adjoint
Chief Manager	☐ Directeur exécutif
Executive Director	☐ Directeur administratif
Managing Director	☐ Administrateur délégué
Chief Executive Officer	☐ Directeur général
Chief Financial Officer	☐ Agent en chef des finances
Chief Information Officer	☐ Directeur général de l'information
Chief Operating Officer	☐ Administrateur en chef des opérations
Chief Administrative Officer	☐ Directeur général de l'administration
Comptroller	☐ Contrôleur
Authorized Signing Officer	☐ Signataire autorisé
Other (Untitled)	☐ Autre (sans titre)

Director Information/Renseignements relatifs aux administrateurs

Resident Canadian/Résident canadien ☐ YES/OUI ☐ NO/NON
(Resident Canadian applies to directors of business corporations only.)/(Résident canadien ne s'applique qu'aux administrateurs de sociétés par actions)

Date Elected/Date d'élection (Year/Année Month/Mois Day/Jour) | Date Ceased/Date de cessation (Year/Année Month/Mois Day/Jour)

Officer Information/Renseignements relatifs aux dirigeants

	PRESIDENT/PRÉSIDENT (Year/Année Month/Mois Day/Jour)	SECRETARY/SECRÉTAIRE (Year/Année Month/Mois Day/Jour)	TREASURER/TRÉSORIER (Year/Année Month/Mois Day/Jour)	GENERAL MANAGER/DIRECTEUR GÉNÉRAL (Year/Année Month/Mois Day/Jour)	*OTHER/AUTRE (Year/Année Month/Mois Day/Jour)
Date Appointed/Date de nomination					
Date Ceased/Date de cessation					

DIRECTOR / OFFICER INFORMATION - RENSEIGNEMENTS RELATIFS AUX ADMINISTRATEURS/DIRIGEANTS

Full Name and Address for Service/Nom et domicile élu

Last Name/Nom de famille | First Name/Prénom | Middle Names/Autres prénoms

Street Number/Numéro civique | Suite/Bureau

Street Name/Nom de la rue

Street Name (cont'd)/Nom de la rue (suite)

City/Town/Ville

Province, State/Province, État | Country/Pays | Postal Code/Code postal

*OTHER TITLES (Please Specify) / *Autres titres (Veuillez préciser)

Chair	☐ Président du conseil
Chair Person	☐ Président du conseil
Chairman	☐ Président du conseil
Chairwoman	☐ Président du conseil
Vice-Chair	☐ Vice-président du conseil
Vice-President	☐ Vice-président
Assistant Secretary	☐ Secrétaire adjoint
Assistant Treasurer	☐ Trésorier adjoint
Chief Manager	☐ Directeur exécutif
Executive Director	☐ Directeur administratif
Managing Director	☐ Administrateur délégué
Chief Executive Officer	☐ Directeur général
Chief Financial Officer	☐ Agent en chef des finances
Chief Information Officer	☐ Directeur général de l'information
Chief Operating Officer	☐ Administrateur en chef des opérations
Chief Administrative Officer	☐ Directeur général de l'administration
Comptroller	☐ Contrôleur
Authorized Signing Officer	☐ Signataire autorisé
Other (Untitled)	☐ Autre (sans titre)

Director Information/Renseignements relatifs aux administrateurs

Resident Canadian/Résident canadien ☐ YES/OUI ☐ NO/NON
(Resident Canadian applies to directors of business corporations only.)/(Résident canadien ne s'applique qu'aux administrateurs de sociétés par actions)

Date Elected/Date d'élection (Year/Année Month/Mois Day/Jour) | Date Ceased/Date de cessation (Year/Année Month/Mois Day/Jour)

Officer Information/Renseignements relatifs aux dirigeants

	PRESIDENT/PRÉSIDENT (Year/Année Month/Mois Day/Jour)	SECRETARY/SECRÉTAIRE (Year/Année Month/Mois Day/Jour)	TREASURER/TRÉSORIER (Year/Année Month/Mois Day/Jour)	GENERAL MANAGER/DIRECTEUR GÉNÉRAL (Year/Année Month/Mois Day/Jour)	*OTHER/AUTRE (Year/Année Month/Mois Day/Jour)
Date Appointed/Date de nomination					
Date Ceased/Date de cessation					

For Ministry Use Only
À l'usage du ministère seulement

Initials/Paraphes
LI ____ QA ____
DE ____ VER ____

6.16 (continued)

COMPLETION OF SCHEDULE A

Complete all applicable items on Schedule A in full, including the Ontario Corporation Number and Date of Incorporation or Amalgamation.

Schedule A must report all information pertaining to directors and the five most senior officers of the corporation and must include all changes that have taken place since the filing of the initial return, special notice, annual return or most recent notice of change.

One director/senior officer information section must be completed for each individual who is a director and/or senior officer of the corporation.

There must be a minimum of one director in a non-offering business corporation and a minimum of three directors in a not-for-profit corporation or an offering business corporation.

Not-for-profit corporations must also have a minimum of two senior officers, namely a president and a secretary, plus three directors.

DIRECTOR/OFFICER INFORMATION

The following two sections must be completed for each individual:

NAME
Complete the name in full, providing last, first, and middle name or initials.

ADDRESS
A full address for service is required for the individual. A box number is not acceptable.

Director Information

If the individual is a director, the next three sections must be completed.

Resident Canadian
This information is required for directors of business corporations only.

Specify whether the individual is a Resident Canadian by checking **yes** or **no**.

Date Elected
Complete the date on which the individual became a director.

Date Ceased
Insert the date the director ceased to hold his/her position.

If the date ceased has been completed, the date the director assumed his/her position must also be completed.

Officer Information

If the individual is one of the five most senior officers, the next two sections must be completed:

Date Five Most Senior Officers Appointed
Complete the date the individual was appointed as a senior officer under the appropriate title(s).
'Other Titles' includes other senior officers, if the senior officer is not the president, secretary, treasurer and general manager. Please note the dates for the position(s) shown on the pre-printed list. If the title is not included on the list, the "Other (untitled)" position title should be selected.

Date Officer Ceased
Insert the date the senior officer ceased to hold his/her position.
Insert the date an officer ceased to be one of the five most senior officers.

If the date ceased has been completed, the date the officer assumed his/her position must also be completed.

The completed form must be mailed or delivered to:

Ministry of Consumer and Commercial Relations
Companies Branch
393 University Ave Suite 200
Toronto ON M5G 2M2

6.17 Annual Return—*Corporations Tax Act*

Ontario Ministry of Finance
Corporations Tax Branch
PO Box 620
33 King Street West
Oshawa ON L1H 8E9

2000 **MCCR Annual Return and Guide**

Corporations Tax Act - Ministry of Finance (MOF)
Corporations Information Act - Ministry of Consumer and Commercial Relations (MCCR)

This **Annual Return** (page 1 and Schedule A or K) is for **Ontario-Business share-capital corporations** or **Foreign-Business share-capital corporations that have a licence to operate in Ontario** that want to file an Annual Return now in hard copy with the Ministry of Finance (MOF) and have either:

1) **filed a CT23 Corporations Tax Return (CT23)** or an **Exempt From Filing Corporations Tax Return Declaration (EFF Declaration)**, but have **not filed an Annual Return (AR)** in respect of that particular taxation year with the MOF or electronically with MCCR; **OR**
2) **have not filed a CT23** or an **EFF Declaration** or an **AR** (with the MOF or MCCR) in respect of a particular taxation year and want to file either a CT23 or EFF Declaration form later.

This return contains non-tax information collected under the authority of the *Corporations Information Act* for the purpose of maintaining a public database of corporate information.

Ministry Use

MCCR Annual Return Required? *(if above applies, check ✓ yes)* ☐ Yes ☐ No

Page 1 of 4

Corporation's Legal Name *(including punctuation)* and Mailing Address

Registered Head Office Address

Name of person to contact regarding this Return (MOF)	Telephone No.	Fax No.

Address of Principal Office in Ontario *(Extra-Provincial Corporations only)* (MCCR)

Former Corporation Name *(Extra-Provincial Corporations only)* ***Not Applicable*** ☐ (MCCR)

Information on Directors/Officers/Administrators must be completed on MCCR Schedule A or K as appropriate. If additional space is required for Schedule A, this schedule only may be photocopied. State number submitted (MCCR). ▶ No. of Schedule(s)

If there is **no change** to the Directors'/Officers'/Administrators' information previously submitted to MCCR, please check ☒ this box. Schedule(s) A and K are not required (MCCR). ▶ ☐ **No Change**

Ontario Corporations Tax Account No. (MOF)

Corporation's Taxation Year (MOF)

Start: year / month / day

End: year / month / day

Date of Incorporation or Amalgamation: year / month / day

Ontario Corporation No. (MCCR)

Canada Customs and Revenue Agency (formerly Revenue Canada) Business No. (MOF)

If applicable, enter: RC

Jurisdiction Incorporated

If not incorporated in Ontario, indicate the date Ontario business activity commenced and ceased:

Commenced: year / month / day

Ceased: year / month / day

(Not Applicable) ▶ ☐

Preferred Language / *Langue de préférence*

English / anglais ☐ French / français ☐

Ministry Use

Certification (MCCR)

I certify that all information set out in the **Annual Return** is true, correct and complete.

Name of Authorized Person *(Print clearly or type in full)*

Title: ☐ Director ☐ Officer ☐ Other individual having knowledge of the affairs of the Corporation

Note: Sections 13 and 14 of the *Corporations Information Act* provide penalties for making false or misleading statements or omissions.

(1) 1872 (00-06)

6.17 (continued)

Guide to the 2000 MCCR Annual Return

Page 2 of 4

The Ministry of Finance (MOF) prefers to have all corporations file a combined return (CT23 Corporations Tax and Annual Return). However, as outlined at the top of page one when this is not possible this stand-alone Annual Return may be used. The MOF is collecting this information on behalf of the Ministry of Consumer and Commercial Relations (MCCR). This collection process applies to corporations that have a taxation year ending on or after January 1, 2000.

How Can You File?

A corporation may complete and submit this Annual Return to the MOF at the address indicated on the top of page 1 or complete the electronic filing version of the Annual Return found through the MCCR website, www.ccr.gov.on.ca/mccr/companies.htm. A corporation that chooses one of these two options must file a CT23 or an EFF declaration form (if exempt from filing (EFF)) for the taxation year with the MOF.

When Must You File?

A corporation, with share capital that is required to file a CT23 (or is EFF) and an Annual Return, is required to deliver an Annual Return within six months after the end of the **corporation's first taxation year (enter start and end date on page 1)** of each calendar year. This applies whether the Annual Return is delivered to the MOF or electronically to the MCCR.

The Annual Return will be considered delivered on the date it is received by the MOF. The effective date of filing for the Annual Return is the date the information is updated in the Ontario Business Information System (ONBIS).

If the Annual Return is filed electronically during MCCR business hours, the date of receipt will be considered to be that day. Otherwise, the date of receipt will be the next business day of MCCR.

An Annual Return is considered filed if it is complete and has been recorded in the ONBIS.

Incomplete Annual Returns are considered to be deficient. MCCR will contact corporations regarding Annual Return deficiencies. The Annual Return will not be considered **filed** until the deficiency is corrected.

What Must You File?

Ontario-Business Corporations (OBCs) and Foreign-Business Corporations (FBCs) must complete all of the information requested on page 1. In addition, OBCs complete MCCR Schedule A and FBCs complete MCCR Schedule K, if there has been a change in the information previously submitted to MCCR.

All information in the Annual Return must be current as of the **date of delivery** to the MOF or to the MCCR.

Each corporation must keep an up-to-date paper or electronic record of the prescribed information set out in the return available for examination at its registered/head office or principal place of business in Ontario.

Complete all of the applicable fields on the appropriate MCCR schedule (A or K), ensuring that the Corporation's name includes all punctuation and that the Ontario Corporation Number (MCCR) is the number assigned by MCCR.

MCCR Schedule A must report current information on all directors and the five most senior officers of the corporation. Senior officers include the following positions or their equivalent: president, general manager, treasurer and secretary. A minimum of one director is required in a non-offering business corporation and a minimum of three directors is required for all others. Space is provided for information on two Director/Officer positions. If the box "Other (specify)" is applicable, in order to cease or change an officer previously reported under "Other Titles", cease the officer, then use a blank schedule "A" to add (if applicable) the new information.

MCCR Schedule K is for reporting current information on the Chief Officer/Manager and the Agent for Service for foreign corporations which have a licence endorsed under the *Extra-Provincial Corporations Act* to carry on business in Ontario.

What If You Need Help to Complete this Annual Return?

If you need help after reading this guide, please contact the Revenue Operations and Client Services Branch of the MOF at: English 1-800-263-7965, French 1-800-668-5821, TTY 1-800-263-7776.

07-1572 (00-04)

6.17 (continued)

MCCR

Schedule A

Page 3 of 4

Schedule A: Information on Ontario Corporations

(Corporations that are incorporated, continued or amalgamated under the *Ontario Business Corporations Act*)

To submit additional Director or Officer Information, please photocopy this page and attach the completed schedules with your return.

Identification

Corporation's Legal Name *(including punctuation)*	Ontario Corporation No. (MCCR)	Date of Incorporation or Amalgamation (year / month / day)

Director/Officer Information

Full Name and Address for Service

Last Name	First Name	Middle Name(s)	
Street Number and Name		Suite	
City/Town/Village	Province/State	Country	Postal/Zip Code

Director

Are you a Canadian resident? *(Applies to directors of business corporations only)*

☐ Yes ☐ No

Date Elected (year / month / day)

Date Ceased (year / month / day)

Officer

Indicate the appointment period for each of the following:

	Date Appointed (year / month / day)	Date Ceased (year / month / day)
President		
Secretary		
Treasurer		
General Manager		
Other *(specify)*		

Other Titles *(please specify)*:

☐ Chair
☐ Chair Person
☐ Chairman
☐ Chairwoman
☐ Vice-Chair
☐ Vice-President
☐ Assistant Secretary
☐ Assistant Treasurer
☐ Chief Manager
☐ Executive Director
☐ Managing Director
☐ Chief Executive Officer
☐ Chief Financial Officer
☐ Chief Information Officer
☐ Chief Operating Officer
☐ Chief Administrative Officer
☐ Comptroller
☐ Authorized Signing Officer
☐ Other (untitled)

Director/Officer Information

Full Name and Address for Service

Last Name	First Name	Middle Name(s)	
Street Number and Name		Suite	
City/Town/Village	Province/State	Country	Postal/Zip Code

Director

Are you a Canadian resident? *(Applies to directors of business corporations only)*

☐ Yes ☐ No

Date Elected (year / month / day)

Date Ceased (year / month / day)

Officer

Indicate the appointment period for each of the following:

	Date Appointed (year / month / day)	Date Ceased (year / month / day)
President		
Secretary		
Treasurer		
General Manager		
Other *(specify)*		

Other Titles *(please specify)*:

☐ Chair
☐ Chair Person
☐ Chairman
☐ Chairwoman
☐ Vice-Chair
☐ Vice-President
☐ Assistant Secretary
☐ Assistant Treasurer
☐ Chief Manager
☐ Executive Director
☐ Managing Director
☐ Chief Executive Officer
☐ Chief Financial Officer
☐ Chief Information Officer
☐ Chief Operating Officer
☐ Chief Administrative Officer
☐ Comptroller
☐ Authorized Signing Officer
☐ Other (untitled)

Note: Sections 13 and 14 of the *Corporations Information Act* provide penalties for making false or misleading statements or omissions.

[illegible]

6.17 (continued)

MCCR

Schedule K: Information on Foreign Business Corporations

Schedule K

(Corporations that are incorporated, continued or amalgamated in a jurisdiction outside Canada)

Page 4 of 4

Only one Schedule K may be submitted. Please DO NOT photocopy.

Identification

Corporation's Legal Name (including punctuation)	Ontario Corporation No. (MCCR)	Date of Incorporation or Amalgamation (year / month / day)

Chief Officer/Manager Information

Name and Office Address of the Chief Officer/Manager in Ontario: *Not Applicable* ☐

Last Name	First Name	Middle Name(s)	
Street Number and Name		Suite	
City/Town/Village	Province: Ontario	Country: Canada	Postal Code

Indicate the appointment period for the position of Chief Officer/Manager: Date Appointed (year / month / day) Date Ceased (year / month / day)

Agent for Service Information

Indicate if the Agent for Service is an individual or a corporation:

Please check ☑ box if applicable ☐ **Individual**

Agent's Last Name	First Name	Middle Name(s)	
Street Number and Name		Suite	
City/Town/Village	Province: Ontario	Country: Canada	Postal Code

Please check ☑ box if applicable ☐ **Corporation** Ontario Corporation No.

Corporation Name *(including punctuation)*			
Care Of			
Street Number and Name		Suite	
City/Town/Village	Province: Ontario	Country: Canada	Postal Code

Note: Sections 13 and 14 of the *Corporations Information Act* provide penalties for making false or misleading statements or omissions.

(A) 1372 (00-04)

6.18 Initial Return/Notice of Change by an Extra-Provincial Corporation—*Corporations Information Act*—Form 2

Ontario | Ministry of Consumer and Commercial Relations | Ministère de la Consommation et du Commerce | Companies Branch, 393 University Ave Suite 200, Toronto ON M5G 2M2 | Direction des compagnies, 393 av. University Bureau 200, Toronto ON M5G 2M2

Page 1/Page 1

FORM 2- EXTRA PROVINCIAL CORPORATIONS/
FORMULE 2 - PERSONNES MORALES EXTRA-PROVINCIALES
Please type or print all information in block capital letters using black ink.
Prière de dactylographier les renseignements ou de les écrire en caractères d'imprimerie à l'encre noire.

INITIAL RETURN/NOTICE OF CHANGE / RAPPORT INITIAL/AVIS DE MODIFICATION
Corporations Information Act/ Loi sur les renseignements exigés des personnes morales

For Ministry Use Only / À l'usage du ministère seulement

2. Ontario Corporation Number / Numéro matricule de la personne morale en Ontario

3. Date of Incorporation or Amalgamation / Date de constitution, ou fusion
Year/Année Month/Mois Day/Jour

1. | Initial Return / Rapport initial | Notice of Change / Avis de modification
Business Corporations/ Société par actions ☐ ☐
Not-For-Profit Corporation/ Personne morale sans but lucratif ☐ ☐

4. Corporation Name Including Punctuation/Raison sociale de la personne morale, y compris la ponctuation

For Ministry Use Only / À l'usage du ministère seulement

5. Address of Registered or Head Office/Adresse du siège social
c/o / a/s
Street Number/Numéro civique | Street Name/Nom de la rue | Suite/Bureau
Street Name (cont'd)/Nom de la rue (suite)
City/Town/Ville | Province, State/Province, État
Country/Pays | Postal Code/Code postal

For Ministry Use Only / À l'usage du ministère seulement

6. Address of Principal Office in Ontario/Adresse du bureau principal en Ontario
☐ Same as Above/ Même que celle ci-dessus ☐ Not Applicable/ Ne s'applique pas
Street Number/Numéro civique
Street Name/Nom de la rue | Suite/Bureau
Street Name (cont'd)/Nom de la rue (suite)
City/Town/Ville **ONTARIO, CANADA**
Postal Code/Code postal

7. Language of Preference / Langue préférée ☐ English/Anglais ☐ French/Français

8. Former Corporation Name if applicable/Raison sociale antérieure de la personne morale, le cas échéant.
☐ Not Applicable / Ne s'applique pas

9. Date commenced business activity in Ontario/ Date de début ces activités en Ontario
Year/Année Month/Mois Day/Jour

10. Date ceased carrying on business activity in Ontario/ Date de cessation des activités en Ontario
Year/Année Month/Mois Day/Jour
Not Applicable/ Ne s'applique pas ☐

11. Jurisdiction of Incorporation/Amalgamation or Continuation. (Check appropriate box) Do not check more than one box.
Ressort de constitution/de fusion ou prorogation (cocher la case pertinente). Ne cocher qu'une seule case.

1. ☐ ALBERTA / ALBERTA
2. ☐ CANADA / CANADA
3. ☐ NEW BRUNSWICK / NOUVEAU-BRUNSWICK
4. ☐ NOVA SCOTIA / NOUVELLE-ÉCOSSE
5. ☐ QUEBEC / QUÉBEC
6. ☐ YUKON / YUKON
7. ☐ BRITISH COLUMBIA / COLOMBIE-BRITANNIQUE
8. ☐ MANITOBA / MANITOBA
9. ☐ NEWFOUNDLAND / TERRE-NEUVE
10. ☐ PRINCE EDWARD ISLAND / ÎLE-DU-PRINCE-ÉDOUARD
11. ☐ SASKATCHEWAN / SASKATCHEWAN
12. ☐ NORTHWEST TERRITORIES / TERRITOIRES DU NORD-OUEST
13. ☐ NUNAVUT / NUNAVUT

If other please specify/ Si autre, veuillez préciser

This information is being collected under the authority of The Corporations Information Act for the purpose of maintaining a public data base of corporate information.
La Loi sur les renseignements exigés des personnes morales autorise la collecte de ces renseignements pour constituer une banque de données accessible au public.

07201(08/99) FOR MINISTRY USE ONLY/À L'USAGE DU MINISTÈRE ☐ See deficiency letter enclosed/Voir l'avis d'insuffisance ci-joint

6.18 (continued)

FORM 2 - EXTRA PROVINCIAL CORPORATIONS/
FORMULE 2 - PERSONNES MORALES EXTRA-PROVINCIALES

Page 2/Page 2

Please type or print all information in block capital letters using black ink.
Prière de dactylographier les renseignements ou de les écrire en caractères d'imprimerie à l'encre noire.

FOR MINISTRY USE ONLY À L'USAGE DU MINISTÈRE SEULEMENT	Ontario Corporation Number/ Numéro matricule de la personne morale en Ontario	Date of Incorporation or Amalgamation Date de constitution ou fusion Year/Année Month/Mois Day/Jour	For Ministry Use Only À l'usage du ministère seulement

12. Name and Office Address of the Chief Officer/Manager in Ontario/
Nom et adresse du bureau du directeur général/gérant en Ontario

☐ Not Applicable/Ne s'applique pas

Last Name/Nom de famille — First Name/Prénom — Middle Name/Autres prénoms

Street Number/Numéro civique

Street Name/Nom de la rue

Street Name (cont'd)/Nom de la rue (suite) — Suite/Bureau

City/Town/Ville — Postal Code/Code postal

ONTARIO, CANADA

Date Effective / Date d'entrée en vigueur — Year/Année Month/Mois Day/Jour

Date Ceased / Date de cessation des fonctions — Year/Année Month/Mois Day/Jour

13. Name and Office Address of Agent for Service in Ontario - Check One box
Nom et adresse du bureau du mandataire aux fins de signification en Ontario. Cocher la case pertinente.

☐ Not Applicable/Ne s'applique pas

Only applies to foreign business corporations
S'applique seulement aux personnes morales étrangères

a) ☐ Individual or / un particulier ou b) ☐ Corporation / une personne morale

Complete appropriate sections below/Remplir les parties pertinentes ci-dessous.

a) Individual Name/Nom du particulier

Last Name/Nom de famille — First Name/Prénom — Middle Name/Autres prénoms

b) Ontario Corporation Number/Numéro matricule de la personne morale en Ontario

Corporation Name including punctuation/Raison sociale, y compris la ponctuation

c) Address/Adresse

c/o / a/s

Street Number/Numéro civique — Street Name/Nom de la rue — Suite/Bureau

Street Name (cont'd)/Nom de la rue (suite) — City/Town/Ville

ONTARIO, CANADA — Postal Code/Code postal

14. (Print or type name in full of the person authorizing filing / Dactylographier ou inscrire le prénom et le nom en caractères d'imprimerie de la personne qui autorise l'enregistrement)

I/Je

certify that the information set out herein, is true and correct.
atteste que les renseignements précités sont véridiques et exacts.

Check appropriate box
Cocher la case pertinente

D) ☐ Director/Administrateur

O) ☐ Officer /Dirigeant

P) ☐ Other individual having knowledge of the affairs of the Corporation/Autre personne ayant connaissance des activités de la personne morale

NOTE/REMARQUE: Sections 13 and 14 of the **Corporations Information Act** provide penalties for making false or misleading statements or omissions. Les articles 13 et 14 de la **Loi sur les renseignements exigés des personnes morales** prévoient des peines en cas de déclaration fausse ou trompeuse, ou d'omission.

This information is being collected under the authority of The Corporations Information Act for the purpose of maintaining a public data base of corporate information.
La Loi sur les renseignements exigés des personnes morales autorise la collecte de ces renseignements pour constituer une banque de données accessible au public.

07201(08/99) FOR MINISTRY USE ONLY/À L'USAGE DU MINISTÈRE ☐ See deficiency letter enclosed/Voir l'avis d'insuffisance ci-joint

6.19 Corporations Tax Return—*Corporations Tax Act*—CT23

Ontario

Ministry of Finance
Corporations Tax Branch
PO Box 620
33 King Street West
Oshawa ON L1H 8E9

2001 CT23 Short-Form Corporations Tax and Annual Return

Corporations Tax Act - Ministry of Finance (MOF)
Corporations Information Act - Ministry of Consumer and Business Services (MCBS) (formerly Ministry of Consumer and Commercial Relations)

This return is a combination of the Ministry of Finance (MOF) CT23 Short-Form Corporations Tax Return and the Ministry of Consumer and Business Services (MCBS) Annual Return. Page 1 is a common page required for both returns. For tax purposes, depending on which criteria the corporation satisfies, it must complete either the **Exempt from Filing (EFF)** declaration on page 2 or file the **CT23 Short-Form Return** on pages 3-6. **Corporations that do not meet the EFF criteria or the Short-Form criteria, must file the regular CT23 return.**

The **Annual Return** (common page **1** and MCBS Schedules A or K on pages 7 and 8) contains non-tax information collected under the authority of the *Corporations Information Act* for the purpose of maintaining a public database of corporate information. This return must be completed by Ontario share-capital corporations or Foreign-Business share-capital corporations that have an extra-provincial licence to operate in Ontario.

Ministry Use

MCBS Annual Return Required? *(Refer to Guide)* Yes ☐ No ☐

Page 1 of 8

Corporation's Legal Name *(including punctuation)* and Mailing Address

Ontario Corporations Tax Account No. (MOF)

This CT23 Return covers the Taxation Year

Start year month day

End year month day

Has address changed since last filed CT23 Return? Yes ☐ Date of Change year month day

Date of Incorporation or Amalgamation year month day

Registered/Head Office Address

Ontario Corporation No. (MCBS)

Location of Books and Records

Canada Customs and Revenue Agency (formerly Revenue Canada) Business No.

If applicable, enter RC

Name of person to contact regarding this CT23 Return Telephone No. Fax No.

Jurisdiction Incorporated

Address of Principal Office in Ontario *(Extra-Provincial Corporations only)* (MCBS)

If not incorporated in Ontario, indicate the date Ontario business activity commenced and ceased:

Commenced year month day

Ceased year month day

Former Corporation Name *(Extra-Provincial Corporations only)* ***Not Applicable*** ☐ (MCBS)

(Not Applicable) ☐

Preferred Language / *Langue de préférence* English *anglais* ☐ French *français* ☐

Information on Directors/Officers/Administrators must be completed on MCBS Schedule A or K as appropriate. If additional space is required for Schedule A, only this schedule may be photocopied. State number submitted (MCBS). No. of Schedule(s)

Ministry Use

If there is **no change** to the Directors'/Officers'/Administrators' information previously submitted to MCBS, please check ☑ this box. Schedule(s) A and K are not required (MCBS). ☐ **No Change**

Certification (MCBS)

I certify that all information set out in the **Annual Return** is true, correct and complete.

Name of Authorized Person *(Print clearly or type in full)*

Title: D ☐ Director O ☐ Officer P ☐ Other individual having knowledge of the affairs of the Corporation

Note: Sections 13 and 14 of the *Corporations Information Act* provide penalties for making false or misleading statements or omissions.

1399B (2001-01)

6.19 (continued)

Taxation Year End
year month day

Exempt From Filing (EFF) Corporations Tax Return Declaration

Page 2 of 8

Corporation's Legal Name	Ontario Corporations Tax Account No. (MOF)

I, ______________________________ declare that:
(Please print name in full)

The above corporation satisfies **all** of the exempt from filing criteria (a) through (f) below for the taxation year and therefore qualifies under the *Corporations Tax Act* as exempt from filing an Ontario Corporations Tax Return.

Criteria for exempt from filing status:

a) has filed a federal Income Tax Return (T2) with Canada Customs and Revenue Agency *(formerly Revenue Canada)* for the taxation year;
b) had no Ontario taxable income for the taxation year (subject to the provisions in NOTE 2 below);
c) had no Ontario Corporations Tax payable for the taxation year;
d) was a Canadian-controlled private corporation throughout the taxation year (i.e. generally a private corporation with 50% or more shares owned by Canadian residents as defined by the *Income Tax Act* (Canada));
e) had provided its Canada Customs and Revenue Agency business number to the Ministry of Finance, Corporations Tax Branch; and
f) is NOT subject to the Corporate Minimum Tax (i.e. alone or as part of an associated group whose total assets exceed $5 million or whose total revenues exceed $10 million for the taxation year).

NOTE 1: Filing of this declaration and the Annual Return does NOT constitute the filing of a Corporations Tax Return under section 75 of the *Corporations Tax Act*.

Signature	Title/Relationship to Corporation	Telephone Number	Date

Please note that making a false statement to avoid compliance with the *Corporations Tax Act* is an offence which can result in a penalty and/or fine.

NOTE 2: EFF corporations filing losses to be carried back and applied to prior years or applied to future years, *must file a tax return* complete with all the related schedules for the taxation year of the loss and for the taxation year to which the loss is being applied.

The following 3 items MUST be completed if the EFF declaration only is being submitted at this time. In cases where the annual return, which includes page 1, is also being filed, completion of these fields is NOT necessary

1. Corporation's Mailing Address	2. Ontario Corporation No. (MCBS)	3. Canada Customs and Revenue Agency (formerly Revenue Canada) Business No.
		If applicable, enter RC

A corporation **must file** an **Exempt From Filing Corporations Tax Return Declaration** form for each taxation year that the corporation is exempt from filing, **within 6 months** after the end of its taxation year, to the address shown at the top of Page 1.

The CT23 Short-Form Corporations Tax Return may be used by corporations that check "Yes" to ALL of the following criteria:

Yes	No	
☐	☐	(a) The corporation is a Canadian-controlled private corporation (CCPC) throughout the taxation year. Indicate Share Capital with full voting rights owned by Canadian Residents ____ % (nearest whole percentage)
☐	☐	(b) The corporation's taxable income for the taxation year is $200,000 or less. For a taxation year with less than 51 weeks, taxable income must be grossed-up. *(Refer to guide)*
☐	☐	(c) The corporation is NOT a member of a partnership/joint venture or a member of an associated group of corporations during the taxation year.
☐	☐	(d) The corporation's taxation year ends on or after January 1, 2000 and its gross revenue and total assets are each $1,000,000 or less and the corporation is not a financial institution; OR The corporation's taxation year ends on or after January 1, 2001, and its gross revenue and total assets are each $1,500,000 or less and the corporation is not a financial institution.
☐	☐	(e) The corporation is NOT claiming a tax credit other than the Incentive Deduction for Small Business Corporations (IDSBC), Co-operative Education Tax Credit (CETC) or Graduate Transitions Tax Credit (GTTC).
☐	☐	(f) The corporation's Ontario allocation factor is 100%.

NOTE: Family Farm or Fishing corporations that have a taxation year ending on or after January 1, 2000 and that are NOT subject to the Corporate Minimum Tax, may also use the **CT23 Short-Form Corporations Tax Return** if the corporation checks "Yes" to (a), (b), (c), (e) and (f) above.

13995 (2001-01)

6.19 (continued)

Corporation's Legal Name	Ontario Corporations Tax Account No. (MOF)	Taxation Year End	Page 3 of 8

CT23 Short-Form Corporations Tax Return

Please check (✓) box(es) if applicable in sections 1 **and** 2 **below:**

1 — 1 ☐ Family Farm Corporation s.1(2) — 2 ☐ Family Fishing Corporation s.1(2) — 14 ☐ Bare Trustee Corporation

2 —
- ☐ First Year of Filing
- ☐ Amended Return
- ☐ Taxation Year End has Changed (Canada Customs and Revenue Agency approval required)
- ☐ Final Taxation Year up to Dissolution (wind-up)
- ☐ Final Taxation Year before Amalgamation
- ☐ Floating Fiscal Year End
- ☐ Transfer or Receipt of Asset(s) involving a corporation having a Canadian permanent establishment outside Ontario
- ☐ Acquisition of Control (fed s. 249(4)) — Date Control was acquired: year / month / day

Was the corporation inactive throughout the taxation year? Yes ☐ No ☐

Has the corporation's Canada Customs and Revenue Agency T2 Return been filed? Yes ☐ No ☐

Ontario Retail Sales Tax Vendor Permit No. (Use Head Office no.) — If applicable, enter

Ontario Employer Health Tax Account No. (Use Head Office no.) — If applicable, enter

Gross Revenue . . . . 480 $

Total Assets (per balance sheet) . . . . 420 $

Summary

(Refer to Guide)

Total Tax Payable (Income Tax from 230) = 950 ________

Subtract: Payments . . . . – 960 ________

Specified Tax Credits 220 – 225 *(Refer to Guide)* . . . – 955 ________

Balance . . . . = 970 ________

If payment due . . . . Enclosed * 990 ________

If overpayment: Refund = 975 ________

Apply to: year / month / day — 980 ________ *(includes credit interest)*

* For payment, please make your cheque (drawn on a Canadian financial institution) or a money order in Canadian funds, ***payable to the Minister of Finance*** and print your Ontario Corporations Tax Account No. (MOF) on the back of cheque or money order.

Certification

I am an authorized signing officer of the corporation. I certify that this **CT23 Return, including all schedules and statements** filed with or as part of this CT23 Return, has been examined by me and is a true, correct and complete return and that the information is in agreement with the books and records of the corporation. I further certify that the financial statements accurately reflect the financial position and operating results of the corporation as required under section 75 of the *Corporations Tax Act*. The method of computing income for this taxation year is consistent with that of the previous year, except as specifically disclosed in a statement attached.

Name of Authorized Person *(Print clearly in full)* — **Signature** — **Date**

Note: Section 76 of the *Corporations Tax Act* provides penalties for making false or misleading statements or omissions.

Request to Carry-Back Losses of the Current Taxation Year to a Prior Taxation Year(s)	Taxation Year Ending (year / month / day)	Non-Capital Losses	Total Capital Losses	Farm Losses	Restricted Farm Losses
Total amount of loss		910	920	930	940
Deduct: Loss to be carried back to preceding taxation years: i) 3rd preceding	901	911	921	931	941
ii) 2nd preceding	902	912	922	932	942
iii) 1st preceding	903	913	923	933	943
Total loss to be carried back and applied to reduce taxable income		From 706	From 716	From 726	From 736
Balance of loss available for carry-forward		919	929	939	949

1399B (2001-01)

6.19 (continued)

CT23 Page 4 of 8

Income Tax

DOLLARS ONLY

Net Income (loss) for Ontario purposes (per reconciliation schedule, page 5)	± From 690		•
Subtract: Charitable donations	−	1	•
Subtract: Gifts to Her Majesty in right of Canada or a province and gifts of cultural property *(Attach schedule)*	−	2	•
Subtract: Taxable dividends deductible, per Federal T2 SCH 3	−	3	•
Subtract: Ontario political contributions *(Attach schedule)*	−	4	•
Subtract: Prior years' losses applied – Non-capital losses	− From	704	•
Net capital losses (page 6) From 715 ____ • X inclusion rate ____ % =	−	714	•
Farm losses	− From	724	•
Restricted farm losses	− From	734	•
Taxable Income (Non-capital loss)	=	10	•

Taxable Income

Number of Days in Taxation Year

From 10 ____ •	X 100% Ontario Allocation X 15.5% X	22 Days before May 2, 2000	÷ 73 Total Days	= + 23	•
From 10 ____ •	X 100% Ontario Allocation X 14.5% X	24 Days after May 1, 2000 and before Jan. 1, 2001	÷ 73 Total Days	= + 25	•
From 10 ____ •	X 100% Ontario Allocation X 14.0% X	26 Days after Dec. 31, 2000	÷ 73 Total Days	= + 27	•

Income Tax Payable (before deduction of tax credits) 23 + 25 − 27 = 40 ____ •

Incentive Deduction for Small Business Corporations (IDSBC) (s.41)

(If section is not completed, IDSBC will be denied.)

Did you claim the federal Small Business Deduction (fed.s.125(1)) in the taxation year? (✓) Yes ☐ No ☐

Income from active business carried on in Canada for federal purposes (fed.s.125(1)(a))		50 ____ •
Federal taxable income, less adjustment for foreign tax credit (fed.s.125(1)(b))	+ 51 ____ •	
Add: Losses of other years deducted for federal purposes (fed.s.111)	+ 52 ____ •	
Subtract: Losses of other years deducted for Ontario purposes (s.34)	− 53 ____ •	
	= ____ • ▶	54 ____ •
Business limit for the year (not exceeding $200,000 for corporations using CT23 Short form)		55 ____ •
Income eligible for the IDSBC	100% Allocation X	56 ____ • = 60 ____ •

Least of 50, 54 or 55

Calculation of IDSBC Rate

Number of Days in Taxation Year

7.0% X	74 Days after Dec. 31, 1998 and before Jan. 1, 2000	÷ 73 Total Days	= + 75	____
7.5% X	76 Days after Dec. 31, 1999 and before Jan. 1, 2002	÷ 73 Total Days	= + 77	____
8.0% X	69 Days after Dec. 31, 2001 and before Jan. 1, 2003	÷ 73 Total Days	= + 79	____

IDSBC Rate for Taxation Year 75 + 77 + 79 = 78 ____

Claim From 60 ____ • X From 78 ____ % = 70 ____ •

Subtotal of Income Tax 40 − 70 = 180 ____ •

Transfer to top of Page 5

Continued on Page 5

6.19 (continued)

Corporation's Legal Name	Ontario Corporations Tax Account No. (MOF)	Taxation Year End	CT23	Page 5 of 8
				DOLLARS ONLY

Continued from Page 4

Subtotal of Income Tax — From [190] ______ •

Deduct Specified Tax Credits *(Refer to Guide)*

Co-operative Education Tax Credit (CETC) (s.43.4) *Applies* to employment of eligible students.

Eligible Credit From [5798] *(Attach Summary Schedule F from the insert to the Short-Form Return/Guide package)* + [192] ______ •

Graduate Transitions Tax Credit (GTTC) (s.43.6) No. of Graduates From [6596]

Applies to employment of eligible unemployed post-secondary graduates. [194] ______

Eligible Credit From [6598] *(Attach Summary Schedule G from the insert to the Short-Form Return/Guide package)* + [195] ______ •

Total Specified Tax Credits [192] + [195] = [220] ______ •

Specified Tax Credits *Applied to reduce Income Tax* = [225] ______ •

Income Tax [190] – [225], **OR Enter NIL if reporting Non-Capital Loss** = [230] ______ •

Transfer to Summary, Page 3

Reconcile net income (loss) for federal income tax purposes with net income (loss) for Ontario purposes if amounts differ

Net Income (loss) for federal income tax purposes, per federal T2 SCH 1 ± [600] ______ •

Add:

Federal capital cost allowance	+ [601]	•
Federal cumulative eligible capital deduction	+ [602]	•
Ontario taxable capital gain	+ [603]	•
Federal non-allowable reserves. Balance beginning of year	+ [604]	•
Federal allowable reserves. Balance end of year	+ [605]	•
Ontario non-allowable reserves. Balance end of year	+ [606]	•
Ontario allowable reserves. Balance beginning of year	+ [607]	•
Federal exploration expenses (e.g. CEDE, CEE, CDE, COGPE)	+ [608]	•
Federal resource allowance	+ [609]	•
Federal depletion allowance	+ [610]	•
Federal allowable business investment loss	+ [620]	•
Total of other items not allowed by Ontario but allowed federally *(Attach schedule)*	+ [614]	•
Subtotal of Additions [601] to [610] + [620] + [614]	=	▶ [640] •

Deduct:

Ontario capital cost allowance	+ [650]	•
Ontario cumulative eligible capital deduction	+ [651]	•
Federal taxable capital gain	+ [652]	•
Ontario non-allowable reserves. Balance beginning of year	+ [653]	•
Ontario allowable reserves. Balance end of year	+ [654]	•
Federal non-allowable reserves. Balance end of year	+ [655]	•
Federal allowable reserves. Balance beginning of year	+ [656]	•
Ontario exploration expenses (e.g. CEDE, CEE, CDE, COGPE) *(Retain calculations. Do not submit.)*	+ [657]	•
Ontario depletion allowance	+ [658]	•
Ontario resource allowance	+ [659]	•

Workplace Child Care Tax Incentive: (*Applies* to qualifying expenditures incurred after May 5, 1998.) *(Refer to Guide)*

Qualifying expenditures: [665] ______ • X 30% X **100% Allocation** = [666] ______ •

Workplace Accessibility Tax Incentive: (*Applies* to qualifying expenditures incurred after July 1, 1998.) *(Refer to Guide)*

Qualifying expenditures: [667] ______ • X 100% X **100% Allocation** = [668] ______ •

Number of Employees accommodated [669] ______

Ontario School Bus Safety Tax Incentive (OSBSTI): (*Applies* to the eligible acquisition of school buses made within the 3 year period commencing after May 4, 1999.) *(Refer to Guide)*

Qualifying expenditures: [670] ______ • X 30% X **100% Allocation** = [671] ______ •

Ontario allowable business investment loss: = [678] ______ •

Total of other deductions allowed by Ontario *(Attach schedule)* + [684] ______ •

Subtotal of Deductions [650] to [659] + [666] + [668] + [671] + [678] + [684] = ______ • ▶ [680] ______ •

Net income (loss) for Ontario Purposes [600] + [640] – [680] = [690] ______ •

1399B (2001-01)

6.19 (continued)

DOLLARS ONLY

Continuity of Losses Carried Forward

	Non-Capital Losses (1)	Total Capital Losses (6) (7)	Farm Losses	Restricted Farm Losses	Listed Personal Property Losses
Balance at Beginning of Year	700 (2)	710 (2)	720 (2)	730	740
Add: Current year's losses	701	711	721	731	741
Losses from predecessor corporations (3)	702	712	722	732	
Subtotal	703	713	723	733	743
Subtract: Utilized during the year to reduce taxable income	704	715 (4)	724	734 (4)	744 (4)
Expired during the year	705		725	735	745
Carried back to prior years to reduce taxable income (5)	706 (2) to Page 3	716 (2) to Page 3	726 (2) to Page 3	736 (2) to Page 3	746
Subtotal	707	717	727	737	747
Balance at End of Year	709	719	729	739	749

Notes:

(1) Non-capital losses include allowable business investment losses, fed.s.111(8)(b), as made applicable by s.34.

(2) Where acquisition of control of the corporation has occurred, the utilization of losses can be restricted. See fed.s.111(4) through 111(5.5), as made applicable by s.34.

(3) Includes losses on amalgamation (fed.s.87(2.1) and s.87(2.11)) and/or wind-up (fed.s.88(1.1) and 88(1.2)), as made applicable by s.34.

(4) To the extent of applicable gains or income only.

(5) Generally a three year carry-back applies. See fed.s.111(1) and fed.s.41(2)(b), as made applicable by s.34.

(6) Total Capital Losses for a year is the excess of 100% of the Capital Losses in the taxation year minus 100% of the Capital Gains (less any reserves) in the taxation year. Total Capital Losses is before the inclusion rate has been applied.

(7) In the 2001 CT23 Short Form, this column now refers to Total Capital Losses (100% of loss), whereas previously the column referred to Net Capital Losses (75% of loss or after the inclusion rate has been applied). Loss amounts that are not carried at 100% of the loss must be grossed back up to 100% by multiplying the balance by 1.333333. No adjustment is required where losses are carried at 100% of the loss amount.

Analysis of Balance by Year of Origin

Year of Origin (oldest year first) year / month / day	Non-Capital Losses	Non-Capital Losses of Predecessor Corporations	Total Capital Losses from Listed Personal Property only (6) (7)	Farm Losses	Restricted Farm Losses
800				850	870
801				851	871
802				852	872
803	820	830	840	853	873
804	821	831	841	854	874
805	822	832	842	855	875
806	823	833	843	856	876
807	824	834	844	857	877
808	825	835	845	858	878
809	826	836	846	859	879
Total	829	839	849	869	889

6.19 (continued)

Schedule A: Information on Ontario Corporations

(Corporations that are incorporated, continued or amalgamated under the *Ontario Business Corporations Act*)

MCBS
Schedule A
Page 7 of 8

To submit additional Director or Officer information, please photocopy this page and attach the completed schedules with your return.

Identification

Corporation's Legal Name *(including punctuation)*

Ontario Corporation No. (MCBS)

Date of Incorporation or Amalgamation: year / month / day

Director/Officer Information

Full Name and Address for Service:

Last Name | First Name | Middle Name(s)

Street Number and Name | Suite

City/Town/Village | Province/State | Country | Postal/Zip Code

Director

Are you a resident Canadian? *(Applies to directors of business corporations only)*

☐ Yes ☐ No

Date Elected: year / month / day

Date Ceased: year / month / day

Officer

Indicate the appointment period for each of the following:

	Date Appointed (year)	(month)	(day)	Date Ceased (year)	(month)	(day)
President						
Secretary						
Treasurer						
General Manager						
Other *(specify)*						

Other Titles *(please specify)*:

☐ Chair ☐ Chief Executive Officer
☐ Chair Person ☐ Chief Financial Officer
☐ Chairman ☐ Chief Information Officer
☐ Chairwoman ☐ Chief Operating Officer
☐ Vice-Chair ☐ Chief Administrative Officer
☐ Vice-President
☐ Assistant Secretary ☐ Comptroller
☐ Assistant Treasurer ☐ Authorized Signing Officer
☐ Chief Manager
☐ Executive Director
☐ Managing Director ☐ Other (untitled)

Director/Officer Information

Full Name and Address for Service:

Last Name | First Name | Middle Name(s)

Street Number and Name | Suite

City/Town/Village | Province/State | Country | Postal/Zip Code

Director

Are you a resident Canadian? *(Applies to directors of business corporations only)*

☐ Yes ☐ No

Date Elected: year / month / day

Date Ceased: year / month / day

Officer

Indicate the appointment period for each of the following:

	Date Appointed (year)	(month)	(day)	Date Ceased (year)	(month)	(day)
President						
Secretary						
Treasurer						
General Manager						
Other *(specify)*						

Other Titles *(please specify)*:

☐ Chair ☐ Chief Executive Officer
☐ Chair Person ☐ Chief Financial Officer
☐ Chairman ☐ Chief Information Officer
☐ Chairwoman ☐ Chief Operating Officer
☐ Vice-Chair ☐ Chief Administrative Officer
☐ Vice-President
☐ Assistant Secretary ☐ Comptroller
☐ Assistant Treasurer ☐ Authorized Signing Officer
☐ Chief Manager
☐ Executive Director
☐ Managing Director ☐ Other (untitled)

Note: Sections 13 and 14 of the *Corporations Information Act* provide penalties for making false or misleading statements or omissions.

13998 (2001-01)

6.19 (continued)

Schedule K:
Information on Foreign Business Corporations

(Corporations that are incorporated, continued or amalgamated in a jurisdiction outside Canada)

MCBS
Schedule K
Page 8 of 8

Only one Schedule K may be submitted. Please DO NOT photocopy.

Identification

Corporation's Legal Name *(including punctuation)*	Ontario Corporation No. (MCBS)	Date of Incorporation or Amalgamation (year / month / day)

Chief Officer/Manager Information

Name and Office Address of the Chief Officer/Manager in Ontario: *Not Applicable* ☐

Last Name	First Name	Middle Name(s)	
Street Number and Name		Suite	
City/Town/Village	Province **Ontario**	Country **Canada**	Postal Code

Indicate the appointment period for the position of Chief Officer/Manager:

Date Appointed (year / month / day)	Date Ceased (year / month / day)

Agent for Service Information

Indicate if the Agent for Service is an individual or a corporation:

Please check ☑ box if applicable ☐ **Individual**

Agent's Last Name	First Name	Middle Name(s)	
Street Number and Name		Suite	
City/Town/Village	Province **Ontario**	Country **Canada**	Postal Code

Please check ☑ box if applicable ☐ **Corporation** — Ontario Corporation No.

Corporation Name *(including punctuation)*			
Care Of			
Street Number and Name		Suite	
City/Town/Village	Province **Ontario**	Country **Canada**	Postal Code

Note: Sections 13 and 14 of the *Corporations Information Act* provide penalties for making false or misleading statements or omissions.

13998 (2001-01)

9. Articles of Amendment

9.1 Articles of Amendment—*Business Corporations Act*—Form 3

DYE & DURHAM CO. INC
FORM 3 (B.C.A.)

Articles of Amendment
Form 3
Business Corporations Act

Instructions for Completing

Articles must be in duplicate in Form 3 prescribed in Ontario Regulations made under the Business Corporations Act. Articles which do not conform to Form 3 cannot be accepted for filing and will be returned to the corporation/agent filing the articles.

FORMAT OF DOCUMENTS

Articles of amendment and any supporting documents which are to be filed with the Ministry must be typewritten, or, if completed by hand, printed in BLOCK CAPITAL letters, and must be legible and compatible with the microfilming process. Supporting documents and supplementary pages must be upon one side of good quality white bond paper 8 1/2" x 11" with a margin of 1 1/4" on the left hand side or the metric equivalent. Documents which do not conform to this standard cannot be accepted for filing and will be returned to the corporation/agent filing the articles.

If additional pages are required due to lack of sufficient space they should be the same size as all other pages, must have a margin of 30 mm. or 1 1/4" on the left side and must be numbered the same as the original with the additional of letters of the alphabet to indicate sequence. For example, supplementary Page 1 would be numbered 1A, 1B, etc.

CHANGE OF NAME

Where articles of amendment are to change the existing name of the corporation, they must be accompanied by a computer printed name search report obtained from a private search house and produced by the NUANS System. The report must be produced not more than 90 days prior to delivery of the articles. Articles accompanied by stale dated search report will not be accepted for filing. Names and addresses of private name search houses are listed in the Yellow Pages of your telephone directory under the heading "Searchers of Records". Name search houses have been established in most of the larger cities and towns in the Province.

The new name set out in the articles must correspond exactly with the name set out in the computer printed name search report from the NUANS System, otherwise the articles will not be accepted for filing. The name must not contain words prohibited by the Regulations or symbols not set out in the Regulations. Where the corporation intends to seek registration/licencing from another government agency the applicant should clear the name with the appropriate Registrar/Licencing Officer prior to delivery of the articles for filing. Failure to obain such clearance may result in inconvenience and expense in having to file subsequent Articles of Amendment to amend a name which is found to be unacceptable by another government agency or another regulatory body.

Where the corporation is changing its name to a "number name" it is not required to obtain a NUANS name search report.

ARTICLES

ARTICLE 1 Set out the present name of the corporation in BLOCK CAPITAL letters.

ARTICLE 2 If the present name of the corporation is being changed set out the new name of the corporation in BLOCK CAPITAL letters. The new name must correspond with the name searched and set out in the NUANS name search report. Where a "number name" is desired, leave the first 9 spaces blank and complete as follows ".........ONTARIO LIMITED or INCORPORATED or CORPORATION or LIMITÉE or INCORPORÉE" or the corresponding abbreviation LTD., or INC., or CORP. or LTÉE.

ARTICLE 3 Set out the date of incorporation/amalgamation, (year, month, day).

ARTICLE 4 In this article set out an extract from the resolution amending the existing articles of the corporation i.e.
Resolved that:
(a) The name of the corporation is changed to ABC INC..
(b) the authorized capital of the corporation is amended by........

ARTICLE 6 Insert the date on which the resolution authorizing the amendment was approved by the shareholders/directors of the corporation, (year, month, day).

CBR 173

9.1 (continued)

<u>EXECUTION</u> Articles must be signed in duplicate by an officer or director of the corporation and signatures on both copies must be original signatures and not photocopies. The present name of the corporation must be set out in BLOCK CAPITAL letters. If the corporation has a corporate seal it should be affixed to the articles next to the signature of the officer/director of the corporation.

Articles (in duplicate), original computer printed name search report (if changing name of corporation), supporting documents and the prescribed filing fee should be mailed or delivered to:

COMPANIES BRANCH
MINISTRY OF CONSUMER AND COMMERCIAL RELATIONS
393 UNIVERSITY AVENUE, SUITE 200, TORONTO, ONTARIO M5G 2M2

or delivered by hand for over-the-counter transaction (in person only) at any one of the following Land Registry Offices: Barrie, Hamilton, Kingston, Kitchener, London, Ottawa, Peterborough, Sarnia, Sault Ste. Marie, Sudbury, Thunder Bay, Welland, Whitby, Windsor.

9.1 (continued)

For Ministry Use Only
À l'usage exclusif du ministère

Ontario Corporation Number
Numéro de la société en Ontario

1.

Form 3
Business Corporations Act

Formule 3
Loi sur les sociétés par actions

ARTICLES OF AMENDMENT
STATUTS DE MODIFICATION

1. The name of the corporation is: *Dénomination sociale de la société:*

2. The name of the corporation is changed to (if applicable): *Nouvelle dénomination sociale de la société (s'il y a lieu):*

3. Date of incorporation/amalgamation: *Date de la constitution ou de la fusion:*

(Year, Month, Day)
(année, mois, jour)

4. The articles of the corporation are amended as follows: *Les statuts de la société sont modifiés de la façon suivante.*

DYE & DURHAM
FORM 3 (B.C.A.)
07/96

CBR 173

9.1 (continued)

2.

5. The amencment has been duly authorized as required by Sections 168 & 170 (as applicable) of the Business Corporations Act.

La modification a été dûment autorisée conformément aux articles 168 et 170 (selon le cas) de la Loi sur les sociétés par actions.

6. The resolution authorizing the amendment was approved by the shareholders/directors (as applicable) of the corporation on

Les actionnaires ou les administrateurs (selon le cas) de la société ont approuvé la résolution autorisant la modification le

(Year, Month, Day)
(année, mois, jour)

These articles are signed in duplicate.

Les présents status sont signés en double exemplaire.

(Name of Corporation)
(Dénomination sociale de la société)

By:/*Par:*

(Signature) *(Signature)* (Description of Office) *(Fonction)*

07/96

CBF 173

10. Annual Meetings

10.1 Minutes of a Meeting of the Board of Directors

MINUTES OF A MEETING OF THE BOARD OF DIRECTORS of

held at
(Place)

on (Day) the day of (year) at (local time).

PRESENT

being of the directors of the Corporation. All of the directors being present in person and/or having waived notice of the meeting as evidenced by their signatures at the bottom of these minutes, notice calling the meeting was dispensed with and the meeting declared to be regularly constituted.

The President took the chair and the Secretary acted as secretary of the meeting.

The minutes of the previous meeting of directors were read and confirmed.

The Chairman presented to the meeting the financial statements of the Corporation for the financial year ending on (year), which had been prepared by the auditor of the Corporation together with the auditor's report to the shareholders on such financial statements. After discussion,

Upon motion duly made and carried unanimously, IT WAS RESOLVED that the

(See Page 2)

10.1 (continued)

said financial statements be and the same are hereby approved as the financial statements of the Corporation for the financial year ending _______ *(year)* _______, and that

(insert names) _______________ and _______________ be and are hereby authorized to sign the balance sheet as evidence of the board's approval.

There being no further business before the meeting, the meeting then terminated.

______________________	______________________
Chairman	Secretary

We, the undersigned, being all of the directors of the Corporation, hereby consent to this meeting being held at the above time and place and do hereby waive notice of this meeting and consent to the transaction of the business conducted at the meeting as evidenced by the foregoing minutes.

______________________	______________________
______________________	______________________

10.2 Minutes of the Annual Meeting of the Shareholders

MINUTES OF THE ANNUAL MEETING OF SHAREHOLDERS of

held at (Place)

on (Day) the day of (year) at (local time).

PRESENT

being of the shareholders of the Corporation. All of the shareholders being present in person and/or having waived notice of the meeting as evidenced by their signatures at the bottom of these minutes, notice calling the meeting was dispensed with and the meeting declared to be regularly constituted.

The President,

took the chair and the Secretary acted as secretary of the meeting.

The minutes of the last annual meeting of shareholders were confirmed as read.

The Chairman then laid before the meeting the financial statements of the Corporation for the financial year ending on (year), which had been prepared by the Corporation's auditor and approved by the directors. At the request of the Chairman, the Secretary read to the meeting the auditor's report on the said financial statements.

(See Page 2)

10.2 (continued)

UPON MOTION duly made and carried unanimously, IT WAS RESOLVED that the financial statements and the report of the auditors thereon for the financial year ending *(year)* be and the same are hereby approved and adopted.

The Chairman stated that it was desirable to review the actions of the board of directors and the officers of the Corporation since the last annual meeting of shareholders.

UPON MOTION duly made and carried unanimously, IT WAS RESOLVED that all by-laws, resolutions, contracts, acts, proceedings and payments of the board of directors and of the officers of the Corporation enacted, made, done or taken since the date of the last annual meeting of shareholders of the Corporation be and they are hereby approved, ratified and confirmed.

The meeting then proceeded to elect directors of the Corporation for the ensuing year. The Chairman called for nominations and the following were nominated:

No further nominations having been received, the nominations were declared closed and the Chairman then declared the said

elected as directors of the Corporation to hold office until the next annual meeting of shareholders or until their successors are elected or appointed.

(See Page 3)

10.2 (continued)

The meeting then proceeded to appoint auditors for the Corporation for the ensuing year, and

UPON MOTION duly made and carried unanimously, IT WAS RESOLVED that

be appointed auditors of the Corporation until the next annual meeting of shareholders or until a successor is appointed, at a remuneration to be fixed by the directors, the directors being authorized to fix such a remuneration.

There being no further business before the meeting, the meeting then terminated.

Chairman	Secretary

WE, the undersigned, being all of the shareholders of the Corporation, hereby consent to this meeting being held at the above time and place and we do hereby waive notice of this meeting and consent to the transaction of the business conducted at the meeting as evidenced by the foregoing minutes.

10.3 Alternative Clauses for Annual Meeting of Shareholders

APPROVAL OF FINANCIAL STATEMENT WHERE CORPORATION EXEMPT

RESOLUTIONS OF THE SHAREHOLDERS

of

FINANCIAL STATEMENTS

BE IT RESOLVED THAT:

the financial statements of the Corporation for the financial year ending

be and the same are hereby approved and adopted.

(year)

CONFIRMATION OF PROCEEDINGS

BE IT RESOLVED THAT:

all by-laws, resolutions, contracts, acts, proceedings and payments of the board of directors and of the officers of the Corporation enacted, made, done or taken since incorporation or the last annual meeting of shareholders of the Corporation be and the same are hereby approved, ratified, sanctioned and confirmed.

ELECTION OF DIRECTORS

BE IT RESOLVED THAT:

the following be and they are hereby elected directors of the Corporation for the ensuing year or until their successors are duly elected or appointed:

(insert names.)

10.3 (continued)

APPOINTMENT OF ACCOUNTANTS AND EXEMPTION FROM AUDIT REQUIREMENTS

BE IT RESOLVED THAT:

be and they are hereby appointed accountants of the Corporation for the ensuing financial year, and the shareholders of the Corporation hereby consent to the exemption of the Corporation from the audit requirements of the Ontario *Business Corporations Act* for the ensuing year.

The undersigned, being all of the shareholders of the Corporation, hereby sign the foregoing resolutions pursuant to subsection 104 (1) of the Ontario *Business Corporations Act*.

DATED the day of

(year)

____

____

10.4 Alternative Set-up for Annual Meeting of Shareholders Where Proxy or Proxies are Present

MINUTES of the ANNUAL MEETING of the SHAREHOLDERS of , held at (the head office of the Corporation/or insert address), (insert city/town) Ontario, on the day of at, the hour of o'clock in the noon.

PRESENT:

REPRESENTED BY PROXY IN
FAVOUR OF :

being (all/a quorum) of the shareholders of the Corporation.

CHAIRMAN AND SECRETARY

occupied the Chair and acted as Secretary to the meeting.

CONSTITUTION OF MEETING

(All/A quorum) of the shareholders being present in person or represented by proxy, notice calling the meeting was waived and consent given to the holding of the meeting as is testified by the signatures of the respective shareholders hereto. The Chairman declared the meeting to be regularly called and properly constituted for the transaction of the business.

PROXY

The undersigned, a shareholder of hereby appoints of as proxy for the undersigned, to act and vote for and on behalf of the undersigned at the Annual Meeting of shareholders of the said Corporation to be held on the day of and at any adjournment thereof.

DATED the day of

(type in name of shareholder)

10.5 Minutes of the Adjourned Meeting of the Board of Directors

MINUTES of an ADJOURNED MEETING of the BOARD OF DIRECTORS of held at , Ontario, on the day of at the hour of o'clock in the noon.

PRESENT:

being (all/a quorum) of the Directors of the Corporation.

CHAIRMAN AND SECRETARY

occupied the Chair and acted as Secretary to the meeting.

CONSTITUTION OF MEETING

The Chairman reconvened the meeting which had been adjourned to permit the holding of the Annual Meeting of the shareholders of the Corporation.

The Chairman declared that a quorum was present and that the meeting was properly constituted to transact the business to come before it.

ELECTION OF OFFICERS

The Chairman informed the meeting that it was now in order to elect or appoint officers of the Corporation for the ensuing year and opened the meeting for nominations.

The following persons were nominated for the offices shown opposite their names:

There being no further nominations, the Chairman declared the nominations to be closed and directed the Secretary to cast a single ballot for the election of those nominated. Such ballot having been cast, the Chairman declared those nominated be elected or appointed officers of the Corporation to hold the offices referred to opposite their respective names until the next Annual Meeting of the shareholders or until their successors are appointed.

*There being no further or other business, the meeting thereupon adjourned.

Chairman	Secretary

*Alternative form which could be substituted would read:

TERMINATION OF MEETING

There being no further business, UPON MOTION duly made, seconded and unanimously carried, IT WAS RESOLVED that the meeting be terminated.

10.6 Resolutions of the Sole Director

RESOLUTION OF THE SOLE DIRECTOR
OF

The undersigned, the sole director of (the "Corporation"), hereby consents to the passing of the following two resolutions by the sole director of the Corporation pursuant to the provisions of the Business Corporations Act (Ontario), as evidenced by the signature of the undersigned hereto.

ANNUAL FINANCIAL STATEMENTS

WHEREAS the sole director of the Corporation has examined the financial statements of the Corporation for the financial year ended , together with the auditors' report thereon;

AND WHEREAS a copy of the financial statements of the Corporation are annexed to these resolutions as Schedule "A";

BE IT RESOLVED

that the financial statements of the Corporation for the year ended consisting of a balance sheet as at that date, *a statement of retained earnings for the year ended on that date and a *statement of income for the year ended on that date together with the auditors' report thereon, be hereby approved and the sole director of the Corporation be authorized to sign the balance sheet on behalf of the board of directors of the Corporation.

ANNUAL MEETING OF SHAREHOLDERS

WHEREAS an annual meeting of the shareholders of the Corporation should be held prior to the end of ;

BE IT RESOLVED

that an annual meeting of the shareholders of the Corporation be held on the day of , at the hour of o'clock in the at the head office of the Corporation, in the Town of , in the County of , and Province of Ontario, for the following purposes:

(a) to receive the financial statements of the Corporation for the year ended ;

(b) to elect directors;

(c) to appoint auditors and to authorize the directors to fix the auditors' remuneration;

(d) to approve the acts of the director and officers of the Corporation since the date of the last annual meeting of shareholders of the Corporation; and

(e) to transact such other business as may properly come before the meeting or any adjournment thereof.

DATED at the day of

____

*Retain/delete as circumstances dictate.

10.7 Minutes of an Annual Meeting of Shareholders

MINUTES of an annual meeting of the shareholders of held at on the day of , at the hour of o'clock in the (local time).

PRESENT IN PERSON:

being all of the shareholders of the Corporation.

CHAIRMAN AND SECRETARY

On motion duly made, seconded and carried unanimously, was appointed Chairman of the meeting and was appointed Secretary of the meeting.

CONSTITUTION OF MEETING

All of the shareholders of the Corporation being present in person and having waived notice of and consented to the holding of this meeting, the Chairman declared the meeting to be regularly constituted for the transaction of business.

MINUTES OF PREVIOUS MEETING OF SHAREHOLDERS

The minutes of the last meeting of the shareholders of the Corporation held on were read and approved and directed to be taken as a correct record.

ANNUAL FINANCIAL STATEMENTS

The Chairman presented to the meeting a statement of for the Corporation's year terminating and a balance sheet of the Corporation showing the financial position of the Corporation as at . On motion duly made, seconded and carried unanimously, the following resolution was passed:

BE IT RESOLVED:

that the *balance sheet of the Corporation showing the financial position of the Corporation as at and the *statement of for the Corporation's financial year terminated , be and the same are hereby approved and adopted.

ELECTION OF DIRECTOR

The Chairman then advised the meeting that it was in order to proceed with the election of the sole director and asked for nominations. The following individual was nominated:

(insert name of person)

---

*Retain/delete as circumstances dictate.

10.7 (continued)

There being no further nominations, the Chairman declared the nominations to be closed and directed the Secretary of the meeting to cast a single ballot for the election of the individual so nominated. Such ballot having been cast, the Chairman declared that he had been duly elected the sole director of the Corporation to hold office until the next annual election of directors or until his successor shall be elected or appointed. He then expressed his consent to act as the sole director of the Corporation.

APPOINTMENT OF AUDITORS

On motion duly made, seconded and carried unanimously, the following resolution was passed:

BE IT RESOLVED

that Messrs. , Chartered Accountants, be and they are hereby appointed auditors of the Corporation to hold office until the next annual meeting of shareholders of the Corporation, at a remuneration to be fixed by the directors of the Corporation, the directors being hereby authorized to fix such remuneration.

CONFIRMATION OF ACTS

On motion duly made, seconded and carried unanimously, the following resolution was passed:

BE IT RESOLVED

that all acts, contracts, options, by-laws, proceedings, appointments, elections and payments enacted, made, done, given and taken by the director and officers of the Corporation since the date of the last meeting of shareholders of the Corporation as the same are set out or referred to in the minutes of the meetings of the board of directors or in the financial statements submitted to this meeting, be and the same are hereby approved, sanctioned, ratified and confirmed.

CONSENT AND WAIVER OF NOTICE

The following memorandum was then read, consented to and directed to be inserted in the minutes of this meeting:

The undersigned, being all of the shareholders of , hereby waive notice of and consent to the holding of this meeting and to the transaction of such business as may come before it as testified by our signatures hereto.

There being no further business to come before it, the meeting on motion duly made, seconded and carried unanimously, adjourned.

Chairman of the meeting	Secretary of the meeting

10.8 Auditor(s) Consent and Waiver of Notice

CONSENT AND WAIVER OF NOTICE

TO:

AND TO: THE DIRECTORS AND SHAREHOLDERS THEREOF

The undersigned, the auditors of , hereby waive notice of and consent to the holding of an annual meeting of the shareholders of to be held on the day of , at the hour of o'clock in the (local time) at and hereby consents to the transaction of such business as may come before the said meeting or any adjournment thereof.

DATED the day of

Per: ______________________________

10.9 Resolution of the Sole Director

RESOLUTION OF THE SOLE DIRECTOR
OF

The undersigned, the sole director of (the "Corporation"), hereby consents to the passing of the following resolution by the sole director of the Corporation pursuant to the provisions of the Business Corporations Act (Ontario), as evidenced by the signature of the undersigned hereto.

ELECTION AND APPOINTMENT OF OFFICERS

WHEREAS it is expedient that officers of the Corporation be appointed for the ensuing year;

BE IT RESOLVED

that the following persons be elected or appointed as officers of the Corporation to hold the office referred to opposite their respective names for the ensuing year or until their respective successors shall be elected or appointed:

(insert offices and names of persons appointed)

DATED at the day of

____

Note: Terms and format used for annual metings will reflect the requirements of the statute and the preferred practice in the individual law office.

11. Extra-Provincial Corporations

11.1 Application for Extra-Provincial Licence—*Extra-Provincial Corporations Act*—Form 1

Ontario Corporation Number
Numéro de la compagnie en Ontario

Form 1
Extra-Provincial Corporations Act

Formule 1
Loi sur les personnes morales extraprovinciales

1.

APPLICATION FOR EXTRA-PROVINCIAL LICENCE/
DEMANDE EN VUE D'OBTENIR UN PERMIS EXTRAPROVINCIAL

1. The name of the Corporation is (Print in UPPER CASE ONLY) :
Dénomination sociale de la compagnie (Écrire en LETTRES MAJUSCULES SEULEMENT) :

2. Business name or style, other than the corporate name, under which the corporation is to be licensed in Ontario, if any (if none, state so): / Nom, autre que la dénomination sociale, sous lequel un permis doit être délivré à la compagnie en Ontario, le cas échéant (si ce n'est pas le cas, veuillez l'indiquer) :

3. Jurisdiction to which subject:/
Compétence législative :

(Name of Province, State or Country) / (Province, État ou pays)

4. Date of incorporation/amalgamation:/
Date de la constitution ou de la fusion :

year / année month / mois day / jour

5. Full address of the head or registered office: / Adresse du siège social :

(Street & Number or R.R. Number & if Multi-Office Building give Room No.) / (Rue et numéro ou numéro de la R.R. et numéro du bureau)

(Name of Municipality or Post Office) / (Municipalité ou bureau de poste)

Postal/Zip Code / Code postal/zip

(Name of State or Country) / (État ou pays)

6. The corporation has been authorized to make this application by a resolution passed by the directors of the corporation at a meeting held on: / La compagnie est autorisée à présenter cette demande au moyen d'une résolution adoptée par ses administrateurs le :

year / année month / mois day / jour

07065(04/01)

11.1 (continued)

2.

7. Full address (including postal code) of the principal office or chief place of business in Ontario, if determined (if not, state so): / Adresse de l'établissement principal en Ontario, si elle est établie (si ce n'est pas le cas, l'indiquer) :

(Street & Number or R.R. Number & if Multi-Office Building give Room No.) / (Rue et numéro ou numéro de la R.R. et numéro du bureau)

(Name of Municipality or Post Office) / (Municipalité ou bureau de poste)

Postal/Zip Code / Code postal/zip

8. Chief officer or manager in Ontario, if determined (if none, state so): /
Premier dirigeant ou gérant en Ontario, s'il est désigné (si ce n'est pas le cas, l'indiquer) :

Name in full, including all first and middle names / Nom et prénoms	Residence address, giving Street & No. or R.R. No. & Municipality or Post Office and Postal Code: / Adresse personnelle y compris la rue et le numéro ou le numéro de la R.R., et le nom de la municipalité ou du bureau de poste et le code postal

9. The business which the corporation intends to carry on in Ontario is: /
Les activités commerciales que la compagnie entend exercer en Ontario sont les suivantes :

07065(04/01)

11.1 (continued)

3

10. The corporate existence of the corporation is not limited in any way by statute or otherwise and the corporation is a valid and subsisting corporation. / La personnalité morale de la compagnie n'est restreinte d aucune manière notamment par l'effet de la loi et la compagnie conserve sa validité et son existence juridique.

11. The corporation has the capacity to carry on business in Ontario. / La compagnie est habilitée à exercer ses activités commerciales en Ontario.

12. The corporation has the capacity to hold land without conditions or limitations. / La compagnie est habilitée à posséder des biens-fonds sans condition ni restriction.

13. The corporation hereby acknowledges that upon the licence being issued the corporation shall be subject to the provisions of the Extra-Provincial Corporations Act, the Corporations Information Act, the Corporations Tax Act and to such further and other legislative provisions as the Legislature of Ontario may deem expedient in order to secure the due management of the corporation's affairs and the protection of its creditors within Ontario. / La compagnie reconnaît par la présente que dès la délivrance du permis, elle sera assujettie aux dispositions de la *Loi sur les compagnies extraprovinciales*, de la Loi sur les renseignements exigés des compagnies et associations, de la *Loi sur l'imposition des personnes morales* ainsi qu'aux autres dispositions législatives ultérieures que la Législature de l'Ontario peut juger opportunes afin d'assurer la saine gestion des affaires de la compagnie et la protection de ses créanciers en Ontario.

This application is executed in duplicate. / La présente demande est signée en double exemplaire.

____
(Name of Corporation) / (Dénomination sociale de la compagnie)

By: / Signé : ______________________________
(Signature) / (Signature)

____
(Description of Office) / (Fonctions)

(Corporate Seal) / (Sceau de la compagnie)

07065(04/01)

11.2 Appointment of/Revised Appointment of Agent for Service—*Extra-Provincial Corporations Act*—Form 2

Form 2
Extra-Provincial Corporations Act
Formule 2
Loi sur les personnes morales extraprovinciales

Check (X) the appropriate box
Cochez (X) la case appropriée

☐ APPOINTMENT OF AGENT FOR SERVICE
DÉSIGNATION DU MANDATAIRE AUX FINS DE SIGNIFICATION

or/ou

☐ REVISED APPOINTMENT OF AGENT FOR SERVICE
MODIFICATION DE LA DÉSIGNATION DE MANDATAIRE

Ontario Corporation Number
Numéro de la société en Ontario

1.

____
(Name of appointing corporation)
(Dénomination sociale de la société désignant le mandataire)

(hereinafter called the "Corporation") hereby nominates, constitutes and appoints
(ci-après appelée la «société») constitue

____
(Name of agent giving first name, initials and surname; or full Corporate Name)
(Mandataire : prénom, initiale et nom de famille; ou dénomination sociale complète)

____
(Business address of the agent, including Street Number, Suite or Room Number and Municipality)
(Adresse d'affaires du mandataire : numéro et rue, bureau et municipalité)

Postal/Zip Code / Code postal/zip

its true and lawful agent for service, to act as such, and as such to sue and be sued, plead and be impleaded in any court in Ontario and generally on behalf of the corporation within Ontario to accept service of process and to receive all lawful notices and, for the purposes of the corporation, to do all acts and to execute all deeds and other instruments relating to the matters within the scope of this appointment. Until due lawful notice of the appointment of another and subsequent agent has been given to and accepted by the Director under the Extra-Provincial Corporations Act, service of process or of papers and notices upon the said agent for service shall be accepted by the corporation as sufficient service.

son mandataire aux fins de signification, qui agira en cette qualité, soutiendra à titre de demandeur ou de défendeur les actions en justice intentées en Ontario et, de manière générale, recevra et acceptera en Ontario, au nom de la société, tous actes de procédure et tous avis requis ou autorisés par la loi, accomplira toutes actions et signera tous actes et autres instruments relativement aux affaires entrant dans le cadre du présent mandat. Tant qu'un avis en bonne et due forme visant à désigner un autre mandataire n'aura pas été donné au directeur et accepté par lui, conformément à la *Loi sur les personnes morales extraprovinciales*, la société accepte comme suffisante la signification au mandataire susmentionné desdits actes de procédure, avis et autres documents.

____
(Name of Corporation / Dénomination sociale de la société)

Dated
Date ______________________________
year/année month/mois day/jour

BY: ______________________________ ______________________________
(Signature) (Description of Officer / Titre)

(Corporate Seal)
(Sceau de la société)

______________________________ ______________________________
(Signature) (Description of Officer / Titre)

CONSENT TO ACT AS AGENT FOR SERVICE
CONSENTEMENT À AGIR EN QUALITÉ DE MANDATAIRE AUX FINS DE SIGNIFICATION

I / Je soussigné(e), ______________________________
(Name of Agent in full; if Corporation, full Corporate Name)
(Nom complet du mandataire; si personne morale, dénomination sociale complète)

of / dont l'adresse d'affaires est : ______________________________
(Business address including Street Number, Suite or Room Number and Municipality)
(Adresse d'affaires : numéro et rue, numéro du bureau et municipalité)

Ontario, hereby consent to act as the agent for service in the Province of Ontario of
en Ontario, consens par les présentes à agir, dans la Province de l'Ontario, en qualité de mandataire aux fins de signification de

____
(Name of Corporation / Dénomination sociale de la société)

pursuant to the appointment executed by the said corporation on the
en vertu du présent mandat que ladite société a signé le

______________ day of / jour de ______________, year / année ______________;

authorizing me to accept service of process and notices on its behalf
ledit mandat m'autorise à recevoir et à accepter au nom de la société
tous actes de procédure, avis et autres documents.

Dated
Date ______________________________
year/année month/mois day/jour

______________________________ ______________________________
(Signature of witness / Signature du témoin)
(Signature of the consenting person or Officer/Director of Corporation)
(Signature du mandataire; si personne morale, signature du dirigeant / administrateur agissant en son nom)

07064(04/01)

11.3 Application for Amendment to Extra-Provincial Licence—*Extra-Provincial Corporations Act*—Form 3

Ontario Corporation Number
Numéro de la compagnie en Ontario

Form 3
Extra-Provincial Corporations Act

Formule 3
Loi sur les personnes morales extraprovinciales

APPLICATION FOR AMENDED EXTRA-PROVINCIAL LICENCE/
DEMANDE EN VUE D'OBTENIR UN PERMIS EXTRAPROVINCIAL MODIFIÉ

1. The name of the Corporation which is currently licensed in Ontario (Print in UPPER CASE ONLY):
Dénomination sociale de la compagnie présentement autorisé en Ontario (Écrire en LETTRES MAJUSCULES SEULEMENT:

2. Name, other than the corporate name, under which the corporation is currently licensed to carry on business in Ontario, if different from above: / Nom, autre que la dénomination sociale, sous lequel la compagnie est présentement autorisée à exercer ses activités commerciales en Ontario, s'il diffère de celui qui est mentionné ci-dessus :

3. Jurisdiction to which subject:/
Compétence législative :

(Name of Province, State or Country) / (Province, État ou pays)

4. Date of incorporation/amalgamation:/
Date de la constitution ou de la fusion :

year/année month/mois day/jour

5. Date of original extra-provincial licence: / Date du permis extraprovincial original :

year/année month/mois day/jour

6. The name of the corporation has been changed in its home jurisdiction to: /
La dénomination sociale de la compagnie, dans la compétence législative de sa constitution, a été modifée de la façon suivante :

and the corporation requests that it be permitted to use this name in Ontario./
et la compagnie demande l'autorisation d'utiliser cette dénomination sociale en Ontario.

07066(04/01)

11.3 (continued)

2.

7. The corporation requests amendments to its provincial licence as follows: /
La compagnie demande que son permis extraprovincial soit modifié de la façon suivante :

8. The corporation has been authorized to make this application by a resolution passed by the directors of the corporation on /
La compagnie est autorisée à faire la présente demande au moyen d'une résolution adoptée par ses administrateurs le

year / année month / mois day / jour

This application is executed in duplicate. / La présente demande est signée en double exemplaire.

(Name of Corporation) / (Dénomination sociale de la compagnie)

By: / Signé :

(Signature) / (Signature)

(Description of Office) / (Fonctions)

(Corporate Seal) / (Sceau de la compagnie)

07066(04/01)

11.4 Application for Termination of Extra-Provincial Licence—*Extra-Provincial Corporations Act*—Form 4

Ontario Corporation Number
Numéro de la personne morale en Ontario 1.

Form 4
Extra-Provincial Corporations Act

Formule 4
Loi sur les personnes morales extraprovinciales

APPLICATION FOR TERMINATION OF EXTRA-PROVINCIAL LICENCE/
DEMANDE DE RÉSILIATION D'UN PERMIS EXTRAPROVINCIAL

1. Name of the Corporation(Print in UPPER CASE ONLY):
Dénomination sociale de la personne morale (Écrire en LETTRES MAJUSCULES SEULEMENT) :

2. Business name or style, other than the corporate name, under which the corporation is licensed in Ontario, if any (if none, state so): / Nom, autre que la dénomination sociale, sous lequel un permis est délivré à la personne morale en Ontario, le cas échéant (si ce n'est pas le cas, veuillez l'indiquer) :

3. Jurisdiction to which subject:/
Compétence législative :

(Name of Province, State or Country) / (Province, état et pays)

4. Date of incorporation/amalgamation:/
Date de la constitution ou de la fusion :

(year month day) / (année mois jour)

5. The corporation has ceased to carry on business in Ontario within the meaning of the Extra-Provincial Corporations Act on: / La personne morale a cessé d'exercer ses activités commerciales en Ontario au sens de la *Loi sur les personnes morales extraprovinciales* le :

(year month day) / (année mois jour)

6. The corporation therefore requests that the extra-provincial Licence and any amended extra-provincial licence obtained by the corporation be terminated. / La personne morale demande par conséquent la résiliation du permis extraprovincial ainsi que de tout permis extraprovincial modifié qu'elle a obtenus.

(Name of Corporation) / (Dénomination sociale de la personne morale)

By: / Signé : ______________________

(Signature) / (Signature)

(Description of Office) / (Fonctions)

(Corporate Seal) / (Sceau de la personne morale)

07067(04/01)

12. Searches

12.1 Registration or Renewal of Business Name or Style—*Business Names Act*—Form 2

Ontario

Ministry of Consumer and Commercial Relations / Ministère de la Consommation et du Commerce

Registration
under the Business Names Act – Corporations

Enregistrement
en vertu de la Loi sur les noms commerciaux (Personnes morales)

Print clearly in CAPITAL LETTERS / Écrivez clairement en LETTRES MAJUSCULES

Form 2

Formule 2

Page___ of /de ___

1. Registration Type / Type d'enregistrement
   BIN / NIE — If B, C or D enter "Business Identification Number" / En cas de B, C ou D, inscrivez «Le n° d'identification de l'entreprise»
   A New / Nouvel — B Renewal / Renouvellement — C Amendment / Modification — D Cancellation / Révocation

2. Business or Identification Name / Nom commercial ou d'identification

3. Mailing Address / Adresse postale
   Street Number / N° de rue — Street name / Nom de la rue — Suite No. / Bureau n°
   City/Town / Ville — Province — Country / Pays — Postal Code / Code postal

4. Business address in Ontario / Adresse d'affaires en Ontario — Same as above / Idem à ci-dessus
   Street Number / N° de rue — Street Name / Nom de la rue — Suite No. / Bureau n°
   City/Town / Ville — Province / Province **Ontario** — Postal Code / Code postal

5. Give a brief description of the **ACTIVITY** being carried out under the business/identification name.
   Résumez brièvement le genre d'**ACTIVITÉ** exercée sous le nom commercial ou d'identification.

6. Corporation Name / Personne morale

7. Ontario corporation number / Numéro matricule de la personne morale en Ontario

8. Jurisdiction in which the corporation was incorporated / Le territoire de compétence où la personne morale a été constituée

9. Address of Head or Registered Office of the corporation / Adresse du siège social ou du bureau enregistré de la personne morale
   Street Number / N° de rue — Street Name / Nom de la rue — Suite No. / Bureau n°
   City/Town / Ville — Province / Province — Country / Pays — Postal Code / Code postal

10. Print name of person authorizing this registration
    (either an officer, or a director, or a person acting under a power of attorney)
    Indiquez en lettres majuscules le nom de la personne autorisant l'enregistrement
    (dirigeant, administrateur ou personne habilitée en vertu d'une procuration)
    Last Name / Nom de famille
    First Name / Prénom
    Middle Name / 2e prénom
    OR / OU
    Additional Information / Renseignements supplémentaires

MINISTRY USE ONLY – RÉSERVÉ AU MINISTÈRE

C7197 (01/96) CD441

MINISTRY COPY / COPIE DU MINISTÈRE
Do Not Separate Copies / Ne pas détacher les copies

#

12.2 Request for Corporation Information

Ontario | Ministry of Consumer and Commercial Relations | Ministère de la Consommation et du Commerce | Companies Branch | Direction des compagnies

Request for Corporation Information
Demande de renseignements sur une personne morale

Please use separate forms for electronic and non-electronic products.
See instructions and description of products on reverse.
Please check appropriate box for product requested and whether uncertified or certified.

Veuillez utiliser des formules distinctes si vous désirez obtenir des documents électroniques et non électroniques.
Les instructions et les descriptions des documents se trouvent au verso.
Veuillez cocher les cases appropriées pour indiquer les documents désirés et s'ils doivent être certifiés ou non.

Electronic Search Products
Documents électroniques

For speedier service, please provide the Ontario Corporation Number below.
Afin d' accélérer le service, veuillez indiquer ci-dessous le numéro de la personne morale.

A: Point-in-Time Report / Rapport «Renseignements à une date déterminée»
B: Profile Report / Rapport de profil
C: Document List / Liste de documents
D: Business Names List / Liste de raison sociales
E: Certificate of Status / Certificat de statut
F: Certificate of No Record / Certificat d'absence de dossier
G: Certificate of Non-Filing / Certificat de non-dépôt

	Corporation Name / Raison Sociale	Ontario Corporation No. / Numéro de la personne morale	Point-in-Time Date / Date déteminée du rapport	A	B	C	D	E	F	G
1.				UNCERTIFIED / NON CERTIFIÉ						
				CERTIFIED / CERTIFIÉ						
2.				UNCERTIFIED / NON CERTIFIÉ						
				CERTIFIED / CERTIFIÉ						
3.				UNCERTIFIED / NON CERTIFIÉ						
				CERTIFIED / CERTIFIÉ						
4.				UNCERTIFIED / NON CERTIFIÉ						
				CERTIFIED / CERTIFIÉ						

Please use separate forms for electronic and non-electronic products.
See instructions and description of products on reverse.
Please check appropriate box for product requested and whether uncertified or certified.

Veuillez utiliser des formules distinctes si vous désirez obtenir des documents électroniques et non électroniques.
Les instructions et les descriptions des documents se trouvent au verso.
Veuillez cocher les cases appropriées pour indiquer les documents désirés et s'ils doivent être certifiés ou non.

Non-Electronic Search Products
Documents non électroniques

For speedier service, please provide the Ontario Corporation Number below.
Afin d' accélérer le service, veuillez indiquer ci-dessous le numéro de la personne morale.

H: Copy of Document/Notice where Profile not available / Copie du document/avis s'il n'y a pas de profil
I: Dossier - TC Files (copies) / Dossier - transf. (copies)
J: Microfiche / Microfiche

		Ontario Corporation No. / Numéro de la personne morale	H	I	J
1.	Corporation Name / Raison Sociale		UNCERTIFIED / NON-CERTIFIÉ		
			CERTIFIED / CERTIFIÉ		
	Name of Document(s) and Date(s) required / Nom du ou des document(s) and date(s)				
2.	Corporation Name / Raison Sociale		UNCERTIFIED / NON-CERTIFIÉ		
			CERTIFIED / CERTIFIÉ		
	Name of Document(s) and Date(s) required / Nom du ou des document(s) and date(s)				
3.	Corporation Name / Raison Sociale		UNCERTIFIED / NON CERTIFIÉ		
			CERTIFIED / CERTIFIÉ		
	Name of Document(s) and Date(s) required / Nom du ou des documen:(s) and date(s)				

Client Name/Nom du/de la client(e) :

Attention / Personne à contacter :

Address / Adresse

Signature / Signature | Date/Date | Telephone No. / N° de téléphone

☐ Mail out/ Envoyer par courrier ☐ Pick-up/Prendre livraison	Pick-up box #/ N° de la boîte	Account #/N° de compte	Sub-Account/Compte auxiliaire	Access I.D./Mot de passe

Ministry use only/Réservé au ministère

Request#/N° de la demande	Pull/Retrait	File/Dossier	Fiche/Fiche	Copies/Copies	Time In/Arrivé	Time Out/Départ	Pages/Pages	Fee/Droits	Clerk/Commis

07249(12/98)

12.3 Industry Canada Purchase Order/Invoice

Purchase Order

Page 1 of 4

Industry Canada Industrie Canada

Canada

For Departmental use only

PURCHASE ORDER / INVOICE

Purchase Order No.

Financial Control No.

For general instructions and codes, see page 2.

Deposit Account No.

Date

Responsible Branch

- ☐ Patents
- ☐ Corporations
- ☐ Trademarks
- ☐ Copyrights and Industrial Designs
- ☐ Registration
- ☐ Lobbyists,

12.3 (continued)

Purchase Order

Code	No. of Copies	Item Number or Description	Quantity	Amount

Canada

GST Registration No.

SUB TOTAL

GST, TPS

TOTAL

Make all payments to the order of the Receiver General for Canada

Date

Validation

K.C.-C.C.

Amount

Validation

K.C.-C.C.

Amount

Validation

K.C.-C.C.

Amount

MAILING

☐ Air mail

☐ Messenger

☐ Pick-up call

☐ Telephone

Mailing address

Name

Street and Number

12.3 (continued)

Purchase Order

City

Province or State

Postal Code

ATTENTION

INDUSTRY CANADA / INDUSTRIE CANADA 9th Floor, Jean Edmonds Towers South / 9ième étage, Tour Jean Edmond Sud 365 Laurier Avenue West / 365, avenue Laurier ouest Ottawa, Ontario K1A 0C8 / Ottawa (Ontario) K1A 0C8

PURCHASE ORDER INSTRUCTIONS

A. GENERAL

1. Indicate the Branch to which the request should be directed by placing an "X" in the appropriate box.

2. In the column entitled CODE, enter the code number or letter which corresponds to the requested service as described in section B below.

3. Under the heading ITEM NUMBER OR DESCRIPTION, enter the appropriate item number of the documents requested, OR, in the case of Corporations Directorate requests, include the complete corporate name, the corporate number and any specific details of the request. NOTE: Separate forms must be used for foreign patents.

4. In the area entitled MAILING, indicate desired method of delivery. NOTE: FOR CORPORATIONS DIRECTORATE CLIENTS: Indicate under ITEM NUMBER OR DESCRIPTION any other delivery instructions not provided in MAILING section.

5. Retain a copy for your records. There are no refunds for material ordered in error.
5.

B. CODE NUMBERS AND DESCRIPTIONS

Corporations Directorate Direction générale des Corporations
A. Filing fee for Articles.
B. Filing fee for Annual Return.
C. Filing fee for Exemptions.
D. Certified Copies (specify documents to be certified).
E. Certificate of Compliance.
F. Ordinary Copies.
G. Other (specify).

Other Branches

12.3 (continued)

Purchase Order

Page 4 of 4

1. Canadian Printed Patents.
*2. Certified Copies.
3. Drawings.
4. Claims.
5. Disclosure.
6. Specifications.
7. Record File.
8. Copy of Grant.
9. Assignments (e.g. Change of Name, Licence, Letters Testamentary, Certificate of Guardianship, Letters of Administration, Power of Letters Probate, Abstracts of Title, etc.).
10. File Covers Only.
11. Letters Patent (Registration Division).
12. Supplementary Letters Patent (Registration Division).
13. Other Items (specify) - In cases where documents requested are not identified by a number, use this code with a specific explanation as to the type of copy to be furnished. This may be typed across the form portion alloted to the purchaser.

* Certified Copies: codes depicting any specific document where certification is required must be coupled with code
2. For example: 4-2 indicates Claims - Certified.

Publication Date: 1999-09-28
Author: Industry Canada

12.4 *Personal Property Security Act*—Financing Statement/Claim for Lien—Form 1C

Ontario

Ministry of Consumer and Commercial Relations / Ministère de la Consommation et du Commerce

Account No. (if applicable) / Nº de compte (si pertinent) | Registration Account Code / Code du compte d'enregistrement

Form / Formule **1C**

Financing Statement / Claim for Lien
État de financement / Demande de privilège

Registration No. (for office use only) / Nº d'enregistrement (usage interne)
YYYY / AAAA MM / MM DD / JJ Time / heure Branch / Bureau Sequence / Séquence

File No / Nº de dossier: 085208769

Caution Filing / Avis de saisie | Page / Page | Total Pages / Nombre de pages | Motor Vehicle Schedule attached / Liste des véhicules automobiles annexée

01 OFF / 86 X

PPSA-P / RSLA-P | Registration Period / Période d'enregistrement

Debtor / Débiteur

02 Individual Debtor / Débiteur particulier — Date of Birth / Date de naissance (DD MM YYYY / JJ MM AAAA) — First Given Name / *Premier prénom* — Initial / Initiale — Surname / *Nom de famille*

03 Business Debtor / Débiteur commercial (Complete lines 02 & 04 or lines 03 & 04 / Compléter les lignes 02 et 04 ou les lignes 03 et 04)

Line 03 cont'd / *Ligne 03 (suite)*

Ontario Corporation No. / Nº matricule de la personne morale en Ontario

04 Address / *Adresse* — City, etc. / *Ville, etc.* — Prov. / Prov. — Postal Code / Code postal

Debtor / Débiteur

05 Individual Debtor / Débiteur particulier — Date of Birth / Date de naissance — First Given Name / *Premier prénom* — Initial / Initiale — Surname / *Nom de famille*

06 Business Debtor / Débiteur commercial (Complete lines 05 & 07 or lines 06 & 07 / Compléter les lignes 05 et 07 ou les lignes 06 et 07)

Line 06 cont'd / *Ligne 06 (suite)*

Ontario Corporation No. / Nº matricule de la personne morale en Ontario

07 Address / *Adresse* (Complete if different from line 04 / *Compléter si différente de la ligne 04*) — City, etc. / *Ville, etc.* — Prov. / Prov. — Postal Code / Code postal

Secured Party / Lien Claimant / Créancier garanti / Créancier privilégié

08 Secured Party / Lien Claimant / *Créancier garanti / Créancier privilégié*

09 Address / *Adresse* — City, etc. / *Ville, etc.* — Prov. / Prov. — Postal Code / Code postal

Collateral / Biens grevés

If PPSA, Section 1 **must** be completed.
If PPSA and only Consumer Goods, Sections 3 & 4 **must** also be completed.
If RSLA, Section 3 **must** be completed.

S'il s'agit de PPSA, la section 1 doit être remplie.
S'il s'agit de PPSA, et de biens de consommation seulement, les sections 3 et 4 doivent aussi être remplies.
S'il s'agit de RSLA, la section 3 doit être remplie.

Section 1: Collateral Classification / Classification des biens grevés. Type 'X' in appropriate box or boxes. Taper 'X' dans la (les) case(s) appropriée(s)

Consumer Goods / Biens de cons. — Inventory / Stock — Equipment / Matériel — Accounts / Comptes — Other / Autre

Section 2: Type 'X' if motor vehicle included / *Taper 'X' si véhicule automobile inclus.*

Section 3: Principal Amount Secured / Amount of the Lien / *Montant principal garanti / Montant du privilège*

Section 4: Date of Maturity / *Date d'échéance* (DD MM YYYY / JJ MM AAAA) — Type 'X' if no Fixed Date of Maturity / *Taper 'X' si la date d'échéance n'est pas déterminée*

10 X X X X X | X | $ .00 | OFF / 86 X

Motor Vehicle Description / *Description du véhicule automobile*
Year / *Année* — Make / *Marque* — Model / *Modèle* — Vehicle Identification No. / *Nº d'identification du véhicule*

11

12

If more than two vehicles, continue on the Motor Vehicle Schedule (Form 4C). / S'il y a plus de deux véhicules automobiles, utiliser la Liste des véhicules automobiles (formule 4C).

General Collateral Description (PPSA optional) / *Description générale du bien grevé (PPSA facultatif)*

13

14

15

Agent / Agent

Registering Agent (if other than Secured Party / Lien Claimant) / *Agent d'enregistrement (si autre que le créancier garanti / créancier privilégié)*

16 Name / *Nom*

17 Address / *Adresse* — City, etc. / *Ville, etc.* — Prov. / Prov. — Postal Code / Code postal

Authorized Signature / Signature autorisée

Name and Signature of Secured Party / Lien Claimant **OR** Name of Secured Party / Lien Claimant **AND** Name and Signature of Agent of Secured Party / Lien Claimant.
Nom et signature du créancier garanti / créancier privilégié **OU** *Nom du créancier garanti / créancier privilégié* **ET** *nom et signature de l'agent du créancier garanti / créancier privilégié.*

10551(10/98) This form must not be reproduced for registration purposes.
Cette formule ne doit pas être reproduite aux fins d'enregistrement.

Central Office Copy / *Exemplaire du bureau central*

12.5 *Personal Property Security Act*—Financing Change Statement/ Change Statement—Form 2C

Ontario

Account No. (if applicable) / N° de compte (si pertinent) | Registration Account Code / Code du compte d'enregistrement

Form / *Formule* 2C

Ministry of Consumer and Business Services | Ministère des Services aux consommateurs et aux entreprises

Financing Change Statement / Change Statement
État de modification du financement / État de modification

Part 1 / *Partie 1*

01 — Caution Filing / *Avertissement* | Page / *Page* | Total Pages / *Nbre de pages* | Motor Vehicle Schedule attached / *Liste des véhicules automobiles annexée* — OF / *DE*

Registration No. (for office use only) / *N° d'enregistrement (usage interne)*: YYYY / AAAA MM / MM DD / JJ Time / Heure Branch / Bureau

PPSA-P
RSLA-R

21 Reference File Number (see reverse) / *N° de dossier de référence (voir au verso)*

22 **Amendments Only / *Corrections seulement*** — Page No. of page to be amended / *N° de la page à corriger* OR / *OU* Type 'X' if no specific page is to be amended / *Taper 'X' s'il n'y a pas de page précise à corriger* | Enter Letter for Change (see reverse) / *Indiquer la lettre - code de modification (voir au verso)* | Enter Number of Additional Years if Renewal (see reverse) / *Indiquer le nombre d'années supplémentaires s'il s'agit d'un renouvellement (voir au verso)* | **Amendments Only / *Corrections seulement*** Type in Total Correct Registration Period (for reduction only) / *Indiquer la période totale exacte d'enregistrement (en cas de diminution seulement)*

23 Debtor Name (as recorded). Complete line 23 or 24 but not both / *Nom du débiteur (tel qu'inscrit). Remplir la ligne 23 ou 24 mais pas les deux.* — Individual Debtor / Transferor / *Débiteur particulier / Cédant* First Given name / *Premier prénom* | Initial / *Initiale* | Surname / *Nom de famille*

24 Business Debtor / Transferor / *Débiteur commercial / Cédant* — Line 24 cont'd / *Ligne 24 (suite)*

Part 2 / *Partie 2*

25 Specify Other Change here / *Préciser l'autre modification ici*

26 Enter below Reasons for Amendment / Other Change Description / *Motifs de correction à écrire ci-dessous / Description de l'autre modification*

27

28

Part 3 / *Partie 3*

02/05 Individual Debtor / Transferee / *Débiteur particulier / Cessionnaire* — Date of Birth / *Date de naissance* DD / JJ MM / MM YYYY / AAAA | First Given Name / *Premier prénom* | Initial / *Initiale* | Surname / *Nom de famille*

OR / *OU*

03/06 Business Debtor / Transferee / *Débiteur commercial / Cessionnaire* — Line 03/06 cont'd / *Ligne 03/06 (suite)* | Ontario Corporation No. / *N° matricule de la personne morale en Ontario*

04/07 Address / *Adresse* | City, etc. / *Ville, etc.* | Prov. / *Prov.* | Postal Code / *Code postal*

Part 4 / *Partie 4*

29 Assignor (as recorded) / *Cédant (tel qu'inscrit)*

08 Secured Party / Lien Claimant / Assignee / *Créancier garanti / Créancier privilégié / Ayant droit*

09 Address / *Adresse* | City, etc. / *Ville, etc.* | Prov. / *Prov.* | Postal Code / *Code postal*

Part 5 / *Partie 5*

10 **Section 1:** Collateral Classification / *Classification des biens grevés* — Type 'X' in appropriate box or boxes. / *Taper 'X' dans la (les) case(s) appropriée(s).* Consumer Goods / *Biens de cons.* | Inventory / *Stock* | Equipment / *Matériel* | Accounts / *Comptes* | Other / *Autre* — **Section 2:** Type 'X' if motor vehicle included / *Taper 'X' si véhicule automobile inclus.* — **Section 3:** Principal Amount Secured / Amount of the Lien / *Montant principal garanti / Montant du privilège* $ .00 — **Section 4:** Date of Maturity / *Date d'échéance* DD / JJ MM / MM YYYY / AAAA OR / *OU* Type 'X' if no Fixed Date of Maturity / *Taper 'X' si la date d'échéance n'est pas déterminée.*

Motor Vehicle Description / *Description du véhicule automobile* — Year / *Année* | Make / *Marque* | Model / *Modèle* | Vehicle Identification No. / *N° d'identification du véhicule*

11

12

If more than two vehicles, continue on the Motor Vehicle Schedule (Form 4C).
S'il y a plus de deux véhicules automobiles, utiliser la Liste des véhicules automobiles (formule 4C).

General Collateral Description / *Description générale du bien grevé*

13

14

15

Part 6 / *Partie 6*

Registering Agent / Secured Party / Lien Claimant / *Agent d'enregistrement / Créancier garanti / Créancier privilégié*

16 Name / *Nom*

17 Address / *Adresse* | City, etc. / *Ville, etc.* | Prov. / *Prov.* | Postal Code / *Code postal*

Authorized Signature / *Signature autorisée*

Name and Signature of Secured Party / Lien Claimant **OR** Name of Secured Party / Lien Claimant **AND** Name and Signature of Agent of Secured Party / Lien Claimant
*Nom et signature du créancier garanti / créancier privilégié **OU** Nom du créancier garanti / créancier privilégié **ET** nom et signature de l'agent du créancier garanti / créancier privilégié.*

10552(09/98) This form must not be reproduced for registration purposes.
Cette formule ne doit pas être reproduite aux fins d'enregistrement.

Central Office Copy /
Exemplaire du bureau central

12.6 *Personal Property Security Act*—Motor Vehicle Schedule—Form 4C

Ontario

Ministry of Consumer and Commercial Relations / Ministère de la Consommation et du Commerce

Form / *Formule* 4C

Motor Vehicle Schedule
Liste des véhicules automobiles

Complete and submit with a Form 1C or a Form 2C only if lines 11 and 12 have been completed.

Completer et présenter avec la formule 1C ou la formule 2C seulement si les lignes 11 et 12 ont été remplies.

01 Page / *Page* OF / *DE* Total Pages / *N^bre de pages*

Registration No. (for office use only) / *N° d'enregistrement (usage interne)*

YYYY / *AAAA* MM / *MM* DD / *JJ* Time / *Heure* Branch / *Bureau* Sequence / *Séquence*

00 Reference File Number (see reverse) / *N° de dossier de référence (voir au verso)*

	Year / *Année*	Make / *Marque*	Model / *Modèle*	Vehicle Identification No. / *N° d'identification du véhicule*
41				
42				
43				
44				
45				
46				
47				
48				
49				
50				
51				
52				
53				
54				
55				
56				

10554(10/98) This form must not be reproduced for registration purposes.
Cette formule ne doit pas être reproduite aux fins d'enregistrement.

Central Office Copy / *Exemplaire du bureau central*

12.7 Personal Property Security Registration Service Request

SERVICE REQUEST WORKSHEET

DATE:_________________________

CUSTOMER:

	NUMBER	FEE ($)	
VERBAL			
CERTIFICATE			
Adm (Total No	X $2) =		
	Total Enquiry Fees		✓

CSRA part/view			
CSRA photo			
PPSR TC/CTC			
Credit Issued			
Other			
Total Miscellaneous Fees			✓

1C's or Renewals (2C/ 3C)	A # of regs	B # OF YEARS	(A x B)	(A x B) x 8	
DISC.				N/C	
AMEND		@ $12 each =			
		Subtotal			
Total No		X 5 = Admin Fees			
		Total Registration Fees			✓

Last sequence			✓✓✓
First sequence		PAYMENT BY	
Last - First + 1		CA ________	
Less non-issues		CH ________	
Total Reg'ns		Cr rec'd________	
		TOTAL ______	

CLERK____________________

12.8 *Personal Property Security Act*—Enquiry Request

Ontario — Ministry Consumer and Commercial Relations / Ministère de la Consommation et du Commerce — Personal Property Registration Branch / Direction de l'enregistrement des sûretés mobilières

Enquiry Request
Demande de renseignements

TYPE (CAPITAL LETTERS ONLY) OR PRINT (BLOCK LETTERS ONLY)
DACTYLOGRAPHIER OU ÉCRIRE EN MAJUSCULES

Date

PAYMENT TYPE/TYPE DE PAIEMENT

☐ Cash/Espèces ☐ Cheque/Chèque ☐ Deposit Account/ Compte de dépôt ☐ Credit Card/Carte de crédit ☐ VISA ☐ Mastercard

Credit Card Number/Numéro de carte de crédit:

Expiry Date/ Date d'expiration:

Applicant's Signature/Signature du demandeur

Amount Paid/Montant payé $ ________ $

DEPOSIT ACCOUNT HOLDERS ONLY/TITULAIRES D'UN COMPTE DE DÉPÔT SEULEMENT

Deposit Account Number/Numéro du compte dépôt

Account Code/ Code du compte

To be completed by PPSR Staff only/Réservé au personnel de la DESM seulement:

Done by Operator#/Effectué par l'opérateur n°: ____________

for TBO use initials/pour le bureau de Toronto, inscrire ses initiales

(COMPLETE ONE FORM FOR EACH ENQUIRY)
(REMPLIR UNE FORMULE PAR DEMANDE DE RENSEIGNEMENTS)

Note: Before making an enquiry, please read the Enquiry Section (Part IV) of the Personal Property Security Registration and Enquiry Guide.

Remarque: Avant de faire une recherche, prière de lire la section traitant des recherches (partie IV) du guide pour l'enregistrement et la recherche des sûretés mobilières.

PART / PARTIE I **Complete A, B, C, or D to show type of enquiry required.**
Cocher la case A, B, C ou D pour indiquer le genre de recherche demandée.

A ☐ Motor Vehicle Identification Number Enquiry
Recherche sur le numéro d'identification du véhicule automobile
Vehicle Identification Number/Numéro d'identification du véhicule

If A complete 1 or 2
Si "A" cocher 1 ou 2
1 ☐ Exact Vehicle Identification Number
Numéro exact d'identification du véhicule
2 ☐ Exact and Similar Vehicle Identification Numbers
Numéro exact et semblade d'identification du véhicule

B ☐ Individual Non Specific Debtor Name Enquiry
Recherche sur le nom d'un particulier débiteur non spécifique
First Given Name/Premier prénom — Surname/Nom de famille

C ☐ Individual Specific Debtor Name Enquiry
Recherche sur le nom d un particulier débiteur spécifique
First Given Name/Premier prénom — Initial/Initiale — Surname/Nom de famille — Date of Birth/Date de Naissance D/J M/M YYYY/AAAA

D ☐ Business Debtor Name Enquiry
Recherche sur le nom d'un débiteur commercial
Business, Corporate, Partnership or Other Name (As Appropriate)/Enterprise, personne morale, société en nom collectif ou autre raison sociale (le cas échéant)

PART / PARTIE II **Complete only if up-date enquiry response required.**
Remplir seulement si une réponse à jour est requise à la suite de la recherche.

A ☐ Include only Registrations Recorded in the System as of:
Inclure seulement les enregistrements entrés dans le système en date du:
Date / Date D/J M/M YYYY/AAAA

PART / PARTIE III **Complete A or B to show type of response required.**
Cocher le case A ou B, pour indiquer le genre de réponse demandée.

A ☐ **Immediately**
Printed Response (Uncertified)
Réponse non certifiée

B ☐ **Overnight**
Certified Response
Réponse Certifée

PART / PARTIE IV **Complete A or B to indicate if English or French response is required. (Headings only).**
Cocher "A" ou "B" pour indiquer si la réponse est requise en anglais ou en français. (Rubriques seulement).

A ☐ English/Anglais B ☐ French/Français

PART / PARTIE V Indicate if response is to be
Indiquez si vous voulez votre réponse A ☐ Mailed/Par la poste B ☐ Picked Up/en personne

Applicant's Name/Nom du demandeur — Attention (If Applicable) Aux soins de (le cas échéant)

To be completed - FOR MAILING RESPONSE
À remplir - POUR RÉPONSE POSTALE

Street Address/Address (Rue et numero)

City, Town, Etc./Ville, Etc. — Province/Province — Postal Code/Code Postal

10512 (06/96)

See Reverse for Application for Used Vehicle Information Package/Pour la Trousse d' Information Sur les Vehicules d'ocassion voyez au verso.

12.9 Notice of Intention—*Bank Act*

NOTICE OF INTENTION **FORM 710 Part 1 (9-80)**

The Firm or Company must be correctly designated, in case of individuals give name in full.

TO WHOM IT MAY CONCERN:

____________________ ____________________

(Name of Person, Firm or Company) **(Post Office Address)**

hereby gives notice that it is my/our intention to give security under the authority of section 427 of the Bank Act, to ____________________ (Name of Bank)

Dated at ________________ this ________________ day of ____________ 19____.

____

____

06702-003

(Only Part 1 of this form needs to be signed by the cusotmer)

NOTICE OF INTENTION **FORM 710 Part 2 (9-80)**

N.B.–This document must be renewed and registered within three years.

The Firm or Company must be correctly designated, in case of individuals give name in full.

TO WHOM IT MAY CONCERN:

____________________ ____________________

(Name of Person, Firm or Company) **(Post Office Address)**

hereby gives notice that it is my/our intention to give security under the authority of section 427 of the Bank Act, to ____________________ (Name of Bank)

Dated at ________________ this ________________ day of ____________ 19____.

____

____

06702-003

(Only Part 1 of this form needs to be signed by the cusotmer)

12.10 Bankruptcy Certificate

Monday, October 22, 2001 Page 1 of 1

Office of the Superintendent of Bankruptcy Canada
An Agency of Industry Canada

Bureau du surintendant des faillites Canada
Un organisme d'Industrie Canada

Canada

INSOLVENCY SEARCH

2001/10/22

Search : Word = ' ', Debtor = 'Both'

Reference :

A name search has been made of the public record kept by the Superintendent of Bankruptcy for all the Districts and Divisions in Canada.

The public record was found to contain no facts nor any reference to the aforementioned name, from 1978 to 2001/10/17.

Canada

OSB • BSF Protecting the Integrity of the Insolvency System / Protéger l'intégrité du système d'insolvabilité

osb-bsf.gc.ca

12.11 Application for Vehicle Record Search

Ontario | Ministry of Transportation | Ministère des Transports | Licensing and Control Branch | Direction des permis et de l'immatriculation

Application for Vehicle Record Search
Demande de recherches au dossier d'un véhicule

Application Date / *Date de la demande* Y/A M D/J

☐ To be picked up / *L'auteur de la demande passera prendre la réponse*

☐ To be mailed / *À expédier par la poste*

Your File No. / *N° de votre dossier*

Telephone No. / *N° de téléphone*

Name and Address of Individual / Company Receiving Information
Nom et adresse de la personne / compagnie recevant les renseignements

State the reason why this information is required.
Donnez la raison pour laquelle vous désirez ces renseignements.

Head Office Use Only
Réservé au bureau principal
Name of Vehicle Owner

Ministry Use Only
Réservé au ministère
Personal Identification Viewed (State name of document)

Report No. | Office No. | Fee Paid $

Please provide all known information about the vehicle being searched.
Veuillez fournir tous les renseignements connus sur le véhicule qui fait l'objet des recherches.

Ont. Licence Plate No. / *N° d'immatriculation de l'Ont.*

Vehicle Identification No. (V.I.N.) / *N° d'identification du véhicule (N.I.V.)*

Name of Vehicle Owner / *Nom du propriétaire du véhicule*

Individual / *Particulier*

Driver's Licence No. / *N° du permis de conduire*

Name / *Nom*

Company / *Compagnie*

Registrant Identification No. (R.I.N.) / *N° d'identification du conducteur (N.I.C.)*

Name / *Nom*

Name / *Nom*

Address of Vehicle Owner / *Adresse du propriétaire du véhicule*

Street Number and Name or Lot, Concession and Twp. / *N° et rue ou lot, concession, canton* | Apt. No. / *App. n°*

City, Town or Village / *Ville ou village* | Postal Code / *Code postal*

Applicant's Signature
Signature de l'auteur de la demande ____________________

The Ministry may decline to supply information unless satisfied that it is required in connection with a matter involving a motor vehicle.

Le ministère peut refuser de fournir les renseignements demandés s'il estime que la demande ne se rapporte pas à une question relative à un véhicule automobile.

Request for Search
Demande de recherches
Check appropriate box(es).
Cochez la ou les cases appropriées.

☐ Current Vehicle, Owner and Plate Information / *Renseignements actuels concernant le véhicule, son propriétaire ou son immatriculation.*

☐ Vehicle, Owner and Plate Information on / *Renseignements sur le véhicule, son propriétaire ou son immatriculation le* Y/A M D/J

☐ History of Vehicle, Owner(s), and Plate(s) for the past 3 years. / *Historique du véhicule, de son ou ses propriétaires ou immatriculation(s) au cours des trois dernières années.*

Request for Document
Demande de documents
Please provide all known information about the document you need. / *Veuillez fournir tous les renseignements connus au sujet des documents dont vous avez besoin.*

☐ Certified copy of each search or document for legal purposes. / *Copie certifiée conforme de chaque recherche ou document à des fins juridiques.*

Fees / Droits Please make cheque or money order payable to the Minister of Finance. / *Libellez les chèques ou mandats à l'ordre du ministre des Finances.*

$12.00	for each search request	*12 $*	*pour chaque demande de recherches*
$6.00	additional each certified request	*6 $*	*de plus pour chaque demande de recherche certifiée*

If vehicle owner has more than 1 vehicle, a $12.00 fee will be required for each vehicle found on the record. / *Si le propriétaire possède plus d'un véhicule, des droits additionnels de 12 $ sont perçus pour chaque véhicule au dossier.*

Send application with fees to:
Envoyez les demandes et les droits au :

Ministry of Transportation
Data Management, East Bldg.
2680 Keele Street
Downsview, Ontario M3M 3E6

Ministère des Transports
Gestion des données
2680, rue Keele, édifice est
Downsview (Ontario) M3M 3E6

SR-LV-61 95-03

M.T.O. - Data Management / *Gestion des données*

13. Federal Incorporations

13.1 Federal Name Granting Policy Compendium

Corporations Database Online

Page 1 of 1

Industry Canada Industrie Canada

Canada

Name Granting Compendium

- Introduction
- I. Absolutely Prohibited
- II. Qualifiedly Prohibited
- III. Obscene
- IV. Lacking Distinctiveness
- V. Confusion
- VI. Deceptively Misdescriptive
- VII. Other Related Policies

Last Modified: 2001-10-01

Important Notices and Disclaimers
Privacy Statement

Canada
http://strategis.gc.ca

13.1 (continued)

Industry Canada Industrie Canada Canada

NAME GRANTING COMPENDIUM

April 22, 1999.

Policy Statement 1.1.

INTRODUCTION TO NAME POLICIES

The *Canada Business Corporations Act* and the *Canada Corporations Act* have almost identical name regulations describing those types of corporate names which are prohibited. Essentially, one cannot have a name that lacks distinctiveness, that is likely to cause confusion with other businesses or that is misdescriptive or obscene.

The policies contained in this document are guidelines for interpreting the name regulations. They try to demonstrate how certain regulations will be applied in certain types of fact situations. Since, however, each name decision requires an exercise of judgment, based on the particular facts of that case, and after considering a number of factors , any one particular regulation and guideline may not necessarily determine the decision.

The following checklist should provide assistance in deciding which policies may be important for a particular corporate name:

1. Have you included an ABSOLUTELY PROHIBITED TERM in your name? Check regulation 16 (page 1.1) regarding the use of "Air Canada", "Trans Canada Airlines" or "Lignes Aeriennes Trans Canada", "Canada Standard" or "CS", "Cooperative", "Co-op" or "Pool", "Parliament Hill" or "Colline du Parlement", "Royal Canadian Mounted Police" or "Gendarmerie Royale du Canada", "RCMP" or "GRC", "United Nations" or "Nations Unies", "UN" or "ONU".

2. Where you are using "CANADA" or the name of a province in your name, check regulation 17(a) and(b) (page 2.1). Your name should not give the impression of being a government sponsored entity.

3. If your corporation will be in a PROFESSIONAL or EDUCATIONAL field, ensure that your name does not mislead or connote affiliation with an existing body. (See regulation 17(c) (page 2.4).

4. If your corporation will have activities of a FINANCIAL nature, make sure that

13.1 (continued)

you are not contravening federal trust, loan, insurance or banking legislation. (See regulation 17 (d)(page 2.5).

5. Your name must have some DISTINCTIVENESS to distinguish your business from that of others. You cannot have a name that merely describes your business or is merely the name of a person or a geographic location. Check regulation 19 (a),(b) and (d) for details (pages 4.1 and 4.4). Keep in mind that the more distinctive your name is, the more protection it will get.

6. If you are using the name of an individual in your corporate name, you may be required to file a CONSENT OF that INDIVIDUAL unless he or she is a director or incorporator. (See regulations 19(c) and 21 (page 4.2).

7. If you are using INITIALS in your proposed corporate name, you should check page 5.3 for guidelines explaining when names with initials are confusing. If you are proposing the use of initials with surnames, see also page 5.9.

8. Your corporation should not appear to be the holding corporation of other, unrelated businesses which happen to use the same distinctive element as yours in their names. The use of the word "GROUP" can give this impression. Check page 5.4 if you are planning to use the word "group".

9. The name you propose will not be found to be available if it seems likely to cause CONFUSION with existing business names (whether or not incorporated) or trade-marks. Confusion can be between names A and B so that A and B are likely to be mistaken for the same company, or it can be between A and B where A misleadingly looks related to B. Both are instances of confusion.

   You are required to obtain and file a Newly Upgraded Automated Name Search (NUANS) report that will list business names and trade-marks which sound the same as your name. Such a search can be obtained from private businesses known as Search Houses, which are listed under "Searchers of Records" in your telephone book. Officers of the Directorate will examine the NUANS search with certain factors in mind: Do any of the names or trade-marks which sound alike appear to be in the same business as yours? Would they likely have the same type of client or territory of operation as yours? How much protection do they deserve?

   Officers of the Directorate will have the INFORMATION listed in the paragraph above only if you provide it to them when making your submission. If you have satisfied yourself that your corporation will not create a likelihood of confusion, give the Directorate the basis for your conclusions. Chances are it will satisfy the Director. Name submissions often must be rejected for lack of this kind of information. For more details concerning how the Directorate determines whether there is a likelihood of confusion, see regulations 13 and 20 (page 5.1). For more detail about what information to file, see page b.1.2. Failure to provide this information with the first submission of your proposed corporate name will likely result in the rejection of your name request. Approval is often not possible until the information is provided.

13.1 (continued)

Introd Page 3 of 7

10. If you are taking the name of a corporation which has been DISSOLVED, check regulation 22 (page 5.4). For a period of two years after the dissolved corporation ceases operations, its memory is thought to stay in the public's mind. You will not be able to have the exact same name during that TWO YEAR PERIOD. As explained in item 12 below, you may choose to resolve this problem by adding some distinguishing feature to your name which can be removed after the two year period has expired.

11. If you are REVIVING a corporation that has been dissolved, check regulation 22 (page 5.4). The name may now be prohibited if another corporation was incorporated since your corporation was dissolved.

12. Under certain conditions, you are permitted to have names that appear to be confusing with an existing business name (i.e.,appear to be the same business as an existing business, or appear to be affiliated with an existing business). Essentially, the EXISTING BUSINESS must CONSENT, (regulation 26) or, must CONSENT AND UNDERTAKE to change its name. Even then, because of the two year period referred to in item 10 above, there may still be confusion unless certain other conditions are met. If you wish to use the name of a corporation which has been INACTIVE FOR TWO YEARS, check regulation 25 (page 5.5.1). If you wish to incorporate AN AFFILIATE of an existing corporation, check regulation 26 (page 5.5.1). If you wish to incorporate a corporation which will TAKE OVER THE BUSINESS of an existing corporation, check regulation 27 (page 5.6). If you are proposing an AMALGAMATION, check regulation 28(1)(page 5.8) for names which are permissible for the amalgamated corporation. In order to use a name identical to the name of an affiliated corporation whose ASSETS your corporation will ACQUIRE, check regulation 28(2) (page5.8). If the existing corporation whose name you wish to take is BANKRUPT, check page 5.9 for the consent that is required.

13. If your proposed name appears to be confusing with a TRADE-MARK which has been registered for 5 or more years, you will have trouble getting approval of that name. (See page 5.5).

14. The Directorate is reluctant to approve names for profit-making corporations which contain words such as "INSTITUTE" or "CLUB". These words are more commonly used in the names of non-profit corporations and may, for that reason, be misleading. (See page 6.1).

15. The same regulations apply in respect of the CONTINUANCE of a corporation as in respect of its incorporation.

16. The legislation and policies with respect to the names of NON-PROFIT corporations are a little different. Generally, it is accepted that non-profit names tend to be more general and descriptive. Non-profit names are less likely to be rejected for being too general or merely descriptive, as set out in item 5 above. (See page 7.1).

13.1 (continued)

17. If you are proposing a BILINGUAL corporate name, you must ensure that the two language forms are not so different from one another that they appear to be two different corporations. (See pages.7.1 to 7.4).

18. If the French and English versions of your corporate name are similar enough you may not need two NUANS search reports. (See page 7.5).

19. For information on how to get PROTECTION FROM TRADE-MARKS which may be registered after your incorporation, check page 5.5 and the Appendix.

What is a Name Reservation?

One can only say that he or she has reserved their proposed corporate name when the following two things have been done:

1. A NUANS search has been run on the proposed name, and
2. The Director, CBCA has determined that the proposed name does not contravene the regulations. In order for the Director to make this determination, the proposed name has to be submitted to the Corporations Directorate accompanied by the NUANS search report. This can be done before articles are filed if it is important that the articles not be rejected (Save yourself time! Use this method!). Otherwise, the Director's decision will be taken when articles of incorporation etc. are filed in a certain proposed name.

Once the director has decided that a particular name is approved, that name is automatically reserved retroactive to the date the NUANS search report was requested, i.e. the date appearing in the right-hand column beside the proposed name. Note that where two consecutive dates appear in the right hand column, the reservation will be retroactive to the earlier of the two dates.

Facts are necessary for a Name Decision

Most name decisions can not be made without at least some information. Even where no confusingly similar names appear on the search report and there is therefore no concern about confusion, the Director can not properly assess whether a name connotes government sponsorship, connotes the business of trust, loan, insurance or banking, misdescribes, or merely describes the business of a corporation unless she is given some information about what that business will be.

Where there are similar names on the search report, even more information becomes necessary, that is, the type of information listed in regulation 20:

- the TYPE OF BUSINESS the proposed company will carry on and how this business is dissimilar to the activities of existing businesses which have similar names

- WHERE THE PROPOSED COMPANY WILL CARRY ON ITS BUSINESS and whether this territory is different from the territory in which other businesses with similar names and similar activities are operating

13.1 (continued)

- with WHAT TYPES OF CLIENT the proposed company will do business and whether they are different from the types of people that existing businesses, with similar names and similar activities in a similar territory, will do business - e.g. deal with retailers, computer programmers or the general public

- the DERIVATION OF THE DISTINCTIVE ELEMENT(S) of the proposed name. If there is a very reasonable sounding explanation for why the client wants that distinctive element, one is less likely to suspect that the client is trying to trade on the goodwill of an existing business with a similar name

- whether the proposed company will be RELATED TO EXISTING BUSINESSES with similar names or trade marks and if so, the consent of some or all of them

- whether the proposed company has a FOREIGN PARENT with a similar name which carries on business or is known in Canada. If so, consent is required and proposed company must add (Canada) or "of Canada".

- whether an EARLIER RESERVATION of a similar name which appears on the search report, was made by the same client.

- the CONSENT OF AN INDIVIDUAL whose name appears in the corporate name, unless that individual is an incorporator or a director. The consenting individual must indicate that he has or had a material interest.

Too often the applicant fails to give us this information and the name must be rejected because the Director has no basis on which to satisfy herself that the new corporate name will not create a likelihood of confusion with existing similar names appearing on the search report.

Without this information it may appear that the proposed name will be likely to be confused with an existing name which appears to be in the same business, in the same territory. With the information, it sometimes becomes clear that the two businesses are, in fact, significantly different, in totally different territories, dealing with different types of people and therefore confusion is not likely.

Generally speaking, if the applicant has reviewed the search report carefully and is satisfied in his/her own mind that the new corporation is not likely to cause confusion, he/she can also satisfy the Director. It is merely a matter of giving to the Director information upon which he/she bases his/her own conclusion. Applicants should always be reasonably cautious in reaching their conclusion however because it is very painful to be sued by an existing business or to be required by the Director to change their corporate name a year later after the Director has been persuaded by an existing business that the new corporation really does create a likelihood of confusion. Of course, the new corporation would always have the opportunity to state its case before the Director's decision was taken.

<u>VOICE INFORMATION SYSTEM FOR THOSE WHO PREFER TO GET THIS INFORMATION ORALLY</u>

The Corporations Directorate has implemented a Voice Information System, providing taped answers to commonly asked questions about federal corporate name-granting issues. The system is intended to

13.1 (continued)

be an alternate method for explaining, orally, to our clients how to get a name approval or what to do when their proposed corporate name has been rejected. The system is fully bilingual and accessible by calling either (613) 946-0147 or (613) 946-0148.

CBCA REGULATIONS AND RELATED POLICIES IN NAME GRANTING PROCESS

What is a corporate name?

Generally, a corporate name is composed of three elements:

A DISTINCTIVE element which is the unique identifier of the name.
A DESCRIPTIVE element which describes the line of business.
A LEGAL element which indicates the legal status of the company as an incorporated body.

TELFAX	**COMMERCIAL COMMUNICATIONS**	**LTD.**
distinctive	descriptive	legal
element	element	element

To decide whether or not a proposed name is available, several guidelines apply. In accordance with the Canada Business Corporations Act and its regulations, one must consider if the proposed name is:

I. absolutely prohibited
II. qualifiedly prohibited
III. obscene
IV. lacking distinctiveness
V. confusing
VI. deceptively misdescriptive

In the following pages, each of the specific Canada Business Corporations Act Regulations is presented with the related policies of the Directorate.

INTERPRETATION

12. In this Part,

"confusing", in relation to a corporate name, means a corporate name the use of which causes confusion with a trade mark or trade name in the manner described in section 13; (prête à confusion)

"distinctive", in relation to a trade name, means a trade name that actually distinguished the business in association with which it is used by its owner from the business of others or that is adapted so as to distinguish them; (distinctif)

"secondary meaning", in relation to a trade name, means a trade name that has been used in Canada or elsewhere by any applicant or his predecessors as to have become distinctive in Canada as at the date of filing an application for a corporate name; (sens dérivié)

13.1 (continued)

"trademark", means a trade mark as defined by the *Trade Marks Act*; (marque de commerce)

"trade name", means the name under which any business is carried on, whether it is the name of a body corporate, a trust, a partnership, a proprietorship or an individual; (nom commercial)

"use" means actual use by a person that carries on business in Canada or elsewhere (emploi)

RESERVATION OF CORPORATE NAME

15.(1) A request, pursuant to section 11 of the Act, to be made by submitting to the Director the original of a Canada-biased NUANS search report dated not more than 90 days before the date of its submission.

(2) Where the corporate name requested has an English form and a French form or a combined English and French form in a single name; and the English and French forms are phonetically dissimilar, the originals of separate NUANS search reports shall be submitted for both the English and French forms.

15.1 For the purpose of section 15, "NUANS search report" means the computer-generated search report that identifies trade names which are phonetically similar to the corporate name in respect of which the search is performed and that is produced by the Newly Upgraded Automated Name Search (NUANS) system, which uses the national data bank of existing and reserved trade names, and registered and applied-for trade-marks, in Canada.

15.2 For the purpose of paragraph 12(1)(a) of the Act, a corporate name is prohibited in respect of a request to reserve if it is the same as, or is confusing with, a corporate name that has, before the date of the request, been reserved by the Director for another person, unless

(a) written consent has been obtained from the person for whom the corporate name was reserved; or

(b) the 90-day reservation period referred to in subsection 11(1) of the Act has expired without the person for whom the corporate name was reserved having made a renewed request to reserve the corporate name.

15.3 Sections 15 to 15.2 apply in respect of an application for revival submitted to the Director in accordance with section 209 of the Act.

Publication Date: 1999-11-19
Author: Industry Canada

13.1 (continued)

Industry Canada Industrie Canada

Canada

NAME GRANTING COMPENDIUM

I. <u>ABSOLUTELY PROHIBITED</u>

16. FOR THE PURPOSES OF PARAGRAPH 12(1)(a) of the Act, a corporate name is prohibited where the name contains any of the following:

a) "AIR CANADA"

b) "TRANS CANADA AIRLINES" or "LIGNES AERIENNES TRANS CANADA"

c) "CANADA STANDARD" or "CS"

d) "COOPERATIVE", "COOPERATIVE, "CO-OP" or "POOL" where it connotes a cooperative venture

e) "PARLIAMENT HILL" or "COLLINE DU PARLEMENT"

f) "ROYAL CANADIAN MOUNTED POLICE", "GENDARMERIE ROYALE DU CANADA", "RCMP" or "GRC"

g) "UNITED NATIONS", "NATION UNIES", "UN" or "ONU"

13.1 (continued)

Industry Canada Industrie Canada

Canada

NAME GRANTING COMPENDIUM

II. QUALIFIEDLY PROHIBITED

17. FOR THE PURPOSES OF PARAGRAPH 12(1)(a) of the Act, a corporate name is prohibited where the name connotes that the corporation

> **a) carries on business under royal, vice-regal or governmental patronage, approval or authority, unless the appropriate government department or agency requests the name in writing**

17. FOR THE PURPOSES OF PARAGRAPH 12(1)(a) of the Act, a corporate name is prohibited where the name connotes that the corporation

> **b) is sponsored or controlled by or is affiliated with the Government of Canada, the government of a province, the government of a country other than Canada or a political subdivision or agency of any such government, unless the appropriate government, political subdivision or agency consents in writing to the use of the name**

Related Policies

Examples of names which connote government sponsorship and control:

"SPORTS CANADA"
"CANADIAN ASSOCIATION OF POSTMASTERS"
"HEALTH & WELFARE PROGRAMMERS ASSOCIATION"
"CANADIAN ARMED FORCES"
"CANADIAN FORCES"

ABBREVIATIONS FOR GOVERNMENT DEPARTMENTS

Some care should be taken when allowing initials that could connote government sponsorship or control in a proposed name. For example: The abbreviation "IC" for Industry Canada would be available with a descriptive feature like "shoes" providing that it is not confusing. The same distinctive element with a descriptive feature like "Corporate Information Services" would be unavailable because of the government connotation implied.

USE OF (ALTA), (ALBERTA), (B.C.), (BRITISH COLUMBIA) AND NOVA SCOTIA,

13.1 (continued)

II. Qu

MANITOBA AND
SASKATCHEWAN IN FEDERAL CORPORATE NAMES

At the request of Alberta and British Columbia Governments, we will no longer allow the use of the terms "(ALTA), "(ALBERTA)", "(B.C.)" or "(BRITISH COLUMBIA)" in a federal corporate name. This format is reserved for companies incorporated in those two provinces as affiliates of an extra-provincial company of the same or similar name. If a client has strong objections, he may wish to contact the respective Alberta and British Columbia Companies Branch to try to obtain clearance.

The terms "ALTA", "ALBERTA", and "OF ALBERTA" will be available unless they give a government connotation to the name in which case consent of the relevant government authority will be necessary.

The terms "B.C.", "BRITISH COLUMBIA" and "OF BRITISH COLUMBIA" will not be available without the approval of B.C. Registrar of Companies.

While the Alberta Companies Branch leaves it up to us to determine when there is governmental connotation, the British Columbia Registrar of Companies wishes all names of this nature to be referred to his office for that determination to be made.

Chart form of the above:

Click here to download the Adobe Acrobat version of the chart.

USE OF NOVA SCOTIA

"Nova Scotia" cannot be used as the first word in a corporate name without consent from the Nova Scotia Companies Branch.

Address:
Registrar of Joint Stock Companies
Department of the Attorney General
Box 1529, Centennial Building
1660 Hollis Street
Halifax, N.S. B3J 2Y4
Tel: (902) 424-7742

USE OF MANITOBA

"Manitoba" cannot be used in the name of a proposed federal company without consent from the Corporations Branch in Manitoba.

Address:
Director
Corporations Branch
Dept. of Consumer and Corporate Affairs and Environment
10th Floor, Woodsworth Building

13.1 (continued)

405 Broadway Avenue
Winnipeg, Manitoba R3C 3L6
Telephone: (204) 945-2500

USE OF SASK., SASKATCHEWAN (SASK), (SASKATCHEWAN) or coined words such as SASKO

1. SASK., SASKATCHEWAN, (SASK), (SASKATCHEWAN)

These words are permitted near the end of a corporate name if:

1) the corporation is an affiliate of an existing corporation and
2) its registered office is located in, or it carries on business in Saskatchewan

2. SASK., SASKATCHEWAN or coined words such as SASKO

These words are not permitted at the beginning of a corporate name unless the applicant has the consent of the Saskatchewan Department of Consumer and Commercial Affairs.

Address:
Director
Corporations Branch
Dept. of Justice
1871 Smith Street
Regina, Saskatchewan S4P 3V7
Telephone: (306) 787-2962

USE OF NEWFOUNDLAND OR NFLD

"Newfoundland" or "Nfld" are not permitted in a name proposed for a federal company without consent from the Registrar of Deeds, Companies and Securities in Newfoundland.

Address:
Registrar of Deeds, Companies and Securities
Department of Justice
Box 4750, Confederation Building
Ground Floor, East Block
St. John's, NFLD A1C 5T7
Telephone: (709) 729-3317

USE OF NEW BRUNSWICK

"New Brunswick" cannot be used at the beginning of a corporate name without consent from the Director, Corporate and Trust Affairs in New Brunswick.

Address:
Director
Corporate and Trust Affairs
Department of Justice

13.1 (continued)

Consumer and Corporate Affairs
P.O. Box 6000, Centennial Building, Suite 475
Fredericton, N.B. E3B 5H1
Telephone: (506) 453-2703

USE OF NAMES OF FOREIGN COUNTRIES

A name such as XYZ (Switzerland) Inc. would be available without consent of the Swiss government.

17. FOR THE PURPOSES OF PARAGRAPH 12(1)(a) of the Act, a corporate name is prohibited where the name connotes that the corporation

> **c) is sponsored or controlled by or is affiliated with a university or an association of accountants, architects, physicians, engineers, lawyers, surgeons or any other professional association recognized by the laws of Canada or a province unless the appropriate university or professional association consents in writing to the use of the name.**

Related Policies

Professional Associations

This regulation should be interpreted liberally, that is to say that we should not require the consent of a certain professional organization every time a proposed name makes reference in any way to a member or members of that profession.

e.g. Heritage Lawyers' Association - no consent required
John Brown Accounting Services Ltd. - no consent required
Black & White Engineers or
Engineering & Consulting Ltd.- no consent required

Rather, consent will be required only when the proposed name is confusingly similar with a particular university or professional association.

e.g. University of Montreal Debating Society - consent required
Upper Canada Lawyers' Debating Society (Law Society of Upper Canada - the professional association) - consent required
Certified General Accountants Debating Society - consent required

(This means that 17(c) will, in fact, be a restatement of the general rule against permitting confusing names.)

Since we are not aware of the names of all professional bodies, in each case where a proposed name refers to an existing profession, the applicant should be specifically asked whether this name is likely to be confusing with any existing professional association. As long as he says "no" (noted on file) we can incorporate. However, because the use of any name granted is subject to the laws of the

13.1 (continued)

jurisdiction where the company carries on business, the applicant may wish to contact the appropriate authorities for more information before using the name. It is to be noted that the various provincial professional bodies have their own remedies against misuse of their professional titles and that a provincial legislature has the power to legislate in such a way to prevent a federal professional association from being able to carry on operations in its province.

Where no professional regulating body exists in a particular field, we can incorporate a body purporting to be such a professional association and the use of the word "professional" in the name should not be prohibited.

e.g. North American Professional Shoemakers' Association

Note: We would also incorporate another body purporting to offer the same professional services (i.e. shoemakers' association) providing that the name proposed for that company is not confusing with the existing professional association.

e.g. North American Professional Shoemakers' Association - existing
Uniso Professional Shoemakers' Society - acceptable

Exception:
The name of a professional association bearing the words "Corporation Professionnelle du Québec" will be refused, unless it is accompanied by the consent of the Office des Professions du Québec, since it connotes an organization approved by the professional code of Quebec.

Use of the term University

Where the name of a proposed corporation uses the term university in a fashion that suggests that the corporation is a degree-granting institution, the name will be rejected as being misleading unless it can be established that the corporation has been authorized by the relevant federal or provincial authority to issue degrees.

e.g. University Painters Inc. - acceptable

e.g. Northern University Inc. - misleading

Use of terms College, School, Adult Education, Research, Applied Research

Where the name of a proposed corporation uses the terms academy, college, school, 'institute', adult education, research, applied research or a like term, and it appears either from the name itself, or from other information we have, that the proposed corporation will grant bachelors, masters or doctorate degrees or a licentiate without the authorization of a relevant authority, the name will be rejected for being misleading.

e.g. Sudbury Typing College (Inc) - acceptable

e.g. Northwest Applied Research (Inc) - unacceptable if it issues degrees without authorization

13.1 (continued)

When an application is received for the incorporation of a post-secondary educational institution, with the aim of granting a bachelors, masters or doctorate degree or a licentiate (as a university or college), the application will be referred to the Association of Universities and Colleges of Canada, 350 Albert St. Suite 600, Ottawa, Ontario, K1R 1B1 for comment. Enquiries (613) 563-1236 ext 345.

17. FOR THE PURPOSES OF PARAGRAPH 12(1)(a) of the Act, a corporate name is prohibited where the name connotes that the corporation

> **d) carries on the business of a bank, loan company, insurance company, trust company, other financial intermediary or a stock exchange that is regulated by a law of Canada or a province unless the appropriate government department or agency consents in writing to the use of the name**

Related policies

In cases where it is not clear whether a particular proposed corporate name connotes the business of loan, trust, insurance or banking, the Corporations Directorate asks the applicant to obtain the advice of the Office of the Superintendent of Financial Institutions (OSFI). OSFI staff will provide this advice to applicants. The following are the guidelines that should be followed for these types of corporate names:

A. When a proposed name intended for a CBCA corporation appears to connote a loan or trust company or a subsidiary of a bank, the applicant should refer to the Office of the Superintendent of Financial Institutions, Rulings and Compliance Division at (613) 990-7251 or (613) 990-0557. Where it appears to connote an insurance company, contact the OSFI Legislation and Precedents Division at (613) 991-2480. For example, the following cases should be referred to OSFI:

i) where a name uses a descriptive term like "guaranty," "warranty," "surety," "life," "casualty" or "indemnity" refer to OSFI at (613) 991-2480.

ii) where any financial terms including any of those mentioned in this section are used with the name of a bank, even if it does not connote the business of banking (e.g. Bank of Montreal Mortgage Corporation), refer to OSFI at (613) 990-7251 or (613) 990-0557.

When they are satisfied, OSFI will confirm by fax to the Name Officers of the Directorate that the referred name does not connote a loan, trust or insurance company, a bank or other financial intermediary.

B. When a proposed name, intended for a CBCA corporation, clearly connotes a financial intermediary, it is not available. Corporations bearing such names could be incorporated only under one of the Acts administered by OSFI. For example, subject to Section C, the following types of names clearly connote a financial intermediary:

i) where a descriptive term like "fiduciary," "trustco," "trust," "loanco," "loan," "mortgage," savings," "assurance," "insurance," "annuity" or "lifeco" is used. These terms are reserved for companies incorporated under the Trust and Loan Companies Act or the Insurance Companies Act administered by OSFI.

13.1 (continued)

ii) where a term like "bank," "banker" or "banking" is used alone or in combination with certain other words (e.g. "bancorp," "banco" or "bankco") in connection with financial activities. These terms are reserved for banks regulated by the Bank Act administered by OSFI and are not permitted for CBCA corporations.

An applicant who intends to incorporate or amend the name of a loan, trust or insurance company or a bank should consult the following sections of OSFI:

For loan and trust companies or banks --
Rulings and Compliance Division
(613) 990-7251

For life insurance companies --
Legislation and Precedents Division
(613) 990-7609

For property and casualty insurance companies –
Property and Casualty Division
(613) 990-5893

C. When a proposed name clearly does not connote a financial intermediary, it does not need to be referred to OSFI. For example, the following situations do not need to be referred:

i) where any of the terms that normally connote the business of a financial intermediary are used in a fanciful way. Examples are "Once in a Life Time Bridal Boutique Inc.," "Piggy Bank Children's Shop Ltd.," "Time Savings Household Cleaner Inc.," "Sam's TrustWorthy Contracting Services Ltd.," "ABC Data Bank Inc."

ii) where the terms "finance," "acceptance," "credit," "fund," "fidelity" and "underwriters" are used.

iii) where a term such as "broker," "agent," "agency" or "service(s)" is added to a name that implies an insurance or mortgage-related service, e.g., "Cartier Insurance Brokers Inc."

iv) where the terms "trust foundation" or "trust society" are used by non-profit corporations.

Note 1:

For the purposes of licensing, some provincial jurisdictions (e.g., Quebec and Ontario) have restrictions on the type of names allowed for companies offering insurance-related services. Since the use of a name granted is subject to the laws of the jurisdiction where the company intends to carry on business, the applicant may wish to contact the appropriate authorities before applying for the proposed name.

In Quebec:

13.1 (continued)

Regarding general insurance:
(514) 282-8765
Regarding personal insurance:
(418) 647-2244

In Ontario:
Regarding use of the word "agent";
(416)250-7250
Regarding use of the word "broker":
(416) 365-1900

Note 2:
Information Re: OSFI Legislation

For your information, we are providing the following information regarding the legislation administered by OSFI. This information is for your interest only and does not directly relate to the operations of the Corporations Directorate under the regulation set out above. As you will see, however, the legislation administered by the Corporations Directorate and by OSFI are quite consistent with one another.

The Insurance Companies Act, the Trust and Loan Companies Act and the Bank Act were amended in June 1996 by Bill C-15 and in June 1997 by Bill C-82. The Insurance Companies Act, the Trust and Loan Companies Act and the Bank Act contain prohibitions regarding the use of certain words subject to an exception for non-financial corporations.

Under subsection 47(2) of the Insurance Companies Act, subject to certain exceptions, no entity incorporated or formed by or under an Act of Parliament may use the word "assurance," "assurances," "insurance" or "lifeco" in its name. Subsection 47(2) provides that these restrictions do not apply to:

- a company or society (a defined term for an insurance company or fraternal benefit society)
- an entity the business of which is not financial activities
- an entity that is primarily engaged in insurance brokerage or insurance agency services
- an entity that is grandfathered from the provision.

Under subsections 47(1) and (2) of the Trust and Loan Companies Act, no entity incorporated or formed by or under an Act of Parliament, other than a trust or loan company, may use the word "fiduciaire," "fiduciary," "fiducie," "trust," "trustco," "loan," "loanco" or "prêt" in its name. However, subsection 47(3) provides that these restrictions do not apply to an entity the business of which is not financial activities.

For both the Insurance Companies Act and the Trust and Loan Companies Act, exemptions to the name use restrictions (such as for a subsidiary of a company or society) may be approved in writing by the Superintendent of Financial Institutions.

13.1 (continued)

Under the Bank Act, an entity other than a bank is prohibited from adopting a name that includes the word "bank," "banker" or "banking" either alone or in combination with other words or any words of import equivalent to these words, unless the words are used in connection with a business that is not engaged in financial services or that is a subsidiary of a bank. The Minister of Finance's approval is not required for these exceptions. For your information, OSFI considers terms such as "bankcorp," "banc," "bancorp," "bankco" and "banco" to be words that have import equivalent to the words referred to above.

The above Note is only a summary of the legislation. Interested persons should refer to the statutes themselves for their specific provisions.

13.1 (continued)

Industry Canada Industrie Canada

Canada

NAME GRANTING COMPENDIUM

III. OBSCENE

18. FOR THE PURPOSES OF PARAGRAPH 12(1)(a) of the Act, a corporate name is prohibited where the name contains a word or phrase that is obscene or connotes a business that is scandalous, obscene or immoral.

Because a contravention of this nature arises so seldom we have no guidance to offer here.

Publication Date: 1999-11-19
Author: Industry Canada

13.1 (continued)

Industry Canada Industrie Canada Canada

NAME GRANTING COMPENDIUM

IV. LACKING DISTINCTIVENESS

Definition of Distinctiveness:

Distinctiveness is defined in the regulations as being that quality that in relation to a trade name means a trade name that actually distinguishes the business in association with which it is used by its owner from the business of others. Distinctiveness can be inherent or acquired (secondary meaning).

14. SUBJECT TO SECTION 19, when determining whether a trade name is distinctive, the name as a whole and not only its separate elements shall be considered.

Generally speaking, the most inherently unique names have distinctive features which are composed of letters or figures which have no generic meaning.

e.g. XLYK
DWIDAG

In addition, unusual combination of generic words can be distinctive.

e.g. Jean Junction

Words composed of parts of other words, surnames, christian names, initials, numbers, geographic location and arbitrary dictionary words make a less inherently distinctive name.

e.g. SUNCRAFT Shoes Ltd.
SMITH Shoes Ltd.
OTTAWA Shoes Ltd.
I.I.L. Shoes Ltd.
STAR Shoes Ltd.

19. FOR THE PURPOSES OF PARAGRAPH 12(1)(a) of the Act, a corporate name is prohibited where the name is not distinctive because

a) it is too general

Related Policies

Names will be found to be "too general" when they are only descriptive of the type of business,

13.1 (continued)

industry, product or service of the corporation. Examples are "Software Inc." and "Car Sales Inc." An acceptable distinctive element would need to be added before such a corporate name could be granted, e.g., "Turner Software Inc." or "Greymark Car Sales Inc."

Names that are merely suggestive of the type of business, industry, product or service, however, would be acceptable. An example of a merely suggestive name is "Tires and Wheels Ltd." for a car sales business. The name "Tires and Wheels Ltd." does not describe the business nor the product produced. It simply suggests the corporation's field of activity. If the corporation manufactured or sold tires and wheels, however, this name would be unacceptable because, in this context, it would be "too general."

Please note that the approval of certain words as a corporate name does not necessarily mean that those words would be registrable as a trade-mark.

19. FOR THE PURPOSES OF PARAGRAPH 12(1)(a) of the Act, a corporate name is prohibited where the name is not distinctive because

> **b) it is only descriptive, in any language, of the quality, function or other characteristic of the goods or services in which the corporation deals or intends to deal**

Related Policies

As a general rule, the Director will not accept names that only describe a quality of the corporation's business or its goods or services, e.g., "Faster Consulting Services Inc."

- However, the Director will accept such names where:
- alliteration gives that name an acceptable level of distinctiveness, e.g., "Better Business Boardrooms Inc."
- the NUANS report demonstrates that the word describing a quality is commonly used as a distinctive feature in business names, e.g., "Superior" in "Superior Machinery Ltd." or "Advanced" in "Advanced Technology Solutions Ltd."
- the descriptive word sounds unusual when used to describe the business of the proposed corporation (for example "Endless Furniture Inc." is acceptable, whereas "Long Lasting Furniture Ltd." is not)

Although these names are descriptive of a quality of the business, they are not "only descriptive" but have some distinctiveness. By reason of alliteration or being unusual, these names are distinguishable from others. Also, where the NUANS search reports show that a descriptive word is extensively used as a distinctive element, we will follow the common practice.

Please note that the approval of certain words as a corporate name does not necessarily mean that those words would be registrable as a trade-mark.

19. FOR THE PURPOSES OF PARAGRAPH 12(1)(a) of the Act, a corporate name is prohibited where the name is not distinctive because

> **c) it is primarily or only the name or surname used alone of an individual who is living or has died within 30 years preceding the date of the request to the**

13.1 (continued)

Director for that name.

Related Policies

How to determine if a name is a surname?

Do you reasonably think of this word or words as a name or surname rather than as something else, e.g. a coined word? If so, Reg. 19 applies and that word or words cannot be used alone unless there is secondary meaning.

e.g. Legault Inc. - unacceptable
S. V. Lee Ltd. - unacceptable
Sarah Legault Inc. - unacceptable
S & R Wolfe Inc. - unacceptable

Corporate names in which this name or surname (as determined in the paragraph above) is not used alone would be available.

e.g. (1) Wilson & Myers Ltd.
Bob & Carol Harris Inc.

(2) Legault Gardening Enterprises Ltd.
Thomas Construction Inc.

Where the added descriptive word is non-specific and gives no indication of the nature of the proposed business* (other such non-specific descriptors are: agency, associates, brothers, distributions, enterprises, industries, group, products, services, sons, Canada, International, etc) the name may be refused for creating a likelihood of confusion with existing similarly named corporations.

e.g. Thomas Construction Inc. - existing
Thomas Enterprises Ltd. - unacceptable
or G. W. Thomas Enterprises Ltd. - unacceptable

Either the applicant must provide information to show that there is in fact no likelihood (based on differences of wares, territory, clientele) with existing companies, or, the applicant should add a more specific descriptive word,

e.g. Thomas Landscaping Inc. - acceptable
or, add a more specific name or surname,

e.g. George W. Thomas Enterprises Ltd. - acceptable

Note: "Associates" or "and Associates" can be used in combination with a name or surname. Although "Associates" is acceptable with a coined word, "and Associates" is not because it could mislead one into assuming that the distinctive element is a surname

e.g. XYLX & Associates - not acceptable

13.1 (continued)

Note: Bankruptcy Branch prefers that trustees who incorporate use only the name(s) of the principal partner(s) in the corporate name. However, if only one person is involved, then a surname used alone may not be acceptable (see surname formats on preceding page). The addition of a descriptive term like "Insolvency Trustee" or Bankruptcy" would overcome any such objection.

Related Regulation

21. FOR THE PURPOSES OF PARAGRAPH 12(1)(a) of the Act, a corporate name is prohibited where an element of the name is the family name of an individual, whether or not preceded by his given name or initials, unless the individual or his heir or legal representative consents in writing to the use of his name and the individual has or had a material interest in the corporation

The Regulation appears to state that every word that is in fact a family name of an individual requires a consent regardless of whether the reasonable person would think of it as a family name. Anyone not providing such a consent would be in contravention of this regulation.

For the purpose of policing this regulation however, the Corporations Directorate will use the same standard as is used for Reg. 19, i.e. only where a reasonable person would look upon that word as a family name. When the word does so connote a family name, a consent will be required, otherwise it will not be required.

e.g. RAN SHOES INC. - no consent
RAN SMITH SHOES INC. - consent of RAN SMITH
RAN, SMITH SHOES INC. - consent of RAN and consent of SMITH

Punctuation such as comma (,), ampersand (&) or hyphen (-) is necessary in a proposed name if the use of two surnames could wrongly connote the name of one individual (e.g. "Robert-Simpson" should become "Robert, Simpson", Robert & Simpson", "Robert-Simpson" if two surnames are intended).

A consent is not required where the word is a dictionary word or a christian name unless it is used in such way as to connote a family name to a reasonable person.

e.g. STAR SHOES LTD. - no consent
STAR, SMITH SHOES LTD. - consents of STAR & SMITH
STAR SMITH SHOES LTD. - consent of STAR SMITH
STARSMITH SHOES LTD. - no consent
STAR ASSOCIATED LTD . - no consent
STAR & ASSOCIATES LTD. - consent of STAR
STAR ASSOCIATES LTD. - no consent
ROSE GREEN'S TOOLS LTD. - consent of ROSE GREEN

Consents would not be required where the word or words are obviously the name of an historical person, literary or fictional character.

e.g. DORIAN GREY FASHIONS INC.

13.1 (continued)

LADY MACBETH COSMETICS INC.

Where the proposed corporate name contains a fictitious name, it will be necessary to file an affidavit of the principal of the proposed company stating that the name in question is a fictitious name and is not the name of a person who is well-known or known to him personnally.

A consent is not required when the family name is the name of the incorporator or a director.

A consent is not required when the family name is the name of a street on which the business is located.

Since it is required by the regulations, the consenting person must have a material interest in the corporation.

19. FOR THE PURPOSES OF PARAGRAPH 12(1)(a) of the Act, a corporate name is prohibited where the name is not distinctive because

d) it is primarily or only a geographic name used alone

Related Policies

for example: "Red Lake Inc."

USE OF NAMES CONTAINING GEOGRAPHIC TERMS

There should be no prohibition against the use of geographic reference in the granting of corporate name if a descriptive feature is added. Some form of substantitation for the use of a geographic location is not required.

for example:

"Red Lake Gold Mines Inc."

would be acceptable providing that it is not confusing.

A street address used alone is considered primarily a geographic name and is not available unless a descriptive term is added.

e.g. 235 St. Catherine Street Inc. - unacceptable

19. FOR THE PURPOSES OF PARAGRAPH 12(1)(a) of the Act, a corporate name is prohibited where the name is not distinctive because

a)

b)

c)

d)

13.1 (continued)

> **unless the person requesting the name establishes that it has, through use, acquired and continues to have <u>secondary meaning</u> at the time of the request**

<u>Definition</u>

> **"secondary meaning", in relation to a trade name, means a trade name that has been used in Canada or elsewhere by any applicant or his predecessor so as to have become distinctive in Canada as at the date of filing an application for a corporate name**

The applicant can escape the prohibitions of Reg. 19(a), (b), (c) and (d) as long as he can show that the trade name has been used in Canada or anywhere else to such an extent that persons in that trade would, on hearing the name, think of it, rather than the primary meaning of the words in its name.

In order to convince us of secondary meaning, the applicant must produce in writing cold, hard facts showing how large and widespread the business is and if necessary, include written statements from others in the trade.

Evidence to support a claim for secondary meaning must be in the form of an affidavit or statutory declaration and must attest to use of the name across Canada, either for significant periods of time or with great intensity.

<u>Note</u>: Reproduced below is a copy of the note which goes out with names rejected by reason of lacking distinctiveness.

<u>NOTE - LACKING DISTINCTIVENESS</u>

This name has been turned down because it lacks distinctiveness.

If we were to approve names which lacked any distinctiveness the task of preventing confusion among business names would be just about impossible. The only way the name attached to business X will not be confused with the name attached to business Y is if there is something in the names to distinguish them. The stronger the distinguishing feature the less likely confusion will occur.

Based on this reasoning our name regulations require that corporate names have a distinguishing feature, and then they draw some arbitrary rules to define where distinctiveness is insufficient or lacking. According to such rules a name lacks distinctiveness and is therefore unavailable when it is too general, only descriptive, primarily a name or primarily a geographic place.

The concept of "too general" is difficult but suffice it to say that a corporate name that only describes the type of business, industry, product or service of the corporation is unavailable, eg., "Car Sales Inc." A name will also be unavailable for being "only descriptive" where it only describes the quality of the corporation's business or its products, eg., Faster Consulting Services Inc.

Some proposed names which appear to lack any distinctiveness may have, in fact, acquired distinctiveness through extensive use. If this, is the case and the applicant can demonstrate it in writing, the name will be available.

13.1 (continued)

Otherwise, the best way to overcome the objection of lacking distinctiveness is:

Only descriptive/Too general
- add a distinctive word
e.g. a coined work like "Spillex"
e.g. a dictionary word that doesn't describe like "Star"
e.g. an individual's name like "Turner"

Primarily a name
- add a descriptive word
e.g. "Manufacturing"

Primarily a place
- add a descriptive word
e.g. " Enterprises"

13.1 (continued)

Industry Canada Industrie Canada Canada

NAME GRANTING COMPENDIUM

V. CONFUSION

(A) METHOD OF DETERMINING CONFUSION

13. A CORPORATE NAME IS CONFUSING WITH

- **a) a trade mark if the use of both the corporate name and the trade mark is likely to lead to the inference that the business carried on or intended to be carried on under the corporate name and the business connected with the trade mark are one business, whether or not the nature of the business of each is generally the same; or**
- **b) a trade name if the use of both names is likely to lead to the inference that the business carried on or intended to be carried on under the corporate name and the business carried on under the trade name are one business, whether or not the nature of the business of each is generally the same**

Factors to consider when determining confusion with existing trade marks or trade names under Reg. 13.

20. FOR THE PURPOSES OF PARAGRAPH 12(1)(a) of the Act, a corporate name is prohibited where the name is confusing having regard to all the circumstances, including

- **a) the inherent distinctiveness of the whole or any elements of any trade mark or trade name and the extent to which it has become known**
- **b) the length of time the trade mark or trade name has been in use**
- **c) the nature of the goods or services associated with a trade mark or the nature of the business carried on under or associated with a trade name, including the likelihood of any competition among businesses using such a trade mark or trade name**
- **d) the nature of the trade with which a trade mark or trade name is associated, including the nature of the products or services and the means by which they are offered or distributed**
- **e) the degree of resemblance between the proposed corporate name and any trade mark or trade name in the appearance or sound or in the ideas suggested by them; and**
- **f) the territorial area in Canada in which the proposed corporate name or an existing trade name is likely to be used**

13.1 (continued)

Often, clients do not supply sufficient information in the name request to apply all of the factors under Regulation 20. In these cases, we can only rely on Regulation 20(a) and (e) to make our name decision. If the requestor should decide to provide more information, the name decision can be re-evaluated in light of the new facts.

A decision of confusing similarity may be based on phonetic similarity alone.

Note that federal incorporation does not in itself give you rights over an existing provincial corporate name or trade name.

(B) TREATMENT OF EXISTING NAMES WITH HIGH DISTINCTIVENESS IN DETERMINING CONFUSION

Our primary concern in enforcing the name regulations should be in ensuring that we cause no confusion. Nowhere do the regulations enshrine the principle that a highly distinctive name should be protected from dilution and so we will have no hard and fast rule with respect to protection of them. In practice, however, the protection principle should complement the principle of avoiding confusion. Where an existing corporation has a highly distinctive name, i.e. unique and imaginative, being a purely arbitrary creation, e.g. DWIDAG (for a food wholesaler), as opposed to an obviously derived composition, e.g. CORTIVET (for the manufacture of costisone veterinarian preparation), one is generally more apt to foresee confusion in granting the same distinctive element to a second company because the distinctive element of the existing company is more likely to linger in the mind of the public. Each case, however, depends on its facts and depending on differences of wares, territory and clientele, we may or may not feel that there is in fact a likelihood of confusion.

Some words are so common that they are used as the distinctive element in many business names. Such wide usage dilutes the impact of the business name and gives it a reduced claim to protection. As a general rule, where a distinctive element is highly diluted, the same distinctive feature may be used in new corporate names that are only slightly different from the existing names. For instance, a different descriptive word might be all that is needed to distinguish the proposed corporate name from similar existing names, even if the descriptive word describes essentially the same business that is carried on under the existing names.

> For example, names such as "Universal Products Inc." or "Universal Bakery Products Inc." would not be prohibited, even though there were existing names like "Universal Food Enterprises Inc.," because the distinctive element "Universal" is highly diluted, and the existing names do not deserve much protection.

We cannot gear our policies to the mere possibility that any given existing company with a highly distinctive name will develop into a famous conglomerate, dealing in a variety of wares and services.

"Famous" names are a case apart. They may originally have been highly distinctive, e.g. KODAK, or alternatively, very lacking in distinctiveness, e.g. GENERAL MOTORS. They are generally conglomerates and we will not approve any corporate name that uses their distinctive feature.

Therefore, the guidelines for initial, front line name decisions (normally without benefit of much detailed information) should be as follows:

13.1 (continued)

Classification	First Decision	Reconsideration
FAMOUS	IBM Draperie Ltd. (UNAVAILABLE)	
HIGHLY DISTINCTIVE	1) IGSAC Toys Inc. - existing IGSAC Bicycles Ltd. - proposed (UNAVAILABLE) IGSAC Drapery Installation Inc. - proposed (AVAILABLE SUBJECT TO RISK ACCEPTED BY THE APPLICANT IN WRITING)	There are circumstances which are not generally known at the time of initial name granting which would make BICYCLES available, or DRAPERY unavailable on Reconsideration or Confusion Allegation.
	2) IGSAC Inc. - existing IGSAC Drapery Installations Inc. UNAVAILABLE BECAUSE YOU DON'T KNOW HOW DIFFERENT THE WARES ARE)	On Reconsideration you might find out amonst other things that IGSAC Inc. is in toys.
LOW DISTINC-TIVENESS	1) Maple Leaf Toys Inc. - existing Maple Leaf Bicycles Ltd. - proposed (AVAILABLE)	There are circumstances which are not generaly known at the time of initial decision which would make BICYCLES unavailable on Reconsideration or Confusion Allegation.
	2) Maple Leaf Inc. - existing Maple Leaf Bicycles - proposed (AVAILABLE)	
	Note: You can substitute "I.I.L" for " MAPLE LEAF".	

N.B. Of course even the unavailable names would be available if the companies were related and consent was provided.

Any detailed information with respect to wares, clientele, territory of existing companies must be provided to us in writing.

(C) INITIALS AND CONFUSION

There is no hard and fast rule with respect to when a name containing initials is likely to cause confusion. Territory of operations and any other relevant information always has to be taken into consideration. What follows is merely a guideline which assumes that the territory of the existing businesses and the proposed business are identical and that the client has produced no other information going to show that confusion is unlikely (e.g. totally different clientele, long co-

13.1 (continued)

existence, existing company inactive for a long period)

(a) If a distinctive feature is made up of two initials, the proposed name will be considered confusing if:

(i) the descriptive feature is the same or confusingly similar, and

(ii) the initials are identical (and in the same order) or if the first initial is the same and the last initial is phonetically similar.

for example:	BN Construction	- confusing with BM Construction - confusing with BN Builders - not confusing with BF Construction

(b)

If three or more initials make up the distinctive feature of a name, the proposed name will be considered confusing if:

(i) the descriptive feature is the same or confusingly similar, and

(ii) all of the initials except for the last one are identical, and

(iii) the initials are in the same order as the initials in the existing corporate name.

(c)

Initials may be acceptable without a descriptive word if it is not confusing.

Because it is difficult to develop a general policy which applies to each case that arises, some judgement must be used for cases not strictly covered by these guidelines. For example, a name like "BNND Construction" or "BMND Building" would be considered confusing with "BNMD Construction" because M and N are very similar in sound and appearance. "A & M Construction Inc." would be found to be confusing with "ANM Construction Ltd." because phonetically there is a little difference between the two.

(D) DESCRIPTIVE TERMS AND CONFUSION

Our present policy, designed to avoid confusion, says that where an existing corporate name has a certain distinctive element, a proposed name with the same distinctive element, if it is available at all, is available only with a specific descriptive feature which demonstrates the difference in the lines of business of the two companies, or, at least, identifies with particularity the wares or services of the proposed company. In

13.1 (continued)

the latter case there is still some risk that the existing company is in the same line of business as the proposed, but this possibility is remote.

e.g. SUNCREST INVESTMENT INC. - existing
SUNCREST TOYS INC. - proposed
(AVAILABLE)

SUNCREST ENTERPRISES INC. - existing
SUNCREST TOYS INC. - proposed
(AVAILABLE)

SUNCREST ENTERPRISES INC. - existing
SUNCREST PRODUCTS INC. - proposed
(UNAVAILABLE)

While this will continue as a good front-line policy for initial name decisions without benefit of many facts, where it becomes apparent from written representations that there are, in fact, substantial differences in wares, territory or clientele, a more general descriptive word, e.g. ENTERPRISES, PRODUCTS, SERVICES, ASSOCIATES etc. may be acceptable, or in some case, even no descriptive word may be required.

The present policy has never been applied to situations where there is an existing trade mark in different wares. Here we have not required the company to have a specific descriptive word. Probably the thinking was that confusion is less likely in this case because at least the trade mark is attached to a specific ware. We will continue not to require the new company to have a specific descriptive word in this case.

NOTE: RE WORD "GROUP"

Where there are no other unrelated companies with the same distinctive feature as the proposed corporate name, the proposed name would be available without further requirement.

If there are other companies with the same distinctive feature as the proposed corporate name but unrelated to the proposed corporation, the applicant must explain why the proposed corporate name will not misleadingly suggest a grouping of those companies.

Examples of possible responses:

- - the business of the proposed corporation and that of the existing unrelated companies are too different for them to

13.1 (continued)

be confused as being affiliated.

- - the proposed corporation will be the umbrella company for related companies using that distinctive feature and the proposed name will connote a relationship with them alone.

The addition of a descriptive word (e.g. textile) modifying the word "group" will likely make the proposed name available as long as the descriptive word clearly distinguishes the business of the proposed company from the business of existing companies with the same distinctive element.

Note: Consents of the "grouped" companies will be required unless the existing parent of those companies is requesting a change of name to "Group".

(E) REVIVALS / DISSOLUTION

22. FOR THE PURPOSES OF PARAGRAPH 12(1)(a) of the Act

a) a corporate name is prohibited where its use is likely to lead to the inference that the business carried on or intended to be carried on under it and the business of a body corporate that is dissolved are one business, whether or not the nature of their businesses is generally the same; and

b) the name of a revived corporation is prohibited where it is confusing with a name acquired by another corporation between the date of dissolution and revival of the revived corporation

REVIVALS - NAMES

Where, either before dissolution or in the interval between dissolution and revival of a federal corporation, another company with an identical name is incorporated, the federal corporation will not be able to revive in that name as long as the identical name is in existence.

Where, in the above circumstances, the new name is only confusingly similar, it is important to know the continuousness of the operation of the applicant for revival. If its operation was continuous during a substantial period of the time that the new

13.1 (continued)

company was in operation, this goes to show that the revival of the federal corporation is unlikely now to cause confusion.

DISSOLUTION - See "Two Year Special Status" (page 5.8)

(F) TRADE MARKS

(i) In order to approve a name for which there are phonetically similar trade mark citations, Corporations Directorate must know in general terms what the proposed company will do and that all phonetically similar trade marks are in substantially different wares or services. In this way we can be satisfied that there is no likelihood of confusion. This information must be provided to us in writing. Where this information is lacking, we will have to assume that the trade mark are the same as that of the proposed corporation.

(ii) The following guidelines provide guidance in situations where there is an existing trade-mark in substantially the same wares or service as the proposed name.

1. Trade-mark (TM) owned by someone other than applicant (i.e. conflicting trade-mark)

- TM registered for five years: Corporate name applicant cannot have the proposed name without consent of TM owner, no matter how long the applicant has used it.

- TM application, or TM registered for less than five years: Determine who had prior use. If the corporate name applicant files an affidavit that satisfies us that the applicant had prior use of a corporate name or a trade name and provides us with an undertaking that the applicant will contest the other party's TM application or registration, we will give the applicant the name.

2. Trade-mark (TM) owned by the applicant (i.e. supporting trade-mark)

13.1 (continued)

- TM registered for five years: Even if there is another business name that is confusing, the corporate name applicant will be given the name because the applicant's TM is not likely to be struck out.

- TM application, or TM registered for less than five years: If there is another business name that is confusing and that appears to have used the name before the corporate name applicant, the applicant's TM is not sufficient reason to grant the name. The name will not be approved.

Note that in these types of trade-mark situations, the important information is:

- the date of first use

- whether the trade-mark has been registered for five years.

(iii) A notice entitled "Protecting Your Corporate Name is attached hereto as an appendix. Clients should be aware that the holder of a corporate name bears the responsibility of ensuring that no new confusing trade-marks are registered by anyone else.

General enquiries concerning trade-marks should be directed to the Trade Marks Branch at (819) 997-1420.

CONFUSION WITH TRADENAMES

We feel that it could be confusing for a tradename and a confusingly similar corporate name to exist at the same time (even if they are owned by the same person) unless both names form part of the same business.

For this reason we will refuse a proposed corporate name where Mr. X is carrying on business in that tradename (even if Mr. X is the applicant for incorporation) unless we get Mr. X's consent and his undertaking to cease carrying on business in that tradename or to transfer his trade name registration to the corporation.

13.1 (continued)

There will, of course, be no need for such a consent and undertaking when a change of corporate name is proposed by a corporation that has already registered a tradename and the proposed name of the corporation will be that tradename. A copy of the tradename registration showing the corporation as the owner should be filed however.

Note re Ontario Business Names on the NUANS report: Ontario Business Names expire after 5 years unless they are renewed. Unrenewed registrations remain on the database however. The Director will assume that all Ontario trade name registrations less than 5 and 1/2 years old and appearing on the NUANS report, are active. Any registrations over 5 and 1/2 years old and not renewed, will be disregarded. The 1/2 year period is a grace period to allow time for renewal after expiry.

Suggested Consent Form from the Owner of an Unincorporated Trade Name

The Director, Corporations Branch
Industry Canada
9th Floor, Jean Edmonds Towers South
365 Laurier Avenue West
Ottawa, Ontario K1A 0C8

Re:

Incorporation of a corporation by the name of
INCORPORATING PARTY'S NAME

(Consenting party's name), owner of the registered trade name (enter trade name),
hereby consents to the incorporation of (name of the proposed corporation).

(Consenting party's name) undertakes to stop carrying on business under the trade name
(or to transfer his/her rights in the trade name to the corporation bearing the proposed name)
before the corporation proposing to use the name begins to carry on business under the
corporate name.

Consent given at (city), this (date) day of (month), (year).

Consenting Party's name

Per: ____________________

Jane Doe, President

13.1 (continued)

CONFUSION WITH EXISTING CORPORATE NAMES AND TRADENAMES WHICH ARE FRANCHISEES

Because the use of the name of a franchise accrues to the franchisor rather than to the franchisee, the consent of existing business and trade names which are franchisee businesses will not be required for the incorporation of a confusingly similar name. Only the consent of the franchisor will be required. In that consent, the franchisor must identify the existing corporate names as franchisees.

CONFUSION WITH OFFICIAL MARKS

Where a proposed name is confusingly similar in sound, appearance and idea with an existing official mark adopted and used pursuant to the provisions of section 9 of the Trade-marks Act, the CBCA name regulations provide no basis for rejecting the proposed corporate name. The Director will therefore approve the proposed corporate name, but will issue a notice to the client warning that he or she might not be entitled to use the name by virtue of the prohibition contained in section 9 of the Trade-marks Act.

(G) OVERCOMING CONFUSION

25. A corporate name that is confusing with the name of a body corporate that has not carried on business in the 2 years immediately preceding the date of a request for that corporate name shall not for that reason alone be prohibited if the body corporate that has that name

a) consents in writing to the use of the name; and

b) undertakes in writing to dissolve forthwith or to change its name before the corporation proposing to use the name commences to use it

26. A corporate name containing a word that is the same as or similar to the distinctive element of an existing trade mark or trade name shall not for that reason alone be prohibited if

a) the person who has the trade mark or trade name consents in writing to the use of the corporate name; and

b) the corporate name is not confusing

Note: such a consent would not be required from a foreign company unless it was known or carrying on business in

13.1 (continued)

Canada.

CONSENTS

Note the difference between consent to a corporate name and consent to the use of certain words as a tradename. The letter will not be sufficient to replace the former.

Note that consents must be unconditional - not "until such time as we give notice" for example:

Suggested consent form --Regulation 25

The Director, Corporations Branch
Industry Canada
9th Floor, Jean Edmonds Towers South
365 Laurier Avenue West
Ottawa, Ontario K1A 0C8

Re:

Incorporation of a corporation by the name of *INCORPORATING PARTY'S NAME.*

(Consenting party's name), a body corporate, consents to the incorporation/amendment of (name of the proposed corporation).

(Consenting party's name) undertakes to dissolve immediately or to change its name before the corporation proposing to use that name begins to carry on business under that name.

(Consenting party's name) confirms that it has not carried on business under its corporate name during the past two years.

Consent given at (city), this (date) day of (month), (year).

CONSENTING PARTY'S NAME

Per: ____________________

JANE DOE, President

Note: The signature of the authorized signing officer must describe him or her as an officer of the consenting corporation.

Suggested Consent Form -- Regulation 26

The Director, Corporations Branch
Industry Canada

13.1 (continued)

9th Floor, Jean Edmonds Towers South
365 Laurier Avenue West
Ottawa, Ontario K1A 0C8

Re:

Incorporation of a corporation by the name of INCORPORATING PARTY'S NAME.

(Consenting party's name, i.e. the name of an incorporated or unincorporated business or the name of the owner of a trade-mark) consents to the incorporation of (name of the proposed corporation).

Consent given at (city), this (date) day of (month), (year).

CONSENTING PARTY'S NAME

Per: ______________________

JANE DOE, President

27. 1) A corporate name that is confusing with the name of a body corporate shall not be prohibited for that reason alone if

a) the corporate name is the name of an existing or proposed corporation that is the successor to the business of the body corporate and the body corporate has ceased or will, in the immeditate future, cease to carry on business under that corporate name and undertakes in writing to dissolve forthwith or to change its corporate name before the successor corporation commences carrying on business under that corporate name; and

b) subject to subsection (2), the corporate name of the existing or proposed corporation sets out in numerals the year of incorporation or the year of the most recent amendment to the corporate name, in parentheses immediately before the word or expression "Limited", "Limitée", "Incorporated", "Incorporée", "Corporation", "Société par actions de régime fédéral" or "Société commerciale canadienne" or the abbreviation "Ltd.", "Ltée", "Inc.",

13.1 (continued)

"Corp.", "S.A.R.F." or "S.C.C".

2) The reference in a corporate name to the year of incorporation or the year of the most recent amendment to the corporate name may be deleted two years after its use is introduced, if the corporate name so changed is not confusing.

Related Policies

Suggested Consent Form -- Regulation 27

The Director, Corporations Branch
Industry Canada
9th Floor, Jean Edmonds Towers South
365 Laurier Avenue West
Ottawa, Ontario K1A 0C8

Re:

Incorporation of a corporation by the name of INCORPORATING PARTY'S NAME.

(Consenting party's name), a body corporate, consents to the incorporation/amendment of (name of the proposed corporation), which is to be a successor corporation and which has the year of incorporation or amendment in parentheses before the legal element.

(Consenting party's name) undertakes to dissolve immediately or to change its name before the corporation proposing to use that name begins to carry on business under that name.

Consent given at (city), this (date) day of (month), (year).

CONSENTING PARTY'S NAME

Per: ______________________

JANE DOE, President

Exception to 27 *(1)b)*

If the existing company has not carried on business for two years preceding the request to use the name, the successor corporation does not need to insert the year of incorporation or amendment but the requirements of Regulation 25 must be met.

Section 27 may apply both in the case where a corporation changes its name and in the case of a proposed new corporation.

13.1 (continued)

In the former case, the date in parenthesis is the date the corporation succeeds to the name and not the date it is incorporated.

Note:

Where a corporation succeeds to a name of a non-federal body corporate whose name is primarily or only the name of an individual, the corporation will not be able to delete the reference to the year in parentheses after two years, unless secondary meaning can be established. The name without the year in parentheses is prohibited under Regulation 19(c) for being primarily or only the name of an individual. At the time of obtaining the successor company name under Regulation 27, the applicant may wish to add another word, in addition to the year in parentheses, so that the year in parentheses can be deleted after two years pursuant to Regulation 27(2).

Note:

Please note that regulation 27 does not override other applicable regulations. Where, for instance, X1, the body corporate which is consenting and undertaking to the incorporation of X1 (1999), pursuant to regulation 27 was, itself, incorporated pursuant to a consent of X in conformity to regulation 26, the consent of X, pursuant to regulation 26 will also be required for the incorporation of X1 (1999).

Or, where X is an individual, the requirement to file the consent to use of family name (Reg 21) will still apply

OTHER USE OF "(1999)" AND SUBSTITUTION OF "(CANADA)" FOR "(1999)"

This policy does not prohibit the use of "(1999)" for the incorporation of a non-successor new company. This will be allowed except where the new corporation is going to be the affiliate of an existing corporation which will remain in existence and "(1999)" is proposed as the distinguishing element. We consider this situation to be misleading as "(1999)" connotes a successor.

As a general rule we will not accept "Canada" or any other term as a replacement for "(1999)" in a successor situation unless the successor company is related to the existing company which has undertaken to dissolve or to change its name in which case we are really dealing with regulation 26 not 27.

The chart below tries to clarify these guidelines.

13.1 (continued)

for example:	ABCD Construction:	- confusing with ABCF Construction - not confusing with DABC Construction

*	
ABC (Canada) or ABC Canada or ABC (1999) or ABC 1999* as newco: no existing company, ABC	Okay
ABC (CANADA) or ABC Canada as newco related to existing company, ABC which will continue to exist (consent - we assume affiliation)	Okay
ABC (1999) as newco related to existing company, ABC which will continue to exist (consent - we assume affiliation ABC 1999 as a newco related to existing company, ABC, which will continue to exist (consent - we assume affiliation)	No (as a general rule not available because it is misleading, however may be permissible where clients of newco, are sophisticated enough to know that newco is not the successor to existing co. ABC even though it looks like it is, and ABC consents) Okay
ABC (1999) as newco related or unrelated to existing company, ABC which is dissolving or changing name (consent & undertaking)	Okay
ABC (CANADA) or ABC Canada or ABC 1999 as newco related to ABC which is dissolving or changing name (consent)	Okay
ABC (CANADA) or ABC Canada or ABC 1999 as newco unrelated to ABC dissolving or changing name	No (as a general rule) (may be permissible where clients of newco are sophisticated to know that newco is not related to existing co. ABC even though it looks like it is.)

* as long as the corporation is not to be a successor to an existing company any reasonable date is permissible, unless it is misleading.

13.1 (continued)

e.g. ABC 1884 Ltd. would be misleading for the name of a corporation which has not been in business since 1884.

Exception to Regulation 27(1) *b)*

"DE FACTO" IMPORT CONTINUANCES

We will permit a company to incorporate with a name that is identical (i.e. without the year of incorporation) to the name of an existing provincial (e.g. Quebec) company where the federal incorporation is to serve as a "de facto" continuance from that province which does not permit exports to the federal jurisdiction.

The applicant must file with us a written undertaking of the provincial company to dissolve forthwith or to change its name before the corporation proposing to use the name carries on business.

There must be a note on file to indicate that the applicant considers this incorporation to be a "de facto" continuance, i.e. the same shareholders and assets will be involved in the federal company as in the provincial company.

Like other import continuances, the availability of this name will be subject to a name search and approval.

28. 1) When two or more corporations amalgamate, the name of the amalgamated corporation shall not be prohibited if

a) it is the same as one of the amalgamating corporations

b) it is a distinctive combination of the names of the amalgamating corporations and is not otherwise confusing or prohibited; or

c) it is a distinctive new name that is not confusing

2) Where an existing corporation has acquired or will, in the immediate future, acquire all or substantially all of the property of an affiliated body corporate, the use by the corporation of the corporate name of the body corporate is not prohibited if the body corporate undertakes in writing to dissolve, or to change its corporate name, before the corporation commences using the corporate name.

13.1 (continued)

3) Where a proposed corporation will, in the immediate future, acquire all or substantially all of the property of a body corporate that is to be an affiliate of the proposed corporation, the use by the proposed corporation of the corporate name of the body corporate is not prohibited if the body corporate undertakes in writing to dissolve, or to change its corporate name, before the proposed corporation commences using the corporate name.

Related Policies

Note: Where the name is granted on the understanding that the applicant will, in the immediate future acquire all or substantially all the property of the affiliated body corporate, the applicant should confirm within a few days that substantially all the property did transfer from the affiliated body corporate.

Upon incorporation of Newco, Corporations Directorate will keep the file open pending receipt of the above-referenced written confirmation. If it is not received without delay, steps will be taken to require Newco to change its name.

Other regulations on name unavailability are overriden by name availability under Regulation 28(1)a) and Regulation 28(2).

Suggested Consent Form -- Regulation 28(2)

The Director, Corporations Branch
Industry Canada
9th Floor, Jean Edmonds Towers South
365 Laurier Avenue West
Ottawa, Ontario K1A 0C8

Re: Incorporation of a corporation by the name of INCORPORATING PARTY'S NAME.

(Consenting party's name), a body corporate, consents to the change of name of (previous name of the corporation) to (proposed name).

(Consenting party's name) confirms that the corporation is affiliated to (consenting party's name) and (has or will immediately) acquire all or substantially all the property of (consenting party's name). (Consenting party's name) hereby undertakes to dissolve immediately or to change its name before the corporation proposing to use the name begins carrying on business under that name.

CONSENTING PARTY'S NAME

13.1 (continued)

Per: ______________________

JANE DOE, President

Suggested Consent Form -- Regulation 28(3)

The Director, Corporations Branch

Industry Canada
9th Floor, Jean Edmonds Towers South
365 Laurier Avenue West
Ottawa, Ontario K1A 0C8

Re: Incorporation of a corporation by the name of INCORPORATING PARTY'S NAME.

(Consenting party's name), a body corporate, hereby consents to the incorporation of (name of proposed corporation).

(Consenting party's name) confirms that the proposed corporation will be affiliated to (consenting party's name) and will immediately acquire substantially all the property of (consenting party's name). (Consenting party's name) undertakes to dissolve immediately or to change its name before the corporation proposing to use the name begins to carry on business under that name.

CONSENTING PARTY'S NAME

Per: ______________________

JANE DOE, President

FAILING TO HONOUR UNDERTAKING

Subsections 12(4.1) and (5) of the Act state that if a corporation acquires a name as a result of a person undertaking to dissolve or to change names, and that undertaking is not honoured, the Director may direct the corporation to change its name in accordance with section 173, unless the undertaking is honoured within the Director's 60 day notice.

TWO YEAR SPECIAL STATUS

Names identical to those of companies that have dissolved or that have amalgamated under another name or that have changed their name are not available (whether related or not) for two years after the date of dissolution, amalgamation or amendment. The purpose of such a period of non-use is to allow the public time to disassociate that name from a specific business.

13.1 (continued)

Within the two year period anyone could, however, incorporate a successor company (i.e. same name but with year of incorporation in brackets), or a company with a slightly varied name (or with an identical name if they meet Reg. 28(2) requirement) as long as the consent of the amalgamated company or the company whose name was amended, is obtained. Because no consent would be obtainable, this would not be possible with the name of a dissolved company unless the applicant for the new corporation could demonstrate that he had acquired from the dissolved corporation prior to its dissolution, the rights to its name.

After two years the name becomes available to anyone as long as no successor companies were incorporated within the two years and as long as the original name has not been perpetuated as a registered trade name.

INITIALS AND GIVEN NAMES

The addition of initials to a surname that is otherwise confusing is not sufficient to overcome that confusion.

for example:
"I.E. SMITH SHOES LTD. would be confusing with "SMITH SHOES INC."

However, given names may be added to corporate names that contain a surname and that may be sufficient to overcome confusion.

for example:
"Smith Shoes Ltd." would not be used to refuse "Robert Smith Shoes Ltd." unless we are aware that their territory of operation is the same.

BANKRUPTCY

For the purposes of Regulations 25, 26 or 27, a name is available, where it is confusing with the name of a bankrupt corporation, if the trustee in bankruptcy consents.

NAMES OF PROVINCES AND CITIES TO REMOVE CONFUSION BETWEEN RELATED COMPANIES

The name of a province or city with or without parentheses is not considered a general term and may be added to a corporate name to overcome confusion with the name of an existing related company.

for example:
"Newton Tool Québec Ltd." would not be considered confusingly similar to "Newton Tool Manitoba Ltd." or "Newton Tool (Canada) Ltd."

13.1 (continued)

However, the consent of the existing company(ies) would be required in order to grant such a similar name. Where there are many existing affiliates, the consent of the geographically closest affiliate or the parent of all affiliates, would be sufficient.

Exception: Use of certain provincial names in federal corporation names.
Refer to pages 2.2, 2.3, 2.4, 2.5

A GENERAL TERM WILL NOT DISTINGUISH UNRELATED COMPANIES WITH CONFUSINGLY SIMILAR NAMES

Example of a case where a general term would not distinguish a proposed name from a confusingly similar name:

"The United MacMillan Construction Co. Ltd." would be considered confusing with the existing name "The MacMillan Construction Co. Ltd."

Proposed names with a general term should be compared to existing names on the basis that the general term is NOT there.

GENERAL TERMS MAY BE USED TO DISTINGUISH RELATED COMPANIES

A distinguishing feature must be used to differentiate a federal company from its provincial, federal or foreign affiliate. For this purpose, the use of general terms such as "Canada", "(Canada)", "Canadian" and the word "International" would be permissible.

CANADIAN SUBSIDIARIES

Where proposed Canadian subsidiaries of foreign, provincial or federal parent use the name of that parent, which name is too general or merely descriptive, the proposed company

a) must add the word "Canada" or equivalent unless there is some other distinguishing feature between parent and subsidiaries and

b) can overcome the objection of generality by showing that the name has acquired some distinctiveness in Canada, (whether or not it has actually been used in Canada, e.g. American advertising which regularly crosses the border)

c) will be prohibited for confusion with an existing Canadian company or trade mark.

13.1 (continued)

Note: A proposed Canadian subsidiary of a foreign parent with the identical name would not be required to add the word "Canada" if it could establish that the foreign company had never carried on business in Canada and is not known in Canada.

Note: Reproduced below is a copy of the Note sent out with names which are rejected by reason of their being confusing.

NOTE - CONFUSING

This name has been turned down because on the basis of the information that we have, it appears to create a likelihood of confusion with the names indicated on the relevant search report. Please note that corporations dissolved less than 2 years ago are considered to be existing for purposes of confusion.

We will reconsider our decision if we are given other information which demonstrates that, in fact, there is no likelihood of confusion.

The kind of information to which we refer is specified in section 20 of the Regulations, that is, details concerning the dissimilarity of the wares, territory, clientele and operative status of the business to be carried on under the proposed name and the business being carried on under the existing name.

Unless the requirements of Regulation 28(2) have been met, a name which is identical to an existing company will not be approved even with the consent of the existing corporation, unless there are very convincing reasons why no one would be confused, or even if confused, why they could not be harmed thereby.

PLEASE NOTE THAT THERE IS NO LONGER A TELEPHONE CONSULTATION SERVICE ON NAMES. ANY REQUESTS FOR RECONSIDERATION OR INFORMATION MUST BE MADE IN WRITING.

Publication Date: 1999-11-19
Author: Industry Canada

13.1 (continued)

Industry Canada Industrie Canada Canada

NAME GRANTING COMPENDIUM

VI. DECEPTIVELY MISDESCRIPTIVE

23. FOR THE PURPOSES OF PARAGRAPH 12(1)(a) of the Act, a corporate name is deceptively misdescriptive if it misdescribes, in any language

- **a) the business, goods or services in association with which it is proposed to be used.**
- **b) the conditions under which the goods or services will be produced or supplied or the persons to be employed in the production or supply of those goods or services; or**
- **c) the place or origin of those goods or services**

Related Policies

USE OF THE WORD "CLUB" IN CORPORATE NAMES

There is no general restriction on the use of the word "Club" in corporate names. The word may be used for business incorporations, but extreme care should be exercised to ensure that the use of the word does not imply to the public a membership corporation. The use of the word should be carefully evaluated before granting the name to profit-making corporations.

for example:

"Rough Riders Football Club" would be acceptable, as the general public would be aware that such a football club is a profit-making organization.

USE OF THE WORD "INSTITUTE", "ASSOCIATION", "FOUNDATION", OR OTHER SUCH WORDS

Since these terms connote a non-profit organization, they are usually restricted to PART II COMPANIES. If strong representations are made for the use of one of these words in names for profit-making companies, the case should be referred to the Director, Compliance Branch, for a decision

USE OF A YEAR - "(1989)" OR "1989" - see Exception to paragraphe 27(1)(b)

13.1 (continued)

13.1 (continued)

Industry Canada Industrie Canada

Canada

VII. OTHER RELATED POLICIES

A. Non-Profit Organizations (Part II Companies)
B. Regulation 24
C. Bilingual Names
D. Use of Words "Broadcasting", "Radio", "Televison"
E. USA - SEC Names
F. Number of Search Reports Required; Is a Search Required?
G. Trade Name
H. Numbered Name
I. Microfiche Supplement of NUANS report for Names with More Than One Distinctive Element
J. Internet Domain Names as Corporate Name
Protecting your Corporate Name

VII. OTHER RELATED POLICIES

(A) NON-PROFIT ORGANIZATIONS (Part II Companies)

NON-DISTINCTIVE NAMES

Corporate names which are refused as too general or only descriptive under Regulations 19(a) and (b) of the CBCA are not for these reasons alone prohibited for non-profit companies.

Because of the nature of the names approved for Part II Companies, there may be a greater likelihood of receiving names which could connote government sponsorship or control. Therefore, more attention should be paid to Regulation 17 when granting names for non-profit companies.

for example:
"Canadian Association of Postmasters"

CHAMBER OF COMMERCE

The term "Chamber of Commerce" is available for use in the name of a non-profit corporation with suitable objects.

LEGAL ELEMENTS

The only legal elements which are permitted for non-profit companies are:

13.1 (continued)

"Incorporated" or "Inc."
"Corporation" or "Corp."

NON-PROFIT CONFUSION

In the past, where the name of a proposed non-profit corporation consisted of a geographical term plus a descriptive term, e.g. "Canada Ultralight Aircraft Association" or "Canada Dance Foundation", and an existing non-profit corporation had the same descriptive words with a different geographical qualification, e.g. "Calgary Ultralight Aircraft Association" and "Toronto Dance Foundation", we required the consent of the existing corporation. This should continue to be the case. However, applicants should be advised that a slight modification of their proposal would probably make it available, e.g. "Canada Ultralight Aircraft Society" or "Canada Dance Funding Society".

(B) Regulation 24 of the Act states that a corporate name is not prohibited only because it contains alphabetic or numeric characters, initials, punctuation marks or any combination thereof.

(C) BILINGUAL NAMES

i) General Rule:

The English and French forms of a corporate name do not have to be literal translations, but a corporation cannot have French and English forms of a corporate name that are so different as to appear to belong to two different corporations. Where there is concern this may be the case, the proposed name will be rejected. (Or the applicant may be permitted to put the name in the articles in the "combined form", which will be defined under proposed amendments to the Act. This will ensure that the two forms will be used together in all the important places).

ii) Guidelines within the General Rule:

The Directorate will permit all words contained in English and French forms of a corporate name to be translated in the following situations:

1) The name is made only of generic words, literally translated. There is no separate distinctive element although the name as a whole is distinctive, e.g., "Think Retail Inc./Pensez Détail Inc."

2) The name consists only of a distinctive element, which is partly translated. The part that is translated is descriptive and the other part is identical in both English and French, e.g., "Techni-Glass (or Techniglass) Inc./Techni-Verre (or Techniverre) Inc."

3) The name consists of both distinctive and descriptive elements, both of which are very literally translated, e.g., "Édition Entre-Nous Inc./Between-Us Publishing Inc."

4) Generally speaking, a corporation with a corporate name whose distinctive feature

13.1 (continued)

VII. O Page 3 of 8

is an acronym may not have an alternate version of the acronym in the other official language even if the acronym is formed by letters which reflect a translation of the descriptive words of the name.

e.g. Service Informatique SI Inc.
CS Computer Service Inc. - (not available without proof of acquired secondary meaning in the acronyms)

The name of a non-profit corporation in which an acronym (relating to the descriptive words of the name) forms a part, may be available although the acronym is different in the English and French versions of the name, if the name would be available without the acronym and the acronym forms a non-substantive part of the name.
e.g. Institut de Recherches Aerospatiale du Canada IRAC

ARIC Aerospace Research Institute of Canada

Note: For corporations operating in Quebec it may be advisable to have a French form of the corporate name.

Note: When selecting a French form for a corporate name, for the purposes of carrying on business in Quebec, it is advisable to check the acceptability of the translation with the Office de la langue française. Where the Office de la langue française advises that a rejected French form is the only French form acceptable for use in the Province of Quebec, every effort will be made to find a way to accept that French form.

BILINGUAL NAME

	Look like 2 different companies		
yes (eg. CMI Inc./MIC Inc.)		No	(e.g. ABC Importex Import Export Corp./
		allow	
	secondary meaning		
exact trans. refused by the Office de la langue française	yes allow		
yes - try to allow no - use more exact translation			

Office de la langue française
Quebec City: (418) 643-8968 ou 69
Hull: (819) 770-7713
Montreal: (514) 873-7734 - (514) 873-5608

iii) Fees

a) There is no fee for the filing of articles of amendment to add the French or

13.1 (continued)

English version of a corporate name.

b) Where a name change application requests that a legal element common to both language versions such as "INC.", replace the existing legal element, e.g. "LTD.", we will assume that this is to create a French version of the name and we will not require the $200.00 fee despite the fact that technically the English version is also being amended.

(iv) Is another search necessary?

Articles filed under both linguistic versions are very often, accompanied by only one search report when two are necessary. This results in rejection of the articles which are considered deficient by the Corporations Directorate.

The intent behind the need for two search reports is strictly to avoid confusion in names and not for bureaucratic or pecuniary reasons. The following criteria should be used to judge whether or not a bilingual name (whether with separate or combined English and French versions) requires two searches:

1) identical names require only one search report:
e.g. AVITEK LTD./AVITEK LTEE
e.g. DUBOIS DISTRIBUTIONS LTD./DISTRIBUTIONS DUBOIS LTEE

2) names which are exact translations with phonetic differences require two searches unless the English and French versions share a substantial, distinctive component and differ only in respect of a minor, everyday descriptive term, in which case the name can be searched in such a way that one search will suffice.
e.g. Placements Protar Holdings Inc. - one search
e.g. Gestion Quadra Inc./Quadra Management Inc. - one search

In other words, where the bilingual name has a short distinctive part with a long and differing descriptive part, two search reports would be required.

e.g. LB Plumbing + Heating Inc.
Tuyauterie et Chauffage LB Inc. - two searches

Similarly, where the descriptive part of a bilingual name is unusual, two search reports would be required.

e.g. Collecte de sang Croix Bleue Inc.
Blue Cross Blood Collection Inc. - two searches

(v) Legal Elements

A corporate name which, in the English version, has the legal element "Limited", must in the French version use the legal element "Limitée". Similarly "Incorporated" and "Incorporée" go together. Where the legal element in the English version is "Corporation", the French version may have either "Corporation" or "société par actions de régime fédéral" but not "La Corporation" as its legal element. Where the legal element in the English version is "Corp.," the French version may have either "Corp."

13.1 (continued)

or "S.A.R.F."

In addition, the legal element for both versions must be either in long form or in the abbreviated form.

Note: We should be denying use of the legal element "S.A.R.F." with the English form of a name.

e.g. Exeter Shoes S.A.R.F. - unacceptable

N.B.: Watch out for "S.A.R.F." as a distinctive element.

(vi) Confusing Descriptive Terms

Because a holding company and an investment company may well be carrying on the same business, i.e. investments, and because applicants are inclined to use the word "Placements" as a translation for both "Holdings" and "Investments", granting names such as below will likely cause confusion.

From now on, the rule of thumb should be not to grant proposed names with the descriptive features of "Holdings", "Placements", "Investments", "Gestion", "Management", "Investissements" when the existing trade names have the same distinctive feature and one of the above descriptive features.

For example:
XYZ HOLDINGS INC. - existing
XYZ PLACEMENTS INC. - proposed (not acceptable)
XYZ INVESTMENTS INC. - proposed (not acceptable)

Both proposed names are not acceptable because there is a likelihood of confusion with the existing company name.

(vii) The distinctive element is the only feature in a corporate name which does not require translation for the alternate linguistic version. In addition, the distinctive element is the only element in a corporate name which could be in a foreign language and in this case a descriptive word may be unnecessary if there is no question of confusion. Where the foreign word has been determined to be a surname, a descriptive word may be necessary however to satisfy the section or the Regulation relating to surnames.

e.g. ETOILE MANUFACTURING LIMITED - acceptable
INVESTISSEMENTS MAPLE LEAF LIMITEE - acceptable
VITELLO RESTAURANTS INC. - acceptable

(viii) Equivalent name in any other language for use outside the country for a CBCA.

When an applicant proposes a corporate name in English or French or both in its Articles of Incorporation, it can also (in item 7 of Form 1) specify an equivalent name in French or English or any other language, for use outside the country. However, it cannot specify another name for use outside the country. This would mislead the public. To be very clear, where an applicant proposes, for example, an English name under item 1, he or she may insert an italian or even a french version of that name under item 7 for use outside the country. Note that English and French forms of the corporate name do not necessarily both have to appear in item 1. This is the client's choice.

13.1 (continued)

(D) USE OF THE WORDS "BROADCASTING", "RADIO", "TELEVISION" ....

In the course of our telephone conversations with some searchouses, the question of requesting consent from "Canadian Radio-Television and Telecommunications Commission" (CRTC) for a proposed name using the words "Broadcasting", "Radio" and "Television" (used in a broadcasting sense) has arisen. A review of our Act reveals that CRTC consent is not required by CCAC when granting such names.

CBCA gives us no authority to deny them the right to broadcast or the right to use the word "Broadcasting". Rather, the CRTC will deny them a licence to operate if they are unqualified.

(E) USA-SEC NAMES

NUANS reports may cite corporate names which originate from the Securities & Exchange Commission - USA. These companies are generally considered to be multi-national corporations doing business in Canada.

It has been our policy to consider such names in the name granting process. If a proposed name is refused because it is confusing with a USA-SEC name, one is advised but NOT required to find out from the available sources (see telephone and address below) whether or not the company is doing business in Canada. If the name is not checked out, it may be granted with full assumption of risk IN WRITING on the incorporator's part.

available source:
Public Records
Securities & Exchange Commission
500 North Capitol
Washington, D.C. 20549
Telephone: (202) 272-2650

(F) NUMBER OF SEARCH REPORTS REQUIRED

There will be cases where one name search will suffice for several name requests.

This is more likely to be the case where the names requested are for proposed affiliated companies distinguished only by the geographical location in brackets.

e.g. XYZ TOOLS (OTTAWA) INC.
XYZ TOOLS (HAMILTON) INC.
XYZ TOOLS (TORONTO) INC.

At the moment, however, there is no firm rule as to when only a single search report will be required. Each case should be referred to the Name Section for individual consideration.

(see also Bilingual Names page 7.1)

Is any search necessary?

13.1 (continued)

VII. O **Page 7 of 8**

No search is required for an application made pursuant to Regulation 28(2) unless the name being taken by the new company is the name of a provincial body corporate.

In the case of an application made pursuant to Regulation 27(1), a NUANS microfiche search is acceptable in place of a NUANS search but only if the body corporate consenting and undertaking is a federal corporation.

In the case of an application made pursuant to Regulation 27(2), a NUANS microfiche search is acceptable in place of a NUANS search.

Where articles of continuance are filed at the same time as articles of amalgamation and where the certificate of amalgamation is to be issued in a name different from the name of the continued corporation and on the same day as the certificate of continuance, a NUANS search report will not be required.

Where articles of continuance are filed at the same time as articles of amalgamation and where the certificate of amalgamation is to be issued in a name different from the name of the continued corporation and within a very short period of time after the certificate of continuance, a NUANS search report will not be required, if the applicant provides a NUANS microfiche search and undertakes:

- to file a NUANS search immediately if the amalgamation does not take effect as planned, and change its name if the Director decides it is necessary
- not to provide a consent under Regulation 28(2) or (3) for another entity to use its continued name, unless that name has been determined to be not confusing by the Directorate on the basis of a NUANS search report obtained by the entity at that time.

Depending on the length of time between the continuance and the amalgamation, the continued company may also be asked to undertake that it will not carry on business between the date of continuance and the date of amalgamation.

In the case of all other applications, a NUANS search is required.

(G) TRADE NAME

A corporation may carry on business under or identify itself by a name other than its corporate name if that other name does not contain, other than in a figuration or descriptive sense, either the word or expression "Limited", "Limitée", "Incorporated", "Incorporée", "Corporation" or "Société par actions de régime fédéral" or the corresponding abbreviation.

(H) NUMBERED NAME

If requested to do so by the incorporators or a corporation, the Director shall assign to the corporation as its name a designating number followed by the word "Canada" and a legal element.

(I) MICROFICHE SUPPLEMENT OF NUANS REPORT FOR NAMES WITH MORE THAN ONE DISTINCTIVE ELEMENT

13.1 (continued)

Very occasionally, when the corporate name that is searched has more than one distinctive element, the NUANS search report will list business names and trade-marks that are similar to only one of those distinctive features. To spare applicants the time and expense of ordering a second NUANS search on the other distinctive element, Names Officers will undertake to carry out a NUANS microfiche search of the other element to see whether there are any confusing names relating to it. The applicant will be asked to accept the risk that the NUANS microfiche search, which, unlike a regular NUANS search, does not list names that are phonetically similar to the one proposed, may not reveal a conflict and that the Name Officer may fail to find a conflict that later comes to light, causing the name to become disallowed, at the applicant's expense.

(J) INTERNET DOMAIN NAMES AS CORPORATE NAME

Suffixes like ".ca" or ".com" will not be treated as distinctive elements of a corporate name. The name will be treated as if it did not have the suffix. If the name has some distinctiveness without the suffix, e.g., "Doc Systems Inc.," and it is not confusing, it will be approved. If the name has no distinctiveness without the suffix, it will be rejected, since the suffix does not add distinctiveness; e.g., "Cars.ca Inc." would not be accepted because the name "Cars Inc." would not be accepted, being "too general."

Publication Date: 1999-11-19
Author: Industry Canada

13.1 (continued)

Industry Canada Industrie Canada

Canada

Protecting Your Corporate Name

The granting of a corporate name by the Director under the *Canada Business Corporations Act* (CBCA) generally confers a degree of protection for that corporate name. However, the granting of names under the CBCA does not in itself confer any rights to those names vis-à-vis corporate names or trade names which may have existed at the time of granting but which did not appear on the NUANS search report or which the Director did not, at the time of granting, consider likely to cause confusion. Similarly, the granting of a corporate name may not protect you from earlier or subsequent trade marks of other parties.

The following gives a succinct overview of the relationship between trade name, corporate name and trade mark rights and some general guidance as to how you can best protect your corporate name and the goodwill associated with it.

1. Before an applicant applies for a corporate name, it is important for him or her to ensure that there are no similar existing corporate names, trade names or trade marks. A NUANS search report, including trade marks which are registered or proposed for registration, is required to be filed with articles of incorporation, amendment, etc. and is usually very reliable. Since, however, the NUANS system is not foolproof, the applicant remains responsible for any likelihood of confusion.

   While a name granted by the Director will appear on future NUANS searches required for incorporation in the federal and most provincial jurisdictions, you may wish to conduct your own NUANS searches on a periodic basis after your name has been approved. This would be done in order to ensure, to your own satisfaction, that no confusing corporate or business name has subsequently been approved in the jurisdiction(s) in which you are carrying on business, and to give you up-to-date information about trade marks that have been applied for or registered subsequent to the granting of your corporate name.

2. Using a corporate name which is similar to a registered trade mark may result in liability for infringement of the registered trade mark, even if the trade mark was registered after the corporate name was granted. This is so because, under trade marks law, the holder of a corporate name bears the responsibility for ensuring that no new trade marks are registered which are confusing with that name. Information on registered and advertised trade marks can be obtained from the *Trade Marks Journal*, distributed weekly by Supply and Services Canada* or by conducting a

13.1 (continued)

search of one of the various electronic trade mark databases.** The holder of a corporate name has the right, in certain circumstances, to oppose the registration of a trade mark or to have a trade mark registration expunged.

3. Registration of a trade mark is the best way to obtain the exclusive right to use the mark in all of Canada in association with the wares and services for which the registration is obtained. While the Trade Marks Office** can provide basic guidance, it is recommended that a specialist (a trade mark agent or trade mark lawyer) be consulted. It should be noted that trade mark registration is not available for corporate names in all circumstances.

* Canada Communications Group - Publishing
Supply and Services Canada
45 Sacré-Coeur Blvd.
Hull QC K1A 0S9
Tel.: 1-800-567-4422

** Trade Marks Office
Industry Canada
Phase I, Place du Portage
Hull QC K1A 0C9
Tel.: (819) 953-8098 (re: on-line databases)
Tel.: (819) 997-1420 (re: general inquiries)

Publication Date: 1996-10-08
Author: Industry Canada - Industrie Canada

14. Incorporation—Federal Jurisdiction

14.1 Articles of Incorporation—*Canada Business Corporations Act*—Form 1

Annex B - Sample Articles of Incorporation: Two Classes of Shares Page 1 of 4

Sample Articles of Incorporation: Two Classes of Shares

Form 1

Industry Canada — Industrie Canada
Canada Business Corporations Act — Loi canadienne sur les sociétés par actions

FORM 1
ARTICLES OF INCORPORATION
(SECTION 6)

FORMULE 1
STATUTS CONSTITUTIFS
(ARTICLE 6)

1 - Name of corporation — Dénomination de la société

ABBA Consulting Inc.

2 - The place in Canada where the registered office is to be situated — Lieu au Canada où doit être situé le siège social

Any Regional Municipality in Canada

3 - The classes and any maximum number of shares that the corporation is authorized to issue — Catégories et tout nombre maximal d'actions que la société est autorisée à émettre

An unlimited number of Class A and an unlimited number of Class B shares with the rights, privileges, restrictions and conditions set out on Schedule A attached.

4 - Restrictions, if any, on share transfers — Restrictions sur le transfert des actions, s'il y a lieu

See attached Schedule I

5 - Number (or minimum and maximum number) of directors — Nombre (ou nombre minimal et maximal) d'administrateurs

Minimum of 1, maximum of 10

6 - Restrictions, if any, on business the corporation may carry on — Limites imposées à l'activité commerciale de la société, s'il y a lieu

None

7 - Other provisions, if any — Autres dispositions, s'il y a lieu

See attached Schedule II

8 - Incorporators - Fondateurs

Address (include postal code)

14.1 (continued)

Annex B - Sample Articles of Incorporation: Two Classes of Shares

Name(s) - Nom(s)	[illegible]	Signature
Jane Smith	555 Any Street Anytown ON M1A 5T6	[J. Smith]

FOR DEPARTMENTAL USE ONLY - À L'USAGE DU MINISTÈRE SEULEMENT Corporation No. - N° de la société	Filed - Déposée

IC 3419 (6/90)

SCHEDULE A TO ARTICLES OF INCORPORATION – SHARE RIGHTS

1. The holders of Class A shares are entitled:

   a. to vote at all meetings of shareholders except meetings at which only holders of a specified class of shares are entitled to vote;

   b. to receive the remaining property of the Corporation upon dissolution; and

   c. subject to the rights and privileges attaching to the Class B shares, to receive dividends as and when declared by the board of directors of the Corporation.

2. The holders of Class B shares are entitled:

   a. in priority to the holders of Class A shares and from the funds declared for the payment of dividends, to receive a maximum annual, preferential and non-cumulative dividend based on the prime lending rate of the bank of the Corporation at the date of the dividend less one percent (1%) as applied to the amount added, in respect of these shares, to the stated capital account maintained for the Class B shares, the date and terms of payment of such dividends to be determined by the board of directors; and

   b. upon dissolution of the Corporation, to repayment of the amount paid for such share (plus any declared and unpaid dividends) in priority to the Class A shares, but not to participate any further in profits or assets of the Corporation.

3. The holders of Class B shares shall not be entitled to vote at meetings of the shareholders except as otherwise specifically provided for by the terms of the *Canada Business Corporations Act*.

SCHEDULE I TO ARTICLES OF INCORPORATION

The right to transfer shares of the Corporation shall be restricted in that no shareholder shall be entitled to transfer any share or shares of the Corporation without the approval of:

a. the directors of the Corporation expressed by resolution passed by the votes cast by a majority of the directors of the Corporation at a meeting of the board of directors or signed by all of the directors of the Corporation; OR

b. the shareholders of the Corporation expressed by resolution passed by the votes cast by a majority of the shareholders who voted in respect of the resolution or signed by all shareholders entitled to vote on that

14.1 (continued)

resolution.

*Restrictions on share transfer are normally limited to the consent of the directors **and/or** the shareholders. If you wish your company to be a private company (referred to in the CBCA as a "non-distributing corporation") and thus not have to comply with prospectus filings or other related procedures set out in the CBCA or provincial securities rules, it is necessary to include in your articles a restriction on the transfer of shares. Many companies also include "private company restrictions" similar to those in sample Schedule II on the next page for the purposes of provincial securities regulation.*

*The CBCA allows for a number of provisions that **may** be included in the articles of incorporation. You may also choose to include clauses to satisfy requirements of other legislation (such as the restriction on the number of shareholders and any distribution of shares to the public, which are aimed at excluding the company from regulation by securities laws) or institutions (the limits on borrowing powers specified below are often included to satisfy lending institutions). These provisions are optional, and the ones below provide sample wording used for the most commonly occurring features.*

SCHEDULE II TO ARTICLES OF INCORPORATION

Other provisions:

a. The number of shareholders in the Corporation, exclusive of employees and former employees who, while employed by the Corporation were, and following the termination of that employment, continue to be, shareholders of the Corporation, is limited to not more than fifty, two or more persons who are the joint registered holders of one or more shares being counted as one shareholder.

b. Any invitation to the public to subscribe for securities of the Corporation is prohibited.

c. If authorized by by-law which is duly made by the directors and confirmed by ordinary resolution of the shareholders, the directors of the Corporation may from time to time:

   i. borrow money upon the credit of the Corporation;
   ii. issue, reissue, sell or pledge debt obligations of the Corporation; and
   iii. mortgage, hypothecate, pledge or otherwise create a security interest in all or any property of the Corporation, owned or subsequently acquired to secure any debt obligation of the Corporation.

   Any such by-law may provide for the delegation of such powers by the directors to such officers or directors of the Corporation to such extent and in such manner as may be set out in the by-law.

   Nothing herein limits or restricts the borrowing of money by the Corporation on bills of exchange or promissory notes made, drawn, accepted or endorsed by or on behalf of the Corporation.

d. The directors may appoint one or more directors, who shall hold office for a term expiring not later than the close of the next annual general meeting of shareholders, but the total number of directors so appointed may not exceed one third of the number of directors elected at the previous annual general

14.1 (continued)


```
meeting of shareholders.
```

Annex C

Table of Contents

Publication Date: 1998-12-14
Author: Corporations Directorate

14.2 Notice of Registered Office or Notice of Change of Registered Office—*Canada Business Corporations Act*—Form 3

Industry Canada / Industrie Canada

Canada Business Corporations Act / Loi canadienne sur les sociétés par actions

FORM 3
NOTICE OF REGISTERED OFFICE
OR NOTICE OF CHANGE OF
ADDRESS
OF REGISTERED OFFICE
(SECTION 19)

FORMULE 3
AVIS DE DÉSIGNATION
OU DE CHANGEMENT D'ADRESSE
DU SIÈGE SOCIAL
(ARTICLE 19)

1 – Name of the Corporation – Dénomination sociale de la société

2 – Corporation No. – N° de la société

3 – Place in Canada where the registered office is situated. (Describe the place in terms of a broad municipal definition. This place must match the place listed in item 2 of the Articles.)

Lieu du siège social au Canada. (Indiquer le lieu selon la définition générale de municipalité. Il doit correspondre au lieu indiqué à l'article 2 des statuts.)

4 – Address of registered office

Adresse du siège social

CAUTION: Address of registered office must be within the place that is described in the Articles and item 3; otherwise an amendment to the Articles is required (paragraph 173(1)(b) of the Act. Use Form 4 in addition to this form.

AVIS : L'adresse du siège social doit se trouver dans les limites du lieu indiqué dans les statuts et à la rubrique 3. Sinon, il faut modifier les statuts (alinéa 173(1)(b) de la Loi) et remplir, outre la présente formule, la formule 4.

5 – Effective date of change

Date de prise d'effet

6 – Previous address of registered office

Ancienne adresse du siège social

Date	Signature	Title – Titre

FOR DEPARTMENTAL USE ONLY – À L'USAGE DU MINISTÈRE SEULEMENT

Filed – Déposée

IC 3420 (5/98)

14.2 (continued)

Canada Business Corporations Act

Notice of Registered Office or
Notice of Change of Address of Registered Office
FORM 3
INSTRUCTIONS

Format
Documents required to be sent to the Director must be in a clear and legible form.

Complete items 1, 3 and 4 for new corporations.
Complete items 1 through 6 for changes.
Note: Where required by the Act, the changes being reported by the filing of this form must be authorized by the director(s).

Item 1
Set out the full legal name of the corporation.

Item 2
Complete only in the case of change of registered office.

Item 3
Set out the place in Canada where the registered office is situated as indicated in the articles of the corporation. The description should be in terms of a broad municipal definition, not a specific street address (e.g. Montreal Urban Community, in the Province of Quebec).

Item 4
Set out in full the address at which the registered office is to be situated or to which it is to be changed.

Item 5
State the date when the change of registered office is to take effect.

Item 6
Set out the previous address of the registered office, if any.

Signature
A director or authorized officer of the corporation shall sign the notice. If a new corporation, an incorporator shall sign the notice.

Completed document is to be sent to:

The Director, Canada Business Corporations Act
Jean Edmonds Towers, South
9th Floor
365 Laurier Ave. West
Ottawa, Ontario
K1A 0C8

Loi canadienne sur les sociétés par actions

Avis de désignation ou
de changement d'adresse du siège social
FORMULE 3
INSTRUCTIONS

Présentation
Tous les documents dont l'envoi au directeur est exigé doivent être clairs et lisibles.

Remplir les rubriques 1, 3 et 4 pour les nouvelles sociétés.
Remplir les rubriques 1 à 6 si des changements sont survenus.
Nota : Lorsqu'exigé par la Loi, les changements rapportés par le dépôt de cette formule doivent être autorisés par les administrateurs.

Rubrique 1
Indiquer la dénomination sociale complète de la société.

Rubrique 2
À remplir seulement dans le cas d'un avis de changement du siège social.

Rubrique 3
Indiquer le lieu au Canada où se situe le siège social, tel qu'il est indiqué dans les statuts de la société. Il s'agit de décrire le lieu en général, en fonction de la municipalité plutôt que par rapport à une adresse municipale précise (ex. dans la Communauté urbaine de Montréal, province de Québec).

Rubrique 4
Indiquer l'adresse complète du siège social ou celle où il doit désormais être situé.

Rubrique 5
Indiquer la date à laquelle le changement du siège social doit prendre effet.

Rubrique 6
Indiquer l'adresse précédente du siège social, le cas échéant.

Signature
Un administrateur ou un dirigeant autorisé de la société doit signer l'avis. S'il s'agit d'une nouvelle société, un fondateur doit signer l'avis.

Le document rempli doit être envoyé au :

Directeur, Loi canadienne sur les sociétés par actions
Tours Jean-Edmonds, sud
9ième étage
365, ave Laurier ouest
Ottawa (Ontario)
K1A 0C8

14.3 Notice of Directors or Notice of Change of Directors—*Canada Business Corporations Act*—Form 6

Industry Canada | Industrie Canada

Canada Business Corporations Act | Loi canadienne sur les sociétés par actions

FORM 6
NOTICE OF DIRECTORS
OR NOTICE OF CHANGE
OF DIRECTORS
(SECTIONS 106 AND 113)

FORMULE 6
LISTE DES ADMINISTRATEURS
OU AVIS DE CHANGEMENT
DES ADMINISTRATEURS
(ARTICLES 106 ET 113)

1- Name of corporation - Dénomination de la société	2- Corporation No. - N° de la société

3- The following persons became directors of this corporation — Les personnes suivantes sont devenues administrateurs de la présente société

Name Nom	Effective Date Date d'entrée en vigueur :	Residential Address - Adresse domiciliaire	Resident Canadian - Y/N Résident canadien - O/N

4- The following persons ceased to be directors of this corporation — Les personnes suivantes ont cessé d'être administrateurs de la présente société

Name Nom	Effective Date Date d'entrée en vigueur :	Residential Address - Adresse domiciliaire

5- The directors of this corporation now are — Les administrateurs de la présente société sont maintenant

Name - Nom	Residential Address - Adresse domiciliaire	Resident Canadian - Y/N Résident canadien - O/N

Date	Signature	Title - Titre
IC 3103 (2/96)		Filed - Déposée

DYE & DURHAM CO. INC.

14.3 (continued)

Canada Business Corporations Act

Notice of Directors or
Notice of Change of Directors
FORM 6
INSTRUCTIONS

Format
Documents required to be sent to the Director must be in a clear and legible form.
Complete items 1 and 5 for new corporations.
Complete items 1 through 5 for changes.

Item 1
Set out the full legal name of the corporation.

Item 2
Always set out the corporation number when filing a Notice of Change of Directors (Form 6).

Item 3, 4 and 5
With respect to each director,
(a) set out first given name, initial and family name;
(b) set out full residential address (not business address), including postal code;
(c) specify occupation clearly - e.g. manager, geologist, lawyer; and
(d) refer to the definition of "resident Canadian" in the *Canada Business Corporations Act* and *Canada Business Corporations Regulations*.

Signature
A director or authorized officer of the Corporation shall sign the Notice. If a new corporation, an incorporator shall sign the Notice.

Completed document is to be sent to:

The Director, Canada Business Corporations Act
Journal Tower South
9th Floor
365 Laurier Ave. West
Ottawa, Ontario
K1A 0C8

The information you provide in this document is collected under the authority of the *Canada Business Corporations Act* and will be stored in personal information bank number IC/PPU-049. Personal information that you provide is protected under the provisions of the *Privacy Act*. However, public disclosure pursuant to section 266 of the *Canada Business Corporations Act* is permitted under the *Privacy Act*.

Loi canadienne sur les sociétés par actions

Liste des administrateurs ou
Avis de changement des administrateurs
FORMULE 6
INSTRUCTIONS

Présentation
Tous les documents dont l'envoi au directeur est exigé doivent être clairs et lisibles.
Remplir les rubriques 1 et 5 pour les nouvelles sociétés.
Remplir les rubriques 1 à 5 si des changements sont survenus.

Rubrique 1
Indiquer la dénomination officielle complète de la société.

Rubrique 2
Indiquer toujours le numéro de la société lors de l'envoi d'un avis de changement des administrateurs (Formule 6).

Rubrique 3, 4 et 5
En ce qui concerne chaque administrateur :
a) indiquer son prénom, ses initiales et son nom de famille;
b) donner l'adresse complète de son domicile (non son adresse d'affaires) en incluant le code postal;
c) spécifier clairement son occupation - par exemple, gérant, géologue, avocat;
d) consulter la définition de "résident canadien" dans la *Loi et le Règlement sur les sociétés par actions de régime fédéral.*

Signature
Un administrateur ou un dirigeant autorisé de la société doit signer l'avis. S'il s'agit d'une nouvelle société, un fondateur doit signer l'avis.

Le document rempli doit être envoyé au :

Directeur, Loi canadienne sur les sociétés par actions
Édifice Journal tour sud
9ième étage
365 ave Laurier ouest
Ottawa (Ontario)
K1A 0C8

Les renseignements que vous fournissez dans ce document sont recueillis en vertu de la Loi canadienne sur les sociétés par actions et seront emmagasinés dans le fichier de renseignements personnels IC/PPU-049. Les renseignements personnels que vous fournissez sont protégés par les dispositions de la *Loi sur la protection des renseignements personnels*. Cependant, la divulgation au public selon les termes de l'article 266 de la Loi canadienne sur les sociétés par actions est permise en vertu de la Loi sur la protection des renseignements personnels.

Canada

14.4 Common Share with Restriction—Canada

DYE & DURHAM

COMMON SHARE CERTIFICATE

Certificate No. ____________

For ____________ Shares

Issued to

____

____

Dated ____________ *(year)*

From whom transferred

____

Dated ____________ *(year)*

No. Original Certificate ____________

No. Original Shares ____________

No. of Shares Transferred ____________

Received Certificate No. ____________

for ____________ Shares

this ______ day of ____________ *(year)*

____

____

____

No. ____________ INCORPORATED UNDER THE CANADA BUSINESS CORPORATIONS ACT ____________ **Shares**

This is to Certify that ....

is the registered holder of .... Common Shares of

The class or series of shares represented by this certificate has rights, privileges, restrictions or conditions attached thereto and the Corporation will furnish to the holder, on demand and without charge, a full copy of the text of,

(i) the rights, privileges, restrictions and conditions attached to the said shares and to each class authorized to be issued and to each series insofar as the same have been fixed by the directors, and

(ii) the authority of the directors to fix the rights, privileges, restrictions and conditions of subsequent series, if applicable.

COMMON

RESTRICTIONS ON TRANSFER. There are restrictions on the right to transfer the shares represented by this Certificate.

IN WITNESS WHEREOF the Corporation has caused this Certificate to be signed by its duly authorized officers this .... day of .... *(year)*

____________ ____________

NO PAR VALUE

D&D "COMMON" 8½ x 11

14.4 (continued)

For Value Received, ______ *hereby assign and transfer unto*

____

______________________________ *Common Shares*

____

represented by the within Certificate.

Dated ______________________ *(year)* __________

In the presence of ______________________

____

NOTICE THE SIGNATURE OF THIS ASSIGNMENT MUST CORRESPOND WITH THE NAME AS WRITTEN UPON THE FACE OF THE CERTIFICATE IN EVERY PARTICULAR WITHOUT ALTERATION OR ENLARGEMENT OR ANY CHANGE WHATEVER

14.5 Preference Share Certificate—Canada

DYE & DURHAM

PREFERENCE SHARE CERTIFICATE

Certificate No. ________ ________

For ______________________ Shares

Issued to

____

____

Dated ______________________ *(year)*

From whom transferred

____

Dated ______________________ *(year)*

No. Original Certificate ______________________

No. Original Shares ______________________

No. of Shares Transferred ______________________

Received Certificate No. ______________________

for ______________________ Shares

this __________ day of ______________ *(year)*

____

____

____

No. ____ INCORPORATED UNDER THE CANADA BUSINESS CORPORATIONS ACT ________ **Shares**

This is to Certify that ....

is the registered holder of .... Preference Shares of

The class or series of shares represented by this certificate has rights, privileges, restrictions or conditions attached thereto and the Corporation will furnish to the holder, on demand and without charge, a full copy of the text of,

(i) the rights, privileges, restrictions and conditions attached to the said shares and to each class authorized to be issued and to each series insofar as the same have been fixed by the directors, and

(ii) the authority of the directors to fix the rights, privileges, restrictions and conditions of subsequent series, if applicable.

RESTRICTIONS ON TRANSFER. There are restrictions on the right to transfer the shares represented by this Certificate.

IN WITNESS WHEREOF the Corporation has caused this Certificate to be signed by its duly authorized officers this .... day of .... *(year)*

______________________ ______________________

NO PAR VALUE

D&D "PREFERENCE" 8½ x 11

14.5 (continued)

For Value Received, ________ *hereby assign and transfer unto*

____

______________________________________ *Preference Shares*

____

represented by the within Certificate.

Dated ______________________ ________

In the presence of

____

____

15. Organization—Federal Corporation

15.1 By-law No. 1

DYE & DURHAM

CANADA CORPORATION

BY-LAW No.1

for use under the Canada *Business Corporations Act*

For corporations with more than 1 director or more than 1 shareholder

Revised 1999

This form of by-law is suitable for use by non-offering corporations incorporated pursuant to the Canada *Business Corporations Act* as amended.

It has been designed for use by the typical small corporation and contains those provisions which have been found to be most applicable for the majority of such companies.

Depending on the requirements, additions to or deletions from this by-law may be necessary prior to its use and the incorporators are advised to consult with legal counsel before completion.

Sections 2.01 ***(Powers)****, 3.09* ***(Casting Vote)****, 6.12* ***(Votes to Govern)****, 9.01* ***(Financial Year)*** *and 13.01* ***(Repeal)*** *of this by-law should be reviewed by the incorporators and completed as the circumstances require.*

15.1 (continued)

BY-LAW NO. 1

A by-law relating generally to the conduct of the business and affairs of

(herein called the "Corporation")

CONTENTS

1. Interpretation
2. Directors
3. Meetings of Directors
4. Remuneration and Indemnification
5. Officers
6. Meetings of Shareholders
7. Shares
8. Dividends
9. Fiscal Year
10. Notices
11. Execution of Documents
12. Effective Date
13. Repeal

BE IT ENACTED as a by-law of the Corporation as follows:

1. INTERPRETATION

1.01 In this by-law and all other by-laws and resolutions of the Corporation, unless the context otherwise requires:

(a) "Act" means the Canada Business Corporations Act together with the Regulations made pursuant thereto and any statute or regulations that may be substituted therefor as amended from time to time;

(b) "articles" means the articles of incorporation of the Corporation as amended or restated from time to time;

(c) "board" means the board of directors of the Corporation;

(d) "by-laws" means this by-law and all other by-laws of the Corporation as amended from time to time, and from time to time in force and effect;

(e) "Corporation" means this Corporation;

15.1 (continued)

(f) "meeting of shareholders" means any meeting of shareholders, whether annual or special; and "special meeting of shareholders" means a special meeting of all shareholders entitled to vote at an annual meeting of shareholders and a meeting of any class or classes of shareholders entitled to vote on the question at issue;

(g) "person" includes an individual, partnership, association, body corporate, trustee, executor, administrator or legal representative;

(h) "recorded address" means, in the case of a shareholder, his address as recorded in the shareholders' register; and, in the case of joint shareholders, the address appearing in the shareholders' register in respect of such joint holding or the first address so appearing if there are more than one; and, in the case of a director, officer, auditor or member of a committee of the board, his latest address recorded in the records of the Corporation; and

(i) "unanimous shareholder agreement" shall have the meaning ascribed to such term under the Act.

1.02 In this by-law where the context requires, words importing the singular include the plural and vice versa and words importing gender include the masculine, feminine and neuter genders.

1.03 Save as aforesaid, words and expressions defined in the Act shall have the same meanings when used herein.

2. DIRECTORS

2.01 Powers - Subject to any unanimous shareholder agreement, the business and affairs of the Corporation shall be managed by a board of directors.

Until changed in accordance with the Act, the board shall consist of

(Delete as applicable.)

a fixed number of directors.

not fewer than the minimum number and not more than the maximum number of directors provided for in the articles.

2.02 Resident Canadians - A majority of the directors and of any committee of the directors shall be resident Canadians as defined in the Act.

15.1 (continued)

2.03 Qualifications - No person shall be qualified for election as a director if he is less than 18 years of age; if he is of unsound mind and has been so found by a court in Canada or elsewhere; if he is not an individual; or if he has the status of a bankrupt.

2.04 Election and Term - The election of directors shall take place at the first meeting of shareholders and at each succeeding annual meeting at which an election of directors is required. The directors shall hold office for an expressly stated term, which shall expire not later than the close of the third annual meeting of shareholders following the election. A director not elected for an expressly stated term ceases to hold office at the close of the first annual meeting of shareholders following his election. Incumbent directors, if qualified, shall be eligible for re-election. If an election of directors is not held at the proper time, the incumbent directors shall continue in office until their successors are elected.

2.05 Removal - Subject to the provisions of the Act, the shareholders may, by resolution passed by a majority of the votes cast at a special meeting of shareholders duly called for that purpose, remove any director before the expiration of his term of office and may, by a majority of votes cast at the meeting, elect any person in his stead for the remainder of his term, failing which such vacancy may be filled by the board.

2.06 Vacation of Office - A director ceases to hold office when he dies; he is removed from office by the shareholders; he ceases to be qualified for election as a director; or his written resignation is sent or delivered to the Corporation, or if a time is specified in such resignation, at the time so specified, whichever is later.

2.07 Vacancies - Subject to the provisions of the Act, a quorum of the board may fill a vacancy in the board, except a vacancy resulting from an increase in the number or minimum number of directors or from failure to elect the number or minimum number of directors required by the articles. If there is not a quorum of directors, or if there has been a failure to elect the number or minimum number of directors required by the articles, the directors then in office shall forthwith call a special meeting of shareholders to fill the vacancy, and, if they fail to do so or if there are no directors then in office, the meeting may be called by any shareholder.

15.1 (continued)

3. MEETINGS OF DIRECTORS

3.01 Place of Meetings - Meetings of the board of directors may be held at any place in or outside Canada.

3.02 Quorum - A majority of the number of directors or minimum number of directors required by the articles constitutes a quorum at any meeting of directors, and, notwithstanding any vacancy among the directors, a quorum of directors may exercise all the powers of the directors.

3.03 Resident Canadians - Directors shall not transact business at a meeting of directors unless a majority of the directors present are resident Canadians.

3.04 Notwithstanding Section 3.03, directors may transact business at a meeting of directors where a majority of resident Canadian directors is not present if,

(a) a resident Canadian director who is unable to be present approves in writing or by telephone or other communications facilities the business transacted at the meeting; and

(b) a majority of resident Canadian directors would have been present had that director been present at the meeting.

3.05 Calling of Meetings - Meetings of the board shall be held from time to time at such place, at such time and on such day as the chairman of the board, the managing director, the president or any two directors may determine, and the secretary shall call meetings when so directed or authorized. Notice of the time and place of every meeting so called shall be given to each director not less than 48 hours before the time when the meeting is to be held, except that no notice of a meeting shall be necessary if all the directors are present or if those absent have waived notice of or otherwise signified their consent to the holding of such meeting. A notice of a meeting of directors need not specify the purpose of or the business to be transacted at the meeting except where the Act requires such purpose or business to be specified, including any proposal to:

(a) submit to the shareholders any question or matter requiring approval of the shareholders;

15.1 (continued)

(b) fill a vacancy among the directors or in the office of an auditor;

(c) issue securities;

(d) declare dividends;

(e) purchase, redeem or otherwise acquire shares of the Corporation;

(f) pay a commission for the sale of shares;

(g) approve a management proxy circular;

(h) approve a take-over bid circular or directors' circular;

(i) approve any annual financial statements; or

(j) adopt, amend or repeal by-laws.

3.06 Regular Meetings - The board may appoint a day or days in any month or months for regular meetings at a place and hour to be named. A copy of any resolution of the board fixing the place and time of regular meetings of the board shall be sent to each director forthwith after being passed, but no other notice shall be required for any such regular meetings except where the Act requires the purpose thereof or the business to be transacted thereat to be specified.

3.07 First Meeting of New Board - Each newly elected board may without notice hold its first meeting following a meeting of shareholders at which such board is elected, provided that a quorum of directors is present.

3.08 Votes to Govern - At all meetings of the board, every question shall be decided by a majority of the votes cast on the question.

3.09 Casting Vote - In the case of an equality of votes on any question at a meeting of the board, the chairman of the meeting *shall / shall not* be entitled to a second or casting vote. *(Delete accordingly.)*

3.10 Disclosure of Interests in Contracts - Every director or officer of the Corporation who is a party to a material contract or transaction or proposed material contract or transaction with the Corporation, or is a director or officer of or has a material interest in any person who is a party to a material contract or transaction or proposed material contract or

15.1 (continued)

transaction with the Corporation shall disclose in writing to the Corporation or request to have entered in the minutes of a meeting of directors the nature and extent of his interest at the time and in the manner required by the Act. Any such contract or proposed contract shall be referred to the board or shareholders for approval even if such contract is one that in the ordinary course of the Corporation's business would not require approval by the board or the shareholders, and a director interested in a contract so referred to the board shall not vote on any resolution to approve the same except as provided by the Act.

3.11 Waiver of Notice - A director may in any manner waive a notice of a meeting of directors; and attendance of a director at a meeting of directors is a waiver of notice of the meeting, except where a director attends a meeting for the express purpose of objecting to the transactions of any business on the grounds that the meeting is not lawfully called.

3.12 Participation by Telephone - A director may, if all the directors of the Corporation consent, participate in a meeting of directors or of a committee of directors by means of such telephone or other communications facilities as permit all persons participating at the meeting to hear each other, and a director participating in such a meeting is deemed to be present at the meeting.

3.13 Adjournment - Notice of an adjourned meeting of directors is not required to be given if the time and place of the adjourned meeting is announced at the original meeting.

3.14 Delegation - Directors may appoint from their number a managing director who is a resident Canadian or a committee of directors and delegate to such managing director or committee any of the powers of the directors. If the directors appoint a committee of directors, a majority of the members of the committee must be resident Canadians.

3.15 Resolution in Lieu of Meeting - A resolution in writing, signed by all the directors entitled to vote on that resolution at a meeting of directors or committee of directors, is as valid as if it had been passed at a meeting of directors or committee of directors. A copy of every such resolution shall be kept with the minutes of the proceedings of the directors or committee of directors.

15.1 (continued)

3.16 One Director Meeting - If the Corporation has only one director, that director may constitute a meeting.

4. REMUNERATION AND INDEMNIFICATION

4.01 Remuneration - Subject to any unanimous shareholder agreement, the directors shall be paid such remuneration as may from time to time be determined by the board. Nothing herein shall preclude any director from serving the Corporation in any other capacity and receiving remuneration therefor. In addition, directors shall be paid such sums in respect of their out-of-pocket expenses incurred in attending board, committee or shareholders meetings or otherwise in respect of the performance by them of their duties as the board may from time to time determine.

4.02 Limitation of Liability - Every director and officer of the Corporation, in exercising his powers and discharging his duties, shall act honestly and in good faith with a view to the best interests of the Corporation, and exercise the care, diligence and skill that a reasonably prudent person would exercise in comparable circumstances. Subject to the foregoing, no director or officer shall be liable for the acts, receipts, neglects or defaults of any other director or officer or employee, or for joining in any receipt or other act for conformity, or for any loss, damage or expense happening to the Corporation through the insufficiency or deficiency of title to any property acquired for or on behalf of the Corporation, or for the insufficiency or deficiency of any security in or upon which any of the monies of the Corporation shall be invested, or for any loss or damage arising from the bankruptcy, insolvency or tortious acts of any person with whom any of the monies, securities or effects of the Corporation shall be deposited, or for any loss occasioned by any error of judgment or oversight on his part, or for any other loss, damage or misfortune whatever, which shall happen in the execution of the duties of his office or in relation thereto, unless the same are occasioned by his own willful neglect or default; provided that nothing herein shall relieve any director or officer from the duty to act in accordance with the Act or from liability for any breach thereof.

4.03 Indemnity of Directors and Officers - Subject to the provisions of the Act, the

15.1 (continued)

Corporation shall indemnify a director or officer of the Corporation, a former director or officer of the Corporation, or a person who acts or acted at the Corporation's request as a director or officer of a body corporate of which the Corporation is or was a shareholder or creditor, and his heirs and legal representatives, against all costs, charges and expenses, including an amount paid to settle an action or satisfy a judgment, reasonably incurred by him in respect of any civil, criminal or administrative action or proceeding to which he is made a party by reason of being or having been a director or officer of such corporation or body corporate if,

(a) he acted honestly and in good faith with a view to the best interests of the Corporation; and

(b) in the case of a criminal or administrative action or proceeding that is enforced by a monetary penalty, he had reasonable grounds for believing that his conduct was lawful.

5. OFFICERS

5.01 Appointment - Subject to the provisions of the Act, the articles or any unanimous shareholder agreement, the board may from time to time appoint a president, one or more vice-presidents (to which title may be added words indicating seniority or function), a secretary, a treasurer and such other officers as the board may determine, including one or more assistants to any of the officers so appointed. The board may specify the duties of and, in accordance with this by-law and subject to the provisions of the Act, delegate to such officers powers to manage the business and affairs of the Corporation. Save for the chairman of the board and the managing director, an officer may but need not be a director and one person may hold more than one office.

5.02 Term, Remuneration and Removal - The terms of employment and remuneration of all officers elected or appointed by the board (including the president) shall be determined from time to time by resolution of the board. The fact that any officer or employee is a director or shareholder of the Corporation shall not disqualify him from receiving such remuneration as may be determined. All officers, in the absence of agreement to the contrary, shall be subject to removal by resolution of the board at any time with or without cause.

15.1 (continued)

5.03 Chairman of the Board - The board may from time to time also appoint a chairman of the board who shall be a director. If appointed, the board may assign to him any of the powers and duties that are by any provisions of this by-law capable of being assigned to the president; and he shall, subject to the provisions of the Act, have such other powers and duties as the board may specify. During the absence or disability of the chairman of the board, his duties shall be performed and his powers exercised by the president.

5.04 Managing Director - The board may from time to time appoint a managing director who shall be a resident Canadian and a director. If appointed, he shall be the chief executive officer and, subject to the authority of the board, shall have general supervision of the business and affairs of the Corporation; and he shall, subject to the provisions of the Act, have such other powers and duties as the board may specify. During the absence or disability of the president, or if no president has been appointed, the managing director shall also have the powers and duties of that office.

5.05 President - The president shall be the chief operating officer of the Corporation and if no managing director has been appointed and, subject to the authority of the board, shall have the general supervision of the business and affairs of the Corporation and shall have such other powers and duties as the board may specify. During the absence or disability of the managing director, or if no managing director has been appointed, the president shall also have the powers and the duties of that office.

5.06 Vice-President - The board may from time to time appoint one or more vice-presidents. A vice-president so appointed shall have such powers and such duties as the board or the chief executive officer may prescribe.

5.07 Secretary - The board may from time to time appoint a secretary. The secretary shall attend all meetings of the directors, shareholders and committees of the board and shall enter or cause to be entered in books kept for that purpose minutes of all proceedings at such meetings; he shall give, or cause to be given, when instructed, notices required to be given to shareholders, directors, auditors and members of committees; he shall be the custodian of the stamp or mechanical device generally used for affixing the corporate seal

15.1 (continued)

of the Corporation and of all books, papers, records, documents and other instruments belonging to the Corporation; and he shall perform such other duties as may from time to time be prescribed by the board.

5.08 Treasurer - The board may from time to time appoint a treasurer. The treasurer shall keep, or cause to be kept proper accounting records as required by the Act; he shall deposit or cause to be deposited all monies received by the Corporation in the Corporation's bank account; he shall, under the direction of the board, supervise the safekeeping of securities and the disbursement of the funds of the Corporation; he shall render to the board, whenever required, an account of all his transactions as treasurer and of the financial position of the Corporation; and he shall perform such other duties as may from time to time be prescribed by the board.

5.09 Other Officers - The duties of all other officers of the Corporation shall be such as the terms of their engagement call for or the board requires of them. Any of the powers and duties of an officer to whom an assistant has been appointed may be exercised and performed by such assistant, unless the board otherwise directs.

5.10 Variation of Duties - From time to time and subject to the provisions of the Act, the board may vary, add to or limit the powers and duties of any officer.

5.11 Agents and Attorneys - The board shall have power from time to time to appoint agents or attorneys for the Corporation in or outside of Canada with such powers of management or otherwise (including the power to sub-delegate) as may be thought fit.

5.12 Fidelity Bonds - The board may require such officers, employees and agents of the Corporation as it deems advisable to furnish bonds for the faithful performance of their duties, in such form and with such surety as the board may from time to time prescribe.

5.13 Conflict of Interest - An officer shall disclose his interest in any material contract or transaction or proposed material contract or transaction with the Corporation in accordance with section 3.10 herein.

15.1 (continued)

6. MEETINGS OF SHAREHOLDERS

6.01 Annual Meetings - The annual meeting of shareholders of the Corporation shall be held at such time and on such day in each year as the board may from time to time determine, for the purpose of receiving the reports and statements required by the Act to be laid before the annual meeting, electing directors, appointing auditors and for the transaction of such other business as may properly be brought before the meeting.

6.02 Special Meetings - The directors may at any time call a special meeting of shareholders, for the transaction of any business which may properly be brought before such a meeting of shareholders. All business transacted at an annual meeting of shareholders, except consideration of the financial statements, auditor's report, election of directors and re-appointment of the incumbent auditor, is deemed to be special business.

6.03 Place of Meetings - Meetings of shareholders shall be held at the registered office of the Corporation, or at such other place within Canada as the directors from time to time determine, or if all the shareholders entitled to vote at the meeting so agree, at some place outside Canada.

6.04 Notice of Meetings - Notice of the time and place of each meeting of shareholders shall be sent not less than 21 days and not more than 50 days before the date of the meeting to the auditor of the Corporation, to each director, and to each person whose name appears on the records of the Corporation at the close of business on the day next preceding the giving of the notice as a shareholder entitled to vote at the meeting. Notice of a meeting of shareholders shall state:

(a) the nature of the business to be transacted at the meeting in sufficient detail to permit the shareholders to form a reasoned judgment thereon; and

(b) the text of any special resolution or by-law to be submitted to the meeting.

A shareholder and any other person entitled to attend a meeting of shareholders may in any manner and at any time waive notice of or otherwise consent to a meeting of shareholders.

6.05 Persons Entitled to be Present - The only persons entitled to attend a meeting of shareholders shall be those entitled to vote thereat, the directors and the auditor of the

15.1 (continued)

Corporation and others who although not entitled to vote are entitled or required under any provision of the Act or by-laws of the Corporation to be present at the meeting. Any other persons may be admitted only on the invitation of the chairman of the meeting or with the consent of the meeting.

6.06 Quorum - Subject to the provisions of the Act, the holders of a majority of the shares entitled to vote at a meeting of shareholders present in person or by proxy constitute a quorum for the transaction of business at any meeting of shareholders.

6.07 One Shareholder Meeting - If the Corporation has only one shareholder, or only one holder of any class or series of shares, the shareholder present in person or by proxy constitutes a meeting.

6.08 Right to Vote - At any meeting of shareholders, unless the articles otherwise provide, each share of the Corporation entitles the holder thereof to one vote at a meeting of shareholders, subject to the provisions of the Act.

6.09 Joint Shareholders - Where two or more persons hold the same share or shares jointly, any one of such persons present at a meeting of shareholders may in the absence of the others vote the shares but, if two or more of such persons who are present in person or by proxy, vote, they shall vote as one on the shares jointly held by them.

6.10 Proxies - Every shareholder entitled to vote at a meeting of shareholders may, by means of a proxy, appoint a proxyholder or one or more alternate proxyholders who are not required to be shareholders to attend and act at the meeting in the manner and to the extent authorized by the proxy and with the authority conferred by the proxy. A proxy shall be in writing and executed by the shareholder or by his attorney authorized in writing and shall conform with the requirements of the Act. The board may specify in a notice calling a meeting of shareholders a time, preceding the time of such meeting by not more than 48 hours exclusive of non-business days, before which time the proxies to be used at such meeting must be deposited. A proxy shall be acted upon only if, prior to the time so specified, it shall have been deposited with the Corporation or an agent thereof specified in

15.1 (continued)

such notice or, where no time is specified in such notice, the proxy has been received by the secretary of the Corporation or by the chairman of the meeting or any adjournment thereof prior to the time of voting.

6.11 Scrutineers - At each meeting of shareholders one or more scrutineers may be appointed by a resolution of the meeting or by the chairman with the consent of the meeting to serve at the meeting. Such scrutineers need not be shareholders of the Corporation.

6.12 Votes to Govern - Unless otherwise required by the Act, or the articles or by-laws of the Corporation or a unanimous shareholder agreement, all questions proposed for the consideration of the shareholders at a meeting shall be decided by a majority of the votes cast thereon. In case of an equality of votes either upon a show of hands or upon a poll, the chairman of the meeting *shall / shall not* be entitled to a second or casting vote.

(Delete accordingly.)

6.13 Show of Hands - Subject to the provisions of the Act, at all meetings of shareholders every question shall be decided by a show of hands unless a ballot thereon be required by the chairman or be demanded by a shareholder or proxyholder present and entitled to vote. Upon a show of hands every person present and entitled to vote, has one vote regardless of the number of shares he represents. After a show of hands has been taken upon any question, the chairman may require or any shareholder or proxyholder present and entitled to vote may demand a ballot thereon. Whenever a vote by show of hands shall have been taken upon a question, unless a ballot thereon be so required or demanded, a declaration by the chairman that the vote upon the question has been carried or carried by a particular majority or not carried and an entry to that effect in the minutes of the meeting shall be prima facie evidence of the fact without proof of the number or proportion of the votes recorded in favour of or against the question. The result of the vote so taken and declared shall be the decision of the Corporation on the question. A demand for a ballot may be withdrawn at any time prior to the taking of the ballot.

6.14 Ballots - If a ballot is required by the chairman of the meeting or is demanded and the demand is not withdrawn, a ballot upon the question shall be taken in such manner as the chairman of the meeting directs.

15.1 (continued)

6.15 Adjournment - The chairman of a meeting of shareholders may, with the consent of the meeting and subject to such conditions as the meeting may decide, adjourn the meeting from time to time and from place to place.

7. SHARES

7.01 Allotment - Subject to the provisions of the Act, the articles and any unanimous shareholder agreement, the board may from time to time allot or grant options to purchase the whole or any part of the authorized and unissued shares of the Corporation at such time and to such persons and for such consideration as the board shall determine, provided that no share shall be issued until it is fully paid as provided by the Act.

7.02 Share Certificates - Every holder of one or more shares of the Corporation is entitled, at his option, to a share certificate, or to a non-transferable written acknowledgment of his right to obtain a share certificate, showing the number and class or series of shares held by him as shown on the records of the Corporation. Share certificates and acknowledgments of a shareholder's right to a share certificate, respectively, shall be in such form or forms as the board shall from time to time approve. Any share certificate shall be signed in accordance with Section 11.01 of this by-law and need not be under the corporate seal; provided that certificates representing shares in respect of which a transfer agent or registrar has been appointed shall not be valid unless countersigned by or on behalf of such transfer agent or registrar. If authorized by resolution of the directors, the corporate seal of the Corporation and the signature of one of the signing officers, or in the case of share certificates representing shares in respect of which a transfer agent or registrar has been appointed, the signatures of both signing officers may be printed or otherwise mechanically reproduced upon share certificates.

7.03 Replacement of Share Certificates - The directors may by resolution prescribe, either generally or in a particular case, the conditions upon which a new share certificate may be issued to replace a share certificate which has been defaced, lost, stolen or destroyed.

15.1 (continued)

7.04 Securities Records - The directors may from time to time appoint an agent to maintain the central securities register for the shares of the Corporation and if deemed advisable one or more branch securities registers.

8. DIVIDENDS

8.01 Declaration - Subject to the provisions of the Act, the articles or to any unanimous shareholder agreement, the directors may from time to time declare dividends payable to the shareholders according to their respective rights and interests in the Corporation. Dividends may be paid in money or property or by issuing fully paid shares of the Corporation.

8.02 Payment - A dividend payable in cash shall be paid by cheque drawn on the Corporation's bankers or one of them to the order of each registered holder of shares of the class in respect of which it has been declared, and mailed by ordinary mail postage prepaid to such registered holder at his last recorded address, unless such holder otherwise directs. In the case of joint holders the cheque shall, unless such joint holders otherwise direct, be made payable to the order of all of such joint holders and mailed to them at their recorded address. The mailing of such cheque as aforesaid shall satisfy and discharge all liability for the dividend to the extent of the sum represented thereby plus the amount of any tax which the Corporation is required to and does withhold, unless such cheque be not paid on presentation.

8.03 Non-Receipt of Cheque - In the event of the non-receipt of any cheque for a dividend by the person to whom it is so sent as aforesaid, the Corporation shall issue to such person a replacement cheque for a like amount on such terms as to indemnity, reimbursement of expenses and evidence of non-receipt and of title as the board may from time to time prescribe, whether generally or in a particular case.

9. FINANCIAL YEAR

9.01 Financial Year - The financial year of the Corporation shall end on the day of in each year, until changed by resolution of the board.

15.1 (continued)

10. NOTICES

10.01 Method of Giving Notice - Any notice, communication or other document to be given by the Corporation to a shareholder, director, officer, or auditor or a member of a committee of the board of the Corportion under any provision of the articles or by-laws or otherwise shall be sufficiently given if delivered personally to the person to whom it is to be given, or if delivered to his recorded address, or if mailed by prepaid post in a sealed envelope addressed to him at his recorded address or if sent to him at his recorded address by means of any prepaid transmitted or recorded communication. The secretary may change the address on the records of the Corporation of any shareholder in accordance with any information believed by him to be reliable. A notice, communication or document so delivered shall be deemed to have been given when it is delivered personally or at the address aforesaid; a notice, communication or document so mailed shall be deemed to have been given when it is deposited in a post office or public letter box; and a notice so sent by means of transmitted or recorded communication, shall be deemed to have been given when it is delivered to the appropriate communication company or agency or its representative for dispatch.

10.02 Computation of Time - In computing the date when notice must be given under any provision of the articles or by-laws requiring a specified number of days' notice of any meeting or other event, the date of giving the notice shall be excluded and the date of the meeting or other event shall be included.

10.03 Omissions and Errors - The accidental omission to give any notice to any shareholder, director, officer or auditor or the non-receipt of any notice by any shareholder, director, officer or auditor or any error in any notice not affecting the substance thereof shall not invalidate any action taken at any meeting held pursuant to such notice or otherwise founded thereon.

10.04 Notice to Joint Shareholders - All notices with respect to any shares registered in more than one name may, if more than one address appears on the records of the Corporation in respect of such joint holding, be given to such joint shareholders at the first address so appearing, and notice so given shall be sufficient notice to all the holders of such shares.

15.1 (continued)

10.05 Persons Entitled by Death or Operation of Law - Every person who by operotion of law, by transfer or the death of a shareholder or otherwise becomes entitled to shares, is bound by every notice in respect of such shares which has been duly given to the registered holder from whom he derives title prior to his name and address being entered on the records of the Corporation (whether such notice was given before or after the happening of the event upon which he became so entitled) and prior to his furnishing to the Corporation the proof of authority or evidence of his entitlement prescribed by the Act.

10.06 Waiver of Notice - Any shareholder (or his duly appointed proxy), director, officer or auditor or member of a committee of the board may at any time waive the sending of any notice, or waive or abridge the time for any notice, required to be given under the Act, the articles or by-laws of the Corporation or otherwise and such waiver or abridgement, whether given before or after the meeting or other event of which notice is required to be given, shall cure any default in the giving or in the time of such notice, as the case may be. Any such waiver or abridgement shall be in writing except a waiver of notice of a meeting of shareholders or of the board or a committee of the board which may be given in any manner.

10.07 Signatures to Notices - The signatures to any notice to be given by the Corporation may be written, stamped, typewritten or printed or partly written, stamped, typewritten or printed.

11. EXECUTION OF DOCUMENTS

11.01 Signing Officers - Deeds, transfers, assignments, contracts and obligations of the Corporation may be signed by two persons, one of whom holds the office of chairman of the board, managing director, president, vice-president or director and the other of whom holds one of the said offices or the office of secretary or treasurer, assistant secretary or assistant treasurer, director or any other office created by by-law or by the board. Notwithstanding this, the board may at any time and from time to time direct the manner in which and the person or persons by whom any particular deed, transfer, contract or obligation or any class of deeds, transfers, contracts or obligations may be signed.

15.1 (continued)

11.02 Seal - Any person authorized to sign any document may affix the corporate seal thereto.

12. EFFECTIVE DATE

12.01 Effective Date - This by-law shall come into force when enacted by the directors, subject to the provisions of the Act.

13. REPEAL

(Delete this section if inapplicable.)

13.01 Repeal - Upon this by-law coming into force, By-law Number of the Corporation is repealed provided that such repeal shall not affect the previous operation of such by-law so repealed or affect the validity of any act done or right, privilege, obligation or liability acquired or incurred under the validity of any contract or agreement made pursuant to any such by-law prior to its repeal.

ENACTED by the board the day of *(year)* .

____________________ President

____________________ Secretary

(Corporate Seal)

CONFIRMED by the sole shareholder day of *(year)* .

____________________ Secretary

(Corporate Seal)

15.1 (continued)

Resolved that the foregoing by-law is hereby enacted by the directors of the Corporation, pursuant to the Canada Business Corporations Act, as evidenced by the respective signatures hereto of all the directors.

Dated the day of *(year)* .

In lieu of confirmation at a general meeting of the shareholders, we the undersigned, being all of the shareholders of the Corporation entitled to vote at a meeting of shareholders, hereby confirm in writing the above by-law in accordance with the Canada Business Corporations Act.

Dated the day of *(year)* .

16. Articles of Amendment

16.1 Articles of Amendment—*Canada Business Corporations Act*—Form 4

Industry Canada — Industrie Canada

Canada Business Corporations Act — Loi canadienne sur les sociétés par actions

FORM 4
ARTICLES OF AMENDMENT
(SECTION 27 OR 177)

FORMULE 4
CLAUSES MODIFICATRICES
(ARTICLES 27 OU 177)

1 - Name of corporation - Dénomination de la société	2 - Corporation No. - N° de la société

3 - The articles of the above-named corporation are amended as follows: — Les statuts de la société mentionnée ci-dessus sont modifiés de la façon suivante :

Date	Signature	Title - Titre
		FOR DEPARTMENTAL USE ONLY - À L'USAGE DU MINISTÈRE SEULEMENT Filed - Déposée

Canada

IC 3069 (2/96)

16.1 (continued)

Canada Business Corporations Act

Articles of Amendment
FORM 4
INSTRUCTIONS

Format
Documents required to be sent to the Director pursuant to the *Canada Business Corporations Act* must conform to sections 5 to 10 of the *Canada Business Corporations Regulations.*

General
(1) Any change in the articles of the corporation must be made in accordance with sections 27 or 177 of the Act. If an amendment involves a change of corporate name, the new name must comply with sections 10 and 12 of the Act. Articles of amendment must be accompanied by a Canada-biased NUANS search report dated not more than ninety (90) days prior to the receipt of the articles by the Director. On request, a number name may be assigned under subsection 11(2) of the Act, without a search.

(2) Each amendment must correspond to the paragraph and subparagraph references of the articles being amended.

(3) A Director or authorized officer of the corporation shall sign the articles.

Other Notices
If applicable, the articles must be accompanied by a Notice of Change of Registered Office (Form 3) and Notice of Change of Directors (Form 6).

Completed documents in duplicate and fees payable to the Receiver General are to be sent to:

The Director, Canada Business Corporations Act
9th Floor, Journal Tower South
365 Laurier Ave. West
Ottawa, Ontario K1A 0C8

Loi canadienne sur les sociétés par actions

Clauses modificatrices
FORMULE 4
INSTRUCTIONS

Présentation
Tous les documents dont l'envoi au directeur est exigé par la *Loi canadienne sur les sociétés par actions* doivent être conformes aux articles 5 à 10 du ***Règlement sur les sociétés par actions de régime fédéral.***

Généralités
(1) Toute modification apportée aux statuts de la société doit satisfaire aux exigences des articles 27 ou 177 de la Loi. Dans les cas où la modification comporte un changement de dénomination sociale, la nouvelle dénomination sociale doit satisfaire aux exigences des articles 10 et 12 de la Loi. Les clauses modificatrices doivent être accompagnées d'un rapport de recherche NUANS couvrant le Canada, dont la date remonte à quatre-vingt-dix (90) jours ou moins avant la date de réception par le directeur des clauses modificatrices. Si un numéro matricule est demandé en guise de dénomination sociale, il peut être assigné, sans recherche préalable, en vertu du paragraphe 11(2) de la Loi.

(2) Chaque modification doit correspondre aux renvois des alinéas et sous-alinéas des statuts modifiés.

(3) Un administrateur ou un dirigeant autorisé de la société doit signer les clauses.

Autres avis
S'il y a lieu, les clauses doivent être accompagnées de l'avis de changement du siège social (formule 3) ou de l'avis de changement des administrateurs (formule 6).

Les documents remplis en double et les droits payables au receveur général doivent être envoyés au :

Directeur, Loi canadienne sur les sociétés par actions
9ième étage, Édifice Journal, Tour sud
365, rue Laurier ouest
Ottawa (Ontario) K1A 0C8

18. Annual Returns

18.1 Annual Return (Section 263)—*Canada Business Corporations Act*—Form 22

DYE & DURHAM CO. INC.

Industry Canada | Industrie Canada

Canada Business Corporations Act | Loi canadienne sur les sociétés par actions

Form 22 **ANNUAL RETURN** (section 263) | Formule 22 **RAPPORT ANNUEL** (article 263)

1. Corporation name and registered office address — **Dénomination de la société et adresse du lieu du siège social**

(and mailing address, if different from that of registered office) — (ainsi que l'adresse postale si elle diffère de celle du siège social)

2. Corporation No - N° de la société

3. Business No - N° d'entreprise

4. Taxation Year End / Fin de l'année d'imposition

Y-A | M | D-J

5. Main types of business - Catégories principales d'activité commerciale

6. Has there been a change of directors? / Y a-t-il eu un changement d'administrateurs ?

☐ Yes / Oui ☐ No / Non

If yes, has Form 6 been: - Si oui, la formule 6 a-t-elle été :

☐ Filed / Déposée ☐ Attached / Annexée

7. Has there been a change of registered office? / Y a-t-il eu un changement du siège social ?

☐ Yes / Oui ☐ No / Non

If yes, has Form 3 been: - Si oui, la formule 3 a-t-elle été :

☐ Filed / Déposée ☐ Attached / Annexée

8. Date of last annual meeting - Date de la dernière assemblée annuelle

9. Does the corporation distribute its securities to the public? / La société émet-elle ses valeurs mobilières par voie de souscription publique ?

☐ Yes / Oui ☐ No / Non

10. Does the corporation have 15 or more shareholders? - La société a-t-elle 15 actionnaires ou plus ?

☐ Yes / Oui ☐ No / Non

11. Does the corporation have in place a unanimous shareholder agreement referred to in subsection 146(2) of the *Act*, that restricts, in whole or in part, the power of the directors to manage the business and affairs of the corporation?

La société dispose-t-elle d'une convention unanime des actionnaires visée au paragraphe 146(2) de la *Loi*, qui restreint en tout ou en partie les pouvoirs des administrateurs de gérer les affaires tant commerciales qu'internes de la société ?

☐ Yes / Oui ☐ No / Non

12. Jurisdictions in which the corporation is carrying on business - Provinces et territoires où la société exerce ses activités

Prov./Territory Prov./Territoire	Address of the principal place of business or address for service Adresse principale de la société ou adresse aux fins de signification

Signature	Title - Titre	Date	Telephone No. N° de téléphone

FOR DEPARTMENT USE ONLY - A L'USAGE DU MINISTÈRE SEULEMENT

Date received Date de réception	Validation	Key code - Code clé	Cheque - Chèque	Amount - Montant

Note: A fee of $50 is required, payable to the Receiver General for Canada

Note : Un droit de 50 $ est requis, payable au a l'ordre du receveur général du Canada

Please see instructions on reverse side

Voir les instructions au verso

18.1 (continued)

Canada Business Corporations Act

ANNUAL RETURN
FORM 22
INSTRUCTIONS

General
In accordance with section 263 of the *Canada Business Corporations Act* and subsection 4(3) of the *Canada Business Corporations Regulations*, a corporation must submit to the Director an annual return with the prescribed fee of $50 within 6 months of its taxation year end as defined by the *Income Tax Act*.

Item 4
State the date of the corporation's taxation year end as defined by the *Income Tax Act*.

Item 5
State the main actual business, or businesses of the corporation, indicating, where possible, the corporation's standard industrial classification code (S.I.C.C.).

Item 6
Indicate whether there has been any change of directors since the last annual return and whether a notice of change of directors (Form 6) has been filed. Note that under subsection 113(1) of the *Act* a notice of change of directors must be filed within fifteen (15) days of a change of directors. Note that where required by the Act, the changes being reported by the filing of this form must be authorized by the director(s) or shareholders.

Item 7
Indicate whether there has been any change of registered office since the last annual return and if a notice of change of registered office (Form 3) has been filed. Note that under subsection 19(4) of the *Act* a notice of change of registered office must be filed within fifteen (15) days after a change of registered office. Note that where required by the *Act*, the changes being reported by filing of this form must be authorized by the director(s) or shareholders.

Item 8
Indicate the date of the last annual meeting.

Item 9
Indicate whether the corporation is a "distributing corporation", that is, a corporation that has made a distribution of its securities to the public within the meaning of subsection 2(7) of the *Act*.

Item 10
Indicate whether the corporation has 15 or more shareholders. Part XIII of the *Act* requires any corporation that has 15 shareholders or more to solicit proxies.

Item 11
Indicate whether a unanimous shareholder agreement is in place. A unanimous shareholder agreement is a written agreement among all the shareholders of a corporation that restricts, in whole or in part, the powers of the directors to manage the business and affairs of the corporation by giving to the shareholders certain powers usually conferred to the Board of Directors.

Item 12
For each provincial/territorial jurisdiction in which the corporation is carrying on business, including the operation of an enterprise, or possesses an immoveable real right, other than a prior claim or hypothec, state the address of the principal place of business or address for service, including the city and the postal code. If there is not enough room, please attach a piece of paper with the additional information. A corporation is presumed to be "carrying on business" if it has an address in the province/territory or having there, either directly or through the agency of a representative acting under a general mandate, an establishment, a post office box or the use of a telephone line, or carrying out in the province/territory any act for the purpose of profit. This information is being collected as part of an initiative which may eventually eliminate the need to register in each province or territory in which the corporation carries on business.

Signature
A director or authorized officer of the corporation shall sign the return.

Completed form to be sent to:
The Director, Canada Business Corporations Act
9th Floor, Jean Edmonds Towers South
365 Laurier Avenue West
Ottawa, Canada
K1A 0C8

Canada

Loi canadienne sur les sociétés par actions

RAPPORT ANNUEL
FORMULE 22
INSTRUCTIONS

Généralités
En vertu de l'article 263 de la *Loi canadienne sur les sociétés par actions* du paragraphe 4(3) du *Règlement sur les sociétés par actions de régime fédéral*, toute société doit soumettre au directeur un rapport annuel accompagné du droit prescrit de 50 $ dans les 6 mois suivant la fin de l'année d'imposition telle qu'elle est définie dans la *Loi de l'impot sur le revenu*.

Rubrique 4
Donner la date de la fin de l'année d'imposition de la société telle qu'elle est définie dans la *Loi de l'impôt sur le revenu*.

Rubrique 5
Donner la ou les principales activités de la société en utilisant, si possible, le code de classification des activités économiques.

Rubrique 6
Indiquer s'il y a eu un changement des administrateurs depuis le dernier rapport annuel et si un avis de changement des administrateurs (formule 6) a été déposé. En vertu du paragraphe 113(1) de la *Loi* un avis de changement des administrateurs doit être fourni dans les 15 jours suivant un changement. Nota : Lorsqu'exigé par la *Loi*, les changements rapportés par le dépôt de cette formule doivent être autorisés par les administrateurs ou les actionnaires.

Rubrique 7
Indiquer s'il y a eu un changement du siège social depuis le dernier rapport annuel et si un avis de changement du siège social (formule 3) a été déposé. En vertu du paragraphe 19(4) de la *Loi*, un avis de changement du siège social doit être fourni dans les 15 jours suivant un changement. Nota : Lorsqu'exigé par la *Loi*, les changements rapportés par le dépôt de cette formule doivent être autorisés par les administrateurs ou les actionnaires.

Rubrique 8
Indiquer la date de la dernière assemblée annuelle.

Rubrique 9
Indiquer si la société a émis de ses valeurs mobilières par voie de souscription publique au sens du paragraphe 2(7) de la *Loi*.

Rubrique 10
Indiquer si la société a 15 actionnaires ou plus. La partie XIII de la *Loi* exige que toute société comptant 15 actionnaires ou plus sollicite des procurations.

Rubrique 11
Indiquer si la société est assujettie à une convention unanime des actionnaires. Une convention unanime des actionnaires est une entente écrite liant tous les actionnaires de la société et qui restreint en tout en ou partie les pouvoirs des administrateurs de gérer les affaires tant commerciales qu'internes de la société, en donnant aux actionnaires certains pouvoirs qui sont normalement conférés aux administrateurs.

Rubrique 12
Donner l'adresse principale de la société ou l'adresse pour fin de signification avec ville et code postal pour chaque province/territoire où la société exerce ses activitiés, incluant l'exploitation d'une entreprise, ou y possède un droit réel immobilier autre qu'une priorité ou une hypothèque. S'il n'y a pas suffisamment d'espace, veuillez joindre une feuille supplèmentaire contenant l'information additionnelle. Une société est présumée exercer une activité ou exploiter une entreprise si elle possède une adresse dans la province/territoire ou qui, par elle-même au par l'entreprise de son représentant agissant en vertu d'un mandat général, possède un établissement ou un casier postal ou dispose d'une ligne téléphonique dans la province/territoire, ou y accomplit un acte dans le but d'en tirer un tirer profit. Cette information est demandée suite à une initiative qui pourrait éventuellement éliminer l'obligation d'enregistrement dans chaque province/territoire où la société exerce ses activités. Pour l'instant, le dépôt des formules au niveau provincial est encore obligatoire.

Signature
Un administrateur ou un dirigeant autorisé de la société doit signer le rapport.

La formule complétée doit être envoyée au :
Directeur, Loi canadienne sur les sociétés par actions
9e étage, Tours Jean Edmonds, sud
365, avenue Laurier Ouest
Ottawa, Canada
K1A 0C8

18.2 T2 Corporation Income Tax Return

Canada Customs and Revenue Agency — Agence des douanes et du revenu du Canada

T2 CORPORATION INCOME TAX RETURN
(2000 and later taxation years)

200

055 **Do not use this area**

This form serves as a federal, provincial, and territorial corporation income tax return, unless the corporation is located in Quebec, Ontario, or Alberta. If the corporation is located in one of these provinces, you have to file a separate provincial corporate return.

Parts, sections, subsections, and paragraphs mentioned on this return refer to the *Income Tax Act*. This return may contain changes that had not yet become law at the time of printing. If you need more information about items on the return, including proposed legislation, see the corresponding items in the *2000 T2 Corporation Income Tax Guide*.

Send one completed copy of this return, including schedules, and the *General Index of Financial Information* (GIFI) to your tax services office or to the tax centre that serves the corporation. You have to file the return within six months after the end of the corporation's taxation year. For more information on when and how to file T2 returns, see items 1 to 5 in the guide.

Identification

Business Number (BN) (item 11) ..... 001 _ _ _ _ _ _ _ _ _ R C _ _ _ _

Corporation's name (item 12)
002 ________

Has the corporation changed its name since the last time we were notified? .... 003 1 Yes ☐ 2 No ☐

If *yes*, do you have a copy of the articles of amendment? ...... 004 1 Yes ☐ 2 No ☐

Address of head office (item 13)
Has the address changed since the last time we were notified? .... 010 1 Yes ☐ 2 No ☐

011 ________
012 ________
City 015 ________ Province, territory, or state 016 ________
Country (other than Canada) 017 ________ Postal code/ZIP code 018 ________

To which taxation year does this return apply? (item 17)
Taxation year start 060 YYYY | MM | DD
Taxation year-end 061 YYYY | MM | DD

Has there been an acquisition of control to which subsection 249(4) applies since the previous taxation year? .... 063 1 Yes ☐ 2 No ☐

If *yes*, provide the date control was acquired .... 065 YYYY | MM | DD

Mailing address (if different from head office address) (item 14)
Has the address changed since the last time we were notified?
020 1 Yes ☐ 2 No ☐

021 c/o ________
022 ________
023 ________
City 025 ________ Province, territory, or state 026 ________
Country (other than Canada) 027 ________ Postal code/ZIP code 028 ________

Is the corporation a professional corporation that is a member of a partnership? (item 18) .... 067 1 Yes ☐ 2 No ☐

Is this the first year of filing after:
Incorporation? (item 19) .... 070 1 Yes ☐ 2 No ☐
Amalgamation? (item 20) .... 071 1 Yes ☐ 2 No ☐
If *yes*, please provide Schedule 24

Has there been a windup of a subsidiary under section 88 during the current taxation year? (item 21)
If *yes*, please provide Schedule 24 ...... 072 1 Yes ☐ 2 No ☐

Location of books and records (item 15)
031 ________
032 ________
City 035 ________ Province, territory, or state 036 ________
Country (other than Canada) 037 ________ Postal code/ZIP code 038 ________

Is this the final taxation year before amalgamation? (item 22) .... 076 1 Yes ☐ 2 No ☐

Is this the final return up to dissolution? (item 23) .... 078 1 Yes ☐ 2 No ☐

Is the corporation a resident of Canada? (item 24)
080 1 Yes ☐ 2 No ☐ If *no*, give the country of residence.
081 ________

Is the non-resident corporation claiming an exemption under an income tax treaty? (item 24)
If *yes*, please provide Schedule 91 ...... 082 1 Yes ☐ 2 No ☐

040 **Type of corporation at the end of the taxation year** (item 16)
1 ☐ Canadian-controlled private corporation (CCPC)
2 ☐ Other private corporation
3 ☐ Public corporation
4 ☐ Corporation controlled by a public corporation
5 ☐ Other corporation (please specify, below) ________

If the type of corporation changed during the taxation year, please provide the effective date of the change .... 043 YYYY | MM | DD

If the corporation is exempt from tax under section 149 tick one of the following boxes: (item 25)
085 1 ☐ Exempt under 149(1)(e) or (l)
2 ☐ Exempt under 149(1)(j)
3 ☐ Exempt under 149(1)(t)
4 ☐ Exempt under other paragraphs of section 149

Do not use this area

091	092	093	094	095	096
097					

18.2 (continued)

Attachments

Financial statement information: For taxation years ending in 2000 and later, use GIFI schedules 100, 125, and 141. * We do not print these schedules.

Schedules – Answer the following questions. For each *yes* response, attach to the T2 return the schedule that applies.

Guide item			Yes	Schedule
27	Is the corporation related to any other corporations?	150		9
28	Does the corporation have any non-resident shareholders?	151		19
29	Is the corporation an associated Canadian-controlled private corporation?	160		23
30	Is the corporation an associated Canadian-controlled private corporation that is claiming the expenditure limit?	161		49
32	Has the corporation had any transactions, including section 85 transfers, with its shareholders, officers, or employees, other than transactions in the ordinary course of business? Exclude non-arm's-length transactions with non-residents	162		11
33	If you answered *yes* to the above question, and the transaction was between corporations not dealing at arm's length, were all or substantially all of the assets of the transferor disposed of to the transferee?	163		44
34	Has the corporation paid any royalties, management fees, or other similar payments to residents of Canada?	164		14
35	Is the corporation claiming a deduction for payments to a type of employee benefit plan?	165		15
37	Is the corporation claiming a loss or deduction from a tax shelter acquired after August 31, 1989?	166		T5004
38	Is the corporation a member of a partnership for which a partnership identification number has been assigned?	167		T5013
40	Did the corporation, a foreign affiliate controlled by the corporation, or any other corporation or trust that did not deal at arm's length with the corporation have a beneficial interest in a non-resident discretionary trust?	168		22
41	Did the corporation have any foreign affiliates during the year?	169		25
42	Has the corporation made any payments to non-residents of Canada under subsections 202(1) and 105(1) of the federal *Income Tax Regulations*?	170		29
43	Has the corporation had any non-arm's-length transactions with a non-resident?	171		T106
47	Has the corporation made payments to, or received amounts from, a retirement compensation arrangement in the year?	172		—
46	Does the corporation (private corporations only) have any shareholders who own 10% or more of the corporation's common and/or preferred shares?	173		50
53	Is the net income/loss shown on the financial statements different from the net income/loss for income tax purposes?	201		1
76-79	Has the corporation made any charitable donations, gifts to Canada or a province, or gifts of cultural or ecological property?	202		2
88,102	Has the corporation received any dividends or paid any taxable dividends for purposes of the dividend refund?	203		3
67-74	Is the corporation claiming any type of losses?	204		4
128	Is the corporation claiming a provincial tax credit or does it have a permanent establishment in more than one jurisdiction?	205		5
54	Has the corporation realized any capital gains or incurred any capital losses during the taxation year?	206		6
100	i) Is the corporation claiming the small business deduction and reporting income from: a) property (other than dividends deductible on line 320 of the T2 return, b) a partnership, c) a foreign business, or d) a personal services business; or ii) is the corporation claiming the refundable portion of Part I tax?	207		7
55	Does the corporation have any property that is eligible for capital cost allowance?	208		8
56	Does the corporation have any property that is eligible capital property?	210		10
57	Does the corporation have any resource-related deductions?	212		12
58	Is the corporation claiming reserves of any kind?	213		13
59	Is the corporation claiming a patronage dividend deduction?	216		16
60	Is the corporation a credit union claiming a deduction for allocations in proportion to borrowing or an additional deduction?	217		17
146	Is the corporation an investment corporation or a mutual fund corporation?	218		18
127	Was the corporation carrying on business in Canada while not a Canadian corporation?	220		20 *
115	Is the corporation claiming any federal or provincial foreign tax credits, or any federal or provincial logging tax credits?	221		21
151	Is the corporation a non-resident-owned investment corporation claiming an allowable refund?	226		26 *
108	Does the corporation have any Canadian manufacturing and processing profits?	227		27
118	Is the corporation claiming an investment tax credit?	231		31
61	Is the corporation claiming any scientific research and experimental development expenditures?	232		T661/T665
121	Is the corporation subject to gross Part I.3 tax?	233		33/34/35
121	Is the corporation a member of a related group with one or more members subject to gross Part I.3 tax?	236		36
121	Is the corporation claiming a surtax credit?	237		37
125	Is the corporation subject to gross Part VI tax on capital of financial institutions?	238		38
125	Is the corporation claiming a Part I tax credit?	242		42
126	Is the corporation subject to Part IV.1 tax on dividends received on taxable preferred shares or Part VI.1 tax on dividends paid?	243		43
126	Is the corporation agreeing to a transfer of the liability for Part VI.1 tax?	244		45
122	Is the corporation subject to Part II – Tobacco Manufacturers' surtax?	249		46
125	For financial institutions: Is the corporation a member of a related group of financial institutions with one or more members subject to gross Part VI tax?	250		39
125	For life insurance corporations: Is the corporation a member of a related group of insurance corporations with one or more members subject to the additional gross Part VI tax?	251		40
125	For deposit-taking institutions: Is the corporation a member of a related group of financial institutions (other than life insurance corporations) with one or more members subject to the additional Part VI tax?	252		41
148	Is the corporation claiming a Canadian film or video production tax credit refund?	253		T1131

page 2

18.2 (continued)

Corporation's name	Business Number	Taxation year-end Year Month Day

Attachments – continued from page 2

Guide item		Yes	Schedule
149	Is the corporation claiming a film or video production services tax credit refund?	☐	T1177
44	Did the corporation have any foreign affiliates that are not controlled foreign affiliates?	☐	T1134-A
44	Did the corporation have any controlled foreign affiliates?	☐	T1134-B
44	Did the corporation own specified foreign property in the year with a cost amount over $100,000?	☐	T1135
44	Did the corporation transfer or loan property to a non-resident trust?	☐	T1141
44	Did the corporation receive a distribution from or was it indebted to a non-resident trust in the year?	☐	T1142
—	Has the corporation entered into an agreement to allocate assistance for SR&ED carried out in Canada?	☐	T1145
—	Has the corporation entered into an agreement to transfer qualified expenditures incurred in respect of SR&ED contracts?	☐	T1146
—	Has the corporation entered into an agreement with other associated corporations for salary or wages of specified employees for SR&ED ?	☐	T1174

Additional information

Is the corporation inactive? (item 48) ... **280** 1 Yes ☐ 2 No ☐

Has the major business activity changed since the last return was filed? (enter *yes* for first time filers) (item 49) ... **281** 1 Yes ☐ 2 No ☐

What is the corporation's major business activity? (item 50) ... **282** ________
(Only complete if *yes* was entered at line 281.)

If the major activity involves the resale of goods, indicate whether it is wholesale or retail (item 51) ... **283** 1 Wholesale ☐ 2 Retail ☐

Specify the principal product(s) mined, manufactured, sold, constructed, or services provided, giving the approximate percentage of the total revenue that each product or service represents. (item 52)

284	________	**285**	____ %
286	________	**287**	____ %
288	________	**289**	____ %

Taxable income

Net income or (loss) for income tax purposes from Schedule 1, financial statements, or GIFI (item75) ... **300** ________ A

Deduct:

Charitable donations from Schedule 2 (item 76)	**311**	________
Gifts to Canada or a province from Schedule 2 (item 77)	**312**	________
Cultural gifts from Schedule 2 (item 78)	**313**	________
Ecological gifts from Schedule 2 (item 79)	**314**	________
Taxable dividends deductible under section 112, 113, or subsection 138(6) from Schedule 3 (item 80)	**320**	________
Part VI.1 tax deduction from Schedule 43 (item 81)	**325**	________
Non-capital losses of preceding taxation years from Schedule 4 (item 82)	**331**	________
Net-capital losses of preceding taxation years from Schedule 4 (item 83)	**332**	________
Restricted farm losses of preceding taxation years from Schedule 4 (item 84)	**333**	________
Farm losses of preceding taxation years from Schedule 4 (item 85)	**334**	________
Limited partnership losses of preceding taxation years from Schedule 4 (item 86)	**335**	________
Taxable capital gains or taxable dividends allocated from a central credit union (item 87)	**340**	________
Prospector's and grubstaker's shares (item 88)	**350**	________

Subtotal ________ ▶ ________ B

Subtotal (amount A minus amount B) ________ C

Add: Section 110.5 additions (item 89) ... **355** ________ D

Taxable income (amount C plus amount D) (item 90) ... **360** ________

Income exempt under paragraph 149(1)(t) (item 91) ... **370** ________

Taxable income for a corporation with exempt income under paragraph 149(1)(t) (line 360 minus line 370) (item 92) ... ________ Z

18.2 (continued)

Small business deduction

Canadian-controlled private corporations (CCPCs) throughout the taxation year

Income from active business carried on in Canada from Schedule 7 (item 93) . . . . 400 ________ A

Taxable income from line 360 or amount Z on page 3, whichever applies, **minus** 10/3 of the amount that would be deductible at line 632*, and 10/4 of line 636 on page 7, and **minus** any amount that, because of federal law is exempt from Part I tax (item 94) . . . . 405 ________ B

Business limit (for associated corporations, enter business limit from Schedule 23) (item 95) . . . . 410 ________ C

Reduction to business limit: (item 96)

Amount C ________ x 415 ** ________ D = ... ________ E

11,250

Reduced business limit (amount C minus amount E) (if negative, enter "0") . . . . 425 ________ F

Small business deduction – 16% of the least of amounts A, B, C, and F . . . . 430 ________ G

(enter amount G on line 9 of page 7)

* Calculate the amount of foreign non-business income tax credit deductible at line 632 without reference to the refundable tax on CCPC's investment income (line 604).

** **Large corporation tax for preceding year** – Enter the total gross Part I.3 tax for the corporation for its preceding taxation year, before deducting the surtax credits, increased to reflect a full-year tax liability if the previous year is less than 51 weeks. For associated corporations, see Schedule 23 for the special rules that apply.

Accelerated tax reduction (item 97)

Canadian-controlled private corporations throughout the taxation year that claimed the small business deduction

Reduced business limit (amount from line 425) . . . . ________ x 3/2 = ________ A

Net active business income (amount from line 400) * . . . . ________ B

Taxable income from line 360 or amount Z on page 3, whichever applies, minus 10/4 of line 636 on page 7 . . . . ________ C

Deduct:

Aggregate investment income (amount from line 440 of page 6) . . . . ________ D

Amount C minus amount D (if negative, enter "0") . . . . ________ ▶ ________ E

The least of amounts A, B, or E above . . . . ________ F

Amount Z from Part 9 of Schedule 27 . . . . ________ x 100/7 = ________ G

Amount QQ from Part 13 of Schedule 27 . . . . ________ H

Resource allowance (amount from line 346 of Schedule 1) . . ________ x 3 = ________ I

Amount used to calculate the credit union deduction (amount E in Part 3 of Schedule 17) . . . . . ________ J

Least of amounts on lines 400, 405, 410, and 425 of the small business deduction . . . . ________ K

Total of amounts G, H, I, J, and K . . . . ________ ▶ ________ L

Amount F minus amount L (if negative, enter "0") . . . . ________ M

Amount M ________ x Number of days in the taxation year after December 31, 2000 ________ = ________ N

Number of days in the taxation year

Accelerated tax reduction – 7% of amount N . . . . ________ O

(enter amount O on line 637 of page 7)

* Specified partnerships need to use Schedule 70 to calculate net active business income, if the amount at line 450 of Schedule 7 is positive.

page 4

18.2 (continued)

General tax reduction for Canadian-controlled private corporations (item 98)

Canadian-controlled private corporations throughout the taxation year

Taxable income from line 360 or amount Z of page 3 .... ______ A

Amount Z from Part 9 of Schedule 27 .... ______ x 100/7 = ______ B

Amount QQ from Part 13 of Schedule 27 .... ______ C

Resource allowance (amount from line 346 of Schedule 1) .. ______ x 3 = ______ D

Amount used to calculate the credit union deduction (amount E in Part 3 of Schedule 17) ..... ______ E

Least of amounts on lines 400, 405, 410, and 425 of the small business deduction on page 4 .. ______ F

Aggregate investment income form line 440 of page 6 .... ______ G

Amount used to calculate the accelerated tax reduction (amount M of page 4) .... ______ H

Total of amounts B, C, D, E, F, G, and H .... ______ ▶ ______ I

Amount A minus amount I (if negative, enter "0") .... ______ J

Amount J ______ x Number of days in the taxation year after December 31, 2000 / Number of days in the taxation year ______ = ______ K

General tax reduction for Canadian-controlled private corporations – 1% of amount K .... ______ L
(enter amount L on line 638 of page 7)

General tax reduction (item 99)

Corporations other than a Canadian-controlled private corporation, an investment corporation, a mortgage investment corporation, a mutual fund corporation, or a non-resident-owned investment corporation

Taxable income from line 360 or amount Z of page 3 .... ______ A

Amount Z from Part 9 of Schedule 27 .... ______ x 100/7 = ______ B

Amount QQ from Part 13 of Schedule 27 .... ______ C

Resource allowance (amount from line 346 of Schedule 1) .. ______ x 3 = ______ D

Amount used to calculate the credit union deduction (amount E in Part 3 of Schedule 17) ..... ______ E

Total of amounts B, C, D, and E .... ______ ▶ ______ F

Amount A minus amount F (if negative, enter "0") .... ______ G

Amount G ______ x Number of days in the taxation year after December 31, 2000 / Number of days in the taxation year ______ = ______ H

General tax reduction – 1% of amount H .... ______ I
(enter amount I on line 639 of page 7)

page 5

18.2 (continued)

Corporation's name	Business Number	Taxation year-end Year Month Day

Refundable portion of Part I tax (item 100)

Canadian-controlled private corporations throughout the taxation year

Aggregate investment income ... 440 ________ x 26 2/3 % = ... ________ A
(amount P from Part 1 of Schedule 7)

Foreign non-business income tax credit from line 632 on page 7 .... ________

Deduct:

Foreign investment income ..... 445 ________ x 9 1/3 % = ... ________
(amount O from Part 1 of Schedule 7) (if negative, enter "0") ________ ▶ ________ B

Amount A minus amount B (if negative, enter "0") .... ________ C

Taxable income from line 360 on page 3 .... ________

Deduct:

Least of amounts on lines 400, 405, 410, and 425 on page 4 ________

Foreign non-business income tax credit from line 632 of page 7 .... ________ x 25/9 = ________

Foreign business income tax credit from line 636 of page 7 .... ________ x 10/4 = ________ ▶ ________

________ x 26 2/3 % = ________ D

Part I tax payable minus investment tax credit refund (line 700 minus line 780 of page 8) ________

Deduct corporate surtax from line 600 of page 7 .... ________

Net amount .... ________ ▶ ________ E

Refundable portion of Part I tax – The least of amounts C, D, and E .... 450 ________ F

Refundable dividend tax on hand (item 101)

Refundable dividend tax on hand at the end of the preceding taxation year .... 460 ________

Deduct dividend refund for the previous taxation year .... 465 ________ ▶ ________ A

Add the total of:

Refundable portion of Part I tax from line 450 above .... ________

Total Part IV tax payable from line 360 on page 2 of Schedule 3 .... ________

Net refundable dividend tax on hand transferred from a predecessor corporation on amalgamation, or from a wound-up subsidiary corporation .... 480 ________ ▶ ________ B

Refundable dividend tax on hand at the end of the taxation year – Amount A plus amount B .... 485 ________

Dividend refund (item 102)

Private and subject corporations at the time taxable dividends were paid in the taxation year

Taxable dividends paid in the taxation year from line 460 on page 2 of Schedule 3 .... ________ x 1/3 ________ A

Refundable dividend tax on hand at the end of the taxation year from line 485 above .... ________ B

Dividend refund – **Lesser of** amounts A and B (enter this amount on line 784 of page 8) .... ________

18.2 (continued)

Corporation's name	Business Number	Taxation year-end Year Month Day

Part I tax

Base amount of Part I tax – 38% of taxable income (line 360 or amount Z, whichever applies) from page 3 (item 103) ... 550 ______ A

Corporate surtax calculation (item 104)

Base amount from line A above	______	1
Deduct:		
10% of taxable income (line 360 or amount Z, whichever applies) from page 3	______	2
Investment corporation deduction from line 620 below	______	3
Federal logging tax credit from line 640 below	______	4
Federal qualifying environmental trust tax credit from line 648 below	______	5

For a mutual fund corporation or an investment corporation throughout the taxation year, enter the least of a, b, and c below on line 6:

28% of taxable income from line 360 of page 3	______	a		
28% of taxed capital gains	______	b	______	6
Part I tax otherwise payable (line A plus lines C and D **minus** line F)	______	c		
Total of lines 2 to 6			______	7
Net amount (line 1 minus line 7)			______	8

Corporate surtax – 4% of the amount on line 8 ... 600 ______ B

Recapture of investment tax credit from line XX in Part 16 on page 8 of Schedule 31 (item 105) ... 602 ______ C

Calculation for the refundable tax on Canadian-controlled private corporation's investment income (for a CCPC throughout the taxation year) (item 106)

Aggregate investment income from line 440 on page 6		______	i
Taxable income from line 360 on page 3	______		
Deduct:			
The least of amounts on lines 400, 405, 410, and 425 of page 4	______		
Net amount	______ ▶	______	ii

Refundable tax on CCPC's investment income – 6 2/3 % of the lesser of amounts i or ii ... 604 ______ D

Subtotal (add lines A, B, C, and D) ______ E

Deduct:

Small business deduction from line 430 of page 4		______	9
Federal tax abatement (item 107)	608	______	
Manufacturing and processing profits deduction from amount BB or amount VV of Schedule 27 (item 108)	616	______	
Investment corporation deduction (item 109)	620	______	
(taxed capital gains 624 ______)			
Additional deduction – credit unions from Schedule 17 (item 110)	628	______	
Federal foreign non-business income tax credit from Schedule 21 (item 111)	632	______	
Federal foreign business income tax credit from Schedule 21 (item 112)	636	______	
Accelerated tax reduction from amount O of page 4 (item 113)	637	______	
General tax reduction for CCPCs from amount L of page 5 (item 114)	638	______	
General tax reduction from amount I of page 5 (item 114)	639	______	
Federal logging tax credit from Schedule 21 (item 115)	640	______	
Federal political contribution tax credit (item 116)	644	______	
Federal political contributions 646 ______			
Federal qualifying environmental trust tax credit (item 117)	648	______	
Investment tax credit from Schedule 31 (item 118)	652	______	
Subtotal		______ ▶ ______	F

Part I tax payable – Line E minus line F (enter amount G on line 700 of page 8) (item 119) ... ______ G

page 7

18.2 (continued)

Summary of tax and credits

Federal tax

Part I tax payable from page 7 (item 120) ... 700 ______
Part I.3 tax payable from Schedule 33, 34, or 35 (item 121) ... 704 ______
Part II surtax payable from Schedule 46 (item 122) ... 708 ______
Part IV tax payable from Schedule 3 (item 123) ... 712 ______
Part IV.1 tax payable from Schedule 43 (item 124) ... 716 ______
Part VI tax payable from Schedule 38 (item 125) ... 720 ______
Part VI.1 tax payable from Schedule 43 (item 126) ... 724 ______
Part XIV tax payable from Schedule 20 (item 127) ... 728 ______
Total federal tax ______

Add provincial and territorial tax:

Provincial or territorial jurisdiction (item 128) 750 ______
(if more than one jurisdiction, enter "multiple" and complete Schedule 5)
Net provincial and territorial tax payable (except Quebec, Ontario, and Alberta) (item 129) 760 ______
Provincial tax on large corporations (New Brunswick and Nova Scotia) (item 143) ... 765 ______
Total tax payable 770 ______ A

Deduct other credits:

Investment tax credit refund from Schedule 31 (item 144) ... 780 ______
Dividend refund from page 6 (item 145) ... 784 ______
Federal capital gains refund from Schedule 18 (item 146) ... 788 ______
Federal qualifying environmental trust tax credit refund (item 147) ... 792 ______
Canadian film or video production tax credit refund from Form T1131 (item 148) ... 796 ______
Film or video production services tax credit refund from Form T1177 (item 149) ... 797 ______
Tax withheld at source (item 150) ... 800 ______
Total payments on which tax has been withheld (item 150) 801 ______
Allowable refund for non-resident-owned investment corporations from Schedule 26 (item 151) ... 804 ______
Provincial and territorial capital gains refund from Schedule 18 (item 152) ... 808 ______
Provincial and territorial refundable tax credits from Schedule 5 (item 153) ... 812 ______
Royalties deductible under Syncrude Remission Order (item 154) 815 ______
Tax remitted under Syncrude Remission Order (item 154) ... 816 ______
Tax instalments paid (item 155) ... 840 ______
Total credits 890 ______ ► ______ B

Refund code (item 156) 894 ☐ Overpayment (item 159) ______

Balance (line A minus line B) ______

If the result is negative, you have an **overpayment**.
If the result is positive, you have a **balance unpaid**.
Enter the amount on whichever line applies.
We do not charge or refund a difference of less than $2.

Balance unpaid (item 159) ______

Enclosed payment (item 158) 898 ______

Direct deposit request (item 160)

To have the corporation's refund deposited directly into the corporation's bank account at a financial institution in Canada, or to change banking information you already gave us, complete the information below:

☐ Start ☐ Change information 910 ______ Branch number

914 ______ Institution number 918 ______ Account number

If the corporation is a Canadian-controlled private corporation throughout the taxation year, does it qualify for the one month extension of the date the balance of tax is due? (item 157) ... 896 1 Yes ☐ 2 No ☐

Certification (item 161)

I, 950 ______ Last name in block letters 951 ______ First name in block letters 954 ______ Position, office, or rank

am an authorized signing officer of the corporation. I certify that I have examined this return, including accompanying schedules and statements, and that the information given on this return is, to the best of my knowledge, correct and complete. I further certify that the method of calculating income for this taxation year is consistent with that of the previous year except as specifically disclosed in a statement attached to this return.

955 ______ Date (yyyy/mm/dd) ______ Signature of an authorized signing officer of the corporation 956 ( ) ______ Telephone number

Is the contact person the same as the authorized signing officer? If *no*, complete the information below ... 957 1 Yes ☐ 2 No ☐

958 ______ Name in block letters 959 ( ) ______ Telephone number

Language of correspondence – Langue de correspondance (item 162)

990 Please indicate the language of your choice.
Indiquer la langue de correspondance de votre choix.
1 English / Anglais ☐ 2 Français / French ☐

18.3 Industry Canada—Annual Return—Canada Business Corporations Act

Canada Customs and Revenue Agency and Industry Canada | Agence des douanes et du revenu du Canada et Industrie Canada

SCHEDULE 80

INDUSTRY CANADA – ANNUAL RETURN – *CANADA BUSINESS CORPORATIONS ACT*

Name of corporation	Business Number	Taxation year end (Year / Month / Day)

Corporations incorporated under the *Canada Business Corporations Act* (CBCA) may satisfy the CBCA requirements to file an annual return with the Director, CBCA, by completing this schedule and filing it with the *T2 Corporation Income Tax Return* (T2 return) within six months of the taxation year end, (as that term is defined under the *Income Tax Act*).

By completing Schedule 80, you are consenting to Revenue Canada's disclosure of the information provided on this annual return, and certain information from the T2 return (i.e., corporation name, Business Number, taxation year end, head office address, mailing address, and the major business activity), to Industry Canada, Director, CBCA, as part of the joint initiative to ease the reporting burden for common clients.

Schedule 80 is deemed to be signed by a director or authorized officer if it is attached to a signed *T2 Corporation Income Tax Return*.

If you do not consent to the above, you can file directly with Industry Canada using their prescribed forms.

Part 1 – Corporate Information

Does the corporation distribute its securities to the public? .... 110 1 Yes ☐ 2 No ☐

Does the corporation have 15 or more shareholders? .... 111 1 Yes ☐ 2 No ☐

Does the corporation have in place a unanimous shareholder agreement referred to in subsection 146(2) of the *Canada Business Corporations Act*? A unanimous shareholder agreement is a written agreement among all the shareholders of a corporation that restricts, in whole or in part, the powers of the directors to manage the business and affairs of the corporation by giving to the shareholders certain powers usually conferred to the Board of Directors .... 112 1 Yes ☐ 2 No ☐

What was the date of the last annual meeting? .... 113 Year Month Day

Part 2 – Director Information

Has there been a change of directors of the corporation? .... 120 1 Yes ☐ 2 No ☐

If *yes*, has Form 6, *Notice of Change of Directors* been filed pursuant to the provisions of the CBCA? .... 121 1 Yes ☐ 2 No ☐

If the answer is *no* at line 121, please indicate if you have completed and attached Schedule 81 – *Notice of Change of Directors* – CBCA with this form .... 122 1 Yes ☐ 2 No ☐

Part 3 – Filing Fee

An annual return filing fee of $40.00 payable to the Receiver General for Canada is prescribed by the regulations to the CBCA. Have you included this payment with this T2 return? .... 130 1 Yes ☐ 2 No ☐

Please use the attached remittance voucher to make your payment.

T2 SCH 80 E (01) (Ce formulaire existe en français.) Canada

18.3 (continued)

Part 4 – Registered Office

Is the Registered Office address of the corporation the same as the Head Office address identified on page 1 of the T2 return? ..... **200** 1 Yes ☐ 2 No ☐

If the answer is *no* at line 200, please provide the address of the Registered Office in the space below:

201 Street		
City	Province / Territory	Postal code

Has there been a change of Registered Office since you last filed your annual return? ..... **210** 1 Yes ☐ 2 No ☐

If *yes*, has Form 3, *Notice of Change of Registered Office* been filed pursuant to the provisions of the CBCA? ..... **211** 1 Yes ☐ 2 No ☐

If the answer is *no* at line 211, you may complete a *Notice of Change of Registered Office* by providing the information in this part. The notice will be deemed to be received by the Director, CBCA, at the time and date that this return is received by Revenue Canada. Where required by the Act, the changes being reported by the filing of this form must be authorized by the director(s) or shareholder(s). If the address of the Registered Office is changed to a place located outside of the area specified in the Articles, an amendment to the Articles, will be necessary.

Effective date of the change of Registered Office ..... **220** Year Month Day

Place in Canada where the Registered Office is currently situated.

221 Place

Previous address of the Registered Office.

231 Street		
City	Province / Territory	Postal code

Part 5 – Jurisdiction In Which The Corporation Is Carrying On Business

For each provincial/territorial jurisdiction in which the corporation is carrying on business, state the address of the principal place of business or address for service, including the city, province, and postal code. A corporation is presumed to be "carrying on business" if it has an address in the province/territory or having there, either directly or through the agency of a representative acting under a general mandate, an establishment, a post office box or the use of a telephone line, or carrying out in the province/territory any act for the purpose of profit.

240

	Address of the principal place of business or address for service	City	Province / Territory	Postal code
1.				
2.				
3.				
4.				
5.				
6.				
7.				
8.				
9.				
10.				
11.				
12.				

Certification

Please complete this area if this schedule is filed separately from the signed T2 return.

I, **950** ____________ (Surname in block letters) **951** ____________ (First name in block letters) **954** ____________ (Position, office, or rank),

am an authorized signing officer of the corporation. I certify that I have examined this schedule, and that the information given on this schedule is, to the best of my knowledge, correct and complete.

955 Year Month Day (Date) ____________ Signature of an authorized signing officer of the corporation **956** ____________ Telephone number

Printed in Canada

18.3 (continued)

Please use this voucher only to pay your Canada Business Corporations Act (CBCA) annual return filing fee. Complete all boxes and the name area on the voucher to ensure we allocate your payment correctly. See the reverse for further instructions.

Canada Customs and Revenue Agency and Industry Canada | Agence des douanes et du revenu du Canada et Industrie Canada

BUSINESS REMITTANCE VOUCHER
Annual Return Filing Fee

Do not use this area
001958

T2 SCH 60 E (01)

9030 | 090

Business Number

Taxation Year End
Year Month Day

Amount Paid
40.00

Corporation's Name

001958 9030 0090 00 000000000 000000 000000004000 8

18.3 (continued)

Return the voucher to your taxation centre with your *T2 Corporation Income Tax Return* and Schedule 80, *Industry Canada - Annual Return*, and your cheque or money order made payable to the Receiver General for Canada. **Do not make your payment at your financial institution.**

To help us credit your payment, write your business number on the back of your cheque or money order.

We will charge a fee for any dishonoured payment.

DO NOT staple, paper clip, tape or fold voucher or your cheque

DO NOT mail cash

18.4 Notice of Change of Directors, Canada Business Corporations Act

Canada Customs and Revenue Agency and Industry Canada | Agence des douanes et du revenu du Canada et Industrie Canada

SCHEDULE 81

NOTICE OF CHANGE OF DIRECTORS, *CANADA BUSINESS CORPORATIONS ACT*

Name of corporation	Business Number	Taxation year end (Year / Month / Day)

If there has been a change of directors since the last annual return filed and *Notice of Change of Directors*, has not been previously submitted, you may do so now by completing this schedule and filing it with Schedule 80, *Industry Canada – Annual Return – Canada Business Corporations Act*. Where required by the Act, the changes being reported by the filing of this form must be authorized by the director(s) or shareholder(s). If the number of directors of the corporation is not within the limits specified in the Articles, an amendment to the Articles will be necessary. This information is collected under the authority of the *Canada Business Corporations Act* and will be stored in personal information bank number IC/PPU–049. Personal information that you provide is protected under the provisions of the *Privacy Act*. However, public disclosure pursuant to section 266 of the *Canada Business Corporations Act* is permitted under the *Privacy Act*.

If you need more space, continue on a separate schedule.

Part 1 – The following persons became directors of this corporation (please print):

	Name 130	Effective date YYYY/MM/DD 131	Complete residential address (including postal code) 132	Resident Canadian Y or N 133
1.				
2.				
3.				
4.				
5.				

Part 2 – The following persons ceased to be directors of this corporation (please print):

	Name 140	Effective Date YYYY/MM/DD 141	Complete residential address (including postal code) 142
1.			
2.			
3.			
4.			
5.			

T2 SCH 81 E (00) (Ce formulaire existe en français.) 1312 Canadä

18.4 (continued)

Part 3 – The directors of this corporation now are (please print):

	Name 150	Complete residential address (including postal code) 151	Resident Canadian Y or N 152
1.			
2.			
3.			
4.			
5.			
6.			
7.			
8.			
9.			
10.			
11.			
12.			
13.			
14.			

Certification

Please complete this area if this schedule is filed separately from the signed T2 return.

I, 950 __________ (Surname in block letters) 951 __________ (First name in block letters) 954 __________ Position, office, or rank ,

am an authorized signing officer of the corporation. I certify that I have examined this schedule, and that the information given on this schedule is, to the best of my knowledge, correct and complete.

955 Year Month Day __________ Date __________ Signature of an authorized signing officer of the corporation 956 __________ Telephone number

Printed in Canada

Appendices

APPENDIX A

FREQUENTLY USED ADDRESSES AND TELEPHONE NUMBERS

COMPANIES BRANCH

Ministry of Consumer and Business Services
Companies Branch
375 University Avenue
Toronto, Ontario
M5G 2M2

Note: Public Office
Companies Branch
2nd Floor at above address

General Enquiries (corporate searches and all other searches, including partnership, sole proprietorship, limited partnership and name/style) .... (416) 314-8880 or 1-800-361-3223

CORPORATIONS TAX — ONTARIO

Ministry of Finance
Corporations Tax Branch
P.O. Box 627
33 King Street West
Oshawa, Ontario
LIH 8H5

General Enquiries 1-800-263-7965

To obtain copies of the *Business Corporations Act,* call Publications Ontario 1-800-668-9938

INDUSTRY CANADA

Corporations Directorate
9th Floor, Jean Edmonds Tower South
365 Laurier Avenue West
Ottawa, Ontario
KIA 0C8 .... (613) 941-9042

FLASHFAX—automated fax information system service, Ottawa ... (613) 941-0199
(613) 941-0200

Industry Canada—Ontario Offices

Industry Canada 9th Floor Jean Edmonds Tower South 365 Laurier Avenue West **OTTAWA, ONT.** K1A 0C8	Phone: (613) 941-9042 Fax: (613) 941-0601	All kits & forms available Document drop off time: before 4:30 p.m. Information and assistance on programs & services
Industry Canada Yonge-Richmond Centre 151 Yonge St., 3rd Floor **TORONTO, ONT.** M5C 2W7	Phone: (416) 954-2714 Fax: (416) 973-8714	All forms & kits available Document drop off time: before 2:00 p.m.
Canada/Ontario Business Service Centre 151 Yonge St. 9th Floor **TORONTO, ONT.** M5C 2W7	Phone: (416) 954-"INFO" (4636) 1-800-567-2345 Fax: (416) 954-8597	Basic kits available

ADDRESS FOR THE OFFICE OF THE SUPERINTENDENT OF BANKRUPTCY (BY PROVINCE)

Nova Scotia

Industry Canada
Office of the Superintendent of Bankruptcy
Maritime Centre
1505 Barrington St., 16th Floor
Halifax, NS, B3J 3K5
Tel: (902) 426-2900
Fax: (902) 426-7275

Quebec

Industrie Canada
Bureau du surintendant des faillites

1141, Route de l'Église, 4e étage
SAINTE-FOY (Québec) G1V 3W5
Tel: (418) 648-4280
Fax: (418) 648-4120

Industrie Canada
Bureau du surintendant des faillites
2665 ouest, rue King - Bureau 600
SHERBROOKE (Québec) J1L 1C1
Tel: (819) 564-5742
Fax: (819) 564-4299

Industrie Canada
Bureau du surintendant des faillites
Pièce 800
5, Place Ville Marie, 8e étage
MONTRÉAL (Québec) H3B 2G2
Tel: (514) 283-6192
Fax: (514) 283-9795

Ontario

Industry Canada
Office of the Superintendent of Bankruptcy
Trebla Building
473 Albert St., 2nd Floor
Ottawa, ON, K1R 5B4
Tel: (613) 995-2994
Fax: (613) 996-0949

Industry Canada
Office of the Superintendent of Bankruptcy
25 St.Clair Avenue East, 6th Floor
Toronto, ON, M4T 1M2
Tel: (416) 973-6486
Fax: (416) 973-7440

Industry Canada
Office of the Superintendent of Bankruptcy
69 John St. South, 4th Floor
Hamilton, ON, L8N 2B9
Tel: (905) 572-2847
Fax: (905) 572-4066

Industry Canada
Office of the Superintendent of Bankruptcy
Federal Building
451 Talbot Street, Room 303

London, ON, N6A 5C9
Tel: (519) 645-4034
Fax: (519) 645 5139

Manitoba
Industry Canada
Office of the Superintendent of Bankruptcy
400 St. Mary Avenue, 4th Floor
Winnipeg, MB, R3C 4K5
Tel: (204) 983-3229
Fax: (204) 983-8904

Saskatchewan

Industry Canada
Office of the Superintendent of Bankruptcy
1020-2002 Victoria Avenue
Regina, SK, S4P 0R7
Tel: (306) 780-5391
Fax: (306) 780-6947

Industry Canada
Office of the Superintendent of Bankruptcy
123 - 2nd Avenue South, 7th Floor
Saskatoon, SK S7K 7E6
Tel: (306) 975-4298
Fax: (306) 975-5317

Alberta

Industry Canada
Office of the Superintendent of Bankruptcy
Standard Life Tower Building
510, 639-Fifth Avenue S.W., 5th Floor
Calgary, AB, T2P 0M9
Tel: (403) 292-5607
Fax: (403) 292-5188

Industry Canada
Office of the Superintendent of Bankruptcy
Suite 725, Canada Place
9700 Jasper Avenue
Edmonton, AB, T5J 4C3
Tel: (780) 495-2476
Fax: (780) 495-2466

British Columbia

Industry Canada
Office of the Superintendent of Bankruptcy

300 West Georgia Street, Suite 1900
Vancouver, BC, V6B 6E1
Tel.: (604) 666-5007
Fax: (604) 666-4610

Corporations Directorate:

Office of the Director General

Director General
Richard G. Shaw .... (613) 941-2837
Fax: (613) 941-5783

Incorporation and Disclosure Services Branch

Director
Marc Leblanc .... (613) 941-8118
Fax: (613) 941-0999

Public and Corporate Services Section

Manager
Réal Fortin .... (613)941-2593
Fax: (613) 941-0999

Information and Certification Section

Head
Françoise Langevin .... (613) 941-5777
Fax: (613) 941-5789

Regional Officers

The Field Officers are responsible for providing information and assistance relating to Corporations Directorate services and programs as well as accepting documents sent to the Directorate. Documents received in the Regional Offices before 2:30 p.m. are forwarded to headquarters for next day delivery.

Region	Name	Telephone / (v) = voice mail	Fax
Montreal	Michel Hall Luc Béliveau Claire Blake Diane Chevrette Fred Lagarde 5 Place Ville Marie 7th Floor Montréal QC H3B 2G2	(514) 496-1797 (v) (514) 496-5734 (v) (514) 496-9630 (v) (514) 496-7214 (v) (514) 496-5734 (v)	(514) 283-2247 (514) 496-9671 (514) 496-9671 (514) 496-2247 (514) 496-2247
Toronto	Luisa Gallo 151 Yonge Street 3rd Floor Toronto ON M5C 2W7	(416) 954-2714 (v)	(416) 973-8714
Vancouver	Richard York (acting) Suite 2000 300 West Georgia St. Vancouver BC V6B 6E1	(604) 666-9875 (v)	(604) 666-4274

Document Production and Information Processing Section

The overall objective of the Section is to provide a range of electronic publication and data processing services for the Corporations Directorate. The Section is also responsible for the Corporations Directorate Site on Strategis. It also performs a variety of tasks related to the maintenance and operation of our database containing information on federally-incorporated corporations. The Section produces our monthly publication, the Canada Corporations Bulletin. Other activities of the Section include responding to general enquiries from the public on the format and content of the SOURCE and NUANS systems, processing internally-generated NUANS search reports, publication in the Canada Gazette and acknowledge receipt of statutory filings. The Section is responsible for the scanning and indexing of the corporate files. The Manager of this Section is also responsible for the Records Office.

Title	Name	Telephone / (v) = voice mail	Fax
Manager	Michelle Beaudry	(613) 941-7636 (v)	(613) 941-4803
Senior Strategis Production Officer	Suzanne Lacasse (Acting)	(613) 941-5723 (v)	(613) 941-4803
Junior Strategis Production Officer	Nathalie Beaulne (Acting)	(613) 941-2592 (v)	(613) 941-4803
Information Processing & Document Control Clerks	Monique Croteau	(613) 946-4440	(613) 941-4803
	Rosemarie Farrell	(613) 946-4439	(613) 941-4803
	Hélène Laberge	(613) 946-4438	(613) 941-4803
	Carol Rosengren	(613) 957-9553	(613) 941-4803
	David Awuy	(613) 946-4436	(613) 941-4803
	Nicole Ricard	(613) 941-5425	(613) 941-4803
	Jessie Vethamuthu	(613) 946-4431	(613) 941-4803
	Heather Billings	(613) 946-4437	(613) 941-4803
	Richard Osborne	(613) 946-6631	(613) 941-4803
	Lise Casselman	(613) 946-6631	(613) 941-4803
	Marie-Marthe Harvey	(613) 941-6631	(613) 941-4803

Records Office

The staff of the Records office is responsible for the creation, maintenance and storage of all hard copy corporate files retained in the building. They also assign and distribute the mail received by the organization.

Title	Name	Telephone / (v) = voice mail	Fax
Manager	Michelle Beaudry	(613) 941-7636 (v)	(613) 941-4803
Senior Records Clerk	Robert Gosselin	(613) 941-0202	(613) 941-4803
Records Clerks	Sharon Basque	(613) 946-8941	(613) 941-4803
	Florence Debassige	(613) 941-0453	(613) 941-4803
	Gilles Gosselin	(613) 941-0205	(613) 941-4803
	Rosa Leung	(613) 941-3927	(613) 941-4803

Informatics Services Section

This Section is responsible for implementing the technology components of the business initiatives. The Section ensures that a technical architecture is in place to support the evolving automated business environment. Technical staff support the smooth functioning of the Directorate's computer systems. Working closely with other staff, they ensure that the Directorate's systems are updated as scheduled, properly secured against unauthorized users, that regular backups are performed, etc. They see to it that all computer equipment, software and other peripherals function as required, are enhanced and/or replaced as required and participate as key members of systems development teams. They must also keep abreast of new developments in information technology both at the departmental level in liaising with central staff, inter-departmentally and generally throughout the industry at large.

Title	Name	Telephone / (v) = voice mail	Fax
Senior Manager	Dominique Roy	(613) 941-5724 (v)	(613) 941-5722
Manager IT Development Services	Louise Bédard	(613) 941-0602 (v)	(613) 941-5722
Manager IT Infrastructure	Brian McDonnell	(613) 952-9298 (v)	(613) 941-5722
IT Specialist System Administration	Martinho Rafael	(613) 941-5725 (v)	(613) 941-5722
IT Specialist, PC Support, Help Desk and LAN Administration	Daniel Turgeon	(613) 941-4945 (v)	(613) 941-5722
IT Specialist Programmer	Lynn Bergeron	(613) 946-2563 (v)	(613) 941-5722
Data Integrity Specialist	Elaine Jacques	(613) 952-9116 (v)	(613) 941-5722

Compliance Branch

This Branch is headed by a Director responsible for the Policy Section and the Corporate Examination Section.

Title	Name	Telephone / (v) = voice mail	Fax
Director	Robert Weist	(613) 941-5756 (v)	(613) 941-5781
Secretary	Ginette Chartrand	(613) 941-5757 (v)	(613) 941-5781

Corporate Examination Section

The Corporate Examination Section is responsible for the examination of certain CBCA applications (complex amalgamations, going-private transactions, etc.) as well as all non-CBCA applications (not-for-profit corporations, co-operatives, boards of trade, etc.). The Section also processes all requests for correction of CBCA certificates which have been issued and all requests that the Director order a change of corporate name. In addition, the Section reviews complaints of non-compliance and reviews applications for arrangements and for exemption from certain requirements of the Act.

Title	Name	Telephone / (v) = voice mail	Fax
Manager re: corporate names, non-profit, Co-op examination, review of complaints of non-compliance, arrangement and exemption applications.	Jean Turner	(613) 941-5754 (v)	(613) 941-5781
Compliance Officer re: review of complaints, arrangements of exemption application.	Joyce Hébert (Acting)	(613) 941-5726 (v)	(613) 941-5781
Corporate Examiners: re: not-for-profit, co-operatives, board of tradeapplications, examination of certain CBCA applications	Marie-Marthe-Soulière-Roussel (Acting)	(613) 941-5751 (v)	(613) 941-5781
	Maurice Séguin (Acting)	(613) 941-5752 (v)	(613) 941-5781
Corporate Examination Clerk: re: to obtain status in respect of all co-op, not-for-profit, BOTA applications	Chantal Wolfe	(613) 941-5758 (v)	(613) 941-5781

Ontario Regional Points of Service

Industry Canada 9th Floor Jean Edmonds Tower South 365 Laurier Avenue West **OTTAWA, ONT.** K1A 0C8	Phone: (613) 941-9042 Fax: (613) 941-0601	All kits & forms available Document drop off time: before 4:30 p.m. Information and assistance on programs & services
Industry Canada Yonge-Richmond Centre 151 Yonge St., 3rd Floor **TORONTO, ONT.** M5C 2W7	Phone: (416) 954-2714 Fax: (416) 973-8714	All forms & kits available Document drop off time: before 2:00 p.m.

Canada/Ontario Business Service Centre 151 Yonge St. 9th Floor **TORONTO, ONT.** M5C 2W7	Phone: (416) 954-"INFO" (4636) 1-800-567-2345 Fax: (416) 954-8597	Basic kits available

GENERAL

Archives of Ontario
77 Grenville Street
Toronto, Ontario
M7A 2R9 .... (416) 327-1600

Ministry of Transportation
1201 Wilson Avenue
East Building, Main Floor
Downsview, Ontario
M3M 1J8
General Enquiries .... (416) 235-4686

LEGAL STATIONERS

Dye & Durham Company Inc.
1060 Tapscott Road
Scarborough, Ontario
M1X 1G3 .... (416) 321-1000
Fax: (416) 321-0222
1-800-668-9011
Canadian Fax: 1-800-263-2772

NAME SEARCH HOUSES

Dye & Durham Company Inc.
Name Search Department
(see above, under Legal Stationers, for particulars)

REGIONAL OFFICES

SEARCH & REGISTRATION SERVICES
393 University Avenue, Suite 1519
Toronto, Ontario
Canada M5G 1E6
Telephone: (416) 595-7177
Fax: (416) 595-1268
Toll Free Telephone: 1-800-668-8208
Toll Free Fax: 1-800-667-3146
E-mail: search_registration@dyedurham.ca

CORPORATE SUPPLIES

Toronto
1060 Tapscott Road
Scarborough, Ontario M1X 1G3
Telephone: (416) 321-1000
Fax: (416) 321-0222
Canada Toll Free Telephone: 1-800-668-9011
Canada Toll Free Fax: 1-800-263-2772

London
506 Newbold Street
London, Ontario Canada N6E 1K6
Telephone: (519) 685-3256
Fax: (519) 685-3256
Toll Free Telephone: 1-800-265-4687
Toll Free Fax: 1-800-567-5814

Ottawa
1665 Russell Road, Unit 3
Ottawa, Ontario Canada K1G 0N1
Telephone: (613) 739-8200
Fax: (613) 739-3500
Toll Free Telephone: 1-800-267-2718
Toll Free Fax: 1-800-563-1085

Winnipeg
1274 Border Street
Winnipeg, Manitoba Canada R3H 0M6
Telephone: (204) 632-8884
Fax: (204) 632-7537
Toll Free Telephone: 1-800-758-1355
Toll Free Fax: 1-800-207-9793

Nova Scotia/Newfoundland
P.O. Box 127
Tantallon, Nova Scotia Canada B0J 3J0
Telephone: (902) 823-1801
Fax: (902) 823-1808

New Brunswick/Prince Edward Island
40 Hennessey Road
Moncton, New Brunswick Canada E1A 4W8
Telephone: (506) 383-8299
Fax: (506) 383-6982

British Columbia
10-620 Royal Avenue
New Westminster, B.C. V3M 1J2
Telephone: (604) 257-1800 800-661-1811
Fax: (604) 257-1888
www.dyedurhambc.com
info@dyedurhambc.com

Dye & Durham Frequent Fax Numbers

Head Office .... (416) 321-0222
Printing Department .... (416) 321-2175
Downtown Toronto .... (416) 595-1268

PERSONAL PROPERTY REGISTRATION BRANCH

375 University Avenue
2nd Floor
Toronto, Ontario
M5G 2M2

General Enquiry and PPSR Searches .... (416) 325-8847
1-800-267-8847

Registrations

P.O. Box 2100 100, Station A
M5W IW6

LAND REGISTRY OFFICES

Services provided: Personal property searches for anything registered in the system pertaining to Personal Property, Corporation Securities Registration and Personal Property Registrations, and Land Registry Services.

Hours: 8:30 — 5:00

Services Provided:
Registry — REG
Land Titles — LT
Personal Property Security Registration — PPSR
Company Incorporation — CO
Registrar General — ORG
Ontario Business Connects — OBC
Automated land registration data base — POLARIS

Glengarry
Land Registry Office — REG
PO Box 668
63 Kenyon Street West
Alexandria ON K0C 1A0
Tel: (613) 525-1315
Fax: (613) 525-0509

Lanark
Land Registry Office — REG, OBC, PPSR
2 Industrial Dr
P.O. Box 1180
Almonte ON K0A 1A0
Tel: (613) 256-1577
Fax: (613) 256-0940

Simcoe
Land Registry Office — REG, LT, PPSR, CO, OBC, POLARIS, ORG
Court House
114 Worsley Street
Barrie ON L4M 1M1
Tel: (705) 725-7232
Fax: (705) 725-7246

Hastings
Land Registry Office — REG, LT, PPSR, ORG
15 Victoria Ave
Belleville ON K8N 1Z5
Tel: (613) 968-4597 — General Inquiry
(613) 968-8261 — PPSR
Fax: (613) 968-3606

Muskoka
Land Registry Office — REG, LT, PPSR, OBC
15 Dominion Street North
Bracebridge ON P1L 2E7
Tel: (705) 645-4415
Fax: (715) 645-7826

Peel
Land Registry Office — REG, LT, PPSR, OBC, POLARIS, ORG
7765 Hurontario St
Brampton ON L6V 2L8
Tel: (905) 874-4008
Fax: (905) 874-4012

Brant
Land Registry Office — LT, REG, PPSR, POLARIS
Court House
80 Wellington Street
Brantford ON N3T 2L9
Tel: (519) 752-8321
(519) 752-5571 — PPSR
Fax: (519) 752-0273

Leeds
Land Registry Office — REG, PPSR, OBC
7 King St
Box 633
Brockville ON K6V 3P7
Tel: (613) 345-5751
Fax: (613) 345-7390

Haldimand
Land Registry Office — REG, PPSR
10 Echo St.
PO Box 310
Cayuga ON N0A 1E0
Tel: (905) 772-3531
Fax: (905) 772-0105

Kent
Land Registry Office — REG, PPSR, LT, POLARIS
40 William Street North
Chatham ON N7M 4L2
Tel: (519) 352-5520
Fax: (519) 352-3222

Northumberland
Land Registry Office — LT, REG, PPSR
1005 William St Suite 105
Cobourg ON K9A 5J4
Tel: (905) 372-3813
Fax: (905) 372-4758

Cochrane
Land Registry Office — REG, LT, PPSR
149 4th Avenue
Court House
PO Box 580
Cochrane ON P0L 1C0
Tel: (705) 272-5791
Fax: (705) 272-2951

Stormont
Land Registry Office — REG, PPSR, OBC
127 Sydney Street
Cornwall ON K6H 3H1
Tel: (613) 932-4522
Fax: (613) 932-4524

Rainy River
Land Registry Office — REG, LT, PPSR
353 Church Street
Fort Frances ON P9A 1C9
Tel: (807) 274-5451
Fax: (807) 274-1704

Huron
Land Registry Office — REG, PPSR, OBC, LT, POLARIS
38 North Street
Goderich ON N7A 2T4
Tel: (519) 524-9562
Fax: (519) 524-2482

Manitoulin
Land Registry Office — REG, LT, PPSR
27 Phipps St
Gore Bay ON P0P 1H0
Tel: (705) 282-2442
Fax: (705) 282-3245

Wellington
Land Registry Office — LT, REG, PPSR, POLARIS
1 Stone Rd W
Guelph ON N1G 4Y2
Tel: (519) 826-3372
Fax: (519) 826-3373

Timiskaming
Land Registry Office — REG, LT, PPSR, OBC
375 Main St PO Box 159
Haileybury ON P0J 1K0
Tel: (705) 672-3332
Fax: (705) 672-3906

Wentworth
Land Registry Office — REG, LT, PPSR, CO, ORG, POLARIS
119 King Street West 4th fl
PO Box 2112
Hamilton ON L8P 4Y7

Tel: (905) 521-7561
Fax: (905) 521-7505

Prescott
Land Registry Office — REG, LT, PPSR
179 Main St. E.
Hawkesbury ON K6A 1A1
Tel: (613) 636-0314
Fax: (613) 636-0772

Kenora
REG, LT, PPSR, OBC
220 Main St S
Kenora ON P9N 3X7
Tel: (807) 468-2794
Fax: (807) 468-2796

Frontenac
Land Registry Office — LT, REG, PPSR, CO, OBC, POLARIS
1 Court Street
Kingston ON K7L 2N4
Tel: (613) 548-6767
Fax: (613) 548-6766

Waterloo
Land Registry Office — ORG, REG, PPSR, CO, OBC, LT, POLARIS
200 Frederick St 3rd Fl
Kitchener ON N2H 6H9
Tel: (519) 571-6043
Fax: (519) 571-6067

Victoria
Land Registry Office — REG, LT, PPSR
Provincial Court Building
440 Kent St W
Lindsay ON K9V 6G8
Tel: (705) 324-4912
Fax: (705) 324-6290

Middlesex
Land Registry Office — REG, PPSR, ORG, CO, LT, POLARIS
Provincial Court Bldg
80 Dundas St Ground Floor J
London ON N6A 6A7
Tel: (519) 675-7600
Tel: (519) 675-7612 – PPSR
Fax: (519) 675-7611

Halton
Land Registry Office — REG, LT, PPSR, POLARIS
491 Steeles Ave E
Milton ON L9T 1Y7
Tel: (905) 878-7287
Fax: (905) 876-8806

Haliburton
Land Registry Office — REG
Newcastle Street Box 270
Minden ON K0M 2K0
Tel: (705) 286-1391
Fax: (705) 286-4324

Dundas
Land Registry Office — REG
5th St PO Box 645
Morrisburg ON K0C 1X0
Tel: (613) 543-2583
Fax: (613) 543-4541

Lennox
Land Registry Office — REG, PPSR
2 Dairy Ave, Unit 10 Dale=s Plaza
Napanee ON K7R 3T1
Tel: (613) 354-3751
Fax: (613) 354-1474

York Region
Land Registry Office — REG, LT, PPSR, ORG, OBC, POLARIS
50 Eagle Street W 1st Fl
Newmarket ON L3Y 6B1
Tel: (905) 895-1561
Fax: (905) 895-6517

Nipissing
Land Registry Office — REG, LT, PPSR, ORG
360 Plouffe Street
North Bay ON P1B 9L5
Tel: (705) 474-2270
Fax: (705) 495-8511

Dufferin
Land Registry Office — REG, LT, PPSR, POLARIS, OBC
10 Louisa St
Orangeville ON L9W 3P9

Tel: (519) 941-1481
Fax: (519) 941-6444

Ottawa-Carleton
Land Registry Office — LT, REG, PPSR, CO, OBC, ORG, POLARIS
Court House
161 Elgin Street 4th fl
Ottawa ON K2P 2K1
Tel: (613) 239-1230
Fax: (613) 239-1422

Grey
Land Registry Office — REG, PPSR, OBC
1555 16th St E, Suites 1 and 2
Owen Sound ON N4K 5N3
Tel: (519) 376-1637
Fax: (519) 376 1639

Parry Sound
Land Registry Office — REG, LT, PPSR
28 Miller Street
Parry Sound ON P2A 1T1
Tel: (705) 746-5816
Fax: (705) 746-6517

Renfrew
Land Registry Office — REG, PPSR, OBC, LT
400 Pembroke St E
Pembroke ON K8A 3K8
Tel: (613) 732-8331
Fax: (613) 732-0297

Peterborough
Land Registry Office — REG, LT, PPSR, CO, OBC, POLARIS
300 Water St., 2nd Fl
P.O. Box 7000
Peterborough ON K9J 8M5
Tel: (705) 755-1342
Fax: (705) 755 1343

Prince Edward
Land Registry Office — REG, PPSR
1 Pitt Street
PO Box 1310
Picton ON K0K 2T0
Tel: (613) 476-3219

Fax: (613) 476-7908

Grenville
Land Registry Office — REG
499 Centre Street
P.O. Box 1660
Prescott ON K0E 1T0
Tel: (613) 925-3177
Fax: (613) 925-0302

Russell
Land Registry Office — REG, LT
1122 Concession St.
PO Box 10
Russell ON K4R 1C8
Tel: (613) 445-2138
Fax: (613) 445-0614

Lambton
Land Registry Office — REG, PPSR, CO, OBC
Court House
700 Christina Street North, Suite 102
P.O. Box 3021
Sarnia ON N7V 3C2
Tel: (519) 337-2393
Fax: (519) 337-8371

Algoma
Land Registry Office — REG, LT, PPSR, CO, OBC, ORG
420 Queen ST E PO Box 550
Sault Ste. Marie ON P6A 5M8
Tel: (705) 253-8887
Fax: (705) 253-9245

Norfolk
Land Registry Office — REG, LT, PPSR
530 Queensway W., 2nd Fl
Court House
Simcoe ON N3Y 4K8
Tel: (519) 426-2216
Fax: (519) 426-9627

Niagara North
Land Registry Office — REG, LT, PPSR, POLARIS, OBC
59 Church St
St. Catharines ON L2R 3C3
Tel: (905) 684-6351

Fax: (905) 684-5874

Elgin
Land Registry Office — REG, LT, PPSR
Court House Block
4 Wellington St.
St. Thomas ON N5R 2P2
Tel: (519) 631-3015
Tel: (519) 633-4471 – PPSR
Fax: (519) 631-8182

Perth
Land Registry Office — REG, LT, PPSR, POLARIS
5 Huron St.
Stratford ON N5A 5S4
Tel: (519) 271-3343
Fax: (519) 271-2550

Sudbury
Land Registry Office — REG, PPSR, LT, CO, ORG, POLARIS, OBC
199 Larch, Ste. 301
Sudbury ON P3E 5P9
Tel: (705) 564-4300
Fax: (705) 564-4148

Thunder Bay
Land Registry Office — REG, PPSR, LT, CO, OBC, ORG
189 Red River Rd., Ste. 201
Thunder Bay ON P7B 1A2
Tel: (807) 343-7436
Fax: (807) 343-7439

Toronto City
Land Registry Office — LT, POLARIS
20 Dundas St W., Ste. 420
Box 117
Toronto ON M5G 2C2
Tel: (416) 314-4430
Fax: (416) 314-4453

Toronto Registry
Land Registry Office — REG, POLARIS
20 Dundas St W Ste 321
Box 108
Toronto ON M5G 2C2
Tel: (416) 314-4400
Fax: (416) 314-5875

Bruce
Land Registry Office — REG, LT, PPSR, OBC
203 Cayley Street
PO Box 1690
Walkerton ON N0G 2V0
Tel: (519) 881-2259
Fax: (519) 881-2322

Niagara South
Land Registry Office — CO, REG, LT, PPSR, OBC, POLARIS
200 Division St
Welland ON L3B 4A2
Tel: (905) 735-4011/13
Fax: (905) 735-2430

Durham
Land Registry Office — REG, LT, PPSR, ORG, CO, OBC, POLARIS
590 Rossland Road E
Whitby ON L1N 9G5
Tel: (905) 665-4007
Fax: (905) 665-5247

Essex
Land Registry Office — ORG, REG, LT, PPSR, CO, POLARIS
250 Windsor Ave 3rd Fl
Windsor ON N9A 6V9
Tel: (519) 971-9980
Tel: (519) 971-9976 – PPSR
Fax: (519) 971-9937

Oxford
Land Registry Office — REG, LT PPSR, OBC, POLARIS
75 Graham Street
PO Box 246
Woodstock ON N4S 6J8
Tel: (519) 537-6287
Fax: (519) 537-3107

APPENDIX B

SCHEDULE OF CURRENT FEES

COMPANIES BRANCH - (SERVICE STANDARDS * & FEES)
As of December 1, 2000

CORPORATE DOCUMENTS: Filing Services	OVER-THE-COUNTER		MAILED-IN SERVICE		PRIMARY SERVICE PROVIDERS (PSP) (see below)	
Corporate Filing Services:		Fee		Fee	- statutory fee; does not include PSP's service fee	FEE
Business Corporations Act (For-Profit)						
Incorporation	Immediate	$360	2 - 4 weeks	$360	Immediate	$300
Amalgamation (10 or fewer amalgamating corporations)	Immediate	$330	2 - 4 weeks	$330	Not Available	----
Amalgamation (more than 10 amalgamating corporations)	Immediate	$500	2 - 4 weeks	$500	Not Available	----
Amendment	Immediate	$150	2 - 4 weeks	$150	Not Available	----
Restated Articles	Immediate	$150	2 - 4 weeks	$150	Not Available	----
Dissolution	Immediate	$25	2 - 4 weeks	$25	Not Available	----
Winding-Up (first filing)	Not Available	----	2 - 4 weeks	$25	Not Available	----
Continuation in Ontario	48 hours	$330	2 - 4 weeks	$330	Not Available	----
Expedited Service for Continuation in Ontario	24 hours	$500	Not Available		Not Available	----
Authorization to Continue in another jurisdiction	Immediate	$330	2 - 4 weeks	$330	Not Available	----
Revival	Immediate	$330	2 - 4 weeks	$330	Not Available	----
Arrangement or Reorganization	48 hours (minimum)	$330	2 - 4 weeks	$330	Not Available	----
Expedited Service for Arrangements	24 hours	$500	Not Available		Not Available	----
Corrected Certificate	Not Available	$500	4 - 6 weeks	$500	Not Available	----
*****Multiple transactions special service.***	Immediate	$25	Not Available		Not Available	----
Corporations Act (Not-For-Profit)						
Incorporation / Amalgamation / Continuation	Not Available		6 - 8 weeks	$155	Not Available	----
Expedited Letters Patent	7 working days (drop off)		7 working days	$255	Not Available	----
Supplementary Letters Patent	Not Available	----	6 - 8 weeks	$130	Not Available	----
Surrender of Charter	Not Available	----	6 - 8 weeks	No Fee	Not Available	----
Revival	Immediate	$100	2 - 4 weeks	$100	Not Available	----
Corrected Letters Patent/Supplementary Letters Patent	Not Available	----	4 - 6 weeks	$155	Not Available	----
Extra-Provincial Corporations Act						
Extra-Provincial Licence (Foreign)	Not Available	----	4 weeks	$330	Not Available	----
Extra-Provincial Licence Amendment	Not Available	----	4 weeks	$150	Not Available	----
Termination of Extra-Provincial Licence	Not Available	----	4 weeks	No Fee	Not Available	----
Corrected Extra-Provincial Licence	Not Available	----	4 weeks	$315	Not Available	----
Corporations within Canada file under the CIA	Not Available	----	25 working days	No Fee	Not Available	----
Corporations Information Act						
Initial Return/Notice of Change	Not Available	----	25 working days	No Fee	Immediate	No Statutory Fee

PLEASE NOTE:

Payment Information

Payments to Companies Branch may be made by cash, Visa, Mastercard, Interac, certified cheque, money order or personal cheque payable to the Minister of Finance. Personal cheques must include pre-printed name, address, bank transit number and account number on the front of the cheque. Please do not send cash in the mail. You cannot pay by Visa or Mastercard when using the mailed in service.

The Federal Goods and Services Tax does not apply to Companies Branch statutory fees.

N.B. A $35.00 fee will be charged for any cheque returned as non-negotiable.

**** Service times are subject to change.***

***** By appointment for filing more than 3 over-the-counter BCA documents. $25 fee in addition to filing fee for each transaction over 3.***

Primary Service Providers are under contract with the Ministry of Consumer and Commercial Relations.
Cyberbahn Inc. www.cyberbahn.ca (416) 595-9522 or 1-800-806-0003
or
Oncorp Direct Inc. www.oncorp.com (416) 964-2677 or 1-800-461-7772

COMPANIES BRANCH - (SERVICE STANDARDS * & FEES)
As of December 1, 2000

BUSINESS NAME, LIMITED PARTNERSHIP, REGISTRATION / FILING SERVICES	OVER-THE-COUNTER		MAILED-IN SERVICE		ONTARIO BUSINESS CONNECTS (Electronic Registration)		ONTARIO BUSINESS CONNECTS (Mailed-in Registration)	
		Fee		Fee		Fee		Fee
Business Names Act								
Registration								
New / Renewal	Immediate	$80	6 - 8 weeks	$80	Immediate	$60	2 weeks	$80
Amendment	Immediate	No Fee	6 - 8 weeks	No Fee	Not Available		Not Available	
Cancellation	Immediate	No Fee	6 - 8 weeks	No Fee	Not Available		Not Available	
Limited Partnerships Act								
Declaration								
New / Renewal	Immediate	$210	6 - 8 weeks	$210	Not Available		Not Available	
Late Renewal ($210 + $150 penalty)	Immediate	$360	6 - 8 weeks	$360	Not Available		Not Available	
Change	Immediate	No Fee	6 - 8 weeks	No Fee	Not Available		Not Available	
Dissolution	Immediate	No Fee	6 - 8 weeks	No Fee	Not Available		Not Available	
Withdrawal	Immediate	No Fee	6 - 8 weeks	No Fee	Not Available		Not Available	

PLEASE NOTE:

Payment Information

Payments to Companies Branch may be made by cash, Visa, Mastercard, Interac, certified cheque, money order or personal cheque payable to the Minister of Finance. Personal cheques must include pre-printed name, address, bank transit number and account number on the front of the cheque. Please do not send cash in the mail. You cannot pay by Visa or Mastercard when using the mailed in service.

The Federal Goods and Services Tax does not apply to Companies Branch statutory fees.

N.B. A $35.00 fee will be charged for any cheque returned as non-negotiable.

* ***Service times are subject to change.***

You may register your business name via the Internet at http://www.ccr.gov.on.ca/obcon/welcome.htm.
The fee for registration via the Internet is $60.

Aussi disponible en français

COMPANIES BRANCH - (SERVICE STANDARDS * & FEES)
As of December 1, 2000

CORPORATE SEARCH PRODUCTS / SERVICES	COMPANIES BRANCH				PRIMARY SERVICE PROVIDERS (PSP) (see below)	
	FEE	OVER-THE-COUNTER SERVICE TIME	FAXED-IN SERVICE TIME	MAILED-IN SERVICE TIME	- Statutory fee; does not include PSP's service fee	FEE
Corporate Search Products and Services:						
Profile Report	$12	Immediate	Not Available	4 - 6 weeks	Immediate	$8
Point-In-Time Report	$12	Immediate	Not Available	4 - 6 weeks	Immediate	$8
Corporate Document List	$5	Immediate	Not Available	4 - 6 weeks	Immediate	$3
Corporate Business Names List	$12	Immediate	Not Available	4 - 6 weeks	Immediate	$8
Certificate of Status	$30	Immediate	Not Available	4 - 6 weeks	Immediate	$26
Certificate of No Record	$30	Immediate	Not Available	4 - 6 weeks	Immediate	$26
Certificate of Non-Filing	$30	Immediate	Not Available	4 - 6 weeks	Immediate	$26
Statement of No Record	$12	Immediate	Not Available	4 - 6 weeks	Immediate	$8
Data Extraction Display	----	Not Available	Not Available	Not Available	Immediate	$8
For certification of all electronic products add $8.00 to the product fee						
Microfiche	$10	3 days	3 days	4 - 6 weeks	3 days (pick-up at Companies Branch)	$10
Certified Microfiche	$36	3 days	3 days	4 - 6 weeks		$36
Photocopy of Notice/Return (Only if Profile Report is not available)	$14	10 days (if film on site)	10 days (if film on site)	4 - 6 weeks	Not Available	
Certified Copy of Notice/Return (from Microfilm only)	$40	10 days (if film on site)	10 days (if film on site)	4 - 6 weeks	Not Available	
TC/RC paper files (old files not kept onsite)	$25	10 days (minimum) - depending on number of copies	10 days	4 - 6 weeks	Not Available	
For certification of TC/RC paper file, add $26.00 to the product fee						

PLEASE NOTE:

Payment Information:

Payments to Companies Branch may be made by cash, Visa, Mastercard, Interac, certified cheque, money order or personal cheque payable to the Minister of Finance. Personal cheques must include pre-printed name, address, bank transit number and account number on the front of the cheque. Please do not send cash in the mail. You cannot pay by Visa or Mastercard when using the mailed in service.

The Federal Goods and Services Tax does not apply to Companies Branch statutory fees.

N.B. A $35.00 fee will be charged for any cheque returned as non-negotiable.

*** Service times are subject to change.**

Primary Service Providers are under contract with the Ministry of Consumer and Commercial Relations.

Cyberbahn Inc. www.cyberbahn.ca (416) 595-9522 or 1-800-806-0003 or Oncorp Direct Inc. www.oncorp.com (416) 964-2677 or 1-800-461-7772

COMPANIES BRANCH - (SERVICE STANDARDS * & FEES)
As of December 1, 2000

BUSINESS NAME, LIMITED PARTNERSHIP SEARCHES	COMPANIES BRANCH				PRIMARY SERVICE PROVIDERS (PSP) (see below)		ONTARIO BUSINESS CONNECTS (OBC)			
	FEE	OVER-THE-COUNTER SERVICE TIME	FAXED-IN SERVICE TIME	MAILED-IN SERVICE TIME	– Statutory fee; does not include PSP's service fee	FEE	Self-Service OBC Workstation	FEE	Mailed-in together with OBC application •	FEE
Business Names & Limited Partnerships Searches:							- Electronic Business Names/ No Match Display	$8		
Business Names Report	$12	Immediate	Not Available	4 - 6 weeks	Immediate	$8	Not Available		2 weeks	$12
Document Replica	$12	Immediate	Not Available	4 - 6 weeks	Immediate	$8	Not Available		Not Available	
BNLP Document List	$5	Immediate	Not Available	4 - 6 weeks	Immediate	$3	Not Available		Not Available	
Certificate of Non-Registration	$30	Immediate	Not Available	4 - 6 weeks	Immediate	$26	Not Available		Not Available	
Partnership Business Names List	$12	Immediate	Not Available	4 - 6 weeks	Not Available		Not Available		Not Available	
Statement of No Match	$12	Immediate	Not Available	4 - 6 weeks	Immediate	$8	Not Available		2 weeks	$12
For certification of all electronic products add $8.00 to the product fee										
Copy of Declaration under the LPA	$12	24 hours	Not Available	4 - 6 weeks	Not Available		Not Available		Not Available	
Certified Copy of Declaration under LPA	$38	24 hours	Not Availabe	4 - 6 weeks	Not Available		Not Available		Not Available	
Expired Search - Registration has expired. The name was registered more than 5 years ago, but less than 10 years prior to date of search.	$40	5 days	5 days	4 - 6 weeks	Not Available		Not Available		Not Available	

Primary Service Providers are under contract with the Ministry of Consumer and Commercial Relations.

Cyberbahn Inc. www.cyberbahn.ca
(416) 595-9522 or 1-800-806-0003

or

Oncorp Direct Inc. www.oncorp.com
(416) 964-2677 or 1-800-461-7772

Aussi disponible en français

Federal Corporations Branch

Canada Business Corporations Act Regulations SOR/79-316, as am.

SCHEDULE II
(*Subsection 82(1)*)
FEES

Item	Column I Filing, Examination or Copying of Documents or Action by the Director	Column II Fees
1.	Issuance by the Director of	
	(*a*) a certificate of incorporation, pursuant to section 8, if the application is made by using Industry Canada's online incorporation feature	$ 200
	(*a*.1) a certificate of incorporation, pursuant to section 8, if the application is made by means other than Industry Canada's online incorporation feature	$ 250
	(*b*) a certificate of amendment, pursuant to subsection 27(5), section 178 or subsection 191(5) (except a certificate of amendment referred to in paragraph 82(2)(*a*) of these Regulations)	$ 200
	(*c*) a restated certificate of incorporation, pursuant to subsection 180(3) (unless issued with certificate of amendment)	$ 50
	(*d*) a certificate of amalgamation, pursuant to subsection 185(4)	$ 200
	(*e*) a certificate of continuance, pursuant to subsection 187(4) (unless subsection 268(8) applies)	$ 200
	(*f*) a document evidencing satisfaction of the Director, as required under subsection 188(1)	$ 200
	(*g*) a certificate of arrangement, pursuant to subsection 192(7)	$ 200
	(*h*) a certificate of revival, pursuant to subsection 209(3)	$ 200
	(*i*) a certificate of revocation of intent to dissolve, pursuant to subsection 211(11)	$ 50
	(*j*) a corrected certificate, pursuant to subsection 265(1)	same fee as would be payable for the certificate it replaces

2.	Sending the annual return to the Director for filing under subsection 263(1)	
	(*a*) using Industry Canada's online filing feature	$ 20
	(*b*) using any means other than Industry Canada's online filing feature	$ 40
3.	Examination by the Director of the corporation's file in connection with a request for a certificate of compliance pursuant to subsection 263(2)	$ 10
4.	Application to the Director for an exemption under subsection 2(8), 10(2), 82(3), 151(1), 171(2) or 187(11)	$ 250
5.	Application to the Director for an exemption under subsection 127(8)	
	(*a*) first application	$ 300
	(*b*) renewal	$ 100
6.	Application to the Director for an exemption under section 156	$ 250
7.	Furnishing by the Director of uncertified copies of documents under subsection 266(2), per page	$ 1
8.	Furnishing by the Director of certified copies of documents under subsection 266(2), per certificate	$ 35

NOTE: All references to provisions are references to provisions of the Act, unless otherwise specified.

Dye & Durham Company Inc.—Corporate Supplies (Prices as at December 2001)

CORPORATE SUPPLIES

DYE & DURHAM STYLE REGISTERS AND MINUTE BOOKS

8312	Corporate Register	$53.50
8312	Cover	$41.00
8312	Index	$13.00
8312	Corporate 'Laser' Register	$56.50
8312	"Laser" Cover	$41.00
8312	"Laser" Index	$13.00
3C1	Corporate Register	$53.50
3C1	Cover	$41.00
3C1	Index	$13.00
3C1	Corporate 'Laser' Register	$56.50
3C1	"Laser" Cover	$41.00
3C1	"Laser" Index	$13.00
76NL	Corporate Register	$53.50
76NL	Cover	$41.00
4085	Corporate Register	$53.50
4085	Cover	$35.00
4085	Index	$13.00
4085	Condominium Register	$57.00
4085	Condominium Index	$17.00
4186	Corporate Register	$59.95
4186	Cover	$39.95
4187	Corporate Register	$64.00
4187	Cover	$45.50
P5006H	Corporate Register (Black or Burgundy)	$56.50
P5006H	Cover	$40.00
P5006H	Index	$13.00
PM118	Corporate Register (with slipcase)	$64.00
PM118	Corporate Register	$53.50
PM118	Cover	$41.50
PM118	Slipcase	$17.00
DURHAM	Corporate Register (with slipcase)	$56.50
DURHAM	Corporate Register	$46.50
DURHAM	Cover	$29.50
DURHAM	Slipcase	$17.00
ATTACHÉ	Corporate Register (no seal)	$69.95
4267	Corporate Register	$61.95
4267	Cover	$41.95
T1185	Minute Book	$161.00
T1185	Cover	$145.00
T1185	Corporate Register	$165.00
T1185	Index	$15.00
F1185	Minute Book (Black or Red)	$161.00
F1185	Cover	$145.00
F1185	Corporate Register	$165.00
F1185	Index	$15.00

RING STYLE REGISTER (784 SERIES)

* Premium quality, pebble finish (black or burgundy)
* 1 1/2" capacity
* 3-D rings
* 8 1/2"x 11" sheet size
* Attractive gold tooling on front and spine

Jurisdictions: ONTARIO * NOVA SCOTIA *NEW BRUNSWICK * NEWFOUNDLAND * ALBERTA BRITISH COLUMBIA * FEDERAL (CANADA) PRINCE EDWARD ISLAND

Corporate Register with Slipcase	$56.50
Corporate Register	$46.50
French Version with Slipcase	$59.95
French Version	$49.95
Slipcase - Standard Size	$17.00
New Long Slipcase - with seal storage compartment	$28.00
Cover Only	$30.00
MB 300M Corporate Register with Long Slipcase	$58.50

POST STYLE REGISTER (362 SERIES)

The 362 is a traditional 4 post register with the following features:

* Fine quality, burgundy pebble finish cover
* Sheet size 8 1/2"x 12 3/4" (suitable for laser printer)

Jurisdictions: ONTARIO * NOVA SCOTIA NEW BRUNSWICK * NEWFOUNDLAND * FEDERAL (CANADA) PRINCE EDWARD ISLAND

Corporate Register with Index & Contents	$53.50
French Version	$56.50
Cover Only	$41.00

CORPORATE SUPPLIES STORAGE BOXES

Also known as transfer cases, these boxes can hold minute books and seals or other documents.

Wide Box - Black - Low Profile #492 15 5/8"L x 5"W x 11 3/4"H	$25.00
Wide Box - Black - High Profile #492D 15 5/8" x 5"W x 12"H	$33.00
Narrow Box - Black - High Profile #492N 15 5/8' x 3 1/2"W x 12"H	$29.00
Wide Box - Walnut - Low Profile #491W 12" x 5"W x 10 7/8"H	$27.00
#492W 15 5/8" x 5"W x 11 3/4"H	$27.00

QUANTITY PRICING AVAILABLE ON ALL CORPORATE BOXES

◆ **Ontario P.P.S.A. Forms**

FINANCING STATEMENT- Form 1C
FINANCING CHANGE STATEMENT - Form 2C
MOTOR VEHICLE SCHEDULE - Form 4C

QUANTITY PRICING AVAILABLE UPON REQUEST

◆ **Ontario Business Corporations Act Forms**

Form 1	Articles of Incorporation	} $8.00
Form 2	Consent to act as a first direct	
Form 3	Articles of Amendment	**$8.00**
Form 4	Articles of Amalgamation	**$8.00**
Form 5	Restated Articles of Incorporation	**$8.00**
Form 6	Articles of Continuance	**$8.00**
Form 7	Application for Authorization to continue in another Jurisdiction	**$8.00**
Form 8	Articles of Arrangement	**$8.00**
Form 9	Articles of Reorganization	**$8.00**
Form 10	Articles of Dissolution	} $8.00
Form 11	Articles of Dissolution	
Form 15	Articles of Revival	**$8.00**
Form 16	Notice concerning winding up	**$8.00**

◆ **Canada Business Corporation Act Forms**

Forms 1,3&6	Articles and 2 Notices (12 of each form)	**$13.00** per set
Form 1	Articles of Incorporation	**$8.00/12**
Form 3	Notice of Registered Office	**$8.00/12**
Form 4	Articles of Amendment	**$8.00/12**
Form 6	Notice of Directors	**$8.00/12**
Form 7	Restated Articles of Incorporation	**$8.00/12**
Form 9	Articles of Amalgamation	**$8.00/12**
Form 11	Articles of Continuance	**$8.00/12**
Form 14	Articles of Reorganization	**$8.00/12**
Form 14.1	Articles of Arrangement	**$8.00/12**
Form 15	Articles of Revival	**$8.00/12**
Form 17	Articles of Dissolution	**$8.00/12**
Form 19	Statement of Intent to Dissolve	**$8.00/12**
Form 22	Annual Return	**$8.00/12**
Form 24	Insider Report	**$8.00/12**
Form 27	Application for Exemption	**$8.00/12**

Personal Property Security Act

Ontario Ministry of Consumer and Commercial Relations

Fee Schedule
Effective October 1, 1997

	Registrations	
1.	For registering of a financing statement or financing change statement designated as a renewal under the Personal Property Security Act: · for 1 - 25 years · for a perpetual period	 $8.00 a year $500.00
2.	For a registration of a claim for a lien or change statement designated as a renewal under the Repair and Storage Liens Act: · for 1 - 3 years	 $8.00 per year
3.	For all other registrations (except discharges) (Discharge continues to be "No Charge". However the Administrative fee of $5.00 applies to paper registrations)	$12.00
4.	**Administrative fee for each registration by paper form, over and above the registration fee** *** Fee is per registration and not per page.**	$5.00
	Enquiries	
5.	For verbal/printed response	$8.00
6.	For a certificate response	$8.00
7.	Administrative fee for each staff assisted enquiry over and above the enquiry fee	$2.00
	Branch Office Documents	
	Branch office documents include: · a chattel mortgage registered under the **Bills of Sale and Chattel Mortgage Act:** · a contract registered under the **Conditional Sales Act**; and · an assignment of book debts registered under **The Assignment of Book Debts Act.**	
8.	For production (retrieval) of a branch office document	$1.00
9.	For a copy of a branch office document	$1.00 per page
	Central Office Statements	
	Central Office statements include: - financing statements - claims for liens - financing change statements - change statements	
10.	For the production (retrieval) and copy of a central office statement	$14.00
11.	For a certified copy of a statement (fee includes production and copying)	$15.00
	Corporation Securities Registration Act (CSRA) Registration	
12.	For inspection of a document registered under the CSRA	$12.00
13.	For a copy of a document registered under the CSRA	$1.00 per page
14.	For certification of a copy of a document registered under the CSRA	$23.00

NOTE: PPSR IS REQUIRED TO CHARGE A FEE OF $35.00 FOR ALL CHEQUES RETURNED BY THE BANK AS NON-NEGOTIABLE

10556 ((09/97)

APPENDIX C

ONTARIO BUSINESS CONNECTS SERVICE LOCATIONS

Greater Toronto Area

Aurora — Government Information Centre
Location: Aurora
Address: 50 Bloomington Road West
Aurora, ON L4G 3G8
Phone: (416) 326-1234 or 1-800-267-8097
Fax: (905) 713-6906
Workstation hours: 8:30 a.m. — 3:30 p.m.

Brampton — Government Information Centre
Location: Brampton
Address: 1st floor
7765 Hurontario Street
Brampton, ON L6V 2L8
Phone: (416) 326-1234 or 1-800-267-8097
Fax: (905) 874-4012
Workstation hours: 8:30 a.m. — 4:00 p.m.

Brampton — Brampton Small Business Enterprise Centre
Location: Brampton
Address: 33 Queen Street West
Brampton, ON L6Y 1L9
Phone: (905) 874-2650
Fax: (905) 874-2670
Workstation hours: Monday-Friday, 9:00 a.m. — 3:30 p.m.

Downsview — Government Information Centre
Location: Downsview
Address: Building A
2680 Keele St.
Downsview, ON M3M 3E6
Phone: (416) 326-1234 or 1-800-267-8097
Fax: (416) 235-3777
Workstation hours: 8:30 a.m. — 3:45 p.m.

Hamilton — Ministry of Finance Retail Sales Tax Office
Location: Hamilton
Address: 119 King Street West
Hamilton, ON L8N 3Z9
Phone: (905) 521-7504 or 1-800-263-9229
Fax: (905) 521-7868
Workstation hours: 8:30 a.m. — 3:45 p.m.

Hamilton — Workplace Safety and Insurance Board Office
Location: Hamilton
Address: 120 King Street West
Hamilton, ON L8P 4V2
Phone: (905) 523-1800
Fax: (905) 521-4502
Workstation hours: 8:30 a.m. — 4:00 p.m.

Hamilton — Government Information Centre
Location: Hamilton
Address: 119 King Street West, Lobby
Hamilton, ON L8P 4Y7
Phone: (905) 521-7825
Fax: (905) 521-7851
Workstation hours: 8:30 a.m. — 3:30 p.m.

Maple — Vaughan Business Enterprise Centre
Location: Maple
Address: Beaverbrook House
9995 Keele Street
Maple, ON L6A 1R6
Phone: (905) 417-0412
Fax: (905) 417-0410
Workstation hours: 9:00 a.m. — 3:30 p.m.

Markham — YMCA Markham Business Centre
Location: Markham
Address: 4855 14th Avenue, Unit 3
Markham, ON L3S 3L6
Phone: (905) 948-9622
Fax: (905) 948-8737
Workstation hours: 9:00 a.m. — 4:30 p.m. (Monday — Friday)

Mississauga — Ministry of Finance Employer Health Tax Office
Location: Mississauga
Address: 1290 Central Parkway West
1st Floor
Mississauga, ON L5C 4R3
Phone: (905) 273-9490
Fax: (905) 949-3389
Workstation hours: 8:30 a.m. — 4:00 p.m.

Mississauga — Mississauga Central Library
Location: Mississauga
Address: 301 Burnhamthorpe Road West
Mississauga, ON L5B 3Y3
Phone: (905) 615-3500
Fax: (905) 615-3615
Workstation hours: 9:30 a.m. - 7:00 p.m.

Newmarket - Land Registry Office
Location: Newmarket
Address: 50 Eagle Street West, 1st Floor
Newmarket, ON L3Y 6B1
Phone: (905) 895-1561
Fax: (905) 895-6517

Newmarket — York Simcoe Community Business Access Centre
Location: Newmarket
Address: The Tannery
465 Davis Drive, Suite 103
Newmarket, ON L3Y 4W3
Phone: (905) 898-5844/6322
Fax: (905) 898-7190
Workstation hours: M-F: 8:30 — 3:30

Oakville — Halton Region Business Development Centre
Location: Oakville
Address: 1151 Bronte Road
Oakville, ON L6M 3L1
Phone: (905) 825-6300
Fax: (905) 825-8839
Workstation hours: Monday-Friday 8:30 — 3:30 p.m.

Oshawa — Ministry of Finance Customer Service Centre
Location: Oshawa
Address: 33 King Street West
Oshawa, ON L1H 8H5
Phone: (905) 433-6096 or 1-800-263-7965
Fax: (905) 436-4445
Workstation hours: 8:30 a.m. — 3:30 p.m.

Pickering — Pickering Public Library
Location: Pickering
Address: One, The Esplanade
Pickering, ON L1V 6K7
Phone: (905) 831-6265 ext. 243
Fax: (905) 831-8795
Workstation hours: Monday-Friday 10 a.m. — 7 p.m., Saturday 10 a.m. — 3 p.m., Sunday 1 p.m. — 4 p.m.

Richmond Hill — Richmond Hill Business Centre-Seneca College
Location: Richmond Hill
Address: 24 Wright Street (at Yonge Street)
Richmond Hill, ON L4C 4A1
Phone: (905) 770-5211
Fax: (905) 780-6541
Workstation hours: 9:00 a.m. — 3:00 p.m., Monday — Friday.

Toronto — Government Information Centre
Location: Toronto
Address: Queen's Park-Macdonald Block
900 Bay Street
Main Lobby
Toronto, ON M7A 1N3
Phone: (416) 326-1234
Fax: (416) 325-3407
Workstation hours: 8:30 a.m. — 4:15 p.m.

Toronto — BUSINESS ACCESS (Licensed Wholesaler)
Location: Toronto
Address: 393 University Avenue
Suite 1519
Toronto, ON M5G 1E6
Phone: (416) 595-7177 or toll-free 1-800-688-8208
Fax: (416) 595-1268 or toll-free 1-800-667-3146

Toronto — Companies Branch Public Office
Location: Toronto
Address: 393 University Avenue, 2nd Floor
Toronto, ON M5G 2M2
Phone: (416) 314-9151
Fax: (416) 314-6533
Workstation hours: 8:30 a.m. — 4:00 p.m.

Toronto — Teranet Legal Services Inc. (Licensed Wholesaler)
Location: Toronto
Address: 123 Edward Street, Suite 600
Toronto, ON M5G 1E2
Phone: (416) 348-0432
Fax: (416) 599-5632

Whitby — Land Registry Office
Location: Whitby
Address: 590 Rossland Road East
Whitby, ON L1N 9G5
Phone: (416) 326-1234 or 1-800-267-8097
Fax: (905) 665-5247
Workstation hours: 9:00 a.m. — 3:30 p.m.

Southwestern Ontario

Brantford — Ministry of Finance Employer Health Tax Office
Location: Brantford
Address: 213 King George Road
Brantford, ON N3R 6S8
Phone: (519) 754-4849
Fax: (519) 758-2239
Workstation hours: 8:45 a.m. — 4:00 p.m.

Cambridge — Business Enterprise Centre
Location: Cambridge
Address: 73 Water Street, Main Floor
Cambridge, ON N1R 5W8
Phone: (519) 740-4536 ext. 4615
Fax: (519) 740-4512
Workstation hours: 8:30 a.m. to 3:15 p.m.

Chatham-Kent — Government Information Centre
Location: Chatham
Address: 315 King Street West
Chatham-Kent Civic Centre
Chatham ON N7M 5K8
Phone: (519) 436-3297
Fax: (519) 436-3227
Workstation hours: 8:30 a.m. — 4:30 p.m.

Chatham — Municipality of Chatham-Kent
Location: Chatham
Address: 445 Grand Ave. West
P.O. Box 944,
Chatham ON N7M 5L1
Phone: (519) 351-7700
Fax: (519) 351-7852
Workstation hours: 9:00 a.m. — 4:00 p.m.

Goderich — Land Registry Office
Location: Goderich
Address: 38 North Street
Goderich, ON N7A 2T4
Phone: (519) 524-9562
Fax: (519) 524-2482
Workstation hours: 8:30 a.m. — 4:00 p.m.

Guelph — Guelph Business Enterprise Centre
Location: Guelph
Address: Stone Road Complex
1 Stone Road West, Atrium
Guelph, ON N1G 4Y2
Phone: (519) 826-4701
Fax: (519) 826-4721
Workstation hours: 8:30 a.m. — 3:30 p.m.

Hanover — Saugeen Business Resource Centre
Location: Hanover
Address: 501 9th Avenue
Hanover, ON N4N 2M4
Phone: (519) 364-0419
Fax: (519) 364-0420
Workstation hours: 9 a.m. – 12 noon (Monday to Friday)

Kitchener — Ministry of Finance Retail Sales Tax Office
Location: Kitchener
Address: 305 King Street West
1st Floor
Kitchener, ON N2G 1B9
Phone: (519) 576-8400
Fax: (519) 571-6100
Workstation hours: 8:45 a.m. — 4:00 p.m.

Kitchener — Land Registry Office
Location: Kitchener
Address: 200 Frederick Street, 3rd floor
Kitchener, ON N2H 6N9
Phone: (519) 571-6043
Fax: (519) 571-6073
Workstation hours: 8:30 a.m. — 4:00 p.m.

Kitchener — Business Enterprise Centre and Government Information Centre
Location: Kitchener
Address: 200 King Street West
Main Floor, City Hall
Kitchener, ON N2G 4G7
Phone: (519) 576-6517 or 1-800-837-0877
Fax: (519) 576-6377
Workstation hours: 8:45 a.m. — 3:45 p.m.

London — Government Information Centre
Location: London
Address: 659 Exeter Road
London, ON N6E 1L3
Phone: (519) 873-4000
Fax: (519) 873-4016
Workstation hours: 8:30 a.m. — 4:00 p.m.

London — Regional Tax Office
Location: London
Address: 130 Dufferin Avenue, Main Floor
London, ON N6A 6G8
Phone: (519) 433-3901 or 1-800-265-1540
Fax: (519) 661-6618

Workstation hours: 8:30 a.m. to 4:00 p.m.

Sarnia — Land Registry Office
Location: Sarnia
Address: Court House
700 North Christina Street
Suite 102
Sarnia, ON N7V 3C2
Phone: (519) 337-2393
Fax: (519) 337-8371
Workstation hours: 8:30 a.m. — 4:00 p.m.

Sarnia — Government Information Centre
Location: Sarnia
Address: 150 Christina Street North
Suite 70 & 71
Sarnia, ON N7T 7W5
Phone: (519) 383-7754
Fax: (519) 383-1648
Workstation hours: 8:30 a.m. — 4:00 p.m.

Seaforth — Huron Business Development Corporation
Location: Seaforth
Address: 138 Main St.
Box 1120
Seaforth, ON N0K 1W0
Phone: (519) 527-0305
Fax: (519) 527-2245
Workstation hours: 9:00 a.m. — 4:30 p.m. (Mon., Tues., Thurs., Fri.), 9:00 a.m. — 6:30 p.m. (Wednesdays)

Simcoe — Simcoe and District Chamber of Commerce
Location: Simcoe
Address: 76 Kent Street South
Simcoe, ON N3Y 2Y1
Phone: (519) 426-5867
Fax: (519) 428-7718
Workstation hours: 8:30 a.m. — 4:00 p.m.

Simcoe — Government Information Centre
Location: Simcoe
Address: 40 Colborne Street South
Simcoe, ON N3Y 4H3
Phone: (519) 426-6655
Fax: (519) 428-0787
Workstation hours: Mon.-Wed. 9:00 a.m. — 4:30 p.m., Thurs.-Friday 9:00 a.m. — 5:30 p.m., Sat. 9:00 a.m. — 3:30 p.m.

Stratford — Government Information Centre
Location: Stratford
Address: 581 Huron Street
Stratford, ON N5A 5T8
Phone: (519) 271-9995
Fax: (519) 271-1007
Workstation hours: 8:30 a.m. — 4:30 p.m.

St. Catharines — Land Registry Office
Location: St. Catharines
Address: 59 Church Street
St. Catharines, ON L2R 3C3
Phone: (905) 684-6351
Fax: (905) 684-5874
Workstation hours: 8:30 a.m. — 4:00 p.m.

St. Catharines — Government Information Centre
Location: St. Catharines
Address: 301 St. Paul Street
Ground Floor
St. Catharines, ON L2R 7R4
Phone: (905) 704-2111
Fax: (905) 704-2003
Workstation hours: 8:00 a.m. — 3:30 p.m.

St. Catharines — St. Catharines/Niagara Business Self-Help Office
Location: St. Catharines
Address: 50 Church Street, 2nd floor
P.O. Box 3012
St. Catharines, ON L2R 7C2
Phone: (905) 688-5601, ext. 1761
Workstation hours: 8:30 a.m. — 3:30 p.m.

Welland — Land Registry Office
Location: Welland
Address: 200 Division Street
Welland, ON L3B 4A2
Phone: (905) 735-4011
Fax: (905) 735-2430
Workstation hours: 8:30 a.m. — 4:00 p.m.

Windsor — Windsor District Tax Office
Location: Windsor
Address: 215 Eugenie Street West
Windsor, ON N8X 2X7
Phone: (519) 250-0066 or 1-800-465-4021
Fax: (519) 972-2950
Workstation hours: 8:30 a.m. — 4:30 p.m.

Windsor — Government Information Centre
Location: Windsor
Address: Dorwin Plaza
2445 Dougall Avenue
Windsor, ON N8X 1T3
Phone: (519) 972-5546
Fax: (519) 972-0067
Workstation hours: 8:30 a.m. — 3:30 p.m.

Northern Ontario

Atikokan — Government Information Centre
Location: Atikokan
Address: 108 Saturn Avenue, Box 940
Atikokan, ON P0T 1C0
Phone: (807) 597-2701
Fax: (807) 597-6185
Workstation hours: 8:30 a.m. — 4:30 p.m.

Blind River — Government Information Centre
Location: Blind River
Address: 62 Queen Avenue
P.O. Box 760
Blind River, ON P0R 1B0
Phone: (705) 356-2226
Fax: (705) 356-7441
Workstation hours: 8:30 a.m. — 5:00 p.m.

Bracebridge — Land Registry Office
Location: Bracebridge
Address: 15 Dominion Street North
Bracebridge, ON P1L 2E7
Phone: (705) 645-4415
Fax: (705) 645-7826
Workstation hours: 8:30 a.m. — 4:15 p.m.

Chapleau — Government Information Centre
Location: Chapleau
Address: 190 Cherry St., Box 488
Chapleau, ON P0M 1K0
Phone: (705) 864-1515
Fax: (705) 864-0681
Workstation hours: 8:30 a.m. — 4:30 p.m.

Cochrane — Government Information Centre
Location: Cochrane
Address: 2 Third Avenue
Cochrane, ON P0L 1C0
Phone: (705) 272-4274
Fax: (705) 272-3489
Workstation hours: 8:30 a.m. — 4:30 p.m.

Dryden — Government Information Centre
Location: Dryden
Address: 479 Government Rd, Box 3000
Dryden, ON P8N 3B3
Phone: (807) 223-8500
Fax: (807) 223-8502
Workstation hours: 8:30 a.m. — 4:30 p.m.

Elliot Lake — Government Information Centre
Location: Elliot Lake
Address: 50 Hillside Drive North
Elliot Lake, ON P5A 1X4
Phone: (705) 848-7133
Fax: (705) 848-2408
Workstation hours: 8:30 a.m. — 4:30 p.m.

Espanola — Government Information Centre
Location: Espanola
Address: Ontario Government Building
148 Fleming Street
Espanola, ON P5E 1R8
Phone: (705) 869-1330
Fax: (705) 869-5602
Workstation hours: 8:30 a.m. — 3:30 p.m.

Fort Frances — Government Information Centre
Location: Fort Frances
Address: 922 Scott Street
Fort Frances, ON P9A 1J4
Phone: (807) 274-5329 or (807) 274-5337
Workstation hours: 8:30 a.m. — 4:30 p.m.

Geraldton — Government Information Centre
Location: Geraldton
Address: 208 Beamish Ave. West
P.O. Box 640
Geraldton, ON P0T 1M0
Phone: (807) 854-0266
Fax: (807) 854-0335
Workstation hours: 8:30 a.m. — 4:30 p.m.

Gore Bay — Government Information Centre
Location: Gore Bay
Address: 35 Meredith St.
P.O. Box 9
Gore Bay, ON P0P 1H0
Phone: (705) 282-2043
Fax: (705) 282-2792
Workstation hours: 8:30 a.m. — 4:30 p.m.

Haileybury — Land Registry Office
Location: Haileybury
Address: 375 Main Street
Haileybury, ON P0J 1K0
Phone: (705) 672-3332
Fax: (705) 672-3906
Workstation hours: 8:30 a.m. — 4:00 p.m.

Hearst — Government Information Centre
Location: Hearst
Address: 613 Front St., Box 1688
Hearst, ON P0L 1N0
Phone: (705) 362-4358
Fax: (705) 362-7011
Workstation hours: 8:30 a.m. — 4:30 p.m.

Huntsville — Muskoka Business Self-help Office
Location: Huntsville
Address: 37 Main Street East 2nd floor
Huntsville, ON P1H 1A1
Phone: (705) 789-6693
Fax: (705) 789-6689
Workstation hours: 9:00 a.m. — 4:00 p.m.

Huntsville — Government Information Centre
Location: Huntsville
Address: 207 Main Street West
Huntsville, ON P1H 1Z9
Phone: (705) 789-4616
Fax: (705) 789-9533
Workstation hours: 8:30 a.m. — 4:00 p.m.

Ignace — Government Information Centre
Location: Ignace
Address: Hwy. 599 at Hwy. 17

Ignace, ON P0T 1T0
Phone: (807) 934-2260
Fax: (807) 934-2304
Workstation hours: 8:30 a.m. — 4:30 p.m.

Kapuskasing — Government Information Centre
Location: Kapuskasing
Address: Hwy. 11 West
Ontario Government Building
Kapuskasing, ON P5N 2X8
Phone: (705) 335-6008
Fax: (705) 335-8765
Workstation hours: 8:30 a.m. — 5:00 p.m.

Kenora — Land Registry Office
Location: Kenora
Address: 220 Main Street South
Kenora, ON P9N 3X7
Phone: (807) 468-2794
Fax: (807) 468-2796
Workstation hours: 8:30 a.m. — 4:00 p.m.

Kenora — Government Information Centre
Location: Kenora
Address: 810 Robertson Street, Suite 104
Kenora, ON P9N 4J2
Phone: (807) 468-2803
Fax: (807) 468-2941
Workstation hours: 8:30 a.m. — 4:30 p.m.

Kirkland Lake — Government Information Centre
Location: Kirkland Lake
Address: 10 Government Road East,
Box 100
Kirkland Lake, ON P2N 3M6
Phone: (705) 568-4550
Fax: (705) 568-4515
Workstation hours: 8:30 a.m. — 4:30 p.m.

Marathon — Government Information Centre
Location: Marathon
Address: 52 Peninsula Road, Centre Block, Suite 105, Box 280
Marathon, ON P0T 2E0
Phone: (807) 229-1153
Fax: (807) 229-1592
Workstation hours: 8:30 a.m. — 4:30 p.m.

Moose Factory — Wakenagun Community Futures Development Corporation
Location: Moose Factory
Address: PO Box 308
Moose Factory, ON 0L 1W0
Phone: (705) 658-4428
Fax: (705) 658-4672

Moosonee — Government Information Centre
Location: Moosonee
Address: Ontario Government Building
Revillon Road North
Moosonee, ON P0L 1Y0
Phone: (705) 336-2987
Fax: (705) 336-2983
Workstation hours: 8:30 a.m. — 4:30 p.m.

New Liskeard — Government Information Centre
Location: New Liskeard
Address: 280 Armstrong Street
New Liskeard, ON P0J 1P0
Phone: (705) 647-7391
Fax: (705) 647-7993
Workstation hours: 8:30 a.m. — 4:30 p.m.

Nipigon — Government Information Centre
Location: Nipigon
Address: 5 Wadsworth Drive
Nipigon, ON P0T 2J0
Phone: (807) 887-3230
Fax: (807) 887-2993
Workstation hours: 8:30 a.m. — 5:00 p.m.

North Bay — Business Self-help Office
Location: North Bay
Address: 200 McIntyre Street East
North Bay, ON P1B 8H8
Phone: (705) 474-0400 x425
Fax: (705) 474-4493
Workstation hours: 8:30 a.m. — 4:00 p.m.

North Bay — Government Information Centre
Location: North Bay
Address: 447 McKeown Avenue
North Bay, ON P1B 9S9
Phone: (705) 497-6822
Fax: (705) 497-5544
Workstation hours: 8:30 a.m. — 4:00 p.m.

Parry Sound — Government Information Centre
Location: Parry Sound
Address: Ontario Government Building
7 Bay Street
Parry Sound, ON P2A 1S4
Phone: (705) 773-4216
Fax: (705) 746-8828
Workstation hours: 8:30 a.m. — 4:00 p.m.

Red Lake — Government Information Centre
Location: Red Lake
Address: 227 Howey Street
Red Lake, ON P0V 2M0
Phone: (807) 727-2870
Fax: (807) 727-2861
Workstation hours: 8:30 a.m. — 5:00 p.m.

Sault Ste. Marie — Land Registry Office
Location: Sault Ste. Marie
Address: 420 Queen Street East

Sault Ste. Marie, ON P6A 5M8
Phone: (705) 253-8887
Fax: (705) 253-9245
Workstation hours: 8:30 a.m. — 4:00 p.m.

Sault Ste. Marie — Community Development Corporation
Location: Sault Ste. Marie
Address: 672 Queen Street East
Sault Ste. Marie, ON P6A 2A4
Phone: (705) 942-9000
Fax: (705) 942-0274
Workstation hours: 8:30 a.m. — 4:30 p.m.

Sault Ste. Marie — Government Information Centre
Location: Sault Ste. Marie
Address: 70 Foster Drive, Main Lobby
Sault Ste. Marie, ON P6A 6V4
Phone: (705) 945-5877
Fax: (705) 945-5958
Workstation hours: 9:00 a.m. — 4:30 p.m.

Sioux Lookout — Government Information Centre
Location: Sioux Lookout
Address: 62 Queen Street
Sioux Lookout, ON P8T 1A2
Phone: (807) 737-1318
Fax: (807) 737-3419
Workstation hours: 8:30 a.m. — 4:30 p.m.

South Porcupine — Government Information Centre
Location: South Porcupine
Address: Ontario Government Complex
P.O. Bag 3060, Hwy 101 East
South Porcupine, ON P0N 1H0
Phone: (705) 235-1667
Fax: (705) 235-1668
Workstation hours: 8:30 a.m. — 5:00 p.m.

Sturgeon Falls — Economic Partners — Sudbury East/ West Nippising Inc.
Location: Sturgeon Falls
Address: 30 Front Street, Highway 17 East
Sturgeon Falls, ON P0H 2G0
Phone: (705) 753-5450 X 229
Fax: (705) 753-3456
Workstation hours: 8:30 a.m. — 4:00 p.m.

Sudbury — Land Registry Office
Location: Sudbury
Address: 199 Larch Street Suite 301
Sudbury, ON P3E 5P9
Phone: (705) 564-4300
Fax: (705) 564-4148
Workstation hours: 8:30 a.m. — 4:00 p.m.

Sudbury — Sudbury Regional Business Centre
Location: Sudbury
Address: 200 Brady Street
Tom Davies Square
Sudbury, ON P3E 5K3
Phone: (705) 673-4161
Fax: (705) 673-7722
Workstation hours: 8:30 a.m. — 4:15 p.m.

Sudbury — Government Information Centre
Location: Sudbury
Address: 199 Larch St., Suite 103
Sudbury, ON P3E 5P9
Phone: (705) 564-0060
Fax: (705) 564-0063
Workstation hours: 9:00 a.m. — 4:30 p.m.

Thessalon — Community Development Centre for East Algoma
Location: Thessalon
Address: 199 Main Street
Thessalon, ON P0R 1L0
Phone: (705) 842-3605
Fax: (705) 842-3742

Thunder Bay — Ministry of Finance Employer Health Tax Office
Location: Thunder Bay
Address: 130 South Syndicate
Thunder Bay, ON P7E 1C7
Phone: (807) 625-5840
Fax (807) 625-5848
Workstation hours: 8:15 a.m. — 4:30 p.m.

Thunder Bay — Land Registry Office
Location: Thunder Bay
Address: 189 Red River Road Suite 201
Thunder Bay, ON P7B 1A2
Phone: (807) 343-7436
Fax: (807) 343-7439
Workstation hours: 8:30 a.m. — 4:00 p.m.

Thunder Bay — Government Information Centre
Location: Thunder Bay
Address: 435 South James Street
Suite 114
Thunder Bay, ON P7E 6S7
Phone: (807) 475-1425
Fax: (807) 475-1763
Workstation hours: 9:00 a.m. — 4:00 p.m.

Timmins — Business Self-help Office
Location: Timmins
Address: 54 Spruce Street South
Timmins, ON P4N 2M5
Phone: (705) 360-8484
Fax: (705) 360-1394
Workstation hours: 8:30 a.m. — 4:15 p.m.

Wawa — Government Information Centre
Location: Wawa
Address: Highway 101

Wawa, ON P0S 1K0
Phone: (705) 856-2354
Fax: (705) 856-7511
Workstation hours: 8:00 a.m. — 4:30 p.m.

Central Ontario

Alliston — Nottawasaga Community Economic Development Corporation
Location: Alliston
Address: 233 Church Street South
P.O. Box 184
Alliston, ON L9R 1V5
Phone: (705) 435-1540
Fax: (705) 435-6907
Workstation hours: 9:00 a.m. — 3:30 p.m.

Barrie — Land Registry Office
Location: Barrie
Address: Court House
114 Worsley Street
Barrie, ON L4M 1M1
Phone: (705) 725-7232
Fax: (705) 725-7246
Workstation hours: 8:30 a.m. — 4:00 p.m.

Barrie — Government Information Centre
Location: Barrie
Address: 34 Simcoe Street
Barrie, ON L4N 6T4
Phone: (705) 737-0823
Fax: (705) 737-5722
Workstation hours: 8:30 a.m. — 3:30 p.m.

Caledon Chamber of Commerce
Location: Bolton
Address: 33 King Street West
Bolton, ON L7E 5T5
Phone: (905) 857-7393
Fax: (905) 857-7405
Workstation hours: 8:30 a.m. — 5:00 p.m.

Caledon Public Library
Location: Bolton
Address: 150 Queen St. South
Bolton, ON L7E 1E3
Phone: (905) 857-1400
Fax: (905) 857-8280
Workstation hours:
Tues., Wed. & Thurs.: 10:00 a.m. -8:00 p.m.
Friday: 10:00 a.m. — 4:30 p.m.
Saturday: 10:00 a.m.–3:30 p.m.
Sunday: 12:00 p.m.–3:30 p.m.

Cobourg — Northumberland Business Self-Help Office
Location: Cobourg
Address: Dressler House
212 King Street West
Cobourg, ON K9A 2N1
Phone: (905) 372-9279
Fax: (905) 372-1306
Workstation hours: 9:00 a.m. to 4:15 p.m.

Collingwood — Georgian Triangle Economic Development Corporation
Location: Collingwood
Address: 450 Hume St., Unit 2
Collingwood, ON L9Y 1W6
Phone: (705) 445-8410
Fax: (705) 444-6082
Workstation hours: 8:30 a.m. — 4:30 p.m.

Keswick — Georgina Job Skills
Location: Keswick
Address: 155 Riverglen Drive, Unit 7
Keswick, ON L4P 3M3
Phone: (905) 476-8088
Fax: (905) 476-5988
Workstation hours: 9:00 a.m. — 3:30 p.m.

Lindsay — Government Information Centre
Location: Lindsay
Address: 322 Kent Street West
Lindsay, ON K9V 4T7
Phone: (705) 324-3849 or 1-877-994-9928 (within area codes 705 and 905 only)
Fax: (705) 324-8440
Workstation hours: 8:30 a.m. — 3:30 p.m.

Midhurst — Midhurst Government Complex
Location: Midhurst
Address: 2284 Nursery Road
Midhurst, ON L0L 1X0
Phone: (705) 725-7500
Fax: (705) 725-7584
Workstation hours: 8:30 a.m. — 3:30 p.m.

Minden — Government Information Centre
Location: Minden
Address: Highway 35, Bypass
PO Box 820
Minden, ON K0M 2K0
Phone: (705) 286-1521
Fax: (705) 286-4355
Workstation hours: 8:30 a.m. — 3:30 p.m.

Orangeville — Orangeville Land Registry Office
Location: Orangeville
Address: 10 Louisa St.
Orangeville, ON L9W 3P9
Phone: (519) 941-1481
Fax: (519) 941-6444
Workstation hours: 8:30 a.m. — 3:30 p.m.

Orillia — Community Development Corporation
Location: Orillia
Address: 6 West Street, North
Orillia, ON L3V 5A7
Phone: (705) 325-4903
Fax: (705) 325-6817
Workstation hours: 8:30 a.m. — 4:30 p.m.

Owen Sound — Land Registry Office
Location: Owen Sound
Address: 1555 Sixteenth Street East
Units 1&2
Owen Sound, ON N4K 5N3
Phone: (519) 376-1637, Fax (519) 376-1639
Workstation hours: 8:30 a.m. — 4:00 p.m.

Peterborough — Land Registry Office
Location: Peterborough
Address: 2nd floor
South Tower
300 Water Street
Peterborough, ON K9J 8M5
Phone: (705) 755-1342
Fax: (705) 755-1343
Workstation hours: 8:30 a.m. — 4:15 p.m.

Port Elgin — Saugeen Shores & Area Small Business Self-Help Office
Location: Port Elgin
Address: 600 Tomlinson Drive
Port Elgin, ON N0H 2C0
Phone: (519) 832-2008
Fax: (519) 832-2140
Workstation available from 9:30 a.m. to 3:00 p.m.

Walkerton — Walkerton Land Registry Office
Location: Walkerton
Address: 203 Cayley Street
Walkerton, ON N0G 2V0
Phone: (519) 881-2259
Workstation hours: 9:00 a.m. — 3:30 p.m.

Eastern Ontario

Almonte — Land Registry Office
Location: Almonte
Address: 2 Industrial Drive
Almonte ON K0A 1A0
Phone: (613) 256-1577
Fax: (613) 256-0940
Workstation hours: 8:30 a.m. — 4:00 p.m.

Bancroft — Government Information Centre
Location: Bancroft
Address: Bancroft District Office
Ministry of Transportation
50 Monck Street
Bancroft, ON K0L 1C0
Phone: (613) 332-5573
Fax: (613) 332-4027
Workstation hours: 8:30 a.m. — 4:15 p.m.

Belleville — Government Information Centre
Location: Belleville
Address: 15 Victoria Avenue, 2nd Floor
Belleville, ON K8N 1Z5
Phone: (613) 968-3769
Fax: (613) 968-3606
Workstation hours: 8:30 a.m. — 4:00 p.m.

Brockville — Land Registry Office
Location: Brockville
Address: 7 King Street West
Market Street Entrance
Brockville, ON K6V 3P7
Phone: (613) 345-5751
Fax: (613) 345-7390
Workstation hours: 8:30 a.m. — 4:00 p.m.

Cornwall – Land Registry Office
Location: Cornwall
Address: 127 Sydney Street
Cornwall, ON K6H 3H1
Phone: (613) 932-4522
Fax: (613) 932-4524
Workstation hours: 8:30 a.m. — 4:00 p.m.

Gloucester – Regional Tax Office Ottawa-Carleton
Location: Gloucester
Address: 1400 Blair Place, 3rd Floor
Gloucester, ON K1J 9B8
Phone: (613) 746-9200
Fax: (613) 842-3593
Workstation hours: 8:30 a.m. to 4:15 p.m.

Hawkesbury — Government Information Centre
Location: Hawkesbury
Address: 692 Main Street East
Hawkesbury, ON K6A 1B4
Phone: (613) 632-2192
Fax: (613) 632-6805
Workstation hours: 8:30 a.m. — 5:00 p.m.

Kingston — Government Information Centre
Location: Kingston
Address: Beechgrove Complex
51 Heakes Lane
Kingston, ON K7M 9B1
Phone: (613) 536-7372
Fax: (613) 531-5730
Workstation hours: 8:30 a.m. — 4:00 p.m.

Nepean — Public Library
Location: Nepean
Address: Nepean Civic Square
101 Centrepointe Drive
Nepean, ON K2G 5K7
Phone: (613) 727-6660
Fax: (613) 727-6677
Workstation hours: Monday-Thursday 10:00 a.m. -7:30 p.m., Friday 10:00 a.m. — 3:00 p.m.

Ottawa — The Entrepreneurship Centre
Location: Ottawa
Address: 110 Laurier Avenue West
Main Floor

Ottawa, ON K1P 1J1
Phone: (613) 560-6081
Fax: (613) 560-2102
Workstation hours: M,T, Thu, Fri 8:30 a.m. — 4:00 p.m., W 8:30 a.m. — 6:00 p.m.

Ottawa — YMCA-YWCA of Ottawa Enterprise Centre
Location: Ottawa
Address: 180 Argyle Street
4th floor
Ottawa, ON K2P 1B7
Phone: (613) 788-5001
Fax: (613) 788-5051
Workstation hours: 8:30 a.m. — 3:00 p.m.

Ottawa — Access Ontario
Location: Ottawa
Address: 161 Elgin Street
Ottawa, ON K2P 2K1
Phone: (613) 238-3630
Fax: (613) 566-2234
Workstation hours: 8:00 a.m. — 4:15 p.m.

Pembroke — Land Registry Office
Location: Pembroke
Address: 400 Pembroke Street East
Pembroke, ON K8A 3K8
Phone: (613) 732-8331
Fax: (613) 732-0297
Workstation hours: 9:00 a.m. — 4:00 p.m.

Pembroke — Government Information Centre
Location: Pembroke
Address: 31 Riverside Drive
Pembroke, ON K8A 6X4
Phone: (613) 732-3661
Fax: (613) 732-6998
Workstation hours: 9:00 a.m. — 3:30 p.m.

Renfrew — Government Information Centre
Location: Renfrew
Address: 315 Raglan Street South
Renfrew, ON K7V 1R6
Phone: (613) 432-4841
Fax: (613) 432-5260
Workstation hours: 8:30 a.m. — 4:00 p.m., Monday-Friday.

INDEX

Accountant, 134, 136, 167 *See also* **Auditor**
report to accountant, 169-170

Annual meetings *See also* **Auditor**
federal corporations, 297-299
notices and matters considered, 298-299
requirements, 297-298
financial statements, 196
minutes and resolutions, 189-192
annual meeting of shareholders, 190-191, Forms 10.2-10.4
preliminary directors' meetings, 189-190, Form 10.1
adjourned/reconvened, 191-192, Form 10.5
requirements, 185-189
conduct of meeting, 186-187
financial statements, 186, 196
minutes or resolutions, 188-189
notice of meetings, 185-186
place of meetings, 187
proxy, 187-188
record date, 186-187
single shareholder corporation, 185
special business, 188
voting rights, 187
sole director/multiple shareholder resolutions, 193, Forms 10.6-10.9
sole director/sole shareholder resolutions, 192

Annual return *See also* **Corporate tax**
combined annual and corporate tax returns, 81, 152, 153, 157, 205, Form 6.19
extra-provincial foreign business corporation (Schedule K), 81, 152, 153, 155, 205
Ontario corporation (Schedule A), 81, 152, 153, 154, 205
corporate records, part of, 153-154
Corporations Information Act, 81, 150-155
electronic filing, 152, 153
electronic or preprinted version, 81
federal corporations, 301-302
requirements, 301-302
combined annual and tax return, 301-302, Form 18.2
Notice of Change of Directors (Sch. 81), 301, Form 18.3
Notice of Change of Registered Office (Sch. 80), Form 18.2
separate annual return, 301, Form 18.1
Standard Industrial Classification Code (S.I.C.C.)
exemption from corporate tax return, 81, 153
generally, 152-153, 167-168
separate annual return, 81, 152, Form 6.17

Articles of amendment *See also* **Special resolution**
certificate of amendment, 183
federal corporations, 295-296
filing, 296
fundamental changes, 181-184, 295-296
change of name, 181, 183
other changes, 182
generally, 99
insolvent corporation, 181-182
introduction, 181
registered office, 183
relocation to different municipality, 99, 183
sample, 183, Form 9.1

Articles of incorporation *See also* **Incorporation process**
federal corporation, Form 14.1 *see also* **Federal corporations**
completion of forms, 272-279, Form 9.1

authorized capital, 273-274
borrowing power, 277
cumulative voting for directors, 277
number of directors, 276
ordinary resolution, 277
other provisions, 278
pre-emptive rights, 275, 277-278
private restrictions, 278
Quebec, carrying on business in, 277
registered office, 272-273
restrictions on share transfers, 275-276
restrictions on type of business, 276
format of documents, 270-272
incorporators, 278-279
Ontario corporation
authorized capital, 98, 101-102
minimum statutory rights, 102
no par value, 98
borrowing powers, 97-98
cancellation for sufficient cause, 184
directors
first directors, 99-100
consent to act as first director, 100
"resident Canadian", majority, 100
number of, 99
drafting generally, 97-98, Form 5.1
filing, 110
name of corporation, 98-99
names and addresses of incorporators, 109
miscellaneous provisions, 95-97
meetings of shareholders, 96, 108
private restrictions, 95, 105-106
purchase or redemption of shares, 96
Quebec, carrying on business in, 95, 98, 106-108
other provisions, 108-109
subject matter of by-law, 108-109
private restrictions, 95, 105-106
registered office, address of, 99, 131, 165-166
relocation to different municipality, 99, 183
relocation within municipality, 99, 183
special resolution, 99, 183
restrictions on business carried on, 100-101
shares, rights and restrictions attaching to, 102-106
dividends, 102-103
special or preference shares, 103-105
voting or non-voting, 103
signed in duplicate, 109

Auditor *See also* **Organization of corporation**, organizational resolutions
annual audit/auditors' report, 134-135, 195
appointment of auditor or accountant, 134, 167, 194
notice of appointment, 194
financial statements, 196
removal of auditor, 194
representations to corporation, 194
report of auditor to shareholders, 135, 195
amending, 195-196
GAAP principles, 135, 196
report to auditor or accountant, 169-170
right to attend meetings, 195
vacancy, 194
waiver of audit
consent of all shareholders, 134, 193
exemptions, 193
generally, 176-177
persons disqualified as auditors, 134, 195

***Bank Act* searches**, 236-239 *See also* **Searches**

Banking resolution, 131, 146-147 *See also* **Organization of corporation**, corporate bank account

Bankruptcy search, 239-244 *See also* **Searches**

Business Identifier Number (BIN)
federal-provincial business registration, 29
general partnership, 16
limited partnership, 18
sole proprietorship, 6, 7

***Business Names Act* registration**
extra-provincial corporation, 202
partnership

additional business name, 15-16
amended registration, 16
Form 1, 15, 16
more than 10 partners, 15, 16
designated partner, 15, 16
10 or fewer partners, 15, 16
power of attorney, 16
dissolution or withdrawal, 16-17
sole proprietorship, 3, 4
cancellation, 7-8
Form 1, 3-4, 5
further filings, 5
Master Business Licence (MBL), 5-6
Ontario Business Registration Application, 4
renewal, 5
restrictions respecting names, 4-5

Business Number (BN)
CCRA programs, 26, 29

Business registration on-line (BRO), 28-29

By-laws, 123-129 *See also* **Organization of corporation**

Canada Customs and Revenue Agency (CCRA), 26, 28-29, 158, 301-302

Contracts *See* **Corporate powers**

Corporate powers
contracts, 84-90
elements of contracts, 84-85
consideration, 84
competent parties, 85
consent, genuine, 85
legal purpose, 85
offer and acceptance, 84
types of contracts, 85-90
contracts in writing not under seal, 87-88
contracts in writing under seal, 85-87
Statute of Frauds, 86, 87
parol contract, 88
power of attorney, 88
pre-incorporation contracts, 88-90
general, 81-82
loans to shareholders, directors, etc., 54-55, 82-84
disclosure not required, 54, 83
disclosure requirements, 54-55, 82-83
extent of disclosure, 83-84
outside powers, acting, 82
power to act outside Ontario, 82
Quebec, carrying on business in, 95
restrictions on powers, 100-101

Corporate records, 115-118, 151 *See also* **Organization of corporation**

Corporate seal, 118-119, 126, 130-131, 149-150 *See also* **Organization of corporation**

Corporate tax
account number, 158, 161
combined annual and corporate tax returns, 152, 153, 157, 161, Form 6.19
extra-provincial foreign business corporation (Schedule K), 152, 153, 155
Ontario corporation (Schedule A), 152, 153, 154
default in complying, 158
notice of dissolution, 158
revival of corporation, 158
destruction of books and records, 158-161
conditions, 159-160
written permission for early disposal, 160
electronic filing, 152, 153
exemption from filing corporate tax return, 153, 156-158, 160, 168
requirements to be met, 156-157
federal T2 income tax return, 158, 301-301, Form 18.2
Notice of Change of Directors, 301, Form 18.3
Notice of Change of Registered Office, 301, Form 18.2
financial year end, 157
"permanent establishment" in Ontario, 155-156
status of filing returns, 161, 168

Corporations generally
advantages of incorporation, 33-34
federal incorporation, 34
Business Corporations Act (BCA), 33, 34
Canada Business Corporations Act (CBCA), 33
extra-provincial corporation, 34
fundamental concepts, 32-33
historical origins of corporations, 31-32
introduction, 31
"offering" and "non-offering" corporations, 34-35
private restrictions, 35

Corporations Information Act (CIA) See also **Corporate tax**
annual return, 81, 152-158
combined annual and corporate tax returns, 152, 153, Form 6.19
extra-provincial foreign business corporation (Schedule K), 152, 153, 155, 205
Ontario corporation (Schedule A), 152, 153, 154, 205
corporate records, part of, 153-154
electronic filing, 152, 153
exemption from corporate tax return, 153
generally, 152-153
separate annual return, 152, Form 6.17
corporate records, part of, 151, 153-154
director information, 154-155
default in filings, 184
cancellation of certificate of incorporation, 184
initial notice, 81
initial return, 150, 151-152, Form 6.15
extra-provincial corporations, 198, 205-206
Schedule A, 152, Form 6.16
notice of change, 43, 81, 99, 150, 151-152, 211
officer information, 155
sanctions for non-compliance, 151

Directors
annual returns
director information, 154-155
board of directors, 39-40
minimum number, 40
"resident Canadian", 40, 43-44
committee of directors, 50-51, 60, 116
limits on authority, 50-51
conduct of business, 50
consent of director at meeting, 57, 137-138
consent to appointment, 44, 100
cumulative voting for directors, 44-46
examples, 45-46
disclosure by director of interest in contracts, 51-53, 287
confirmation by shareholders, 52-53
contract falling within "ordinary course of business", 52
first meeting after director interested in contract, 51-52
general notice of interest, 52, 53
material interest, 51
refrain from voting, 52
setting aside contract, 53
dissent, notification of, 137-138
duties, 50
election of directors, 44
federal corporations, 283-287
notice of change of directors, 280
notice of directors, 279-280, 284
first directors, 40-41, 99-100
consent to act as first director, 100, 110, 137
term of office, 40-41
vacancy, 41
whether quorum, 41, 47
introduction, 39, 59
liability of directors, 53-56
commission contrary to s. 37, 55
compelling repayment, 56
contribution from other directors, 56
dividend payment contrary to s. 38, 55-56
financial assistance
contrary to s. 20, 54, 84
disclosure not required, 54, 83
disclosure requirements, 54-55, 82-83
extent of disclosure, 83-84
indemnity payment contrary to s. 136, 56
issuance of shares, 53

limitation of liability, 57-58
payment to shareholder, 56
purchase or redemption of shares, 55
wages, for, 57
managing director, 50-51, 60, 116
limits on authority, 50-51
meetings
calling meetings, 49
notice, 49-50
definition of "day", 50
place of, 48-49
telephone or other communication facilities, by, 49
number of directors
increasing or decreasing, 41-43
articles of amendment, 41, 42
directors resolution, 42, 48
fixed number, 42-43
minimum to maximum number, 42, 43
special resolution, 42, 47-48
delegation to directors, 42, 48
filing certified copy, 42
minimum number, 40
notice of change, 43
qualifications of directors, 43-44, 137, 284
individual, 43
minimum age, 43
not disqualified, 43
"resident Canadian", majority, 43-44, 100
deemed "resident Canadian", 43-44
quorum of directors, 46-47
vacancy, 41, 47
special meeting where no quorum, 41, 47, 48
removal of directors, 58
ordinary resolution, 58
special resolution, 58
unanimous shareholders agreement, 60, 61, 178-179
restriction on powers, 60, 61, 178-179
vacancies, 41, 47-48
minimum to maximum number of directors, 47-48
right of remaining directors to fill vacancy, 48
right of shareholders to elect director(s), 48
special meeting where no quorum, 41, 47, 48

Dividends *See also* **Shares**
cumulative, 91-92, 102-103
fixed, preferential cash, 102-103
non-cumulative, 92, 103
partially cumulative, 92

Electronic Corporate Index (ECI), 67-68, 79

Extra-provincial corporations
annual returns
combined annual and corporate tax returns, 81, 152, 153, 157, 161, 205, Form 6.19
Class 1 and 2 corporations (Schedule A), 205
extra-provincial foreign business corporation (Schedule K), 152, 153, 155, 205
Extra-Provincial Corporations Act, 81, 152, 155, 197
certificates, 204-205
classes of extra-provincial corporations, 197-200
foreign corporations, 198
agent for service, 198
appointment of agent for service, 198, Form 11.2
carrying on business in Ontario, whether, 200
licence, 198, Form 11.1
application for amended licence, 198-199, Form 11.3
application for termination of licence, 199, Form 11.4
cancellation of licence, 199
certificates, 204-205
not required for corporations of other provinces, 199
generally, 197-198
initial return, 198
power to hold land, 199
other provincial or Canada corporations, 199

forms on internet, 71, 204
initial return, 198, 205-206
licence applications, Class 3, 198-199, 202-204
  application for amended licence, 198-199, 202, 203-204, Form 11.3
  application for extra-provincial licence, 198, 202-203, Form 11.1
  application for termination of licence, 199, 202, 204, Form 11.4
  appointment of agent for service, 203
  cancellation of licence, 199
  not required for corporations of other provinces, 199
  signatures on documents, 204
name clearance, 200-202
  foreign corporations (Class 3)
    name other than corporate name, 201-202
      business name registration, 202
      licenced only with corporate name, 201-202
    NUANS search report, 201
    refusal of licence, 201
    generally, 200-201
notice of change, 205
power of attorney, 88

Extra-provincial limited liability partnership, 25 *See also* **Limited liability partnership (LLP)**

Extra-provincial limited partnership, 21-22 *See also* **Limited partnerships**

Federal corporations
advantages of federal incorporations, 268-270
Canada Business Corporations Act
  generally, 267
  objectives, 268
corporate searches, 219-222
directors liability, 269-270
directors and officers, 283-287
  notice of directors, 279-280, 284, 301, Forms 14.3, 18.3
  qualifications, 284
electronic filing centre, 282-283
filing of documents, 280-282
glossary of terms, 253-255
incorporation process, 255-265, 270-283
  articles of incorporation, 270-279, Form 14.1
    completion of forms, 272-279
      authorized capital, 273-274
      borrowing power, 277
      cumulative voting for directors, 277
      number of directors, 276
      ordinary resolution, 277
      other provisions, 278
      pre-emptive rights, 275, 277-278
      private restrictions, 278
      Quebec, carrying on business in, 277
      registered office, 272-273
      restrictions on share transfers, 275-276
      restrictions on type of business, 276
        format of documents, 270-272
    incorporators, 278-279
  name and NUANS search, 255-258
    information added to database on continuing basis, 256-257
    key to reading computer printout, 258-259
    name clearance, 259-265
      change of name, directing, 265
      designating number, 264-265
      prohibited names, 261-264, 265
      regulatory requirements, 259-265
      reserving name, 264
      statutory requirements, 259
    Name Granting Compendium, 255, Form 13.1
    search houses, 257
    search report, 256, Form 13.3
      additional searches, 258
      where not required, 257-258
  notice of directors, 279-280, 284, 301, Forms 14.3, 18.3
    notice of change, 280
  notice of registered office, 279, 301, Forms 14.2, 18.2
  shares and securities, 287-289

share certificates, 288-289, Form 14.4-14.5
introduction, 253, 267-268
unanimous shareholders agreement, 269

Federal-provincial business registration *See also* **Ontario Business Connects (OBC)**
business number (BN), 26, 29
business registration on-line (BRO), 28-29
Canada Customs and Revenue Agency (CCRA), 26, 28-29

FLASHFAX, 222

Incorporation process *See also* **Articles of incorporation**, **Federal incorporations**, and **Shares**
articles of incorporation generally
filing, 110
miscellaneous provisions, 95-97
meetings of shareholders, 96, 108
private restrictions, 95
purchase or redemption of shares, 96
restrictions on right, 96
Quebec, carrying on business in, 95, 106-108
other provisions, 108-109
fees, 80-81
form of documents, 79-80
name clearance, 73-81
documentation requirements, 77
Newly Updated Automated Name Search (NUANS), 73-74
clearance of name, 73-74
Corporations Act, 74
documentation requirements, 77
filing requirement, 77
not filed where electronic filing of articles of incorporation, 70
number name, 78
preliminary checks, 78-79
prescribed documents, 79-80
private search houses, 79
recommended steps, 78
requirements for corporate name, 75-79
elements of name, 75
language of corporation, 75-76
"likely to deceive", whether, 76
setting out name, 76
restrictions on names, 74-75

Initial return *See* ***Corporations Information Act***

Limited liability partnership (LLP), 23-25 *See also* **Partnerships**
Business Names Act registration, 24
more than 10 partners, 24
designated partner, 24
10 or less partners, 24
extra-provincial , 25
"LLP" designation, 24
Partnership Act, 23-24
partnership practising profession, 24

Limited partnerships *See also* **Partnerships**
bank account, 23
declaration, 17-19
additional business name, 18
Business Identifier Number (BIN), 18
dissolution or withdrawal, 18
failure to file renewal, 18-19
general partners, 18
extra-provincial limited partnership, 21-22
carrying on business in Ontario, 21
declaration, 21
cancellation, 22
sanction for non-compliance, 22
power of attorney, 22
Limited Partnership Act, 17
records, 22-23
rights of limited partner, 19-21
assignment and substitution, 20
contribution, demand and receive return of, 20
dissolution, 20-21
settling of accounts, 21
limited liability, 19
person both general and limited partner, 19
rights generally, 19-20

Master Business Licence (MBL)
sole proprietorship, 5-6

MyBIS
Business Information Service, 71

Name search *See* **Newly Updated Automated Name Search (NUANS)** and

Newly Updated Automated Name Search (NUANS)
change of name, 181
clearance of name, 73-74
Corporations Act, 74
extra-provincial corporations, 201
federal incorporations, 255-265
name and NUANS, 255-258
information added to database on continuing basis, 256-257
key to reading computer printout, 258-259
Name Granting Compendium, 255, Form 13.1
name clearance, 259-265
change of name, directing, 265
designating number, 264-265
prohibited names, 261-264, 265
regulatory requirements, 259-265
reserving name, 264
statutory requirements, 259
search report, 256, 257-258
filing requirement, 77
not filed where electronic filing of articles of incorporation, 70
French version of corporate name, 96
requirements for corporate name, 75-79
restrictions on names, 74-75

NUANS *See* **Newly Updated Automated Name Search**

Officers *See also* **Directors**
annual returns
officer information, 155
choice of officers, 60
committee of directors, 60
conflict of interest, 59-60
fiduciary capacity, 61
introduction, 59
managing director, 60
material interest in contract, 59-60
disclosure of interest, 59-60
standard of care, 60-61
unanimous shareholders agreement, 61

Ontario Business Information System (ONBIS)
accessing system, methods of, 214
automated process, 66-67
CIDREQ, 69
client survey, 63
conversion to automation, 67
Corporations on Microfiche (COM) index, 214, 215, 216
current conversion status, 67-69
Electronic Corporate Index (ECI), 67-68, 79, 214-215
electronic filing, 69-70
articles of incorporation, 70
extra-provincial corporations, 205-206
forms, 70-71
microfiche records, 213, 214, 215
MyBIS, 71
name search, 6
private service providers, 209
public record, 66
Certificate of Status, 68, 80-81
Corporate Business Names List, 68
Corporate Document List, 68, 213
Corporate Profile Report, 68, 69, 213
Electronic Corporate Index (ECI), 67-68, 79, 214, 215
searches generally, 208-209
system
introduction, 63-64
special notices, 64-65
failure to file, 65-66

Ontario Business Registration Application
amendment application, 27, 28
cancellation application, 27-28
clearing path, 25
confirmation of registration, 28
federal-provincial business registration, 28-29
business number (BN), 26, 29
business registration on-line (BRO), 28-29

Canada Customs and Revenue Agency (CCRA), 26, 28-29
four applications, 26
name search, 29-30
Ontario Business Connects (OBC), 26-28, 29
website, 26
private-sector service providers, 28
self-help workstations, 25-26
sole proprietorship, 4
submitting application, 27

Organization of corporation *See also* ***Corporations Information Act*** and **Reports**
by-laws, 123-129
federal corporation, 291
generally, 123
multiple director by-laws, 124-128
appointment of officers, 125
by-law no. 2, 127
by-law no. 3, 127-128
casting vote, 125
corporate seal, 126
financial year, 126
lien for indebtedness, 125
powers of directors, 124-125
repeal, 127
signing officers, 126
preparing, 123-124, 129
single director by-law, 128-129
banking by-law (by-law no. 2), 128
confirmation clauses, 128
financial year, 129
corporate bank account, 145-150
banking resolution, 131, 146-147
certificate of incumbency, 147
corporate seal, 149-150
generally, 145-146, 176
Proceeds of Crime (Money Laundering) Act, effect of, 148-149
safety deposit box, 150
service charges and fees/financial services, 147
specimen signature card(s), 148-149
corporate records, 115-118
accounting records, 116-117
destruction of books and records, 158-161
conditions, 159-160
general consent, 158-160
notice of revocation, 160
written permission for early disposal, 160
disposal of records, 118, 145, 160
examination, right of, 117
registers, 115-116, 117, 140-145
directors register, 141
general requirements, 140-141
location of registers, 145
register of transfers, 142-143, 145
shareholders ledger, 143-144
shareholders, list of, 145
shareholders register, 143
securities register, 141-142
transfer agent, 145
location of records, 117, 145
name wrongly entered, 118
required records, 115-116
shareholders, list of, 117-118, 145
corporate seal, 118-119, 126, 130-131, 149-150
adoption of, 130-131
by-law, 126
corporate embosser, 119
desk seal, 119
generally, 118-119
pocket seal, 119
organizational resolutions, 129-138
banking resolution, 131, 146-147
confirmation that resolutions passed, 132-133
corporate seal, adoption of, 130-131
directors, 137-138
consent at meeting, 137-138
consent to act as first director, 137
disqualified from acting as, 137
dissent, notification of, 137-138
financial/fiscal year end, 131-132
generally, 129
officers, election or appointment of, 129-130
pre-incorporation contract, 133
registered office, site of, 131
share certificate form, approval of, 130

shareholders, rights of, 133-137
accountant, appointment of, 136
audit, waiver of, 134-136
annual audit/auditors' report, 134-135
appointment of auditor, 134
consent of all shareholders, 134
persons disqualified as auditors, 134
report of auditor to shareholders, 135
financial statement, 135
GAAP principles, 135
confirmation clause, 136-137
director(s), election of, 133
signed by all shareholders, 136
shares issued to incorporator(s), 130
subscription for shares, 132
summary, 139-140
federal corporations, 291-294
by-laws, 291
corporate supplies, 291
organizational resolutions of directors, 292-293
organizational resolutions of shareholders, 293
registers, 294
report to client, 294
post-organizational resolutions of directors, 138-139, 293
federal corporations, 293
standard matters, 138
subscription for shares, 138-139
declaration of trust, 138-139
share certificates, 119-123, Forms 6.1-6.3
approval of, 130
entitlement to, 122
fully paid, 122-123
information required on face of certificate, 120-121
restrictions on transfer of share, 121-122
non-offering corporation, 121, 122
offering corporation, 121-122
right to claim lien, 121, 125
manually signed, 122
non-assessable, 122
ordering certificates, 120
pre-emptive rights, 122
share certificate book, 119-120
both preference and common shares, 120
common shares, 120
preference shares, 120

Partnerships

general partnership, 14-17
Business Names Act registration, 14-16
additional business name, 15-16
amended registration, 16
Form 1, 15, 16
more than 10 partners, 15, 16
designated partner, 15, 16
10 or fewer partners, 15, 16
power of attorney, 16
dissolution or withdrawal, 16-17
introduction, 14
introduction, 9-10
limited liability partnership (LLP), 23-25
Business Names Act registration, 24
more than 10 partners, 24
designated partner, 24
10 or less partners, 24
extra-provincial , 25
"LLP" designation, 24
Partnership Act, 23-24
partnership practising profession, 24
limited partnerships, 17-23
bank account, 23
declaration, 17-19
additional business name, 18
Business Identifier Number (BIN), 18
dissolution or withdrawal, 18
failure to file renewal, 18-19
general partners, 18
extra-provincial limited partnership, 21-22
carrying on business in Ontario, 21
declaration, 21
cancellation, 22
sanction for non-compliance, 22
power of attorney, 22
Limited Partnership Act, 17
records, 22-23
rights of limited partner, 19-21
assignment and substitution, 20

contribution, demand and receive return of, 20
dissolution, 20-21
settling of accounts, 21
limited liability, 19
person both general and limited partner, 19
rights generally, 19-20
Partnership Act, 9, 10-13
business relationship within partnership, 11-13
dissolution of partnership, 12, 13, 16
liability of partners, 10- 11
limited liability partnership (LLP), 23-24
searches, 209-210

Personal Property Security Act (PPSA) *See* **Searches**

Pre-incorporation contracts *See also* **Corporate powers**
adoption of, 89, 133
introduction, 88-89
non-adoption of, 89
personal liability of person involved, 89
exception, 89-90

***Proceeds of Crime (Money Laundering) Act*, effect of**, 148-149

Proxy, 187-188 *See also* **Annual meetings**

Registered office *See also* **Articles of incorporation**
notice of change, 99, Form 16.18
relocation to different municipality, 99, 183
relocation within municipality, 99, 183

Registers, 115-116, 117,140-145 *See also* **Organization of corporation**, corporate records

Reports
legal account for services rendered, 168-169
report to auditor or accountant, 169-170
report to client, 163-168
annual returns, 167-168
auditors/accountants, 167
authorized capital, 164-165
corporate records, 168
corporate tax status, 168
directors and officers, 166
execution of instruments, 167
financial year, 167
generally, 163
incorporation process, 164
issued shares, 167
organization, 166
registered office, 165-166
restrictions on business, 165

Searches
Bank Act searches, 236-239
assignment under s. 427, 239
Canadian Securities Registration System (CSRS), 239
"in person" search, 239
letter search, 239
notice of intention, 239, Form 12.9
security under s. 427, 239
types of security upon which bank authorized to lend, 236-238
bankruptcy search, 239-244
bankruptcy methods, 240
conducting search, 241-244
bankruptcy court offices, 241-243
bankruptcy certificate, 243, Form 12.10
on-line personal searches or certificate searches, 243
online insolvency name search, 243
client account, 243
Official Receiver, 242, 243
Superintendent of Bankruptcy, offices of, 242, App. A
online insolvency name search, 243
consumer guide, 243-244
effect of bankruptcy, 240
general, 239-240
priority of creditors, 240
corporate search, 210-223
federal corporations, 219-222
automated fax information sources, 221-222
deposit account, 220-221

financial statements, 220
letter delivery, 221
notice of directors, 219
notice of registered office, 219
on-line services, 222
searching options, 219
Ontario corporations, 210-219
accessing ONBIS system, methods of, 214-215
alphabetical listing of corporations, 215
bonds/debentures, 211-212
Certificate of Status, 218
certified copies, 218-219
corporate document list, 214
corporate profile report, 214
Corporations on Microfiche (COM) index, 214, 215, 216
Electronic Corporate Index (ECI), 67-68, 79, 214-215
microfiche records, 213, 215-216
request for corporate information, 212-213, Form 12.2
types of searches, 216
default in filings, 216
financing, 216
litigation matter, 216
summary of required information, 216-218
when required, 211
other jurisdictions, 223
executions, 247
motor vehicle search, 248-249, Form 12.11
name/style registration search, 210
OBC self-serve workstations, 210
ONBIS and automation, 208-209
Ontario Securities Commission (OSC) searches, 244-247
Micromedia, 244-247
CanCorp Financials, 245
guidebooks, 244-245
official document agent for OSC, 244
demand documents service, 245
monitoring service, 245
OSC Bulletin PLUS, 245-247
Prospectus Researcher PLUS, 245-247
U.S. Securities Exchange Commission filings, 245
stock exchanges, 244
overview, 207
partnership or proprietorship/business search, 209-210
services requisition, 209, Form 1.6
patents search, 247-248
Personal Property Security Act (PPSA) search, 223-235
collateral, 225
deposit account, 224
electronic filing, 226-227
enquiry process, 231-235
bilingual, 232
certified copies, 235
guidebook, 235
in-person search, 234
introduction, 231-232
procedure in making PPSA search, 232-234
up-to-date search, 234-235
written enquiries, 234
errors in registered statement, 230
fee schedule, 228, App. B
Financing Change Statement/Change Statement
Form 2C, 225, 226, 229, 230-231, Form 12.5
Form 3C
discharge or renewal, 226, 229-230
verification statement, 226, 228, 229, 230
Financing Statement/Claim for Lien (Form 1C), 225, 226, 229, 230-231, Form 12.4
introduction, 223
Motor Vehicle Schedule (Form 4C), 225, 230-231, Form 12.6
Personal Property Security Registration (PPSR) System, 223-224
electronic filing, 227
registry offices, 228, App. A
PPSA not applying to, 224
preparation of prescribed forms, 228
Repair and Storage Liens Act (RSLA), 224, 225, 226, 228-229
registration number, 227

linking registrations, 226, 230
registration particulars, 227
registration period, 228
security agreement, copy of, 227, 228
"security interest" defined, 225
notice of security interest, 225
search fees, 207-208

Share certificates, 119-123, 288-289, Forms 6.1-6.3, 14.4-14.5 *See also* **Organization of corporation**

Shareholders' agreement
contents check-list, 172-177
arbitration clause, 177
auditor, waiving appointment of, 176-177
board of directors, 175
corporate bank account, 176
employment contracts, 176
financing, 175-176
general preamble, 172
miscellaneous provisions, 177
restrictions on transfer, 175
shareholder defaults, 177
specific clauses, 173-175
compulsory buy-sell arrangements, 173-174
definitions, 173
first right of refusal, 173
other, 174-175
pre-emptive rights, 173
special voting arrangements, 174
purpose, 171-172
unanimous shareholder agreements, 178-179
defined, 178
provisions of BCA subject to, 60, 61, 178-179
provisions of CBCA, 269

Shares *See also* **Organization of corporation**, share certificates
authorized capital, 90, 101-102
declaration of trust, 138-139
equality of shares of class, 94-95
no par value, 90
shareholder rights, 90-91
shares within class equal, 91-94
common shares (Class A), 91
voting rights, 91
conversion rights, 93
dividends, 91-92, 102-103
cumulative, 91-92, 102-103
non-cumulative, 92, 103-104
partially cumulative, 92
preference shares (Class B), 91
preferences, 92
voting rights, restricted, 94
dissolution or sale of substantial assets, 94
redeemable shares, 93
restrictions on redemption rights, 93-94
transfer of shares, 91
pre-emptive rights, 122, 173
private restrictions, 95, 105-106
rights and privileges attaching to shares, 102-105
dividends, 102-103
special shares, 103-105
voting or non-voting, 103

Sole proprietorship
bank account, 8-9
business name registration, 3-6
Business Names Act, 3, 4
cancellation, 7-8
Form 1, 3-4, 5
further filings, 5
Master Business Licence (MBL), 5-6
Ontario Business Registration Application, 4
renewal, 5
restrictions respecting names, 4-5
cancellation of registration, 5, 7-8
introduction, 3
licensing or permits, 5-6, 8
name search and its importance, 6-7
Business Identifier Number (BIN), 6
Business Names Act
sanctions for non-compliance with, 6-7
Ontario Business Information System (ONBIS), 6
"passing off", common law action of, 7

services requisition in respect of unincorporated businesses, 6, 209, Form 1.6

Special resolution
confirmation of interested director contract, 52-53
federal corporations, 296, Form 16.1
number of directors
delegating to directors, 42, 48
fixing, 47-48
increasing or decreasing, 42
registered office
relocation to different municipality, 99, 183
removal of directors, 58

Unanimous shareholder agreements, 178-179, 269 *See also* **Shareholders' agreement**